fourth edition

Mastering Public Speaking

George L. Grice
Radford University

John F. Skinner
San Antonio College

W9-AZC-278

Allyn and Bacon
Boston   London   Toronto   Sydney   Tokyo   Singapore

To Wrenn, Evelyn, Carol, and Leanne

*To Suzanne, Drew, and Devin;
Gertrude and Beverley;
and the rowdy Skinner girls:
Meghan, Katy, Taylor, and Stevi*

&

*To the memory of Robert C. Jeffrey,
our teacher and friend*

Editor: Karon Bowers
Vice President, Editor in Chief: Paul Smith
Developmental Editor: Carol Alper
Editorial-Production Administrator: Joe Sweeney
Editorial-Production Service: Heckman & Pinette
Composition Buyer: Linda Cox

Manufacturing Buyer: Megan Cochran
Cover Administrator: Linda Knowles
Text Designer: Glenna Collett
Photo Researcher: Sue C. Howard
Text Composition: Omegatype Typography, Inc.

Copyright © 2001, 1998, 1995, 1993 by Allyn & Bacon
A Pearson Education Company
160 Gould Street
Needham Heights, Massachusetts 02494
www.abacon.com

Between the time Web site information is gathered and then published it is not unusual for some sites to have closed. Also, the transcription of URLs can result in typographical errors.

Library of Congress Cataloging-in-Publication Data
Grice, George L.
    Mastering public speaking / George L. Grice, John F. Skinner.--4th ed.
      p. cm.
    Includes bibliographical references and index.
    ISBN 0-205-31808-8
      1. Public speaking. I. Skinner, John F. II. Title.

    PN4121 .G719 2000
    808.5'1--dc21

                                 00-028391

Printed in the United States of America
10 9 8 7 6 5 4 3 2   VHP 03 02 01 00

brief contents

contents

Responding to Speeches   66

Analyzing Your Audience   92

Selecting Your Speech Topic   120

Researching Your Topic   142

Supporting Your Speech   174

Organizing the Body of Your Speech   198

Introducing and Concluding Your Speech   218

Appendix A   **A Classroom Speech and Speaker's Journal**   457

Appendix B   **Sample Speeches**   464

preface to the student

The word began as the spoken word. Long before anyone devised a way to record messages in writing, people told one another stories and taught each other lessons. Societies flourished and fell, battles were waged and won on the basis of the spoken word. Ancient storytellers preserved their cultures' literature and history by translating them orally to eager audiences. Crowds might wander away from unprepared, unskilled speakers, but the most competent, skilled storytellers received widespread attention and praise.

After the development of script and print, people continued to associate marks on the page with the human voice. Even today, linked as we are by radio, television, and computer networks, a speaker standing at the front of a hushed room makes a special claim on our attention and our imagination. As you develop and deliver speeches in class—and in future years as you deliver reports, sell products, present and accept awards, or campaign for candidates—you are a part of an ancient oral tradition. This book is about the contract that always exists between a speaker and an audience and about the choices you make in your roles as speaker and listener.

We developed this book with two principles in mind. First, public speaking, like ancient storytelling, requires a level of competence that develops from skills handed down from patient teacher to interested student. Yet this is more than a skills course. Although a working knowledge of skills is fundamental to your mastery of public speaking, the master speaker is principled as well as skilled. We want to instruct you in how to make wise choices as you choose topics and then research, organize, practice, and deliver your speeches. Just as important, we want to spur you at each point in the speech-making process to think about why you make the choices you do.

Our second guiding principle has been most economically stated by British journalist and author Gilbert K. Chesterton: "There are no uninteresting subjects, there are only uninterested people." This book is for those who believe, as we do, that the lessons we have to teach one another can enrich the lives of every listener. The student of art history can learn from the business major, just as the business student learns from the art historian. This course will give you the chance to investigate subjects that appeal to you. We challenge you to develop speech topics creatively and to listen to one another's speeches expecting to learn.

Public speaking is an important part of communication, and communication is not only part of your education but also the way you gain and apply your learning. A liberating and lifelong education occurs only through communication, with ourselves and those around us. We wish each of you the kind of education Steven C. Beering, former president of Purdue University, described so eloquently in a speech inaugurating his university's School of Education:

> Education is dreaming, and thinking and asking questions. It is reading, writing, speaking, and listening. Education is exploring the unknown, discovering new ideas, communicating with the world about us. Education is finding yourself, recognizing human needs, and communicating that recognition to others. Education is learning to solve problems. It is acquiring useful knowledge and skills in order to improve the quality of life. Education is an understanding of the meaning of the past, and an inkling of the potential of the future. Education represents self-discipline, assumption of responsibility and the maintenance of flexibility, and most of all, an open

mind. Education is unfinishable. It is an attitude and a way of life. It makes every day a new beginning.[1]

An Invitation

We are interested in hearing your feedback about this new edition of *Mastering Public Speaking.* Please contact us by e-mail at the following addresses:

ggrice@runet.edu

jskinner@accd.edu

We look forward to hearing from you.

GEORGE L. GRICE and JOHN F. SKINNER

---

[1]Steven C. Beering, "The Liberally Educated Professional," *Vital Speeches of the Day* 15 April 1990: 400.

preface to the instructor

In 1993 we published the first edition of *Mastering Public Speaking* to show students both the hows and the whys of public speaking. Ours was the first major public speaking textbook to devote an entire chapter to speaker and listener ethics and another to managing speaker nervousness. We also introduced students to the 4 S's, a practical mnemonic device for organizing each major idea in a speech.

The text's instructional approach mirrored our view of the public speaking instructor as a "guide on the side" rather than a "sage on the stage." Our goal is to empower students with responsibility for their own learning by challenging them to make all the decisions required of public speakers. By incorporating into our text many credible examples, both actual and hypothetical, we hoped to inspire and encourage students to achieve the full potential of public speech.

In support of our goals, we also wanted to help instructors shape the public speaking classroom into a community of caring, careful thinkers. We sought to improve the quality of feedback in the classroom by analyzing in our text the elements of sound critiques and providing a helpful model for discussing speeches.

In our view, little of consequence has changed in the discipline since that first edition. Although new media have altered our expectations of what a public speech can accomplish, and new research tools and visual arts media have sent us scrambling to ensure that we know as much about these emerging technologies as do most of our students, the fundamentals remain the same. Sensitive audience analysis, adequate research, clear organization, and forceful delivery remain the key ingredients for an effective speech. Therefore, our basic instructional approach in this text has also remained constant: We seek to engage students in the principles, practice, and ethics of public speaking—both as speakers and listeners.

Changes in the Fourth Edition

Although our basic approach remains the same, we have made significant changes and improvements to strengthen it. Instructors who have taught from previous editions suggested some of these changes. We made others to help students navigate through the technological advances that have broadened the menu of research and presentational aid options for public speakers.

Two new features reinforce the text's basic instructional emphases:

- "Speaking with Confidence," a boxed feature that appears in most chapters, spotlights the words of students who used the third edition of *Mastering Public Speaking*. Students were invited to describe aspects of their course work that helped them develop increased confidence.
- Sidebar features citing Internet sources throughout the book direct students to Web sites that we consider especially interesting or useful.

We have revised one feature, collecting the Speaker's Journal entries that were highlighted in various chapters of the third edition and placing them after Daniel Sarvis's classroom speech in Appendix A.

You will notice far more Exercises at the ends of chapters than in previous editions, expanding your options for possible assignments.

We have replaced and updated many student and professional examples throughout the text, using authentic speakers for most of these examples, as in previous editions. In addition to updating examples, the most significant changes are as follows:

- Chapter 2, "The Ethics of Public Speaking," continues to warn students of the seriousness of plagiarism, especially in these days of "cut-and-paste" Internet research. Significantly, the chapter expands the discussion of ethics by also explaining the fair use provision of copyright law. This section examines the conditions under which students may be able to use even copyrighted materials in their speeches without securing permission from the copyright holder.

- Chapter 3, "Speaking Confidently," now contains James McCroskey's "Personal Report of Public Speaking Anxiety," along with instructions for scoring and interpreting individual results on the questionnaire. The chapter now has a stronger theoretical emphasis with its discussion of cognitive restructuring and visualization.

- Chapter 4, "Responding to Speeches," the most thorough discussion of critiquing speeches in any textbook, contains an additional guideline, "Target a Few Key Areas for Improvement."

- Chapter 5, "Analyzing Your Audience," now introduces students to the VALS2 typology, developed at Stanford University, as another way of analyzing and conceptualizing members of a speech audience.

- Chapter 7, "Researching Your Topic," is expanded and updated to reflect the profound effects that the Internet is having on methods of research. No longer a limited alternative to traditional library work, online research is the first choice of many college students. The lists of Web sites and their URLs in Chapter 7 provide a ready reference for students logging onto the Internet.

- Both Chapter 7 and Chapter 8, "Supporting Your Speech," contain more thorough discussions of the importance of evaluating information provided by Internet sources. "Evaluating Electronic Information" in Chapter 8 provides an expanded checklist of questions to consider about Web and Internet sources.

- Chapters 9 and 10 provide new focus and insights for organizing a speech. Chapter 9, "Organizing the Body of Your Speech," now consolidates most of the methods of organizing informative and persuasive speeches, including problem–solution and need–plan patterns. Chapter 10, "Introducing and Concluding Your Speech," now includes an additional step of a speech conclusion, emphasizing the importance of activating an audience response.

- Chapter 11, "Outlining Your Speech," features a new extended example of the stages of outlining undertaken by one person developing a speech.

- Chapter 12, "Wording Your Speech," now discusses the importance of using inclusive, not just nonsexist, language and contains an expanded treatment of metaphor.

- Chapter 13, "Delivering Your Speech," is reorganized to emphasize the various methods of speech delivery and to stress the advantages of extemporaneous delivery. This chapter also incorporates recent research on the functions of gestures.

- Chapter 14's new title, "Using Presentational Aids," reflects a more contemporary approach to studying supplements to the spoken word. The chapter now also includes expanded guidelines for designing presentational aids.

- Chapter 15, "Speaking to Inform," now ends with Emelyn Carley's speech on quilts, a favorite of ours. In previous editions we have included that speech in an appendix or at the end of Chapter 10 to illustrate the principles of effective organization. At the end of Chapter 15, it provides an appropriate example of a well-organized, well-documented, informative speech that incorporated effective presentational aids.

- Chapter 16, "The Strategy of Persuasion," and Chapter 17, "The Structure of Persuasion," enhance an already extensive coverage of persuasion with expanded discussion of persuasion theory, additional fallacies of reasoning, and more detailed illustration of Monroe's motivated sequence. Chapter 17 now ends with a student speech, annotated to illustrate the steps of Monroe's popular organizational pattern.

- Chapter 19, "Speaking in and as a Group," now includes the work team as one type of task-oriented group and discusses an additional guideline for developing a group presentation.

- Appendix B includes four new sample speeches, retaining two from previous editions.

Supplements

For this edition, we have enlisted the help of a number of talented colleagues in revising existing supplements and developing new ones. The following resources are available to help instructors plan and teach the public speaking course.

- The *Instructor's Manual/Test Bank* was prepared by a team of three professionals: Trudy Hanson, West Texas A&M University, and Jason Teven, NW Missouri State University, prepared the instructor's materials, and Tom Diamond, Montana State University, prepared the test questions. This comprehensive guide provides suggestions for constructing the course syllabus, assignments, sample exercises and activities, critiquing strategies, techniques for conducting in-class reviews, and detailed chapter outlines. Also included are more than 1200 test questions, including multiple choice, true/false, short answer, and essay questions, also available in a computerized version.

- *A Guide for New Public Speaking Teachers: Building Toward Success,* by Calvin L. Troup, Duquesne University, covers such topics as preparing for the term, planning and structuring your course, evaluating speeches, utilizing the textbook, integrating technology into the classroom, dealing with challenges, and much more.

- The *Allyn & Bacon Communication Studies Digital Media Archive,* available on CD-ROM, offers more than 200 still images, video excerpts, and PowerPoint™ slides that can be used to enliven classroom presentations.

- The *PowerPoint™ Package,* prepared by Mary Kaye Krum, formerly of Florence Darlington Technical College, consists of a collection of lecture outlines and graphic images keyed to every chapter in the text and is available on the Web at www.abacon.com/ppt.

- The *Allyn & Bacon Public Speaking Transparency Package,* containing 100 public speaking transparencies created with PowerPoint™ software, is also available to provide visual support for classroom lectures and discussion on a full range of course topics. An expanded version is available at www.abacon.com/ppt.

- *Mastering Public Speaking Video: A Student Speech with Critiques, Fourth Edition,* prepared by Julie Benson-Rosston, Red Rocks Community College, is designed to provide a model for students and instructors to learn to provide effective speech critiques. Included are guidelines for effective speech critiques, an informative student speech, an interactive session offering student and instructor feedback on the speech, and the improved student speech.

- An array of other video materials is also available. The *Allyn & Bacon Student Speeches Video Library* includes three two-hour American Forensic Association videos of award-winning student speeches and one video with a range of student speeches delivered in the classroom. The *Allyn & Bacon Public Speaking Video* contains excerpts of classic and contemporary speeches as well as student speeches to illustrate the public speaking process. The *Allyn & Bacon Communication Video Library* contains a collection of communication videos produced by Film for the Humanities and Sciences.

- *Custom Solutions* is a special program offered by Allyn & Bacon that allows instructors to create a Web page specifically for their course combining information on Allyn & Bacon sites with their own course information.

In addition, there are many resources available to help students get the most out of their public speaking course. Several are presented as electronic resources.

- The *Interactive Companion Web Site,* prepared by Thomas E. Jewell of Marymount College and Elsa Peterson, offers materials for students to enrich their learning and study for exams. This electronic text companion includes Web links to hundreds of related Internet sites, video excerpts from student speeches to illustrate key points, audio clips that expand upon key information, and activities—many tied to the video and audio materials—designed to reinforce learning. The final section in each chapter expands on the Internet feature in the text by providing hot links to all the sites mentioned. Practice tests for each include answers and feedback. Students receive a PIN code and access to the Interactive Companion Web Site upon purchase of a new text.

- The *Companion Web Site with Online Practice Tests,* accessed at www.abacon.com/grice, was prepared by Linda Anthon, Valencia Community College. It provides a wealth of activities to help students practice their critiquing techniques by linking to archived speeches on the Internet and learn to identify effective evidence and support for their speeches by critically evaluating scholarly Web sites. Web links include sites with speeches in text, audio, and video formats. The site also contains online learning objectives, practice tests, and interactive discussions.

- The *Allyn & Bacon Public Speaking Web Site,* prepared by Terrence Doyle, Northern Virginia Community College, is designed to help students use the Internet along with their public speaking textbook to learn about the process of public speaking and to prepare speeches. It can be accessed at *www.abacon.com/pubspeak.*

- Interactive Speechwriter, Version 1.1, by Martin R. Cox, is an interactive software package for student purchase providing supplemental material, including templates for writing speeches and sample speeches, and enhancing students' understanding of key concepts discussed in the text.

There are also many traditional print products (and one audio product) designed for student use.

- The *Study Guide,* prepared by Terry Perkins, Eastern Illinois University, contains a set of comprehensive review questions for each chapter in *Mastering Public Speaking.*

- *Speech Communication on the Net,* by Terrence Doyle, Northern Virginia Community College, includes the basics of using the Internet, conducting Web searches, and critically evaluating and documenting Internet sources. It also contains Internet activities and URLs specific to the discipline of speech communication.

- *Speech Preparation Workbook,* by Jennifer Dreyer and Gregory H. Patton, San Diego State University, takes students through the various stages of speech creation—from audience analysis to writing the speech—and provides guidelines, tips, and easy-to-fill-in pages.

- *Preparing Visual Aids for Presentations,* Second Edition, by Dan Cavanaugh, is a 32-page booklet providing a host of ideas for using today's multimedia tools to improve presentations including suggestions for how to plan a presentation, guidelines for designing visual aids, storyboarding, and a walkthrough that shows how to prepare a visual display using PowerPoint^{TM}.

- *Public Speaking in the Multicultural Environment,* Second Edition, by Devorah A. Lieberman, includes activities and helps students think about the effects that the diverse backgrounds of audience members can have, not just on how speeches are prepared and delivered but also on how those speeches are perceived.

Acknowledgments

We are, first and foremost, grateful to the many university, college, and community college educators whose enthusiasm contributed to the success of previous editions of this textbook. This edition of *Mastering Public Speaking* is the product of more than just two coauthors. Though we have tried to speak with one voice for the sake of our readers, the truth is that many voices resonate throughout this text—the voices of our teachers, our colleagues, our editors, and our students. What we know, what we value, and what we write is shaped in part by their influence and insights. Wherever possible we have tried to acknowledge their contributions. For all their influence on this manuscript, we are thankful.

Significantly, our collaboration began at the urging of a former student, Pam Lancaster, when she was a sales representative at Prentice Hall. We are grateful to Prentice Hall and Allyn & Bacon for allowing us to make previous editions of *Mastering Public Speaking* the book we wanted it to be. We are especially indebted to Steve Dalphin, Virginia Feury-Gagnon, Carla Daves, Helane Manditch-Prottas, and Marlene Ellin for their faith in the project, their patience, and their suggestions.

We would like to thank the entire editorial and production staffs at Allyn & Bacon for their contributions to this fourth edition. We are proud to have been one of the first Allyn & Bacon books to carry the name of Paul Smith, Editor-in-Chief. We have benefited from his enthusiasm and support, as well as from the unflagging encouragement and accommodation of Karon Bowers, acquisitions editor. We are especially grateful to Carol Alper, developmental editor, for her guidance and suggestions and for carefully supervising the editing process. Her professionalism and patience provided us the time to explore and evaluate new ideas, while keeping the project on schedule. These colleagues in cyberspace were always just an e-mail away from providing us their input and support. Carol, Karon, and Paul, thanks for helping to make writing fun.

Jennifer Becker, editorial assistant, completed many tasks along the way with efficiency and enthusiasm. Joe Sweeney, production administrator, orchestrated the process very capably. We are grateful to our careful copyeditor, Margaret Pinette, who also masterfully guided our manuscript into page proofs. Thanks for keeping all the plates spinning. Many students, authors, and publishers graciously allowed us to quote material in this book. We thank James McCroskey for permission to reprint his Personal Report of Public Speaking Anxiety, featured in Chapter 3. We are especially indebted to

Daniel Sarvis for granting us permission to print his speech and his comments on its development in Appendix A. Jennifer A. Brown, thanks for your careful work checking URLs of magazines and newspapers for Chapter 7. Cori Bunn, Rebekah Compton, and Jennifer Noah, thanks for investigating and monitoring many of the Web sites we feature in this edition. We also appreciate the many contributions of Dolly Conner, who tracked down hard-to-find sources, tested our ideas in her classrooms, and coordinated feedback from students.

A number of students responded to our call for feedback about classroom experiences or topics in *Mastering Public Speaking* that increased their confidence. We thank them all, particularly the students selected for the "Speaking with Confidence" feature in this edition: Joey Bell, Radford University; Anne Bergstrom, Eastern Illinois University; Jennifer A. Brown, San Antonio College; Rometta Carrico, Radford University; Jacob Casey, Clark College; Elizabeth Cleaver, Clark College; Brian Collins, Clark College; Terri Easley, Sam Houston State University; Allison Holt, Eastern Illinois University; Amy Landry, San Antonio College; Kenneth Martinez, San Antonio College; and Benjamin Wilson, Radford University.

Five reference librarians read this and previous versions of our research chapter closely: Caroline Gilson, Jane Schillie, Linda Farynk, and Larry Pollard of Radford University's McConnell Library, and Ralph Domas of the San Antonio College Learning Resource Center. We thank all of them for their expert advice and encouragement.

We have benefited immensely from the encouragement and advice of some former colleagues and from our fellow faculty members at Radford University and San Antonio College: Maresa Brassil, Mary Crow, Bruce Dorries, Merrill Jones, J. Drew McGukin, Rick Olsen, Ray Penn, Janet Stahl, and Richard Worringham. We are especially grateful to Gwen Brown, Mike Cronin, Cynthia Cone, Barbara Strain, Suzanne Skinner, Carolyn DeLecour, Charles Falcon, and David Mrizek, who gave us their insights, suggestions, and encouragement.

In addition, *Mastering Public Speaking* has been shaped and refined by the close readings and thoughtful suggestions of a number of reviewers in this and in previous editions:

Linda Anthon, Valencia Community College
Barbara L. Baker, Central Missouri State University
Elizabeth Bell, University of South Florida
Jim Benjamin, University of Toledo
Tim Borchers, Moorhead State University

Carl R. Burgchardt, Colorado State University
Pamela Cooper, Northwestern University
Tom Diamond, Montana State University
Terrence Doyle, Northern Virginia Community College
John Fritch, Southwest Missouri State University
Trudy L. Hanson, West Texas A&M University
Dayle C. Hardy-Short, Northern Arizona University
Deborah Hatton, Sam Houston State University
Kimberly Batty Herbert, Clovis Community College
Leslie A. Klipper, Miramar College
Mary Kaye Krum, formerly of Florence-Darlington Technical College
Bruce Loebs, Idaho State University
Patricia Palm McGillen, Mankato State University
David B. McLennan, Peace College
Eileen Oswald, Valencia Community College
Rosemarie Rossetti, Ohio State University
Jim Roux, Horry-Georgetown Technical College
Edward H. Sewell, Virginia Tech University
Frances Swinny, professor emerita, Trinity University
Cory Tomasson, Illinois Valley Community College
Beth M. Waggenspack, Virginia Tech University
Doris Werkman, Portland State University
Dianna R. Wynn, Midland College

For the first time we have enlisted the help of several talented individuals to prepare the supplemental materials for *Mastering Public Speaking*. We would like especially to thank Trudy L. Hanson of West Texas A&M University, Jason Teven of NW Missouri State University, and Tom Diamond of Montana State University for preparing the *Instructor's Manual/Test Bank;* Terry Perkins of Eastern Illinois University, for preparing the printed study guide; Linda Anthon of Valencia Community College, for her work on the Companion Web Site; Thomas Jewell of Marymount College and Elsa Peterson for preparing the *Interactive Companion;* Julie Benson-Rosston of Red Rocks Community College, for her work on the *Mastering Public Speaking Video: A Student Speech with Critiques,* Fourth Edition; and Mary Kaye Krum, for her work on the PowerPoint™ Package.

Finally, we are indebted to all our public speaking students, who have crafted their messages, walked to the front of their classrooms, and informed, persuaded, entertained, and challenged us. Without their ideas and experiences, writing and revising this book would have been impossible, just as without tomorrow's students it would have been unnecessary.

An Invitation

We are interested in hearing your feedback about this new edition of *Mastering Public Speaking*. Please contact us by e-mail at the following addresses:

ggrice@runet.edu

jskinner@accd.edu

We look forward to hearing from you.

GEORGE L. GRICE and JOHN F. SKINNER

Mastering Public Speaking

Speech is civilization itself. The word, even the most contradictory word, preserves contact—it is silence which isolates.

—*Thomas Mann*

An Introduction to Public Speaking

Why Study Public Speaking?

By anyone's standards, Deep Springs College is an unusual two-year school. A self-sustaining cattle ranch and alfalfa farm in a remote, far eastern California valley, its entire student body is a couple of dozen young men; its faculty, half a dozen residents. The nearest town of significant size is an hour's drive away. The average combined SAT score for applicants exceeds 1400, making it "second among the nation's institutes of higher learning with respect to the aptitude of the students it admits."[1] After two, sometimes three, years at Deep Springs, students transfer to the "safety net" schools that accepted them fresh out of high school: Harvard, Cornell, Berkeley, Swarthmore, Princeton, or MIT, for example.[2] Students, who attend free of tuition in return for 20 hours a week of labor, govern the school, evaluate the progress of their peers, and select each year's incoming students.

L. L. Nunn, industrialist and founder of Deep Springs, wanted to prepare young people of exceptional aptitude for lives of public service. He knew that would require them to be articulate. For that reason, the only two required courses are English composition and public speaking. Deep Springs president L. Jackson Newell says that

> [e]ven today every student is required to take public speaking each term he is in residence. The requirement benefits the college in ways that Nunn may not have anticipated. Monday evenings have become major events in the community as faculty, staff, and their families gather to hear students speak on topics ranging from international affairs to institutional concerns. Always lively, these sessions provide a natural setting for the exchange of ideas and the unification of the community.[3]

Public speaking required each semester? That, you may think, is the most unusual fact of all. Yet the people of Deep Springs—past and present—seem keenly aware of how important public speaking can be, both in the college classroom and beyond.

Today, beyond the relative security of the college or university classroom, nearly 7,000 speakers will stand in front of American audiences and deliver speeches.[4] And during those same 24 hours, people will make more than 30 *million* business presentations.[5] These speakers will express and elaborate their ideas, champion their causes, and promote their products or services. Those who are successful will make sales, enlist support, and educate and entertain their listeners. Many will also enhance their reputations as effective speakers. To achieve these goals, each will be using the skills, principles, and arts that are the subject of this textbook.

Consider, too, that somewhere on a college campus right now is the student who will one day deliver an inaugural address after being sworn in as president; the student who will appear on national television to accept the Heisman Trophy, the Tony Award for Best Actress, or the Academy Award for Best Director; and the student who will present breakthrough medical research findings to a national conference of doctors and medical technicians, or whose words will usher passage of important legislation.

You may be taking this course as an elective because you want to improve your public speaking skills in the relative security of a classroom. Chances are, however, that, like the students at Deep Springs, you are in this class because it is a requirement for graduation. If that's the case, you may rightfully be asking, "Why should I take a course in public speaking?" The answer, suggested in the preceding real-life examples, has three parts: Studying and practicing public speaking benefits you personally, professionally, and publicly.

Personal Benefits of Studying Public Speaking

This course can benefit you personally in three ways.

1. Studying public speaking helps you to succeed in college.
2. Studying public speaking increases your knowledge.
3. Studying public speaking helps build your confidence.

First, mastering public speaking can help you acquire skills important to your success in college. According to a Carnegie Foundation report,

> To succeed in college, undergraduates should be able to write and speak with clarity, and to read and listen with comprehension. Language and thought are inextricably connected, and as undergraduates develop their linguistic skills, they hone the quality of their thinking and become intellectually and socially empowered.[6]

Look at some of the chapter titles in this textbook. They include words such as *analyzing, researching, organizing, wording,* and *delivering.* These are skills you will use in constructing and delivering your speeches. They are also *transferable* skills; they can help you throughout your academic studies, as well as in your chosen career.

Second, public speaking can help you become more knowledgeable. According to one study, we remember:

10 percent of what we read,
20 percent of what we hear,
30 percent of what we see, and
70 percent of what we speak.[7]

Consider for a moment two different ways of studying lecture notes for an exam. One method is to read and reread your notes silently. An alternative is more active and makes you a sender of messages. You stand in your room, put your lecture notes on your dresser, and deliver the lecture out loud, pretending you are the instructor explaining the material to the class. Which method do you think promotes better understanding and retention of the course material? You will not be surprised to learn that it's the second method.

Speaking is an active process. You discover ideas, shape them into a message, and deliver that message using your voice and body. The act of speaking is a crucial test of your thinking skills. As author E.M. Forster observed, "How do I know what I think until I've seen what I've said?" The process of developing and delivering an idea clarifies it and helps make it uniquely your own. In this course, you will learn a lot about the topics on which you choose to speak. By learning how to construct an effective public speech, you will also become a better listener to others' speeches, oral reports, and lectures, and this will further increase your learning.

A third personal benefit of this course is that it can help build your confidence and self-esteem. We devote Chapter 3 to discussing the most common fear of adult Americans: the fear of speaking to a group of people. In this course, you will learn how to turn this apprehension into confidence. You will do so by reading this textbook, by listening to your instructor, and, most important, by doing. The confidence and poise you gain as you begin to master public speaking will help you when you give that oral report on "Gender Roles in the Plays of Shakespeare" in your British literature class, when you address your school board urging them to expand the district's arts education program, or when you are asked to say a few words upon receiving the Outstanding Community Service award for your work at a local food bank. As the Emerson quotation at the beginning of this chapter suggests, great speaking requires practice, but your efforts will bring you these three rewards.

Professional Benefits of Studying Public Speaking

Studying communication, and specifically public speaking, is important to you not only personally but also professionally. In fact, numerous studies document a strong relationship between communication competence and career success. Effective speaking skills enhance your chances of first securing employment and then advancing in your career. In a 1999 report, the National Association of Colleges and Employers listed characteristics employers consider most important when hiring an employee. At the top of the list was communication skills.[8]

In another study three speech and business professors surveyed 1,000 randomly selected human resource managers to determine the "factors most important in helping graduating college students obtain employment." Oral communication skills ranked first with written communication second and listening third.[9] The researchers concluded:

> From the results of this and the previous study, it appears that the skills most valued in the contemporary job-entry market are communication skills. The skills of listening, oral communication (both interpersonal and public), written communication, and the trait of enthusiasm are indicated to be the most important. Again, it would appear to follow that university officials wishing to be of the greatest help to their graduates in finding employment would make sure that basic competencies in oral and written communication are developed. Courses in listening, interpersonal, and public communication would form the basis of meeting the oral communication competencies.[10]

This course will instruct you in two of those vital skills: public speaking and listening.

Once you are hired, your speaking skills continue to work for you, becoming your ticket to career success and advancement. Researchers Roger Mosvick and Robert Nelson found that managers and technical professionals spend approximately twice as much time speaking and listening as they do reading and writing.[11] A survey of 500 executives found that speaking skills "rated second only to job knowledge as important factors in a businessperson's success." That same study also showed that effective communication helped improve company productivity and understanding among employees.[12]

Although you are likely to spend only a small portion of your communication at work giving presentations and speeches, your ability to stand in front of a group of people and present your ideas is important to your career success. One survey of 66 companies found that 76 percent of executives gave oral reports.[13] Another survey found that while on-the-job public speaking accounted for only 6 percent of managers' and technical professionals' time, it nevertheless ranked as more important to job performance than did time spent reading mail and other documents, dictating letters and writing reports, and talking on the phone.[14] Oral communication and public speaking clearly play a critical role in your professional life.

Public Benefits of Studying Public Speaking

Finally, public speaking can help you play your role as a member of society. As Thomas Mann noted in the quotation preceding this chapter, it is communication that connects us with each other. Public speaking is an important part of creating a society of informed and active citizens.

A democratic society is shaped, in part, by the eloquence of its leaders:

Franklin Delano Roosevelt, who rallied a nation during the Great Depression by declaring, "The only thing we have to fear is fear itself";

John F. Kennedy, who urged citizen involvement, exhorting us to "ask not what your country can do for you; ask what you can do for your country";

Martin Luther King, Jr., who challenged us to dream of a day when people will be judged not "by the color of their skin but by the content of their character";

Oprah Winfrey, who urges people to change their lives by reading and discussing books.

But a democratic society is also shaped by the quiet eloquence of everyday citizens:

the police officer who informs residents of a crime-plagued area how to set up a neighborhood watch program;

the social worker who addresses the city council and secures funding for a safe house for abused and runaway children;

the elementary school teacher who speaks to civic clubs, generating their support for a meals-on-wheels program for elderly citizens confined to their homes;

the student who consoles grieving students and faculty at an assembly remembering classmates fatally shot at their school.

In each of these instances, the speaker used the power of the spoken word to address a need and solicit an appropriate audience response.

While we recognize effective speaking when we meet the person who always says "just the right thing" or who says things in funny and colorful ways, few of us have been trained to speak well. To appreciate the power of communication you must understand just what it is. That requires a look at some definitions of communication and at some of its essential components.

Definitions of Communication

The word *communicate* comes from the Latin verb *communicare,* meaning "to make common to many, share, impart, divide."[15] This concept of sharing is important in understanding communication and is implicit in our definition of the term. Simply stated, when you communicate you share, or make common, your knowledge and ideas with someone else.

You can understand communication best when you view it as both a *process* and a *product.* Some scholars believe that communication is basically a process. For example, Thomas Scheidel provides a process perspective when he defines communication as "the transmission and reception of symbolic cues."[16] Other scholars see communication as an outcome or a product and define it simply as shared meaning. We believe both of these perspectives offer insights into the concept of communication. **Communication,** then, *is the sharing of meaning by sending and receiving symbolic cues.*

You can understand how meaning is shared by studying Figure 1.1, Charles Ogden and I. A. Richards's triangle of meaning.[17] This figure illustrates the three elements necessary when someone communicates; those elements are interpreter, symbol, and referent. The word interpreter refers to both the sender and the receiver of a message. The **interpreter** is simply the person who is communicating, with words or other symbols.

The second element of this model, the **symbol,** is anything to which people attach or assign a meaning. Symbols can be pictures, drawings, or objects. We know, for example, that a sign in an airport showing a fork, a spoon, a glass, and an arrow means that we can find a restaurant or a snack bar in the direction the arrow points. The police officer's uniform and squad car are symbols of the authority of the police. The most familiar symbols, however, are words in a particular language. Many words refer to particular objects, places, and people: *chair; Long Beach, California;* and *Eudora Welty,* for example. Some words refer to concepts, such as *freedom of expression, existentialism,* and *fair play.*

The third and final element of the triangle of meaning is the **referent,** the object or idea for which the symbol stands. Both the sender and the receiver of a message have a referent for the symbols used. This referent depends upon each individual's knowledge

communication: the process of sharing meaning by sending and receiving symbolic cues.

interpreter: any person using symbols to send or receive messages.

symbol: anything to which people attach meaning.

referent: the object or idea each interpreter attaches to a symbol.

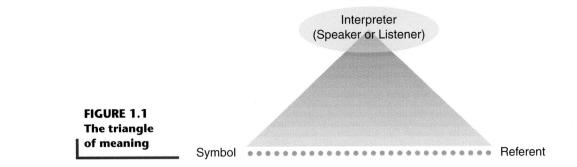

**FIGURE 1.1
The triangle
of meaning**

Interpreter
(Speaker or Listener)

Symbol ● Referent

and experience. People cannot exchange referents in the way they can exchange objects. For example, someone can hand you a paper clip, and that paper clip is the same in your hand as it is in your friend's. Your friends, however, cannot transfer their ideas or information to you. All they can do is to code their ideas into symbols and hope that as you decode them, the ideas you receive will be similar to the ones they intended. In short, as senders we select a symbol based on our referent. That symbol, in turn, triggers the receiver's referent. To check your understanding of how interpreters, symbols, and referents interact, consider an incident one of us experienced.

> A father casually asked his son one evening, "How's your homework coming?" The boy, a seventh grader taking his first computer class, said, "I have to summarize some articles on computers. I've got three, and I need four." The father, planning to go to a bookstore later that night, said, "OK, I'll buy you a new computer magazine." However, the next morning when his father showed him the magazine with the article on computers, the boy asked, "Where are the others? I told you I need four."

The interpreters in this case, the boy and his father, obviously had a communication problem centering around the symbols, "I've got three, and I need four." The son's referent, the idea he had in mind, was, "I've got three articles, and I need four more." The father's referent, however, was, "He's got three of the four articles he needs."

As this example demonstrates, communication is successful only when the interpreters involved attach similar referents to the message being communicated. The *New Yorker* cartoon illustrates the consequences of speaker and listener having different referents. You can, no doubt, think of similar experiences you have had when people misinterpreted what you said because they attached different referents to your words. The most important thing to remember about the triangle of meaning and the process of communication is this: *Words and other symbols have no inherent meaning. People have meaning; words do not.* The word takes on the meaning that the interpreter attaches to it.

Public meetings provide citizens with a forum for public debate, an essential ingredient for a democratic society.

What does the triangle of meaning have to do with public speaking? As you will discover throughout this book, this model applies to public speaking just as it does to all other forms of communication. If speakers and listeners always used specific symbols, interpreted them objectively, and attached similar referents to them, we would experience few if any communication problems arising from the content of the message. As a result, your work in a public speaking class could be limited to improving your organization and polishing your style of delivery. Yet many of our communication problems can be traced directly to difficulties in the relationships between interpreters, the symbols they use, and the referents behind those symbols.

As a public speaker, you must try to ensure that the message your audience hears matches as closely as possible the message you intended. You do that by paying particular attention to your content, organization, and delivery, major subjects of this book. To understand the complexity of public speaking, you need to realize how it relates to other levels of communication.

Levels of Communication

Communication can occur on five different levels:

1. intrapersonal
2. interpersonal
3. group
4. public
5. mass communication

Each of these levels is distinguished by the number of people involved, the formality of the situation, and the opportunities for feedback. One of these levels, public communication, is the subject of this book and the focus of the course you are now taking. Yet public speaking incorporates elements of the other four levels of communication, and a brief look at each of them will help you better understand public speaking.

Intrapersonal Communication

Simply stated, **intrapersonal communication** is communication with yourself. The prefix *intra-* means "within." Intrapersonal communication serves many functions, and we all practice it every waking moment. If you woke up late this morning, for example, and panicked because you overslept for a class, you were communicating intrapersonally. If you sit in class worrying about a problem, or reminding yourself to do something later in the day, or daydreaming about someone or something, you are communicating intrapersonally. If in the middle of a public speech you tell yourself, "This is really going well," or "I can't believe I just said that," you are also communicating intrapersonally.

> Intrapersonal Communication
> http://www.adm.uwaterloo.ca/infocecs/CRC/manual-home.html
> The communication that is central to your career success begins with effective intrapersonal communication. If you're uncertain about your ultimate career, the University of Waterloo's *Career Development Manual* will help you assess your strengths and interests, research various occupations, decide on career objectives, make employment contacts, measure your success at work, and reevaluate your goals in later life.

As these examples demonstrate, much intrapersonal communication is geared toward a specific, conscious purpose: evaluating how we are doing in a particular situation, solving a problem, relieving stress, or planning for the near or distant future. Though we all have probably uttered something aloud to ourselves at times of stress, joy, puzzlement, or discouragement, intrapersonal communication is typically silent. We sit quietly as we reflect on a speaker explaining the difference between ambient and progressive jazz. We are attentive as we hear another speaker explain the preparations necessary for a first sky dive. These examples show the connection between public speaking and intrapersonal communication. Both as public speakers and as audience members for others' speeches, we communicate intrapersonally a great deal. Key features of intrapersonal communication to keep in mind are that it is a continuous process of self-feedback and that it involves only one person.

Interpersonal Communication

As soon as our communication involves ourselves and one other person, it moves to a second level, that of interpersonal communication. **Interpersonal communication** occurs between people, usually two of them. Interpersonal communication is sometimes called dyadic communication; *dyad* is Latin for "pair." Conversations between friends, colleagues, or acquaintances are a common form of interpersonal communication. Yet even strangers communicate interpersonally: A police officer questioning a witness to a crime, a company interviewer meeting a job applicant, and a new student talking to a teacher are all communicating interpersonally.

Whenever two communicators are face to face or speaking over the telephone, the opportunity for verbal interaction always exists. Consider, for example, your last conversation with your best friend, and how easily and naturally you interacted. In fact, if someone had secretly tape-recorded that conversation and typed a transcript of it for you to read, you would probably be surprised by the number of incomplete sentences you and your friend spoke. Ideas that do not appear to make much sense in writing were likely quite clear in conversation. Your best friend is someone who is really on your wavelength, often knows how you are going to finish a sentence, and either finishes it for you or nods agreement and switches to another idea.

In some interpersonal situations, of course, the verbal interaction is less frequent and more self-conscious. We do not interrupt the interviewer sizing us up for a job or the police officer who has just pulled us over for a traffic violation as easily as we do a close friend. Yet the opportunity for verbal interaction exists in even those relatively stressful situations, and is always a characteristic of spoken interpersonal communication.

intrapersonal communication: cognition or thought; communicating with oneself.

interpersonal communication: communication between individuals in pairs; also called dyadic communication.

As we add to the number of people involved, the next level is group communication. Although we discuss group interaction more thoroughly in Chapter 19, we will present some important points about it here. **Group communication** generally takes place with three or more people interacting and influencing each other to pursue a common goal. Although researchers place varying limits on the size of a group, everyone recognizes that a sense of cohesion or group identity is essential to any definition of this level of communication.

Seven students who get together and spend half the night reviewing material and quizzing one another for an upcoming exam are obviously engaged in group communication. A restaurant's owners and managers meeting to revise the menu are similarly involved in a process of group communication. When you present your speeches in class, you will not be engaged in group communication. However, if your presentation on a particularly interesting topic generates questions and discussion, your public speaking class might qualify as an example of group communication.

The important thing to remember about group communication is that the people involved must have a sense of group identity. A group of 14 people, for example, is not just seven dyads or pairs of people. They must believe and accept that they belong together for some reason, whether they face a common problem, share similar interests, or simply work in the same division of a company.

Group communication may be informal, with all group members free to discuss issues as they wish, or formal, operating under the rules of parliamentary procedure. As long as members are relatively free to contribute to the discussion, what occurs is clearly

group communication: three or more people interacting and influencing one another to pursue a common goal.

Courtesy of Patrick O'Connor/*Daily Kent Stater.*

group communication. However, once someone stands up and begins to present a report or make a speech, the communication shifts to the fourth level, public communication.

Public Communication

Public communication, the subject of this course, occurs when one person speaks face to face with an audience. That audience may be as small as your public speaking class or as large as the masses of people who fill stadiums and other public areas to hear certain speakers. As the size of the audience grows, the flow of communication becomes increasingly one-directional, from speaker to audience. When the audience is large, individual members have less opportunity for verbal interaction with the speaker.

For example, your public speaking class is probably small enough that you feel free to have your instructor answer any questions you have during class. In a lecture class of several hundred students, however, you might feel more pressure to keep silent, even if you had a legitimate question. If you were part of an audience of several thousand people, not only would you feel pressure to keep quiet during a speech, but even if you did voice a question the speaker probably could not hear it.

The key characteristics of public communication, therefore, are a more one-directional flow of information and a more formal feeling than the other types of communication we have discussed so far. Whether the audience is as small as a class of 20, or as large as a convention assembly of 2,000, or a congregation of 200,000 standing outside the Vatican to hear an Easter message from the Pope, public communication always involves one person communicating to an audience that is physically present.

Mass Communication

But what happens if we sit in front of our television sets and see videotape clips from that Easter service at the Vatican or a telecast of an Academy Awards ceremony? In such a situation we have entered the fifth and final level of communication, **mass communication.** Once the audience becomes so large that it cannot be gathered in one place, some type of print or electronic medium—newspaper, magazine, radio, television, or computer, among others—must be placed between speaker or writer and the intended audience. The physical isolation of speaker and audience severely limits the possibilities for spontaneous interaction between them. In fact, an important characteristic of mass communication is that audience feedback is *always* delayed. Assume, for example, that a magazine or newspaper article inspires or angers you enough that you write a letter to the editor. Your response will be slowed by the necessities of composing the letter and mailing or e-mailing it. Then, before your response can be shared with the magazine or newspaper readership, someone must review it, decide to publish it, have it typeset and printed, and distribute it to readers. You have the opportunity to send feedback, but it is delayed.

A second characteristic we should consider about mass communication is that the method of message transmission can become very important. Advertising agencies, political consultants, and the people who use them know very well that the *way* a message is sent can be as important as the *content* of that message, something public speakers should also remember. Advertisements for products, services, and political candidates reach different sizes and types of audiences via radio, television, billboards, magazines, newspapers, or Internet Web sites. We devote a portion of Chapter 18 to the special challenges of speaking before a video camera, because future technology will surely expand the importance of mass media in getting messages across to the public.

You will master public speaking skills more quickly and easily if you remain aware of the connections between public communication and the four other levels of communication. In this class, you may use interpersonal and group communication to determine your speech topics and how you approach them. You may interview an expert on a topic you are considering for a speech. Through informal conversations with your

public communication: one person communicating face to face with an audience.

mass communication: one person or group communicating to a large audience through some print or electronic medium.

classmates, you will form a clearer picture of your audience by discovering their interests, attitudes, and values. You may offer others feedback on their speeches and receive their comments regarding your speech. If you have the opportunity to videotape one or more of your speeches, you will gain experience with one of the important electronic media of mass communication, even if your speech is not broadcast publicly. Certainly, you will consult print or electronic media resources as you research your speech. And, all the time you are delivering your public speeches, you will be giving yourself intrapersonal feedback about the job you are doing and the positive responses we hope you are receiving.

Components of Communication

Now that you have an understanding of the different levels of communication, we will look at the various components common to any type of communication and, specifically, to public speaking. Remember, the better you understand how communication works in general, the better you will be able to make communication work for you in specific speaking situations. A brief look at the elements in two communication models will allow us to develop a more accurate view of this complex phenomenon. Just as important, these models will let us see where some common communication problems arise.

> **Comparing Communication Models**
> http://www.sfc.keio.ac.jp/~masanao/Mosaic_data/com_model.html
> Visit this site, maintained by Keio University in Japan, to view and compare a variety of communication models. The site includes linear, interactional, and transactional models. For explanations of each model, you will need to consult the sources cited.

Linear Model of Communication

The earliest models devised by scholars show three basic elements of communication: a speaker sending a message to a listener (see Figure 1.2). The **speaker** may also be called the sender, the source, or the encoder. **Encoding** is the process of putting ideas into symbols, and we encode so much and so well that we are aware of the process only when we find ourselves "at a loss for words" while either speaking or writing. The ideas of the **message** originate with the speaker, who determines the form that the message will take. Unless the communication is intrapersonal, the message is sent to a **listener**—the decoder or receiver. This person then begins **decoding** the message, attaching meanings to the words, gestures, and voice inflections that are received.

Those three elements are important to communication. So what was wrong with the early, linear models of communication? First, they assumed that a person is either a sender or a receiver of messages. The truth is that we perform both of these roles simultaneously. The early one-directional model of communication shown in Figure 1.2 does not account for this.

The second weakness of this simple model is its suggestion that communication involves only one message. Yet remember our earlier discussion of the triangle of meaning. The truth is that there are as many messages as there are communicators involved. The message the speaker intends is never identical to the one received. As long as they are similar, communication will usually be effective.

speaker: the sender, encoder, or source of the message.

encoding: the process of selecting symbols to carry a message.

message: ideas communicated verbally and nonverbally.

listener: the receiver or decoder of the message.

decoding: the process of attaching meanings to symbols received.

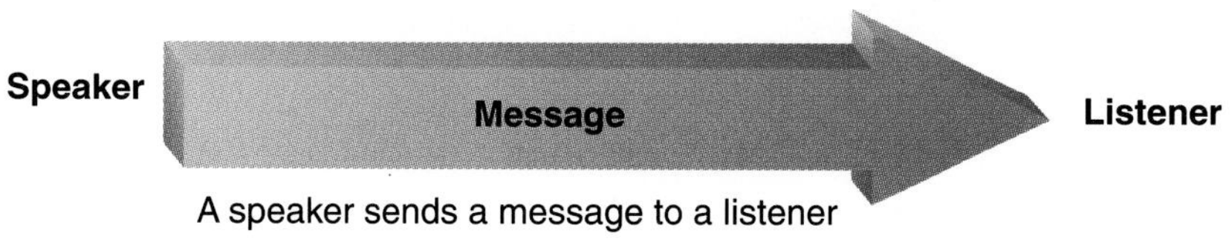

Speaker → Message → Listener

A speaker sends a message to a listener

FIGURE 1.2
Linear model of communication.
Simple, early models of communication depicted a speaker sending a message to a listener.

Interactive Model of Communication

Once communication scholars began to see the limitations of this early linear, three-element model, they began to add other components. Today, the most instructive and widely accepted model of communication has seven elements. To the three elements already mentioned—speaker, message, and listener—we add channel, feedback, environment, and noise. Figure 1.3 illustrates this more complete model of communication.

The first element we need to add is the **channel** or medium, which refers to the way the message is sent. In public speaking, the medium is vibrations in the air between speaker and listener, set in motion by the speaker's voice. The message could also be written in any language, put into some code known to both speaker and listener, tape-recorded or videotaped, put into sign language, translated into Braille, or even sent by smoke signal, among other methods. As you realize, voice and words are not our only media for communication. In fact, communication scholar Albert Mehrabian has estimated that when cues conflict, nonverbal cues are more important than verbal cues in communicating our feelings or attitudes to others. He summarized his research in the following equation:

Total feeling = 7% verbal feeling + 38% vocal feeling + 55% facial feeling[18]

Mehrabian's formula suggests that when you communicate with someone, the majority of the feeling behind your message is carried by visual elements such as facial expression, eye contact, gestures, and movement. More than one-third of your message is carried paralinguistically, that is, by vocal elements such as rate, volume, voice quality, and changes in pitch level. Your actual words carry less than 10 percent of the message

channel: the way a message is sent.

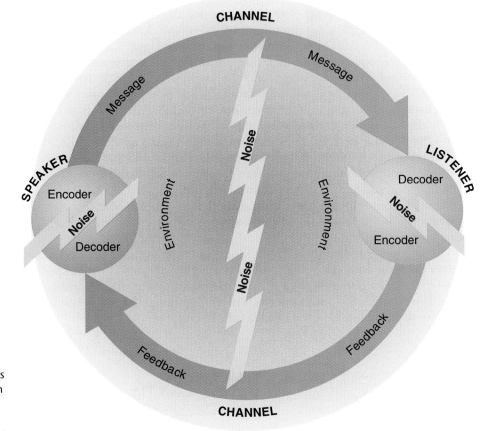

FIGURE 1.3
Interactive model of communication.
A speaker encodes a message, sending it through a channel to a listener, who decodes it. The listener provides feedback, sending it through a channel to a speaker. This interaction takes place in an environment with varying levels of internal and external noise.

Comparing Channels
http://cnn.com/
ALLPOLITICS/1996/
analysis/back.time/9610/
03/index.shtml
For an interesting example
of the impact that different
channels of communica-
tion can have, read the
brief *Time* article on this
page. Written just after the
first televised presidential
debate in October 1960, it
compares the responses of
radio listeners and television viewers and discusses
the immediate effects on
the Kennedy and Nixon
campaigns.

about how you feel. As a public speaker, you must learn to manipulate and control all three of these channels: visual, vocal, and verbal. As you can see, public speaking, like every other level of communication, is more complicated than just saying the right words.

A second element added to that preliminary model of communication is feedback. **Feedback** includes all messages, verbal and nonverbal, sent by listeners to speakers. If you tell a joke, your listeners will tell you through vocal (laughter), verbal, and visual feedback whether they understood the joke and how they evaluated it. If you are paying attention, you will know who liked it, who didn't, who hasn't understood it, and who was offended by it. "If you are paying attention" is the particularly important phrase, for, in order to be effective, feedback must be received and interpreted correctly.

Because public speaking is an audience-centered activity, you as speaker must be sensitive to feedback from your audience. Some feedback is deliberate and conscious; some is unintentional and unconscious. But your audience will always provide you with feedback of some kind. If you are paying attention to it, you will know when they appreciate your humor, understand the point you are making, disagree with the position you advocate, or are momentarily confused by something you have said.

Importance of Nonverbal
Communication
http://uts.cc.utexas.edu/
%7Eadgrad/importance.
html
Many people have cited
Mehrabian's formula since
he published it. Visit this
Web page to read a brief
critique of his study and
to get the citation for an
article examining the limitations of Mehrabian's
methodology.

The third element we need to add to make a more accurate model of communication is the **environment.** Two factors shape a communication environment: (1) the occasion during which communication occurs, and (2) the physical setting or site where communication occurs. The occasion refers to the reasons why people have assembled. Circumstances may be serious or festive, planned or spontaneous. Occasions for communication may be as relaxed and informal as a party with friends, as rule-bound as a college debate, or as formal and traditional as a commencement address at a graduation ceremony.

The physical setting for your classroom speeches is probably apparent to you. You know the size of the room and the number of people in the audience. You know whether the seating arrangement is fixed or changeable. You know whether a lectern, a chalkboard, or a computer are available. You know, or will soon discover, potential problems with the room: The table at the front of the room is wobbly; the air seems stuffy about halfway through each class meeting; one of the fluorescent lights flickers. Each of these distracting elements is a form of noise, a fourth element for which any accurate model of communication must account.

Noise is anything that distracts from effective communication, and some form of noise is always present. We will discuss three different forms. First, much noise is **physical;** that is, it occurs in the physical environment in which people are communicating. When we think of noise, we usually think of physical noise: the sounds of traffic, the loud whoosh of an air conditioner or a heater, the voices of people talking and laughing as they pass by your classroom. Some physical noise may not involve a sound at all, however. If your classroom is so cold that you shiver or so hot that you fan yourself, then its temperature is a form of noise. If the lighting in the room is poor, then that form of noise will certainly affect the communication occurring there. If your

feedback: verbal and nonverbal responses between communicators about the clarity or acceptability of messages.

environment: the physical setting and the occasion for communication.

noise: anything that distracts from effective communication.

physical noise: distractions originating in the communication environment.

The mass medium of television allows politicians to share their views with millions of people. That diverse audience may also motivate political candidates to use vague and noncommittal language to avoid alienating different segments of society.

classroom is near a construction site and the heavy, acrid smell of creosote is nauseating you, then that odor is a form of noise. Anything in the immediate environment that interferes with communication is physical noise.

A second type of noise is **physiological:** A bad cold that affects your hearing and speech, a headache, or an empty, growling stomach are examples. Each of these bodily conditions can shift your focus from communicating with others to thinking about how uncomfortable you feel, a form of intrapersonal communication.

A third and final type of noise is **psychological.** This type of noise refers to mental rather than bodily distractions. Anxiety, worry, daydreaming, and even joy over some recent event can distract you from the message at hand. Each of these forms of noise—physical, physiological, and psychological—can occur independently or in combination, and as we have said, some form of noise is always present. Music lovers continually search for better audio equipment—a compact disc player, for example—to reduce the noise involved in playing recorded music. As a speaker, you must make similar efforts to minimize the effects of noise in public communication: by varying your rate, volume, and pitch, for example, or through lively physical delivery that combats noise and rivets the audience's attention to your message.

As the interactive model of communication suggests, public speaking is a complex activity. Although we can identify the seven different elements of the communication process, we cannot assess them in isolation. Contemporary scholars emphasize the transactional nature of the communication process: Each component simultaneously influences, and is influenced by, the others. Speech communication scholar Karlyn Kohrs Campbell depicts this dynamic relationship when she writes:

> Ideas do not walk by themselves; they must be carried—expressed and voiced—by someone. As a result, we do not encounter ideas neutrally, objectively, or apart from a context; we meet them as *someone's* ideas.[19]

physiological noise: distractions originating in the bodies of communicators.

psychological noise: distractions originating in the thoughts of communicators.

Part of mastering public speaking begins with basic skills: organizing a presentation with an identifiable introduction, body, and conclusion; providing previews, summaries, and transitions; deciding whether the oral message needs the support of visual aids; and using appropriate grammar, pronunciation, and articulation.[20] To design, develop, and deliver a speech that is appropriate to you, your audience, and the communication context requires some higher-order thinking, however. Public speaking involves choices, and to choose appropriately you must sharpen your thinking skills.

The Public Speaker as Critical Thinker

We began this chapter by discussing benefits you gain from studying and practicing public speaking. One of those benefits is that public speaking not only uses but also *develops* your critical thinking ability. **Critical thinking** is "reasonable reflective thinking that is focused on deciding what to believe or do."[21] Is it important? If you are perfectly satisfied with your daily routine, with dealing with others in relative isolation, and with accepting the obvious without question, then critical thinking may seem unimportant to you. If, however, you have ever questioned obvious answers you were offered, viewed yourself as part of a larger group, looked for patterns you thought no one else had noticed, or followed a hunch to solve a problem in your own way, you have already begun to cultivate your critical thinking ability.[22] You probably also recognize its importance to your personal and professional life.

> In a world overloaded with information, both a business and a personal advantage will go to those individuals who can sort the wheat from the chaff, the important from the trivial. . . . Quality of life is directly tied to our ability to think clearly amid the noise of modern life, to sift through all that competes for our attention until we find what we value, what will make our lives worth living.[23]

Drawing from the works of Stuart Rankin and Carolyn Hughes, Robert Marzano and his colleagues have identified eight categories of critical thinking skills. As a public speaker you will exercise all of these as you develop and deliver your speech.

This skill . . .	enables you to . . .
Focusing	Define problems, set goals, and select pieces of information
Information Gathering	Formulate questions and collect data
Remembering	Store information in long-term memory and retrieve it
Organizing	Arrange information so that it can be understood and presented more effectively
Analyzing	Clarify existing information by examining parts and relationships
Generating	Use prior knowledge to infer and elaborate new information and ideas
Integrating	Combine, summarize, and restructure information
Evaluating	Establish criteria and assess the quality of ideas[24]

You *focus* when you select your topic, narrow it to key points, and set goals for your speech. You *gather information* to develop your speech content. From your research, you determine your key ideas and how you will support them. You *remember* as you call up information stored in your memory that may be relevant to your topic. You also exercise these skills when you practice with a set of speaking notes, relying on key words to trigger your ideas and explanations.

critical thinking: the logical, reflective examination of information and ideas to determine what to believe or do.

You *organize* as you outline your key ideas and develop the introduction, body, and conclusion of your speech in a logical way. Throughout the speech-making process, you must *analyze.* You interpret your audience's needs and values; you identify key points from the research you've collected; and you select supporting materials that contribute to sound reasoning.

You use *generating* skills when you brainstorm a list of possible speech topics, when you draw conclusions from your evidence, and when you predict the effects of what you propose. You *integrate* when you synthesize your ideas and supporting material to reinforce your specific purpose, and when you summarize your speech for your listeners. Finally, you *evaluate* when you assess the validity of what you say and your effectiveness in saying it.

Consider the way one student applied these eight skills in developing a particular speech. Wanda's first assignment in her public speaking class was to prepare and deliver a speech about someone she admired. She immediately began *generating* a list of names: her mother, who held down two jobs to help raise five children; a high school teacher who inspired Wanda to go to college; Coretta Scott King, First Lady of the Civil Rights Movement; and Thurgood Marshall, the first African American to serve on the U.S. Supreme Court. Wanda was a high school student when Marshall died in 1992, and she recalled how his commitment to justice for all was one of the reasons she decided to become a prelaw major. So Wanda decided to *focus* her speech on Marshall.

She devised a research plan and began to *gather information. Remembering* the moving tributes following Marshall's death, Wanda located some of these articles and also found several books about him.

She *analyzed* her audience, the occasion, and the information she had collected, and began to focus her speech further. Wanda decided that a biography of Marshall's life was far too encompassing for a three- to five-minute speech. She also chose not to discuss his more controversial decisions on abortion and capital punishment. Rather, she *organized* her key ideas and *integrated* her supporting materials around two central images: closed doors and open doors.

First, she would describe some of the doors closed to African Americans during much of Marshall's life: equal education, housing, public transportation, and voting. She would recount that Marshall, the great-grandson of a slave, was denied admission to the University of Maryland Law School.

Second, she would tell how Marshall fought to open these doors by expanding access to housing, public transportation, and voting. And she would, of course, note that it was Marshall who successfully argued the *Brown v. Board of Education of Topeka* case (1954) which declared racial segregation in public schools unconstitutional. She would conclude her story by observing that it was Marshall who litigated the admission of the first African American to graduate from the University of Maryland Law School. Wanda *evaluated* each of these examples as she prepared her speech to ensure that her ideas were well supported.

As she constructed her speaking notes, Wanda used only a brief outline to help her *remember* her ideas. And after delivering her speech, she *evaluated* her speaking strengths and weaknesses to help her improve her next speech.

Wanda obviously cared about developing an interesting, accurate speech and delivering it well. But is it necessary to *care* in order to think critically? Educator Barbara Thayer-Bacon states that position forcefully:

> Caring is a necessary characteristic of critical thinkers for ideas and arguments do not have a life of their own; they are generated by people and critical thinking is an activity performed by people. *What* a knower brings to the knowing and *how* a knower relates to the knowing is as important as the knowing itself.[25]

Caring helps us both as speakers and as listeners. Caring means "being receptive to what another has to say, and open to hearing the other's voice more completely and fairly" than we otherwise might.[26] The fact that you are reading this sentence—so close to the end of the chapter—is evidence that you care to expose yourself to all of our message, that you care about being able to answer any exam question about this chapter, or both. The critical thinker is, then, a person who cares enough to be reasonable and to think clearly. These abilities can help overcome prejudices and foster a community of caring, careful thinkers in your classroom. We can't imagine a better climate in which to exercise your critical thinking as you study the remainder of this textbook and put its principles into action.

Summary

Public speaking offers personal, professional, and public benefits for the individual. On a personal level, public speaking teaches you skills you can use in other courses of study. It is also an active form of learning and can increase your retention of information. Finally, gaining public speaking skills and experience will build your confidence and self-esteem. On a professional level, public speaking is an important form of communication, and excellent communication skills increase your chances of getting the job you want and advancing in it. On a public level, public speaking binds people into groups and propels social movements and social change.

We may view *communication* as either a process or a product, but the most accurate definition of the term probably includes both perspectives. Effective communication is the sharing of meaning by sending and receiving symbolic cues.

Public communication, the focus of this textbook, is one of five levels of communication. *Intrapersonal communication* refers to the communication we do with ourselves individually. *Interpersonal communication* is that carried out between pairs of people. *Group communication* involves three or more people communicating for some purpose and with a clear sense that they belong together. *Public communication* occurs when one person speaks face to face with an audience, either large or small. *Mass communication* involves one person communicating to a large audience through some print or electronic medium. These five levels of communication are differentiated by the numbers of people involved, the direction of communication flow, and the opportunities for audience feedback.

Terms to be used throughout this book include seven components of communication. The *speaker* or sender is the person originating and encoding the *message,* the ideas communicated. The *listener* is the person receiving and decoding the message. The *channel* or medium of communication is the way the message is sent. Public speaking involves verbal, vocal, and visual channels. *Feedback* refers to all verbal and nonverbal responses from listener to speaker, either intentional or unintentional. The *environment* includes the speaking occasion and the setting where communication occurs. Finally, *noise* is the name given to anything that interferes with communication. Noise can be physical (environmental), physiological (bodily), or psychological (mental).

The process of developing and delivering a public speech requires you to sharpen and use eight categories of critical thinking skills. You use *focusing* skills as you select your speech topic and narrow it to key points. You use *information gathering* skills as you conduct research, identify your key ideas, and decide how you will support them. You use *remembering* skills as you tap personal knowledge and experience relevant to your topic and as you practice speaking only from key words and phrases. You use *organizing* skills as you outline your key ideas and develop your speech introduction, body, and conclusion in a logical way.

Throughout the speech-making process, you use *analyzing* skills as you study your audience, your research, your main points, your supporting materials, and the ideas or arguments you develop. As you brainstorm for topic ideas, draw conclusions from your evidence, and predict the effect of what you propose, you are using *generating* skills. You use *integrating* skills as you arrange your supporting material to reinforce your specific purpose and as you summarize your main points for your listeners. Finally, you use *evaluating* skills as you assess the validity of what you say and your effectiveness in saying it. Caring enough to think clearly, to be reasonable, and to remain open to other people's ideas is the quality that activates all of these critical thinking skills. A community of caring and careful listeners is the ideal environment for improving public speaking.

Exercises

1. If your class includes international students, ask them to describe the roles speaking plays in their native cultures. Are students encouraged to speak in class? Or are such behaviors discouraged? Are speaking skills considered more important for one gender than for the other? What differences do international students notice in the speaking skills of U.S. students compared with those of their own nationalities?

2. Select a business or professional person to interview. From this interview, gather information about the importance of oral communication to job performance and career advancement. Specifically, inquire about the value of public speaking skills. Write a brief report on your findings, and discuss in class what you have discovered.

3. Jot down a few of your most embarrassing experiences. Review your list, noting incidents that resulted from a breakdown in communication because you did not share similar referents with someone else. Can you think of other examples of miscommunication based on individuals' having different referents for the same message?

4. List examples of words that trigger referents that are different because of the users' ages, genders, religious experiences, educational backgrounds, political affiliations, economic status, and so forth. Discuss how a speaker could enhance shared meaning in each of these examples.

5. Create a list of careers you are considering. Then write how the different levels of communication may be important to success in each of those careers. Discuss the role that good public speaking skills may play in your career success.

6. Using the interactive model of communication as a guide (Figure 1.3), analyze a lecture given by an instructor in one of your classes. Focus specifically on the listeners and feedback. Was the instructor attentive to the verbal and nonverbal behaviors of the students? If you answer is no, what could the instructor have done to make the communication event more of a two-way experience? If your answer is yes, give examples to illustrate the instructor's attentiveness to student feedback.

7. Find an article in a magazine or journal discussing speech communication in business and professional environments. Write a one-page summary, and attach it to the article.

8. Use the components of communication listed in your text (and any others you wish to add) to design your own model of communication. Draw or construct your own model of communication.

9. Analyze the physical noise present in your classroom. As a listener, how does this affect your reception of your instructor's message? As a speaker, how might you minimize the effect of this noise? If you were redesigning the classroom, what changes would you make to minimize this type of noise?

10. On a sheet of paper make two lists: "My Communication Strengths" and "My Communication Weaknesses." In the first list, indicate those strengths you think will help you in this public speaking course. In the second list, note those weaknesses you would most like to improve in this course. Keep the lists, and refer to

them at the conclusion of this course. What changes would you make to the lists at that time?

 Notes

1. L. Jackson Newell, "Deep Springs College: Loyal to a Fault?," *Deep Springs College* 12 June 1999 <http://www.telluride.cornell.edu/deepsprings/whatis/newell.html>.

2. Jim Doherty, "The Cattle Ranch That Doubles as a School for Doers," *Smithsonian* April 1995: 115–17.

3. Newell.

4. Robert Johnson, "For One Reagan, You Can Get Many Mikki Williamses," *Wall Street Journal* 30 January 1992: A1.

5. "Critical Link between Presentation Skills, Upward Mobility," *Supervision* October 1991: 24.

6. Ernest L. Boyer, *College: The Undergraduate Experience in America* (New York: Harper, 1987) 73.

7. Cited in William E. Arnold and Lynne McClure, *Communication Training and Development,* 2nd ed. (Prospect Heights, IL: Waveland, 1996) 38.

8. *Planning Job Choices: 2000,* 43rd ed. (Bethlehem, PA: National Association of Colleges and Employers, 1999) 20.

9. Jerry L. Winsor, Dan B. Curtis, and Ronald D. Stephens, "National Preferences in Business and Communication Education: II." Speech Communication Association Convention, Marriott Hotel & Marina, San Diego. 26 Nov. 1996: 17.

10. Winsor 11.

11. Roger K. Mosvick and Robert B. Nelson, *We've Got to Start Meeting Like This!* (Glenview, IL: Scott, 1987) 225.

12. This survey was conducted by Communispond, Inc., and is reported in "Executives Say Training Helps Them Speak Better," *Training: The Magazine of Human Resources Development* October 1981: 20–21, 75.

13. James Wyllie, "Oral Communications: Survey and Suggestions," *ABCA [American Business Communication Association] Bulletin* June 1980: 15.

14. Mosvick 224.

15. *The Oxford English Dictionary,* 2nd ed. (Oxford: Clarendon, 1989) 577.

16. Thomas M. Scheidel, *Persuasive Speaking* (Glenview, IL: Scott, 1967) 2.

17. C. K. Ogden and I. A. Richards, *The Meaning of Meaning,* 9th ed. (New York: Harcourt, Brace, 1953) 10–12. Chapter 1, "Thoughts, Words and Things" (pp. 1–23), explains in detail the relationships between symbols, referents, and interpreters.

18. Albert Mehrabian, *Silent Messages: Implicit Communication of Emotions and Attitudes,* 2nd ed. (Belmont, CA: Wadsworth, 1981) 77.

19. Karlyn Kohrs Campbell, *The Rhetorical Act,* 2nd ed. (Belmont, CA: Wadsworth, 1996) 119.

20. National Center for Educational Statistics. *National Assessment of College Student Learning: Identifying College Graduates' Essential Skills in Writing, Speech and Listening, and Critical Thinking.* NCES 95-001. (Washington, DC: GPO, May 1995) 122.

21. Robert Ennis, "A Taxonomy of Critical Thinking Dispositions and Abilities," in *Teaching Thinking Skills: Theory and Practice,* ed. Joan Boykoff Baron and Robert Sternberg (New York: Freeman, 1987) 10.

22. June Stark, "Critical Thinking: Taking the Road Less Traveled," *Nursing 95* November 95: 55.

23. National Assessment of Educational Progress. *Reading, Writing and Thinking: Results from the 1979–80 National Assessment of Reading and Literature.* Report No. 11–L–01 (Washington, DC: GPO, October 1981) 5.

24. Adapted from Robert J. Marzano, Ronald S. Brandt, Carolyn Sue Hughes, Beau Fly Jones, Barbara Z. Presseisen, Stuart C. Rankin, and Charles Suhor, *Dimensions of Thinking: A Framework for Curriculum and Instruction* (Alexandria, VA: Association for Supervision and Curriculum Development, 1988) 66, 70–112. Copyright © 1988 by ASCD. Reprinted with permission of the publishers.

25. Barbara J. Thayer-Bacon, "Caring and Its Relationship to Critical Thinking," *Educational Theory* Summer 1993: 323. Our emphasis.

26. Thayer-Bacon 325.

Knowledge is not a loose-leaf notebook of facts. Above all, it is a responsibility for the integrity of what we are, primarily of what we are as ethical creatures.

—Jacob Bronowski

The Ethics of Public Speaking

ommercial cartographers will sometimes produce maps into which they have injected symbols representing features that they know do not exist: streets or bodies of water, for example. Why would such professionals, who should certainly value accuracy, place deliberate mistakes in their works? Those who make such intentional errors call them "copyright traps" and use them to establish grounds for legal action if other cartographers copy the maps without permission.[1] This unusual practice emphasizes the value both of the original work and of the reputations of people producing it. Unlike these mapmakers, who produce printed or electronic maps, you as a classroom public speaker will produce a product that leaves no permanent record, except possibly in the memories of some of your listeners. Nevertheless, the speeches you deliver will reflect your originality, the creativity of your critical thinking, and your credibility. Your work will have a unique value that depends in large part on your own reputation.

In Chapter 1 we observed that ideas cannot be separated from the people who voice them. Everything you do or say affects the credibility your audience assigns you; that credibility in turn affects the believability of your ideas. Of course, as important as the *perceived* credibility you have with various audiences is the *actual* credibility of your character. Whether you speak to inform or to persuade, one of your goals as a speaker, in this class and beyond, should be to make choices that develop and maintain your integrity.

As you strive to develop the individual skills described in the chapters of this text, keep in mind that your goal in mastering public speaking is not simply to develop those skills as ends in themselves, but to use them to serve the various audiences that you may face throughout your life. Effective and ethical public speakers understand and respect their audiences. They demonstrate this respect by entering into and honoring an unwritten contract with their listeners. Terms of this contract require that audience members listen expecting to learn, that they listen without prejudging you or your ideas, and that, ultimately, they evaluate the messages you present to them and provide feedback. As a speaker, you assume responsibility for being well prepared, communicating ideas clearly in order to benefit the audience, and remaining open to feedback that will help you improve as a speaker. In this chapter we focus on these mutual responsibilities as we examine issues related to ethical speaking and listening and to plagiarism. Because each speech you make will reveal aspects of your personality and your values, you should study and consider these issues before even planning your first speech.

Definition of Ethics

It is virtually impossible to read a newspaper or listen to a newscast today without encountering the topic of ethics. We hear of politicians selling out to special interest groups, stockbrokers engaged in insider trading, laboratories charging Medicare millions of dollars for blood tests doctors never ordered, contractors taking shortcuts in construction projects, and college officials illegally recruiting student athletes. We read stories of people who agonized over the decision to allow, and in some cases even to help, a terminally ill loved one to die. We watch news clips of rallies and demonstrations by constituents accusing their elected officials of abusing the public trust. Society is so concerned with unethical behavior that many professions even include the term *ethics* as a component: We have all heard of medical ethics, business ethics, bioethics, journalistic ethics, environmental ethics, and so forth.

When we talk about **ethics,** we are referring to the standards we use to determine right from wrong, or good from bad, in thought and behavior. Television's fictional Frasier Crane has offered a surprisingly serious and useful definition: "Ethics is what you do when no one is looking."[2] Our sense of ethics guides the choices we make in all aspects of our professional and private lives. You should not be surprised that your aca-

ethics: standards used to discriminate between right and wrong, good and bad, in thought and action.

demic studies include a discussion of ethics. You are, after all, educating yourself to function in a world where you will make ethical decisions daily. You may be surprised to learn, however, that colleges throughout the United States offer more than 11,000 courses in ethics.[3] In Chapter 1, we established the importance of speech communication in our lives. We will now examine why it is important for you to ensure that you communicate ethically.

Principles of Ethics

In discussing communication ethics, Donald Smith notes that "speaking skill is frequently studied as an ethically neutral instrument. . . ." He compares communication skills to the skill of shooting a rifle. It is not wrong to practice your marksmanship shooting skeet; ethical concerns arise, however, when your target is another human being. "From this point of view," Smith writes, "speaking skill per se is neither good nor bad. The skill can be used by good persons or bad persons. It can be put to the service of good purposes [or] bad purposes. . . ."[4] In this course you will learn fundamental communication skills that will empower you as both a speaker and a listener, just as the act of picking up a gun empowers an individual. How you exercise these skills will involve ethical choices and responsibilities.

Two principles frame our discussion of ethics. First, *we contend that all parties in the communication process have ethical responsibilities.* Assume, for example, that one of your instructors had been denied promotion or a requested leave of absence or had some other reason for holding a grudge against your college administrators. Assume as well that this instructor, without revealing his or her true motives, used class time to provoke and anger you about inadequate parking or poor food quality in the student center at your school, then led you across campus to take the school president hostage, barricade yourselves in the administration building, and tear up the place.

Anyone who knew the facts of this case would agree that the instructor acted unethically; it is wrong to manipulate people by keeping your true motives hidden from

From SHRINK WRAP, collected cartoons by P. S. Mueller © 1991. Reprinted by permission.

them. Yet we contend that any students who let themselves be exploited by participating in such a violent and destructive episode would also share ethical responsibility for what happened. College students, no matter what their age, know that their actions have consequences. As this outlandish example demonstrates, all parties involved in communication share ethical obligations.

In spite of this, public speaking textbooks often discuss ethics only from a speaker's perspective, presenting ethical standards as a list of dos and don'ts for the sender of the message. Certainly, a speaker has ethical responsibilities, but a speaker-centered approach to ethics is incomplete. Communication, as we suggest throughout this textbook, is an activity shared by both the speaker and listener. As such, both parties have ethical responsibilities. For that reason, we will discuss the ethics of speaking and listening.

Second, *we contend that ethical speakers and listeners possess attitudes and standards that pervade their character and guide their actions before, during, and after their speaking and listening.* In other words, ethical speakers and listeners do more than just abstain from unethical behaviors. Ethics is as much a frame of mind as it is a pattern of behavior. Ethics is not something you apply to one speech; it is a working philosophy you apply to your daily life and bring to all speaking situations. Consider the actions of the speaker in the following incident that one of us witnessed in a classroom.

> Lisa presented a persuasive speech on the need for recycling paper, plastic, and aluminum products. To illustrate the many types of recyclables and how overpackaged many grocery products are, she used as an effective visual aid a paper grocery bag filled with empty cans, paper products, and a variety of plastic bottles and containers. After listening to her well-researched, well-delivered speech, with its impassioned final appeal for us to help save the planet by recycling, the class watched in amazement as she put the empty containers back in the bag, walked to the corner of the room, and dropped the bag in the trash can! After a few seconds, someone finally asked the question that had to be asked: "You mean you're not going to take those home to recycle them?" "Nah," said Lisa. "I'm tired of lugging them around. I've done my job."

You may or may not believe that people have an ethical responsibility to recycle. But regardless of your views on that issue, you likely question the ethics of someone who insists, in effect, "Do as I say, not as I do." Lisa's actions made the entire class question the sincerity with which she spoke. Ethical standards cannot be turned on and off at an individual's convenience.

Ethical Speaking

Maintaining strong ethical attitudes and standards requires sound decision making at every step in the speech-making process. In this section we present seven guidelines to help you with these decisions.

Speak Up about Topics You Consider Important

First, ethical public speakers make careful decisions about whether or not to speak. In many public discussions outside of the classroom, silence is often an option, and if the issue is trivial, it is sometimes the best option. There are times, though, when people have an ethical obligation to convey information or when they feel strongly about an issue or an injustice. *Ethical communicators speak up about topics they consider important.* Our nation's history has been shaped by the voices of Thomas Jefferson, Frederick Douglass, Susan B. Anthony, Martin Luther King, Jr., Cesar Chavez, and other advocates. That shaping continues today in the voices of Jesse Jackson, Marian Wright Edelman, Colin Powell, and Elie Wiesel, among many others. You may not have the impact of those famous speakers, but you do have an opportunity to better the communities of which you are a part. This class provides you with an opportunity to share information your classmates can use to help them get more from their college experience or to help them function better in their careers and personal lives. You also have a chance to educate others about problems you feel need to be confronted. We remember one student who showed special sensitivity in addressing a topic she opposed on ethical grounds.

Pam, a sophomore public relations major, had been an animal welfare advocate for a long time, but she knew from class discussions and conversations before class that a number of her classmates hunted for sport or for food. She realized that if she turned her ten-minute persuasive speech into a general sermon against killing animals she would only make a number of her classmates feel defensive. She wanted to speak on some aspect of animal welfare but knew she had to narrow and focus the topic.

As a volunteer worker for several animal protection agencies, Pam had become aware of the problems associated with the use of steel leg-hold traps. Inside city limits, they posed a threat to pets, children, and adults who did not know where they had been set. She also opposed their use in the wilderness because, she said, they inflict pain and suffering and kill nontarget animals. Pam delivered a well-documented speech to persuade her listeners that the use of these traps should be outlawed. Her carefully worded thesis was not that killing animals is wrong, but that use of this particular trap is cruel and inhumane. She even discussed two other types of traps as humane alternatives. The class listened intently to Pam, and toward the end of the speech she was gratified to see that many of her classmates, hunters included, were nodding in apparent agreement with her.

Much of your speaking in this class and later in life may not be on significant social or political issues. Yet this class provides you with the training ground to hone your skills as speaker and listener. Use these skills as you move from involvement in class and campus issues to improvement of your community.

> *A speech is a solemn responsibility. The man who makes a bad thirty-minute speech to 200 people wastes only a half hour of his own time. But he wastes 100 hours of the audience's time—more than four days—which should be a hanging offense.*
>
> *—Jenkin Lloyd Jones*

Concentration camp survivor Elie Wiesel often warns his listeners about the implications of indifference to genocide, and, in doing so, acts as a public conscience for society.

Choose Topics That Promote Positive Ethical Values

Second, *ethical speakers choose topics that promote positive ethical values*. Selecting a topic is one of the first ethical choices you will make as a speaker. Unless you are assigned a topic, you can choose from a wide range of subjects. In a real sense, you give your topic credibility simply by selecting it. As an ethical speaker, your choice should reflect what you think is important for your audience.

In the course we teach, many student speeches have expanded our knowledge or moved us to act on significant issues. But consider this list of informative speech topics:

How to get a fake I.D.

How to "walk" (avoid paying) a restaurant check

How to get a faculty parking permit

How to beat police radar

How to get out of a speeding ticket

We have heard speeches on each of these topics. Even though they were informative rather than persuasive speeches, each of these how-to topics implies that its action is acceptable. We do not know why students chose these topics, but we suggest that all of those speakers disregarded their listeners, failed to consider the values they were promoting, and presented unethical speeches.

Speak to Benefit Your Listeners

Third, *ethical public speakers communicate in order to benefit their listeners*. Speakers and listeners participate in a transactional relationship; both should benefit from their participation. As the Jones quotation on page 27 suggests, listeners give speakers their time; speakers should provide information that is interesting or useful in return.

You may often speak for personal benefit, and this is not necessarily unethical. You may, for instance, speak to a group, urging them to support you for president of the student body. There is nothing wrong with pursuing such personal goals, but ethical speakers do not try to fulfill personal needs at the expense of their listeners. As one popular book on business ethics states, "There is no right way to do a wrong thing."[5] Speakers whose objective is to persuade, for example, should do so with the goal of benefiting both the audience and themselves. Even informative speakers have an ethical obligation to benefit their audiences. Here's an example of how this can work in your public speaking class.

Assigned to give an informative speech demonstrating a process or procedure, plant lover Evelyn decided to show how to plant a seed in a pot. Her instructor, who had asked students to write down their topic choices, was privately worried that this subject was something everyone already knew about. Evelyn was, after all, speaking to college students who presumably could read the planting instructions on the back of a seed packet. The instructor did not want to discourage Evelyn but wanted the class to benefit from her speech.

Without saying, "You cannot speak on this topic," the instructor shared her concerns with Evelyn. She found out that Evelyn had several other plant-related topics in mind. Evelyn agreed that a more unusual topic would be more interesting to the class and more challenging for her to deliver. On the day she was assigned to speak, Evelyn presented an interesting speech demonstrating how to propagate tropical plants by "air layering" them. Evelyn got a chance to demonstrate her green thumb, and her classmates learned something most had never heard of before.

Notice how Evelyn finally paid attention to her audience. At her teacher's suggestion, she rejected the simple, familiar topic that would probably not have taught her audience anything.

Use Truthful, Accurate Supporting Material and Valid Reasoning

Fourth, *ethical speakers use truthful, accurate supporting materials and valid reasoning.* Listeners have a right to know not only the speaker's ideas but also the material supporting those claims. Ethical speakers are well informed and should thus test their ideas for validity and support. They should not knowingly use false information or faulty reasoning. Unlike the commercial cartographers we mentioned at the beginning of this chapter, they should not deliberately include false information in their speeches. Yet we sometimes witness students presenting incomplete or out-of-date material, as in this example:

> Janet presented an informative speech on the detection and treatment of breast cancer. Her discussion of the disease's detection seemed thorough, but when she got to her second point, she said that the only treatments were radical mastectomy, partial mastectomy, radiation therapy, and chemotherapy. She failed to mention lumpectomy, a popular surgical measure often combined with radiation or chemotherapy. Her bibliography revealed that her research stopped with sources published in the early 1980s, explaining the gap in her speech content.

Janet did not necessarily act unethically; she was simply uninformed and ended up being embarrassed. But what if Janet had known of the lumpectomy procedure and had just not wanted to do further research to find out about it? Then we would question her ethics.

In this case, certain listeners did not notice the factual errors and the lapses in content while others did. Not getting caught in a factual or logical error does not free the speaker of ethical responsibility to present complete, factual information. If you speak on a current topic, you need to use the most recent information you can find and to try to be as well informed as possible.

Reveal Your True Motives for Speaking

Fifth, *ethical speakers make their intentions clear to the audience.* In other words, they do not intentionally manipulate the audience. Allan Cohen and David Bradford define manipulation as "actions to achieve influence that would be rendered less effective if the target knew your actual intentions."[6]

We are familiar with one company whose sales strategy certainly matched that definition of manipulation. This company relied on door-to-door salespersons, especially college students, and instructed new employees to make a list of friends who might be interested in purchasing the product. The employees were told to contact these friends and tell them the good news about their new job. The company also coached employees to say that part of the job involves making presentations to potential customers and to ask if they could practice giving their presentation to the friend in order to get some helpful feedback. In addition, because the company wanted to encourage its workers to succeed, employees offered each volunteer "critic" a gift. However, the company also told their salespeople confidentially that the presentations were

Truth and Lies
http://cnn.com/ALLPOLITICS/1997/10/06/back.time/
This site features a thought-provoking 1992 *Time* article by Paul Gray on the relationship between lying and the truth. Gray discusses three types of lies and their place in the "etiquette of lying."

actually a test to see if they could sell the product, and that they should take advantage of these sales opportunities.

We consider this strategy manipulative and unethical. The salespersons made the appointments under false pretenses. The company exploited its employees' friendships; the employees in turn exploited their friends' willingness to be helpful. These helpful critics might not have participated if they knew their friends' real intent. A public speaker may try to inform, convince, persuade, direct, or even anger an audience. Ethical speakers, however, do not deceive their listeners. They are up-front about their intentions, and those intentions include benefiting the audience.

Consider the Consequences of Your Words and Actions

Sixth, *ethical speakers concern themselves with the consequences of their speaking.* Mary Cunningham observed, "Words are sacred things. They are also like hand grenades: Handled casually, they tend to go off."[7] Ethical speakers have a respect for the power of language and the process of communication.

It is difficult to track, let alone to predict, the impact of any one message. Statements you make are interpreted by your immediate audience and may be communicated by those listeners to others. Individuals may form opinions and behave differently because of what you say or what you fail to say. Incorrect information and misinterpretations may have unintended, and potentially harmful, consequences. If you provide an audience with inaccurate information, you may contaminate the quality of their subsequent decisions. If you persuade someone to act in a particular way, you are, in part, responsible for the impact of the person's new action.

Strive to Improve Your Public Speaking

Finally, *ethical speakers strive to improve their public speaking.* Speakers who use the guidelines we have presented accept their obligation to communicate responsibly in the communities of which they are a part. Their ideas have value, are logically supported, and do not deceive their listeners. We would argue, however, that this is not enough.

Ethical speakers are concerned not only with *what* they speak but also with *how* they speak. As a result, they work actively to become more effective communicators. This course provides you with an opportunity to begin mastering public speaking. You will learn how to select, support, evaluate, organize, and deliver your ideas. Your professional and public life beyond the classroom will extend your opportunities to speak publicly. Speakers have "the opportunity to learn to speak well, and to be eloquent [advocates of] truth and justice." If they fail to develop these abilities, they have not fulfilled their "ethical obligation in a free society."[8]

key points

Responsibilities of an Ethical Speaker

1. Speak up about topics you consider important.
2. Choose topics that promote positive ethical values.
3. Speak to benefit listeners.
4. Use truthful, accurate supporting material and valid reasoning.
5. Let the audience know your true motives for speaking.
6. Consider the consequences of your words and actions.
7. Strive to improve your public speaking.

Ethical Listening

The guidelines for ethical speaking we've just discussed probably make perfect sense to you. If some seem intimidating, if you feel that the future of free expression in a democratic society rests squarely on your shoulders, remember that no individual bears such a responsibility alone. Members of your audience also have obligations as ethical listeners, and you share these same four ethical responsibilities as you listen to the speeches of others.

> *A mind that is stretched to a new idea never returns to its original dimension.*
>
> —*Oliver Wendell Holmes*

Seek Exposure to Well-Informed Speakers

The ethics of listening involves four basic principles. First, *ethical listeners seek out speakers who expand their knowledge, increase their understanding, introduce them to new ideas, and challenge their beliefs.* These listeners reject the philosophy, "My mind's made up, so don't confuse me with the facts." A controversial speaker visiting your campus can expand your knowledge or intensify your feelings about a subject, whether you agree or disagree with the speaker's viewpoint. Even in situations in which students are a captive audience for other students' speeches, such as this class, ethical listening should be the standard.

> Ethical Decision Making
> http://www.scu.edu/
> SCU/Centers/Ethics/
> Ethical speakers and listeners should consider the values that shape their decision making. The Markkula Center for Applied Ethics at Santa Clara University is devoted to the study of ethics. The "Practicing Ethics" section of their Web site offers guidelines and resources for ethical problem solving.

Listen without Prejudging Speakers or Their Ideas

Second, *ethical listeners listen openly without prejudging speakers or their ideas.* This may be difficult. Listening without bias requires that we temporarily suspend impressions we have formed from the other person's past actions. But the rewards of doing so can be great, as in this example.

> Linda's first speech in class completely confused her classmates. She seemed nervous and unsure of herself and what she was going to say, and the point of her speech really eluded everyone. Class discussion after the speech focused primarily on Linda's delivery, and some of the distracting mannerisms she exhibited and needed to control. When she went to the front of the room to begin her next speech weeks later, no one was really expecting to be impressed. But they were.
>
> Linda's second speech dealt with the problem of homelessness. Her opening sentence told the class that three years before she had been living on the street for a time. She had their attention from that point on. In addition to citing recent newspaper and magazine articles, Linda had conducted a great deal of original research. She had interviewed the directors of local shelters and a number of the homeless people who took refuge there, and she quoted these individuals. Her speech was well organized and well delivered. It was both educational and inspiring.
>
> When discussing the speech later, classmates kept referring to her first speech and noting the remarkable improvements Linda had made. One person was blunt, but apparently summed up the feelings of a number of listeners that day: "Linda, I wasn't expecting much from you because your first speech was so unclear to me, but today you had a topic that you obviously care about, and you made us understand and care about it, too. I can't get over the difference between those two speeches!"

When listening to your classmates, you should assume that you may learn something important from each speaker and therefore listen intently. Information and ideas are best shared in such an atmosphere of mutual respect.

Evaluate the Speaker's Logic and Credibility

Listening eagerly and openly does not imply a permanent suspension of evaluation, however. A third standard is that *ethical listeners evaluate the messages presented to them.* A listener who accepts a premise without evaluating its foundation is like someone who buys a used car without looking under the hood. The warning "let the buyer beware" is good advice not only for consumers of products but also for consumers of messages. As a listener, you should critically evaluate the ideas of the speaker. Is each idea logically constructed? Is each supported with evidence that is relevant, sufficient, and authoritative?

Ethical speakers and listeners read and listen critically. To see how some students listen more critically than others, consider the example of the following persuasive speaker.

> Sharon presented a speech arguing that all of the problems high school students face today—drug use, gang violence, teenage pregnancy, lack of discipline in class, academic failure—resulted from the Supreme Court decision that ended prayer in school. She had two primary supporting materials: quotations from a local religious leader and a comparison of school conditions in the 1950s with conditions in the 1990s.
>
> Sharon argued her case with a great deal of conviction. As she spoke, many listeners indicated agreement with her by nodding their heads and looking concerned. But after her speech, several students asked, "Sharon, aren't there other differences between schools in the '50s and the '90s? There are more students today and more peer pressure. Drugs that were not even known in the '50s are readily available today. Could it be that teachers in the '50s expected more of students than they do today?" Finally one student said, "I personally agree with you. I think prayer or at least a moment of silence for voluntary prayer might encourage students to be more reverent or thoughtful. But you haven't proved to me that all of these problems you mentioned are a direct result of lack of school prayer. There's a logical flaw in your speech."

Whether offered a product, an idea, or a proposed course of action, ethical listeners evaluate critically.

Beware of the Consequences of Not Listening Carefully

Fourth, *ethical listeners concern themselves with the consequences of their listening.* As the following example illustrates, listeners who assimilate only part of a public speaker's message because they fail to listen actively are responsible for the distorted message that results.

> Hank listened to his classmate Jeff deliver a speech about problems with their college's registration procedures. As Jeff spoke, Hank remembered problems he had encountered: long lines, inconvenient registration times, filled classes. At one point Hank heard Jeff talking about experimental phone registration the school was offering next semester to students with last names beginning from A to L. At the next class meeting, Hank said to Jeff, "I called the registrar's office yesterday to register by phone. They asked for my last name. When I said it was Thompson,

Assessing the Effects of Ethics
http://www.people-press.org/trustrpt.htm
Visit this site administered by the Pew Research Center for the People and the Press to read their report on how Americans perceive the ethics of elected officials. "Deconstructing Distrust: How Americans View Government" discusses how these perceptions have changed since 1964.

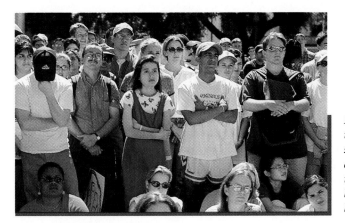

Ethical listening involves thinking critically about a speaker's message. How often do you make a conscious effort to evaluate the meaning and logic behind the messages you hear and read each day?

they told me phone registration this semester was only for students with last names beginning from A to L." "I told you that in my speech," Jeff said. "Weren't you listening?"

Hank may have been embarrassed, but he did not suffer greatly as a result of not listening carefully to Jeff. In other cases, however, the consequences of not listening are more serious. When you fail to listen to someone's directions and are late for an interview, you miss an employment opportunity. In both of these examples, the listener, not the speaker, bears responsibility for the breakdown in communication.

Checking Fairness in News Reporting
http://www.fair.org/whats-fair.html
Interested in journalistic ethics? Visit this Web site maintained by Fairness and Accuracy in Reporting (FAIR) for critiques of the stories you may be getting in mainstream media. A media watch group, FAIR works aggressively to highlight bias and censorship in establishment media and to advocate greater diversity in the press.

At other times, listener and speaker may share responsibility for unethical behavior. For example, audience members who become victims of "scams" because they did not listen critically share with the speaker responsibility for their behavior. Voters who tolerate exaggerated, vague, and inconsistent campaign statements from those who ask to represent them similarly become part of the problem and not the solution.

Most of us begin learning ethical principles as children: "It's wrong to lie." "It's wrong to deceive others." "It's wrong to blame others for what we say and do." In the past, views of communication ethics implied a dotted line across the front of a classroom, with ethics being solely the speaker's responsibility. In contrast, we view ethics as a shared responsibility of the speaker and each listener. An absence of ethical motives among speakers and listeners devalues the currency of communication. Two aspects of ethics, however, do begin as the speaker's responsibility: understanding fair use guidelines and avoiding plagiarism. These two topics deserve special attention.

Responsibilities of an Ethical Listener

1. Seek exposure to well-informed speakers.
2. Listen openly, without prejudging the speaker or the speaker's ideas.
3. Evaluate the logic and credibility of the speaker's ideas.
4. Beware of the consequences of not listening carefully.

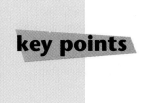

key points

Fair Use Guidelines

If the person behind the counter in a copy shop has ever made you feel like a criminal for asking to have a magazine or journal article copied—never mind a few pages or photographs from a book—you have experienced one of the quirks of copyright law. The copy shop operates to make a profit; you probably don't have any commercial use of the material in mind. "[A] nonprofit educational institution may copy an entire article from a journal for students in a class as a fair use; but a commercial copyshop would need permission for the same copying."[9] As a result, the person behind the print shop counter may direct you to a self-service copy machine, where you assume full responsibility for respecting copyright law. That law places restrictions on uses of copyrighted materials but also grants you important rights to specific uses of them. Section 107 of the Copyright Law of the United States, commonly called the **"fair use provision,"** says that the fair use of a copyrighted work— "including such use by reproduction in copies or phonorecords or by any other means . . . , for purposes such as criticism, comment, news reporting, teaching (including multiple copies for classroom use), scholarship, or research—is not an infringement of copyright."[10]

The law also specifies four factors to consider in determining whether your specific use of copyrighted material is fair. The law is ambiguous and can vary depending upon the specific nature of the work you wish to use. We are not lawyers and cannot offer assurances that will apply to every case. However, attorney Georgia Harper, copyright expert and manager of the intellectual property section of the General Counsel's office for The University of Texas system, has translated these four factors into rules of thumb that "describe a 'safe harbor' within the bounds of fair use."[11] If you are planning to use any copyrighted material in a speech, ask the following four questions:

Fair Use
http://www.utsystem.edu/ogc/inellectualproperty/copypol2.htm
Georgia Harper, copyright and intellectual property expert, offers the most comprehensive discussion of fair use that we have found online. In addition to covering the four factors of fair use, she discusses special issues such as performing, digitizing, and electronically storing copyrighted materials for use in face-to-face teaching and distance learning. The site includes links to guidelines and reports by other groups.

- *What is the character of the use I plan?* If your intended use is personal, educational, or nonprofit, chances are it is fair use. Use of copyrighted material for purposes of criticism, commentary, or even parody also weighs in favor of fair use.

- *What is the nature of the work I plan to use?* Use of a published work that merely reports facts weighs in favor of fair use. You need to seek permission, however, if you are planning to use an unpublished, creative work, such as a story or poem.

- *How much of the work do I plan to use?* Noncommerical use of a small portion of a copyrighted work—or even more than a small portion—likely qualifies as fair use. Commercial uses that exceed strict length limits, however, require permissions.

- *If the use I plan were widespread, what effect would it have on the market value of the original?* This question can become particularly important if you use copyrighted material in a presentation that is preserved electronically or transmitted by electronic means for distance learning.[12]

fair use provision: section of U.S. copyright law allowing limited noncommercial use of copyrighted materials for teaching, criticism, scholarship, research, or commentary.

Using these guidelines can help ensure that your use of copyrighted material in a speech is fair. Note, though, that the fair use provision does *not* give you the right to use another's work without crediting that person. Unattributed use—even fair use—of someone else's work leaves you open to charges of plagiarism, an issue that seems to grow more important in these days of cut-and-paste Internet research.

Plagiarism

The word *plagiarize* comes from a Latin word meaning "to kidnap," so in a sense a plagiarist is a kidnapper of the ideas and words of another. A modern definition of **plagiarism** is "literary—or artistic or musical—theft. It is the false assumption of authorship: the wrongful act of taking the product of another person's mind, and presenting it as one's own."[13]

You must renounce imagination forever if you hope to succeed in plagiarism. Forgery is intention, not invention.

—Horace Walpole

When you write a paper and submit it to a teacher, you are in effect publishing that work. If, in that paper, you copy something from another source and pass it off as your own work, you are plagiarizing. This act is such a serious offense that in most colleges and universities it is grounds for failing the course or even for dismissal from the school. Yet recent history has shown us numerous examples of politicians, educators, and other public figures caught plagiarizing materials, either consciously or unconsciously. An offense serious enough to derail a candidate's campaign for office, to force the resignation of a corporate officer, or to end a student's academic career certainly deserves the attention of students in a public speaking class.

Your manuscript is both good and original; but the part that is good is not original, and the part that is original is not good.

—Samuel Johnson

Just as you publish the paper you write and submit to your teacher, when you deliver a speech in this class or on any other occasion you are also "publishing" your material. Even without putting your words in print or placing a copyright notice on them, you hold the copyright on your ideas expressed in your own words. The current copyright law is interpreted to say, "Even if a speech has merely been delivered orally and not [formally] published, it is subject to copyright protection and may not be used without written permission."[14] Plagiarism of well-known speeches or speakers is both unethical and foolish, as the following example shows.

> Some years ago one of us judged a high school speech tournament event that called upon contestants to speak to entertain. Even though the contest rules stipulated that the speech must be the student's original work, one student copied virtually his entire speech word for word from a George Carlin concert recording. Of course, that blatant plagiarism, noted by several judges, led to the student's prompt disqualification from the competition.

As we have said, repeating a joke a friend tells you is one thing; memorizing and reciting a comedy routine by George Carlin, Caroline Rhea, or Robin Williams is quite another. Repeating distinctive, well-known material as though it were your own may be the most foolish type of plagiarism. No less serious, however, is plagiarizing from obscure sources. If you deliver a speech someone else has researched, organized, and worded, you are presenting another's work as your own. You are plagiarizing.

Plagiarism applies to more than simply the copying of another's words, however. You may also plagiarize another's ideas and organization of material. For example, if you presented a speech organized around the five stages of dying (denial, anger, bargaining, depression, and acceptance) and did not give credit to Elisabeth Kübler-Ross, you would be guilty of plagiarism. On the other hand, if your speech analyzed the

plagiarism: the unattributed use of another's ideas, words, or pattern of organization.

political, economic, and social implications of a pending piece of legislation, you would probably not be guilty of plagiarism. Kübler-Ross developed, explained, and published her framework or model in her book *On Death and Dying,* whereas the second example relies on a commonly accepted pattern of analyzing public policy initiatives. As you can see, the line between legitimate appropriation of material and plagiarism is sometimes unclear. As a speaker, you must always be on guard to credit the source of your ideas and their structure.

As another example of potential plagiarism, suppose a speaker, after reading *Game Plans: Sports Strategies for Business,* selected as his or her specific purpose to explain business management using sports as models. Using three chapter titles from that book, the speaker could word the major ideas of the speech as follows:

   I. Filling Out the Lineup Card (Baseball)
  II. Preparing the Game Plan (Football)
 III. Managing the Flow (Basketball)[15]

Such a speaker would be guilty of plagiarism if he or she did not attribute the ideas to Robert W. Keidel, the author of *Game Plans: Sports Strategies for Business.* Keidel not only supported these ideas, he created them. To avoid plagiarism, the speaker could change the wording of his or her specific purpose: to explain to the audience Robert Keidel's use of sports models for business management. In this way, the speaker clearly attributes the ideas in the speech to Keidel.

As we noted earlier, plagiarism can be intentional or unintentional. **Intentional plagiarism** occurs when speakers or writers knowingly present another person's words, ideas, or organization as their own. **Unintentional plagiarism** is "the careless paraphrasing and citing of source material such that improper or misleading credit is given."[16] Intentional plagiarism is considered the more serious offense. Widespread use of the Internet for research may be blurring the distinction between deliberate and accidental plagiarism, however. Web pages are ephemeral; page content and design can change from one day to the next. That quality, together with the ease of browsing numerous sites in a short time, lets readers pick up phrases, ideas, or even organizational patterns almost unconsciously. If a researcher has not printed, bookmarked, or jotted down the URLs for key sites, retracing steps and finding those sites again may be difficult. Unintentional plagiarism may be committed due to ignorance or sloppy research methods, but the effect is still the same: One person is taking credit for the work of another.

Unintentional plagiarism sometimes occurs because of a common misconception that by simply changing a few words of another's writing you have paraphrased the statement and need not cite it. Michael O'Neill refers to this "hybrid of half textual source, half original writing" as a "paraplage."[17] Note the differences and similarities in the original and adapted passages of the following statement by Peter F. Drucker.

Copyright Violations http://www.benedict.com/ The Copyright Website contains some interesting recent examples of alleged copyright violations in the visual, audio, and digital arts. Enter the site at this address, and then click on the buttons to see and hear these examples, read about the allegations, and discover how they were resolved.

intentional plagiarism: the deliberate, unattributed use of another's ideas, words, or pattern of organization.

unintentional plagiarism: the careless or unconscious, unattributed use of another's ideas, words, or pattern of organization.

Statement by Peter F. Drucker
[T]he Information Revolution has routinized traditional processes in an untold number of areas.

The software for tuning a piano converts a process that traditionally took three hours into one that takes twenty minutes. There is software for payrolls, for inventory control, for delivery schedules, and for all the other routine processes of a business. Drawing the inside arrangements of a major building (heating, water supply, sewerage, and so on) such as a prison or a hospital formerly took, say, twenty-five highly skilled draftsmen up to fifty days; now there is a program that enables one draftsman to do the job in a couple of days, at a tiny fraction of the cost. There is software to help people do their tax returns and software that teaches hospital residents how to take out a gall bladder. The people who now speculate in the stock market online do exactly what their predecessors in the 1920s did while spending hours in a brokerage office. The processes have not been changed at all. They have been routinized, step by step, with a tremendous saving in time and, often, in cost.[18]

Speaker's Paraplage of Peter F. Drucker

The technology of the Information Age has made jobs that once required training and intuition seem almost routine. Tuning a piano no longer takes three hours. Basic knowledge of the computer software for that task makes it a 20-minute job. Architects no longer rely on bands of people spending months drawing plans. Design specifications for a building even as large as a hospital are a two-day job for an individual who knows computer-aided drafting software. Speculators in the stock market now do in minutes online what their ancestors did over many hours in a brokerage firm.

Speaker's Appropriate Citation of Peter F. Drucker

Peter F. Drucker, professor of social science and author of more than 30 books, notes that the Information Revolution has made jobs that once required training and intuition seem almost routine. In an article in the October 1999 issue of *The Atlantic Monthly,* he offers some examples. Tuning a piano no longer takes three hours. Basic knowledge of the computer software for that task makes it a 20-minute job. Architects no longer rely on bands of people spending months drawing plans. Design specifications for a building even as large as a hospital are a two-day job for an individual who knows computer-aided drafting software. Speculators in the stock market now do in minutes online what their ancestors did over many hours in a brokerage firm. In all of these instances, Drucker says, the process is the same, though now routine, quick, and often cost-effective.

Notice that the appropriate citation above not only tells the listener who Peter F. Drucker is, but also explains exactly where his words appeared in print. With that information, any listener wanting to read the entire article could find it quickly.

The ability to paraphrase effectively tests your critical thinking skills of analyzing, integrating, and generating. To improve your paraphrasing, consider the following guidelines from the Purdue University Online Writing Lab.

1. Reread the original passage until you understand it fully.

2. Set the original aside; write your paraphrase on a notecard or on paper or type it into a computer file.

3. Below your paraphrase write a few words to remind you later how you might use this material in your speech. Near your paraphrase write a key word or phrase in all capital letters to indicate its subject.

4. Check your version against the original to make sure that your paraphrase accurately expresses all the essential information in a new form.

5. Use quotation marks to identify any unique terms or phrases you have borrowed exactly from the source.

6. Record the source on your note card so that you can credit it easily if you decide to incorporate the material in your speech.[19]

To avoid plagiarizing, let the following five simple rules guide you.

1. *Take clear and consistent notes while researching.* As you review your notes, you should be able to discern which words, ideas, examples, and organizational structures belong to which authors.

2. *Record complete source citations on each sheet of notes, or write this information on each photocopied article.*

3. *Clearly indicate in your speech any words, ideas, examples, or organizational structures that are not your own.* If you cite a source early in your speech and then use another idea from that author later, you must again give that author credit. You need not, however, repeat the complete citation. The statement "Drucker says" in the appropriate citation of Peter Drucker signals the listener that the speaker is again quoting or paraphrasing his words.

4. *When you paraphrase ideas, credit their originator.* Remember that another's statements are characterized by both content and structure. When paraphrasing, you should use not only your words but also your own language style and thought structure.

5. *When in doubt, cite the source.* At times, you will be unsure whether you need to acknowledge a source. It is always wise to err on the side of caution.

We have discussed some reasons *not* to hide the true authorship of words and ideas. There are also at least two reasons why speakers *should* mention their sources. The first reason may seem self-serving, but it is nevertheless true that speakers who cite their sources increase their credibility or believability with the audience. When you quote from a book, an article, or an interview and name the author or speaker of those words, you show the audience that you have researched the topic and that you know what you are talking about. Second, and far more important, acknowledging your sources is the right thing to do. It is honest. Good ideas and memorably worded thoughts are rare enough that the original writer or speaker deserves credit.

Guidelines to Avoid Plagiarism

1. Take clear and consistent notes while researching.
2. Record complete source citations for notes or photocopied pages.
3. Indicate any quoted material as you deliver the speech.
4. Credit the source of any ideas you paraphrase.
5. Cite the source when in doubt.

Summary

Ethics and plagiarism are topics of concern to students and teachers of public speaking. *Ethics* refers to fundamental questions of right and wrong in thought and behavior. We offer some positive observations on ethics from the viewpoints of both speaker and listener. Ethics is not a standard for acceptable practice that we turn on before speaking and off after the speech is over; it is a value system pervading our lives. We believe that everyone involved in public communication should be guided by the following ethical considerations.

First, ethical speakers choose to speak about topics and issues they consider important. They make the decision to speak out, even when remaining silent might be easier. Second, ethical speakers choose topics that promote positive ethical values.

Third, ethical speakers speak to benefit their listeners, not merely to fulfill their personal needs. Fourth, ethical speakers present audiences with ideas backed by logical reasoning and authentic, up-to-date supporting materials. Fifth, ethical speakers make their intentions clear to their audiences and avoid conscious manipulation. Sixth, ethical speakers care about the consequences their words and actions may have for their listeners. Finally, ethical speakers seek to improve their public speaking.

Listening should be guided by four ethical principles. First, ethical listeners welcome challenges to their beliefs just as they embrace learning. Second, ethical listening means listening openly, without prejudging the speaker's ideas. Third, ethical listeners evaluate the speaker's ideas before acting upon them. Finally, ethical listeners care about and accept responsibility for the consequences of their listening.

Speakers planning to use copyrighted materials in their speeches need to be aware of the *fair use* provisions of copyright law. The four factors to consider in determining whether a particular use is fair are (1) the purpose of your use, (2) the nature of the work you want to use, (3) the quantity of the entire work that you want to use, and (4) the effect that widespread use such as you intend would have on the market value of the work. Both speakers and listeners also need to be aware of the issue of *plagiarism,* the unattributed use of another's ideas, words, or organization. Plagiarism may be either *intentional* or *unintentional.* To avoid plagiarizing sources, speakers should (1) establish a clear and consistent method of notetaking; (2) record a complete source citation on each page of notes or each photocopied article; (3) clearly indicate in the speech any words, ideas, or organizational techniques not their own; (4) orally cite sources for paraphrased, as well as quoted, materials; and (5) when in doubt, acknowledge the source. Careful source citation not only increases a speaker's credibility with the audience but is also ethically right.

Exercises

1. Select two individuals prominent on the international, national, state, or local scene whom you consider ethical speakers. What characteristics do they possess that make them ethical? Select two people you consider unethical. What ethical standards do you think they abuse?

2. Consider the following scenario. State representative Joan Richards is running for a seat in the state senate. She worked hard as a legislator and was voted the best representative by the Better Government League (BGL). The BGL voted her opponent, incumbent Mike Letner, as one of the ten worst senators in the state. Many political analysts think Richards would be the superior senator. Letner has taken a "no new taxes" pledge and has challenged Richards to do the same. Richards personally thinks taxes may have to be raised in order to keep the state solvent. Nevertheless, she knows that unless she promises to oppose any new taxes, she will lose the election. What should Richards do?

3. Answer each of the following questions and be prepared to defend your position.
   a. Should a speech instructor have the right to censor topics students select for their speeches?
   b. Should students have the right to use profanity and obscenity in their speeches in this class?
   c. Should the Ku Klux Klan be allowed to hold a rally on your campus?
   d. Should public prayers be a part of opening ceremonies at athletic contests at publicly supported schools?
   e. Should lawyers defend clients they know are guilty?

4. Find an article on any subject written by an expert. Summarize the article in one or two paragraphs. Use appropriate source citation, paraphrasing, and quotations to avoid plagiarism.

5. Suppose you read an article by a noted medical expert. The author reports a study supporting your claim that the shortage of nurses is a serious problem. She begins her next paragraph, though, with the statement, "However, there are several significant limitations to this study, not the least of which is sample size." Should you present just the researcher's initial claim and make your case seem stronger, or should you acknowledge the study's limitations?

6. Some public access cable television stations have caused controversy by airing programs that show how to make explosives or how to jam automatic teller machines. Are such messages, which could harm individuals or lead them to crime, ethical? Is it ethical to suppress this kind of speech?

7. In researching your speech on discrimination against women in the workplace, you discover two polls reaching conflicting conclusions. One shows that experts generally agree with your position; the other shows that they disagree. Is it ethical to present your listeners only the poll that supports your position, or should you acknowledge the other? On what basis should you make this decision?

8. Many speakers say simply, "experts say," or "research shows," when supporting their positions. Do speakers have an ethical obligation *always* to identify their sources or the data for their conclusions?

9. Develop a list of nonverbal behaviors of speakers and listeners that may be unethical. Consider physical and vocal elements such as appearance, facial expressions, eye contact, gestures, rate, and tone of voice.

10. Politicians often do not write the speeches they deliver, instead relying on the words of speechwriters. Lyndon Johnson used 24 writers for his State of the Union address in 1964.[20] Journalist Ari Posner laments this tradition, observing, "If college or high school students relied on ghosts the way most public figures do, they'd be expelled on charges of plagiarism."[21] Be prepared to defend your answers to the following questions: Is the practice of ghostwriting in politics unethical? What are the advantages and disadvantages of politicians' relying on speechwriters? Should students be permitted to use ghostwriters for their classroom speeches?

11. Ethical behavior is something we should demand in national, state, and local political campaigns. We should also expect it of candidates and the electorate in campus politics. Develop a code of ethics that you think should govern speech in student government campaigns on your campus.

Notes

1. Mark Monmonier, *Mapping It Out: Expository Cartography for the Humanities and Social Sciences* (Chicago: U of Chicago P, 1993) 140. We are grateful to Professor Jeremy Crampton of George Mason University for directing us to this source.

2. *Frasier*, NBC, 18 Feb. 1999.

3. James A. Jaksa and Michael S. Pritchard, *Communication Ethics* (Belmont, CA: Wadsworth, 1988) xi.

4. Donald K. Smith, *Man Speaking: A Rhetoric of Public Speech* (New York: Dodd, 1969) 228.

5. Kenneth Blanchard and Norman Vincent Peale, *The Power of Ethical Management* (New York: Fawcett-Ballantine, 1988) 9.

6. Allan R. Cohen and David L. Bradford, *Influence without Authority* (New York: Wiley, 1990) ix.

7. Mary Cunningham, "What Price 'Good Copy'?" *Newsweek* 29 Nov. 1982: 15.

8. James C. McCroskey, *An Introduction to Rhetorical Communication* (Englewood Cliffs, NJ: Prentice, 1968) 237.

9. Georgia Harper, "Using the Four Factor Fair Use Test," *Fair Use of Copyrighted Materials,* 5 Jan. 1998, U of Texas, Austin, 6 July 1999 <http://www.utsystem.edu/ogc/intellectualproperty/copypol2.htm>.

10. USCS, Sect. 107, Limitations on Exclusive Rights: Fair Use.

11. Harper.

12. Harper.

13. Alexander Lindey, *Plagiarism and Originality* (New York: Harper, 1952) 2.

14. *Prentice Hall Author's Guide* (Englewood Cliffs, NJ: Prentice, 1978) 9.

15. Robert W. Keidel, *Game Plans: Sports Strategies for Business* (New York: Berkley, 1987) vii, 17, 36, 52.

16. John L. Waltman, "Plagiarism: Preventing It in Formal Research Reports," *ABCA [American Business Communication Association] Bulletin* June 1980: 37.

17. Michael T. O'Neill, "Plagiarism: Writing Responsibly," *ABCA Bulletin* June 1980: 34, 36.

18. Peter F. Drucker, "Beyond the Information Revolution," *The Atlantic Monthly* October 1999: 50.

19. *Write it in Your Own Words: Paraphrase,* no. 30, Purdue OWL (Online Writing Lab), Purdue U Writing Lab, 30 June 1999 <http://owl.english.purdue.edu/Files/30.html>.

20. Jo Ann Tooley, "Database," *U. S. News & World Report* 28 Jan. 1991: 10.

21. Ari Posner, "The Culture of Plagiarism," *New Republic* 18 April 1988: 19.

*The best speakers know enough to be scared. Stagefright is
the sweat of perfection. The only difference between the pros and
the novices is that the pros have trained the butterflies to fly
in formation.*

—*Edward R. Murrow*

Speaking Confidently

Recognize the Pervasiveness of Speaker Nervousness

Seinfeld may be playing a bit fast and loose with his facts and his logic, but the point of his humor is sound. **Communication apprehension,** the perceived "fear or anxiety associated with either real or anticipated communication with another person or persons," is widespread.[2] One form of communication apprehension, public speaking anxiety, affects even people with a great deal of public speaking experience. Carol Burnett, another accomplished comedian and actor, has appeared in her own television series, in movies, and as host of various televised award shows. Nevertheless, she has said, "The idea of making a speech does more than make me a nervous wreck; it terrifies me. . . . I'd rather scrub floors—without knee pads."[3]

Burnett would probably be able to scrub those floors quickly with help from a number of men and women who would make the same choice. Meryl Streep, one of America's most versatile actors, has said, "It's odd: I have this career that spans continents, but the pathetic thing is that I can't get up in front of people and speak. I get really, really nervous."[4] Lee Iacocca, former chief executive officer of the Chrysler Corporation, confesses that "to this day I still get a little nervous before giving a speech."[5] And the list of performers and public figures who have disclosed their nervousness about public speaking includes former president Ronald Reagan, Barbra Streisand, Tom Selleck, and former NFL quarterback Joe Montana.

Garrison Keillor, author and host of National Public Radio's *A Prairie Home Companion,* reflected on his teenage years in terms that may seem familiar:

> I had an awful rough time in high school. I was such a shy person. I was so terrified of everything, so afraid of being embarrassed in front of other people, afraid to speak up in class, afraid that I might have the wrong answer to a question that everybody else had the right answer to. . . . I was able to get up in speech class only because I could take off my glasses, and when I did I could no longer see faces. It was just a kind of an Impressionist tapestry.[6]

It is worth noting that, aside from his potential radio audience, Keillor was sharing these thoughts with hundreds of people from the stage of the 996-seat Fitzgerald Theater in St. Paul, Minesota. Keillor has obviously managed his fear of speaking in public.

These examples demonstrate that if you are nervous about public speaking and experience what we sometimes call "platform panic," you are in good company. In fact, the first edition of *The Book of Lists* reported a survey that asked 3,000 Americans, "What are you the most afraid of?" "Speaking before a group" came in first, ahead of heights, insects, financial problems, deep water, sickness, and, yes, even death.[7] Psychiatrists John Greist, James Jefferson, and Isaac Marks contend that public speaking anxiety is "probably the most common social phobia."[8] Today, when so many people are apprehensive about even striking up a conversation with a stranger, is it any wonder that the fear of public speaking is so widespread?

Our experience and research confirm the prevalence of this common fear among college students. When asked to list their communication weaknesses, a clear majority of our students rank speaking before a group of people as their primary fear. James McCroskey has studied the anxieties of public speaking extensively. McCroskey's Personal Report of Public Speaking Anxiety (Figure 3.1) assesses the fear college students have about giving public speeches. His data, collected from several thousand students, confirm that public speaking generates greater apprehension than other forms of communication and that this fear spans several levels:

communication apprehension: perceived fear or anxiety associated with real or anticipated communication with another person or persons.[2]

high anxiety	40%
moderately high anxiety	30%
moderate anxiety	20%
moderately low anxiety	5%
low anxiety	5%

Note that nearly three-fourths of college students fall into the moderately high to high anxiety range! This means that even the person who always has the quick response, who can make others in the class laugh, and who always looks together may be just as worried as you are right now about getting up in front of this class to give a speech. Mc-Croskey and coauthor Virginia Richmond conclude: "What this suggests, then, is that it is 'normal' to experience a fairly high degree of anxiety about public speaking. Most people do. If you are highly anxious about public speaking, then you are 'normal.' "9

What is this platform panic and how does it affect us? Chemically and physiologically, we all experience stage fright in the same way. Adrenaline is suddenly pumped into the bloodstream. Respiration increases dramatically. So do heart rate and "galvanic skin response"—the amount of perspiration on the surface of the skin. All these things occur so that oxygen-rich blood can be quickly channeled to the large muscle groups. You may have heard stories of a 135-pound person who lifts the front of a car to help rescue someone pinned under it. Such incidents happen because the body is suddenly mobilized to do what must be done.

Yet the body can be similarly mobilized in stressful situations that are not life threatening. Musicians waiting for the start of the opening selection, athletes for the game to begin, actors for the curtain to go up, and speakers for their call to the lectern often feel their bodies marshalling all their resources either to perform to capacity or to get away from the threatening situation. This phenomenon is called, appropriately, the "fight-or-flight" syndrome.

Although our bodies' chemical and physiological responses to stress are identical, the outward signs of this anxiety vary from person to person. As the time approaches for your first speech in this class, you may experience any of several symptoms to varying degrees. Our students tell us that their symptoms include blushing or redness, accelerated heart rate, perspiring, dry mouth, shaking, churning stomach, increased rate of speech, forgetfulness and broken speech, and nervous mannerisms such as playing with jewelry, tapping fingers, and clutching the lectern.

As we indicated earlier, it is important to realize that these symptoms are typical, not atypical, of a public speaker. If you experience any of these symptoms, you have plenty of company.

Control Speaker Nervousness

Before discussing what your goal should be regarding speaker nervousness, it is important to note what it should not be. Do *not* make your goal to eliminate nervousness. Such a goal is counterproductive for at least two reasons. First, as we have noted, nervousness is natural. Attempting to eliminate it is therefore unrealistic and probably undesirable. Speakers having far more experience in front of the public have failed to do so—remember Burnett, Streep, and Iacocca. In fact, the more you concentrate on your nervousness, the more nervous you may become.

A second reason why you should not try to eliminate nervousness is that some nervousness can actually benefit a speaker. Nervousness is energy, and it shows that you care about performing well. Use that nervous energy to enliven your delivery and to give your ideas impact. Instead of nervously tapping your fingers on the lectern, for

DIRECTIONS: This instrument is composed of thirty-four statements concerning feelings about communicating with other people. Indicate the degree to which the statements apply to you by marking whether you (1) strongly agree, (2) agree, (3) are undecided, (4) disagree, or (5) strongly disagree with each statement. Work quickly; record your first impression.

_____ 1. While preparing for giving a speech, I feel tense and nervous.

_____ 2. I feel tense when I see the words "speech" and "public speech" on a course outline when studying.

_____ 3. My thoughts become confused and jumbled when I am giving a speech.

_____ 4. Right after giving a speech I feel that I have had a pleasant experience.

_____ 5. I get anxious when I think about a speech coming up.

_____ 6. I have no fear of giving a speech.

_____ 7. Although I am nervous just before starting a speech, I soon settle down after starting and feel calm and comfortable.

_____ 8. I look forward to giving a speech.

_____ 9. When the instructor announces a speaking assignment in class, I can feel myself getting tense.

_____ 10. My hands tremble when I am giving a speech.

_____ 11. I feel relaxed while giving a speech.

_____ 12. I enjoy preparing for a speech.

_____ 13. I am in constant fear of forgetting what I prepared to say.

_____ 14. I get anxious if someone asks me something about my topic that I do not know.

_____ 15. I face the prospect of giving a speech with confidence.

_____ 16. I feel that I am in complete possession of myself while giving a speech.

_____ 17. My mind is clear when giving a speech.

_____ 18. I do not dread giving a speech.

_____ 19. I perspire just before starting a speech.

_____ 20. My heart beats very fast just as I start a speech.

_____ 21. I experience considerable anxiety while sitting in the room just before my speech starts.

_____ 22. Certain parts of my body feel very tense and rigid while giving a speech.

_____ 23. Realizing that only a little time remains in a speech makes me very tense and anxious.

_____ 24. While giving a speech, I know I can control my feelings of tension and stress.

_____ 25. I breathe faster just before starting a speech.

_____ 26. I feel comfortable and relaxed in the hour or so just before giving a speech.

_____ 27. I do poorer on speeches because I am anxious.

_____ 28. I feel anxious when the teacher announces the date of a speaking assignment.

_____ 29. When I make a mistake while giving a speech, I find it hard to concentrate on the parts that follow.

_____ 30. During an important speech I experience a feeling of helplessness building up inside me.

_____ 31. I have trouble falling asleep the night before a speech.

_____ 32. My heart beats very fast while I present a speech.

_____ 33. I feel anxious while waiting to give my speech.

_____ 34. While giving a speech, I get so nervous I forget facts I really know.

SCORING: To determine your score on the PRPSA, complete the following steps:

Step 1: Add the scores for items 1, 2, 3, 5, 9, 10, 13, 14, 19, 20, 21, 22, 23, 25, 27, 28, 29, 30, 31, 32, 33, and 34.

Step 2: Add the scores for items 4, 6, 7, 8, 11, 12, 15, 16, 17, 18, 24, and 26.

Step 3: Complete the following formula:

PRPSA = 132 – Total from Step 1 + Total from Step 2.

Your score should range between 34 and 170. If your score is below 34 or above 170, you have made a mistake in computing the score.

(continued)

FIGURE 3.1 Personal Report of Public Speaking Anxiety (PRPSA)
From COMMUNICATION: Apprehension, Avoidance, and Effectiveness 5th ed. by Virginia P. Richmond and James C. McCroskey. Copyright © 1998 by Allyn & Bacon. Reprinted by permission.

example, you can gesture. Rather than shifting your body weight from foot to foot, incorporate motivated movement into your speech.

Your goal, then, is not to eliminate nervousness but to control and channel it. The coping strategies we suggest in the next section and in Chapter 13 will enable you to control the symptoms of nervousness and to channel that energy into dynamic, effective vocal and physical delivery.

Learn How to Cope with Nervousness

One popular, nonacademic book on public speaking suggests this "quick fix" for reducing stage fright:

> Take an orange crate to a busy downtown street where you're not known, get up on the crate and, using all your lung power, proceed to exhort the passersby with the speech you're preparing. I'm serious. This works because you can't continue feeling the really paralyzing fear of stage fright over and over—your nervous system rebels against going through all that turmoil for no reason.[10]

DILBERT BY SCOTT ADAMS

Before you panic further, note that we do *not* suggest that you try this. In fact, we disagree with this exercise as well as its rationale. If you are nervous about speaking in front of your classmates, wouldn't you be even more nervous shouting to strangers on a street corner? You might even risk arrest and still not reduce your nervousness.

We advocate a far less dramatic approach to ease your nervousness. We offer 12 suggestions to help you become a more confident communicator. If you consider each suggestion seriously, you will control your nervousness and learn to channel it into a dynamic and effective public speaking style.

Know How You React to Stress

We have already noted that nervousness affects different people in different ways. Perhaps you feel that your hands or knees shake uncontrollably as you speak in public. The people sitting next to you may not ever experience those symptoms of nervousness, but they may have difficulty breathing comfortably and feel that their voices are shaky or quivery. Whatever your individual responses to stress, don't wait until you are delivering a public speech to discover them.

Knowing your reactions to stressful situations helps you in two ways. First, this knowledge lets you predict and cope with these physical conditions. Your dry mouth or sweaty palms will not surprise you. Second, because you are anticipating these physical conditions, you will be better able to mask them from the audience. How do you do this? Try these techniques.

If you know that your hands shake when you are nervous, don't hold a sheet of paper during the speech; the shaking paper will only amplify the movement of your hands and will telegraph this sign of nervousness to your audience. If your voice is likely to be thin and quivery as you begin speaking, take

> Relaxation Techniques
> http://ourworld.
> compuserve.com/
> homepages/har/les1.htm
> Visit this site to study Bernd Harmsen's step-by-step directions for "Progressive Muscle Relaxation," a technique invented by Edmund Jacobson. The site also links to directions for a shortened version of the exercises.

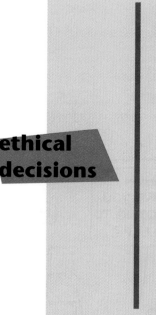

ethical decisions

Sondra is preparing a speech on defensive driving. A drama major, she is comfortable playing all sorts of characters on stage, but the thought of standing in front of an audience and delivering a speech terrifies her. She has visions of herself clutching the lectern, staring blankly at her notes, and mumbling inaudibly. "I'll feel so exposed—I don't think I can get through it just being my ordinary self," Sondra confides to her friends. She asks their help in brainstorming ways to steel herself before she comes to class on speech day.

"I bet a couple of glasses of wine would relax you," suggests her friend Amy.

"Amphetamines would perk you up; you'd zip right through your speech before you even had time to get scared," offers Edward.

"Maybe you could borrow some blood pressure medicine. My dad says it makes him feel less nervous," adds Michal.

"Or you could dress like a car crash dummy and deliver your speech in character," jokes her boyfriend, Steve.

What do you think of these suggestions? In Chapter 2 we noted that ethical speakers enter into and honor an unwritten contract with their listeners. How should the terms of that contract guide Sondra as she wrestles with how to control her nervousness? Could she follow any of her friends' advice and still "be herself" as she speaks? What advice would you offer if you were her friend?

several deep, slow breaths before you begin to speak. If you get tense before speaking, try some muscle relaxation techniques: Tense your hands, arms, and shoulders, and then slowly relax them. If you get flustered before speaking, make sure you arrive on time or even a little early—never late. If looking at an audience intimidates you, talk to audience members before class, and when you speak, look for friendly faces in the audience.

Guidelines for Building Speaker Confidence

1. Know how you react to stress.
2. Know your strengths and weaknesses.
3. Know speech principles.
4. Know that it always looks worse from the inside.
5. Know your speech.
6. Believe in your topic.
7. View speech making positively.
8. Visualize success.
9. Project confidence.
10. Test your message.
11. Practice.
12. Learn from experience.

Know Your Strengths and Weaknesses

Surgeons spend many hours learning how to use the equipment they need to perform operations. Each surgeon knows just what each instrument is capable of doing and can use it to maximum effectiveness. As a public speaker, your instruments are your voice, body, mind, and personality. You will use all these instruments together to create and communicate messages.

To know yourself, you must honestly appraise both your strengths and your weaknesses. Use your strengths to communicate your message with force and impact. If you are a lively and enthusiastic person, channel that energy to reinforce your speech physically and enliven your listeners. If you have a talent for creating memorable phrases, allow that creativity to help your listeners attend to and remember your ideas. Just as

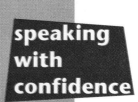

In all my years of high school and college, I was told before making a speech by my friends and teachers, "You'll be fine up there; don't be nervous." Now finally a book that tells me being nervous is okay, in fact it's good. Because I know it's okay to be nervous, and that even nervous energy shows you care about doing well, it eliminated all the pressure. I even learned how to channel this energy into hand gestures and motivated movement. I really wish I had been told a long time ago that being nervous is okay, because I would have looked at things a whole different way, with confidence and peace of mind that everything's going to work out. Nervousness is not only normal but a positive flow of energy.

—Kenneth Martinez, San Antonio College

Nervous energy is a sign that you care about your speech performance. Try to channel that energy into gestures and body movements that will enhance your message.

you can tap your strengths in these ways, you can minimize or avoid your weaknesses if you know them. If you are not effective in delivering humor, you probably should not begin your speech with a joke. To do so would risk failure at this critical point in the speech, and that would make you even more nervous.

The more you understand your strengths and weaknesses, the better you will be able to craft your speech to your abilities. The more confident you are that you can accomplish what you set out to do, the less nervous you will be. One note of caution, however: Don't be too critical of yourself and construct a "safe" speech because you have exaggerated your weaknesses. Instead, expand your abilities by incorporating new strategies into your speech making. Only through thoughtful, measured risk taking will you develop as a public speaker.

Know Speech Principles

If you are confident that you have constructed an effective speech, you will be more confident as you step to the lectern. This textbook and your instructor will assist you in learning speech principles. What are the five functions of an effective speech introduction? How should you construct the body of your speech, and how should you develop each key idea? What strategies help you conclude your speech? How can you use your voice and body to communicate your ideas dynamically? What strategies help you word ideas correctly, clearly, and vividly? We address all these questions, and many others, in this book. As you begin to answer these questions and apply what you learn, you will feel more confident about the content, organization, and delivery of your ideas.

Know That It Always Looks Worse from the Inside

Keep in mind the adage that it always looks worse from the inside. Because you feel nervous, you focus on your anxiety, exaggerate it, and become more nervous. Remember, though, your audience cannot see your internal state! Many times our students have lamented their nervousness after concluding a speech, only to learn that classmates envied them for being so calm and free from stage fright. The authors of a study of 95 speakers found that "untrained audiences are not very good at detecting the self-perceived anxiety of beginning speakers."[11] Even if you feel extremely nervous, then, your audience probably does not realize it. Knowing this should make you more secure and lessen your nervousness.

One of our students, Susan, wrote the following in her self-evaluation of her first graded classroom speech:

Too fast, too rushed. I forgot ½ of it. Yuck! Yuck! Yuck! I used to think I was a good public speaker. People ask me to speak—I'm not going to do it ever again. I was so nervous my insides were on fire. I got up to give my speech, and I felt like I went "mind blank." I looked out at my audience, and I just knew they could feel my fear as I gripped the lectern and my mouth went dry.

The truth is that Susan experienced her speech in a radically different way than her instructor and classmates did. In fact, here are a few of her peers' comments about her speech:

"Wow! You seemed really relaxed! Your speech was organized, informative, and interesting."
"I really saw no weakness in the speech."
"Definitely the best speech given so far."
"She seemed to know what she was talking about."

When the instructor gave Susan her classmates' written comments, he asked her to write how she felt as she read them. Here is some of what Susan wrote:

Dr. Grice. Excuse me, Dr. Grice. You've given me the wrong feedback sheets. These just can't be mine. This person, they all say, seemed relaxed, well organized, interesting, and informative. These just can't be mine. If only I could get with this person, maybe she could help me with my upcoming speech. . . . Are you sure, Dr. Grice, that these [critiques] are mine?

Susan concluded her reaction paper, "Wow! What you said is definitely true. It does look worse from the inside."

If Susan had not received feedback from her audience, she would probably have retained her high level of fear of public speaking, perhaps even avoiding future opportunities to share her ideas with others. By offering honest evaluation, her classmates let her see her speech from "the other side," lessened some of her anxieties, and motivated her to continue to improve her public speaking skills.

In addition, remember our earlier statement about the pervasiveness of nervousness. Your fellow classmates are also apprehensive about speaking to a group of people. View your listeners as supportive individuals who want only the best for you. They know it's their turn next!

If you choose a subject you love, whether it be a favorite hobby, job, class, or poet, you will become deeply involved in developing your speech. This involvement, in turn, may reduce your inhibitions about speaking in public.

Know Your Speech

Knowing your strengths and weaknesses, speech principles, and your audience gains you little, however, if you do not know your speech. This textbook will acquaint you with strategies that will enable you to remember the ideas and supporting material of your speech. If you don't know what you want to say, you won't say it. If you think you will forget, you probably will. The more confident you are about your message, the less nervous you will be.

Keep in mind that we certainly do not believe you need to memorize the entire speech. Yet, if you are well prepared, you should have memorized the outline of major points for your speech and the order in which they are to be presented. If you forget your notes, or drop them on the way to the lectern and cannot get them back into proper order, you should still be able to deliver the speech. (Take a minute to number your notecards, of course, and you have one less worry.)

Believe in Your Topic

If you are giving an informative speech, you must believe that what you say will benefit your listeners—that hearing your speech will improve them in some way. If you are giving a persuasive speech, be committed to the belief you attempt to instill or the action you attempt to initiate in your audience. Convincing your audience that they should listen to your speech is easier if you believe that the topic is important. The more you believe in your topic, the more earnestly you will want to inform or convince your listeners. In short, if you doubt the importance of the topic, you will feel and seem tentative.

Poet Howard Nemerov has said about perception, "What we know is never the object, but only our knowledge."[12] In other words, we do not experience the world directly, but only through the various labels we have attached to things and experiences. More and more we are discovering and investigating the mind's ability to affect behavior. Doctors have learned, for example, that patients' attitudes about their illnesses significantly affect their speeds of recuperation or their chances for recovery.

Cognitive Therapy
http://site.health-center.
com/brain/therapy/
types/cognitive.htm
This Web site presents the rationale for managing speaker nervousness through *cognitive restructuring*—by changing how you think about public speaking. You may also link to a discussion of *behavior therapy* techniques therapists use to reduce anxiety.

One method for reducing communication anxiety is called **cognitive restructuring.** This approach recognizes that nervousness is, in part, caused by illogical beliefs. If speakers can restructure their thinking and focus on positive rather than negative self-statements, anxiety can be reduced. Cognitive restructuring involves two steps. First, you identify your negative self-statements ("Everyone will laugh at me when I give my speech"). Second, you replace the negative thoughts with positive ones ("My classmates understand what it's like to be nervous and will support my speaking efforts").

If you view public speaking as a tedious chore, your audience will sense it from your vocal and physical delivery and perhaps even from your choice of speech topic. On the other hand, if you look upon public speaking as an opportunity, your positive attitude will help you control your nervousness. The following examples illustrate how you can replace negative thoughts with positive ones.

Replace the negative thought . . .

"When I get up to speak, my mind will probably go blank and I'll have nothing to say."

. . . with a positive thought

"I've rehearsed my speech and I have a good set of speaking notes. If I momentarily forget a point, I'll just look at my notecards and then continue."

Replace the negative thought . . .

"My audience will probably be bored with my speech."

. . . with a positive thought

"I found the topic of how 3-D films are made interesting, and my audience will, too."

Thinking positively can help turn anxiety into anticipation. Genuine enthusiasm about the chance to speak in public will guide your choice of topic and will reveal itself to the audience through your lively delivery. Seek out opportunities to test and develop your communication skills. Volunteer for oral reports in classes; speak out at organizational meetings; offer to introduce a guest speaker at your club's banquet. This positive attitude, coupled with practice and experience, will help make you less apprehensive and more confident.

Visualize Success

In football games, place kickers are called upon to attempt field goals and extra points after touchdowns. Before taking the field, they stand on the sidelines, usually in deep

cognitive restructuring:
a strategy for reducing communication anxiety by replacing negative thoughts and statements with positive ones.

concentration and away from the other players. They visualize the football being snapped and placed. They imagine themselves approaching the ball and kicking it. As they watch the football go through the goalposts, the referee lifts his arms to signal a field goal, and the crowd cheers. Through this ritual, place kickers focus on their task, visualizing how they can accomplish it.

Like athletes, public speakers have also used **visualization** to reduce their nervousness and improve their performance. A study of 430 college speech students revealed lowered speech anxiety among those who visualized themselves delivering an effective presentation.[13] Rodney describes how he used positive visualization to help build his confidence:

> The week before I gave my speech, I would find quiet spots where I could relax. I would close my eyes and visualize myself giving an effective presentation. I saw myself arriving at my classroom on the day I was to speak. Calmly, I would walk to my seat. I'd sit down, check my speaking notes to see that they were in order, and collect my thoughts. When Mrs. Conner called my name, I got up from my seat and walked confidently to the front of the room. I put my notes on the lectern, looked at my classmates, and smiled. I paused, took a breath, and then began. I visualized myself being relaxed and delivering my speech as I had planned, with clarity and poise. I felt good talking about a topic that was so important to me. I visualized my classmates smiling at my humor and nodding in agreement as I explained my ideas. I concluded with a dramatic story that really drove home my point. I paused, then walked to my seat. My classmates applauded, and one of them even whispered to me, "Great speech, Rod!"

Project Confidence

Daryl Bem's theory of self-perception states that if you perceive yourself acting a particular way, you will assume that you feel that way.[14] Thus, if you want to feel confident, act confident. Begin by identifying characteristics of speakers who seem confident to you; then incorporate those behaviors into your own speaking. For example, instead of walking tentatively to the lectern, approach it confidently. Instead of avoiding eye contact with your listeners, look directly at them. Instead of leaning on the lectern or shifting your weight from foot to foot, stand erect and still. Instead of tapping your fingers on the lectern or jingling the change in your pocket, use your hands to gesture emphatically. Displaying confident behaviors such as these will not only make you *appear* more confident, it will also help you *feel* more confident.

Test Your Message

A confident speaker must believe that the content of a speech will interest or satisfy a need of the audience. If your listeners are bored with your topic, you will sense it, and that will make you more nervous. If the audience is interested in the content of your speech, they will be attentive.

Advertisers know the importance of message testing. Before they print an ad or air a commercial, they test the message to gauge public reaction. As a speaker, you can test your message by practicing your speech in front of friends. Can they restate your main points after listening to you? Do they find your supporting material believable? Is your vocal delivery lively and varied? Does your physical delivery detract from or reinforce your message? Answers to these questions will guide your subsequent practice sessions. The more confident you are that your message will achieve the desired effect on your audience, the less nervous you will be.

visualization: a strategy for reducing communication anxiety by picturing yourself delivering a successful speech.

Practice

In discussing the previous coping strategies, we have implied the importance of practice. Practicing your speech is so important, however, that it deserves a separate category. Jack Valenti, former presidential speechwriter and now president of the Motion Picture Association of America, correctly observes, "The most effective antidote to stage fright and other calamities of speech making is total, slavish, monkish preparation."[15]

Reducing Anxiety
http://www.all-biz.com/
articles/anxiety.htm
This article, "Overcoming Speaking Anxiety in Meetings and Presentations" by Lenny Laskowski, a Connecticut speech consultant, lists and briefly discusses ten steps for reducing speech anxiety.

Your approach to your practice sessions will vary, depending on how your presentation develops. Sometimes you may practice specific sections of your speech that give you difficulty. But you should also practice your speech several times from start to finish without stopping. Too often when students mess up in practice, they stop and begin again. This is not a luxury you have when you address an audience, so as you practice, practice recovering from mistakes. Knowing that you can make it through your speech despite blunders in practice should make you more confident.

We also recommend that you occasionally practice your speech in an environment laden with distractions. Students who practice only in the silence of an empty classroom may not be prepared for distractions that arise when they actually deliver their speeches—for example, a student coming into the classroom during the speech, a lawnmower passing by the window, two students talking in the back of the room, or a classmate inadvertently pushing books off a desk. These distractions, especially those stemming from rudeness, should not occur; in reality, though, they sometimes do. Practicing with the television on in the background or in your room with noise in the hallway forces you to concentrate on what you are saying and not on what you are hearing. You develop poise as a speaker only through practice.

Learn from Experience

You've heard the expression, "Experience is the best teacher." Well, there's some truth in that folk wisdom. After your speech, assess your performance. What did you try that worked? What didn't work? How did you react when you walked to the front of the room, turned, and looked at the audience looking at you? Did you remember what you planned to say? Did you have trouble finding your place in your notes? How nervous did you feel? Did you get more or less nervous as the speech progressed? Your instructor will give you feedback to help you answer some of those questions; others you will need to answer for yourself, because you alone know the true answers. This is difficult for most of us to do. Especially if you think you made mistakes, your reaction may be to put the whole episode out of your mind. Resist this temptation. You can learn a great deal from reviewing your performance.

On the other hand, don't be too critical as you evaluate your performance. You will do some things well, and this should build your confidence. Other aspects of your speech you can improve, and you should work on these. Suppose, however, that you do encounter a serious problem: You completely lose your place, your mind goes blank, and so you bury your head in your notes and race to the end of your speech. Rather than trying to forget this, use it as a learning experience. Ask yourself why you forgot. Did you try to memorize your speech instead of speaking from a set of notes? Were your notes disorganized, or did they contain too little or too much information?

Did you focus too much on your instructor and not enough on the entire audience? Once you face the problem and determine its cause, you will be better able to plan so that it does not occur again.

These 12 coping strategies will help you channel your nervous energy into a confident and dynamic delivery. In the "Speaking with Confidence" boxes throughout this book, you will read how other public speaking students developed their confidence by using some of these principles. You can begin training those butterflies to fly in formation, however, as you prepare for your first speech in this class.

Prepare Your First Speech

This class will undoubtedly require you to give your first speech before you have read much of this textbook. What is absolutely necessary to know, then, in order to be able to deliver that first speech successfully? Preparing your first speech will be easier if you keep in mind two principles of public speaking. First, the more effectively that you prepare, the better the speech you will deliver and the more confident you will feel. Only then can you recognize what you already do competently and begin to identify skills you want to improve. In addition, your confidence will grow with each speaking experience throughout this course and later in your life.

The second principle is that every public speech is a blend of *content, organization,* and *delivery*. Each of these aspects affects the others. For example, choosing a topic you already know well or have researched thoroughly should easily translate into animated, confident delivery. Elements of speech delivery such as pause and movement can emphasize your speech's organization. Moreover, as you will soon learn, we believe that any speech on any topic should be well organized. The more you know about the principles of speech content, organization, and delivery, then, the better your first speech will be. The following seven guidelines will help you toward that goal.

key points

The Speech-Making Process

1. **Understand the assignment.**
2. **Develop your speech content.**
3. **Organize your speech.**
4. **Word your speech.**
5. **Practice your speech.**
6. **Deliver your speech.**
7. **Evaluate your speech.**

Understand the Assignment

For your first speech assignment, your instructor may prescribe a specific purpose or leave that choice to you. Often your first speech assignment is to introduce yourself or a classmate, and so is informative rather than persuasive. The speech may be graded or ungraded; if graded, it may count less than or as much as speeches you will deliver later. Whether your instructor is trying an innovative assignment or using one that has been tested and proven, he or she is your first and final authority for the specific details of the assignment.

A primary, vital requirement for preparing any speech is to know exactly what you are to do. You must clearly understand the assignment your instructor has given you. The following questions can help you identify your goals for the speech.

- What am I supposed to do in this speech: inform, persuade, or entertain?
- What are my minimum and maximum time limits for the speech?
- Are there special requirements for the delivery of the speech? If so, what are they?

Develop Your Speech Content

As you select a speech topic, you need to decide the number of main ideas you will cover. To determine what those ideas will be, think about what you would want to hear if you were in the audience. If your instructor assigns you a topic, the specific things you say and the order in which you say them will be uniquely your own. If you are asked to choose your topic, you have even greater creative latitude, of course. In either of these cases, you need to keep your audience in mind. The topic you select or the way you approach an assigned topic should be guided by what you think your listeners will find most interesting or useful.

If your assignment is to introduce yourself, begin by jotting down as many aspects of your life as you can. Audit your history, assess your current circumstances, and project your future goals. Among others, topics that apply to your life and the lives of all your listeners include:

accomplishments	people who have been significant influences
career plans	unusual life events
educational backgrounds	personal values
skills or aptitudes	prized possessions
hobbies	pet peeves
special interests	aspirations

In addition, you may have a particularly interesting work history or may have traveled to unusual places. You could decide to limit your speech to one of the preceding areas or to combine several that you think your listeners will find most interesting.

If the ideas you disclose are truly unusual, your speech will be memorable. But don't be intimidated or worried if your experiences seem fairly tame and ordinary. Some of your listeners will be relieved to find that they have backgrounds similar to yours. Whether ordinary or extraordinary, your background and your classmates' will provide the basis for conversation before class, for classroom discussion, and for audience analysis as you prepare for future speeches.

If you are asked to select the subject for your first speech, brainstorm for topics that are of interest to you and those that you think would benefit or be of interest to your audience. Your speaking occasion, the time of year that you speak, and upcoming or recent holidays can also suggest topic ideas. In addition, consider subjects that you discover as you conduct research. Don't settle for the first topic that comes to mind, however. If you generate a number of possible topics and spend some time reflecting on them, the subject you finally choose will probably be more satisfying for you and more interesting to your listeners. To make sure that you have a clear grasp of your speech topic, answer questions such as these:

- What is my speech topic, and why have I chosen it?
- Who are the people in my audience?
- What do I want my listeners to know or remember when I'm finished speaking?

The best way to answer that last question is to ask, "What aspects of my topic interest me and are likely to interest my audience?" Select only a few points to discuss. A time limit of two to four minutes, for example, may seem endless to you right now. It's not; it goes by very quickly. As you develop your speech content, check to be sure that everything you say is relevant to your purpose and to those few main points you want your listeners to remember. Limiting your number of main ideas should give you enough time to develop them with adequate supporting materials—definitions, stories, statistics, comparisons, and contrasts—that are interesting and relevant to your listeners. Once you have done this preliminary work, you are ready to assess your speech content by asking questions such as:

- Have I selected a few key points that I can develop in the time allowed?
- Do I use a variety of specific supporting materials, such as examples and stories, to develop my key points?
- Will my supporting materials be clear and interesting to my classroom audience?
- Do I acknowledge sources for anything I quote or paraphrase from other speakers or writers?
- Is everything that I say relevant to my topic?

Once you begin to generate the main ideas of your topic and then to limit yourself to the ones you think the audience will find most interesting, you have begun to organize your content.

Organize Your Speech

Organizing a speech is similar to writing an essay. Every essay must have an introductory paragraph, a body, and a concluding paragraph. A speech has the same three divisions: an introduction, a body, and a conclusion. To determine whether your ideas are clearly organized and easy to follow, you must consider the organization of each of those three parts of your speech.

Organize Your Speech Introduction. Though usually brief, your speech introduction serves five vital functions. First, it focuses the audience's attention on your message. You want to command the audience's attention with your first words. How can you do this? Question your audience, amuse them, arouse their curiosity about your subject, or stimulate their imaginations.

Second, your introduction should clarify your topic or your purpose in speaking. If your listeners are confused about your exact topic, you limit their ability to listen actively. To minimize any chances of this, state your purpose clearly in a well-worded sentence.

A third function of your introduction is to establish the significance of your topic, explain your interest in it, or reveal any special qualifications you have for speaking on your topic. Fourth, your introduction should help establish your credibility as a speaker on that topic. Your words, voice, and body should instill confidence in your listeners that you have prepared thoroughly. Finally, your introduction should highlight or preview the aspects of your subject that you will discuss in the body. Well-planned and well-delivered opening remarks will make the audience want to listen and will prepare them for what comes next. To check the integrity of your speech introduction, answer the following questions:

- Does my speech have an introduction?
  What is my attention-getter?
  What is my statement of purpose?

What rationale do I provide for speaking about this topic?

How do I establish my credibility to speak on this topic?

What are the points I will cover in my speech?

Organize the Body of Your Speech. The body of your speech is its longest, most substantial section. Though it follows your introduction, you should prepare the body of your speech first. Here you introduce your key ideas and support or explain each one of them. You should develop only a few main ideas, probably between two and five, in any speech that you give. Why? You can more easily develop two to five ideas within your time limit. Your audience will also more easily grasp and remember a few well-developed ideas. Restricting your main points to a few is particularly important in a first speech, because it may be the shortest presentation you make during the semester or quarter.

Your organizational goal in the body of your speech should be to structure your main points so clearly that they are not just distinct but unmistakable to your listeners. To help you do so, we recommend a four-step sequence—the "4 S's"—for organizing each of your main ideas. First, *signpost* each main idea. Typical signposts are numbers ("first" or "one") and words such as *initially* or *finally*. Second, *state* the idea clearly. Third, the step that will take you the most time, *support*, or explain, the idea. Finally, *summarize* the idea before moving to your next one. Those four steps will help you highlight and develop each of your main ideas in a logical, orderly way. The following questions and outline form should help you determine whether the body of your speech is well organized.

- Do I have the body of my speech organized clearly?
    - I. What is my first main idea?
        - A. What will I say about it?
        - B. How will I summarize it?
    - II. What is my second main idea?
        - A. What will I say about it?
        - B. How will I summarize it?
    - III. What is my third main idea?
        - A. What will I say about it?
        - B. How will I summarize it? and so forth.

Organize Your Speech Conclusion. Your speech conclusion is a brief final step with three main functions. The first function, the summary, is a final review of the main points you have covered. Summarizing may be as simple as listing the key ideas you discussed in the body of the speech. Your summary may require more elaboration than a simple listing, but you should not introduce and develop any new ideas in the conclusion. When you summarize, you bring your speech to a logical close.

The second function of a conclusion is to activate an audience response by letting your listeners know whether you want them to accept, use, believe, or act upon the content of your speech. Whether your speech is informative or persuasive, you want the audience to have been involved with your information and ideas. This is your last opportunity to highlight what you want your listeners to take away from your speech.

Finally, your conclusion should provide your speech with a strong sense of closure. To do this, end on a positive, forceful note. You can use many of the same techniques here that you used to get the audience's attention at the very beginning of the speech: Question the audience, amuse them, stimulate their imaginations, and so forth. Your final remarks should be carefully thought out and extremely well worded. Ask and answer these questions to test your speech conclusion:

- Does my speech have a conclusion?

   How have I summarized my main ideas?

   What am I asking my audience to remember or do?

   What will my closing statement be?

If you answer each of the questions we've posed so far, you should have an interesting, well-developed speech that is easy to follow. Both your content and your organization are in good shape. Up to this point, you have spent most of your time thinking about the speech and jotting down ideas. Now you have to word those ideas and practice getting them across to your audience through your vocal and physical delivery.

Word Your Speech

Unless your instructor requests that you do so, avoid writing out your first speech word for word. Even though having the text of your speech in front of you may make you feel more secure, our experience has been that students who deliver speeches from manuscripts early in the semester or quarter often suffer two consequences. One is that what they say tends to sound like writing rather than speech. Our speaking differs from our writing in several significant ways. We speak in shorter sentences than those we write. We use a simpler vocabulary, and we also use more first- and second-person plural pronouns ("we" and "you") when we speak. Finally, we use more repetition and more colloquial language than we usually employ in writing.

A second problem you may encounter if you deliver your speech from manuscript is a lack of eye contact. Effective speakers make eye contact with their listeners. If you are reading, you can't do this. Therefore, if you have a choice, speak from just a few notes, rather than from a prepared manuscript. If you are required to compose and submit a manuscript of your speech, make sure that it sounds like something you would say, not just write.

The language of your speech should be correct, clear, and vivid. To illustrate this, assume that you have been assigned a practice speech of self-introduction early in the course. Assume, too, that you have decided to make your travels one of your main points. "I've traveled quite a bit" is a vague, general statement. Without supporting materials, the statement is also superficial. But suppose you said, instead:

> I've traveled quite a bit. I had lived in five states before I was in middle school, for example. When I was seven, my father worked in the booming oil business, and my family even got a chance to live in South America for more than a year. My brother and I went to an American school in the tiny village of Anaco, Venezuela; we were students 99 and 100 in a school that taught grades one through eight. Instruction in Spanish started in the first grade, and by the time we returned to the States, I was bilingual. I have vivid memories of picking mangoes and papayas off the trees, swimming outdoors on Christmas day, and having my youngest brother born in Venezuela.

The second statement is a great deal clearer and more vivid than the first. It begins with the general comment, but then amplifies it with a more detailed story. The language is personal, conversational, and crisp. Notice how vivid language enhances the content of your speech. The following questions should help you test the language of your own speech:

- Does my speech sound conversational?
- Is the language of my speech correct?
- Will the language of my speech be clear to my listeners?
- Will the language of my speech be vivid for my listeners?

Practice Your Speech

Mental rehearsal is no substitute for oral and physical practice. Merely thinking about what you plan to say will never adequately ready you to deliver a prepared speech in class. As we said toward the beginning of this chapter, speech making is an active process. You gain a heightened knowledge of what you plan to say, as well as increased confidence in your abilities, just by practicing your speech out loud. Before you can do that, however, you must create the notes you will use to practice and deliver the speech.

Prepare Your Notes. Make certain that your speaking notes are in the form of key words or phrases, rather than complete sentences. Remember, you want your listeners to remember your main *ideas,* not necessarily your exact wording. Your goal in preparing your notes should be the same: You should need only a word or phrase to remind you of the order of your ideas. As you elaborate those points, your specific wording can change slightly each time you practice your speech. Make sure that your notes are easy to read. If your speaking notes are on notecards, be certain to number the cards and have them in the correct order before each practice session.

Practice Productively. Most of your practice will probably be done in seclusion. Practice any way that will help you, being sure to stand as you rehearse. Visualize your audience, and gesture to them as you hope to when giving the speech. You may even want to record and listen to your speech on audiotape or videotape, if you have access to that equipment. Give yourself the opportunity to stop for intensive practice of rough spots in your speech. Just make sure that you also practice the speech from beginning to end without stopping.

As valuable as solitary practice is, you should also try your speech out on at least a few listeners, if at all possible. Enlist roommates and friends to listen to your speech and help you time it. The presence of listeners should make it easier to practice the way that you approach your speaking position before you speak and the way you will leave it after finishing. Your rehearsal audience can tell you if there are parts of your speech that are so complex that they are hard to grasp. They may also be able to suggest clearer, more colorful, or more powerful ways of wording certain statements you make. A practice audience can point out strengths of your delivery, as well as help you eliminate distractions that draw their attention away from your message. Most importantly, serious practice in front of others should focus your attention on the important interaction involved in delivering a speech to an audience. The following questions make up a checklist for your speech practice:

- Have I practiced my speech as I intend to deliver it in class?
- Have I made my speaking notes concise and easy to use and read?
- Have I recorded my speech and made changes after listening to or viewing it?
- How many times have others listened to my speech, and what suggestions have they offered for improving it?
- Have I timed my speech? Is the average time within my overall time limit?
- What adjustments can I make in my speech if it is too long or too short?

Deliver Your Speech

The biggest differences between speaking and writing become apparent as you say your speech aloud. Your "delivery system" for something you write includes the typeface you choose, punctuation marks, organization into paragraphs, and even the paper on which you print or type your text. As you deliver the words of your speech to an audience, however, you must provide all of that information with your voice and body.

Your speech delivery is made up of your language, your voice, and your body. Remember that speaking in public should feel natural to you and seem natural to your audience. You want to be conversational and to talk with your listeners, not at them. Use a presentational style with which you are comfortable but which also meets the requirements of your audience, your topic, and your speaking occasion.

Effective vocal delivery is energetic, easily heard, and understandable. Your voice should also show that you are thinking about what you are saying as you deliver your speech. With practice, your voice can communicate humor, seriousness, sarcasm, anger, and a range of other possible emotions behind your words. Check your vocal delivery by answering the following questions:

- Do I change the pitch of my voice enough to create a lively vocal delivery?
- Do I speak with enough volume to be heard easily?
- Do I vary my rate of speaking to match my audience's comprehension of what I am saying?

The message your listeners see should match the one they hear. Effective physical delivery is direct and immediate; effective speakers demonstrate their involvement in their topics and in their speaking situations by interacting with their audiences. You must make eye contact with listeners in all parts of your audience. Your facial expression should signal that you are thinking moment to moment about what you are saying. Physical delivery is not limited to your face, however. Gestures with your arms and hands and selective movement from place to place can emphasize what you say and mark important transitions in your speech.

If you are concentrating on your message and your audience's nonverbal feedback, your physical delivery will likely seem most natural. To gauge your directness, immediacy, and involvement, answer the following questions about your physical delivery:

- Do I look at members of my audience most of the time I am speaking? Do I look at listeners in all parts of the room?
- Do my gestures add emphasis to appropriate parts of the speech? Do my gestures look and feel natural and spontaneous?
- Do my facial expressions show that I am thinking about what I am saying, rather than about how I look or sound?
- Are my clothing and other elements of my appearance appropriate to my topic, my audience, and the speaking occasion?
- If I include place-to-place movement, does it serve a purpose?

Your goal should be delivery that looks and sounds effortless. Yet, ironically, that will require significant practice and attention to the vocal and physical elements of your delivery.

Evaluate Your Speech

Don't forget your speech as soon as you deliver your final words and return to your seat. While the experience is fresh in your memory, evaluate what you said, your organization, and how you delivered your speech. What sorts of feedback did you get from your listeners? What did you do well? What aspects of your speech can you target for improvement? In short, how did you respond to the challenge of preparing and delivering a speech? To evaluate the kind of speaker you are now and the kind of speaker you can become, answer the following questions:

- What did I do well?
- What areas can I target for improvement in this class?
- What specific efforts do I need to make in order to improve my next speech?

No matter what your level of public speaking experience, you will benefit from recognizing two concerns that you probably share with everyone in class. First, most of your classmates are probably as apprehensive as you are about the first speech. Almost everyone worries about questions such as, "Will I be able to get through my speech? Will I remember what I wanted to say? Will I be able to make my listeners understand what I want to say? Will I sound OK and look as though I know what I'm doing?" Your nervousness is natural, typical, and healthy. In fact, your nervousness is a good sign that you have reasonably high expectations of yourself and that you care about doing well.

Do not approach the first speech expecting perfection of yourself or of others. You already may be apprehensive about the prospect of standing at the front of the room and speaking for the first time. Why compound your nervousness by holding unrealistic expectations about your performance? Keep a positive, realistic attitude about how you will do.

Second, you should know that public speaking is a teachable skill, much like math, reading, and writing. So, yes, you can *learn* to speak well. We share responsibility for part of that learning with your instructor. You are also responsible for much of your learning through your own effort and initiative. If you skipped the preface to this book, we urge you to take the few minutes necessary to turn back and read it. Written primarily for you, not just for your instructor, the preface condenses our philosophy about this course and about education in general.

We began this chapter by focusing on speaker nervousness because we know that it is a real worry for most people. We have suggested some techniques to help manage and channel your platform panic into a lively, enthusiastic speech. We have also sketched in broad strokes the process of developing and delivering an effective speech. If you stop to think about public speaking for a moment, though, you will realize that the worst thing that could happen to you is that you might embarrass yourself. Stop and ask yourself, "Have I ever embarrassed myself before?" Unless you never leave your house, the answer to that question will be yes. You may have even embarrassed yourself so badly that you thought, "I'll never be able to face them again" or "I'll never live this down." But you do. The sun rises the next day. None of us is perfect, and it is unreasonable to expect perfection of ourselves or the people around us. So the best advice of all may be, "Keep public speaking in perspective." Your audience is made up of colleagues. They are pulling for you. Use this friendly atmosphere as a training ground to become a more effective speaker.

Summary

The topic of this chapter is the widespread and normal phenomenon of speaker nervousness or stage fright. Caused by the body's preparation to perform to capacity, stage fright is a condition the speaker should try not to eliminate but rather to control. We offer 12 suggestions for controlling nervousness: (1) Know how you react to stress. (2) Know your strengths and weaknesses. (3) Know basic speech principles. (4) Know that it always looks worse from the inside. (5) Without memorizing your speech, know what you plan to say in it. (6) Believe in your topic. (7) Have a positive attitude about speech making. (8) Visualize yourself speaking successfully. (9) Project confidence. (10) Test your message prior to delivering it in class. (11) Practice as much as possible in a variety of situations. (12) Learn from your experience, and keep public speaking in its proper perspective.

You can also lessen your nervousness about your first speech by preparing thoroughly. To do so, you must understand the speaking assignment, develop adequate content of a narrow topic, organize the various sections of the speech, word your ideas effectively, practice productively, deliver the speech, and evaluate your performance. Preparing your first speech will also be easier if you realize that your nervousness is normal and that you can learn to be an effective speaker. Only by reflecting on your performance and on criticisms given by others can you develop as a speaker and deliver your next speech with less anxiety.

Exercises

1. Complete McCroskey's Personal Report of Public Speaking Anxiety (Figure 3.1), and determine your score. Into which group does your score place you, and how do you compare with other college students whose survey results were discussed early in this chapter? Which coping strategies discussed in this chapter seem most promising in building your confidence?

2. Divide a sheet of paper into two columns. In Column A, list nervous symptoms you experience when speaking to a group of people. In Column B, list ways you can control each symptom. For example:

Column A	Column B
Play with ring on my finger, turning it while speaking	Remove ring before speaking Keep hands apart by gesturing more often

3. Again, divide a sheet of paper in two columns. In Column A, list ten of your strengths. In Column B, state how those strengths can benefit you in your public speaking. For example:

Column A	Column B
Like to read a lot	Have lots of ideas for possible speech topics Can put this skill to good use when I start researching my speech

4. Interview someone who occasionally gives public speeches, asking how he or she handles speaker nervousness. Based on your interview, compile a list of suggestions for controlling nervousness. How does that list compare with the one in this chapter?

Notes

1. Jerry Seinfeld, *SeinLanguage* (New York: Bantam, 1993) 120.

2. Virginia P. Richmond and James C. McCroskey, *Communication: Apprehension, Avoidance, and Effectiveness,* 5th ed. (Boston: Allyn, 1998) 41.

3. "Ask Them Yourself," *Family Weekly* 28 January 1979: 2.

4. Wendy Wasserstein, "Streeping Beauty: A Rare Interview with Cinema's First Lady," *Interview* Dec. 1988: 90.

5. Lee Iacocca with William Novak, *Iacocca: An Autobiography* (New York: Bantam, 1984) 16.

6. Garrison Keillor, "Monologue," *A Prairie Home Companion,* 13 Feb. 1999, NPR, 16 Mar. 1999 <http://www.phc.mpr.org/>.

7. David Wallechinsky, Irving Wallace, and Amy Wallace, *The Book of Lists* (New York: Morrow, 1977) 469–70.

8. John H. Greist, James W. Jefferson, and Isaac M. Marks, *Anxiety and Its Treatment* (New York: Warner, 1986) 33.

9. Richmond and McCroskey 45. The "Personal Report of Public Speaking Anxiety (PRPSA)" and directions for interpreting the scored results, reprinted in this chapter, appear on pages 135–136 and page 45, respectively, of Richmond and McCroskey.

10. Ed McMahon, *The Art of Public Speaking* (New York: Ballantine, 1986) 4.

11. Ralph B. Behnke, Chris R. Sawyer, and Paul E. King, "The Communication of Public Speaking Anxiety," *Communication Education* 36 (1987): 140.

12. Howard Nemerov, *Figures of Thought: Speculations on the Meaning of Poetry and Other Essays* (Boston: Godine, 1978) 19.

13. Joe Ayres and Theodore S. Hopf, "Visualization: A Means of Reducing Speech Anxiety," *Communication Education* 34 (1985): 321.

14. Daryl J. Bem, *Belief, Attitudes, and Human Affairs* (Belmont, CA: Brooks/Cole, 1970) 57.

15. Jack Valenti, *Speak Up with Confidence* (New York: Morrow, 1982) 19.

. . . [L]istening requires something more than remaining mute while looking attentive—namely, it requires the ability to attend imaginatively to another's language. Actually, in listening we speak the other's words.

—*Leslie H. Farber*

Responding to Speeches

Listening is a magnetic and strange thing, a creative force. The friends who listen to us are the ones we move forward toward, and we want to sit in their radius. When we are listened to, it creates us, makes us unfold and expand.

—*Karl A. Menninger, Love Against Hate*[1]

Effective public communication occurs in the charged space between a speaker and an audience, with each party leaning slightly toward the other. Within that space, for the duration of a speech, the contract binding public speakers and their audiences is in effect. We discussed that contract in Chapter 2. We maintained that as members of a community of learners in the classroom, each speaker and each listener bear ethical responsibilities. Among the commitments of the ethical speaker are being well prepared, communicating information and ideas clearly in order to benefit the audience, and remaining open to feedback and criticism that will improve future speeches. Among the responsibilities of ethical listeners are listening openly, listening critically, and providing feedback to assist the speaker's thinking on the topic and to help him or her improve as a public speaker. If the mutual respect implicit in this speaker–listener contract exists, as we believe it should, then listening is the paper on which participants write their contract, and criticism is their ink.

In this chapter we focus on the related topics of listening and speech criticism. As we look at the process, problems, and potential of listening, we will provide you with the tools you need to improve your listening skills. We'll then discuss the nature of criticism, offer guidelines for making helpful critical comments, and suggest some ways that you can maximize the benefits of speech critiques you receive from others.

Listening
http://www.listen.org/
Visit the Web site of the International Listening Association to find a host of excellent quotations about listening, as well as links to resources on the topic of listening.

The Importance of Listening

You probably remember playing the game of "telephone" when you were a child. Someone whispered a phrase or sentence to another person, who whispered it to the next one, and so on. The last person to receive the message then said it aloud. Usually, the final message bore little resemblance to what the first person whispered, and the group laughed at the outcome.

Unfortunately, examples of poor listening exist in areas of life where the results are often far from humorous. In fact, researchers estimate that U.S. businesses lose billions of dollars each year simply because of ineffective listening:

> Because of poor listening, letters have to be retyped; appointments have to be rescheduled; shipments have to be reshipped; individuals and organizations are unable to understand and respond to customers' and clients' real needs; employees feel ignored, disgruntled, and ultimately alienated from management; ideas are distorted by as much as 80 percent as they travel through communication channels; unnecessary conflicts disrupt operations and decrease production; and entire organizations are manipulated by propaganda techniques.[2]

Of course, ineffective listening is not confined to commercial settings. You can probably think of several examples of problems, or at least embarrassing situations, caused by your own ineffective listening. You went to the wrong building to begin registering for classes, or you went to the right place at the wrong time. You asked a question the teacher had just answered. You didn't realize that the biology exam covered your lab notes as well as the lecture material, or that a complete sentence outline of your informative speech on the causes and cures of snoring was due a week before you were scheduled to speak. You arrived at a party dressed in jeans, a T-shirt, and Doc Martens® only to find everyone else dressed formally.

Each day, you send and receive both oral and written messages. Of the four roles you perform—speaker, listener, writer, and reader—you spend more time listening than doing any of the other actions. College students, for example, spend approximately 53 percent of their communication time listening.[3] You listen to your parents, teachers, and friends; to television, radio, and movies; and to many other sounds around you. Yet, despite listening's monopoly on your time, you probably know less about this activity than about other forms of communication. While you have taken several courses teaching you to read and write, you have probably never taken a course in listening. In short, you have received the least training in what you do the most!

It will probably not surprise you, then, to learn that most of us are inefficient listeners. In fact, immediately after listening to your classmates' speeches, chances are high that you will remember, at most, only 50 percent of what you heard, and two days later only 25 percent. This doesn't surprise listening expert Robert Montgomery, who summarizes the sad plight of listening:

> Listening is the most neglected and the least understood of the communication arts. It has become the weakest link in today's communications system. Poor listening is a result of bad habits that develop because we haven't been trained to listen.

But there is good news, as Montgomery adds: "Fortunately, it is a skill that can be learned."[4]

Listening vs. Hearing

Does the following situation sound familiar? You are watching *The Late Show with David Letterman,* listening to a Joe Satriani CD, or doing economics homework when one of your parents walks by and tells you to put out the trash. Fifteen minutes later, that person walks back to find you still preoccupied with television, music, or homework, and the trash still in the kitchen. Your parent asks, "Didn't you hear me?" Well, of course you did. You *heard* the direction to put out the trash just as you heard Letterman joking with Paul Shaffer, Satriani playing a riff, the dog barking at a passing car, and the air conditioner clicking on in the hall. You heard all of these things, but you might not have been *listening* to any of them.

What is the difference between **listening** and **hearing?** Listening differs from hearing in at least four important ways.

Listening Is Intermittent

Listening is not a continuous activity, but occurs only from time to time when we choose to focus and respond to stimuli around us. Hearing, on the other hand, is a continuous function for a person having normal hearing ability.

listening: the intermittent, learned, and active process of giving attention to aural stimuli.

hearing: the continuous, natural, and passive process of receiving aural stimuli.

Listening Is a Learned Skill

Listening must be taught and learned. Unless you were born with a hearing loss, however, hearing is a natural capacity for which you need no training. We hear sounds before we are born; fetuses grow accustomed to certain voices, noises, and music. For this reason, pediatricians advise new parents not to tiptoe or whisper around the infant they have just brought home from the hospital. The child is already used to a lot of noise and must grow accustomed to the rest of it. Throughout our lives, we hear sounds even as we sleep.

Listening Is Active

Hearing means simply receiving an aural stimulus. The act of hearing is passive; it requires no work. Anytime the tiny bones of the inner ear are set in vibration, we are hearing something, and the activity requires no expenditure of energy. We can limit hearing only by trying to reduce or eliminate the sources of sound in the environment or by covering our ears.

Listening, in contrast, is active. It requires you to concentrate, interpret, and respond—in short, to be involved. You can hear the sound of a fire engine as you sit at your desk working on your psychology paper. You listen to the sound of the fire engine if you concentrate on its sound, identify it as a fire engine rather than an ambulance, wonder if it is coming in your direction, and then turn back to your work as you hear the sound fade away.

Listening Implies Using the Message Received

Audiences assemble for many reasons. We choose to listen to gain new information; to learn new uses for existing information; to discover arguments for beliefs or actions; to assess those arguments; to laugh and be entertained; to provide emotional support for a speaker; to celebrate a person, place, object, or idea; and to be inspired.

We are attracted to novel ideas and information just because we may have some future use for that data. There are literally thousands of topics you could listen to: for example, characteristics of gangsta rap, regulating the Internet, the history of blue jeans, crimes of ethnic intimidation, the ethics of criminal entrapment, preparing lemongrass chicken, fantasy league football and baseball, digital photography, and the life of Arthur Ashe. Some of these topics might induce you to listen carefully. Others might not interest you, so you choose not to listen. The perceived usefulness of the topic helps

Peanuts by Schultz. Copyright © 1993 United Features Syndicate. Reprinted with the permission of United Media.

determine how actively you will listen to a speaker. Listening implies a choice; you must choose to participate in the process of listening.

The Process of Listening

In Chapter 1, we introduced the listener as one component of communication. Indeed, the listener is vital to successful communication; without at least one listener, communication cannot occur beyond the intrapersonal level. Remember that any time two people communicate, two messages are involved: the one that the sender intends and the one that the listener actually receives. As we discussed in Chapter 1, these messages will never be identical because people operate from different frames of reference and with different perceptions. As you examine the six steps in the process of listening shown in Figure 4.1, you will better understand this concept.

Receive

The first step in listening is to *receive* sounds. In face-to-face communication, we receive sound waves set in motion through the air by the speaker; on the telephone, those same sound waves are transmitted electronically. In both cases, the first step in listening to the speaker is receiving the sounds, the auditory stimuli. In other words, hearing is the first step in effective listening.

You may have heard people say, "I can't hear without my glasses." What they usually mean is that they hear better when they can clearly see the person speaking. Normally, we validate one sense by checking it against others. Thus, even if you recognize the voice of a classmate behind you asking a question, you are likely to turn around and

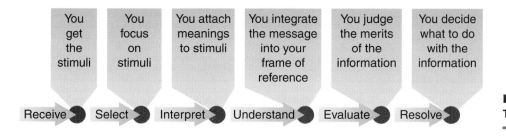

| You get the stimuli | You focus on stimuli | You attach meanings to stimuli | You integrate the message into your frame of reference | You judge the merits of the information | You decide what to do with the information |

Receive ▶ Select ▶ Interpret ▶ Understand ▶ Evaluate ▶ Resolve ▶

FIGURE 4.1
The process of listening

look to make sure. At other times, we may use our senses of taste, smell, or touch to confirm or contradict the auditory message we have received.

Some people unintentionally filter or leave out part of the stimulus. People with a hearing loss, for example, unintentionally filter parts of the messages around them. Whenever we filter, parts of the messages available to us will be lost.

Select

Individuals *select* different stimuli from those competing for their attention, a phenomenon sometimes called selective perception. When the police gather reports from various witnesses to a traffic accident, they often find conflicting information. Each bystander's report will be shaped by where the person was standing or sitting, what the person was focusing on at the moment of impact, how the person was feeling, and a host of other factors. Each witness had a selective perception of the event.

In public speaking situations, the audience reacts in a similar way. One person in the audience may focus primarily on what speakers are saying, another on their tones of voice or their gestures, still another on what they are wearing, or even the distracting hum of the heating system. If you are intrigued by the speaker's accent, you have selected to focus on that element of speech delivery, and you will probably hear a slightly different speech than the person sitting next to you. You may even be distracted by internal noise, such as worrying about an upcoming chemistry exam or trying to resolve a conflict with your roommate. As William James said over 100 years ago, our view of the world is truly shaped by what we decide to heed.

Millions of items of the outward order are present to my senses which never properly enter into my experience. Why? Because they have no interest for me. My experience is what I agree to attend to.[5]

—William James

Tests of Listening Habits
http://www.listencoach.com/LHProfile.html
http://www.isdesignet.com/isdesignet/magazine/Apr'96/commentary.html
To test your own listening habits, visit either of these sites. The first, maintained by Richard Bommelje, lets you complete a ten-item questionnaire. Once you submit it, a second page immediately tells you your score and how to interpret it. The isdesignet site contains a 25-item questionnaire with directions for self-scoring developed by Richard Ensman, Jr., a Rochester, New York, communication consultant.

Interpret

Not only do individuals choose differently among stimuli competing for their attention, they also *interpret* those stimuli differently. Interpreting is the process of decoding the message. When you interpret, you attach meanings to the cluster of verbal and nonverbal symbols the speaker provides—words, tone of voice, and facial expression, for example. At this stage, the listener is paying careful attention to those verbal and nonverbal symbols and their meanings. When a speaker introduced her speech on euthanasia, one listener heard "youth in Asia." Only after correcting this misinterpretation was the listener prepared to understand the speaker's message. As we noted in our discussion of the triangle of meaning in Chapter 1, the speaker's frame of reference must be similar to the listener's if communication is to be clear and effective.

Understand

Once you have decoded, or attached meanings to, a speaker's symbols, you begin fitting the message into your framework of existing knowledge and beliefs. To *understand* a speaker, you must consider both a message's content and its context. Is the speaker attempting to inform or persuade you? Is the speaker serious or joking? In short, what is the speaker trying to do?

It is easier to judge the context of communication when you listen to friends rather than to strangers. When you communicate with your friends, you can tell whether they are joking, upset, or teasing by their facial expressions or tones of voice, but you cannot always tell with strangers. You know your friends well and are more familiar with their cues. Communication from friends provides you cues to understand the context of the message. As you learn more about speakers, then, you enable yourself to understand their messages more accurately.

Evaluate

Before acting upon the message you have decoded and understood, you *evaluate* it. Evaluating is the process of judging both the reliability of the speaker and the quality and consistency of the speaker's information. If the speaker is someone you know, you reflect on the history of that person's interactions with you. Has the person ever tried to deceive you? Or does the speaker have a track record of honest, open communication with you? If the speaker is a stranger, you often gauge the person's credibility based on the nonverbal cues of communication. Is the speaker making eye contact with you? Does he or she speak fluently, without unnecessary pauses or filler words? Do the speaker's gestures and other body language seem relaxed and spontaneous? In short, does the person seem well prepared, confident, and sincere? If your answer to any of these questions is no, you may wonder whether the speaker has ulterior motives for speaking to you. As you evaluate the speaker's message, you decide whether you believe the data presented, and whether you agree or disagree with the position the speaker advocates.

Resolve

The final step in listening, resolving, involves deciding what to do with the information we have received. As listeners, we can *resolve* to accept the information, reject it, take action on it, decide to investigate further, or just try to remember the information so that we can resolve it later.

If you were unable to sense when your friends were serious or joking, you'd have a hard time interpreting and understanding what they told you.

Obviously, we do not consciously go through and dwell upon each of these six steps each time we listen to someone. As the significance of the message increases for us, however, we become more involved in the process of listening—a point each speaker should remember.

Obstacles to Effective Listening

Speakers and audience members should recognize some of the reasons why effective listening is so difficult. Learning to listen better is easier if you know what you're up against. For this reason, you need to identify the major obstacles to effective listening. We list and discuss five barriers to listening in this section.

Physical Distractions

Have you ever told someone that he or she was being so loud that you couldn't hear yourself think? If so, you were commenting on one obstacle to effective listening: physical distraction. **Physical distractions** are interferences coming to you through any of your senses, and they may take many forms: glare from a sunny window, chill from an air conditioner vent, or the smell of formaldehyde in your anatomy and physiology lab. Like a diner whose enjoyment of a meal is spoiled by cigar smoke, you may have trouble focusing on the message of a speech on toxic waste if you concentrate on the speaker's outlandish clothing, on a PE class playing a vigorous game of touch football outside, or on the overpowering smell of aftershave on the person near you.

Physiological Distractions

Physiological distractions have to do with the body. Any illness or unusual physiological condition is a potential distraction to effective listening. A bout of flu, a painful earache, or a sleepless night all place obvious and familiar limitations on our willingness and ability to listen.

Psychological Distractions

Your attitudes also affect your listening behavior. **Psychological distractions,** such as a negative attitude toward the speaker, the topic, or your reason for attending a speech, can all affect how you listen. If you are antagonistic toward the speaker or the point of view the speaker is advocating, you may resist or mentally debate the statements you hear. If you are coerced to be in the audience, you may also be more critical and less open-minded about what is being said. In short, if you are concentrating on thoughts unrelated to what the speaker is saying, you will receive less of the intended message.

Factual Distractions

College students, who should be among the most adept listeners in our society, find that they are often hampered by **factual distractions,** such as listening disturbances caused by the flood of facts presented to them in lectures. You may be tempted to treat each fact as a potential test question. But this way of listening can pose problems for you. For example, have you ever

physical distractions: listening disturbances that originate in the physical environment and are perceived by the listener's senses.

physiological distractions: listening disturbances that originate in a listener's illness, fatigue, or unusual bodily stress.

psychological distractions: listening disturbances that originate in the listener's attitudes, preoccupations, or worries.

factual distractions: listening disturbances caused by attempts to recall minute details of what is being communicated.

Active Listening
http://home.earthlink.
net/~hopefull/active.htm
http://home.earthlink.
net/~hopefull/active1.htm
Visit the first of these pages to review 12 blocks to effective listening and to read a suggestion for breaking that pattern. The second site briefly discusses three activities necessary to active listening: paraphrasing, questioning for clarification, and offering feedback.

taken copious notes in your world civilization class only to find when you reread them that, although you have lots of facts, you missed the key ideas? Students and other victims of factual distractions sometimes listen for details, but miss the general point that the speaker is making.

Semantic Distractions

Semantic distractions are those caused by confusion over the meanings of words. Listeners may be confused by a word they have never before seen or heard, one they have seen in print but have never heard spoken, or a word the speaker is mispronouncing. If a student gave a speech about her native country, Eritrea, without showing that word on a visual aid, the typical American listener would probably begin wondering, "How do I spell that?" "Have I ever seen that word on a map before?" "Is this a new name for an established country?" "Is the speaker pronouncing correctly a word I've always heard mispronounced?" These thoughts divert you from the serious business of listening to a speech filled with new and interesting information. In Chapter 12, "Wording Your Speech," we will discuss some ways speakers can minimize misunderstandings about the meanings of words.

Promoting Better Listening

Once you understand the obstacles to effective listening, you can develop a plan of action to improve your listening behavior and that of your audience. A major theme of this book, as you no doubt are now aware, is that each party in the communication process has a responsibility to promote effective communication. Promoting better listening should be a goal of both the sender and the receiver of the message. How can you encourage better listening?

As a speaker, you can use many of the suggestions in the following chapters to help your audience hear and retain your message. You enhance the audience's retention, for example, when you select your ideas carefully, organize your ideas clearly, support your ideas convincingly, word your ideas vividly, and deliver your ideas forcefully.

As a listener, you must also work hard to understand and remember the speaker's message. So far in this chapter we have examined the process of listening and have discussed the obstacles to effective listening. The following nine suggestions will help you become a more effective listener. As you master these suggestions, you will find yourself understanding and remembering more of what you hear.

Guidelines to Promote Better Listening

1. Desire to listen.
2. Focus on the message.
3. Listen for main ideas.
4. Understand the speaker's point of view.
5. Withhold judgment.
6. Reinforce the message.
7. Provide feedback.
8. Listen with the body.
9. Listen critically.

key points

Desire to Listen

Your attitude will determine, in part, your listening effectiveness. In this class you have the opportunity to learn a great deal of information from your classmates' speeches. Some topics will interest you; others, no doubt, will not. Good listeners, however, begin

semantic distractions: listening disturbances caused by confusion over the meanings of words.

with the assumption that each speech can potentially benefit them. You may not find a speech on how financial institutions determine a person's credit rating of great interest right now. Nevertheless, the first time you apply for a loan you may be happy that you paid attention and prepared for your visit to the bank.

Some speeches you hear in this class will be excellently prepared and delivered; others will not. Again, good listeners can learn something from any speech, even if it is poorly prepared and awkwardly delivered. For example, you can determine what the speaker could have done to improve the poorly developed speech. This experience enables you to apply speech principles you have learned and to improve your own speaking.

In your class you may also have the opportunity to offer helpful suggestions to your colleagues who present speeches. You will want to listen carefully so that you can help them improve. If you have a genuine desire to listen to a speaker, you will understand and remember more.

Speakers can promote better listening by demonstrating early in their speeches how the information will benefit their listeners. Let your audience know quickly just why it is in their interest to listen carefully to your speech. We believe this step is so important that we discuss it in Chapter 10, "Introducing and Concluding Your Speech," as one of the five functions of an effective speech introduction.

Focus on the Message

Your first responsibility as a listener is to listen attentively to the speaker's message. Yet, a speaker's message competes with other, often quite powerful, stimuli for your attention. One of us once conducted a seminar entitled "First Impressions—Lasting Impressions" in a large room adjacent to a hallway that was being painted. The smell of the paint became a powerful distraction for both speaker and audience. During the presentation, one of the audience members opened a door allowing outside air to freshen the room. In addition, the speaker moved from behind the lectern and enlivened his delivery by changing his speaking tone and using more varied gestures. In this situation, both the speaker and the audience worked together to focus more on the message and less on the distracting smell.

Often speakers themselves create distractions. They may play with change or keys in their pockets, dress inappropriately, sway nervously from side to side, use offensive language, or say "um" throughout their speeches. These quirks can be very distracting. We have had students, for example, who actually counted the number of "ums" in a speech. After a classmate's speech, they would write in their critiques, "You said 'um' 31 times in your speech." While this may have provided the speaker with some valuable feedback, we suspect these listeners learned little else from the speaker's message. You may not be able to ignore distractions completely as you listen, but you can try to minimize them.

Active Listening
http://www2.tltc.ttu.edu/
Zanglein/ADR/active.htm
This site, maintained by Professor Jayne Zanglein of Texas Tech University, contains links to 25 sites dealing with active listening.

As we discussed earlier, messages may be both verbal and nonverbal. For this reason, listeners should listen with their eyes as well as their ears. We have all heard someone begin a statement, "I'm not saying this to be critical, but. . . ." That preface often reveals more about the speaker's intent than about the words that follow; usually, the person is being critical. When we perceive a discrepancy between a person's verbal and nonverbal messages, we tend to believe the nonverbal message, and this response may be justified. People are better at disguising their emotions with their words than with their bodies. You can often read body and voice cues to evaluate both what speakers think is important and their degree of commitment to what they are saying.

Speakers, of course, can help listeners focus on the message by eliminating distracting mannerisms and by incorporating nonverbal behaviors that reinforce rather than contradict their ideas. For example, appropriate gestures can make a speech easier to remember by describing objects, providing directions, and illustrating dimensions.

Listen for Main Ideas

You are familiar with the cliché that sometimes you can't see the forest for the trees; well, that saying applies to listening. A person who listens for facts often misses the main point of the message. While it is important to attend to the supporting material of a speech, you should be able to relate it to the major point being developed. As in the simple game of tic tac toe, in which the evolving strategy is most important, "Listening for just the facts is like paying attention to only one O or one X without seeing the relationship or pattern that is emerging. You'll get beaten every time."[6]

When listening to a speech, pay close attention to the speaker's organization of the material. The structure of a speech provides a framework for both speaker and listeners to organize the supporting points and materials of the speech. Speakers who clearly enumerate their key ideas and repeat them at several points in their speeches give their audience a better opportunity to be attentive listeners than do disorganized speakers. We discuss organizational techniques in Chapters 9 and 10.

Understand the Speaker's Point of View

As we discussed in Chapter 1, each of us has different referents for the words we hear or speak because we have different life experiences. These life experiences affect how we view our world.

Speaking in favor of agricultural programs that would preserve the family farm, our student Cathy tried to involve her audience in her speech by tapping their memories. She asked her classmates to think of the houses they grew up in and the memories created there.

> Think of Thanksgiving and Christmas gatherings. Think of slumber parties and birthday celebrations. Of how you changed your room as you moved from child to teenager to young adult. Think of your feelings as you left home to come to college, and of your feelings when you return to those comfortable confines.

After the speech several students said they were moved by Cathy's eloquence and passion. She had tapped memories important to them. Others in the audience, however, said they were unable to relate to the topic in the way the speaker intended. Several had grown up in more than one house. Some were in military families and had moved often. Still others said they had lived in rented townhomes or apartments. And a few commented that their childhood memories were not fond ones. Both speakers and listeners need to remember that different experiences shape and limit our understanding of another's message.

When speakers and listeners come from different cultures, the chances for misunderstanding increase. Differences in language, education, and customs challenge listeners to work especially hard at understanding the speaker's message and intent. These differences are often evident in today's multicultural classroom. Some foreign students, for example, come from educational environments that are more structured and formal than the typical American college classroom. They may interpret a speaker's casual dress and use of humor as an indication that the speaker is not serious about the speech. On the other hand, some American students may perceive the more formal presentations of some of their foreign counterparts as stiff and indicating a lack of interest in the topic. Understanding each other's frame of reference minimizes this distortion.

Speakers should do two things to clarify their points of view in speeches. First, explain early in the speech if you have some particular reason for selecting your topic, or some special qualifications to speak on the subject. If you choose to speak on radio formats because you work at your campus radio station or because you are a radio-television-film major, tell the audience a little about your background. If you are a registered gemologist and decide to speak on the subject of emeralds, be sure to tell the audience about your qualifications. Second, try to relate your subject to your listeners' frames of reference. Your use of technical jargon or complex explanations may limit their ability to listen effectively. Use examples and language your audience will understand.

Withhold Judgment

You have probably listened to some political debates and heard discussions of them afterwards. You and a friend may even have discussed the pros and cons of each candidate and differed over who won. What was important and memorable to you may have been quite different from what your friend found impressive. You may even have wondered if you had been watching the same debate.

In a sense, you and your friend did watch two different debates. Two people with contrasting perspectives receive two different messages while watching one communication event. You filtered what you heard through your set of beliefs and values. You began judging the candidates and the debate before it ever took place. This is quite common. Many of us have a problem withholding judgment. We hear something and immediately label it as right or wrong, good or bad. The problem is that once we do that, we cease to listen objectively to the rest of the message.

It is difficult for you to withhold judgment, of course, when you listen to a speech advocating a position you strongly oppose. The following list includes topics student speakers sometimes discuss: legalization of drugs, capital punishment, mandatory drug testing, abortion, flag burning, euthanasia, gun control, and hiring quotas. We suspect you have some fairly strong opinions on most of these issues. You may even find it difficult to listen to a speech opposing your view without silently debating the speaker. Yet, as you mentally challenge these arguments, you miss much of what the speaker is saying. If you can suspend evaluation until after speakers have presented and supported their arguments, you will be a better listener.

Some speakers present views that are highly divisive. Whether or not we agree with them, we should learn to withhold judgment until after listening to what they say.

Most Americans speak at rates between 125 and 190 words per minute. Those numbers may seem high to you, but consider the average speaking rates of the following people. You might think that Ronald Reagan, our oldest president when he began his first term, would have slowed his rate of speaking. In fact, he averaged 170 words per minute.[7] Former president Jimmy Carter, often described as a plodding speaker, averages 160 words per minute. Bill Clinton averages 120 words per minute. Gene Shalit, the *Today* show's cantankerous movie critic, speaks very fast but very clearly. He rarely strays from an average rate of 190 words per minute. If you communicate simple ideas at a rate between 120 and 140 words per minute, your listeners may think you ill, reluctant, or uncertain.[8] Why? As listeners, we can process 400 to 500 words per minute. This means that, depending on the situation, we may be able to listen at a rate four times faster than a particular person speaks! As a result, we can get bored and move our attention back and forth between what the speaker is saying and some extraneous message, perhaps a personal problem that concerns us. Sometimes, the unrelated thought takes over and psychological noise, which we discussed earlier, drowns out the speaker's message. To be a better listener, you must make better use of this extra time.

You can fill some of this time and better focus on the message by mentally repeating, paraphrasing, and summarizing what the speaker is saying. You use *repetition* when you state exactly what the speaker has said. Consider, for example, a speaker who argues that a tuition increase is necessary to preserve educational excellence at your college or university. The first reason she offers is this: "A tuition increase will enable us to expand our library." If, after the speaker makes this claim, you mentally repeat her argument, you are using repetition to help you remember the speaker's message.

Using *paraphrase* is a second way of helping yourself remember the message. By putting the speaker's ideas into your own words, you become actively involved in message transmission. Suppose the same speaker offers this statement to justify one benefit of a tuition increase:

> A tuition increase would generate funds that could be used to enhance our library facilities and resources. In the chancellor's budget proposal, one-third of the tuition increase would go directly to the library. The chancellor estimates that this would enable us to increase our library holdings of books, periodicals, and audiovisual resources by 10 percent. Also, projected construction would create at least 12 new study rooms.

Obviously, it would be difficult to restate the speaker's explanation word for word. Yet you could paraphrase and summarize her message this way:

> A tuition hike would increase our library holdings by 10 percent and expand the number of study rooms by 12.

You use *summary* when you condense what a speaker says. The above paraphrase includes summary as it leaves out some of the specific information the speaker presented. As a speaker concludes his or her message, you should recollect the key points of the speech. Your summary might be, for example: "A tuition increase will help us

Paraphrasing
http://owl.english.purdue.edu/Files/30e.html
http://www.wisc.edu/writing/Handbook/QuoSuccessfulSummary.html
The Purdue University Online Writing Lab and the University of Wisconsin–Madison Writing Center each offer several exercises that allow you to practice paraphrasing the ideas of others. Both provide guidelines for paraphrasing and examples of appropriate and inappropriate paraphrases. Each site also illustrates how to introduce quotations.

expand the library, increase the number of faculty, and renovate some of the older dormitories." By getting you actively involved in the communication process, repetition, paraphrase, and summary increase your chances of understanding and remembering the message.

Provide Feedback

A listener can enhance the communication process by providing feedback to the speaker. Although there is greater opportunity for *verbal* feedback in interpersonal and group environments, it is nevertheless also possible in public speaking contexts. The effective speaker will especially read the *nonverbal* cues of the audience to assist in the presentation of the speech. If you understand and accept the point of the speaker and nod in agreement, the speaker can move to the next idea. If you appear perplexed, that signal should prompt the speaker to explain the idea more fully before moving to the next point.

Listen with the Body

We listen with more than our ears. In a sense, we listen with our entire bodies. If, as your instructor lectures, you lean back, stretch your legs, cross your arms, and glance at a fellow classmate, you detract from your listening effectiveness. Part of listening is simply being physically ready to listen.

You can ready yourself for listening if you sit erect, lean slightly forward, and place both feet flat on the floor. As you listen, look at the speaker. As important as the message you hear is the message you see. Remember, you want to detect any nonverbal messages that intensify or contradict the speaker's verbal message.

Listen Critically

Even though listeners should understand a speaker's point of view and withhold judgment, they should nevertheless test the merits of what they hear. If you accept ideas and information without questioning them, you are in part responsible for the consequences. If the speaker advocating a tuition increase quotes from the chancellor's budget proposal before it has even been submitted, you have every right to be skeptical. "Will the final budget actually earmark one-third of the tuition increase for library use? Will the board of regents accept the chancellor's proposal? Or is this all speculation?" Decisions based on incorrect or incomplete data are seldom prudent and sometimes disastrous.

Critical listeners examine what they hear by asking several questions: Is the speech factually correct? Are sources clearly identified, and are they unbiased and credible? Does the speaker draw logical conclusions from the data presented? Has the speaker overlooked or omitted important information? Speakers help listeners answer those questions by presenting credible information, identifying their sources, and using valid reasoning.

John Marshall, Chief Justice of the United States from 1801 to 1835, once stated, "To listen well is as powerful a means of communication and influence as to talk well." If you use these nine suggestions you will become a better listener.

Critiquing Speeches

Almost as important as the speeches you deliver in your public speaking course are the kinds of comments you can offer about the speeches others give. This textbook and your instructor will show you how to prepare and deliver an effective speech. You should use this knowledge as you comment on the speeches you hear others deliver. Appropriate feedback is crucial to your development as a public speaker. What you learn from your instructor and classmates about distractions caused by language, voice, or body will help you polish your speaking skills. You, in turn, want to be an incisive and sensitive critic when you write or speak about others' speeches.

For the purposes of this section, we define **criticism** as information (feedback) given to others in a way that enables them to use it for self-improvement.[9] Whether written or spoken, criticism, then, includes both positive comments that reinforce what a speaker did well and negative comments that point to potential improvements. If you say, "Your speech was well within the time limit at seven minutes and twelve seconds," you function as a speech critic as you spotlight a positive aspect of the speech. If you write or say, "I liked your speech a lot," you are also providing speech criticism. Notice, however, that while this last comment would no doubt make most speakers happy, it doesn't really teach them anything. In fact, finding out how long they spoke is probably more instructive for speakers than hearing simply, "I liked it." There is nothing wrong with saying to your classmates, "I enjoyed your speech," or, "I didn't care for this speech as much as your last one." Just don't stop there. Explain why.

All criticism contains three parts: *judgments, reasons,* and *norms.*[10] Figure 4.2 illustrates the relationships between these parts. The most familiar and superficial level of critical comments consists of **judgments.** We make them frequently about many different subjects: "I don't like Christie's restaurant," "I loved the movie *Saving Private Ryan,*" "Dr. Hudson is an excellent teacher," or "I always enjoy your speeches."

Underlying those judgments, whether we voice them or not, are **reasons** of some sort: "I don't like Christie's restaurant because the seafood tastes mushy and the service is slow," "*Saving Private Ryan* really made me think about the sacrifices my generation didn't have to make," "Dr. Hudson is an excellent teacher because her lectures make a course I dreaded lively and interesting," or, "I always enjoy your speeches because you choose such unusual topics." Statements such as these specify reasons for the critics' judgments.

The statements in the preceding paragraph are instructive and useful because they help others infer your **norms,** the values you believe make something "good" or "effective" or "desirable." Such statements tell us that the individual critics value good

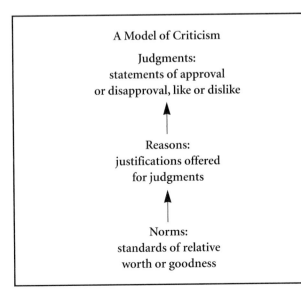

**FIGURE 4.2
A Model of Criticism**

A Model of Criticism

Judgments:
statements of approval
or disapproval, like or dislike

↑

Reasons:
justifications offered
for judgments

↑

Norms:
standards of relative
worth or goodness

criticism: feedback offered for the purpose of improving a speaker's speech.

judgments: a critic's opinions about the relative merits of a speech; the most common and superficial level of speech criticism.

reasons: statements that justify a critic's judgments.

norms: the values a critic believes necessary to make any speech good, effective, or desirable.

seafood and prompt service in a restaurant, emotion and positive messages in movies, liveliness in class lectures, and unusual topics in public speeches. We may, of course, argue with the critics about whether these norms are actually valid. That is healthy and productive. The lesson for us as speech critics is to provide reasons for our judgments; only by doing so do we tell the speaker the basis of our reactions.

Here are some examples of helpful comments made by students about their class-mates' speeches:

> Karen, your concern for children certainly shows in this speech on rating day care centers. Your personal examples really helped make the speech interesting.

> Adele, I liked your speech about the constellations a lot. The introduction was very interesting and piqued my curiosity. Your organization was clear, and you had ex-cellent transitions from one area to the next. You used a good speaking style in easy-to-understand language, and you defined unfamiliar terms. You also seemed really interested in what you were talking about and that made me interested, even though I thought you spoke rather quickly in places.

> Michael, your speech was interesting, but you need to slow down. I thought you also seemed to be distracted because you were looking out the windows or over to-ward the door occasionally.

> John, your speech on how to improve study habits was the best I heard. It was ap-propriate and beneficial to everyone in the class. Your language was simple and co-herent. You explained just what we needed to know in the time you had.

> Lettie, one problem I saw was your use of visual aids. Once you have finished with the visual aid, you should put it away rather than leave it where the audience can see it. That way, the audience will focus their attention on you rather than on the object.

One value of receiving written or oral comments from classmates about your speeches is that repetition of a criticism will reinforce it. If your instructor or an indi-vidual classmate tells you that you need to speak louder, you may discount the advice as one person's opinion. If 12 people in the class write or say that they had trouble hearing you, however, the criticism gains impact, and you are likely to give it more attention.

A second value of receiving criticism from many people is that different people value different aspects of a speech. Some people put a premium on delivery, others on speech content, and still others on organization. Individual classmates may no-tice different aspects of your speech simply because of where they sit in the class-room. With such a variety of perspectives and values, it would be a shame if all their criticism were reduced to "Good job!" or "I liked it." To provide the best criticism you can, just remember to specify the reasons for your judgments; ask yourself why a speech has the effect it does on you, and then try to communicate those reasons to the speaker.

We should also make a final note about the spirit in which you give speech criti-cism in this class. Your instructor may invite you to make oral or written comments about the speeches you hear others give. If your comments are written, they may be signed or unsigned. But whether your comments are written or oral, and whether your written critiques identify you or retain your anonymity, you should never make criticisms that are designed to belittle or hurt the speaker. Target the speech, not the speaker. Focus on specific behaviors rather than the person exhibiting those behav-iors. You will probably never hear a speech so fine that the speaker could not make some improvement; and you will never hear a speech so inept or ill-prepared that it does not have some redeeming value. *Listen evaluatively* and then *respond empatheti-*

cally, putting yourself in the speaker's place, and you should make truly helpful comments about your classmates' speeches.

To help you become a better critic for your classmates, we offer 10 suggestions you can use as you evaluate their speeches. One of our students, Susan, delivered an informative speech on three major tenets of the Amish faith. The text of that speech is included in Appendix B. We asked other students to critique Susan's speech, and we have used their comments to illustrate our suggestions.

Guidelines for Critiquing Speeches

1. Begin with a positive statement.
2. Target a few key areas for improvement.
3. Organize your comments.
4. Be specific.
5. Be honest but tactful.
6. Personalize your comments.
7. Reinforce the positive.
8. Problem-solve the negative.
9. Provide the speaker with a plan of action.
10. End with a positive statement.

key points

Begin with a Positive Statement

Do you remember being told, "If you can't say something nice, don't say anything at all"? Well, that's good advice to follow when you critique your classmates' speeches. Public speaking is a personal experience. You stand in front of an audience expressing *your* thoughts in *your* words with *your* voice and *your* body. When you affirm the positive, you establish a healthy climate for constructive criticism. Demonstrate to speakers that what they said or how they said it was worthy. Fortunately, you can always find something helpful to say if you think about it. Be positive—and be sincere!

Three of our students began their critiques of Susan's speech with the opening statements below.

> I found your speech on the Amish to be very interesting; their beliefs are fascinating. They seem very simple but very committed to their group—what a unique way of living.

> It was great that you brought back and displayed certain items from your trip to the Amish settlement. As a result, you were able to *show* something about the Amish lifestyle and not just *speak* of it.

> I have lived near the Amish in Pennsylvania. Your speech explained the reasons for their behavior. You clearly explained why they do what they do.

Notice that in addition to complimenting the speaker, the third critic also demonstrates her involvement in the topic.

Target a Few Key Areas for Improvement

Sometimes students (and instructors!) think that the more mistakes they can point out to a speaker, the more helpful their critiques will be. However, seldom is this true. Imagine how you would react if your instructor told you, "There are 17 areas you need to work on for your next speech." You'd probably feel overwhelmed: *How can I possibly do all that in time for my next speech? Which of the 17 suggestions should I focus on first?* Notice that Susan's critics focused on the most important strengths and weaknesses of her speech. In so doing, they provided her with manageable goals for her next speech. After accomplishing them, she could begin to improve other aspects of future speeches.

Organize Your Comments

A critique, just like a speech, is easier to follow if it is well organized. You can select from several options to frame your comments, and you should select the one that is most appropriate to you, the speaker, and the speech.

For example, you can organize your comments topically into the categories of speech *content, organization,* and *delivery.* A second option is chronological; you can discuss the speech's *introduction, body,* and *conclusion.* A third option is to divide your comments into speaking *strengths* and *weaknesses* (remember, give positive comments first). You could even combine these options. You could discuss the speaker's introduction, body, and conclusion, and within each of these categories discuss first the strengths and second the weaknesses.

Be Specific

Suppose instead of this list of ten suggestions for offering criticism, we simply said, "When you critique your classmates' speeches, be as helpful as possible so that they can improve their speaking." Although that is good advice, it's not very helpful, is it? By being more specific and detailing ten guidelines, we hope to provide you a handle on how you can improve your critiquing skills. Similarly, you will help your classmates if you provide them with specific suggestions for improvement.

In order for speakers to become more proficient, they need to know *what* to improve and *how* to improve. One of our students told Susan: "I liked the way you presented the speech as a whole." That statement provides a nice pat on the back, but it doesn't give Susan much direction. It certainly doesn't reflect what the listener had in mind. Is this a comment on Susan's vocal and physical delivery? Or does the verb *presented* include content and organization as well? The qualifying phrase "as a whole" seems to suggest that the listener noticed small problems that were minimized by the generally positive effect of Susan's speech. What were those problems, and what could Susan have done to minimize them? Remember, provide reasons for your judgments. In the two statements below, the listeners' comments are specific.

> I was really impressed with the fact that you did not use your notecards while you delivered the introduction or the conclusion. That suggests that you were confident and well prepared.

> Susan, you used good transitional phrases or words to move from subtopic to subtopic within each main point. An example of this was when you said, "Not only do the Amish have simple ways of dressing, but they also provide very simple toys for their children."

Be Honest but Tactful

Providing suggestions for improvement tests your interpersonal skills. At times you may be reluctant to offer criticism because you think it may offend the speaker. If you are not honest, however, the speaker may not know that the topic was dull, the content superficial, and the delivery uninspiring. Still, you must respect your classmates' feelings. The statement "Your speech was dull, superficial, and uninspiring" may be honest, but it is hardly tactful. It may provoke resistance to your suggestions or damage the speaker's self-esteem.

> *Do not remove a fly from your friend's forehead with a hatchet.*
> *—Chinese proverb*

One of our students thought Susan's speech content and organization were excellent but her delivery was mechanical and lifeless. The student could have said, "Your delivery lacked excitement." Instead, she wrote: "The only problem I saw with your speech was a lack of enthusiasm. Maybe the speech was too rehearsed. It just sounded kind of like a newscast. I think it needed some humor to break the monotony of your voice."

Personalize Your Comments

The more interest and involvement your critique conveys, the more likely the speaker is to believe in and act on your advice. You can personalize your comments in three ways. First, use the speaker's name occasionally, as in: "Susan, your hand gestures would be more effective if you used them less. I found myself being distracted by them."

A second way of reducing a speaker's defensiveness and establishing speaker–critic rapport is by using "I-statements" in place of "you-statements." Tell how the speech affected you. Instead of saying, "Your organization was weak," say, "I had trouble following your key ideas," and then give some examples of places where you got lost. The following is an example of what one of our students could have said and what she actually did say in her critique of Susan's speech:

> *She could have said:* "You lost my attention during the first part of your speech because you spoke so fast that I couldn't keep up with you."

> *Instead, she said:* "I had difficulty following your words at first because your rate seemed fast to me. After you settled down into the speech, though, I could listen with more attention."

A third way of personalizing your comments is by stating how you have benefited from hearing the speech. The following statements from two student critiques let Susan know that her speech was interesting and helpful.

> I found myself interested and saying, "Hmm," all through your speech. It especially caught my attention when you showed the toys, the quilt, and the artwork. And putting the visual aids down after explaining them helped in keeping me interested in the next area.

> Your topic was new and exciting information, which made the speech easy to listen to. I have always been curious about why the Amish live differently. Now I know why.

Reinforce the Positive

Sometimes we want so much to help someone improve that we focus on what the speaker did wrong and forget to mention what the speaker did well. As you enumerate how speakers can improve, don't forget the things they did well and should continue doing. One student was impressed with Susan's language and vocal delivery. She made the following comment:

> Susan, your delivery was excellent. You used your voice to emotionally color your message. I really felt as if I was living in the pictures that your descriptions created.

Problem-Solve the Negative

If you are serious about wanting to improve your speaking, you will want to know the weaknesses of your speech. Only then can you improve. As a critic, you have a responsibility to help your classmates become better speakers. Don't be afraid to let them know what went wrong with a speech.

> As she listened to Jeff's speech on the importance of rap music, Crystal found some of the lyrics he recited to be obscene and sexist. As she continued listening, she thought to herself, "These lyrics are offensive. I refuse to listen to them at home, so why should I be forced to listen to them now?" So, Crystal stood up and walked out of the classroom during Jeff's speech.
>
> Was it appropriate for Crystal to leave the classroom? Should audience members in your class have the freedom to listen or not to listen to certain speeches? Are there some topics for which walking out is an acceptable form of feedback to the speaker? If so, what are some of these topics? What should guide a listener's decision to take such action?

As a general rule, though, you should not criticize behaviors that the speaker cannot correct. On the day she spoke, Susan was suffering an allergic reaction to molds and pollen in the air. As a result of antihistamines she was taking, her throat was dry. Even if this had detracted significantly from her message, it would have been inappropriate for a student to comment, "I had trouble listening to what you said because your mouth seemed dry. Avoid that in your next speech." Such a request may well be beyond the speaker's control. On the other hand, it would be useful to suggest that Susan take a drink of water immediately before speaking, and several of our students did offer that advice.

You will help speakers improve their speaking if you follow two steps in your criticism. First, point out a specific problem; and, second, suggest ways to correct it. Remember the title of this section is not "List the Negatives" but "Problem-Solve the Negative." You want to propose ways to overcome problems.

One student was impressed with Susan's visual aids, but offered her the following advice about one of them:

> You said that the Amish don't like to have their pictures taken, and yet you used a picture of an Amish man as a visual aid. Next time, if you'd explain how or where you got the picture, it wouldn't leave picky people like me wondering during the rest of your speech how you got that picture.

Notice how another student offered a solution to a problem with one aspect of Susan's appearance.

> I liked your dress, but it tends to blend into the curtain behind you. Try wearing a lighter color dress next time, if at all possible.

Provide the Speaker with a Plan of Action

When you give your comments, include a plan of action for the speaker. What should the speaker concentrate on when presenting the next speech? One student focused Susan's attention on her next speaking experience by suggesting the following action plan:

> Susan, your overall speech and style of presentation were very good. However, I detected two minor things that could be improved upon. First, except when you were moving toward or away from a visual aid, you remained in one place. I believe that taking a few steps when you begin a subtopic would emphasize your transitions and enhance your message. Second, take more time to demonstrate and talk about the boy's toy that you showed us. You said, "It has marbles and fun moving parts," but I didn't really get a chance to see how it operates. Your

organization, your vocal emphasis and inflection, your eye contact, and your knowledge of the topic were all terrific. You're an effective speaker, and if you use these suggestions for your next speech, you will be even more effective.

End with a Positive Statement

Conclude your critique on a positive note. Speakers should be reminded that both you and they benefited from this experience. One of the highest compliments you can give a speaker is that you learned something from the speech. Two of our students concluded their critiques of Susan's speech as follows:

> Great job, Susan! You were very specific and enthusiastic about your subject, and your visual aids reinforced what was already thorough.

> Susan, you did an outstanding job. Your speech was well organized and very informative. You showed some signs of nervousness, but more practice will alleviate most of them. Whenever and wherever you will be speaking next, I'd like to be there.

Acting on Criticism

If your classmates follow these ten guidelines for offering criticism, you will receive honest, tactful, and specific comments that are well organized. Your critics will begin and end with positive evaluations of your speech. Their comments will offer suggestions and plans of action for solving problems in your speech. Listening to or reading such critiques of your speeches will be helpful and reassuring. Your listeners' critiques will never be identical, however. Remember, listening is a complex activity, and each member of your audience may have heard a slightly different speech. You may receive contradictory comments, and some with which you flatly disagree. Reading or hearing those comments can be intimidating and frustrating. What should you do in such situations?

Most of us dislike receiving criticism, yet such feedback is important to our success as public speakers. If you want to communicate more effectively, you must seek feedback from your listeners. Ethical speakers respect their audiences. Consideration for the audience means, in part, trusting their opinions and advice. If you respect your listeners, you will value their questions and suggestions about your speech. The following suggestions will enable you to get the most out of this process.

Guidelines for Acting on Criticism

1. Focus on *what* your critics say, not *how* they say it.
2. Seek clear and specific feedback.
3. Evaluate the feedback you receive.
4. Develop a plan of action.

key points

Focus on *What* Your Critics Say, Not *How* They Say It

In other words, listen to the content of the feedback, not the way in which it was presented. Too often, we become defensive when someone critiques us. Remember that offering criticism is not easy, and your critic may not have mastered the suggestions we've presented in the previous section. Avoid reacting emotionally to feedback, even if it is poorly worded and insensitive. Instead, focus on the content of the suggestions you receive.

Seek Clear and Specific Feedback

In order to improve your speaking, you must be aware of specific areas for improvement. Suppose a critic says, "Your organization could be improved." That may be an honest and valid statement, but it isn't very helpful. Ask the critic to be more specific. Is the problem with the introduction, body, or conclusion of the speech? What specific strategies could you use to improve your organization? It may take some good interpersonal communication to elicit the feedback you need to become a better public speaker.

Sometimes, you may receive conflicting feedback. Don't dismiss criticisms simply because they seem contradictory. For example, one critic may comment that your eye contact was good, another that it was poor. Both may be right. Perhaps you spoke only to those in the center of the room; they may have liked your eye contact, while others felt excluded. Perhaps some critics made their judgments early in your speech when you were interacting well with your listeners, and others reacted to the conclusion of your speech when you relied too much on your notes. Or, a critic's reaction may have been based on cultural norms; some cultures value eye contact more than others. It's important to learn the reasons behind a critic's judgment before you can improve your public speaking. In other chapters, we'll examine ways that critiquing applies to specific aspects of delivering and responding to speeches.

Evaluate the Feedback You Receive

It's not enough just to receive and understand feedback. You must use your critical thinking skills to analyze and evaluate that feedback. Repetition is one standard of judgment. If only one classmate thought your attention-getting step was weak, don't be too concerned. However, if your instructor and the majority of your classmates thought it deficient, you should target that as an area for improvement.

Develop a Plan of Action

After receiving feedback, summarize and record those comments. Then rank those areas needing improvement according to their importance. Rather than tackling every criticism, select a few to work on for your next speech. Write a plan of action that states your goals and the strategies you will use to achieve them.

Some of us are just generally thin-skinned—easily hurt by anything that seems to be a negative criticism—and at times all of us can become defensive. But don't be too quick to dismiss the feedback others give you about your speeches. Remember that your goal as you move from one speech to the next in a public speaking classroom is not consistency but consistent improvement. So, rather than defending what you said or did in your speech, listen carefully and act upon those suggestions for improvement that you receive most frequently. If you have doubts about the validity of suggestions your classmates are making, discuss the matter with your instructor. You will make the most accelerated improvement if you graciously accept the compliments of your peers and your instructor, and then work quickly to eliminate problems that they bring to your attention.

We began this chapter by talking about the contract that we believe always binds public speakers and their audiences. Speech criticism is further recognition of that commitment between speaker and listener. The ultimate aim of speech criticism is not just to improve a speaker's skills, or just to make a particular speech more enjoyable or instructive for an audience. Speech criticism should amplify and clarify the terms of the contract that any individual speaker will enter with all of his or her future audiences.

Summary

Poor listening costs American businesses billions of dollars yearly. The personal costs of poor listening include lost opportunities, embarrassment, financial losses, and, probably most important, lost time. We spend more time listening than we do involved in any other communication activity. Yet, ironically, we receive less instruction in listening than we do in reading, writing, or speaking. Luckily, we can teach and learn effective listening.

Listening differs from *hearing* in four ways. First, we listen only from time to time throughout the day, while hearing is continuous. Second, listening is a learned behavior, while hearing is a natural capacity for most people. Third, listening is active, hearing passive. Finally, listening implies doing something with the message received.

The complex act of listening contains six steps or phases. First, the listener *receives* sound stimuli from various senders or sources. Second, the listener *selects* particular parts of the total stimulus field for attention. Third, the listener *interprets* or decodes the message, attaching meanings to the various symbols received. The fourth step, *understanding,* involves matching the speaker's message with the listener's frame of reference. In the fifth step, the listener *evaluates* the reliability of the speaker and the speaker's message. Finally, after the reflection involved in the previous steps, the listener *resolves,* or decides what to do with, the information received.

Physical distractions from any part of the environment are one type of obstacle to effective listening. *Physiological distractions,* a second category, arise from conditions in the listener's body. A third obstacle is formed by *psychological distractions,* such as worry or preconceived attitudes toward the speaker or the message. *Factual distractions* are caused by our tendency to listen for small supporting details, even when we miss the main point the speaker is trying to make. Fifth and finally, listeners may be victims of *semantic distractions,* or confusion over the meanings of words.

Both speakers and listeners can contribute to effective listening in nine ways. First, listeners should develop a genuine desire to listen. Speakers promote this openness to listening by expressing a sincere desire to communicate. Second, they should focus on the speaker's message rather than on distracting elements of delivery. Speakers assist listening when they minimize or eliminate distracting behaviors and employ forceful delivery to underscore their messages. Third, listeners should listen for the speaker's main ideas. Speakers make this task much easier by careful speech organization. Fourth, listeners should try to understand the speaker's point of view. Speakers ought to reveal their credentials and explain their reasons for speaking on a particular topic. Fifth, listeners should withhold judgment about the speaker and the message until after hearing and considering both. Sixth, listeners should reinforce the speaker's message by using repetition, paraphrase, and summary. Seventh, effective listeners should provide the speaker with feedback. Speakers should adapt to those responses. Eighth, listeners should be ready to listen with the whole body. Finally, though we have urged you to listen objectively to avoid prejudging speakers and their ideas, effective listening is ultimately critical listening. Gauging the credibility of the speaker's information is easier if the speaker has presented logically supported ideas and has cited credible sources.

You master public speaking faster and easier if you can rely on helpful criticism from your classmates and offer them helpful advice. Criticism consists of *judgments, reasons,* and *norms.* To be helpful, criticism must be balanced between positive and negative aspects of the speech but should begin and end with positive comments. Criticism should be well organized. Critics should reinforce positive aspects of the speech and problem-solve the negative. In addition, criticism should target a few key areas for improvement, be specific, be honest but tactful, be personalized, and should provide the speaker with a plan of action for future speeches.

To act effectively on the speech criticism you receive, you should focus on *what* your critics say rather than on *how* they say it. Seek clear, specific feedback about comments that seem vague. Evaluate the feedback you receive. Finally, target a few areas for improvement. Develop a plan of action that sets goals for your target areas and states the strategies you will use to make those improvements. Our years of teaching experience have convinced us that following these guidelines will pay big dividends as you give, receive, and act on constructive, beneficial speech criticism.

Exercises

1. On a sheet of paper, list your listening strengths and weaknesses. Beside each weakness, indicate specific strategies that could minimize or eliminate the problem.

2. Listen to a speech or lecture, paying particular attention to the five types of distractions discussed in this chapter. Give examples of distractions you encountered. What could you or the speaker have done to minimize these interferences? Discuss these options.

3. Analyze how your classroom's physical environment affects the delivery of student speeches. How does it promote effective listening? How does it inhibit it? What can you do to adapt to any of the limitations?

4. Select a speech you've seen on television or videotape, heard on radio, or read in print or electronic form. Using the guidelines presented in this chapter, write a one-paragraph critique of that speech's organization. You may want to review pages 58–60 in Chapter 3 to stimulate your thinking about clear organization.

5. Suppose you are asked to speak to a group of students at a local high school on the topic "What College Offers to You." Half of the audience plans to attend college; the rest does not. All the students have been requested to stay after school on the first sunny day this spring to attend the assembly. What are your listeners' likely psychological distractions with which you must contend? What strategies could you use to minimize them in your speech?

6. Sit in a different seat and next to a different classmate each class for the next two weeks. After this time period, analyze whether your location affected your listening attentiveness. If so, how?

7. If you've already had the opportunity to present a speech in this class, write a critique of your vocal and physical delivery. Be sure to mention your delivery strengths as well as areas for improvement. Also, write a plan of action for your next speaking assignment.

Notes

1. Bernard E. Farber, comp. *A Teacher's Treasury of Quotations* (Jefferson, NC: McFarland, 1985) 186.

2. Meada Gibbs, Pernell Hewing, Jack E. Hulbert, David Ramsey, and Arthur Smith, "How to Teach Effective Listening Skills in a Basic Business Communication Class," *The Bulletin of the Association for Business Communication* 48.2 (1985): 30.

3. Larry Barker, Renee Edwards, Connie Gaines, Karen Gladney, and Frances Holley, "An Investigation of Proportional Time Spent in Various Communication Activities by College Students," *Journal of Applied Communications Research* 8 (1980): 101–9.

4. Robert L. Montgomery, *Listening Made Easy* (New York: AMACOM, 1981) n.p.

5. William James, *The Principles of Psychology,* vol. 2 (Cambridge: Harvard UP, 1981), 380. This is a reprint of the original 1890 Henry Holt edition.

6. Michael Cronin, Rick Olsen, and Jan Stahl, *Mission Possible: Listening Skills for Better Communication,* computer software, Oral Communication Program, Radford University, Radford, VA, 1992.

7. Lyle V. Mayer, *Fundamentals of Voice and Diction,* 8th ed. (Dubuque, IA: Brown, 1988) 178.

8. Lyle V. Mayer, *Fundamentals of Voice and Diction,* 10th ed. (Dubuque, IA: Brown, 1994) 229.

9. This definition is adapted from Hendrie Weisinger and Norman M. Lobsenz, *Nobody's Perfect: How to Give Criticism and Get Results* (New York: Warner, 1981) 9–10.

10. This model of criticism is adapted from Beverly Whitaker Long, "Evaluating Performed Literature," *Studies in Interpretation,* vol. 2, eds. Esther M. Doyle and Virginia Hastings Floyd (Amsterdam: Rodopi, 1977) 267–81. See also her earlier article: Beverly Whitaker, "Critical Reasons and Literature in Performance," *The Speech Teacher* 18 (November 1969): 191–93. Long attributes this three-part model of criticism to Arnold Isenberg, "Critical Communication," *The Philosophical Review* (July 1949): 330–44.

There are some who speak well and write badly. For the place and the audience warm them, and draw from their minds more than they think of without that warmth.

—Blaise Pascal

Analyzing Your Audience

We have all heard stories so amazing that they seem to take on the qualities of legends. One well-known example is that of Abraham Lincoln and the Gettysburg Address. As the story goes, Lincoln was such a fine man and such a great thinker that he wrote his now-famous speech on some scraps of paper while on the train to Gettysburg, Pennsylvania.[1] Repeated for many, many years, the story seemed plausible because the speech is only 272 words long. Like many other stories that seem too good to be true, however, this one is false. Today, we have a better picture of how Lincoln composed the Gettysburg Address and why it is as brief as it is.

Lincoln was asked to speak at a ceremony dedicating a memorial cemetery for soldiers who had died in the Civil War battle at Gettysburg. He was not to be the main speaker on this occasion, however: Edward Everett, the most famous orator of his day, had top billing. Everett spoke for an hour and 57 minutes to an audience estimated at between 15,000 and 50,000 people seated and standing outdoors.[2] Afterward, Lincoln rose and, holding two pieces of paper, spoke ten sentences in less than three minutes.[3] Why were Lincoln's remarks so brief?

The answer is that Lincoln had done some excellent analysis of the audience and the speaking occasion. He knew, first, of Everett's reputation for making very long speeches. Lincoln undoubtedly knew that if he also delivered a long speech, he would lose either much of his audience's attention or even their presence. Remember, the speech was to be given outdoors, with audience members free to leave whenever they chose!

Second, Lincoln knew, as did his audience, that he was not the featured speaker on this occasion and was, therefore, not expected to make a major address. He had been asked only two weeks ahead of time to make "a few appropriate remarks." Everett, on the other hand, was invited six weeks earlier, and the date for the dedication had actually been changed to fit his schedule. Even though he was president, Lincoln was losing popular support by 1863 and knew that a long speech would seem an inappropriate challenge to the importance of Everett's.

The third and final reason for the length of Lincoln's Gettysburg Address was that he had been anticipating for some time an occasion for an important speech on the same theme. The words of the speech began to take shape in his mind long before he wrote them on paper. For example, Lincoln began his speech at Gettysburg by saying, "Four score and seven years ago our fathers brought forth on this continent a new na-

Speech Texts
http://douglass.speech.nwu.edu
To compare the texts of Abraham Lincoln's and Edward Everett's speeches at Gettysburg, as well as many other speeches from the mid-1600s to the present, visit the Douglass Archives of American Public Address at Northwestern University. You can view the list of featured speeches chronologically, by speaker, by title, or by issue. A sidebar of links at the side of each text will connect you to related speeches or study materials.

(Source: *Frank and Ernest.* Copyright © by Bob Thaves. Reprinted with permission of Bob Thaves.)

tion, conceived in liberty and dedicated to the proposition that all men are created equal." Yet Thomas Scheidel points out that, in informal remarks four months before delivering the Gettysburg Address, Lincoln had said:

> How long ago is it?—eighty-odd years since, on the Fourth of July for the first time in the history of the world a nation by its representatives, assembled and declared as a self-evident truth, that "all men are created equal." . . . Gentlemen, this is a glorious theme, and the occasion for a speech; but I am not prepared to make one worthy of the occasion.[4]

Making speeches "worthy of the occasion" requires meticulous audience analysis today, just as it did in Lincoln's time. Lincoln's careful audience analysis helped him decide the topic, length, and scope of his remarks at Gettysburg. Smart speakers today must also conduct careful listener analysis.

Recognize the Value of Audience Diversity

In interpersonal communication you adapt your message to one other person. The quantity and character of your communication depend on your relationship to that other individual. Your task as a public speaker is more challenging, however, for each added person compounds the dynamics of the communication event. Each additional person increases the diversity that is present in any audience. Listeners may differ from one another in terms of age, gender, ethnicity, educational background, beliefs, values, and a host of other characteristics. In short, each audience member is unique. The challenge for you as a public speaker is not only to recognize these differences but also to understand, respect, and adapt to this diversity as you develop and deliver your speeches.

Rather than thinking of diversity as an obstacle, consider it an opportunity. If you are fortunate to have a high level of diversity in your public speaking class, you can use it as an opportunity to learn about others and yourself. Robert Berdahl, chancellor of the University of California, discusses how diversity affects learning when he writes:

> Education is the process of encountering that which we are not, that with which we are unfamiliar, that which we do not know. Out of that encounter comes the understanding and assimilation of that other, or modification and rejection of it—some response that allows us to know and grasp more than if we had not had that encounter. That process constitutes education.[5]

Our culture, in particular, shapes our values and behaviors. Today the college classroom, like most other segments of American life, is increasingly multicultural. Our differences simultaneously strengthen and threaten to divide us. The truth of the "melting pot" image of America is that no group melted completely, but neither did any resist melting to some degree. Australian Robert Hughes offers an alternative view of the United States' many cultures: "Reading America is like scanning a mosaic. If you look only at the big picture, you do not see its parts—the distinct glass tiles, each a different color. If you concentrate only on the tiles, you cannot see the picture."[6]

If you value your listeners and want to communicate successfully, then you must view public speaking as an audience-centered activity. How can you accomplish this? An audience-centered speaker must develop three important approaches. First, you must *recognize your own place as part of the audience.* You must be ready to admit that you are only one part of the total audience, a fact that should make you want to learn as much as possible about the other parts. Second, as we mentioned in discussing ethics in Chapter 2, you should *respect your listeners.* Respect and care for the audience means wanting to enhance their knowledge and understanding by providing interesting or useful information. In order to do this, you must recognize and appreciate their beliefs, values, and behaviors. This, in turn, leads to a third aspect of audience-centeredness: You should *recognize and act on feedback from your audience,* whether that feedback is

Ethical public speakers consider the diversity of their audiences and use appropriate channels to communicate with as many of them as possible. Here an interpreter renders a message from spoken English to American Sign Language, making it accessible to members of the Deaf community.

verbal or nonverbal. Speakers who are attuned to their audience members will try to discover and cultivate interests their listeners already have as well as challenge them with new, useful topics.

In this chapter we will examine some audience characteristics that may affect the way that you develop a particular speech. Some of these characteristics are social or cultural; others deal with audience thoughts, feelings, and behaviors. Audience analysis is more than gathering statistics and making inferences about your audience, however. Diversity is more than just a collection of calculated audience profiles. When Vivian Sykes thinks about cultural diversity, she recalls the songs she hums in her head.

> The songs blend new age wisdom with Brazilian percussion, Native American flutes, South African folk tunes, inner-city rap, and country music's fiddle. For me, multiculturalism goes beyond trends and statistics; for me diversity has a human face.[7]

As you take and develop a photograph of your audience's "human face," you will exercise the critical thinking skills of information gathering, remembering, analyzing, and evaluating. You will engage in *information gathering* as you collect data to develop an increasingly clearer picture of who your listeners are. As you exercise the skill of *remembering,* you'll tap your memories of what you have heard your listeners say and do. You will *focus* on elements of the picture that seem most relevant to topic areas you are considering for your speeches. As you combine, summarize, and restructure pieces of information about your listeners, you will exercise the critical thinking skill of *integrating.* Finally, you will *analyze* the information you have collected by examining individual characteristics of your listeners and the relationships between those characteristics.

We believe audience analysis is a process that shapes and molds the preparation, delivery, and evaluation of any well-thought-out public speech. In other words, audience analysis occurs before, during, and after the act of speaking. Let's consider more closely how this process works.

Analyze Your Audience *before* the Speech

You will spend more time analyzing your audience before you speak than during or after your speech. Your speech may last only five or ten minutes, for example. Yet if you care about doing well, your audience analysis before the speech will take more than five or ten minutes.

Your public speaking class is a special type of audience and provides you with unique challenges and opportunities. At the beginning of the semester or quarter, you may know few if any of your classmates. As with any general, unfamiliar audience you are preparing to address, you initially analyze your classroom audience by active sleuthing as well as by using your own common sense. As you prepare your first speech, you could ask around about people's knowledge of or interest in a particular subject area. This is a good way to gauge your listeners' interest when you still do not know them well.

On the other hand, this class provides you the rare opportunity to "live" with your audience for the duration of the course. From the comments they make in and outside of class, from the questions they ask other student speakers or your instructor, and from their nonverbal feedback while listening to classroom speeches, you will gradually assemble an increasingly accurate portrait of this group of people. They will disclose, or you will deduce, information about their beliefs, values, interests, likes, and dislikes. Your audience analysis will be a semester- or quarter-long process, and by the time you deliver your final speech in the class, your audience analysis should be both easier and more accurate than it was at the beginning of the term.

Analyze Audience Demographics

Your first step as a speaker is to discover and evaluate as many specific characteristics of your audience as possible. **Demographics** is the term for those characteristics. Discovering the specifics about your audience will help you answer the question, "Who is my target audience?"

Demographic analysis helps you tailor a message to a specific audience. You will never know everything about your listeners, and so you will make generalizations from the information you do know. One note of caution is in order, however: Be careful not to turn these generalizations into stereotypes about audience members. This will undermine your speech-making efforts. For example, we have observed speakers who assumed that audiences of similar demographic makeup inherently have similar interests. They selected topics they thought would fit those groups. Sometimes the audience accepted the speech favorably; other audiences perceived some speeches as patronizing or even insulting.

Some topics may be appropriate to only one type of audience; most subjects, however, can have broader appeal. A speech on the Seneca Falls Declaration of Sentiments is not just a women's topic—it could be informative to both men and women. A speech on gender bias in language can also have wide appeal. The solvency of the social security

demographics: characteristics of the audience, such as age, gender, ethnicity, education, religion, economic status, and group membership.

When we prepared for our first speeches, our speech class examined the characteristics of college freshmen and made a list of our common interests. Then we conducted an audience survey to find out more about our specific class. Based on the information I gathered, I decided that "What to Do on a Friday Night When You Can't Drink" would be a good topic. There are a lot of interesting things to do on and off campus besides drinking. It turned out to be a really good speech because it directly affected my audience—all of them were under the age of 21. Doing audience analysis before the speech really paid off because I was able to include a lot of information that benefited and interested my audience. During the speech I looked for active listeners. I could see that my classmates were interested because they were nodding and making eye contact with me. That feedback gave me a vote of confidence and made me feel that what I was saying was important to them.

—Anne Bergstrom, Eastern Illinois University

speaking
with
confidence

system may be of immediate concern to someone approaching retirement, but with some creative thinking you can make it interesting to anyone who is a taxpayer or who plans to retire some day. The economic plight of the American farmer should interest not only the agriculture major but also anyone who eats.

The function of education is to introduce us to new ideas and information. As a speaker, you defeat that goal when you stereotype an audience and choose only topics you think they will find familiar and comfortable. As a listener, you similarly undermine the goal of education when you tune out speeches on topics you do not find immediately interesting.

Your audience may be highly multifaceted. If so, part of your audience analysis will involve discovering what you can about the various divisions, sections, or subgroups that constitute your listeners. Advertisers and public relations people call this process **audience segmentation.** You might then choose a topic that you believe you can relate to all segments of your audience. However, sometimes speakers choose to speak only to one or more segments of a larger audience, a strategy called **audience targeting.**

For example, if you know that some of your listeners love to travel but are on tight budgets, you could inform them about the option of becoming airline couriers. An informative speech on the dangers of heatstroke and heat exhaustion might be appropriate for athletes in your audience. If you know there are cigarette smokers in your class, they are an obvious target for a persuasive speech on the hazards of smoking. But smokers are common targets lately, so part of your audience analysis needs to consider their prior exposure to your message and their willingness to listen objectively.

In each of these cases, your target audience is a subgroup of the audience as a whole; you direct your speech to them, hoping that others will also be interested or find your information useful. Notice, though, that even this strategy requires careful audience analysis. You must be sure that your target audience does exist and that it is sufficient in size to justify giving them your primary focus. Generally, the more you know about your audience, the more secure you will be and the better speech you will deliver.

Seven of the most common characteristics you will want to analyze about your potential audience are age, gender, ethnicity, education, religion, economic status, and group membership. You will not always be able to learn this much information about your audience. Keep in mind, however, that the more you know, the better prepared you will be to present a successful speech.

Age. The late Terry Sanford, former U.S. senator and North Carolina governor, once made an observation that may mean more to you as you age. He noted, "Communicating with college students is always somewhat of a challenge. It is not that I have too much difficulty understanding your changing expressions and attitudes. It is that I forget what you never saw."[8] One of the most obvious concerns you have as you research your audience is their age. You may need to find out not only what the average age of your audience is, but also what the age range will be. Your public speaking class may include first-year college students, people returning to college to change careers, and others pursuing interests after retirement. People who are 18 to 20 years old today relate to the assassination of Martin Luther King, Jr., the Vietnam War, and Watergate only as important topics of history. While that means that they may be eager to learn more about those topics, it also means they may not understand most casual references to these. If you compare the long gasoline lines of 1973 to food rationing during World War II, an audience of 18-year-olds won't remember either of those events. Ask a college classroom audience today, "Do you remember where you

Demographic Profiling
http://www.ipl.org/ref/RR/static/ref1500.html
Looking for a demographic profile of people in a particular country, state, county, city, or even zip code? The Internet Public Library's "Census Data and Demographics Reference" list is a great place to start your search. It links to nearly 30 other sites, with useful descriptions of the kinds of information you will find at each.

audience segmentation: the strategy of dividing an audience into various subgroups based on their demographic and psychographic profiles.

audience targeting: the strategy of directing a speech primarily toward one or more portions of the entire audience.

were on July 20, 1969, when Neil Armstrong stepped onto the moon's surface?" and only a few of your listeners will have a positive answer. Many in your audience were not yet born. To make a clear speech on one of the preceding topics, a speaker must use supporting materials that are familiar to the audience, and age is one of the most obvious influences on the audience's frame of reference.

Gender. The next factor you need to consider in your audience analysis is gender. It is obviously easier to determine gender than age. Some students run into difficulties with stereotyping when they take gender into consideration for speech making, however. For example, we remember college men who would deliver speeches with purposes such as "to inform you girls about the rules of football so that you don't drive your boyfriends crazy by asking silly questions when you watch a game with them." Most women today would listen to such a speech only under protest.

Yet even today what seems to be consideration for the gender of audience members sometimes turns out to be disguised sexism. We remember a speech informing women how to change a flat tire. While a speaker with genuine safety concerns might be able to deliver such a speech effectively, this particular speaker patronized the women in his audience by repeatedly talking down to them: "Take off your pretty little high heels and put on the pair of running shoes I told you to put in the trunk." "Cover up your fancy little dress with that work shirt I told you to carry in the trunk." Women in the class bristled at the speaker's suggestion that they didn't know enough to change a tire.

As this example shows, speakers make a mistake if they stereotype listeners according to their gender. You would be wise to *disregard* the advice found in one college public speaking text published in the mid-1960s:

> Generally, women are more interested than men in subjects related to the feminine gender, such as women's clothing, cosmetics, housework, the rearing of children, the local ladies' aid society, home decoration, etc. On the other hand, men show strong masculine interests in rough competitive sports like football. More than women, men tend to enjoy technical and scientific subjects, particularly those related to mechanics, electronics, and engineering. Since more men than women serve as chief breadwinners for their families, they are more apt to be interested in matters pertaining to occupations and professions—but remember the possible exceptions.[9]

Effective speakers need to consider the individual life experiences of their audience members to avoid stereotyping and possibly offending some individuals.

Today, those "possible exceptions" are ordinary and routine. As society continues to remove barriers based on gender, gender-specific topics will become fewer. Audience-centered speakers need to remember that.

Ethnicity. Ethnicity means the classification of a subgroup of people who have a common cultural heritage with shared customs, characteristics, language, history, and so on. Members of an ethnic group may share a collective heritage and exhibit strong ethnic pride; speakers appropriately tap these common experiences and feelings as they construct their speeches for audiences having similar ethnic backgrounds. For example, John Jacob, president of the National Urban League, spoke to an audience of African Americans and observed: "Too often, we approach racial issues in a conceptual vacuum. We take a historical view. We forget that while most Americans' forebears came to this nation seeking freedom and opportunity, ours came in chains and were enslaved and oppressed."[10] Jacob's statement was entirely appropriate for his audience, yet he would not have said the words "our forebears" were he speaking, for example, to listeners of diverse ethnic backgrounds.

As with the issue of gender, speakers should avoid ethnic stereotypes. Never assume that because individuals share the same ethnicity they also share similar experiences and attitudes. If you have a working-class Irish Catholic ancestry, do not assume that others having Irish surnames are working-class or Catholic. Two people of the same ethnicity may have diverse attitudes, interests, and experiences because of differences in their ages, education, income levels, and religion.

Education. The educational level of your audience affects not only what subjects you can choose, but also how you approach those particular subjects.

> John, a computer and information sciences major and a math whiz, wanted to deliver an informative speech on the binary number system. His initial outlines for the speech focused on binary theory and Boolean algebra, abstract topics that fascinated him. He planned to discuss the concept of binary existence and to demonstrate some complicated mathematical operations. Yet he knew from conversations he had overheard that more than a few classmates were struggling with their math classes. As a result, he refocused his speech, demonstrating simple conversions from decimal to binary numbers and emphasizing the application of such math in computer programming and CD technology. Audience questions after his speech showed that John met his goals without intimidating or talking down to his audience.

Like John's audience, the college students in your class have a variety of educational backgrounds. Some may have attended private schools, had home schooling, or earned graduate equivalency degrees after interruptions in their high school educations. Others may have lived and studied overseas. Smart speakers will find out as much as they can about the levels and types of education their listeners have.

Remember, also, that education can be informal as well as formal. Just as a high school diploma is unfortunately no guarantee of a solid educational background, listeners who have not completed high school or college are not necessarily uneducated. They may in fact have a wealth of "book" knowledge obtained through personal reading and study, as well as specialized practical knowledge and training.

If you have the opportunity, find out not only what your audience knows about a potential speech topic, but also whether audience members have experience relevant to that topic. The speaker in the following example put such knowledge to good use:

> Demographic Profiling
> http://www.census.gov/
> cgi-bin/gazetteer/
> Using data from the most recent census, this site allows you to customize and print a table of information about people in a particular zip code.

Matt, a movie buff, decided to speak on how to audition for a movie. He went to the library, prepared a research bibliography, and began collecting information. The week before he was to give his speech, he learned that Sarah, a classmate and drama major, had auditioned for a role in a movie that was shot in town last summer. Matt decided to talk with Sarah about the experience. Although she was not cast in the part, Sarah talked excitedly about her auditioning experience. This information helped Matt fill in some of the gaps in his research. In addition, mentioning Sarah's experience in his speech connected the topic to the audience and made it seem more immediate.

Religion. Your college public speaking class may contain members of various Protestant denominations, Catholics, Jews, Muslims, Hindus, Buddhists, and members of other religious groups, as well as agnostics and atheists. Native American classmates may have religious beliefs with which you are not familiar. Students from other countries may also practice religions you do not know about, or they may practice familiar religions in a different way. Even among people who belong to the same denomination, religion will be very important to some and relatively unimportant to others. You have formulated your religious beliefs, whatever they are, over a period of time and you may feel defensive about those beliefs when they are challenged.

Stereotyping people on the basis of what you know of their religious views is as potentially inaccurate and harmful as making generalizations based on other demographic characteristics. Do all Catholics oppose birth control and the ordination of women as priests? Do all Jews observe Hanukkah and Yom Kippur, or observe them in the same way? Do all Protestants interpret scripture in the same manner? Clearly, the answer is no, and this should remind you of the limitations of simply finding out the religious denominations represented in your audience. If your audience's religious views are truly important to a topic you are considering, you will need to find out more about the beliefs behind the denominational labels they prefer.

Economic Status. Economic status is another key factor affecting audience attitudes and behaviors. If a family earns barely enough to subsist, they will probably be more concerned with filling basic life needs than with social or status needs. For that reason, they may readily relate to a speaker who advocates expanded health care benefits and automatic cost-of-living adjustments. They may be more receptive to a progressive income tax than to a flat-rate sales tax on products and services. Analyses of survey data and voting behavior suggest that, generally, the higher the income of a family, the more conservative their political attitudes. Even though many students in your class may not yet have significant incomes, their political attitudes are often similar to those of their parents. Just don't assume that all families who have substantial wealth hold conservative views.

Judging the range of incomes of your classmates' families may be difficult. Certainly, it would be impolite to ask. However, you can probably locate or construct several general profiles of the typical students at your college, as the following speaker did.

For her first informative speech, Julie decided to discuss demographics of students at her college. Her primary sources were student profiles based on registration surveys released by the administration. This proved to be a subject her classmates enjoyed because it was about them and their friends. Some of the information Julie presented was surprising but seemed reasonable; other items were so funny that they seemed to be mistaken. Julie's research provided her information to analyze her own classroom audience. In addition, it helped her classmates in their audience analysis for future speeches.

If you speak on significant national concerns, consult public opinion surveys on those issues. Such polls categorize responses according to several demographic characteristics, and one of them is often income.

Overall, be realistic, be fair, and be sensitive when choosing topics dealing with economic issues. We remember one student who was offended when a speaker said that students shouldn't go home for spring break but should travel with friends to different parts of the United States to expand their historical and cultural knowledge. The offended student argued that some students simply did not have that option. They needed to work in order to remain in college. Speeches that urge college students to consider investing in the stock market or in real estate usually ignore one important fact: Most college students do not have money to spend for these purposes. On the other hand, we have observed student speakers generate lively audience interest on topics such as how to select an excellent yet inexpensive wine, summer employment opportunities at national parks and historic sites, and how to negotiate the price of a new or used car. Although money may be of greater concern to some people than to others, few people want to spend money needlessly.

Demographic Profiling
http://www.census.gov/ftp/pub/population/www
Want a profile of the social or economic characteristics of people in a particular area? Need an estimate of the nation's or the world's population at this minute? This Census Bureau site will provide community profiles for particular voting precincts, and its "PopClock" gives a minute-by-minute estimate of U.S. and world populations. Links from this site can give you valuable demographic and historical information from census studies.

Group Membership. Today we join groups in order to spend time with others who enjoy our hobbies and pastimes, to learn more about subjects that can help us, or to further our political and social goals. Many of these groups are voluntary, such as the IBM computer users club, the art guild, the karate club, Amnesty International, the Young Democrats, the Young Republicans, honor societies, and social fraternities or sororities. We may also belong to some groups—labor unions and professional associations, for example—because we are required to in order to get or keep jobs or special licenses.

Political parties are also important groups. Knowing your listeners' political affiliations can be particularly helpful as you prepare persuasive speeches. How you develop your persuasive appeal, as well as the supporting material you select, will reflect assumptions you have made about your audience. You can make an educated assumption, for example, that an audience composed mainly of Republicans will accept statements from Republican sources more readily than from Democratic ones. We usually identify with a political party because of its positions on significant issues, and it shouldn't be too hard for you to locate positions associated with key political parties. Both major parties prepare position papers on key issues. Newspapers, magazines, and

People have different needs at different stages of their lives. Speakers need to identify those needs and to adapt their speech topics to address them.

electronic media gather polling data. Publications such as the *Gallup Poll Monthly* and a variety of Internet Web sites may provide useful information as well.

You can also presume that audience members who belong to the Sierra Club, Greenpeace, the Nature Conservancy, or the Audubon Society have environmental concerns. Members of People for the Ethical Treatment of Animals, the World Wildlife Federation, and the Animal Liberation Front share a concern for animal welfare. Yet some of those groups have diverse goals and different methods of achieving them. If you are speaking to an organization—local, regional, or national—your audience analysis will require you to research the nature of that group as thoroughly as you can.

Analyze Audience Psychographics

Just as you should develop a demographic profile of your audience, you should also generate a psychological profile. **Psychographics** is a term for characteristics of the audience such as values, beliefs, attitudes, and behaviors. These elements help us understand how our listeners think, feel, and behave. If you look at Figure 5.1, you will see that, typically, our behavior is shaped by our attitudes, which are based on our beliefs, which are validated by our values. In order to understand better the interaction among these elements, we will look at each level of the pyramid, beginning with values and moving upward.

Values. We value something because we deem it to be desirable or to have some inherent goodness. A **value** expresses a judgment of what is desirable and undesirable, right and wrong, or good and evil. Values are usually stated in the form of a word or phrase. For example, most of us probably share the values of equality, freedom, honesty, fairness, justice, good health, and family. These values compose the principles or standards we use to judge and develop our beliefs, attitudes, and behaviors.

If we value honesty, for example, we are probably offended when we learn that a political leader has lied to us. If we value equality and fairness, we will no doubt oppose employment practices that discriminate on the basis of gender, ethnicity, religion, or age. While our actions may not always be consistent with our values, those

psychographics: characteristics of the audience, such as values, beliefs, attitudes, and behaviors.

value: judgment of what is right or wrong, desirable or undesirable, usually expressed as words or phrases.

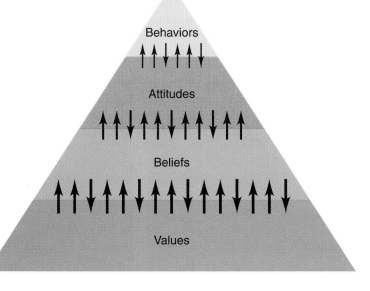

FIGURE 5.1
Levels of Influence

standards nevertheless guide what we believe and how we act. When we act contrary to our values, we may experience conflict or even guilt. That perceived inconsistency or dissonance will often motivate us either to change our behavior to match our beliefs and values or to change our beliefs by rationalizing our behavior.

Beliefs. A **belief** is something you accept as true, and it is usually stated as a declarative sentence. We probably do not think about many of our beliefs because they are seldom challenged: Brushing your teeth regularly reduces your chances of getting cavities; observing speed limits saves lives; sexual abuse is psychologically harmful to children; illiteracy in the United States undermines economic productivity; and so on.

Other beliefs are more controversial, and we often find ourselves defending them. Each of the statements below is debatable.

- Placement of toxic landfills discriminates against poor and ethnic minority populations.
- Colleges place too much emphasis on athletics.
- The benefits of surveillance technology in the workplace outweigh its harms.
- The English language is gender-biased.
- Use of the Internet improves the quality of student research.
- Sweepstakes junk mail is deliberately deceptive.
- The influence of network television programming is decreasing.

There are, no doubt, statements on this list with which you agree and disagree. Those you accept as true are part of your beliefs.

Attitudes. **Attitudes** are expressions of approval or disapproval. They are our likes and dislikes. A statement of an attitude makes a judgment about the desirability of an individual, object, idea, or action. Examples of statements of attitude include the following: I endorse Bob Estrada for Student Government Association president; I favor a decrease in defense spending; I support capping enrollment at our college; I like broccoli; I prefer classical music to jazz; I favor a pass-fail grading system for our school.

Attitudes usually evolve from our values and beliefs. Several values and beliefs may interact to complicate our decision making. When two values or two beliefs collide, the stronger one will generally predominate and determine attitudes. You may value both the right to privacy and the right to good health. If a speaker convinces you that a proposed government action will diminish the right to privacy, you may oppose the action. If another speaker demonstrates that the plan is necessary to gather information to contain the spread of a deadly disease, you may support the proposal. A single belief, then, in and of itself, is not a reliable predictor of a person's attitude. Again, when values collide, the stronger value usually takes precedence.

> Analyzing Psychographics
> http://www.abacon.com/pubspeak/analyze/pubpolls.html
> What do *you* think? To find out what everyone else thinks, access Allyn & Bacon's "Public Opinion Polls" Web site. This site, which provides links to media polls and polling organizations, offers information to assist you in analyzing public opinions and trends on a variety of topics.

belief: a statement that people accept as true.

attitude: a statement expressing an individual's approval or disapproval, like or dislike.

behavior: an individual's observable action.

Behaviors. A **behavior** is an overt action; in other words, it is how we act. Unlike values, beliefs, and attitudes, which are all psychological principles, behaviors are observable. You may feel that giving blood is important (attitude) because an adequate blood supply is necessary to save lives (belief) and because you respect human life (value). Your behavior as you participate in a blood drive and donate blood is a logical and observable extension of your outlook.

If you understand the foregoing components of psychology, you begin to understand the audience you intend to inform, persuade, or entertain. Your knowledge of those principles will help you as you work to analyze your audience and will help you develop their psychological profile. How do you obtain information about your audience's values, beliefs, attitudes, and behaviors? You have two options, both requiring some work.

The first is to use your powers of observation and deduction. You can make educated guesses about people's values, beliefs, and attitudes by observing their behaviors. For example, what are your classmates talking about before and after class? What subjects have they chosen for classroom speeches? How do they respond to various speeches they hear? What do you guess their age range to be? How do they dress? What books do they carry with them to class? The answers to these and many other questions help you infer a psychological profile of your audience. The longer you are around your classmates, the less this profile will be based on stereotypes and the more accurate it will become.

The second way to gather information about your audience's values, beliefs, attitudes, and behaviors is to conduct interviews or administer questionnaires. Interviews and questionnaires may be informal or, if you have the time and resources, formal. You could interview classmates informally during conversation before or after class. Questionnaires administered during class may be as simple as asking for a show of hands to answer a question ("How many of you have access to a personal computer?") or as formal as asking classmates to answer a written questionnaire you have photocopied and distributed. It's true that audience interviews and questionnaires are somewhat artificial; you don't often have the luxury of using them for presentations outside your college classroom. Still, if you are invited or required to address a group of strangers, you would be wise to ask your contact person lots of questions about the audience you will be facing.

Analyze Audience Needs

Demographic and psychographic analyses are not ends in themselves; you waste your time if you do not move beyond discovering these characteristics of your audience. Some of these factors may be irrelevant to the topic you choose for a classroom speech; others may be vital. Your task is to discover the significant items and then explore them more completely. Once you have considered your audience's demographic and psychographic profiles, you will be in a better position to determine your listeners' needs or what motivates them. Two particular models, Maslow's hierarchy and the VALS2 system, will get you thinking about audience needs in an organized way.

Maslow's Hierarchy. The sociologist and psychologist Abraham Maslow (1908–1970) is best remembered for a model of human needs commonly referred to as **Maslow's hierarchy.**[11] Hierarchy means an arrangement of items according to their importance, power, or dominance. Maslow's thesis was that all human needs can be grouped into five categories, based on the order in which they must be filled.[12] These categories, represented in Figure 5.2, are (1) physiological needs, (2) safety needs, (3) belongingness and love needs, (4) esteem needs, and (5) self-actualization needs. As a public speaker, you should be aware of the needs dominating any particular audience you address. To do that you must consider the five categories of needs in more detail.

Maslow's hierarchy: a model of five basic human needs—physiological, safety, belongingness, esteem, and self-actualization—in an ordered arrangement.

The *physiological,* or *physical, needs* refer to basic human requirements for water, food, and sleep. These needs are the most basic and are ordinarily satisfied before any of the others. As Maslow and others have observed, hungry people don't play; in other words, we can occupy ourselves with trivial matters only as long as we have the luxury of taking our food, drink, and rest for granted. Maslow included sex among the physiological needs because, while people can live without sexual contact, sex is necessary for the survival of the species.

After those physiological needs have been largely met, a new category of needs begin to emerge to concern us: the *safety needs.* This category includes everything that contributes to the "safe, orderly, predictable, lawful, organized world" upon which we depend.[13] Having safe roofs over our heads and reliable transportation obviously contribute to the predictable routines of our lives. These and any other items necessary to keep us from physical or mental harm make up the safety needs.

Once we feel relatively secure about a predictable, orderly world, we begin to look to the people around us—friends, spouses, children, parents—and our relationships with them. The third category of Maslow's needs, the *belongingness and love needs,* provides us with a sense of community, of fitting in. According to Maslow, the precise group we choose does not matter. Members may be colleagues at work, a group of people we see socially, friends at church, our family members, or even members of an antisocial gang. What matters is that we all need to feel that we belong to a group of some sort, and that we give affection to and receive affection from those people. Every human needs human contact.

From the people with whom we associate, each of us forms a picture of our worth or value. With his fourth category of needs, the *esteem needs,* Maslow reminds us that we all need reasonably high self-evaluation. We all need a pat on the back from time to time. The people around us often satisfy this need: the boss who gives us a promotion, a compliment, or a bonus of some kind; or the teacher who rewards our work with high grades or praise for our effort and improvement. Some of the time, of course, we master things on our own, such as speaking a foreign language, learning a computer program, or playing a musical instrument, and these achievements give us feelings of competence. But such feelings are confirmed and validated when other people recognize and appreciate them in us.

FIGURE 5.2
Maslow's Hierarchy of Needs
From MOTIVATION AND PERSONALITY by Abraham H. Maslow. Copyright © 1970 by Abraham H. Maslow. Reprinted by permission of Prentice-Hall, Inc., Upper Saddle River, NJ.

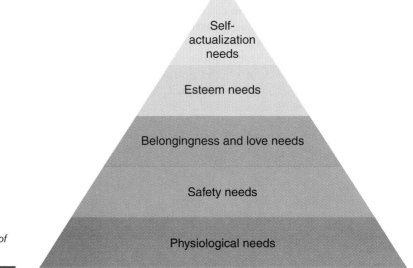

Once we have achieved reasonably high self-evaluation in the endeavors that are important to us, we are motivated by the fifth and highest level of Maslow's categories of needs. *Self-actualization,* or self-fulfillment, means becoming what you were destined to become. The athlete must compete; the novelist must write; the pianist must play music; the mechanic must fix things.

Many people live their lives without reaching their self-actualization goals. In fact, reaching the goal may be less important than trying. Self-actualization needs are the "carrot" we hold ahead of ourselves to keep us working toward a goal. A good way to identify your own self-actualization needs is to imagine that you have reached the end of your life and you are reflecting, "I wish that I had. . . ." The ways you complete that sentence will reveal the range of your own self-actualization needs.

The VALS2 Survey
http://future.sri.com/ VALS/vals2desc.shtml
If you're interested in the VALS2 model and curious about the group(s) to which you belong, you can take the survey and get an immediate report of your primary and secondary "types." Just start from this address and click on *the VALS survey.*

VALS2 Typology. In 1978 the Stanford Research Institute built on Maslow's hierarchy of needs to develop a **VALS (Values and Lifestyle) typology** to categorize American consumers. In 1989 they introduced a slightly modified system, VALS2, that considers individuals' lifestyles, psychological characteristics, and consumption patterns. VALS2 is "the most recent refinement in psychographic segmentation."[14] The VALS2 model consists of eight categories of people, from those with the lowest resources to those with the highest.

- *Strugglers* are poor, ill-educated, low-skilled, without strong social bonds, elderly, and passive. They feel powerless and avoid risk. Limited by the necessity of meeting the urgent needs of the present moment, their chief concerns are for security and safety.

- *Makers* are practical people who have constructive skills, value self-sufficiency, and have enough income, skill, and energy to carry out their projects successfully. They live within a traditional context of family, practical work, and physical recreation. Makers are politically conservative, suspicious of new ideas, respectful of government authority, but resentful of government intrusion on individual rights.

- *Strivers* seek motivation, self-definition, and approval from the world around them. They measure success by wealth and often feel that life has dealt them a bad hand because they have too little money. Strivers are impulsive, politically apathetic, and easily bored. Many of them seek to be stylish by copying those who own more impressive possessions.

- *Believers* are conservative, deeply moral, conventional people with concrete beliefs based on traditional values. They follow established routines, organized in large part around home, family, and the social or religious organizations to which they belong. Their income, education, and energy are modest but sufficient to meet their needs.

- *Experiencers* are young, enthusiastic, impulsive, and rebellious. They seek variety and excitement but are politically uncommitted, uninformed, and highly ambivalent about what they believe. Their energy finds an outlet in exercise, sports, outdoor recreation, and social activities.

- *Achievers* are successful career and work-oriented people who like to feel in control of their lives. They value consensus, predictability, and stability. Deeply committed to work and family, their personal and social lives center around

VALS2 typology: a model that segments eight categories of people based on their lifestyles, psychological characteristics, and consumption patterns.

family, church, and career. Achievers are politically conservative, and they respect authority and the status quo.

- *Fulfilleds* are mature, well-educated, professional people with incomes that provide them satisfaction and comfort. They stay current with world and national events and are open to chances to increase their knowledge. Fulfilleds often seem calm and self-assured because they base their decisions on firmly held principles.

- *Actualizers* are successful, active people with high self-esteem and abundant resources. They are guided both by principle and by the desire to have an effect on the world around them. Independent, open to change, and socially conscious, they have a wide range of interests and tend to be leaders in government and business.[15]

The Importance of Audience Needs. But what do Maslow's hierarchy and the VALS2 system of categorizing individuals mean for you in your public speaking class? Do these models of needs apply to your listeners, and, if so, how? We can suggest several ways to make these systems work for you.

First, the people sitting around you in class are not likely to be strugglers. That is, they probably already have most of their physiological and safety needs met. If not, they would be working at a job, or a second job, in order to provide these life necessities for themselves and their families. This does not mean that you cannot appeal to them on the physiological or safety needs levels. You could certainly adapt a speech to your audience, whatever their VALS2 categories, by targeting those concerns. If you alert listeners to the harms of aggressive driving, dangerous food additives, or potentially deadly drug interactions, for example, you move them to focus on basic issues of survival. In fact, no matter how prosperous and healthy they are, everyone in class would likely be interested in a topic showing them how to save money or demonstrating the health hazards of certain products or practices.

Second, if many of your classmates entered college directly from high school, they are probably interested in being well liked and in fitting in. Consider some of the ways members of the Stanford Research Institute describe experiencers: "young"; fond of "the new, the offbeat, and the risky"; expending energy in "exercise, sports, outdoor recreation and social activities"; and spending a lot of their incomes on "clothing, fast food, music, movies, and video."[16] In other words, Maslow's third category, social needs, is extremely important at this point in such people's lives. If many or most of the people in your class are in their first year of college, their self-esteem may depend partly upon whether they succeed or fail in college, and speeches on scholastic success may easily hold their attention.

Finally, although many college students are unsure of the careers they will undertake upon graduation, most people have formed or are forming self-actualization needs by the time they are in their teens or twenties. Older students may be reassessing and reformulating their self-actualization needs. Those goals are changeable and will adapt as the individual discovers new talents, interests, and abilities. For that reason, a college-age audience is likely quite receptive to speeches showing how various topics can provide personal rewards or self-fulfillment.

It is critical for you to understand, however, that you cannot easily place all of your listeners into a single VALS2 category or ascribe a specific set of Maslow's needs to all of them. In fact, as Maslow admits, all of us probably have unmet needs at each of the five levels of his hierarchy. We move from one level to another more frequently than we suspect. Whether you employ Maslow's model or the VALS2 system, *your challenge as a speaker is to identify and emphasize audience needs that are relevant to your topic.*

For example, if you feel secure in your surroundings, you may take your safety needs for granted. However, if you read in your school newspaper reports of several nighttime attacks on campus, your concern for your own and others' safety will increase. This concern for personal safety may not be on your mind as you walk to your classes during the day, but it may surface as you walk back to the dorm or to your car in the evening. If you choose to address this issue in a persuasive speech, you would want to stress this need for safety, bringing it to the front of your listeners' awareness. Once the situation is evident to your listeners, you can point out ways to satisfy that need. You might advocate better campus lighting, more security patrols, or personal escort services. Successful speakers identify the unmet needs of their listeners and respond appropriately in an informative, persuasive, or entertaining speech.

Using Maslow's hierarchy or the VALS2 typology can also help the speaker facing an unfamiliar audience outside the college classroom. Even though you may initially know little about such an audience, your goal will be to find out as much relevant information as possible about them before the speech. Knowing what motivates them, what they need or want to hear, is an excellent starting point in your audience analysis. It will also help you avoid unfortunate, unnecessary situations such as speaking on the joys of skydiving to a group of people barely able to provide food and clothing for themselves.

Analyze Specific Speaking Situations

Types of Audiences. In terms of their reasons for attending a speech, audiences fall into two categories: voluntary and captive. A **voluntary audience** has assembled of its own free will. Most adults who attend a worship service or a political rally are there voluntarily. Similarly, you may be taking this class as an elective, just because you believe it will benefit you. The **captive audience,** in contrast, feels required to be present. Chances are that you have been part of a captive audience at many school assemblies during your education. You may even be taking this class to fulfill a requirement. You may attend a speech by someone visiting your campus because you are required to do so for this or some other course. Your reasons for attending a speech, a presentation, or a class may have a significant effect on your disposition as you listen.

voluntary audience: a group of people who have assembled of their own free will to listen to a speaker.

captive audience: a group of people who are compelled or feel compelled to assemble to listen to a speaker.

Several years ago, one of your authors received a letter from a major publishing company that began: "When you're called on to give a speech, do you have time enough to prepare? If you're like most school administrators, probably not. Wouldn't it be great if some, or perhaps all, of your speechwriting had been done for you in advance?" The letter offered for purchase a collection of "158 ready-to-use speeches on virtually every subject related to education." These "audience-tested speeches" were "ready to use 'as is' or to adapt to fit the occasion," and "your success is virtually guaranteed."

Is it ethical for school administrators to purchase and use these speeches? Does delivering an "as is" speech written by someone unfamiliar with the actual audience violate the speaker–listener contract? Is it ever ethical for speakers to deliver speeches that they did not write? If so, what principles of audience analysis should guide the use of these speeches?

ethical decisions

Audience Disposition. **Audience disposition** describes how listeners are inclined to react to a speaker and his or her ideas. Listeners may have any of three general attitudes toward speakers or their ideas: *favorable, unfavorable,* or *neutral.* Each of these categories, however, looks deceptively simple. Listeners can be slightly, moderately, or strongly favorable or unfavorable toward your topic, and you should try to determine this level of intensity. A listener who only slightly opposes your position that home schooling is a desirable method of instruction will probably be easier to persuade than one who strongly opposes it.

If you sense that some of your listeners are neutral toward your topic, you should try to uncover the reasons for their neutrality. Some may be *uninterested* in your topic, and you will want to convince these listeners of its importance. Other listeners may be *uninformed* about your topic, and your strategy here should be to introduce your listeners to the data they need to understand and believe your ideas. Still other listeners may simply be *undecided* about your topic. They may be both interested and informed, aware of the pros and cons of your position. They may not have decided, however, which position they support. Your strategy in this instance should be to bolster your arguments and point out weaknesses in the opposition's case. As you can see, evaluating your audience's disposition is a complex activity. The more you know about your listeners, the easier this process becomes.

Listeners can be favorable, unfavorable, or neutral not only to speakers and their topics, but also to the reason for assembling to hear a speech. We are often tempted to view voluntary audiences as friendly and captive ones as hostile, and those situations certainly do occur. A person may go listen to a public lecture at a museum because of interest in the subject or out of respect for the speaker's reputation. On the other hand, members of captive audiences may be so antagonistic about having to be present that they listen to any speaker through a filter of hostility. The connection between the audience's reasons for attending and their attitudes toward the speaker is not this simple and predictable, however.

An audience that has assembled freely may well be unfavorable to the speaker or the speaker's organization. As examples, consider the people who attend a political speech to protest or to heckle the speaker. Alternatively, a captive audience, instead of being hostile because they feel coerced into attending, may actually look forward to a speech. Audience dynamics get even more complicated when a voluntary, favorable audience is forced to listen to other speakers before the person they came to hear. Members of a captive audience initially unsympathetic to the speaker may find themselves becoming friendly as a result of the speaker's interesting message or engaging style of delivery.

Because attendance is a requirement of most college courses, you face a captive audience when you stand before your classmates. That shouldn't frighten you, though; as we've said, a captive audience is not necessarily unfavorable toward the speaker or the speaking occasion. As a matter of fact, your colleagues in this class will be especially friendly because they share some of your concerns and apprehensions. However, the situation does pose an added challenge for you and makes your audience analysis especially important. You have a responsibility to choose novel, interesting topics for informative speeches, to choose significant topics for persuasive speeches, and to be thoroughly prepared for any speech you give. Listeners may develop an unfavorable impression of you if they perceive that you are taking your speech too lightly or exploiting the occasion to preach your own political or religious views. Remember that public speaking is an audience-centered activity; keep your listeners' needs and concerns in mind as you construct your message.

When you use the techniques discussed in this chapter, you will be able to construct an **audience profile.** As you do this, however, be aware of the following points. First, your understanding of your audience will never be complete. It is simply impos-

audience disposition: listeners' feelings of like, dislike, or neutrality toward a speaker, the speaker's topic, or the occasion for a speech.

audience profile: a descriptive sketch of listeners' characteristics, values, beliefs, attitudes, and/or actions.

sible (and probably illegal!) to discover everything about your listeners. Sometimes you have to make educated guesses based on incomplete data. Second, remember our earlier point that much of the information you gather may be of little or no help in preparing your speech. How important is it, for example, to know your listeners' religious affiliations if you are informing them about the benefits of interactive video instruction? On the other hand, if you are discussing the issue of prayer in school, your listeners' religious beliefs may be extremely important.

Finally, keep in mind that your audience is not a uniform mass but a collection of individual listeners having different experiences, values, beliefs, attitudes, behaviors, and personalities. While opinions may overlap, do not think of your audience as having one opinion toward your topic. Rarely will you be able to say, "This audience opposes converting the intramural athletic field to a multistory parking facility." More likely, your audience analysis statement will show that your audience has a variety of opinions about your topic. If you need more precise information, you may want to construct a questionnaire, distribute it to your classmates, and then collect, compile, and interpret the results, as Nakisha did.

> When Nakisha was a freshman, she received a gift just for applying for a credit card at one of the sign-up tables on campus. One year later she was in serious credit card debt. As she wrote her monthly check for the minimum payment on her bill, Nakisha decided on her topic for her upcoming persuasive speech: the problems and solutions of credit card debt. She read several articles on the topic and soon learned that student debt was widespread. She even found a study that linked student credit card debt to increased stress and increased stress to lower grades.
>
> To help her construct her speech, Nakisha decided to prepare and distribute to her classmates the questionnaire shown in Figure 5.3. She compiled and analyzed her classmates' responses to help her develop the topic for her particular audience. Eighty-two percent of her classmates owned at least one credit card, and almost half did not pay their full balance each month, had missed payments, and had felt stress due to credit card debt. Nakisha was convinced that her topic was important.
>
> Before she conducted her survey, Nakisha had planned to propose a simple solution to the problem of student debt: Her school should more tightly regulate credit card marketers who engage in on-campus solicitation. Her survey, however, found that only 36 percent of her audience had acquired their credit cards by signing up on campus. So Nakisha expanded her proposed solution: Credit card marketers should be restricted from soliciting in open areas of the campus and should not offer gifts to encourage students to sign up for credit cards. In addition, the Student Government Association should sponsor personal finance workshops and distribute brochures with suggestions on how to use credit cards responsibly. Nakisha shared some of these suggestions in her speech and distributed a sample brochure to her classmates after she finished. Her hard work paid off. She delivered a speech that was adapted to her specific audience. Her classmates were impressed with Nakisha's hard work and enjoyed being included in her speech.

You may not always have the opportunity to get as much detailed information as Nakisha did before you prepare your speech. The more specific and accurate your audience analysis, however, the better you can develop your ideas and accomplish your specific purpose. You need to use the demographic and psychological information you have gathered about your listeners to develop your audience profile.

Size of the Audience. In Chapter 1, we stated that the greater the number of people involved in speech communication, the less chance there is for verbal interaction between the speaker and individual listeners. In speaking before a small group, a speaker may be frequently interrupted with questions. The situation may be so informal that the

Please take a few minutes to answer the following questions. The information gathered will be used to assist me in preparing for my persuasive speech. To maintain confidentiality, do not include your name. Thank you for your assistance.

_____ Male   _____ Female   (Please indicate your gender.)

1. Do you own a credit card? (If not, skip to #14.)

2. If so, how many credit cards do you own?

3. How long have you had credit card(s)?

4. What type of credit cards do you own? (major, department store, gas, etc.)

5. How did you acquire your credit card(s)?

   _____ sign-up/gift offer on campus

   _____ received information in the mail

   _____ went to the bank

   _____ at the business site (store, etc.)

   _____ other _____

6. Do you pay off the balance on your credit card monthly?

7. If not, do you pay more than the minimum payment?

8. Do you know your interest rate on your credit card?

9. What is your credit limit on your credit card?

10. Have you ever missed a payment on your credit card?

11. Have you ever been called by a collection agent about your credit card?

12. Do you ever feel stressed due to debt accumulated from credit cards?

13. Do you feel confident you can pay your credit card debt?

14. If you do not own a credit card:

    Have you considered getting a credit card?

    Why have you not gotten a credit card?

FIGURE 5.3
Audience
Questionnaire

speaker sits in a chair or on the edge of a table during the presentation. A speaker in such a situation may use jargon and colloquial language, prepared visual aids (as well as those devised on the spot with transparencies and chalkboards), and a relaxed, conversational style of delivery.

As the audience grows larger, however, the speaker will have to use greater volume and larger gestures. The language of the speech may become more formal, especially if the speaker knows that the speech will be published or videotaped. As the distance between the speaker and the last row of audience members increases, the speaker's volume must increase, gestures and facial expression must be exaggerated slightly, and presentational aids must be projected in order to be seen. Unless the audience is encouraged to ask questions after the speech, they will likely remain silent. As you can see, the size of your audience affects both the type of speech you deliver and your manner of presentation.

Occasion. The occasion, the reason for the speaking event, is a critical factor in determining what type of audience you will be facing. You need to ask yourself (and maybe even some members of the group), "Why is this audience gathering? What special circumstances bring them together?" A class, an annual convention, a banquet, a party, a competition, a reunion, and a regular meeting of an organization are all examples of occasions. Occasions can be formal or informal, serious or fun, planned or spontaneous, closed to the public or open to all.

In addition to a simple description of the occasion, you as a speaker may need to know about the history of the occasion or about the recent history of the group you will address. Say, for example, that the officers of an organization have invited you to speak to their entire organization. If there has been recent conflict between the members and the officers, the majority of your audience may look upon you and your speech skeptically. To understand any occasion, you must know both the purpose and the circumstances of the gathering.

Physical Environment. In previous chapters, we discussed the forms of noise that speakers and listeners must battle. Every physical environment or setting contains unique obstacles to communication. The size of the room itself may impede communication. You may be speaking as some audience members finish a meal. You may be speaking to a large audience through an inadequate or defective public address system. You may compete with a variety of physical noise: the sounds of another meeting next door, a room that is too warm, interruptions from caterers bringing in carts of ice water. Just as it makes good sense to practice a speech in the classroom where you will speak, you should always try to find out something about the physical location where you will be speaking to a group.

Time. If you had your choice, would you rather take a college class at 9:00 A.M. or 1:00 P.M.? If you're typical, you'll choose the 9:00 A.M. class, even though you might not consider yourself a morning person. Both students and faculty seem to agree that classes at 1:00 P.M. are particularly difficult to attend and to teach because everyone's energy seems low.

The time at which you deliver your speech is an obvious part of your analysis of the speaking occasion. An address given at 4:00 P.M. on Friday will almost surely find an audience more fatigued and restless than will one given Tuesday at 9:30 A.M. If you are scheduled to speak first in a class that meets at 8:00 A.M., you may face an audience half asleep, so you may need to boost your own energy to enliven them.

Your speech's placement in a program may also affect how your audience receives it. If you follow several other speakers, you may need to work harder at getting and keeping the attention of your listeners. In short, if your listeners are not at their best, plan on working extra hard to enliven your delivery. Think about your class and when you will present your speech. The time factor may not cause you to change your topic, but it may affect how you deliver your speech.

Analyze Your Audience *during* the Speech

If your audience analysis before the speech has been careful and thorough, you will approach any speaking situation—both in this class and outside it—with a fairly complete and accurate picture of your audience. Your analysis to this point will have guided your selection of a topic and the specific ways that you have developed that topic and plan to deliver the speech. Yet even the most scrupulous, conscientious audience analysis will not guarantee that your speech will be compelling and effective. Whether you speak from notes, from a manuscript, from memory, or on the spur of the moment, your audience analysis must continue during the delivery of your speech if you are to make that vital connection with your listeners. Communication scholars suggest that, as a speaker, you must be aware of three things about your listeners as you speak.

First, you must be aware of the audience's *attention* or interest. Do their eye contact, posture, and other body language indicate to you that they are concentrating on you and your message? Are there physical distractions in the speech setting that are competing with you for the audience's attention? Do you seem to have the audience's attention throughout some parts of the speech, only to lose it during other parts? If you are concentrating on your message and on your listeners, rather than on how you sound and look, you will know the answers to these questions about the audience's attention.

If you detect a lapse of audience attention during your speech, how can you solve this problem? You could address some of your listeners by name. You could also make a connection between your speech and another one that the audience has already heard. You can also recapture your audience's attention with statements such as "The most important point to remember is. . . ." Recovering your listeners' attention might also be as simple as changing some aspect of your delivery: speaking more loudly or softly, for example, or moving away from the lectern for part of the speech so that you are closer to the audience. Any change in your established pattern of delivery will be likely to rekindle audience attention and interest. In addition, changing your usual style of delivery may be essential to overcome the distractions of a stuffy room, a noisy heater, or the coughs and other audience noise that occur whenever people assemble.

A second characteristic of your audience that you must try to assess is their *understanding* or comprehension of your message. If you have ever produced a false and hollow sounding laugh when you didn't really understand the joke that was just told, you know how difficult it is to fake comprehension. No matter how hard most of us try to cover up a lack of understanding, something about our voices or our bodies signals to others that we didn't really get it.

Of course, your audience may not try to hide their incomprehension. Members may deliberately tell you with puzzled expressions and other nonverbals that they are confused. The worst thing a speaker can do under either circumstance is to continue as if there were no problems. Clarifying something for the audience may be as simple as repeating or rephrasing the problem statement. If a particular word seems to be the source of confusion, defining the word or writing it on the board may solve the problem.

The third and final component of audience analysis during the speech is your listeners' *evaluation* of you and your message. Sensitive speakers attuned to their audiences are able to gauge the reactions of those listeners. Do members of the audience seem to agree with what you are saying? Do they approve of the suggestions you are making? Answers to these questions are particularly important when you are seeking to persuade your audience.

Sometimes the answer to such questions will be no. You may be delivering bad news or taking what you know will be an unpopular stand on an issue. Having the audience disagree with the content of your message doesn't necessarily mean that your speech has been a failure. Simply knowing that many listeners agree or disagree with you at the end of a persuasive speech shows that you are an audience-centered speaker, and that's an accomplishment in itself.

Analyze Your Audience *after* the Speech

Too often speakers assume that the speech-making process concludes as you utter your final statement and walk to your seat. Your influence on audience members can continue for some time, however. We encourage you to add one additional step: *post-speech analysis.* Part of this step should be self-reflection as you analyze your performance. Did you accomplish what you hoped you would? What do you sense were the strongest aspects of your speech? What were the weakest? How would you rate the content, organization, and delivery of the speech? What can you do to improve these aspects of your next speech?

Your answers to these questions provide a very subjective evaluation of your speech efforts. You may be much more critical than your listeners were because only you know how you planned to deliver the speech. For that reason, you should also consider your audience's assessment of your speech content, organization, and delivery.

In this class, that information may come from oral or written critiques from your peers, or from comments some of them give you after class. If you have given a good speech on an interesting topic, one of the pleasant rewards in a college classroom is that audience members may have questions to ask you. The tone and content of those questions will tell you a great deal about how the audience received your message. You will also receive helpful suggestions from your instructor. If you expect to improve as a public speaker, pay attention to the feedback given you by all your listeners and act upon the comments that are particularly relevant.

Summary

The best speeches are those that seem exactly right for the audience to whom they are delivered. They focus on interesting topics, use colorful but familiar language and supporting materials, are delivered with enthusiasm, and are the right length for the topic and the occasion. Such an accomplishment requires careful audience analysis before, during, and after delivery of the speech.

Before the speech, a speaker should consider audience demographics, audience psychographics, and audience needs. *Demographics* refers to characteristics of the audience, including age, gender, ethnicity, education, religion, economic status, and group membership. Information you gather about these characteristics can help you select a topic and then develop and support it for a particular group of listeners. Realize, however, that simply stereotyping listeners in terms of one or more of these characteristics may not only be incorrect but may also cause a speaker to offend the audience.

Speakers can use information about audience demographics to analyze the way those listeners think. *Psychographics* is a term for audience psychology and how their thoughts influence their actions. Four key components of audience psychology are values, beliefs, attitudes, and behaviors. *Values,* such as freedom and honesty, are expressions of worth or rightness. Our values are the basis for the development of beliefs and attitudes. *Beliefs* are statements we accept as true. They may be either provable or open to debate. *Attitudes* express our approval or disapproval of individuals, objects, ideas, or actions. Several values or beliefs may interact to form our attitudes. When these values or beliefs conflict, the stronger one usually predominates. A fourth element is *behavior,* an overt action that may *reflect* our values, beliefs, and attitudes.

Maslow's hierarchy of needs is a useful tool for analyzing audience motivation. That model ranks five human needs in terms of their predominance. The *physiological needs,* the most basic, include our needs for food, water, and rest. The *safety needs* include everything that contributes to a predictable, orderly existence—secure housing, reliable transportation, and freedom from civil unrest or war, for example. Once these needs are largely met, we begin to concentrate on our community of friends and associates and the ways that they fulfill our *love and belongingness needs.* Feeling that we fit in, that we give and receive affection from a group of people, contributes to our *esteem needs.* This fourth level is important, Maslow says, because we all need a pat on the back from time to time. The highest level of needs, the *self-actualization needs,* refers to our desire to fulfill our potential as human beings.

The VALS2 model provides a way of segmenting people into eight categories based on their lifestyles and psychological characteristics. In the VALS2 profiles, *strugglers* are people working with very limited resources. *Makers* are traditional, practical people who possess skills that they use toward the goal of self-sufficiency. *Strivers* are people who lack confidence, measure success by wealth, and look to others for approval and validation. *Believers* are deeply moral, conservative people who feel most comfortable following established routines. *Experiencers* are young people, often rebellious, who seek variety and excitement in their lives. *Achievers* are successful, career-oriented people who enjoy feeling in control of their lives. *Fulfilleds* are mature, well-educated people with high incomes who value order and knowledge. *Actualizers* are successful, active individuals with high self-esteem and abundant resources.

Gathering information about your audience's values, beliefs, and attitudes can be formal or informal. You can simply observe their behaviors and infer the thoughts behind them. Or you may need and have the opportunity to question the audience, orally or in writing, by administering questionnaires and surveys to gauge their feelings.

A final part of audience analysis before the speech focuses on the specific speaking situation. Will you be facing a *captive* or a *voluntary audience*? Are they likely to be favorable, unfavorable, or neutral to you and your topic? What is the nature of the speaking occasion? Where will the speech take place? What time is it to be delivered? Considering the answers to these questions is the final step in audience analysis before the speech.

During a speech, the speaker should pay attention to listeners' interest or *attention,* their *comprehension* or understanding of the message, and their *evaluation* of the speech. Speakers can influence each of these elements. Lively, sincere delivery helps generate audience interest in the topic. A speaker can help ensure the audience's comprehension of the message by defining unusual terms, slowing down the delivery of technical materials, and using repetition.

Finally, after delivering the speech, a speaker should continue to analyze the audience for signals about their evaluation of the message. What comments do audience members make about the speech, orally or in writing? What questions do they ask? What suggestions does the class instructor offer? Any student who is serious about improving as a public speaker must be aware of and act upon audience feedback after the speech is over.

practice critique

Evaluating a Speaker's Audience Analysis

Effective public speakers adapt their messages to specific audiences. Sarah Meinen, for example, developed her speech, "The Forgotten Four-Letter Word," to be delivered to other college students and judges at several intercollegiate speech tournaments. Read the transcript of that speech in Appendix B. Write a critique to Sarah commenting on how well she did or did not incorporate audience analysis in developing her speech. Suppose your instructor invited Sarah to give her speech in your speech class. What suggestions would you give Sarah for adapting her speech to you and your classmates?

Exercises

1. Select several topics that on first glance appear to be of interest primarily to people of one particular age group, gender, economic status, etc.—for example, the Lamaze method of childbirth, sports and male bonding, and expensive wines. Discuss how speakers could justify these topics as important to a broader audience.

2. Select a speech from *Vital Speeches* or some other published source or electronic database. Read the speech to discern how the speaker adapted, or failed to adapt, the message to the specific audience. Mark examples of audience adaptation strategies, writing in the margins of a copy of the speech the specific appeal or strategy used. Indicate where the speaker could better have adapted to the audience.

3. Using the speech you selected in the above exercise, discuss how the speaker would need to adapt the purpose, content, organization, and language if he or she were speaking to your class.

4. Use a newspaper index to prepare a two- to three-minute newscast of events that happened on the day you were born. Look at local, national, and international news, but also check the classified ads, grocery and clothing prices, and the movie ads and television log. For assistance in this assignment, you may wish to refer to the section on researching newspapers in Chapter 7.

5. Prepare an audience profile of your class using the seven demographic characteristics discussed in this chapter. After this analysis is prepared, answer the following questions: Which categories were easiest to determine? Which required more guesswork? Which characteristics do you think will be more important for most speeches given in this class?

6. Based on your analysis of students in this class, predict their opinions on the following questions.
    a. Should tax dollars be used to support men-only or women-only colleges and universities?
    b. Is a private college education superior to a public college education?
    c. Should the U.S. Constitution be amended to require a balanced budget?
    d. Should women have the right to have an abortion?
    e. Do social fraternities and sororities do more harm than good?

    After you have made your predictions, poll the class to determine their responses to the above questions. Were your predictions fairly accurate? Were you surprised at some of the answers? What factors caused you to predict as you did?

7. Choose a specific brand-name product advertised in several magazines. Analyze how the product is promoted in each publication. Are there differences in the ads' headlines, body copy, and visuals? If so, what do these distinctions reveal about how the advertisers viewed their audiences? If the ads are identical, suggest ways that the product appeal could be tailored to each audience.

8. Each issue of *Congressional Digest* poses a specific policy question on topics such as human cloning, physician-assisted suicide, and administration of our national parks. Each issue presents several speeches, affirming and negating the question. Select a copy of *Congressional Digest,* and read the speeches included. Discuss the differences between the pro and the con sides in terms of the values supporting each side's arguments.

9. Listen to a broadcast debate or discussion on a controversial issue. You can usually find heated discussions on CNN's *Crossfire,* PBS's *NewsHour with Jim Lehrer,* Sunday morning network talk shows, and Bill Maher's *Politically Incorrect.* Discuss the differences in positions based on the values supporting each person's arguments.

10. To give you some experience in analyzing off-campus audiences, select one of the following groups or organizations, find out what you can about it, and report back to the class.
    a. Humane Society
    b. United Way
    c. B'nai B'rith
    d. Veterans of Foreign Wars
    e. League of Women Voters
    f. NAACP
    g. Rotary Club

11. Collect print ads that illustrate Maslow's hierarchy of needs. Draw Maslow's model on a large sheet of posterboard, and create a collage showing the ads' appeals to various needs. Be prepared to present and discuss your collage.

12. Analyze your public speaking class using the VALS2 typology. What categories of people are represented in your class? Brainstorm some topics you think your classmates would find interesting and helpful. Select one of these topics, and discuss some of the needs and values you would tap in your audience.

13. Construct an audience questionnaire pertaining to the topic of an upcoming speech. Distribute it to your classmates, and then collect, compile, and interpret the results. Write an audience profile based on the results.

Notes

1. Mary Raymond Shipman Andrews, *The Perfect Tribute* (New York: Scribner's, 1906) 1–9.

2. Carl Sandburg, *Abraham Lincoln: The Prairie Years and the War Years* (New York: Harcourt, 1954) 443–44.

3. Newspaper reporters the next day began to reflect widely different public views of the president's surprisingly brief speech. The *Chicago Times* referred to "the silly, flat, and dish-watery utterances" of Lincoln; the *Harrisburg* [Pennsylvania] *Patriot and Union* simply reported, "We pass over the silly remarks of the President . . ." (Sandburg 445). Other newspapers, however, made entirely positive evaluations of Lincoln's speech. The *Chicago Tribune* predicted, "The dedicatory remarks of President Lincoln will live among the annals of man" (Sandburg 445). The *Philadelphia Evening Bulletin* noted that thousands who would not wade through Everett's elaborate oration would read Lincoln's brief remarks, "and not many will do it without a moistening of the eye and a swelling of the heart" (Sandburg 446). The *Providence Journal* reminded its readers of the adage that the hardest thing in the world is to make a good five-minute speech, and said, "We know not where to look for a more admirable speech than the brief one which the President made at the close of Mr. Everett's oration" (Sandburg 446).

4. Thomas M. Scheidel, *Persuasive Speaking* (Glenview, IL: Scott, 1967) 97. For a fuller account, see Mark E. Neely, *The Last Best Hope of Earth: Abraham Lincoln and the Promise of America* (Cambridge: Harvard UP, 1993) 154–55. Neely notes that Lincoln made these remarks to acknowledge a serenade celebrating recent Union victories at Gettysburg and Vicksburg.

5. Robert M. Berdahl, "Understanding *Hopwood,*" *Texas Alcalde* July/August 1996: 17.

6. Robert Hughes, *Culture of Complaint: The Fraying of America* (New York: Oxford UP, 1993) 14.

7. Vivian Sykes, "Perspectives on Cultural Diversity," in *Cultural Diversity in Libraries,* ed. Donald E. Riggs and Patricia A. Tarin (New York: Neal-Schuman) 1.

8. Terry Sanford, quoted in "Commencement Remarks: Learning to Care and Share," *Representative American Speeches 1988–1989,* ed. Owen Peterson (New York: Wilson, 1989) 154.

9. Win Kelley, *The Art of Public Address* (Dubuque, IA: Brown, 1965) 25.

10. John Jacob, "Racism and Race Relations: To Grow Beyond our Racial Animosities," *Vital Speeches of the Day* 15 January 1990: 214.

11. Abraham H. Maslow, *Motivation and Personality,* 2nd ed. (New York: Random, 1970) 35–47.

12. Maslow 38.

13. Maslow 41.

14. Michael Pfau and Roxanne Parrott, *Persuasive Communication Campaigns* (Boston: Allyn, 1993) 70.

15. Descriptions of categories are adapted from The VALS Segment Profiles, 1997, Stanford Research Institute, 12 June 1999 <http://www.future.sri.com/vals/vals.segs.html>.

16. <http://www.future.sri.com/vals/experiencers.html>.

. . . [T]here is no such thing as a boring subject. . . . [W]hether it's the plastics industry or the mating habits of a certain insect, you will always find that there are people out there who have devoted their entire lives to the subject. . . . Well, if it can fascinate one person, then you can extract a kind of enthusiasm from that person and transfer it to others out there.

—Ted Koppel

6

Selecting Your Speech Topic

Generate Ideas
    Self-Generated Topics
    Audience-Generated Topics
    Occasion-Generated Topics
    Research-Generated Topics
Select Your Topic
Focus Your Topic

Determine Your General Purpose
    Speeches to Inform
    Speeches to Persuade
    Speeches to Entertain
Formulate Your Specific Purpose
Word Your Thesis Statement
Develop Your Speech Title

If I write what you know, I bore you; if I write what I know, I bore myself; therefore, I write what I don't know.

—*Robert Duncan*[1]

The successful writer begins with a blank sheet of paper or a clear computer screen. The successful director begins with an empty stage. In order to achieve a finished product—a book or a play—both must go through several complicated steps. For example, directors must study the literary form, understand its dynamics, research the script, generate ideas, focus and organize those ideas, and then translate them into performance. In so doing, they give the finished product their individual signatures. Writers follow a similar process to complete a project.

As a public speaker, you are both author *and* director, and you seek to fill two voids: a blank sheet of paper and an empty space before an audience. Speech making is an artistic process that needs the spark of creativity to live. You cannot use a template or other formula to produce an effective speech. As an artist, you will use your creativity as well as your research and organizational skills to transform your ideas into a living speech. Before you can exercise your artistry with language, your persistence as a researcher, or any other talents you possess, however, you must have a topic. Selecting that topic with your audience, your own interests, and your speaking occasion in mind provides your first opportunity to exercise the creativity that will make the speech uniquely yours.

Selecting a topic for a speech is more complex than you may think. Students often fail to choose a topic wisely because they adopt counterproductive strategies. For example, some students select too quickly. They pick up a magazine, find an interesting article, and decide to use its subject as their topic. Much later, they discover that the topic is really inappropriate for the audience or the occasion, or they find no more information on the topic. If they keep the hastily chosen topic and approach the assignment half-heartedly, the quality of the speech suffers. If they change topics, they lose valuable speech preparation time. Either option presents a no-win situation.

Eric had three weeks to prepare his informative speech, and he wanted to select a topic that would excite him, his audience, and his instructor. Because he enjoyed watching the street performers near campus, he thought this would make an excellent speech topic. He went to the library, looked at a couple of indexes, but couldn't find anything listed under the topic of street performers. So he changed topics. In the library reading room, Eric found and skimmed through several magazines. He came across an article in *Discover* magazine on 3-D music. "Everybody's interested in music," Eric said to himself, so he photocopied the article and stuffed it in a notebook.

A couple of days later, he took out a pencil, a notepad, and the article. As he began reading, however, he encountered words such as *psychoacoustics, transponder, binaural imaging,* and *Convolvotron.* Eric realized that the topic as presented in the article was too technical for his audience (and for him!), and he began thinking of other interests he had that he could turn into a speech topic. Eric enjoyed airbrush artwork, but worried that others might find the topic boring. In his psychology class, he was studying dream interpretation, but Eric reasoned that others might have taken the course and would already know much of his information. There had recently been an earthquake in an adjacent state, and he thought this might be a timely topic. But because it had been in the news, he was afraid that someone else would choose the same topic. As the day of his speech quickly approached, Eric was still selecting and rejecting speech topics.

Students like Eric spend far too much time searching for the perfect topic. They jump from one idea to another because none seems quite right. As you can see, this se-lect-and-reject syndrome wastes valuable time that could be devoted to researching and developing a topic. As the speaking date nears, the student usually panics and selects any topic, develops it hastily in the limited time that remains, and never feels really comfortable with the topic. Unfortunately, this lack of preparation and commitment usually shows up in the speech presentation. At some point in the selection process, you must pick your best topic and commit yourself to developing it. Each of Eric's topics, for example, *could* have been both interesting and informative if he had committed his time to it.

The example of Eric should help you see that you cannot treat choosing your speech topic too lightly. Determining your speech topic, then, is an important part of speech making that should not be slighted. If you select a topic of interest to you and your audience for which you can find authoritative supporting material, you greatly enhance your chances of a successful speaking experience. You will also probably find it easier to construct your speech.

Right about now you may be asking yourself, "How am I ever going to pick the right topic?" Choosing your topic involves several steps. You should (1) generate a list of ideas for possible topics, (2) select a topic, (3) focus the topic, (4) determine your general purpose, (5) formulate your specific purpose, and (6) word your thesis state-ment. Depending on the specific speaking situation, you may also want or be asked to develop a speech title.

Generate Ideas

The first step in the process of selecting a speech topic is **brainstorming.** Brainstorm-ing requires you to use the critical thinking skill of generating, discussed in Chapter 1. With this technique, you list all the ideas that come to your mind with-out evaluating or censoring any of them. Too often, a speaker spends insufficient time generating a list of potential topics. Yet, as Dr. Pauling suggests, in order to select a good topic you must generate many top-ics. Author John Steinbeck compared ideas to rabbits, saying, "You get a couple and learn how to handle them, and pretty soon you have a dozen." As a rule, the larger your list of possible topics, the better the topic you will fi-nally select. Remember, do not evaluate or criticize your list as you brainstorm. What may seem silly to you at first can turn out to be an unusual speech subject with a lot of potential to interest your audience.

> *You can't have good ideas if you don't have a lot of ideas.*
>
> —*Linus Pauling*

For example, Angelita brainstormed topics for her informative speech by listing her interests and activities. She had played the saxophone in her high school band and was reminded that President Clinton had elevated the attention given to that instrument. She decided to inform her classmates how to play the saxophone. When she shared this idea with her instructor, however, the teacher cautioned her that such a goal was probably unrealistic in the five- to seven-minute time limits. Hadn't it taken her years to learn how to play the sax? Still interested in this topic area, Angelita consulted encyclopedias and found that this hybrid instrument was popular in military and American jazz bands. She began researching military bands and found the topic fascinating.

She learned that in the early 1600s, when European nations began to create standing armies, those troops started to need to march together. Musical com-posers wrote marches for this purpose. The military band played at outdoor cele-brations and demonstrations, environments requiring instruments, such as the saxophone, that were louder than many string instruments. What began as a

brainstorming: non-criti-cal free association to generate as many ideas as possible in a short time.

Thinking about your own hobbies and interests is one way to brainstorm for speech topics.

speech on how to play the saxophone eventually became a very interesting speech on the history of military bands. The topic expanded Angelita's knowledge in one of her fields of interest and also taught her listeners something new.

You can turn brainstorming into productive work toward your speech by asking and then answering these four questions:

1. What topics interest *you*?
2. What topics interest your *listeners*?
3. What topics develop from the *occasion*?
4. What topics develop from your *research*?

Your answers will help you devise a list of many topics from which you can then select the most appropriate.

Self-Generated Topics

Self-generated topics come from you—your memory, your notes, your interests, your experiences, and your personal files. Take out a sheet of paper, and jot down your hobbies, your favorite courses, books you have read, your pet peeves, names of people who intrigue you, and issues and events that excite you. What are your likes and dislikes? On what topics do you consider yourself knowledgeable? Review your list, writing beside each item possible speech topics. If you enjoy listening to music, perhaps a speech on the history of jazz would be informative. If you are irritated by people who are late, you could inform your audience about why people procrastinate or about how to set and meet goals. Are you uncomfortable in enclosed places? A speech on claustrophobia might interest you and your audience. If you are nearing graduation and have been reading books on how to land your first job, a speech on how to construct a résumé or dos and don'ts for the employment interview may be fitting.

Self-generated topics may also include subjects you *need* to know. If, for example, you expect to travel soon and will be making your own arrangements for the first time, you may find yourself riding in taxis, staying in hotels, and dining in some good restaurants. But are you familiar with tipping etiquette for cab drivers, baggage carriers, and waiters? Researching and delivering a speech on tipping will not only serve your needs but can be an interesting and informative topic for your listeners.

Consider the following topics generated by our students, using just their personal interests and knowledge:

self-generated topics: speech subjects based on the speaker's interests, experiences, and knowledge.

Anger management   Black history in textbooks
Artificial reefs   Calligraphy

Cluster headaches
Colleges of the future
Drying flowers
Hazing
Indian silver jewelry of the Southwest
Jet-skiing
Marshall, Thurgood
Music software

Parachuting, importance to military
Photograph restoration
Rappelling
Robotics
Sleep disorders
Spelunking
Tejano music
Wilderness therapy

Use what you know as a starting point in your topic selection process. Don't worry that you don't know enough about each topic at this stage to construct a speech. Research will help you later in focusing, developing, and supporting your topic. *What is important is that you have a list of possible topics that interest you.* Because these topics come from *your* knowledge, experience, and interests, your commitment to them is usually strong. Your interest and knowledge will motivate you in preparing your speech. In addition, your enthusiasm for your topic will enliven and enhance your speech delivery.

As you can see, self-generated topics can provide you with interesting ideas. However, they can also pose some difficulties for a speaker. One potential pitfall of self-generated topics is the use of overly technical language and jargon. If your topic is technical, be especially attentive to the language you choose to convey your meaning. The speaker in the following example forgot that advice.

Caryn, a pre-med student with a double major in biology and chemistry, found an interesting article that explained how some animals survive winter by freezing and then thawing in the spring.[2] She chose this as an informative speech topic and did further research. She reasoned correctly that many of her classmates wouldn't know of this phenomenon or how it occurs.

Yet most of her listeners knew they were in trouble when Caryn said in her introduction: "Today I want to explain how some animals such as the wood frog, the

My informative speech was entitled "Codicology: Not Just for Bookworms." The topic I originally chose was books as objects, not as tomes of information. This was a self-generated topic that could be spiced up with a little research. Two weeks into the assignment, I concluded that this topic seemed far too broad and a bit juvenile for a class of people who, as students, must have been around books for more than a decade. This sudden clarity had me at a loss. I mean the clock was ticking away, and I thought I had wasted all of my time. Then I discovered something. In my research, I was repeatedly running across this odd, scientific sounding word—*codicology.* I remembered what this chapter said about research-generated topics, so I decided to check this word out. I discovered that *codicology* (from *codex,* Latin for book, and *-ology,* indicating a science) was the name for *the science of manuscript study.* Adopting this interesting field of study as my new topic gave me renewed confidence because the problems inherent to my first topic had been solved. Manuscripts, as opposed to mass-produced books, were fascinating to me, and I was reasonably sure my audience wouldn't be well versed in the subject. Also, this topic was more manageable and had sharper impact.

—Brian Collins, Clark College

speaking with confidence

gray tree frog, painted turtles, and gallfly larvae use so-called antifreeze proteins, ice-nucleating proteins, trehalose, proline, and cryoprotectants to maintain the integrity of cells while their extracellular fluid freezes."

The audience never recovered. The remainder of her speech contained words and phrases such as *colligative cryoprotectants, polyhydroxyl alcohols, cytoplasm,* and *recrystallization.*

Caryn's problem was not with her topic; indeed, it's a fascinating subject. With simplified language and clear visual aids, she could have made that topic accessible to her listeners and drawn them into the speech. But the technical vocabulary and jargon that she found understandable only confused and alienated most of her classmates who were not pre-med majors. Remember that your speech on any technical topic will lose its intended impact if you fail to define key terms clearly for listeners less knowledgeable about the subject. You will create semantic distractions, one of those major obstacles to listening that we discussed in Chapter 4.

A second potential problem with self-generated topics is the speaker's lack of objectivity about the subject. If you become too involved with a topic, you cannot always develop it objectively. Researching your subject is a process of discovery. When you begin with rigid preconceptions, you may disregard important information that doesn't match your preconceived ideas. Take the example of Ken and his proposed speech topic on the legal drinking age.

> When the time came to develop and deliver a persuasive speech for his public speaking class, Ken decided to try to persuade his classmates, most of them first-year students, that the legal drinking age should be lowered from 21 to 18. He was committed to this point of view. He had been mentally rehearsing his arguments since his eighteenth birthday: "If I'm old enough to register with Selective Service and defend my country, I'm old enough to drink if I care to." "If I'm old enough to marry without my parents' consent, I should be able to buy and consume any beverage I want."
>
> Yet two days before his speech was due, Ken asked his speech teacher for an extension. The reason, he explained, was that all of the published sources he had researched *supported* the increased legal drinking age. "Some of the sources even had graphs showing decreases in traffic fatalities among 18- to 21-year-olds or reductions in juvenile crimes since the drinking age was raised," he complained. Ken's instructor prodded him, "If all the evidence says that the new law is a benefit in these ways, have you considered changing your view?" Ken's answer was no. He remained sure that, given more time, he could find the evidence that supported his position.

Ken's predicament is typical of people who form rigid expectations of what their research will reveal. If, after doing some research, he still supported lowering the drinking age, Ken probably should have abandoned the traffic safety and juvenile crime issues altogether. Instead, he could have pursued those philosophical arguments he believed strongly. His primary argument could have centered on the theme that society sends mixed messages by treating 18-year-olds as mature and responsible in many areas of life and irresponsible in others. Make sure you don't follow Ken's example. Gather some good supporting data before you commit yourself to a specific focus for your topic.

Finally, lack of objectivity about a self-generated topic can take a second form: excessive devotion to the speech topic. You may choose as a topic an interest or hobby that has been a passion of yours for years. You are enthusiastic about the topic, you already have a wealth of information on it, and doing further research will seem a pleasure rather than a chore. What could possibly go wrong?

"The audience will love this topic," you think. Be careful. Your audience may not share your enthusiasm for aardvarks or restoring Studebaker cars. Your interest in a topic is just one criterion in the selection process. For most speech topics, you must also work to generate audience interest. We are not suggesting that you avoid self-generated topics of great interest to you. Just do not assume that your audience already has the same level of interest. They may not initially share your enthusiasm for aardvarks (or Bob Marley or the history of fireworks or optical illusions), but if you *work* at it, you can *make* them interested. Be prepared to work hard to do so.

In addition, be prepared to listen openly to others' speeches. Remember that ethical listeners do not prejudge either a speaker or that speaker's ideas. You may encounter some students who seem skeptical of any information that won't help them make the car payment. Granted, some topics seem so narrow or so offbeat that you can imagine thinking, "Who cares about aardvarks?" But can't you also imagine a *terrific* speech on aardvarks by a speaker who was genuinely interested in them and who had lots of vivid supporting material? Much of the value of education is that it makes you a better (smarter, happier, more well-rounded) person. Some information is intrinsically rewarding and just plain fun to know. Don't dismiss information presented in a speech (or anywhere else) just because it won't make you more money, save you time, or whiten your teeth.

Audience-Generated Topics

Pursuing **audience-generated topics** is a second way of triggering speech subjects. What topics are of interest or importance to your listeners? If you are asked to speak to a group, you are often asked because of your expertise in a particular area. Topic selection, in this case, may be predetermined.

On other occasions, such as in this class, you are not provided with topics or topic areas. How can you find out what interests your classmates? There are three ways to do this. First, *ask them*. In this class, ask some of your classmates in casual conversation about topics they would like to hear discussed. If allowed the opportunity, you could also use a formal questionnaire to seek topic suggestions from the entire class. When you speak outside class to an organization, ask the person who contacted you about issues of probable interest to the group.

Second, *listen and read*. What do your classmates discuss before and after class? Articles in your campus or local paper, or letters to the editor, may suggest issues of concern. Finally, *use the audience analysis strategies* detailed in Chapter 5 to generate topics. Consider your listeners' needs. If your class is composed primarily of students just entering college, a speech on the history of your school would be interesting, informative, and appropriate. If your class is composed primarily of seniors, a speech on establishing a good credit history may be timely.

You may even find that most members of your audience seem to feel one way about a controversial topic while you take the opposite view. You may choose to use this situation to develop and deliver a persuasive speech aimed at winning support for your side of the issue.

The following topics were generated by our students using an audience-centered approach:

Barter systems	Horror movies, appeal of
Car-jackings	Internet access, price comparisons
Coca-Cola, history of	Interviews, dressing for
Country and western line dancing	Mnemonic (memory) devices
Critical incident stress	Online scholarship searches
Cruise vacations	Palmistry (palm reading)
Ethereal music	Pre-Columbian artifacts

audience-generated topics: speech subjects geared to the interests and needs of a speaker's listeners.

Prescription drugs, price comparisons	Step aerobics
Reupholstering furniture	Superwoman syndrome
Self-defense for women	Test anxiety, how to control
Small businesses, how to start	Used cars, how to buy

Occasion-Generated Topics

Occasion-generated topics constitute a third source of speech subjects. When and where a speech is given may guide you in selecting a topic. For example, our student Adam gave a speech on mountain biking on the July day when that sport first became an Olympic event at the 1996 games. A speech on setting goals may benefit your classmates more at the beginning of the semester or quarter, whereas a speech on stress management may be particularly relevant preceding midterm or final examinations. A speech on the dangers of overexposure to the sun will have more impact if it is given in the spring or the summer rather than in the fall.

If you are scheduled to speak near a particular holiday, a speech on the history or importance of that holiday may be appropriate. If you have a speech scheduled on or near Victoria Day, for instance, you can take the opportunity to introduce your classmates to a part of Canadian history. To find examples of other holidays, look at your calendar, or examine different calendars at a bookstore. Specialty calendars or almanacs list unusual but interesting holidays, birth dates of notable and notorious people, or anniversaries of important historical events.

Online reference works can greatly aid your search for occasion-generated topics. For example, we explored "Britannica's Lives," part of the online version of the *Encyclopædia Britannica*. We typed the date October 28 and generated a list of 39 noteworthy individuals born in 11 different countries on this day in October. Among those people were William Gates, computer programmer and cofounder of Microsoft Corporation; Jonas Salk, medical researcher who developed a vaccine for polio; Eliphalet Remington, firearms manufacturer and inventor; and Levi Coffin, abolitionist who helped thousands of runaway slaves flee to freedom through the Underground Railroad. By clicking on the name William Gates, we generated a three-paragraph summary of his life, his accomplishments, and additional related topics.

We truly are a people who love to celebrate occasions, whether they are established national holidays or quirky, lesser-known ones. Many of these occasions can suggest possible speech topics. A speech detailing cable television's impact on the viewing habits of the American family would seem appropriately timed during National Cable Month. Banned Book Month may be the ideal occasion for a speech on censorship. Consider some of the possible speech topics suggested by the following: Women's History Month, National Cigar Lovers Day, American Beer Week, International Left-Handers Day, National Pasta Week, Straw Hat Day, National Relaxation Day, American Chocolate Week, National Singles Week, and Mailbox Improvement Week. There are even months to celebrate ice cream, baked beans, and the hot dog.

Occasion-Generated Topics
http://shoga.wwa.com/~mjm/almanac2.html
This site, Daily Almanacs, can help you search for occasion-generated speech topics. You can select any day in the current year to explore the important events that happened on that day. The almanac also lists names and biographical notes about people who were born or who died on that particular day.

Occasion-Generated Topics
http://www.festivals.com
Speaking near a particularly festive occasion, or wondering whether you are? This site is a worldwide guide to festivals. You can search by topic, month, or geographical region, or just browse by clicking the buttons for arts, sports, children, music, motor, or culture.

occasion-generated topics: speech subjects derived from particular circumstances, seasons, holidays, or life events.

A ritual or special occasion can provide an excellent speech topic. Here, parents give their children "lucky money" for Tet, the Vietnamese Lunar New Year.

Somewhere in your schooling you may recall a math teacher discussing the mathematical construct of pi—that's the number expressing the ratio of the circumference of a circle to its diameter (3.14159 . . . *ad infinitum*). Doesn't sound like an exciting speech topic, does it? That's what Corey thought until he read an article on the front pages of his newspaper. He learned that every March 14 at 1:59 P.M. (that's 314159) "thousands of people around the world will unite to sing songs, recite poetry, perform bizarre rites, and eat ritual food in honor of their favorite number." The article stimulated his interest with bizarre facts about the number. Corey learned that "piets"—the devotees of the number—had created Web sites that contained "formulas for calculating pi, . . . pi carols, poems, and other utterly useless bits of trivia for honoring the day."[3] By the time Corey had finished his research, he knew more about this intriguing number, its history, and its cult of followers. His speech informed and interested not only him but his classmates.

Our students generated the following topics as they focused on different occasions for speeches:

Bat mitzvah (female equivalent of bar mitzvah)	Hurricanes
	Juneteenth
Black Music Month	*Oktoberfest* in Germany
Charreada (Mexican rodeo)	Punxsutawney Phil (Groundhog Day)
Conjuto Festival	Ramadan
Dia de los Muertos	Running of the Bulls in Pamplona, Spain
Festival of the Lanterns	
Fireworks, designing displays	Summer internships, finding
Hispanic Heritage Month	Telethons, success of
Home childbirth	Wildflowers, excursions to view

Note that an occasion-generated topic can often lead you to other interesting topic possibilities. Thinking about a current labor strike may spark your interest in the history of labor unions. From there you could decide to focus your informative speech on child labor. Drought conditions in your area may lead you to consider the subjects of cloud seeding or desalting sea water. The occasion of Memorial Day may get you thinking about The Wall, the Vietnam Veterans Memorial in Washington, D.C. You may then decide to focus on the competition for the design of the monument; on Maya Lin, whose design won that competition; or on the aesthetics of the wall and the stirring effect it has on visitors.

Research-Generated Topics

Research-generated topics, a fourth strategy for sparking speech ideas, require you to explore a variety of sources. First, you could consult some of the indexes we list in Chapter 7. Look at the listing of subjects, and jot down those that interest you. A second research strategy is to browse through some magazines or journals in the current periodical section of your library or at a local newsstand. Just remember that this exploration is the first step in selecting a speech topic. Don't leap at the first interesting topic you find, as Eric did in the earlier example. A third strategy for generating topics is to peruse book titles at a good bookstore, noting those that interest you. Bookstores are convenient places to discover speech topics because the books are grouped by general subject area and are arranged to catch your eye. By using these three research tools—indexes, magazines and journals, and books—you can not only discover a speech topic but may also locate your first source of information.

> **Researching College News**
> http://beacon-www.asa.utk.edu/resources/papers.html
> Maintained by *The Daily Beacon* at the University of Tennessee, this site features hypertext links to other college newspapers available online. This resource may be particularly useful in choosing a topic or investigating how other campuses are dealing with an issue you have already selected as a speech topic.

Consider the following topics. You might not have thought of these on your own, but they all have the potential to be excellent topics and they all came from resources our students found.

Adams, Ansel	Movies, how they are rated
Amish life	Nightmares
Artwork, airbrush	*Noh* (Ancient Japanese) theater
Behavior modification	Nuclear medicine, future of
Color's effects on moods	Obsessive-compulsive disorder
Computer-generated music	O'Keeffe, Georgia
Curanderismo (Mexican folk healing)	*Origami* (Japanese paper art)
Fingerprints, features of	Parenting styles
Forensic hypnosis	Political cartoons, history of
Genetic mapping	Pyramids, Aztec
Home schooling	Roller coasters
Hot air balloons	Sleep apnea
Indian folklore	Stonehenge
Insomnia, treatment of	Tattoo removal
Jet lag, cures for	Tomb sculptures
Landscape design	Tuskeegee Airmen, the
Marley, Bob	Williams Syndrome
Medicinal herbs	Yoga techniques

research-generated topics: speech subjects discovered by investigating a variety of sources.

It is important that you use all four of these strategies to generate possible speech topics. If you end your topic generation process too quickly, you limit your options. A substantive list of self-, audience-, occasion-, and research-generated topics gives you maximum flexibility in selecting a topic.

Once you have selected your topic area, we suggest that you use a technique called **visual brainstorming** to investigate the range of possibilities within that topic. Take out a sheet of paper, and write your topic in the center. Now, think of how you might divide and narrow that topic. It may help you to think of some generic categories such as "causes," "types," and "solutions" that are appropriate to numerous topics. As you think of subtopics, draw a line from the center in any direction, and write the narrower topic.

As your thinking suggests additional topics, you will probably be surprised at the web of potential speech topics you have created just from your brainstorming. Figure 6.1 illustrates the end product of a visual brainstorming exercise on the topic of "advertising." Certainly, you can add to this list, but in just a few minutes we were able to provide several options for focusing the subject of advertising. Some of these, such as comparing how television ads depicted families in the 1960s with how they are depicted now, are excellent topics that would probably not have come to mind without this brainstorming exercise.

Topic Search
http://www.abacon.com/pubspeak/assess/topic.html
Need a topic? Drawing a blank? Allyn & Bacon's Web site "Finding a Topic" may help you generate ideas and gather information on a wide variety of topics. Links are provided to general and specific topic areas such as science, health, social problems, technology, and legislative issues.

You can incorporate library research into your discovery and focusing process. For example, if you are interested in advertising awards and conducted some research on that topic, you would discover that awards for outstanding television ads include the CLIOs and LIONs. If you are considering the topic of phobias, for example, you could consult indexes to see how they divide this topic. In just a few minutes, you could narrow your topic area to more manageable topics, such as: the causes of phobias; panic-prone personality; the prevalence of phobias across cultures; akousticophobia, the fear of sounds; hypnophobia, the fear of sleep; phonophobia, the fear of speaking aloud; and phobophobia, the fear of fears. Most of these topics would make excellent informative speeches.

Select Your Topic

Once you have generated a list of possible speech topics, you must then select the best one. Determining what is best is an individual choice; neither a classmate, a friend, nor your instructor can make that choice. However, you can apply some criteria to each of your options to help you make a wise selection.

Four questions should guide your choice of topics. First, *"Am I interested or likely to become interested in the topic?"* The more enthusiastic you are about a topic, the greater the time and attention you will give to researching, constructing, and practicing your speech. When you enjoy learning, you learn better. As a result, speakers motivated by their topics are almost always more productive than those bored with their topics.

Second, ask, *"Is the topic of interest or importance to my audience?"* This question helps you avoid choosing a topic that you love but that your audience will never care about. Speech making is easier when your listeners are potentially interested in what you have to say. When your audience is more attentive and receptive, you can relax and make your delivery livelier. Sometimes, topics seem to be of little initial interest to audience members but may, nevertheless, be important to their personal or career

visual brainstorming: informal written outline achieved by free associating around a key word or idea.

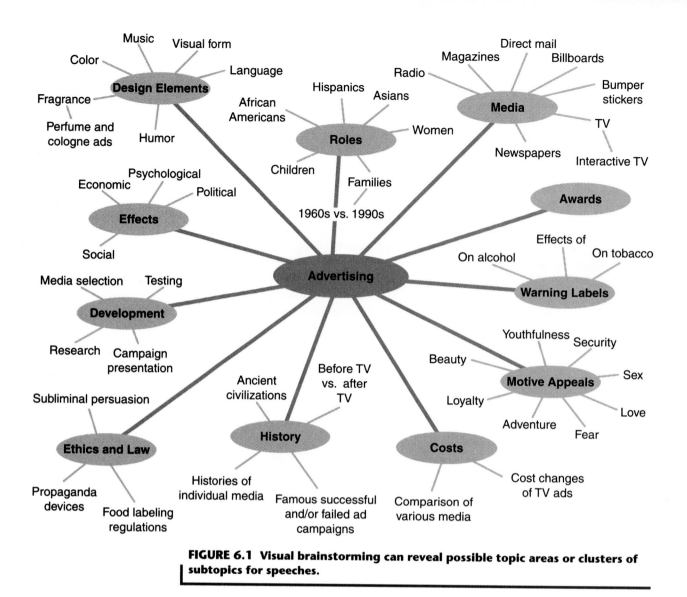

FIGURE 6.1 Visual brainstorming can reveal possible topic areas or clusters of subtopics for speeches.

success. As long as you can demonstrate the importance and relevance of the topic to them, you will motivate your audience to listen.

A third question you should answer in selecting your speech topic is, *"Am I likely to find sufficient authoritative supporting material in the time allotted for researching and developing the speech?"* Rarely do students select topics so narrow that they cannot find sufficient accessible information. You may, however, select a topic so recent that your library has not yet received adequate information. Often, because of your research deadline, you cannot obtain information on your topic through the mail. Occasionally, students contact us just before their speeches are scheduled and tell us that they are unable to complete their speeches because information they ordered has not arrived. That's usually a sign that the student's research started too late or progressed too slowly. In researching your speech, remember the adage that if something can go wrong, it will. Build some flexibility into your schedule so that you can adapt to any crisis that may arise.

Finally, consider the question, *"Do I understand the topic enough to undertake and interpret my research?"* A speaker arguing the merits of a tax increase must have an understanding of economics in order to assess research data. When you inform the audience about music therapy, you need some understanding of psychological treatment techniques and procedures. A speaker may misinterpret the reasons that violent crime in the United States is higher than in Japan if he or she does not understand Japanese culture. You do not need to know much about your topic as you begin your research, but you must know enough to be able to make sense of the data you discover.

Questions to Guide Topic Selection

1. Does this topic interest me or have the potential to do so?
2. Is this topic interesting or important to my listeners?
3. Am I likely to find sufficient supporting materials on this topic?
4. Do I know enough about this topic to start researching it and to interpret what I discover?

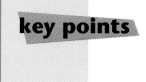

Focus Your Topic

Once you have selected your topic, you must focus it. Even though we have heard students speak on topics that were too narrow, this is rare. More commonly, students fail to narrow their topics sufficiently, leaving too little time to develop their ideas. The result is a speech that is more surface than substance.

When you decide on a topic area, use visual brainstorming to determine some of its divisions, or subtopics. The subject of "loneliness," for example, could focus on any of the following topics: the causes of loneliness, the relationship between loneliness and depression, loneliness and the elderly, loneliness as a cause of teenage suicide, characteristics of the lonely person, the differences between being alone and being lonely, or strategies for coping with loneliness. You could never discuss all of these topics meaningfully in a short speech. Narrowing the scope of your inquiry gives direction to your research and allows you sufficient time to support the ideas you will present to your audience.

A colleague of ours had a long and distinguished career teaching communication. After class one day, she returned to her office visibly upset. When questioned by her colleagues, she said one of her students had announced in his speech introduction that his purpose was to teach the class how to make a lethal poison using ingredients people already had in their homes or could easily buy. "Moreover," she said, "to stress the significance of the topic, he assured us that this substance would kill any living animal, certainly even the heaviest human being."

"What did you do?" her colleagues asked. "I sat there thinking of the rash of teenage suicides, even copycat suicides, we've been hearing about lately, and all the other meanness in the world," she replied. "I wrestled with my conscience for about a minute and a half, and then, for the first time since I started teaching, I interrupted a speaker. I told the student I didn't think we needed to hear this information, and asked him to be seated."

Was this teacher's action justified? Did she violate the student's freedom of speech? Placed in that teacher's position, what would you have done?

Visual brainstorming is an excellent way of focusing your topic. A second way is through research. The more you read about your topic, the more you will likely discover its many aspects. Some may be too narrow for a complete speech, but others may be suitable for an entire speech or may be combined to form a speech.

For a five- to seven-minute informative speech assignment, Rob developed three main points in the body of his speech on baseball:

I. The history of baseball
II. How the game is played
III. The uniform and equipment used

As you might guess, Rob found himself rushing through the speech, and he still did not finish it within the time limit. You probably noticed that each of his main points is too broad. Rob's problem was that he needed to focus his topic further.

One possibility for Rob was to concentrate on the history of baseball and maybe focus on a specific era that interested him. For example, he could have surprised and enlightened his listeners by discussing baseball during the Civil War. Or he could have focused on the all-black leagues operating from the 1920s until the integration of baseball during the 1950s. Rob could have used the popular movie *A League of Their Own* as backdrop and spoken about the All-American Girls Professional Baseball League formed during World War II when many professional baseball players were being drafted. Each of these topics would probably have interested and informed Rob's listeners, regardless of their fondness for baseball. Notice, too, that each of these narrower topics also places baseball in a sociological context. Rob's speech on the history of baseball could have thus become a lesson in a particular period of American history, having appeal even for listeners not especially interested in baseball.

Determine Your General Purpose

Broadly speaking, a speech may have one of three purposes: to inform, to persuade, or to entertain. The general purpose of your speech defines your relationship with the audience. You play the role of mentor when you provide information. You are an advocate when you seek to change beliefs, attitudes, values, or behaviors through a persuasive speech. Your speech to entertain is meant to amuse your audience. As the entertainer, you set a mood to relax your audience using your delivery style, tone, and content.

You may find it difficult at times to distinguish these purposes. Because information may affect both what we believe and how we act, the distinction between informative speaking and persuasive speaking is sometimes particularly blurred. A speech meant to entertain is frequently persuasive because it may make a serious point through the use of humor. Despite the overlap between these general purposes, you must be secure about your primary purpose any time you speak in public. A closer look at the objectives and intended outcomes of each general purpose will help you distinguish them.

Speeches to Inform

A **speech to inform** has as its objective to impart knowledge to an audience. You convey this information in an objective and unbiased manner. Your goal is not to alter the listeners' attitudes or behaviors but to facilitate their understanding of your subject and their ability to retain this new information. We discuss the speech to inform in greater detail in Chapter 15. A speech on any of the following topics could be informative:

Art therapy
Cloning

speech to inform: a speech designed to convey new and/or useful information in a balanced, objective way.

Hispanic film industry
History of science fiction movies
The middle child syndrome
Muralist movement in Mexican art
Poetry slams
Shopping addiction

Speeches to Persuade

A **speech to persuade** seeks to influence either beliefs or actions. The former, sometimes called a **speech to convince,** focuses on audience beliefs and attitudes. A speech designed to persuade audience members to embrace a belief stops short of advocating specific action. A speaker may argue, for example, that polygraph testing is unreliable without suggesting a plan of action. Another speaker may try to convince listeners that women have been neglected in medical research without offering a plan to solve the problem.

A speech designed to persuade to action, or a **speech to actuate,** attempts to change not only the listeners' beliefs and attitudes but also their behavior. A speech to actuate could move the audience to boycott a controversial art exhibit, to contribute money to a charity, to enroll in a specific course, or to urge their elected officials to increase funding for women's health research. In each of these cases, the speaker's goal would be first to intensify or alter the audience's beliefs and then to show how easy and beneficial taking action could be. We discuss the speech to persuade in Chapters 16 and 17.

Speeches to Entertain

A third general purpose of speech is to entertain. A speech to entertain differs from speaking to entertain. *Speaking to entertain* is a general phrase covering several types of speaking. It includes humorous monologues, stand-up comedy routines, and story-telling, for example. When you tell your friends jokes or recount a humorous anecdote, you are trying to entertain them. You are probably not trying to develop a key point in an organized, methodical way.

A **speech to entertain** is more formal than simply speaking to entertain because it is more highly organized and its development is more detailed. Speeches to entertain are often delivered on occasions when people are in a festive mood, such as after a banquet or as part of an awards ceremony. For that reason, we discuss the speech to entertain in more detail in Chapter 18, "Speaking on Special Occasions." Remember that all speeches, including those to entertain, should develop a central thought through an organized presentation of supporting material and ideas. Though the ideas in a speech to entertain will be illustrated and highlighted by humor, a mere collection of jokes does not qualify as a speech. We agree with the communication scholars who contend that a speech to entertain is actually either a speech to inform or a speech to persuade, usually the latter.

Formulate Your Specific Purpose

When you are asked to state the **general purpose** of your speech, you will respond with two words from among the following: *to inform, to persuade* (or *to convince* or *to actuate*), or *to entertain*. When asked to state your specific purpose, however, you will need to be more descriptive. A **specific purpose** statement has three parts.

speech to persuade: a speech designed to influence listeners' beliefs and/or actions.

speech to convince: a persuasive speech designed to influence audience beliefs and attitudes rather than behaviors.

speech to actuate: a persuasive speech designed to influence audience behaviors.

speech to entertain: a speech designed to make a point through the creative, organized use of humorous supporting materials.

key points

To Develop Your Specific Purpose Statement

1. State your general purpose.
2. Name your intended audience.
3. State the goal of your speech.

First, you begin with the general purpose of the speech, stated as an infinitive; for example, "to convince." Second, you name the individuals to whom the speech is addressed. This is usually phrased simply as "the audience" or "my listeners." Third, you state what you want your speech to accomplish. What should the audience know, what should they believe, or what should they do as a result of your speech? You may want to establish the belief that alcoholism is hereditary. In this example, then, the complete specific purpose statement would be: To convince the audience that alcoholism is hereditary. A speech advocating compulsory national service for all U.S. citizens may have this as its specific purpose: to persuade the audience to write Congress urging the passage of a compulsory national service program. Other examples of specific purpose statements are:

- To inform the audience on how to communicate constructive criticism.
- To inform the audience on seasonal affective disorder.
- To convince the audience that use of cellular phones while driving is a serious problem.
- To convince the audience that publically funded professional sports stadiums are a misuse of taxpayers' money.
- To move the audience to draft and sign a living will.
- To move the audience to spend their spring break building a house for Habitat for Humanity.

Word Your Thesis Statement

A **thesis statement** presents the central idea of the speech. It is a one-sentence synopsis of your speech. The thesis statement of the persuasive speech on compulsory national service, mentioned earlier, could be this: "Compulsory national service would benefit the nation by promoting the national spirit, promoting the national defense, and promoting the national welfare." This statement is the central idea of the speech, a proposition the speaker will support with evidence and argument.

Notice that the process of topic selection has, up to this point, enabled you to focus your subject on something specific and manageable. You are now ready to construct a *working thesis:* a statement that, based on your current research and thinking, summarizes what you will say in your speech.[4] Although a thesis statement is designed to keep you focused, it may change as you continue to work on and develop your speech. It gives you a handle on your subject and, as you begin to develop your key ideas, you will be able to determine whether you can support your thesis statement. In organizing the body of the speech, you may realize that your ideas are not balanced or that two of your main points should be collapsed into one. As you research your speech, you may discover additional ideas that are more important than some you had planned to present. That was the experience of our student who spoke on compulsory national service.

Stuart was developing a persuasive speech advocating a system of compulsory national service (CNS). As he began his research, he planned to focus only on the national security that compulsory military service would provide. He imagined that his thesis statement would be, "Compulsory national service would benefit the nation

general purpose: the broad goal of a speech, such as to inform, to persuade, or to entertain.

specific purpose: a statement of the general purpose of the speech, the speaker's intended audience, and the limited goal or outcome.

thesis statement: a one-sentence synopsis of a speaker's message.

by ensuring its military readiness." Yet his research quickly revealed many other benefits of CNS.

Some programs of compulsory national service that have been proposed include a domestic volunteer service that would address issues other than military readiness. For example, Stuart learned that such a program could help conservation and recycling efforts. By training doctors' assistants, CNS could also extend quality health care into rural areas. CNS could serve millions of elderly people who need only light assistance in order to be able to live independently in their own homes.

By the time he had completed his research, Stuart had broadened the focus of his speech and felt he had developed a much stronger case for instituting a CNS program. When he delivered his speech, he presented three main arguments:

I. CNS would promote the national spirit.

II. CNS would promote the national defense.

III. CNS would promote the national welfare.

Stuart made certain to revise his working thesis to reflect his new organization. (Remember, you will also need to modify your thesis statement any time you revise the content and structure of your speech.)

The following examples illustrate how you can narrow a topic's focus from a general area to the speech's thesis statement.

Topic Area: Music

Topic: The marketing of rap music

General Purpose: To inform

Specific Purpose: To inform the audience on alternative strategies of marketing rap music.

Thesis Statement: Rap music is marketed through the use of street teams, "mix tapes," and club deejays.

Topic Area: Sculpture

Topic: Works by Andy Goldsworthy

General Purpose: To inform

Specific Purpose: To inform the audience about Andy Goldsworthy's sculptures.

Thesis Statement: Andy Goldsworthy sculpts wood, ice, and leaves into intricate works in their natural settings.

Topic Area: Police oversight

Topic: Mandatory videotaping of police

General Purpose: To persuade

Specific Purpose: To persuade the audience that all police actions in police stations should be videotaped.

Thesis Statement: Videotaping all police actions in police stations will deter police misconduct, deter false charges of police misconduct, and restore public confidence in police work.

Topic Area: U.S. currency

Topic: Dollar coins

General Purpose: To persuade

Specific Purpose: To persuade the audience that the U.S. government should replace dollar bills with coins.

Thesis Statement: Dollar coins are less costly over their lifetime, are more difficult to counterfeit, and are more functional.

Develop Your Speech Title

Some speeches do not require titles. Many public speaking instructors, for example, do not require titles for speeches delivered in class. In most formal public speaking situations, however, the audience knows the speaker and topic beforehand. The title is often included in a printed program or mentioned by the person introducing the speaker. Therefore, whenever you have the opportunity, you should title all your speeches, including your classroom speeches.

A well-crafted title accomplishes three purposes. First, it generates audience interest in your speech. A speech title disclosed to the audience should arouse interest, secure attention, and make people want to listen. By appealing to the needs and interests of your audience, a title can encourage active listening.

Interesting titles may also enhance your image as a communicator and make the audience want to listen to you specifically. When you speak to an audience that does not know you, your title may generate the audience's first impression of you. Creative titles engender more interest than general, technical, or overused ones. A speech about the All-American Girls Baseball League, for example, could be titled "A History of the All-American Girls Baseball League" or "A Diamond Is a Girl's Best Friend." Which title do you you think is more interesting? Which title would interest you more in hearing a speech on tedium in the workplace: "Job Burnout" or "Making Your Work Relaxing and Rewarding"?

A second purpose of a title is to make your message more memorable. While there is an up side to creativity, you should avoid the temptation of selecting a title simply for the sake of creativity. If, in the process, you sacrifice clarity, you may actually divert audience attention from your central thesis. Remember, when you encapsulate the point of your speech in the title, you prepare the audience to listen for its development or to use it as a reference point when they explain to others what you discussed.

If you study print advertisements, you will see that they usually use this strategy successfully. The headline usually contains a selling promise designed to capture the attention of those likely to buy the product or service. Speech titles such as "Converting Anger to Action" or "Making Your Anger Work for You" are clear and direct. A person who frequently experiences anger can expect to learn how that negative emotion can become a positive option. These titles identify the audience (those who experience anger) and include a promise (anger can work for you). A speech describing the healing nature of the grieving process, for example, could be titled simply "Good Grief!" The title is short, attention-getting, and easy to remember, and it highlights the concept that grief can be good.

We found the following titles of student speeches printed in recent volumes of *Winning Orations,* an annual publication of the Interstate Oratorical Association. You probably have an idea of what each speech is about even though you have not heard or read it.

> Clearing the Air about Cigars
>
> Charities' Telesolicitation: Fundraising or Fraud?
>
> 911: Is Anyone Listening?
>
> Flunking Lunch: The Failure of Public School Lunch Programs
>
> Overdosing from A to Zinc: The Problems with Vitamin Toxicity
>
> Identity Fraud: What's in a Name

If you accomplish the objectives of securing your listeners' interest and enhancing the memorability of your key ideas before you utter your first word, you have gone a long way toward ensuring the success of your speech.

A third and final benefit of a good speech title is primarily for you, the speaker. When you give your speech a title, you are forced to state your point clearly and concisely. If you have difficulty constructing a title that encapsulates your key ideas, your speech probably lacks a clear central thought, or you have strayed from your intended thesis. It is better to discover this before you speak so you have time to make proper adjustments.

There is no one best way to develop a title for a speech, but consider these three options. First, if your speech contains a key phrase or sentence that is used repeatedly, that statement may be your title. Martin Luther King, Jr., used the repeated theme *I have a dream* for the title of his "I Have a Dream" speech. (See Appendix B.) A speech arguing the harm of plastic surgery performed just to make a person feel more beautiful could be titled, "Making Stars, Leaving Scars." The title contrasts the search for physical beauty with the scars it may leave behind. The use of rhyme also makes the title easy to remember.

A second strategy for developing a good speech title is to promise your audience something beneficial in the title. A speech on the benefits of exercise could be titled "Living Longer, Feeling Better." Titles that begin with "How to" follow this strategy, and are particularly appropriate when you know the audience is interested in acquiring a skill you can teach them. "How You Can Pass This Course without Spending Any More Time Studying" may not be the most creative title for a speech, but we bet you and your classmates would listen with rapt attention to it!

Finally, a third strategy is to word your title as a question. A speech investigating laughter therapy could be titled "Is Laughter Really the Best Medicine?" Asking the question signals to the audience what they will know by the end of the speech. Keep in mind that your listeners will expect to be able to answer the question by the end of your speech. We remember one speech professor who titled a speech convention paper on the effects of humor "Can Humor Increase Persuasion, or Is It All a Joke?" The title used humor because the paper was *about* humor, and the fact that we still remember the title attests to its effectiveness.

Summary

By selecting topics for their speeches, students in public speaking classes determine the majority of what they will hear during the course. Six steps can simplify the important process of choosing an appropriate speech topic.

First, brainstorm a list of potential topics focused around your own interests, the needs and interests of your audience, and the occasion for your speech. Your research adds a fourth category of possible topics. Having a large list of subjects gives you the freedom and flexibility to make an appropriate selection.

The second step is to select your topic. Making this decision is easier if you ask yourself four questions while reviewing your topic list: "Am I already interested or likely to become interested in this topic as I develop the speech?" "Is the topic already interesting or important to my audience, or can I interest them in it?" "Am I likely to find adequate, quality supporting materials on this topic in the time I have?" And "Do I know enough about the topic to start researching it and to interpret what I discover?"

The third step is to focus or narrow the subject you've selected. Two ways to accomplish this are *visual brainstorming* and initial research on the topic. Focusing the topic is important in guiding your research and helping you stay within the time limit for the speech.

The fourth step is to determine your *general purpose:* to inform, to persuade, or to entertain. The general purpose may be predetermined, as in most classroom speech assignments, or left to the judgment of the speaker. Whether you are determining the purpose or just reminding yourself of it, having that goal clearly in mind will keep you on target as you research and organize the speech.

The fifth step of selecting a topic is to formulate your *specific purpose.* That statement should specify three things: the general purpose in infinitive form ("to inform," for example), the intended audience, and what you want your listeners to know, believe, or do as a result of your speech.

The sixth step, wording your *thesis statement,* means distilling the message of the speech into one sentence. This step must come last, because it depends upon your initial research and tentative organization of the speech. With the thesis statement in mind, a speaker is ready to conduct in-depth research and to proceed with the development of the speech.

A possible final step, not always required, is to title the speech. Creative, provocative titles achieve three goals. First, they intrigue the audience and make them want to listen to you. Second, they make your message more memorable. Third, they help speakers check to see that the speech has a central focus or thesis.

practice critique

Evaluating Titles

Read the transcript of Martin Luther King, Jr.'s speech in Appendix B. Discuss how "I Have a Dream" fulfills, or fails to fulfill, the three purposes of an effective title. (Using a key phrase that is repeated in the speech illustrates the first option for developing a speech title.) Think of alternative titles for Dr. King's speech using the other two strategies discussed in the chapter. Discuss the strengths and weaknesses of these alternative titles.

Exercises

1. After conducting the necessary brainstorming and research, list eight self-generated, eight audience-generated, eight occasion-generated, and fifteen research-generated topics on a sheet of paper. Place an *I* by the topics you would develop as informative speeches and a *P* by those that are persuasive. Place an asterisk (*) by five informative topics and five persuasive topics you think would make the best speeches. Bring your list to class. Meeting in small groups, share your list with your classmates, having them decide the five best topics in each category. Now review your list, and decide the topics on which you would like to speak.

2. Choose a broad subject area, and write that topic in the middle of a blank page. Use the technique of visual brainstorming to generate a list of specific topics. Continue diagramming as long as it is productive. Review the topics you generated, and identify the best topics for a speech in this class.

3. Using what you know (or think you know) about your classmates, generate lists of topics you believe would interest or be important to them. Share some of these topics with the class, as instructed. This activity provides an opportunity to see how class members perceive each other.

4. Using the topic areas listed below, narrow each subject, and write a specific purpose statement for an informative speech and a persuasive speech on each topic.
   a. Fast foods
   b. Funerals
   c. Illiteracy
   d. Natural disasters
   e. Stress

5. Use any list in this chapter to help you learn more about what interests your class-mates. You can do this by indicating the topics that interest or are important to you or your classmates and those topics that are not. What would a speaker have to do to generate interest in the topics not selected?

6. Select and read a speech in Appendix B. Determine its general purpose. Word its specific purpose and thesis statement.

7. Construct at least two titles for a speech on each of the specific purposes listed below. Word the title so that it attracts audience interest or captures the central ideas of the speech.
    a. To inform the audience on how to interpret their dreams.
    b. To inform the audience on how the stock market works.
    c. To inform the audience on the uses of light therapy to reduce depression.
    d. To inform the audience on the problems of being a single parent.
    e. To persuade the audience that the federal government should no longer mint the penny.
    f. To persuade the audience that professional boxing should be outlawed.
    g. To persuade the audience that IQ tests are culturally biased.

Notes

1. Ralph Fletcher, *What a Writer Needs* (Portsmouth, NH: Heinemann, 1993) 101.

2. Kenneth B. Storey and Janet M. Storey, "Frozen and Alive," *Scientific American* Dec. 1990: 92–97.

3. K. C. Cole, "Math Mavens Thank God It's Pi Day," *Roanoke Times* 14 March 1998: Al, 4.

4. Leonard J. Rosen and Laurence Behrens, *The Allyn & Bacon Handbook,* 4th ed. (Boston: Allyn, 2000) 68.

If we would have knowledge, we must get a world of new questions.

—Susanne K. Langer

Researching Your Topic

Whether you are headed toward pharmacy school, studying architecture, or majoring in economics, you possess or are in the process of acquiring certain knowledge in your chosen field. By the time you graduate, you will know about the history of pharmacology, will be able to identify various architectural styles, or will understand the interplay of forces that drive an economy. In Samuel Johnson's words, you will "know a subject." Yet your field of study will not stop evolving and developing on the day that you graduate from college. Learning information that becomes a part of who you are makes up only a fragment of your education. An "educated" college graduate in the 21st century "will no longer be defined as someone who has absorbed a certain body of factual information, but as one who knows how to find, evaluate, and apply needed information."[1]

As people who were born into or have lived through the dawn of the Information Age, you probably already understand the reason that information literacy is so important. This year more than 65,000 books will be published in the United States.[2] Add to this the information provided by millions of pages printed in newspapers, magazines, and other periodicals; volumes of public and private agencies' reports, hearings, and pamphlets; and countless hours of news and opinions broadcast through television and radio. Much of this information will appear in some form on the Internet, to be archived or argued in that global medium where anyone with a Web page can publish anything. Consider these statistics that highlight the rapidly snowballing accumulation of information:

> The sum total of humankind's knowledge doubled from 1750–1900. It doubled again from 1900–1950. Again from 1960–1965. It has been estimated that the sum total of humankind's knowledge has doubled at least once every 5 years since then.
> . . . It has been further projected that by the year 2020, knowledge will double every 73 days![3]

In light of these circumstances, it may be smarter to think of being educated more as *knowing how to access* information rather than *possessing* or acquiring it. No one needs to feel "out of the loop" today. Indeed, for public speakers the challenge is selecting from the wide range of available data the information most appropriate for their speeches. That requires knowing how to research, how to scratch "an intellectual itch."[4] Today, as Professors Wayne Booth, Gregory Colomb, and Joseph Williams put it bluntly, "In any field, you will need the skills that only research can help you master, whether you expect to design the production line or to run it."[5]

In Chapter 6, we discussed how to select a topic. In this chapter we consider the second step—how to research a topic. **Research** is the gathering of evidence and arguments you will need to understand, develop, and explain your subject. Remember that research is not one step of the speech construction process. Research should occur throughout that process. For example, we have already seen in Chapter 6 how research can help you select your topic. Once you have chosen your topic, additional research helps you focus it and determine your specific purpose. As you move to the next step and begin to construct the body of your speech, you may need to develop some of your ideas further with additional research. Your research continues even as you consult dic-

research: the process of gathering evidence and arguments to understand, develop, and explain a speech topic.

tionaries, thesauruses, and books of quotations to help you word the ideas of your speech before you deliver it in class.

Students often wonder how much research to conduct for a classroom speech. Obviously, there is no one answer to this question. Research your topic until you have enough authoritative evidence for you to make an informative or a persuasive statement to your listeners. You need to back up your ideas with credible sources. Your instructor may specify a minimum number of sources you are to cite during your speech. Does that mean your research is finished when you have reached that magic number? The answer is, not necessarily. Sometimes the information you have collected may be insufficient to support your intended central idea or may even contradict it. In these cases you must continue research to gain additional information. You may find that you have to shift your focus or change your topic altogether. Research can also lead you to discover new aspects of your subject that you had not considered. These new aspects may be more interesting and worthwhile than your original topic. The excellent public speaker, then, does not view research as a phase preceding the construction of the speech but as an evolving process. We research so that excellent evidence supports excellent ideas that can, in turn, be excellently organized and delivered.

Online Research Help
http://www.
researchbuzz.com/news
Check out ResearchBuzz if you are serious about using the Internet for research. Tara Calishain produces a lively weekly newsletter detailing innovations on the Web, press releases from service providers, and magazine and newspaper articles about Internet research. Each free issue contains links to each item mentioned, as well as clear instructions for subscribing and unsubscribing.

As you might guess, conducting research exercises and develops all of your critical thinking skills. Research is not necessarily a linear process. You may be using a number of your critical thinking skills simultaneously throughout. If you have some experience with or knowledge about the topic area you have chosen, however, you'll begin by *remembering* and assessing your knowledge. You'll be *information gathering* as you formulate questions you want your research to answer and then collect your data. You will use your *generating* skills as you develop new lines of inquiry based on the research you have completed. Throughout the process you'll be *analyzing* whether and how information from your different sources fits together. As you connect items of information, you'll be *integrating* and *organizing*. As you measure the quality and quantity of your research results, you'll be *evaluating*. And because you will often find more information than you can use, your entire research process will have you *focusing* your speech topic more and more narrowly.

Occasionally, if you are lucky, you may stumble onto one or two sources of great help as you craft your speech. But most of the time you will work hard on your research to ensure that you collect the information pertinent to your topic. Your research strategy will depend on your particular topic and the available research facilities. However, the following general five-step sequence can assist you in generating excellent ideas and supporting material, regardless of the topic of your speech.

1. Assess your personal knowledge of the topic.
2. Develop your research plan.
3. Collect your information.
4. Record your information.
5. Conclude your search.

Let's look more closely at each phase of the research process.

Assess Your Personal Knowledge

Samuel Johnson correctly noted that personal knowledge is the starting point of research. The first question you should ask and answer is, "What do I know that will help me develop my topic?" When you begin your research, do not make the mistake of confining yourself only to published materials. Your personal memory has been shaped by what you have read, heard, observed, and experienced. Use that knowledge as a starting point for researching your topic.

The concept of mastering public speaking we sketched in the preface to this book requires a public speaker to have an ongoing commitment to public communication. Establishing a personal information base is important for any speaker who wants to be informed and credible. You already have a great deal of personal knowledge. Don't be afraid to tap this resource as you select and develop your speech topic. For example, a student who worked as a plainclothes security guard for a major department store drew from personal experience in his speech on detecting and apprehending shoplifters. A student who assisted her father in administering polygraph tests chose as her speech topic the use and misuse of lie detectors. A person whose hobby was playing the bagpipes informed his audience about the history of this musical instrument. A vegetarian decided to persuade others to consider her diet. These speakers used their personal knowledge and experiences as starting points for their research. Each developed and delivered an interesting speech.

Throughout your life, you will occasionally, perhaps often, be called upon to share your expertise and opinions with others in public speeches. Therefore, you should consider developing a personal filing system of information you can retrieve for those occasions. We have found three kinds of files helpful in constructing our speeches: an article file, a quotation file, and a speech file.

An **article file** includes informative articles on topics that interest you. These can be cut, photocopied, or scanned from newspapers and magazines. You can also cut and paste items from online sources. This type of file gives you a head start in selecting a topic and researching your speech. When you read a provocative passage in a book or an interesting magazine article, photocopy it, download it onto a disk, or print it. Record the complete source citation on the page, and file it in a labeled folder. When you are asked to speak to a group, consult your article file for possible topics appropriate to the occasion and audience.

A second useful file is a **quotation file.** Many good books of quotations are available online, in the reference section of your library, or in a local bookstore. They can assist you in wording and explaining your speech. (See a partial list on page 159.) You may also find it helpful to generate your own collection of quotations. When you read or hear a memorable statement, write it and the name of the speaker or writer on a notecard or type them into a computer file. As your collection grows, you can divide the quotations into categories. When preparing your speech, consult your file for statements that illustrate or highlight your ideas.

Quotations can also serve as excellent attention-getting or concluding statements. For example, Jodi began her speech with the statement: " 'Memory,' it has been said, 'is the power to gather roses in winter.' " She used that quotation to underpin her thesis that the tragedy of Alzheimer's disease is that, by destroying memory, it eliminates one's past. We have also heard several students urge their listeners to action by quoting Edmund Burke: "The only thing necessary for the triumph of evil is for good men to do nothing."

A third file, the **speech file,** contains a folder or an electronic file for each speech you have given or have started to prepare. After you present a speech to one audience, a

article file: a collection of articles, from print and electronic sources, that a speaker finds interesting or important.

quotation file: a collection of passages a speaker finds memorable or important, together with the source citation for each passage.

speech file: a personal collection of materials about the research, preparation, and delivery of speeches completed or initiated.

listener may ask you to speak on the same topic to another group. Therefore, save and file your speaking notes or manuscript. This file should also include your research notes. You may want to refocus your topic to adapt to the new audience, but you will still have saved valuable research and preparation time if you can review your original research notes and articles. It is important to remember, however, that every student speaker should research and develop his or her own speech. One speaker's files should never be used by another speaker to construct a speech.

Winston Churchill was once asked how long he had prepared for one of his speeches. He replied, "For forty years." In discussing this incident, Robert Jeffrey and Owen Peterson observe, "In a sense, a speaker spends his or her entire life preparing for a speech. Everything we have learned and experienced, as well as the attitudes we have developed, shapes and influences our speech."[6] Your knowledge and personal files give you a head start in selecting and developing your topic.

Develop Your Research Plan

Someone once posed this question: "If you don't know where you're going, how will you know when you get there?" Experienced explorers focus on a destination while equipping themselves with detailed plans of action and appropriate tools to reach the target. Similarly, speakers should develop research plans and marshal the tools necessary to achieve their targets—well-presented speeches. Your research plan begins as you answer several questions:

1. What information do I need?
2. Where am I most likely to find it?
3. How can I obtain this information?
4. How will time constraints affect my research options?

Your research plan depends, in large part, on your topic and specific purpose. As we mentioned earlier, many speech topics require library research. Topics such as the electronic encyclopedia, mathematical illiteracy, environmental racism, or the history of graffiti would rely heavily on library resources. Other speech topics rely on personal interviews for most of their information. If, for example, your purpose is to inform your classmates of your school's new registration procedures, your library may be of little assistance. More helpful would be an interview with your college's registrar. A speech explaining new breakthroughs in cancer research could benefit from collecting information from the American Cancer Society. In short, different topics demand different research strategies. A good research plan accounts for these differences. Keep a running list of what you need and where you can obtain it.

Not only should you prepare a list of what you need and where you can obtain it, but you should also prepare a timetable for constructing your speech. If you are going to speak two weeks from now, you still have time to go to the library and work. You may even have time to set up an interview with an expert, conduct it, and transcribe key quotations. However, two weeks is not enough time to write for information and be assured of its arrival in time to integrate it into your speech.

Although you should explore all appropriate options, much of your research will probably take place in or through your college or community library. Today the notion of a college or university library restricted to use by currently enrolled students, faculty, and staff during limited hours of operation may seem fairly old fashioned to you. The personal computer has expanded the library walls and extended its hours of access to 24 each day. Yet the library still exists, and it contains many resources that you can't find anywhere else. One of the most helpful sources of information to assist you in creating your research plan is also one of the least often used: the library staff, particularly those members who work in the reference department. A good reference librarian can: (1) acquaint you with the services and holdings of the library, (2) guide you to particular sources of information helpful for your research, and (3) instruct you in the use of library equipment.

Although all libraries have much in common, each is organized to serve its specific constituency. No college library can subscribe to all periodicals and newspapers, for example. Don't waste your time copying index citations for periodicals that are not in your library. Your reference librarian can guide you to the library's areas of strength, thus making your research more efficient.

One of your library's strengths these days is surely the access to huge electronic **databases** that it provides. As a registered student, you can use such indexes from a library computer or through your library's Web page from a remote computer free of charge. (That's what part of your library use fee provides.) Or your school's computer technology department may have site licenses giving you Internet access and technicians who are skilled researchers to help you navigate your research from a campus computer lab. In the following sections, we'll highlight some of these databases and the research sources they provide you.

In many ways you learn to research just as you learn to drive a car. A good driver receives instruction on driving principles and the workings of an automobile before soloing. The driver's goal is not to remain dependent on the instructor but to become proficient so that he or she can venture out alone. Similarly, the effective researcher receives valuable instruction on research principles and the workings of the library from an experienced researcher. Together they work to develop a research plan. If pursued aggressively, that research plan can yield excellent supporting materials for a public speech.

Collect Your Information

Once you have developed a research plan, begin to collect the information you need to understand and develop your topic. Students who complain, "I can't find any information on my topic," usually do not know where to look. For most topics, more information probably exists than you can locate and read in the time allotted for your research. Two basic approaches to research are: (1) accessing databases and then retrieving the information to which they have directed you, and (2) launching out onto the Internet on your own. The advantage of using database indexes is that the information you get has presumably been evaluated and checked by the magazine, journal, newspaper, or other source that published it. Out in cyberspace, you often lack such quality assurance, and we'll discuss the attractions and aggravations of information published on the Internet a little later.

database: a huge collection of information arranged for quick retrieval by computer using keywords stipulated by a researcher.

URL (Uniform Resource Locator): the standard notation for each Internet Web site's unique address, often beginning with http://www.

In this chapter we cannot list all or even most of the resources available to you. We discuss magazines and journals, newspapers, government documents, books, reference works, electronic media, and some alternative research sources. Even as we write, however, the information landscape continues to undergo revolutionary changes. Partnerships between information providers form and dissolve, changing **URL** (**Uniform Resource Locator**) Web site addresses and the routes by which you retrieve information. Some such changes will no doubt occur between the time we write this and the time you try to make use of it. We have taken great effort to provide accurate information about electronic sources in this chapter. Just remember that http:// in front of any Web site address that we provide stands not only for "hypertext transfer protocol," but also for "hope this text pops up."

Experienced college librarians can help you navigate your way through the research process.

Magazines and Journals

Magazine and journal articles are probably the most common source of information for student speeches. With more than 70,000 magazines from which to choose, however, how do you keep from being overwhelmed with information?[7] Using an index will help you filter useful from extraneous information. Hundreds of excellent indexes of periodicals exist, and many standard indexes are now available on compact disk or online. These indexes can guide you as you focus your search even more.

Research Source
http://www.
newsdirectory.com/
Access more than 8,000 newspapers, magazines, and television stories. Searching by country, type of publication, or even by area code, you can obtain information on newsworthy topics from all over the world.

One of the most commonly used indexes for researching magazines is the *Readers' Guide to Periodical Literature*, available in print, on CD-ROM, and online. This index references more than 250 English-language periodicals, including those most frequently found in libraries. Another useful index is the *Public Affairs Information Service (PAIS) Bulletin*, which indexes articles from periodicals as well as selected books, government publications, pamphlets, and reports of public and private agencies. Although smaller libraries may not have all these publications, check with your librarian about obtaining those you need through interlibrary loan.

Your library probably also subscribes to a group of online magazine and journal indexes. Because they are easier to revise, computerized indexes are generally more current than those published in print. Some of the larger, more familiar magazine and journal indexes include the following:

Database/Index	What It Provides
ABI/Inform	Abstracts and some full text of articles in 1,000+ business and management journals
Dow Jones Interactive	Full-text databases of 5,000+ magazines, newspapers, trade journals, and newswires
ERIC	Indexes to 700,000+ citations, including journal articles of interest to education students, teachers, and policy makers
Expanded Academic Index	Indexes to 1,500 journals in science, social sciences, and the humanities
Lexis-Nexis	Full-text database of 5,000+ journals, magazines, and other sources
OCLC FirstSearch	Fifty databases indexing articles on the arts, books, business, education, humanities, law, medicine, science, and technology
PAIS International Periodical Abstracts	Citations for articles and other sources from 1972; abstracts of articles 1985–present
Periodical Abstracts	Abstracts and some full text of general and academic periodicals, 1986–present
ProQuest Direct	Indexes to 4,000+ magazines and newspapers for business, news, and professional topics
Social Work Abstracts	Index to 450+ journals, 1977–present, in the fields of social work and human services
Wilson Web	Indexes to *Book Review Digest, Art Index, Biography Index,* and *Education Index*

Once you have selected your topic, you may also wish to consult an index to magazines and periodicals in that specific area. Specialized indexes exist for almost every academic field and can make your research more efficient. A few of the many such indexes include the following:

American Statistics Index
Business Periodicals Index
Consumer Health and Nutrition Index
Education Index
General Science Index

Hispanic American Periodicals Index
Humanities Index
Index to Legal Periodicals
Index to Periodicals by and about Blacks
Music Index
Social Sciences Index

Remember that, because these indexes are so specialized, the periodicals and journals they lead you to will likely be written for a specialized audience and may use jargon and technical language familiar only to people in the field. Even if you understand these articles easily, you may have to simplify their language and ideas for the more diverse audience of your classroom.

How can the computerized index help you research your speech topic? A computerized index allows you to tap the resources of hundreds of periodicals, to customize a bibliography specific to your topic, and to print it, thus saving you much time tran-

Title	URL	Site Features
General Interest		
Advertising Age	http://www.adage.com/	Search/Full text
Atlantic Monthly	http://www.theatlantic.com/search	Search/Abstracts/Full text
Business Week	http://www.businessweek.com/	Full text/Subscription required
Car and Driver Online	http://www.caranddriver.com/	Search/Full text
The Economist	http://www.economist.com/	Registration required/Search/Full text
George	http://www.georgemag.com/	Available only on AOL
Maclean's	http://www.macleans.ca	Archives vailable to subscribers only
Mother Jones	http://www.mojones.com	Search/Full text
National Geographic	http://www.nationalgeographic.com	Search/Web site links/Full text
Newsweek	http://www.newsweek.com/	Search/Full text
People Online	http://www.pathfinder.com/people	Current issue articles only
Premiere Magazine	http://www.premieremag.com	Archives by year/No search
Reader's Digest	http://www.readersdigest.com/	Archives/No search
Smithsonian Magazine	http://www.smithsonianmag.si.edu	Full text/Abstracts of articles
Sports Illustrated	http://search.cnnsi.com/index.html	Search/Full text
Time Magazine	http://www.time.com	Search/Full text
USNews Online	http://www.usnews.com/	Archives/Full text
Wired Magazine	http://www.hotwired.com/wired	Search/Full text/Abstracts
Alternative Press		
Denizine	http://www.denizine.com	No search/Full text current articles only
Feed	http://www.feedmag.com	Search/Full text
George, Jr.	http://www.georgejr.com	Search/Full text
Salon Magazine	http://www1:salon.com	Search/Full text
Swanky	http://www.swanky.org	Current issue articles only
Third Age	http://www.thirdage.com	Full text
The Village Voice	http://www.villagevoice.com/	Search/Full text
Utne Reader Online	http://www.utne.com	Current issue articles only
Science & Technology		
Archaeology	http://www.archaeology.org	Search/Full text
Astronomy	http://www2.astronomy.com/astro/	Search/Full text
Discover	http://www.discover.com/archive/	Search/Full text
Invention and Technology	http://www.americanheritage.com	Archives/No search
Nature	http://www.nature.com	Registration required/Full text for subscribers only
Popular Science	http://www.popsci.com	Search/Full text
Science News Online	http://www.sciencenews.org	Search/Full text/Abstracts
Scientific American	http://www.sciam.com	Search/Full text/Abstracts
21st Century	http://www.21net.com/	Current articles/Link to metasearch engine

FIGURE 7.1 Online Magazines

scribing source citations. Probably the greatest advantage of computerized searching is that you can search by keywords, allowing you to locate information not accessible through traditional author, title, or subject searches. Invest the brief time necessary to learn how to use any electronic indexes your library has. Your effort will pay big dividends when you begin your research.

If you have particular magazines and journals in mind at any stage in your research, you can also check the online versions of these publications directly. Particularly helpful are those with search functions. Figure 7.1 gives a sampling of online magazines, their Internet addresses, and brief notes about their site features.

Newspapers

Including articles on topics from aardvarks to zoos, newspapers offer abundant information that can be local, national, or international in scope. Use the newspaper indexes to guide you to your specific topic. Newspapers are usually transferred to microfilm or microfiche for easy storage; consequently, most libraries can house many years' worth of newspapers in a few filing drawers. The *New York Times,* the *Washington Post,* and the *Christian Science Monitor* are all indexed and may be helpful in your research.

Available on computer, InfoTrac's *National Newspaper Index,* UMI's *Newspaper Abstracts Ondisc,* and FirstSearch's *Newspaper Abstracts* provide bibliographic references to a collection of newspapers from throughout the United States. Many newspapers now have sites on the World Wide Web and provide indexes to back issues. At some libraries, you can even download text to your own computer disk.

Other indexes will guide you to newspapers targeted at specific ethnic, professional, and geographical audiences. The *Black Newspapers Index,* for example, references newspapers oriented to African-American audiences and often contains stories not found in more mainstream newspapers. The *Wall Street Journal Index* is a source of information on business and economic topics. Your library may also subscribe to the indexes and newspapers of major city papers.

If your city's newspaper is not indexed, it may still be in your library on microfilm. Without an index, however, its usefulness is limited, unless you know the actual or approximate date of the article you want.

Another excellent guide to newspapers is *NewsBank.* Articles on political, economic, social, scientific, legal, health, and international issues are selected, organized, and recorded on microfiche. The *NewsBank Index,* available on computer as well as in hard copy, puts at your fingertips articles from more than 450 newspapers and regional business publications it references. Included in the front of the bound volumes of the index is an easy to understand, step-by-step guide to locating articles in *NewsBank.*

If you are interested in a localized topic, you may want to launch out onto the Internet and research online newspapers directly. Figure 7.2 lists a number of national and local newspapers, their URLs, and key site features. Note that many of these charge a fee to let you access full-text articles, particularly older ones. Yet it may be worth it to you to use a credit card and shop for research materials from the comfort of home.

Government Documents

The most prolific publisher of information in the United States is the federal government. Much of our bureaucracy is devoted to collecting, cataloguing, and disseminating information. The U.S. government generates a wealth of information on a wide range of topics from its many congressional, executive, and judicial agencies.

Online, the Library of Congress offers *THOMAS: Legislative Information on the Internet.* Named "in the spirit of Thomas Jefferson," *THOMAS* provides texts

Government Documents
http://thomas.loc.gov
This Library of Congress Web site helps you obtain information from the U.S. Congress. You can download House and Senate committee reports, summaries of bills being considered and notes about their status, copies of laws enacted, and even remarks recorded in the *Congressional Record.* Especially helpful is the FAQ (frequently asked questions) feature that describes how to conduct a search in *THOMAS,* how to download a bill or committee report, how to contact your representative or senators, how to cite the documents you find, and other information that will enhance your research skills.

Title	URL	Site Features
National Dailies		
Christian Science Monitor	http://csmonitor.com	Search/Abstracts/Fee for full text
New York Times	http://www.nytimes.com	Search/Archives/Registration required/Fee for full text
USA Today	http://www.usatoday.com/	Search/Fee for full text
Washington Post	http://www.washingtonpost.com	Search/Full text/Current articles only
Washington Times	http://www.washtimes.com/	Search/Full text/Current articles only
Major U.S. Metropolitan Newspapers		
Atlanta Journal-Constitution	http://www.accessatlanta.com/ajcl	Search/Full text available to subscribers
Austin American-Statesman	http://www.statesmen.com	Search/Fee for full text
Baltimore Sun	http://www.sunspot.net/	Archives/Fee for articles more than 2 weeks old
Boston Globe	http://www.boston.com/globe/search/	Search/Abstracts free/Full text for fee
Charlotte Observer	http://www.charlotte.com/observer	Archives/Abstracts free/Full text for fee
Chicago Sun-Times	http://www.suntimes.com	Search/Full text
Chicago Tribune	http://www.chicago.tribune.com	Search/Abstracts free/Full text for fee
Cincinnati Enquirer	http://cincinnati.com/search/	Search/Full text
Cincinnati Post	http://www.cincypost.com	Search/Full text
Cleveland Plain Dealer	http://www.cleveland.com	Search/Full text
Columbus Dispatch	http://www.cd.columbus.oh.us	Search/Recent articles/Full text
Dallas Morning News	http://www.dallasnews.com	Search/Abstracts free/Fee for full text
Denver Post	http://www.denverpost.com	Search current articles/Full text
Denver Rocky Mountain News	http://www.denver-rmn.com	Search/Abstracts free/Fee for full text
Detroit Free Press	http://www.freep.com	Search/Archives/Full text
Detroit News	http://detnews.com	Search/Full text
Fort Lauderdale Sun-Sentinel	http://sun-sentinel.com/archive.htm	Search/Abstracts free/Fee for full text
Fort Worth Star-Telegram	http://www.startext.net	Search/Full text
Hartford Courant	http://www.ctnow.com/search/	Search/Abstracts/Full text
Houston Chronicle	http://www.chron.com	Search/Archives for subscribers only
Indianapolis Star and News	http://www.starnews.com	Search/Archives/Full text
Jacksonville Florida Times-Union	http://jacksonville.com	Search/Archives/Full text
Los Angeles Times	http://www.latimes.com/HOME/ARCHIVES/	Search/Abstracts free/Full text for fee
Miami Herald	http://www.herald.com	Search/Archives/Full text for fee
Milwaukee Journal Sentinel	http://www.jsonline.com	Search/Abstracts/Full text
Minneapolis–St. Paul Pioneer Press	http://www.pioneerplanet.com	Search/Full text/Articles from last 7 days
Minneapolis–St. Paul Star Tribune	http://www2.startribune.com	Fee for articles older than 3 weeks
New York Daily News	http://www.mostnewyork.com	Search/Abstracts/Full text
New York Newsday	http://www.newsday.com/searchit.htm	Search/Archives/Full text
New York Post	http://www.nypostonline.com	Search/Archives/Full text

(continued)

FIGURE 7.2 Online Newspapers

Title	URL	Site Features
Norfolk Virginian-Pilot	http://www.virginianpilot.com	Search/Registration and fees apply
Oakland Tribune	http://www.oaklandtribune.com	Search/Abstracts/Full text
Orlando Sentinel	http://www.orlandosentinel.com	Search/Abstracts free/Fee for full text
Philadelphia Inquirer & Daily News	http://www.philly.com/newslibrary	Search/Abstracts free/Fee for full text
Phoenix Arizona Republic	http://www.arizonarepublic.com	Search/Archives/Full text
Pittsburgh Tribune-Review	http://www.tribune-review.com	Search/Fee for full text
Providence Journal-Bulletin	http://www.projo.com	Search/Abstracts/Some articles for fee
Rochester Democrat & Chronicle	http://www.rochesterdandc.com	Search/Full text
Sacramento Bee	http://www.sacbee.com	Search/Abstracts free/Fee for full text
St. Louis Post-Dispatch	http://archives.postnet.com	Search/Fee for full text
St. Petersburg Times	http://www.sptimes.com	Search Archives by Date Only
Salt Lake City Deseret News	http://www.desnews.com	Recent article search free/Fee for articles over 6 months old
Salt Lake Tribune	http://www.sltrib.com	Search/Full text
San Antonio Express-News	http://www.express-news.com/archives/search.shtml	Search/Abstracts free/Fee for full text
San Diego Union-Tribune	http://www.uniontribune.com	Search/Full text/Registration required
San Francisco Chronicle	http://www.sfgate.com	Search/Recent articles only
San Francisco Examiner	http://www.examiner.com	Search/Full text
San Jose Mercury News	http://www.mercurycenter.com	Search/Fee for full text
Seattle Times	http://www.seattletimes.com/web/	Search/Full text
Tampa Tribune	http://www.tampatrib.com	Search/Fee for full text

FIGURE 7.2 Online Newspapers *continued*

of pending legislation, the *Congressional Record*, committee information, and historical documents, as well as links to other government Internet resources. The Government Printing Office furnishes similar and related information through *GPO Access*. The White House Home Page offers executive publications, presidential speeches, cabinet-level agency information, and press briefings, in addition to virtual tours of the White House. Online, you can read full texts of Supreme Court decisions, hear audio clips of unedited arguments before the court, and read biographies and ruling records of individual justices. In short, almost every federal agency has a World Wide Web site. All of this means that you can see texts of legislation, reports, court decisions, and presidential speeches long before they appear in print.

Accessing printed government documents from a federal depository library may initially seem more intimidating to you than finding them on the Internet. But learning how to locate this information is well worth your time and effort.

Two publications can help you find information in government documents: the *CIS/Index* and the *Monthly Catalog of U.S. Government Publications*. The Congressional Information Service publishes the *CIS/Index* and *CIS Abstracts* to help you select from the more than 800,000 pages of information produced by Congress each year.

In book form, the *CIS/Index* is superior to the *Monthly Catalog* because it is more specific and easier to use. The *CIS* is, however, limited to congressional publications.

Branch/Agency/Document	URL
Budget of the United States Government	http://w3.access.gpo.gov/ usbudget/index.html
Catalog of U.S. Government Publications	http://www.access.gpro.gov/ su_docs/dpos/adpos400.html
Congressional Bills	http://www.access.gpo.gov/ congress/cong009.html
Congressional Record	http://www.access.gpo.gov/ su_docs/aces/aces150.html
Federal Register	http://www.access.gpo.gov/ su_docs/aces/aces140.html
The Library of Congress	http://lcweb.loc.gov/
Statistical Abstract of the United States	http://www.census.gov/statab/ www/
THOMAS	http://thomas.loc.gov/
U.S. Census Bureau	http://www.census.gov/
U.S. House of Representatives	http://www.house.gov/
The United States Senate	http://www.senate.gov/
U.S. Supreme Court Opinions	http://fedbs.access.gpo.gov/ court01.htm
Weekly Compilation of Presidential Documents	http://www.access.gpo.gov/nara/ nara003.html
White House	http://www.whitehouse.gov

**FIGURE 7.3
Government
Documents Online**

The *Monthly Catalog* references documents from all branches of government and is also available in a CD-ROM version known as *Marcive GPO CAT/PAC.* For access to federal statistical publications, you can consult the *American Statistics Index,* published by the Congressional Information Service.

Even if you are not using a library database, you can still access a wealth of government documents online. Figure 7.3 lists Web sites for some key government agencies and the documents they produce.

Books

Books, of course, are excellent sources of information. Because they are longer than magazine and newspaper articles, books allow authors to discuss topics in greater depth and often provide an index to key ideas and a bibliography of sources consulted. Recognize, however, that if your speech topic requires the most up-to-date data you can find, information in magazines may be more current and accessible than what you can find in books. Despite this limitation, books can be an integral part of your research plan.

Today most academic libraries have online catalogs, although some libraries still use the card catalog for parts of their collections. The *online catalog* (Figure 7.4) permits you to access subject, title, and author listings without having to move from one station to another. The online catalog usually provides better cross-referencing of related topics than does the card catalog. An additional feature is the "status" column, which indicates whether the book is on the library shelves, checked out, or on order.

SUBJECTS list subject headings used for this item. Do a SUBJECT search with one of these subjects, and you will find this and other items on the same subject.

CALL#/VOL/NO/COPY The call number is used to locate items on the shelf.

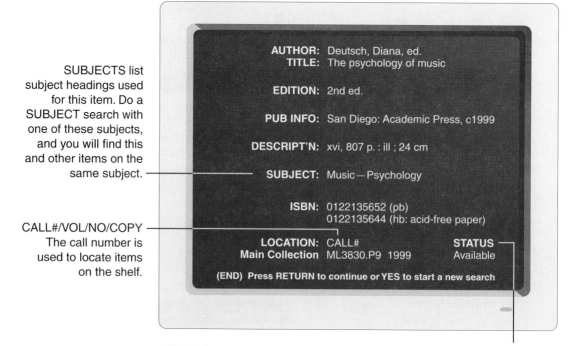

AUTHOR: Deutsch, Diana, ed.
TITLE: The psychology of music

EDITION: 2nd ed.

PUB INFO: San Diego: Academic Press, c1999

DESCRIPT'N: xvi, 807 p. : ill ; 24 cm

SUBJECT: Music—Psychology

ISBN: 0122135652 (pb)
0122135644 (hb: acid-free paper)

LOCATION: CALL#   STATUS
Main Collection ML3830.P9 1999   Available

(END) Press RETURN to continue or YES to start a new search

STATUS tells whether a book is available, checked out, on order, etc. If a book is checked out, the due date will appear under STATUS.

FIGURE 7.4 Online catalog
(Source: Radford University Library Catalog, McConnell Library, Radford, VA.)

Many online catalogs also have printers attached, allowing you to print entries for items you want to find on the library shelves.

The *card catalog,* familiar to many of us since we first began to use libraries, may be completely foreign to young researchers. This system consists of index cards filed alphabetically according to subject, title, and author.

On the Internet, full-text literary works are well represented by Literature Online (LION), a searchable database of more than 250,000 British and American books. If you love books and like browsing on the Internet, we highly recommend *The Book Lover's Guide to the Internet,* revised and updated, by Evan Morris (New York: Fawcett Columbine–Ballantine, 1998).

Reference Works

There are times when I think that the ideal library is composed solely of reference books. They are like understanding friends—always ready to meet your mood, always ready to change the subject when you have had enough of this or that.

—*J. Donald Adams*

Perhaps the heart of any library is its reference section. These resources, usually available for use only in the library, include many types of collections to aid you in your research. Today many reference works have moved online. Your school library has probably purchased site licenses giving you and other registered students free access to various reference works from the library or from remote sites. Whether you are using hard-copy versions in the library, accessing databases through your library's Web page, or logging on to the Internet, a few of the reference works you will find most helpful are dictionaries, encyclopedias, almanacs, yearbooks, and books of quotations.

Dictionaries. Dictionaries help you clarify the meanings of words and their spellings and pronunciations. There are many good general dictionaries, and you undoubtedly use these regularly. A number of more specialized dictionaries covering a wide range of topic areas are also available. A list of a few of these follows.

The Dictionary of Advertising   *A Dictionary of Slang and*
A Dictionary of Bad Manners   *Unconventional English*
Dictionary of Business and Economics *A Dictionary of Statistical Terms*
A Dictionary of Color   *A Feminist Dictionary*
A Dictionary of Dates

Many hundreds of electronic dictionaries exist on the Internet. Robert Beard of Bucknell University maintains a Web site linked to more than 800 dictionaries in 160 different languages (http://www.facstaff.bucknell.edu/rbeard/diction.html). His "Web of Linguistic Fun" includes links to the following dictionaries:

Biographical Dictionary	http://www.s9.com/biography/
Dictionary of Botanical Terms	http://www.botany.com/index.16.htm
Dictionary of Management and Technology	http://www.euro.net/innovation/ Finance_Base/Fin_encyc.html
Dictionary of Terminology: Advertising	http://advertising.utexas.edu/research/terms/
The English-to-American Dictionary	http://english2american.com/
The New Hacker's Dictionary	http://www.tuxedo.org/~esr/jargon/html
Symbols.Com	http://www.symbols.com/index.html

Even a quick glance through these lists should tell you that some of these dictionaries would be good places to begin your search for a speech topic.

Encyclopedias. You have, no doubt, used general encyclopedias, such as *Encyclopedia Americana, Encyclopædia Britannica,* and *World Book,* to prepare reports and papers in elementary and high school. These multivolume sets of books exist today along with their electronic counterparts, such as *Britannica Online,* the *Video Encyclopedia of the 20th Century,* and the *Encyberpedia.* Some electronic encyclopedias, such as *Encyclopedia.Com,* are free. Unless you access others from a library or through a library Web site, however, you may have to pay for a subscription. Subscribing to two popular electronic encyclopedias is possible at the following sites:

Encyclopædia Britannica Online	http://subscribe.eb.com
Microsoft Encarta©	http://encarta.msn.com

Encarta allows you one seven-day free trial, while *Britannica* permits you to try a sample search.

Either in print or as electronic files, encyclopedias organize information on many branches of knowledge. However, you may be less familiar with encyclopedias such as the following, that focus on specific bodies of knowledge.

Encyclopedia of American Humorists   *Encyclopedia of Ethics*
Encyclopedia of American Shipwrecks   *Encyclopedia of Jazz*
Encyclopedia of Black America   *Encyclopedia of Medical History*

Examining some of these volumes can both generate topics for future speeches and give you background information about your current topic.

Advances in database programs and CD-ROM technology make extensive amounts of information readily available.

Almanacs. "Almanacs and Bibles were the first books to come to the United States," writes Lois Horowitz:

> At a time when there were few newspapers, the settlers used almanacs for a melange of valuable information and entertainment. Almanacs predicted the weather for the coming year; gave advice on crops and planting; listed home remedies, multiplication tables, interest charts, and even stagecoach schedules. They also included inspirational verse and stories.[8]

Almanacs have changed over the years—certainly, they no longer publish stagecoach schedules—but their character remains the same. Almanacs contain a wide range of specific and statistical information about topics including education, politics, sports, entertainment, and significant events of a particular year. Almanacs are excellent sources when you need specific facts and background information. What is the exact wording of Amendment II of the United States Constitution? Who is the head of state of Zambia? In what year did Mother Teresa win the Nobel Peace Prize? How many hazardous waste sites operate in the state of New Jersey? A good almanac answers these questions and many others. If you selected the history of space flights as your speech topic, an almanac would be a ready reference for the dates, duration, and description of those flights.

General almanacs include the *World Almanac and Book of Facts, Information Please Almanac, The Universal Almanac,* and the *New York Public Library Desk Reference.* Specialized almanacs cover a wide range of subjects, as illustrated by these examples: *Almanac for Computers, Almanac for American Politics, Almanac of Higher Education,* and *Almanac of World Crime.*

Today you can find a host of searchable almanacs online. You can use the online version of the *Information Please Almanac* at www.infoplease.com. There you will find more than 50 almanacs grouped into categories ranging from sports to business to science and technology. The Internet Public Library (http://www.ipl.org/ref/RR/static/ref0500.html) gives you access to half a dozen almanacs. At Desk Reference (http://www.deskreference.com), a hypertext link will take you to more than 20 almanacs, including the *CIA World Factbook, Almanac of Politics and Government, Daily Almanacs, Living Almanac of Disasters,* and the *Old Farmer's Almanac.*

Yearbooks. Yearbooks are usually published annually and include information pertinent to that year or the previous year. Encyclopedia publishers, for example, often offer yearbooks as supplements to their main set of books. Yearbooks enable researchers to update information on a particular topic. *Facts on File Yearbook,* for example, digests and catalogs world news originally published in the weekly publication *Facts on File.* The diversity of topics covered in yearbooks is illustrated by the following titles: *Yearbook of Agriculture, Yearbook of Higher Education, Yearbook of Emergency Medicine, Yearbook of School Law,* and the *World Yearbook of Robotics Research and Development.*

Books of Quotations. Captivating quotations, both serious and funny, can enliven the language of your speech. As we noted earlier, they are particularly appropriate in speech introductions and conclusions. Quoting another person also adds authority to your comments and thus can strengthen the development of your ideas. Fortunately, many excellent books of quotations are available in bookstores and libraries. Some, like the long popular *Bartlett's Familiar Quotations,* are now available online (http://www.columbia.edu/acis/bartleby/bartlett). Some of our other favorites follow.

A Dictionary of Economic Quotations
The Dictionary of War Quotations
Famous Last Words
Famous Phrases from History
The International Thesaurus of Quotations
My Soul Looks Back, 'Less I Forget: A Collection of Quotations by People of Color
The New International Dictionary of Quotations
The New Quotable Woman: The Definitive Treasury of Notable Words by Women from Eve to the Present
Oxford Dictionary of Quotations
Peter's Quotations
A Treasury of Jewish Quotations

In books or online, collections of quotations are organized alphabetically by author or subject. Almost all of them have indexes, allowing you to find a quotation by a specific person or about a specific subject.

Television and Radio

You can find ideas for excellent speech topics and materials to support them among the investigative reports on television and radio. Many programs provide transcripts for purchase, with ordering information given at the show's conclusion. Even better, transcripts of a number of these shows now appear on the networks' Web sites. You can print them or save them to a disk. If you require older transcripts, you may have to order them online or by phone and pay a charge. For example, ABC posts transcripts of *This Week* for seven days following broadcast; after that you must order and pay for transcripts. Many programs on National Public Radio are archived for downloading and listening after their initial broadcast. The Web sites for a number of television and radio networks will link you to the Federal Document Clearing House (http://www.fdch.com). There you can request transcripts, audiotapes, and videotapes. To check out television and radio Web sites, the following mostly searchable URLs should be helpful.

Network	URL
ABC	http://abcnews.go.com
CBS	http://www.cbs.com

CNN	http://cnn.com
CNN/SI	http://www.cnnsi.com
C-SPAN	http://www.c-span.org
Fox News	http://foxnews.com
MSNBC	http://www.msnbc.com/news
NBC	http://www.nbc.com
NPR	http://www.npr.org
PBS	http://www.pbs.org

Your library and video rental stores may have copies of special televised broadcasts such as the PBS documentary series *Lewis and Clark* or Bill Moyers's *A Walk through the 20th Century.* Through videotapes, you can research topics such as military battles, McCarthyism, and space exploration, to name just a few. Informational videotapes (as well as sites on the World Wide Web) can take you on tours of museums such as the Louvre or the Museum of Modern Art and of distant places such as Australia and Italy. Instructional tapes can teach you how to garden, refinish furniture, and make a sales presentation.

The World Wide Web

So far, we have been talking about researching sources that have been "quality checked" by others. We ordinarily take some comfort in the fact that an article we want to mention in a speech has been reviewed before publication in the *Journal of the American Medical Association,* or that the editor of the *New York Times* apparently stands behind a story in that publication. Rare stories about forged study results or plagiarized articles may ruffle us for a while, but they also underscore our confidence that most published sources have been appropriately checked, verified, and screened. However, we cannot be that naive and complacent when when we venture out onto the Internet.

Both the quality and the quantity of your Internet search results depend upon your ability to focus and narrow a search. You are, no doubt, familiar with some of the larger, more widely used **search engines:** Alta-Vista, HotBot, Lycos, MetaCrawler, WebCrawler, and Yahoo, for example. Each of these offers search tips that you can click and study to make your search more productive. It may also help you to use a category-specific search engine. Searchpower (http://search-power.com) is a site with links to more than 1,600 different search engines arranged into more than 60 categories. In addition to providing support for the speech you will eventually give, electronic sources that you find can also help shape your topic. For example, once you have chosen a broad topic area, you can search for a list serv, a newsgroup, or even a live chat group to investigate your subject in more detail.

List servs are interest groups that use e-mail to distribute messages among members. Your research librarian (or computer lab instructor) can show you how to locate and subscribe to a list serv on your topic. Once you have joined, you will receive all messages sent to the list, so you can read questions, responses, and ongoing discussions on your topic. Because most list serv members take a serious interest in their subject matter, it is probably best for you to "lurk" (simply read the group's exchanges for a while)

Maximizing Your Search
http://www.savvysearch.com
http://mamma.com
http://profusion.com
Meta-engines such as these can save you a lot of research time by utilizing a variety of search engines simultaneously to answer your query. Using either natural language or Boolean structure, these tools are especially helpful if you are trying to locate a site you have visited before. Most of them eliminate duplications of identical sites.

search engine: a tool for locating information on the Internet by matching items in a search string with pages that the engine indexes.

before posting messages of your own. Some lists maintain a posting of frequently asked questions on their topic so that new members can catch up on background information. After you have read through these questions, if you decide to pursue the topic area for your speech you can join in the ongoing conversation and ask targeted questions that should produce knowledgeable responses.

Newsgroups also focus on a topic of interest to all participants, but they are more like interactive bulletin boards. The group posts information—sometimes from professional news services—that readers can respond to with their own messages. Each time a new piece of information is posted, a "thread" of inquiry and debate begins to develop among users. Again, ask your librarian or computer lab instructor to help you locate a newsgroup on your topic; then read and study the group's posting of frequently asked questions before you contribute to an ongoing thread.

> **Evaluating Internet Sources**
> http://www.sccu.edu/
> faculty/R_Harris/evalu8it.htm
> How do you know if you've found a good source of information for your speech? If it's an online source, guidelines and tips provided by *this* Web site will tell you if *your* Web site is worthwhile. Is the source credible? Is the information timely? These are a few of the questions you must pose to make your decision. Screen your source based on these criteria listed by Dr. Robert Harris from the English Department of Vanguard University of Southern California.

You may also want to participate in live chat sessions that you find on your topic. In these sessions, participants exchange messages instantaneously online, so chat resembles spontaneous conversation. However, many chats are unmonitored and somewhat unfocused, so they are likely to be less useful than newsgroup and list serv discussions. If you do begin exchanging ideas with other list serv or newsgroup participants, be sure to save on disk or print any information you may want to use in your speech.

In addition, many college and university speech communication departments, publishers, and other organizations offer general advice and resources for speechmakers through their home pages on the World Wide Web. Allyn & Bacon, the publisher of this textbook, has a public speaking Web site at http://www.abacon.com/pubspeak that will help guide you through the speech-making process and offers many links to reference sites, including some that contain the text of current speeches. Once you become adept at "cruising the Net" on your own, you will discover many more sources of information for ideas and support.

What do you do with material that you get from a productive Internet search? Even as you are reading documents for the first time, you must begin evaluating

Jeanine was researching a speech on the problem of child sexual abuse. While she was cruising the Internet, she discovered a series of forums devoted to this topic, including a newsgroup, a list serv, and a live chat group. She found thought-provoking and useful discussions in the newsgroup and list serv, but the chat discussions were the most intimate and revealing. There, sexual abuse survivors described their memories of actual incidents and talked about how the trauma affected their adult lives.

Jeanine took notes on some of the most remarkable stories and decided to recount one in her speech to add drama. Is this a legitimate way for Jeanine to use her research? Should stories told on the Internet be considered public property, available for anyone to write or speak about? Should Jeanine try to find out whether the speaker would feel comfortable about having the story repeated in a speech? Should she try to verify that the story is true?

ethical decisions

them. One of the great strengths of the Internet—that it levels the playing field and gives anyone who really wants it a voice—is also one of its greatest dangers. As one writer recently noted, "The ability to access information—and lots of it—does not create an ability to evaluate it."[9] On the Internet the medical researcher working in a respected lab may seem to be on equal footing with the person selling magic rocks for you to put under your pillow to prevent cancer. "Anything and everything gets circulated in electronic form, including wild rumors, junk science, appalling misinformation, and naive gibberish." Yet "some people believe as gospel anything that comes out of a computer."[10]

> We are inundated with information, most of it packaged to meet someone else's commercial or political self-interest. More than ever, society needs people with critical minds, people who can look at research, ask their own questions, and find their own answers. Only when you have experienced the uncertain and often messy process of doing your own research can you intelligently evaluate the research of others.[11]

In Chapter 8 we'll provide a checklist of questions to help you weigh the relative quality of information you find on the Internet.

Interviews

You can find a wealth of information outside your library, much of it not confined to the written word. Depending on your topic, an interview may be the best source of firsthand information. Today you can interview people by e-mail or in electronic chat rooms, as well as by telephone or in person. The personal interview can aid you in four ways. First, if published sources are inaccessible, the personal interview may be your only option. The topic you have chosen may be so recent that sufficient information is not yet in print or, if it is, it has not arrived in your library. Your topic may also be so localized as to receive little or no coverage by area media.

Suppose, for example, that your college announces that it will adopt a telephone registration procedure next year. You decide that this will make a timely topic for your informative speech to your classmates. You could make an appointment with the college registrar to learn more about the new procedure. If you learn that other colleges have tried a system similar to the one proposed at your school, you could call officials at those institutions and solicit additional information. Using telephone, computer, or face-to-face interviews, you could generate much of the supporting material you need for your speech, information that would probably not be available at your library.

A second advantage of the personal interview is that it permits you to adapt your topic to your specific audience. Take, for example, the topic of recycling. Your audience would probably be interested in data estimating the amount of resources and landfill space the United States could save annually from recycling. If you interview the director of your school's physical plant to find out how much trash custodians collect and dispose of each day, you give your speech a personal touch. You could take your speech one step further by figuring out how much your college could contribute to resource conservation. What you have done is show your audience how this topic, recycling, affects them directly. You will grab their attention.

Third, personal interviews provide opportunities for you to secure expert evaluation of your research and suggestions for further research. The experts you interview may challenge some of your assumptions or data. If this happens, encourage such feedback, and do not get defensive. Knowing all the angles can only help you give a more thoughtful speech. Near the end of your interview, ask your interviewee to suggest additional sources that will help you better research and understand your topic.

Finally, personal interviews can enhance your image as a speaker. Listeners are usually impressed that you went beyond library research in preparing your message for them. Think of the speech topic we just discussed on recycling. Your classmates will probably see your extra effort as confirmation of your commitment to the topic and the speech-making process.

Preparing for the Interview

1. Determine whom you want to interview.
2. Decide the format for the interview.
3. Schedule the interview.
4. Research the person to be interviewed.
5. Prepare a list of questions.

key points

Prepare for the Interview.

Two days before her speech was due, Marie began thinking of a topic. She remembered reading in the campus newspaper that the school of business at her college was seeking accreditation. Because a majority of students in her public speaking class were business majors, she decided to inform them on the benefits of receiving accreditation and the steps in the accreditation process. She called her accounting professor and arranged for an appointment the next afternoon.

Arriving ten minutes late, she apologized and then explained the reason for the interview. She took out a tape recorder, but Professor Saunders said that he'd rather not be recorded. Because she hadn't prepared a list of questions, Marie began the interview by saying, "Just tell me anything you can about this accreditation thing and how it will benefit the university." Saunders said that he was not involved in the process and didn't think he could be too helpful. He added that he thought accreditation would help the university recruit better students and faculty. After the interview, a disappointed Marie went to the library, found an encyclopedia, photocopied an article on reptiles indigenous to Florida, and went back to the dorm to prepare her speech for the next day's class.

What went wrong during this phase of Marie's speech preparation? Her original topic—accreditation—was a good one; it was timely and relevant to her audience. The personal interview was an appropriate research strategy. Unfortunately, Marie's plan of action was poorly conceived, planned, and executed. Once you decide to conduct a personal interview, you must take several steps in preparation. First, determine whom you want to interview. Your interviewee should be someone who is both knowledgeable on the topic and willing to speak with you. Marie did not bother to find out if her accounting professor was the most knowledgeable person on her topic before she set up the interview.

Second, decide on the format for the interview. Will you conduct it face to face, by phone, or on the computer? A face-to-face interview may give you the most information. People tend to open up more when they interact verbally and nonverbally. As a face-to-face interviewer, you can both listen to what the interviewee says and observe the nonverbal messages. An interview over the phone is another possibility when you cannot travel to the expert. A third option, conducting an interview by e-mail or computer chat room, has both advantages and disadvantages. The e-mail interview is time-consuming because you must prepare a set of questions, send it to the interviewee, and wait for a response. It has the added disadvantage of not allowing for immediate follow-up questions. If something needs clarification, you must e-mail another question. An interview in a chat room eliminates this time lag. Moreover, the e-mail or chat room interview often results in more thoughtful and better worded responses than face-to-face or telephone interviews.

The third preparation step is to schedule the interview. When requesting an interview, identify yourself and the topic on which you seek information. Let the person know how you intend to use that information, the amount of time needed for the interview, and any special recording procedures you plan to use. Some people may object to being quoted or to having their comments recorded. If this is the case, it is best to find that out ahead of time rather than at the interview, as Marie did. You are likely to discover that most people you seek to interview are flattered that you selected them as experts and are therefore happy to cooperate.

Fourth, research the person to be interviewed before you show up at his or her doorstep. Obviously, your selection of the interviewee suggests that you already know something about him or her. In addition, read any articles the interviewee has published on your topic before the interview. This enables you to conduct the interview efficiently. You won't ask questions that the person has already answered in print, and your prior reading may prompt some specific questions on points you would like clarified. Also, your research will show that you are prepared. The interviewee will take you and the interview seriously. Marie did not do this.

Fifth, prepare a list of questions. Always have more questions than you think you will be able to ask, just in case you are mistaken. Mark those that are most important to your research, and make sure you ask them first. You may want to have some closed and some open questions, as Joel did when he interviewed a professor of recreation for his speech on how American adults spend their leisure time. *Closed questions* are those that can be answered with a "yes," a "no," or a short answer. For example, Joel asked, "Do American adults have more time for leisure activities today than they did a generation ago?" and "How many hours per week does the typical adult spend watching TV?" The first question can be answered by a "yes" or a "no"; the second, with a specific figure.

Open questions invite longer answers and can produce a great deal of information. Joel asked the open question: "How do American adults typically spend their leisure time?" When you ask open questions, sit back and prepare to listen for a while!

Open-ended questions, such as those that begin with the phrase, "How do you feel about," can elicit more substantive responses from interviewees than do closed "yes" or "no" questions.

The less time you have for the interview, the fewer open questions you should ask. Open questions can sometimes result in rambling, unnecessary information. At other times, the interviewee's rambling will trigger questions you would not have thought of otherwise. Joel was surprised to learn that American adults spend approximately two hours a week in adult education, a venture he had not included on his initial list of adult leisure activities. When you and the interviewee have plenty of time, and particularly if you are tape recording the interview, open questions can provide the richest information.

Conduct the Interview. The face-to-face interview is an excellent opportunity to practice your interpersonal communication skills. Specifically, you should follow these guidelines. First, introduce yourself when you arrive, thank the person for giving you time, and restate the purpose of the interview.

Second, conduct the interview in a professional manner. If you interview the president of the local savings and loan, don't show up in cut-off jeans, sandals, and your favorite flannel shirt. Make sure you arrive appropriately dressed, ready and able to set up and handle any recording equipment with a minimum of distractions. Try to relax the interviewee, establish a professional atmosphere, pose questions that are clear and direct, listen actively, take notes efficiently, and follow up when necessary. You should control the interview without appearing to be pushy or abrupt.

Third, thank the person again for the interview when you have finished.

Follow up on the Interview. After the interview, review your notes or listen to your tape recording. Do this as soon as possible after the interview, when your memory is still fresh. If you are unclear about something that was said, do not use that information in your speech. You could call your subject to clarify the point if you think it will be important to the audience's understanding of the topic.

As a matter of courtesy, you should write to the people you interviewed, thanking them for the time and help they gave you. You may even want to send them a copy of your finished speech if it is in manuscript form.

Calling, Writing, and E-mailing for Information

Some years ago, one of us taught a student, Lindahl, who wanted to develop an informative speech on the savant syndrome. This was long before Dustin Hoffman's portrayal of Raymond in the film *Rain Man* made many people aware of the special talents and disabilities of savants. Lindahl had seen a *60 Minutes* segment on the syndrome but could not find recent written sources in the local libraries she visited. Her best source, she said, was an article from a three-year-old issue of *Time*. Others might have abandoned their research and switched topics, but Lindahl followed a hunch that paid off for her.

The *Time* article quoted several university professors and medical doctors who were engaged in ongoing research on the savant syndrome. Lindahl got their office telephone numbers through directory assistance. She called these experts to see if they could recommend new sources she had been unable to locate. Lindahl found that the people she called were all flattered by her attention and complimented her perseverance as a researcher. One psychologist mailed her a photocopy of a book chapter she had written on the savant syndrome; a medical doctor mailed Lindahl a packet of journal articles, including the galleys of an article of his that was about to be

> *In America today, you are three or four phone calls away from any expert—a librarian, an industry expert, an editor of a key publication, and so on—and if they don't have the answer, they'll probably know who does.*
>
> —*Jeff Davidson*[12]

"Who is the fairest one of all, and state your sources!"

published; a psychology professor mailed her a tape of savants who had incredible musical talents playing piano concertos they had heard for the first time only moments before. In short, Lindahl received a gold mine of new, expert research as a result of her few long-distance calls. If Lindahl were to conduct such a search today, she might find that e-mail would be an effective way to contact the experts.

Lindahl was lucky that she began her research more than a month before her speech was due. To take advantage of pamphlets and brochures available through the mail, you will need to plan ahead as well. But thousands of organizations, such as the American Cancer Society and the United Way, publish their own informational literature. Political parties and lobbying groups prepare position papers on issues that affect them. Corporations distribute annual reports to their stockholders and will share these with people who request them. You can write to any of these organizations. Some have toll-free phone numbers; for others you would have to pay long-distance charges. Increasing numbers of organizations have home pages on the World Wide Web. You may be able to locate e-mail addresses for companies or groups through search indexes available online. Unfortunately, no index comprehensively catalogs the information available from such groups, so you must take the initiative in tracking down what you need. One source that can be helpful is the *Encyclopedia of Associations*. This publication is divided into three volumes: National Organizations of the U.S.; International Organizations; and Regional, State, and Local Organizations. Each volume lists names, addresses, telephone numbers, e-mail addresses, and URLs for Web sites, along with descriptions of the organizations. The information is also available on computers at some libraries. Remember, this research source will not help you if you have five days left before your deadline. But if time permits and research warrants, writing, calling, or e-mailing these organizations to request information can add relevant primary research to your speech.

Record Your Information

Once you have located information, you must determine what to record and how to record it.

What to Record

When in doubt, record more rather than less. Certainly, it is possible to copy too much information. If you find everything potentially important, your topic probably needs better focus. Without some focus, you run the risk of becoming so bogged down in research that you leave little time for organizing and practicing your speech.

On the other hand, if you are too selective, you may be inefficient. As you research your speech, you may shift your topic focus, and hence the supporting material you previously thought was irrelevant becomes important. Discarding unnecessary information is easier than trying to remember a source, retracing your steps, hoping that the information is still on the library shelves, or that the Internet source is still live, and then recording that information.

How to Record Information

Traditional advice to researchers is to record each piece of information on a separate notecard, along with the source citation, as you find it. With this strategy, you can organize your speech visually and experiment with different structures. The disadvantage of this method of recording information is that it consumes a great deal of library time that might be better devoted to searching for other sources. In addition, much of what you record on notecards may not be used in your speech at all.

Another, more common method is to photocopy material at the library and read it later. Sometimes the simplest and most thorough way to record research information is to photocopy pages from books, documents, reference works, or even entire articles. Later, at your leisure and in more comfortable surroundings, you can review, evaluate, and select from the photocopied materials. However, be aware that photocopies may lull you into a false sense of accomplishment. What you have copied may later turn out to be of little or no use. How can you avoid this problem? Read your material before or very shortly after photocopying it. Do not wait until the night before your speech to read the pile of information you have been collecting on the role of women pilots in World War II.

Also, remember to note your sources on the copied pages. You'd be wise to photocopy the table of contents of each magazine or journal from which you use an article. Copy the page or pages containing publication information for each book you use. If you follow these simple directions, photocopying has two additional advantages over using notecards. First, you may not know what you want to use from an article at the time you first find it. If the focus of your speech changes, a different part of the article may become important. Indeed, sometimes your research forces you to

> **Citing Electronic Sources**
> http://www.mla.org/style/sources.htm
> http://www.apa.org/journals/webref.html
> Both the Modern Language Association and the American Psychological Association have Web sites, with examples of documentation that may be more current than those in their published style manuals. The only Internet guidelines for MLA documentation authorized by the MLA are available at their site. The APA site features their guidelines for citing information from the Internet and the World Wide Web.

refocus the speech topic. Second, if you are quoting from or paraphrasing one specific part of an article, you may need to check later to make sure that you are not quoting the author out of context. Having a photocopy of the book chapter, the journal article, or the encyclopedia entry lets you check the context and the accuracy of your quotation.

If you are gathering information from an electronic source such as a CD-ROM database or the Internet, be sure to print out the pages you will need or transfer the information to a disk. Remember that what appears on the Internet is ephemeral—it disappears quickly. If you do not capture it in print or store it in a file on the day you find it, you may have to forego using the information in your speech because you will not be able to locate it again. If you do not know how to create a storage file for Internet material, ask your librarian or computer lab instructor for help.

It is important to record full citations of sources you have consulted in your research in a bibliography at the end of your speech. Your **bibliography** is simply a list of works you have consulted in developing your speech. Most writer's handbooks will recommend a particular bibliographic form. Two popular forms are those presented

bibliography: an orderly list of works consulted or cited during the preparation and delivery of a speech.

Book with One Author	Markson, Elizabeth W. *Aging in the 21st Century: Issues and Inequalities.* Los Angeles: Roxbury, 2000.
Book with Two or More Authors	Grice, George L., and John F. Skinner. *Mastering Public Speaking.* 4th ed. Boston: Allyn, 2001.
Article in Weekly Magazine	Edwards, Tamala M. "A Day at the Spa." *Time* 18 Oct. 1999: 84–85.
Article in Monthly or Bimonthly Magazine	Drucker, Peter F. "Beyond the Information Revolution." *Atlantic Monthly* Oct. 1999: 47–57.
Newspaper Article	Kolata, Gina. "Scientists Find Enzyme Linked to Alzheimer's." *New York Times* 22 Oct. 1999, natl. ed.: A1+.
Article in Online Magazine	Confessore, Nicholas. "Heard It through the Grapevine." *Atlantic Unbound* 7 Oct. 1999. 19 Oct. 1999 <http://www.theatlantic.com/unbound/citation/wc991007.htm>
Government Document	Commercialization of space. Hearing before the Subcommittee on Science, Technology, and Space of the Committee on Commerce, Science, and Transportation, Senate, 105th Cong., 2nd sess. 1 (1999).
Internet Web Site	Arnett, Bill. *The nine planets: A multimedia tour of the solar system.* 31 July 1999. 21 Oct. 1999 <http://seds.lpl.arizona.edu/nineplanets/nineplanets/nineplanets.html>
Interview	Gilson, Caroline. Personal interview. 14 Oct. 1999.
E-mail	Alper, Carol. "Re: Questions from San Antonio." E-mail to George L. Grice. 18 Oct. 1999.

**FIGURE 7.5
MLA Form for
Some Common Types
of Sources**

Book with One Author	Markson, E. W. (2000). *Aging in the 21st century: Issues and inequalities.* Los Angeles: Roxbury.
Book with Two or More Authors	Grice, G. L., & Skinner, J. F. (2001). *Mastering public speaking* (4th ed.). Boston: Allyn & Bacon.
Article in Weekly Magazine	Edwards, T. M. (1999, October 18). A day at the spa. *Time, 154,* 84–85.
Article in Monthly or Bimonthly Magazine	Drucker, P. F. (1999, October). Beyond the information revolution. *Atlantic Monthly, 284,* 47–57.
Newspaper Article	Kolata, G. (1999, October 22). Scientists find enzyme linked to Alzheimer's. *The New York Times,* pp. A1, A20.
Article in Online Magazine	Confessore, N. (1999, October 7). Heard it through the grapevine. *AtlanticUnbound.* Retrieved October 19, 1999 from the World Wide Web: http://www.theatlantic.com/unbound/citation/wc991007.htm.
Government Document	*Commercialization of space: Hearing before the subcommittee on science, technology, and space of the committee on commerce, science, and transportation,* Senate, 105th Cong., 2d Sess. 1 (1999).
Internet Web Site	Arnett, Bill. (1999, July 31). *The Nine Planets: A Multimedia Tour of the Solar System.* Retrieved October 21, 1999 from the World Wide Web: http://seds.lpl.arizona.edu/nineplanets/nineplanets/nineplanets.html.
Interview and E-mail	APA specifies that interviews and e-mails should be mentioned as personal communications but should not be listed in a bibliography.

**FIGURE 7.6
APA Form for Some Common Types of Sources**

in the *Publication Manual of the American Psychological Association* and the *Modern Language Association Handbook for Writers of Research Papers.* Be sure to check with your instructor, who may have a preference for one of these or some other bibliographic form.

Copies of the two style manuals we just listed are probably in your library's reference section. Figures 7.5 and 7.6 compare the bibliographic forms each presents. Whether you want to cite a segment of National Public Radio's *All Things Considered,* a stop-smoking videotape, or lecture notes you took in an anthropology class last week, the most recent editions of these reference books are likely to give you a pattern to follow.

Conclude Your Search

As you prepare your speech, you must make choices. Your goal is to support your ideas with the most compelling evidence and arguments you can find. The adage

"Knowledge is power" certainly applies to speech making; the more you know about your topic, the greater your flexibility in determining its content and, subsequently, its impact. This concept of choice may make your task more complex, but it will also produce a more effective speech.

There is a limit, however, to the time you can spend researching. An important part of effective research is knowing when to stop accumulating materials and when to start using them. In his book *Finding Facts Fast,* Alden Todd provides the following guideline for research projects:

> If the last 10 percent of your planned research time has brought excellent results, you are doubtless on a productive new track and should extend the project. But if the last 25 percent of your scheduled time has brought greatly diminished results, this fact is a signal to wind up your research.[13]

Although Todd's 10/25 formula may not be wholly applicable to your researching a speech for this class, it does highlight an important issue: At some point you must stop researching and start structuring your speech.

In the next chapter, "Supporting Your Speech," we discuss the purposes and types of supporting material. Understanding these topics will help you evaluate your research and select the best information to support the ideas of your speech.

Summary

Research is the process of gathering information and evidence to understand, develop, and explain your topic. Learning to research is fundamental to mastering public speaking. Even if you are not required to use outside sources for a particular speech, knowing your subject thoroughly greatly reduces your speech anxiety. Of course, knowing your subject probably demands knowing how to use the best library in your area. An agenda for thorough research of a subject involves five steps.

First, assess your knowledge of the subject and begin to organize that knowledge. Chances are good that you chose the topic because you were interested in it or already knew something about it. Keeping *an article file* and a *quotations file* on subjects that interest you gives you a head start in your research. As you prepare the speech and after you deliver it, keep your research notes and speaking notes or manuscript in a *speech file.*

Second, develop a research plan for your topic. What information do you need? Where can you find it? How can you get it in the time you have? Your topic may lead you to interview people or collect printed information from businesses and organizations. Sooner or later, however, you will probably need to learn to use a local library efficiently. Reference librarians can teach you the strengths and limitations of the library you select.

The third step in research is to collect information from a variety of sources. Potential sources include magazines and journals, newspapers, government documents, books, and reference works, including dictionaries, encyclopedias, almanacs, yearbooks, and books of quotations. Many of these sources are now available online. Sources outside the library include interviews and electronic media resources such as radio, television, and videotape. Interviews allow you to collect authoritative, unpublished information on your subject, but they require special planning and preparation. You must select the best interviewee, decide on the format, schedule the interview, research the interviewee you have selected, and prepare a list of questions. After conducting the interview in a competent, professional manner and promptly recording the information you have gathered from it, you should send a note of thanks to the person you interviewed.

The fourth step in research is to record the information you consider important and useful. You may choose to take notes on notecards or to photocopy your information. In either case, be sure to record the source of the information—author, title, and publication information—using a current *bibliography* form.

The fifth and final step in research is to conclude your search. The quality and quantity of the information you collect will not only help you focus and organize the subject, but should also signal you when you have exhausted your research efforts.

Evaluating Research

Suppose that the International Olympic Committee just declared public speaking to be a new event for the Olympic Games. You've been hired as a coach for the U.S. Olympic Public Speaking Team. Suppose, further, that Susan Chontos has entered her speech "The Amish: Seeking to Lose the Self" in the competition. Read the transcript of this speech in Appendix B. Then, write Susan a letter to help her develop a research plan for revising her speech. What information should remain in her speech? What information needs to be updated, clarified, and/or improved? Where could she search for this information?

practice critique

Exercises

1. Make a list of subjects on which you feel especially qualified to speak. In developing this list, you should answer the following questions: Do I have greater knowledge and expertise in this area than my listeners do? Is this expertise sufficient to support the ideas of my speech? If not, where can I find additional information?

2. Select a topic for one of your speeches, then answer the following questions:
   a. What information do I need?
   b. Where am I most likely to find this information?
   c. How can I obtain the information?
   d. How will time constraints affect my research options?

3. Conduct searches on the topics "urban legends" and "clairvoyance," noting the number of hits you get with each of the following search engines: AltaVista (http://www.altavista.com), Northern Light (http://www.northernlight.com), HotBot (http://www.hotbot.com), and Google (http://www.google.com). Which search engine yields the most hits on each subject? The least? Do some of these search engines have features that make them easier to use than others? If so, what are those features?

4. Locate and look at a recent issue of each of the following magazines: *Mother Jones, National Review, New Republic, Newsweek, The Progressive, Time,* and *U.S. News & World Report.* Based on their content, rank the seven magazines from most liberal to most conservative. Which would you classify as liberal, which as conservative, and which as middle of the road? What information helped you decide your rankings? Were similar topics treated in different ways in these publications?

5. Using any magazine or journal index listed in this chapter, construct a bibliography of at least seven sources for an upcoming speech. Locate at least three of these articles.

6. Using a print or an online newspaper index, construct a bibliography of at least five sources for an upcoming speech. Locate at least three of these articles.

7. Using the *CIS/Index* and *CIS Abstract* or the *Monthly Catalog,* locate a congressional document on a topic that would be appropriate for a speech in this class.

8. Which of the reference works discussed in this chapter could you consult to find the answers to the following questions?
   a. What is the derivation of the word *deadline*?
   b. The Speaker of the U.S. House of Representatives comes from what district and state?
   c. In what year was Henrik Ibsen's play *A Doll's House* published?
   d. What are the chief crops of Cameroon?
   e. On what date did the Alexander Hamilton–Aaron Burr duel occur? Who won?
   f. What color is the flag of Libya?
   g. Who was the last U.S. major league baseball player to bat over .400 for the year? What was the year, and what was his batting average?
   h. What is the elevation of Mount Rainier?
   i. What is the preferred pronunciation of the word *data*? In how many other ways can it be pronounced correctly?
   j. Who received the Oscar for Best Actor in 1942? In what movie did he star?
   k. What is the meaning of the Greek words from which *dinosaur* is derived?
   l. How and for whom was the word *boycott* coined?

9. Using books of quotations, such as those listed in this chapter, prepare a list of at least two quotations on each of the following topics:
   a. The Art of Conversation
   b. The Importance of Teachers
   c. Overcoming Failure
   d. The Dangers of Apathy
   e. Turning Problems into Opportunities

   Bring your list to class, and be prepared to discuss how you could use some of the quotations in a speech. Which would contribute to a good introduction or conclusion? Which could be used to illustrate an idea in the body of the speech?

10. Consult the *Encyclopedia of Associations,* and locate at least three organizations you think may have information pertaining to ideas you are considering for upcoming speeches. Write letters requesting relevant information.

11. Select an expert to interview for an upcoming speech. Using suggestions in the chapter, arrange, prepare for, and conduct an interview, and follow up on it.

Notes

1. Patricia Senn Breivik, *Student Learning in the Information Age* (Phoenix, AZ: Oryx P, 1998) 2.

2. Gary Ink, "Book Title Output and Average Prices: 1996 Final and 1997 Preliminary Figures," *The Bowker Annual Library and Book Trade Almanac,* ed. Dave Bogart, 43rd ed. (New Providence, NJ: Reed Elsevier, 1998) 521.

3. Breivik 1.

4. Wayne C. Booth, Gregory G. Colomb, and Joseph M. Williams, *The Craft of Research* (Chicago: U of Chicago P, 1995) 35.

5. Booth, Colomb, and Williams 3.

6. Robert C. Jeffrey and Owen Peterson, *Speech: A Text with Adapted Readings,* 2nd ed. (New York: Harper, 1983) 169.

7. Bill Katz and Linda Sternberg Katz, *Magazines for Libraries,* 7th ed. (New Providence, NJ: Bowker, 1992) ix.

8. Lois Horowitz, *Knowing Where to Look: The Ultimate Guide to Research* (Cincinnati: Writer's Digest, 1988) 115.

9. Deborah C. Sawyer, "The Pied Piper Goes Electronic," *The Futurist* (Feb. 1999) 45.

10. Sawyer 43.

11. Booth, Colomb, and Williams 3.

12. Jeff Davidson, "The Shortcomings of the Electronic Age," *Vital Speeches of the Day* 1 June 1996: 501.

13. Alden Todd, *Finding Facts Fast,* 2nd ed. (Berkeley: Ten Speed, 1979) 14.

A fact in itself is nothing. It is valuable only for the idea attached to it, or for the proof which it furnishes.

—Claude Bernard

c h a p t e r 8

Supporting Your Speech

olo rock climbing is a sport for serious-minded, physically fit people. Before tackling the face of a cliff, climbers study their routes and carry the proper equipment: adequate water, food, and clothing for the conditions they are likely to encounter. All of this helps them proceed more safely from one particular point to another on the face of the rock. Just as rock climbers use their planning, strength, and equipment to secure themselves to points on the face of a cliff, you will use the supporting materials in your speech to provide specific points of reference for your audience. Your goal is to present a clear, memorable, and believable message to your audience. Effective supporting materials help you anchor your ideas in the minds of your listeners.

When you think of argument, you likely think of two people trying to persuade each other. In a real sense, however, all public speaking is argument. We should speak and accept ideas only if they are supported with sufficient evidence and reasoning. Speakers must prove what they assert in informative speeches as well as in persuasive ones. For example, when Susan Chontos tells her audience in her speech in Appendix B, "The second major tenet of the Amish faith is the desire to be simple, or plain," she introduces an idea that they may accept or reject. Listeners should think critically and evaluate the merits of that statement based on the evidence Susan offers for its support. Later we'll look at the types of supporting materials she used to develop that key idea.

Toward the end of Chapter 3, we recommended a formula for structuring each major idea in your speech. This pattern, called the "4 S's," consists of *signposting, stating, supporting,* and *summarizing* each of your key ideas. In Chapter 9, "Organizing the Body of Your Speech," we will explain this pattern in detail and show examples of how to use it. In this chapter, however, we'll focus on the third of these four S's: *supporting* your major ideas. In supporting an idea, you apply the results of your research and original thinking about your speech topic in the form of examples, comparisons, and statistics, among other methods. In this chapter, you will learn more about the purposes of supporting materials. We will also discuss and show you examples of seven types of supporting materials you can use. Finally, we'll suggest ways to evaluate your evidence in order to ensure that you communicate your ideas clearly, memorably, and authoritatively.

Purposes of Supporting Materials

Supporting materials in a speech serve a variety of purposes. They help give your ideas clarity, vividness, and credibility.

Clarity

When the space shuttle *Challenger* exploded within minutes of its liftoff on January 28, 1986, the world recognized that a tragedy had occurred. President Ronald Reagan referred to it as a disaster in his eulogy for the crew members three days later. Yet NASA called the explosion an "anomaly." During the investigation into the cause of the explosion, Arnold Aldrich, manager of the National Space Transportation Systems Program at Houston's Johnson Space Center, said, in part:

> The normal process during the countdown is that the countdown proceeds, assuming we are in a go posture, and at various points during the countdown we tag up on the operational loops and face to face in the firing room to ascertain the facts that project elements that are monitoring the data and that are understanding the situation as we proceed are still in the go condition.[1]

Is it any wonder that it took NASA a while to discover the likely cause of the explosion?

As a speaker, your first goal is to communicate clearly. *Clarity* refers to the exactness of a message. The clarity of any message you send results partly from your language, as we discuss in Chapter 12, "Wording Your Speech." In addition, the supporting material you choose will help make your message clear. As you develop your speech, ask yourself the question, "Does my supporting material really explain, amplify, or illustrate the point I am trying to make?" If it does not, disregard it and continue your search for relevant material. Clear supporting materials help listeners better understand your ideas.

Vividness

Which of the following makes a stronger impression on you?

Mike Wallace takes people into his confidence and disarms them,

or

Mike is interviewing this bad-ass accountant, and there are . . . forty million people watching this broadcast. And only Mike would say to a guy whom he interviews, "Just between you and me. . . ." Now this guy forgets; he thinks it is just between him and Mike. Mike has a way of doing that.[2]

The first comment is something Don Hewitt, executive producer of CBS's *60 Minutes,* might have said about Mike Wallace. The second is what Hewitt actually did say to explain why Wallace is such a successful interviewer for the show. Which statement do you think is more vivid?

Most people would choose the second sentence as the more vivid and memorable. Why? The first remark is general; the second, specific. In a speech on Mike Wallace's interviewing techniques, the first statement could be one of your main ideas. The second is something you could say to support that main idea because it is both clearer and more vivid.

In this chapter, we use several excerpts from speeches to illustrate various types of supporting materials. Once you finish reading the chapter, you will no doubt remember some of the examples and forget others. Those you remember will be ones you found particularly vivid. *Vivid* supporting materials are striking, graphic, intense, and memorable. A major purpose of supporting materials, then, is to help your audience remember the key points in your speech. You will accomplish this best by using vivid forms of support chosen with your unique audience in mind.

Credibility

You gasp as you see the headline "Scientists Discover Microbial Life on Mars." Would it make a difference whether you saw this on the cover of *Scientific American* or the *National Enquirer*? Of course it would. "Microbial life" is nothing to the folks who write for the tabloids; they've shown photographic evidence of human faces carved into the Martian landscape! On the other hand, a scientific article reviewed and selected for publication by a panel of experts is significantly more believable than an article from any tabloid weekly. **Credibility** refers to the dependability or believability of a speaker or that speaker's sources.

Many ideas in the speeches you prepare will require simple supporting materials: short definitions, brief examples, or quick comparisons, for example. In other instances, you may present complex or controversial ideas that require several types of supporting materials. A speech with all of its ideas and support taken from a single source is too limited. Using several sources to corroborate your ideas and facts can be a valuable and persuasive tool. Your main points will be more credible if you present evidence that these ideas are shared by several experts.

You establish clarity by explaining your idea so that listeners *understand* it. You establish vividness by presenting your idea so that listeners will *remember* it. Finally, you establish credibility by presenting the idea so that listeners *believe* it. If the supporting

credibility: the believability or dependability of speakers and their sources.

materials in your speech get the audience to understand, remember, and believe what you say, you have done a good job selecting them.

Accomplishing these goals will require you to use four critical thinking skills. You will *focus* and *evaluate* as you select specific pieces of information and measure their quality. You will *analyze* as you examine different supporting materials to see how they fit together to clarify your message. Finally, you will *integrate* as you combine and restructure your information in a way that is both appropriate to your listeners and uniquely your own.

You know that you want to present clear, vivid, and believable supporting materials. But how do you make sure people understand, remember, and believe your message? You have a wide range to choose from as you organize your supporting materials. Below we discuss the most common types of supporting materials and show you how they can work effectively in your speech.

Types of Supporting Materials

To help you achieve clarity, vividness, and credibility in your speaking, consider seven types of supporting material available to you: examples, definition, narration, comparison, contrast, statistics, and testimony. Keep in mind that there is no one best type of support for your ideas. Select what is most appropriate to your topic, your audience, and yourself.

Finding Supporting Materials
http://www.ukans.edu/ cwis/units/coms2/vpa/ vpa3.htm
Visit this site, maintained by the Communication Studies Department at the University of Kansas, for links to a variety of popular media and reference resources available on the Web. This is a good place to start your online search for supporting materials.

Examples

An **example** is a specific illustration of a category of people, places, objects, actions, experiences, or conditions. In other words, examples are specimens or representations of a general group. The sound of the word itself gives perhaps the easiest definition to remember, however: An *example* is a *sample* of something. Measles, mumps, and chicken pox are examples of common childhood illnesses. New York, Los Angeles, and Miami are examples of the largest cities in the United States. *E.T.—The Extra-Terrestrial, Schindler's List,* and *Saving Private Ryan* are examples of Steven Spielberg movies. Soccer, football, and baseball are examples of popular team sports. Using examples that are familiar to listeners is an excellent way to make your points more clear and memorable. This, of course, requires you to have done some good audience analysis.

example: a sample or illustration of a category of people, places, objects, actions, experiences, or conditions.

(Source: Calvin & Hobbes. Copyright © 1987 by Bill Watterson. Reprinted with permission of Universal Press Syndicate. All rights reserved.)

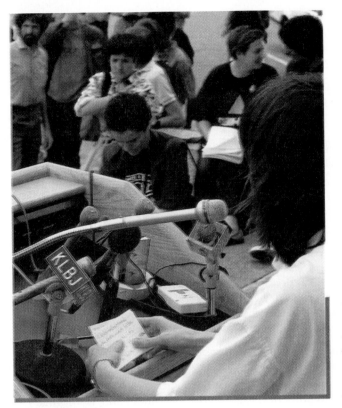

*Supporting materials clarify,
enliven, and add credibility to
your speech. When you prepare
for delivery, ensure accuracy by
recording in complete form any
quotations or definitions you
plan to use.*

Brief Examples. In your speech you can use either brief examples, such as those just noted, or extended ones. Brief examples are short, specific instances of the general category you are discussing. They may be used individually, but are often grouped together. Notice how Jocelyn combined a number of brief examples early in her speech on the attractions of New York City:

> Your walking tour of midtown Manhattan could take you to places as diverse as St. Patrick's Cathedral, Rockefeller Center, the Gotham Book Mart, and the Museum of Modern Art. Try not to gawk as you look at some of the most famous architecture in the world—the Chrysler Building, the Empire State Building, and Grand Central Station. Tired of pounding the pavement? Slip into a chair in the Algonquin Hotel's dim lobby, soak up the literary history, ring the bell on your table, and order something to drink. Hungry? You've got the world's table to choose from—everything from four-star restaurants to little holes in the wall serving the best ethnic dishes: Chinese, Vietnamese, Indian, Mexican, Thai.

Extended Examples. Extended examples are lengthier and more elaborate than brief examples. They allow you to create more detailed pictures of a person, place, object, experience, or condition. Later in her speech, Jocelyn developed an extended example of one of her favorite New York City attractions:

> Beginning with my second visit to New York, one of my first stops has usually been the Museum of Modern Art. If you're like me, you'll need to give yourself at least a couple of hours here, because for a small admission price you're going to get a chance to see up close art that you've only seen before as photographs in books. Upstairs on my last visit, I saw works such as Vincent Van Gogh's *Starry Night* and Roy Lichtenstein's huge pop art paintings of comic strip panels. My favorite Lichtenstein was one called *Oh, Jeff, I Love You Too, But. . . .* On a wall with a number of other paintings was a canvas so small that I almost missed it. I'm glad I didn't. It was Salvador Dali's famous surrealist work, *The Persistence of Memory,* with its melting

clock and watch faces. Then over in a corner is a special room that holds only one painting. As you walk in, you see an expanse of gray carpet and several uphol-stered benches. One wall is glass, two others are white and bare, but the fourth one holds the three panels of Claude Monet's massive painting, *Waterlilies.*

Notice how vividly this extended example suggests a scene and recreates an experience. But whether your examples are brief or extended, they can be of two further types: actual and hypothetical.

Actual Examples. An **actual example** is real or true. Each of the examples we've used so far is an actual example. Steven Spielberg did direct the three films listed. Soccer, football, and baseball are familiar, established team sports. The Chrysler Building and the Empire State Building are famous New York landmarks.

In the following example, notice how Lucas tells a real story to illustrate the danger of infections patients contract in hospitals:

Ted Zahr is a 72-year-old man who was in perfect health until he reached Bracken Ridge Hospital in order to get a benign brain tumor removed. The surgery went without a hitch. In fact, Ted Zahr's first six days in the hospital recovery room went well, until the night of the sixth day when Ted Zahr's condition turned for the worst. His temperature began to rise, and he lost consciousness. On the morning of the seventh day, Ted Zahr found himself paralyzed from the neck down.[3]

Zahr's condition is an actual example of symptoms experienced by those who contract infectious bacteria in hospitals.

Hypothetical Examples. A **hypothetical example,** on the other hand, is imaginary or fictitious. A speaker often signals hypothetical examples with phrases such as, "Suppose that," "Imagine yourself," or "What if." Hypothetical examples clarify and vivify the point you are making, but they do not prove the point.

Notice how the following introduction mentions actual products but places them in a hypothetical situation. The speaker chose this method knowing that not all listeners would have all the products listed. The speaker then generalizes from these examples to support the claim that we live in an electronic world.

We wake up in the morning to soothing music coming from our AM/FM digital clock radio equipped with a gentle wake-up feature. We stumble downstairs, enticed by the aroma of coffee brewed by a preset coffee maker with 24-hour digital clock timer and automatic shut-off function. We zap on our 27-inch color TV with on-screen display of current time and channel and with 139-channel cable-capable tuner. As we sit in our six-way action recliner, we use our 26-function wireless remote to perform the ritual of the morning channel check. Finding nothing that captures our interest, we decide instead to watch the videotape of last week's family reunion recorded with our 12X power zoom, fully automatic camcorder with self-timer, electronic viewfinder, and "flying erase head for 'rainbow'-free edits." Oh dear! What would our grandparents think? Certainly, we live in an electronic world!

actual example: a true instance or illustration.

hypothetical example: an imaginary or fictitious instance or illustration.

definition: an explanation of the meaning of a word, phrase, or concept.

Definition

A **definition** tells us the meaning of a word, a phrase, or a concept. Definitions are essential if your audience is unfamiliar with the vocabulary you use or if there are multiple definitions of a particular term. You want to clarify terms early in your speech so you don't confuse your listeners and lose their attention. In a speech on Internet etiquette, for example, you would need to define bad behaviors such as "flaming," "trolling," and "spamming."

Definitions can take several forms. Four of the most common are definition by synonym, definition by etymology, definition by example, and definition by operation. Choose the form most appropriate to your audience and to the term you want to clarify, and your audience will remember it.

Definition by Synonym. The first type of definition is **definition by synonym.** Synonyms are words that have similar meanings. You have probably used a thesaurus when writing a term paper or report. A thesaurus is simply a dictionary of synonyms. Consider these pairs of words:

mendacity and *dishonesty*	*pariah* and *outcast*
plethora and *excess*	*anathema* and *curse*
mitigate and *lessen*	*surreptitious* and *secret*

Each word is coupled with one of its synonyms. The first word of each pair is probably not a part of your listeners' working vocabulary. As a speaker, you would want to use the second word in each pair; those words are more familiar and thus more vivid. The second word of each pair communicates more clearly. If you suffer from "thesaurusitis," a disease causing you always to choose a fancy word over a simple, more appropriate one, you will be more likely to confuse your listeners. As the joke goes, never use a big word when a diminutive one will do.

Online Dictionaries
http://www.onelook.com
The OneLook Dictionaries Web site has a search box where you can type in a word and search the Internet for a dictionary with the word. It indexes nearly 3,000,000 words in 589 dictionaries. When you call up a definition, it gives you several dictionaries to choose from—a medical dictionary or a general dictionary, for example.

A student in one of our introductory public speaking classes used definition by synonym in his speech on the ritual of bullfighting. After introducing each Spanish term, he provided its English translation. Notice how unobtrusively he defines terms in the following excerpt describing the parade to the bullfighting ring: "The *matadores* enter the ring as the band strikes up a *paso doble,* or two-step. Each matador is followed by a *guardia,* or a team of helpers. . . ." By using two languages, the speaker gave his speech a Spanish flavor, yet his English-speaking audience understood his description clearly.

Definition by Etymology. A second type of definition is **definition by etymology.** Etymology is the study of word origins. You may find that describing how a word has developed clarifies its meaning. For example, the word *decimate* means "to destroy a large portion of," as in, "The hailstorm decimated the soybean crop." You may not know that *decimate* comes from the Latin word for *ten* or *tenth*. The word *decim* was a common military term used by the ancient Romans. If soldiers mutinied against their generals, the entire group was punished. The troops were lined up and every tenth soldier was killed, whether guilty or innocent. This arbitrary punishment made others think twice before trying similar action against their leaders. Not only a word's origin but also the history of a word's use can be fascinating.

Most of the time we use definitions to make an unfamiliar term familiar. However, you can also use definition by etymology to highlight the unusual nature of a familiar term. The following etymological definition of the word *debate* is from John Ciardi's *A Browser's Dictionary*. Notice how Ciardi captures both the meaning and the flavor of the word as he traces its historical evolution:

> **debate:** Now signifies a formal presentation of arguments and counterarguments within parliamentary guidelines and time limits. As the formal rules of debate are lost, the discussion descends to wrangling. [Yet wrangling is the root sense.

definition by synonym: substituting a word having similar meaning for the word being defined.

definition by etymology: explaining the origin of the word being defined.

<L. *de-*, down (also functions as an intensive); *battere*, to beat (BATTERY, ABATE). This root sense is nicely expressed by the colorful It. word *battibecco*, hot argument; lit. "a beating of beaks" (as if two birds are fencing).][4]

That image of birds fighting with their beaks certainly enlivens this definition. The reference section of your library and a variety of Web sites will have a number of dictionaries of word origins and histories of word usage. We enjoy browsing in them, and in Chapter 17, "The Structure of Persuasion," we use definition by etymology to explain the red herring and bandwagon fallacies of reasoning (see pages 400, 402–03).

Definition by Example. As we mentioned earlier, an example is a specific instance or illustration of a larger group or classification. **Definition by example** uses a specific instance to clarify a general category or concept. Cactus Pryor, a popular radio personality in Austin, Texas, chose definition by example to explain what he meant when he used the word *Bubba:*

> Bubba is a good ol' boy. Bubba likes the NRA and Bubba dips snuff and Bubba likes Ollie North and Bubba likes to fish and hunt and eat barbecue and talk about women and frequently is found in Texas politics. Dallas is full of Bubbas, but they dress better. Bubbas are hard to not like because they're friendly. They hate Yankees. Bubba wears cowboy clothes.[5]

Pryor's definition not only clarifies the word *Bubba,* it also makes the concept more vivid.

You need not confine your definitions by example to language, however. Often audible and visual examples can be your quickest and most vivid ways to define a term or concept.

Audible examples are those you let your audience hear. Speeches on types of music, voice patterns, or speech dialects could define key terms by audible examples. For example, if you were using the word *scat* in a speech on jazz, you could offer a dictionary definition of the term: "jazz singing with nonsense syllables."[6] But wouldn't a taped example of Ella Fitzgerald, Al Jarreau, or Bobby McFerrin singing scat be more memorable to your audience? Other terms appropriate for audible definitions include the following:

bird calls	nasality and denasality
Boston Brahmin dialect	straight-ahead jazz
conjunto music	stuttering and cluttering
counterpoint	vocalese
industrial music	yodeling

Visual examples define a term by letting the audience see a form of it. Speeches on styles of architecture or painting could benefit from visual definition, as could any of the following terms:

Abstract Expressionism	Cubism
Art Deco	emoticon [:-o]
caricature	Fauvism
complementary colors	optical illusion
concrete poetry	photorealism

definition by example: providing an instance or illustration of the word being defined.

definition by operation: explaining how the object or concept being defined works, what it does, or what it was designed to do.

Definition by Operation. Sometimes the quickest and liveliest way to define a term is to explain how it is used. **Definition by operation** clarifies a word or phrase by explaining how an object or concept works, what it does, or what it was designed to do.

The terms *wok, radar detector, fax machine, food processor,* and *laser scalpel* are but a few of the physical objects best defined by explaining their operation.

You can also define concepts, actions, or processes by operation. To define magnetic resonance imaging, you would have to explain how that technology operates. Notice how the following person defines virtual reality by explaining how musicians and composers of the near future will use it:

> You're ready to enter an alternate reality. You slip on a pair of headphones, a helmet with a tiny video screen for each eye, and a special glove. Three-dimensional, generated images are projected onto your eye screens. Video "hands" match the movements of your own limbs. Sound seems to be coming from all around, not just inside your head, as you'd normally expect with 'phones.
>
> There's a mixing console floating before you. The music is coming from an apparent distance of a couple yards, but when a channel is "soloed," that sound moves to a point inches from your ear, while the rest of the mix stays put. By grabbing the edge of the board and pulling, you get as many input channels as you need, stretching away to infinity.[7]

Definition by operation is often livelier and more complete than most dictionary definitions. And, as the example above illustrates, it is especially useful in the case of new technologies whose dictionary definitions have yet to be written.

Narration

Narration is storytelling, the process of describing an action or a series of occurrences. If you come to school on Monday and tell a friend about something you did during the weekend, you are narrating those events.

Personal Narrative. As a participant in the events, you will probably speak in first person at least part of the time, using the pronouns *I* or *we.* Such a story is called a **personal narrative.** We have suggested that you draw upon your own experiences as you select and develop a speech topic, and personal narratives can be rich and interesting supporting materials.

Sultana, a student whose husband is Muslim and who had herself converted to the Muslim religion, used a personal narrative effectively. She told the story of her first experience with the celebration of Ramadan, a period of daylight fasting during the ninth month of the Muslim year:

> My first Ramadan I was a bit nervous. I had just become a Muslim, and I thought, "There is no way I can go from sunup to sunset without food. It's not even logical." I like to eat, as some of you may have noticed. And I thought, "There's no way that I can do this." Also, I was a student at the time, and it was finals. I honestly believe that you can't function if you don't eat. I mean, how can you think and pass a final? But I was determined at least to begin Ramadan; it goes for thirty days. So I set out and the first few days were a bit difficult. You can get hungry; there's no denying that. Your stomach growls out loud in class. But after about three days, the body adjusts. You don't really need as much food as most of us consume. You can live a long time on that stored up fat we have and survive quite well. But the experience provides a lot of self-confidence, because if you can spend thirty days fasting, you can do just about anything.

Her classmates laughed along with Sultana as she poked fun at students' eating habits during the stress of final exams, as well as at her own tendency to be finishing a snack as her speech class started. In addition to creating interest in the topic, Sultana's story reinforced her credibility to speak on the topic of Ramadan. We tend to believe the accounts of people who have experienced events firsthand. That is an important reason for using personal narratives.

narration: the process of describing an action or series of occurrences; storytelling.

personal narrative: a story told from the point of view of a participant in the action and using the pronouns *I* or *we.*

Third-Person Narrative. Narratives, of course, need not be personal but may relate a series of incidents in the lives of others. When you speak from the point of view of a witness and use the pronouns *he, she,* or *they,* you are telling a **third-person narrative.**

In the following example, notice how Tara used third-person narrative to illustrate the danger of the drug Halcion:

> It was a hot summer night in Hurricane, Utah, when Ilo Grundberg, restless and unable to sleep, took a single dose of what the June 1, 1996, *Dallas Morning News* describes as "the world's top-selling sleeping pill." Hours later she found herself lightheaded and devoid of reason and proceeded to walk down the hall of her small suburban home. In the horrific moments that followed, Ilo methodically pumped eight bullets into the face of her sleeping 83-year-old mother. Not only did Grundberg never stand trial for her mother's death, court-ordered psychiatrists found her "involuntarily intoxicated" at the time of the murder, and she was able to successfully sue Upjohn, the makers of this sleeping pill, for $21 million. Grundberg, along with millions of Americans, according to *ABC World News Tonight* on May 31, 1996, was taking Halcion without being aware of the evidence that this sleeping pill causes memory loss and violent psychotic behavior. In fact, the FDA reports that when they "tallied the number of hostile acts reported in association with prescription drugs, Halcion ranked number one."[8]

Comparison and Contrast

Comparison is the process of depicting one item—person, place, object, or concept—by pointing out its similarities to another, more familiar item. **Contrast** links two items by showing their differences. We use comparison and contrast to clarify that less familiar term or concept by relating it to a more common one. Your listeners must be familiar with one of the items involved in your comparison or contrast in order for either strategy to serve its purpose and have impact.

Literal Comparison and Contrast. Just as examples can be actual or hypothetical, comparisons and contrasts can be literal or figurative. A **literal comparison** associates items that share actual similarities. In her persuasive speech, "Information Apartheid," Alyse used a literal comparison as she described the problem of discrimination in an information age.

> A hundred years ago, the lack of a local railroad stop condemned many towns to a slow death. Thirty years ago, interstate interchanges and highways helped many communities prosper, while those on the back roads stagnated. Now the information superhighway is coming—how will it affect your neighborhood?
>
> Just as railroads and interstates brought prosperity to some communities and left others to become ghost towns, the information superhighway offers promise to those it reaches and threatens to leave others to slowly die, cut off from the information society in which we live. . . . I'm talking about an entire segment of our society, who because of their socioeconomic status, the quality of the education they received, and the decisions of businesses and government, are being denied access into the information age. Recently, Vice President Al Gore warned that out of the nation's 93 million households, the bottom third, 20 million families, are being left behind, cut off from the advancement of the information age . . . [9]

In a persuasive speech on the dangers of overexposure to the sun, another student, Patricia, made equally effective use of a **literal contrast:**

> Sunblocks are either chemical or physical. Oils, lotions, and creams that claim a certain SPF factor all contain chemical blocks. On the other hand, zinc oxide, the white or colored clay-looking material you see some people wearing, usually on their noses, is a physical sunblock.

third-person narrative: a story told from the point of view of a witness and using the pronouns *he, she,* or *they.*

comparison: the process of associating two items by pointing out their similarities.

contrast: the process of distinguishing two items by pointing out their differences.

literal comparison or contrast: associations or distinctions between two items that share actual similarities or differences.

Figurative Comparison and Contrast. When you draw a **figurative comparison or contrast,** you associate two items that do not necessarily share any actual similarities. The purpose of figurative comparisons is to surprise the listener into seeing or considering one person, place, object, or concept in a new way.

In his persuasive speech Stephen urged his listeners to protect their health by performing the simple act of washing their hands. He used a figurative comparison from one of his sources to make his point:

> Microbiologist Robert Massung stated in his 1996 research that your hands are like limousines; they collect germs and deliver them to the door, the door being the mucous membranes in your eyes, nose, and mouth, which are like moistened carpets, granting microbes quick access to your bloodstream and the rest of your body.[10]

Effective figurative comparisons must contain an element of surprise, as well as a spark of recognition. In a speech of self-introduction in which students were to explain some of the events occurring the year they were born, one student, Carolyn, mentioned the low prices advertised for girdles in a 1946 newspaper she had consulted. She then said, "For those of you women who have never had the pleasure of putting on and wearing a girdle, let me tell you that getting into a girdle was the aerobic dancing of 1946." The figurative comparison evokes a vivid and funny image.

One student, describing the density of a neutron star, quoted from *Sky & Telescope* magazine that "your bathroom sink could hold the Great Lakes if the water were compressed to the density of a neutron star."

You can use comparison and contrast together in your speech. If you clarify a term by showing how it is similar to something the audience knows, you can often make the term even clearer by showing how it is different from something the audience also knows.

Statistics

Statistics are collections of data. Broadly speaking, any number used as supporting material is a statistic. Used appropriately, statistics, too, can make your ideas clear and vivid, increase your credibility, and prove your point.

We place a great deal of trust in statistics that we feel have been accurately gathered and interpreted. Think of how much trust politicians as well as the general public put in preference polls gathered before elections. Statistics can predict certain events in our daily lives, such as price increases or decreases on certain goods and services. When you use statistics in your speech, you can demonstrate trends or compare a situation today with one in the past.

figurative comparison or contrast: associations or distinctions between two items that do not share actual similarities.

statistics: data collected in the form of numbers.

Supporting materials such as those in the diagram this speaker is using can help make a complicated concept clearer and easier for your audience to grasp.

However, you must be careful about how you use statistics in your speech. Used inappropriately, statistics may baffle or even bore your audience. The following five suggestions should guide you in presenting statistical material.

Do Not Rely Exclusively on Statistics. If statistics are your only form of supporting material, your audience will likely feel bombarded by numbers. Remember, your listening audience has only one chance to hear and assimilate your statistics. As a speaker, then, use statistics judiciously and in combination with other forms of support. A few key statistics combined with examples can be quite powerful. Too many statistics will confuse your audience.

Notice in the following speech excerpt how Professor Louis Rader successfully joins statistics with comparison to argue that American industry must commit itself to increasing product quality:

> Many of our CEOs felt that 99 percent good was good enough. If this figure (99 percent good) were converted into our daily non-industrial life, what would it mean? More than 30,000 newborn babies would be accidentally dropped by doctors and nurses each year. There would be 200,000 wrong drug prescriptions each year. Electricity would be off for fifteen minutes each day. Ninety-nine percent good means 10,000 bad out of 1 million.[11]

Round Off Statistics. A statistic of 74.6 percent has less impact and is more difficult for your audience to remember than "nearly three-fourths." No one in your audience will remember the statistic of $1,497,568.42; many, however, may be able to remember "a million and a half dollars." Rounding off statistics for your listeners is neither deceptive nor unethical. Instead, it reflects your concern for helping your audience understand and retain key statistical information.

Locating Statistics
http://www.fedstats.gov
Need a statistic to document the extent of a condition or problem? The Federal Interagency Council on Statistical Policy maintains this Web site containing information and statistics provided by more than 70 government agencies. The site also includes links to other national and international statistical sites.

Use Units of Measure That Are Familiar to Your Audience. In her speech on worker incomes in China, Kim cited the example of the Yue Yuen company, which makes sports shoes for Adidas, Nike, and Reebok. "According to an August 1996 issue of *Far Eastern Economic Review*," she claimed, "junior high school graduates are paid, on average, 600 renminbi a month. That's approximately $72 in U.S. dollars and is a typical wage for that region. In addition," she continued, "the company estimates that non-cash income such as dormitory, food, and medical benefits amount to another 600 renminbi a month—or another $72." Six hundred renminbi would probably have been a meaningless figure to most of her listeners. Kim helped her audience to understand that statistic by translating it to U.S. dollars and by indicating how it compared with other salaries in the region.

Use Presentational Aids to Represent or Clarify Relationships among Statistics.
Suppose you wanted to use the following paragraph in a speech about baseball players:

> Since professional baseball began, in 1876, California has produced 1,282 major leaguers and Pennsylvania has produced 1,260. These states are followed by New York (943), Illinois (859), Ohio (858), and Texas (541).[12]

If you're a baseball fan, you probably find these facts interesting. But remember, even the most avid fans in your audience would probably not remember all these numbers. Your listeners would be more likely to remember the information if you presented the facts both orally and visually. In this case you could construct a chart ranking the states, with the number of players each produced beside the state's name.

Stress the Impact of Large Numbers. Former Surgeon General C. Everett Koop used statistics effectively to make his point that tobacco-related diseases cause significant deaths. Notice how he used repetition and helped his audience visualize the enormity of these deaths.

> Let's start with a factual description of the problem. Based on the calculations of the finest statistical minds in the world and the World Health Organization, they have predicted that by 2025, 27 years from now, 500 million people worldwide will die of tobacco-related disease. That's a numbing figure. It is too large to take in, so let me put it in other terms for you. That's a Vietnam War every day for 27 years. That's a Bhopal every two hours for 27 years. That's a Titanic every 43 minutes for 27 years.
>
> If we were to build for those tobacco victims a memorial such as the Vietnam Wall, it would stretch from here [Washington, D.C.] 1,000 miles across seven states to Kansas City. And, if you want to put it in terms per minute, there's a death [every] 1.7 seconds, or about 250 to 300 people since I began to speak to you this afternoon.[13]

Testimony

Examples, definition, narration, comparison, contrast, and statistics are discrete types of supporting materials. Each is a different strategy for validating the ideas of a speech. Speakers sometimes generate these types of support themselves. Other times, they glean them from their research, citing their sources but justifying the point in their own words. Still other times, speakers find the words and structure of the original source so compelling that they quote directly or paraphrase the source. This latter strategy is known as **testimony**. Testimony, sometimes called quotation, is another method of presenting types of supporting material. When you quote or paraphrase the words and ideas of others, you use testimony. Look at the two examples below of a speaker making the same basic statement:

> A second characteristic of American families today is that they have two incomes. The days of Ricky and Lucy Ricardo, Ward and June Cleaver, and Archie and Edith Bunker are over. In fact, nearly two-thirds of couples with children are supported by incomes from the husband and wife, many of whom work full-time.

Suppose a speaker, instead, phrased and supported the idea like this:

> A second characteristic of American families today is that they have two incomes. The days of Ricky and Lucy Ricardo, Ward and June Cleaver, and Archie and Edith Bunker are over, at least according to Eugene Fram, a research professor at Rochester Institute of Technology, and Joel Axelrod, president of an international marketing research organization. They write in the October 1990 issue of *American Demographics*, "In 1988, almost two-thirds of married couples with children—16 million families—had two incomes. In 8 million of these families, both husband and wife worked full-time, year-round."[14]

As you can see, the key idea in each of the examples is the same: The typical American family has two incomes. Both examples rely on statistics to support the key idea. However, by quoting a source in the second example, the speaker has added an additional element of support. The expert testimony increases the credibility of the idea. In this example, testimony or quotation has not changed the *type* of support; it has merely enhanced its *believability*.

Testimony sometimes draws its effectiveness from the content of the quotation, as in the example above. Other times, testimony relies largely on the reputation of the

testimony: quotations or paraphrases of an authoritative source to clarify or prove a point.

person making the statement. In her speech on "road rage" Sandy listed four causes of this phenomenon. Sandy's own expertise in this area was insufficient to prove her point, so she quoted the statement of a psychologist reported in a reputable magazine to give her ideas credibility.

> Naturally, the phenomenon of road rage has given rise to its own therapeutic movement, whose leading practitioner is Whittier, California, psychologist Arnold Nerenberg. Dr. Nerenberg refers to himself as "America's Road Rage Therapist" and, as reported in *Newsweek,* June 2, 1997, he has identified the four stimuli which he believes provoke road rage: (1) feeling endangered by someone else's driving; (2) resentment at being forced to slow down; (3) righteous indignation at someone who breaks traffic rules; (4) anger at another driver who takes their road rage out on you.[15]

Notice how in all these examples the speakers used the words and ideas of others to enhance the credibility of their ideas. Expert testimony, however, is not limited to the statements of other people. As a speaker, you use *personal testimony* when you support your ideas with your own experiences and observations. Many students select a speech

Type of Support	Use
Example	Provides instances or samples of people, places, objects, actions, conditions, or experiences.
Actual example	Provides clarification and proof.
Hypothetical example	Provides clarification, but does not alone provide proof.
Definition	Clarifies an unfamiliar word or phrase.
Definition by synonym	Substitutes a familiar word for the one defined.
Definition by etymology	Explains the origin of the word defined.
Definition by example	Provides an illustration or sample of the word defined.
Audible example	Lets listeners hear sample of the term defined.
Visual example	Lets listeners see sample of the term defined.
Definition by operation	Explains use, function, or purpose of the object or concept defined.
Narration	Describes action or event.
Personal narrative	Describes action from participant's point of view; uses *I* and *we.*
Third-person narrative	Describes action from witness's point of view; uses *he, she,* and *they.*
Comparison	Clarifies term by showing its similarity to a more familiar term.
Literal comparison	Associates items having actual similarities.
Figurative comparison	Associates items not having actual similarities.
Contrast	Clarifies term by showing its difference from a more familiar term.
Literal contrast	Distinguishes items having actual differences.
Figurative contrast	Distinguishes items not having actual differences.
Statistics	Clarify or prove a point with numbers.
Testimony	Clarifies or proves a point using the speaker's words or those of an expert.

**FIGURE 8.1
Supporting materials: types and uses.**

topic because they have some special knowledge or experience with the subject. One of our students, for example, gave a speech comparing retail prices at large supermarkets to those at convenience stores. He was careful to explain his credentials and establish his expertise in the subject. Not only did he wear his store apron and manager's name tag, but he also said early in his introduction, "As a former receiving control manager, I was in charge of purchasing products for the store, so I have some knowledge of how wholesale prices are translated into the retail prices you and I pay." The speaker enhanced his credibility both verbally and nonverbally.

Remember our reference to Susan Chontos's speech early in this chapter? In that informative speech, "The Amish: Seeking to Lose the Self" (see Appendix B), Susan used a variety of the supporting materials discussed in this chapter. To support her idea that "a major tenet of the Amish faith is the desire to be simple, or plain," she used *examples* of toys the Amish use and clothes that they wear. She also used *definition* when she described their use of *Fraktur* art. Her spoken and visual definition readily communicated this type of art to her listeners. She used *contrast* to support her claim that the Amish "desire to be separate from this world": "Today, however, they [the Amish] are permitted to ride in automobiles, although they can't own one. Similarly, they may use a telephone, but they can't have one in their home. In addition, they may use modern farm equipment, but only if it's pulled by their plow horses." And throughout her speech, Susan used testimony as she quoted from several authoritative sources.

Tests of Evidence

Speakers should choose supporting materials carefully and ethically. The positions you develop in your speech will be only as strong as the evidence supporting them. Seven guidelines will help you evaluate the validity and strength of your supporting materials. These suggestions will also aid your evaluation of evidence you hear others present in their speeches.

Tests of Evidence

1. Is the evidence quoted in context?
2. Is the source of the evidence an expert?
3. Is the source of the evidence unbiased?
4. Is the evidence relevant to the point being made?
5. Is the evidence specific?
6. Is the evidence sufficient to prove the point?
7. Is the evidence timely?

key points

Is the Evidence Quoted in Context?

Evidence is quoted *in context* if it accurately reflects the source's statement of the topic. Evidence is quoted *out of context* if it distorts the source's position on the topic.

For example, suppose Joyce was preparing a speech on the topic of hate crimes on campus. She has read in the campus paper the following statement by the president of her college:

> We've been fortunate that our campus has been relatively free of bias-motivated crimes. In fact, last year, only two such incidents were reported—the lowest figure in the past five years. Yet, no matter how small the number is, any hate crime constitutes a serious problem on this campus. We will not be satisfied until our campus is completely free from all bias-motivated intimidation.

Now, suppose Joyce used the following statement to support her position that hate crimes are prevalent on campus:

> We need to be concerned about a widespread and growing problem on our campus: the prevalence of hate crimes. Just this past week, for example, our president argued that hate crimes constitute, and I quote, "a serious problem on this campus."

The president did say those words, but Joyce did not also mention the president's position that hate crimes on campus are few and decreasing. By omitting this fact, she has distorted the president's message. Joyce has presented the evidence out of context. The evidence you cite in your speech should accurately represent each source's position on the topic.

Is the Source of the Evidence an Expert?

An expert is a person qualified to speak on a particular topic. We trust the opinions and observations of others based on their position, education, training, or experience. The chairperson of a committee that has just completed a study on the effects of a community-based sentencing program is knowledgeable about the facts concerning that issue. A person completing graduate study on the effects of a local Head Start program on literacy has also developed an area of expertise. As a speaker, select the most qualified sources to support your position.

For a persuasive speech condemning the growth of tabloid news, which source would you find more credible: a cub reporter or a Pulitzer Prize–winning journalist? In an informative speech comparing the philosophies of various environmental action groups, would you be more impressed by testimony from a local member of a small environmental organization or from a nationally acclaimed environmental expert? If you delivered a speech advocating the licensing of law clerks to draft wills and conduct other routine legal business, would you rather quote a first-year lawyer or a senior law partner of a major legal corporation? Of course it would depend on the specific individuals and what they said, but you would probably place more trust in the latter, more experienced person in each of these examples.

Our student who compared the pricing policies of large supermarkets and convenience stores was careful to establish his own credibility both verbally and nonverbally. When you as a speaker fail to present your qualifications, or the qualifications of those you quote, you give listeners little reason to believe you.

> **Political Information**
> http://www.democrats.org/index.html
> http://www.rnc.org/
> http://www.reformparty.org/
> The Democratic, Republican, and Reform parties—as well as other political parties—maintain Web sites to promote issues and candidates. These sites offer information and links to party platforms, issues, polls, press releases, and news stories. Although political parties may provide much supporting material for your ideas, remember to evaluate the quality and objectivity of the evidence.

Is the Source of the Evidence Unbiased?

When Markdown Marty of Marty's Used Cars tells you he has the best deals in town, do you accept that claim without questioning it? Probably not. Marty may be an expert on used cars, but he's understandably biased. When individuals have a vested interest in a product, service, or issue, they are often less objective about it.

You expect representatives of political parties, special-interest groups, business corporations, labor unions, and so forth to make statements advancing their interests. It will probably not surprise you, for example, that the supermarket receiving control manager we quoted earlier concluded his speech by stating that it is more economical to shop at large supermarkets than at convenience stores. When you include testimony and quotations in your speeches, try to rely on objective experts who do not have a vested interest in sustaining the position they voice.

Evidence should relate to the speaker's claim. Sounds pretty obvious, doesn't it? However, both speakers and listeners often fail to apply this guideline in evaluating evidence. A speaker who contends that amateur boxing is dangerous but presents only evidence of injuries to professional boxers has clearly violated the relevance criterion. But many times irrelevant evidence is more difficult to detect.

Ryan's speech called for increased funding of medical trauma centers. Throughout his speech, he cited the need for the specialized care provided in these facilities. Yet, when he estimated the demand for this care, he used statistics of emergency room use. Trauma centers are not the same as emergency rooms. Therefore, Ryan's evidence was irrelevant to his argument. As you construct your speech, identify your key points and make certain your evidence relates specifically to them.

Is the Evidence Specific?

Which of the following statements is more informative?

The new convention center will increase tourism a lot.
The new convention center will increase tourism by 40 percent.

What does "a lot" mean in the first statement? Twenty percent? Fifty percent? Eighty percent? We don't know. The second statement is more precise. Because it is more specific, we are better able to assess the impact of the new convention center. Words such as *lots, many, numerous,* and *very* are vague. When possible, replace them with more specific words or phrases.

In her speech "Debunking the Vitamin Myth," Dana discussed the problem of misuse of vitamins. She stated:

An article entitled "The Real Power of Vitamins" in the April 6, 1992, issue of *Time* magazine suggests that misuse of and misconceptions about vitamins can be harmful and even deadly. In fact, the vitamin problem plagues many Americans.

If Dana had stopped there, her audience might have asked: "Is the problem really that harmful? How many people have actually died because of it? How many is 'many Americans'?" But Dana wisely continued:

According to the October 23, 1991, issue of the *New York Times,* on any given day 80 percent of the American population will consume a vitamin, 37 percent will

---

You probably wouldn't be surprised that a Gallup study sponsored by Motorola found that people who use cellular phones are more successful in business than those who don't, or that a Gallup poll sponsored by the zinc industry revealed that 62% of Americans want to keep the penny. These are just two examples that *Wall Street Journal* writer and editor Cynthia Crossen uses in her book, *Tainted Truth: The Manipulation of Fact in America,* to illustrate the difficulty of distinguishing between neutral research and commercially sponsored studies.

Assume that you are preparing to give a speech on hormone replacement therapy to counteract the effects of aging. Through an electronic database search, you find a study that shows the substance melatonin prevents cancer, boosts the immune system, and improves the quality of sleep. When you look for the source, you see that the study was sponsored by a pharmaceutical company that produces melatonin. What course of action should you follow? Should you disregard the findings because the study was commercially sponsored, use the findings without mentioning the study's sponsor, mention the findings and acknowledge the study's commercial sponsorship, or treat the findings in some other way?

ethical decisions

overindulge, and 19 percent will reach toxic levels. They go on to report that 1,752 people lost their lives in 1991 due to the overconsumption of vitamins. Clearly, this subject warrants further examination.[16]

Dana's specific evidence better informed her listeners and made her point: The problem of vitamin misuse is serious.

Is the Evidence Sufficient to Prove the Point?

In her speech on rap music, Lea played excerpts from two rap songs, one of which she characterized as antiwoman and the other as antipolice. She encouraged her listeners to boycott rap music because "it demeans women and law enforcement officers." Lea did not apply this sixth guideline to her evidence. Two examples do not justify a blanket indictment of rap music.

When considering the guideline of sufficiency, ask yourself, "Is there enough evidence to prove the point?" One unpleasant experience at Fred's Cafe is insufficient to conclude that it's a bad bistro. Three examples of college athletes graduating without acquiring basic writing skills are insufficient to prove that athletes are failing to get a good education. One example may illustrate a claim, but it will rarely prove it. Make certain you have sufficient evidence to support your points.

Is the Evidence Timely?

If you were preparing a travel budget for a trip overseas, which would you find more helpful: an airline ticket pricing schedule you had from last year or one your roommate picked up at the airport this week? Of course, you would want to rely on your roommate's more recent information. The timeliness of information is especially important if you are speaking about constantly changing issues, conditions, or events. What you read today may already be dated by the time you give your speech.

Some speech topics, however, are timeless. If you speak about the gods of Mount Olympus, no one would question your use of Thomas Bulfinch's books about mythology, even though they were published in the mid-1800s. Both Edith Hamilton's *Mythology,* published in 1940, and Robert Graves's *Greek Gods and Heroes,* published in 1960, would also add credibility to your speech. As scholars of mythology, Bulfinch, Hamilton, and Graves earned reputations that time is not likely to diminish. Similarly, if you deliver a speech on the ancient Olympic Games, your most authoritative sources may be history textbooks. If, however, your topic concerns current drug-testing procedures in Olympic competition, it would be vital for you to use the most recent sources of the best quality you can find. The date of your evidence must be appropriate to your specific argument.

Evaluating Electronic Information

Testing the quality of your evidence using the preceding questions exercises a number of your critical thinking skills. When you use the Internet for research, however, those skills may get not just exercise but a full-tilt workout. This is because anything can get posted and quickly communicated to millions of people online. Some messages posted on Web sites may just be nutty hoaxes (stories about expensive cookie recipes or fictitious computer virus alerts, for example). Other Internet sites, however, spread dangerous information; fan suspicion, fear, and prejudice; or just lie with other malicious intent.

You'll likely be finding a number of the supporting materials discussed in this chapter through research that you do on the Internet. The most user-friendly part of the Internet, the World Wide Web, is a powerful tool that makes research seem extravagantly easy. For example, assume that you sit down at the computer to begin your research after selecting the Guggenheim Museum in Bilbao, Spain, as your topic for an upcoming speech. After selecting Northern Light as your search engine, you do a subject search by entering "Guggenheim Museum Bilbao." Your results: 663 items match your query. Comforted, you sit back thinking that all the information you will need—and more—is just a series of mouse clicks away. You may very well be right. But for all the convenience that it provides, the Internet forces us to take on a lot of the evaluation of information that other people used to do for us.

Evaluating Internet Sources
http://milton.mse.jhu.edu:8001/research/education/net.html
This site, one of many library sites on the topic "Evaluating Information Found on the Internet," provides a particularly thorough checklist of criteria. Maintained by Elizabeth E. Kirk of Johns Hopkins University, it includes links to related subtopics.

A number of those 663 items will no doubt be articles that appeared first in printed magazines and newspapers. That information will have been filtered several times. The newspaper probably had a fact checker to verify the writer's information. The magazine may have had expert reviewers who had to be convinced of the truth and value of the article before it was selected for publication. Online versions of such magazines and newspapers, as well as government documents, are now regarded on a par with their print counterparts.[17] Today most educational, governmental, or organizational sites also have a review process for materials posted under their sponsorship.[18] Yet as we noted in Chapter 7, anyone with access to a Web page can publish anything on the World Wide Web. As a result, many sites you access on any topic have never been edited, fact-checked, or reviewed. In addition, they may appear today and be gone tomorrow.

A real advantage of the Internet is that so many sites are interesting to look at and fun to navigate. Aside from issues of design and aesthetics, however, what do you need to ask yourself about sites that you are considering using to support your speech? Hundreds of college and university library Web sites now have links to guidelines for evaluating Internet sources. Basic questions you may need to ask are as follows.

Purpose

- What seems to be the purpose of this site: to provide information? to promote a position? to sell a product or service?
- What type of site is it: educational (.edu), commercial (.com), nonprofit organization (.org), governmental (.gov), or military (.mil), for example?
- Is there an institution, agency, or organization identified as sponsoring the site?
- Does the site contain advertising? If so, by whom?
- Who is the author's apparent audience, as reflected by the vocabulary, writing style, and point of view? Students? Professionals? Consumers? Advocates?

Expertise

- Is the author, compiler, or Web master identified?
- Does the author have apparent expertise on the subject?
- Are the author's or compiler's credentials provided?
  - Do you know the author's occupation?
  - Do you know the author's educational background?
  - Do you know the author's organizational affiliation?
- Does the author provide contact information, such as e-mail address, phone number, or mailing address?

- If the site is a compilation, are sources and authors of individual works identified?
- If the site is a research project, does the author explain data, methodology, and interpretation of results?
- If the site is a research project, does the author refer to other works? Provide notes?
- If links to other works are provided, are they evaluated in any way?
- Is the site linked to another site that you already trust or value?
- Are sources or viewpoints missing that you would expect to be present?
- What does this page offer that you could not find elsewhere?

Objectivity

- Does the author's affiliation with an organization, institution, or agency suggest a bias?
- Does the site's sponsorship by an organization or institution suggest an inherent bias?
- Are opposing views represented or acknowledged?
- Are editorial comments or opinions clearly distinguished from facts?

Accuracy

- Can you corroborate the facts using either other Internet sources or library resources (reference works or indexed publications)?
- Is the site inward-focused (providing only links to other parts of the site) or outward-focused (providing links to other Web sites)?
- Has the author expended the effort to write well, with correct spelling and proper grammar?
- Does the author solicit corrections or updates by e-mail?

Timeliness

- Is the date of publication important to this subject matter?
- Can you tell when the site was created?
- Can you tell when the site was last updated?
- Are links from this site current or broken?[19]

Summary

We use supporting materials in a speech to achieve three purposes: *clarity, vividness,* and *credibility.* Clarity helps the audience understand your ideas. Vividness assists them in remembering your ideas. Credible supporting materials make your ideas believable.

Types of material you can use to support the main ideas of your speech include examples, definition, narration, comparison, contrast, statistics, and testimony. *Examples* are samples or illustrations of a category. Those categories may be people, places, objects, actions, experiences, or conditions. Examples may be *brief* or *extended* and actual or hypothetical. *Actual examples* are real or factual. *Hypothetical examples* are imaginary or fictitious. Both types of examples make a general or abstract term more specific and vivid for the audience.

Definitions are explanations of an unfamiliar term or of a word having several possible meanings. We can define terms by synonym, by etymology, by example, or by operation. *Definition by synonym* offers a word or phrase that is the rough equivalent of the word being defined. *Definition by etymology* shows the origin of the word being defined. *Definition by example* gives an illustration or sample of the word in question. *Definition by operation* explains how something works or what it was designed to do. Definitions are crucial if you are using words you suspect your audience will not know, or if you want them to adopt one particular meaning for a term.

Narration is storytelling. Narratives may be personal or third-person. *Personal narratives* originate from the speaker's experience; they use the first-person pronouns *I* or *we. Third-person narratives* are stories about other people, and they are delivered using either people's names or the third-person pronouns *she, he,* or *they.*

Comparisons associate two or more items to show the similarities between or among them. Comparisons can be either literal or figurative. A *literal comparison* links two items that share actual similarities. A *figurative comparison* associates items that do not share any actual similarities.

Contrasts function like comparisons except that their purpose is to distinguish or show differences between two or more items.

Statistics are data collected in the form of numbers. Used properly, statistics can bolster a speaker's credibility and lend vivid support to the ideas of the speech. To ensure your proper use of statistics, you should follow five guidelines. First, don't rely exclusively on statistics, but combine them with other supporting materials. Second, round off statistics to help your listeners remember them. Third, use units of measure familiar to your audience. Fourth, use visual aids to clarify the relationships among various statistics. Fifth, stress the impact of large numbers.

The final form of support is testimony. You use *testimony* when you cite, quote, or paraphrase authoritative sources. The authorities you cite may employ examples, definitions, narration, comparison, contrast, or statistics.

To help ensure that your supporting materials are credible, you should ask seven questions about each piece of evidence you consider using: Is the evidence quoted in context? Is the source of the evidence an expert? Is the source of the evidence unbiased? Is the evidence relevant to the point you are making? Is the evidence specific? Is the evidence sufficient to prove your point? Is the evidence timely?

Evaluating information you collect from the Internet or the World Wide Web requires you to ask and answer additional questions. What is the apparent *purpose* of the Web site providing the information? What evidence of the author's *expertise* do you find? What evidence of the author's *objectivity* do you find? Can you confirm the *accuracy* of the site's information? Is the information *timely*? Based on your answers to these questions, is the information appropriate for your purposes?

Evaluating Evidence

A transcript of a speech by Jennifer Deem is included in Appendix B. After reading the speech, write a critique to Jennifer evaluating the evidence she uses to support her ideas. What types of materials does she use to support her assertions? Are there better choices she could have made to support these ideas? Use the tests suggested in this chapter for evaluating evidence. Does Deem include assertions for which she does not offer adequate support? If so, what other types of evidence should she provide to make her arguments more convincing?

practice critique

Exercises

1. Rewrite the following sentences to make them more vivid.
   a. The food at the Cozy Café is very good.
   b. I have a lot of homework to do.
   c. The students in my speech class are interesting people.
   d. We have a good time at the beach.

2. Select a key idea of a speech you are preparing for this class. Try developing it using three different types of supporting materials. What are the advantages and disadvantages of each? Is the idea best developed by combining two or three of these methods?

3. Locate a transcript of a speech in *Vital Speeches of the Day* or in some other publication or electronic database. Read it, and note in the margins the different types of supporting materials the speaker used. Discuss the materials used most effectively, and account for their effectiveness. Discuss those used least effectively, and suggest ways the speaker could improve them.

4. Read a newspaper, keeping in mind the types of supporting materials presented in this chapter. Select the best and worst example you find for each type of support. Justify your choices.

5. Read the five statements below, indicating those with which you agree and disagree. Discuss the type(s) of supporting materials you would likely use to support your positions.
   a. Soccer is a more popular sport than football.
   b. The fear of giving a speech can be reduced.
   c. Art is more important than science.
   d. Life in the country is more fun than life in the city.
   e. This state is an excellent place to visit.

6. Think of someone who is known to you but unknown to your classmates. Describe this person (personality traits, physical features, attitudes, etc.) by comparing and contrasting him or her with people in your class.

7. Discuss a method of definition you could use for each of the following terms:
   a. Modem
   b. Aphorism
   c. Contralto
   d. Palpable
   e. Chlorophyll
   f. Autocad drafting
   g. Pandemic
   h. Contour map

8. On the World Wide Web, locate two pieces of information on the same topic, and print them. Choose one authoritative source and one whose validity you doubt. Be prepared to discuss what features made you trust the first source and doubt the second.

Notes

1. William Lutz, *Doublespeak: How Government, Business, Advertisers, and Others Use Language to Deceive You* (New York: HarperCollins, 1990) 223.

2. Jack Huber and Dean Higgins, "Mike Wallace," in *Interviewing the World's Top Interviewers: The Inside Story of Journalism's Most Momentous Revelations* (New York: S.P.I.—Shapolsky, 1993) 27.

3. Lucas F. Tatham, "America, a Nation on the Fast Track to Destruction," *Winning Orations, 1998* (Mankato, MN: Interstate Oratorical Association, 1998) 137.

4. John Ciardi, *A Browser's Dictionary* (New York: Harper & Row, 1980) 206–07.

5. Cactus Pryor, in Elizabeth A. Moize, "Austin: Deep in the Heart of Texas," *National Geographic* June 1990: 63.

6. *Webster's Tenth New Collegiate Dictionary* (Springfield, MA: Merriam Webster, 1993) 1043.

7. David Trubitt, "Into New Worlds: Virtual Reality and the Electronic Musician," *Electronic Musician* July 1990: 31.

8. Tara Kubicka, "Halcion," *Winning Orations, 1997* (Northfield, MN: Interstate Oratorical Association, 1997) 1.

9. Alyse Nelson, "Information Apartheid," *Winning Orations, 1995* (Northfield, MN: Interstate Oratorical Association, 1995) 47.

10. Stephen Barnett, "Coming Clean," *Winning Orations, 1998* (Mankato, MN: Interstate Oratorical Association, 1998) 50.

11. Louis T. Rader, "Outstanding Engineering Achievements of the Past," *Vital Speeches of the Day* 1 July 1990: 566.

12. Nancy Ten Kate, "Batter Up," *American Demographics* October 1990: 16.

13. C. Everett Koop, address, National Press Club, Washington, DC, 8 September 1998.

14. Eugene H. Fram and Joel Axelrod, "The Distressed Shopper," *American Demographics* October 1990: 44.

15. Sandy Betlan, "Untitled," *Winning Orations, 1998* (Mankato, MN: Interstate Oratorical Association, 1998) 11.

16. Dana M. Perino, "Debunking the Vitamin Myth," *Winning Orations, 1992* (Mankato, MN: Interstate Oratorical Association, 1992) 15.

17. D. Scott Brandt, "Evaluating Information on the Internet," *Computers in Libraries* May 1996: 45.

18. Caroline L. Gilson, "Evaluating Information Resources," 3 June 1999, McConnell Library, Radford Univ., 2 July 1999 <http://lib.runet.edu/hguide/Evaluating.html>.

19. This checklist was adapted from Serena Fenton and Grace Reposa, "Evaluating the Goods," *Technology & Learning* Sept. 1998: 28–32; Caroline L. Gilson, "Evaluating Information Resources," 3 June 1999, McConnell Library, Radford Univ., 2 July 1999 <http://lib.runet.edu/hguide/Evaluating.html>; Esther Grassian, "Thinking Critically about World Wide Web Resources," 10 Oct. 1997, UCLA College Library, 10 March 1999 <http://www.accd.edu/SAC/LRC/gis/critical.htm>; Stephanie Michel, "Evaluating Information on the World Wide Web," 9 June 1999, McConnell Library, Radford Univ., 2 July 1999 <http://lib.runet.edu/libserv/handout/evaluation.html>; Keith Stanger, "Criteria for Evaluating Internet Resources," 30 Nov. 1998, University Library, Eastern Michigan Univ., 4 March 1999 <http://online.emich.edu/~lib_stanger/ineteval.htm>.

If you want me to talk for ten minutes, I'll come next week. If you want me to talk for an hour, I'll come tonight.

—*Woodrow Wilson*

Organizing the Body of Your Speech

The seventeenth-century mathematician and philosopher Blaise Pascal once wrote to a friend, "I have made this letter longer than usual, because I lack the time to make it short."[1] Have you ever furiously written several pages to answer an essay question on an exam only to discover that the answer requires just one brief paragraph? Or perhaps you have given a driver long-winded directions for getting to a particular location, then remembered a shortcut. If you have had experiences similar to these, Pascal's comment probably makes a great deal of sense to you. It takes time to organize your thoughts to write a coherent letter, give a succinct answer to an essay question, or give clear directions. Spending the time to organize, however, simplifies the task in the end. Getting organized will also simplify your speech preparation and make your speech more vivid and memorable for your listeners. Chapters 9 and 10 are your blueprints for organizing the various parts of your speech.

By the time you enter college, you have already had a good deal of experience with written communication. On the receiving end, you have read numerous essays, short stories, and novels. As a sender, you have written essays, reports, and term papers. You have learned that a good essay or term paper has a clear beginning, middle, and end. When you write an essay, you seek to interest the reader and introduce the topic in the opening. The middle develops your ideas through examples, comparison, contrast, statistics, and other forms of supporting material. The end ties the ideas together and provides closure. If you have learned to do these things well in your writing, you have a head start in speech making. Even if this is your first experience with constructing a speech, you have already mastered some basic organizational skills. If you think you are not good at writing essays and reports, don't despair. The steps we describe in this chapter will help you develop a well-organized speech.

A coherent speech is similar to a written essay because it also has a beginning, middle, and end—what we call the introduction, body, and conclusion. Orally, you seek to achieve goals similar to those you set when writing. Many speech textbooks and instructors summarize the overall strategy of a speech as follows: *Tell us what you are going to tell us. Tell us. Then, tell us what you told us.* Use this organizational perspective in every speech.

Though the organization of speech and writing is similar, these two channels of communication also have significant differences. When you write, for example, you can highlight ideas by using subheads, paragraph indentations, capitalization, boldface type, punctuation, and italics. Note how we use all of these cues in this text to organize our ideas for you. An audience listening to a speech, however, cannot rely on these visual cues. As a speaker, you must supply these missing elements with a clear organizational pattern and effective delivery.

Another difference between writing and speaking is the audience's control over the flow of information. As a reader, you can pause, reread a sentence, think about it, take a break, and come back to your reading when you feel fresher. As a listener, you lack the freedom to do any of these things: You are at the mercy of the speaker. Of course, a sensitive speaker can make the task of listening easier by highlighting key ideas to help the audience remember them during and after the speech.

A speaker supplies the information a reader would get from visual cues with a clear organizational pattern and effective delivery. Good organization maximizes a speaker's information and arranges ideas so that an audience will remember them. In

Sample Speeches
http://www.ukans.edu/cwis/units/coms2/vpa/vpa9.htm
In addition to links to sites addressing public speaking topics such as organization, the "Virtual Presentation Assistant," an online service provided by the Communication Studies Department of the University of Kansas, offers The History Channel's Great Speeches Archive. You can hear audio versions of the speeches with *RealAudio*.

Chapter 13, we suggest techniques of delivery to help you further reinforce the ideas of your speech.

A well-organized, well-delivered speech can have as great an impact on your listeners as a well-written essay has on readers. In this chapter we will teach you how to organize the body of your speech. In Chapter 10 you will learn how to organize the introduction and the conclusion. You may find this an unusual order in which to organize the parts of a speech. Be assured that by the end of Chapter 10 you will see the logic of this sequence.

Although you deliver it after the introduction, organize the body of your speech first, for in order to "tell us what you are going to tell us," you must first determine what to tell us. In constructing the body of a speech, your best strategy is to formulate an organizing question, to divide the speech into key ideas, and then develop each idea.

Formulate an Organizing Question

If your research is productive, you'll gather more information than you can use in your speech. Some of that information will be relevant to your topic; some of it will not. You may also be missing some information that you need to develop your topic fully. Deciding what is relevant, irrelevant, or missing requires you to use your critical thinking skill of *analyzing* as you examine items of information and the relationships among them. You will also be *integrating* as you combine and restructure the different pieces of information, and *organizing* as you arrange your information so that you can present it effectively, in a way your listeners can understand.

How can you begin assessing what you have, how it fits together, and what you still need? Begin by constructing an **organizing question,** a question that, when answered, indicates the ideas and information necessary to develop your topic. Write the question on a notecard or sheet of paper, and keep it visible as you begin sifting through your research. Ask yourself periodically, "What information helps answer that question?" As you continue to work on your speech, you may change your organizing question; usually it will become more specific, helping you focus your speech further.

You should find that your organizing question suggests a pattern, perhaps several possible patterns, of organization. Consider these examples:

- What effects do golf courses have on communities where they exist?
- What does it take to brew a great cup of coffee?
- What does the U.S. National Holocaust Memorial Museum contain?
- Why do some people favor and others oppose political action committees?

The first question suggests that you'll need to examine different positive or negative aspects of golf courses. Answering the second question will probably require you to discover a formula or procedure. The third question calls for description of the different parts of the museum, based on your memory, your research, or both. Answering the fourth question will require you to study and organize the arguments for and against political action committees.

As a final example, Esperanza, a student, was taking and enjoying an ethnic studies course. She wanted to encourage her classmates to take such courses as well. Yet she soon discovered that her preliminary organizing question, "What does research tell us about ethnic studies courses?" was too broad. Esperanza reworded her question: "Why should all students be required to take ethnic studies courses?" To answer this question, Esperanza needed to develop specific arguments from the evidence she collected. Later in this chapter, we'll see how Esperanza answered her organizing question and developed the main points of her speech.

organizing question: a question that, when answered, indicates the ideas and information necessary to develop your topic.

Divide the Speech into Key Ideas

In the body of the speech, you develop your key ideas according to a specific organizational pattern. Public speakers employ a wide variety of organizational structures. We will discuss eight patterns most commonly used: topical, chronological, spatial, causal, pro–con, mnemonic or gimmick, problem–solution, and need–plan. The first six of these patterns are appropriate for either informative or persuasive speeches. Problem–solution and need–plan patterns, however, are appropriate only for persuasive speeches.

Keep in mind as you consider these patterns that no one of them is best. In order to achieve the best results, you must select the structure that best achieves the purpose of your speech. In other words, fit the organization to your topic rather than your topic to the organization. Study these patterns of organization carefully, and you should have no difficulty in finding one that works for any topic you speak on in this class.

key points

Patterns for Dividing Your Speech into Key Ideas

1. Topical division
2. Chronological division
3. Spatial division
4. Causal division
5. Pro–con division
6. Mnemonic or gimmick division
7. Problem–solution division
8. Need–plan division

Topical Division

The **topical division** is the most common organizational pattern for public speeches. This strategy creates subtopics, categories that constitute the larger topic. For example, a speech on graffiti is divided topically if it focuses on graffiti as artistic expression, as political expression, and as vandalism. A speech on the American Indian tribal colleges is arranged topically if the speaker's main points include the history of the tribal colleges, examples of the tribal colleges, and success of the tribal colleges.

As further examples of topical organization, consider these students' experiences. Rowena enjoyed a good cup of coffee. Waiting at the airport for a connecting flight, she sipped a Starbuck's coffee and read some of their brochures about coffee. She found them interesting and thought coffee would make a good topic for an informative speech. When she returned to campus, she did some additional research and organized her speech to cover the following points:

> Organizational Patterns
> http://www.abacon.com/pubspeak/organize/patterns.html
> You can find explanations and examples of organizational patterns for speeches on this Allyn & Bacon Web site. It also provides activities and exercises to assist you in applying various types of organizational strategies. In addition, you can access complete written texts of speeches and listen to *RealAudio* examples.

Specific Purpose: To inform the audience on the types and tastes of coffee.

Key Ideas:
I. Types of coffee
   A. Dark roasts
   B. Blends
   C. Decaffeinated
   D. Specialties

topical division: organizes a speech according to aspects, or subtopics, of the subject.

    II. Tastes of coffee
       A. Acidity
       B. Aroma
       C. Body
       D. Flavor

Rodney, an avid golfer, followed with interest the debate about whether the city should build a new golf course. He collected newspaper editorials, letters to the editor, news reports, and articles that discussed the impact golf courses had on communities similar to his. He discovered many opinions and statistics as to how golf courses affected a city's economic development, tax base, population growth, racial and economic diversity, housing patterns, and wildlife sanctuaries. Rodney organized these and other issues and used a threefold topical organization.

Specific Purpose: To inform the audience on the impact of golf courses on communities.

Key Ideas: I. Sociological effects
          II. Environmental effects
         III. Economic effects

As these examples suggest, topical organization is particularly appropriate as a method of narrowing broad topics, and that may explain its popularity and widespread use. In addition to helping you stay within your time limits, the topical pattern is also attractive because it lets you select subtopics to match your own interests and the interests and needs of your audience.

Chronological Division

The **chronological division** pattern follows a time sequence. Topics that begin with phrases such as "the steps to" or "the history of" are especially appropriate to this organization. Examples of such topics might include the history of your university, the biography of author Toni Morrison, the stages of intoxication, the process of silk screening, steps to getting your first job, or how a product is marketed.

The following ideas are developed chronologically.

Specific Purpose: To inform the audience of the evolution of the piano.

Key Ideas: I. The clavichord
          II. The harpsichord
         III. The piano

Specific Purpose: To inform the audience of Elisabeth Kübler-Ross's five stages of dying.

Key Ideas: I. Denial
          II. Anger
         III. Bargaining
         IV. Depression
         V. Acceptance

Specific Purpose: To inform the audience of the steps to a successful job interview.

Key Ideas: I. Prepare thoroughly.
          II. Arrive promptly.
         III. Enter confidently.
         IV. Communicate effectively.
         V. Follow up immediately.

chronological division: organizes a speech according to a time sequence.

Chronological organization works best if you are explaining procedures or processes. A simple and familiar example of chronological organization is a recipe. Any well-written recipe is organized in a time sequence: First, make sure that you have these ingredients; second, preheat the oven; and so forth. For her speech on coffee, used earlier as an example of topical organization, Rowena could have organized her ideas chronologically if her main points were (1) selecting the coffee, (2) grinding the coffee, (3) brewing the coffee, (4) serving the coffee, and (5) storing unused coffee.

Although the key ideas of a speech should follow a single method of division, you can use another pattern as you develop one of the key ideas. For example, a speech on ventriloquism could be divided topically to include (1) the history of ventriloquism, (2) the types of ventriloquism, and (3) the psychology of ventriloquism. Developing the first idea, however, is best accomplished by a chronological format: The speaker could discuss the history of ventriloquism beginning in Ancient Greece and then show its development in the Middle Ages, the Renaissance, and in modern times.

Spatial Division

You use **spatial division** when your main points are organized according to their physical proximity or geography. This pattern is appropriate for a speech discussing the parts of an object or a place. For example, a speech on the Mazda Miata might discuss the engine, the interior, and the body exterior.

Other examples of spatial division are:

Specific Purpose: To inform the audience about the halls and palaces of the Forbidden City in Beijing, China.

Key Ideas: I. The Halls of Harmony

            II. The Palace of Heavenly Purity

          III. The Palace of Earthly Tranquility

         IV. The Hall of the Cultivation of the Mind

Specific Purpose: To inform the audience of the parts of the U.S. National Holocaust Memorial Museum.

Key Ideas: I. Four classrooms, two auditoriums, and two galleries for temporary exhibits occupy the lower level.

           II. The permanent exhibit occupies four floors of the main building.

        III. The library and archives of the U.S. Holocaust Research Institute occupy the top floor.

spatial division: organizes a speech according to the geography or physical structure of the subject.

speaking with confidence

I used to consider myself organized, but after this class I'm pretty sure that I've made major improvements that I didn't even know I needed. Before, I *kinda* knew what I wanted to say, and I had an *idea* how to say it. Now, using the 4 S strategy, I know *exactly* what I want and need to say to get my point across, and I know *exactly* how to say it in a straightforward manner. Just knowing that everyone could follow where I was going in my speech really helped lessen my nervousness and boost my confidence. The great thing is that I know that the 4 S's will help me organize other things as well, such as term and research papers.

—Jennifer A. Brown, San Antonio College

You would choose a **causal division** pattern when you want to trace a condition or action from its causes to its effects, or from effects back to causes. Medical topics, in which a speaker discusses the symptoms and causes of a disease, can be easily organized using this method of division. Informative speeches on topics such as hurricanes, lightning, earthquakes, and other natural phenomena may also use this pattern. The following speech outline illustrates the causal pattern.

Specific Purpose: To inform the audience about the effects and causes of sports-victory riots.

Key Ideas: I. Effects
    A. Death and injuries
    B. Vandalism
    C. Law enforcement costs

   II. Causes
    A. The competitive nature of sports
    B. Mob psychology
    C. Unfavorable economic conditions
    D. Inadequate police presence

Because the causal pattern may be used any time a speaker attributes causes for a particular condition, it is suitable for persuasive as well as informative speeches. A speaker could attempt to prove that certain prescription drugs are, in part, responsible for violent behavior among those who use them; that the availability of handguns fosters needless death; that televising executions would lead to a call for an end to capital punishment; or that new antibiotic-resistant bacteria are increasing infections once thought to be under control. The causal pattern would work well for speeches on any of these topics.

causal division: organizes a speech from cause to effect, or from effect to cause.

Dynamic speakers combine words and gestures to provide signposts that guide listeners through their speeches.

Pro–Con Division

The **pro–con division** presents both sides of an issue. You explain the arguments for a position and the arguments against. Because it is balanced in perspective, this pattern is more appropriate for an informative speech than a persuasive one. After discussing each side of an issue, however, you may choose to defend the stronger position. In this case, your division becomes *pro–con–assessment*, a pattern more appropriate for a speech to persuade than a speech to inform.

Brian decided to inform his classmates on "snapping." Also known as "cracking," "dissing," and "playing the dozens," this game of insults is part of African-American history and culture. In the book *Snaps*, Brian found examples of this war of words, such as Quincy Jones's snap: "Your house is so small, you have to go outside to change your mind."

At first, Brian thought he'd use a topical division and discuss (1) the history of snaps, (2) how the game is played, (3) common topics, and (4) sample snaps. As he continued to research his topic, however, he discovered that there is a lively debate as to whether snapping is constructive or destructive. Brian decided to use a pro–con division to tell his listeners about the debate:

> I. Snapping should be encouraged.
>   A. It is part of African-American history and culture.
>   B. It is a nonviolent way of expressing hostility.
>   C. It encourages imagination and creative wordplay.
> II. Snapping should be discouraged.
>   A. It is demeaning.
>   B. It can provoke violence.
>   C. There are better ways of expressing anger.

An advantage of the pro–con pattern is that it sets an issue in its broader context and provides balance and objectivity. A disadvantage, however, is the time required to do this. You need plenty of time to discuss both sides of an issue in sufficient detail. Therefore, you will probably want to use this strategy only in one of your longer speeches for this class. If you do not devote sufficient time to each idea, a pro–con or pro–con–assessment development may seem simplistic or superficial to your audience.

The following outlines demonstrate pro–con analyses of two controversial issues.

Specific Purpose: To inform the audience of the arguments for and against an increase in the minimum wage.

Key Ideas: I. Increasing the minimum wage would be beneficial.
>   A. The number of poor would decrease.
>   B. The number of people on welfare would decrease.
>   C. The concept of social justice would be affirmed.
> II. Increasing the minimum wage would be harmful.
>   A. Unemployment would increase.
>   B. Inflation would increase.
>   C. Business bankruptcies would increase.

Specific Purpose: To inform the audience of the pros and cons of limiting campaign contributions by political action committees (PACs).

Key Ideas: I. Limitations on PAC money are desirable.
>   A. PAC money undermines the concept of equal representation.
>   B. PAC money undermines the concept of local representation.
>   C. PAC money promotes public cynicism.
> II. Limitations on PAC money are undesirable.
>   A. Limitations would decrease political participation.
>   B. Limitations would strengthen the advantage of the incumbent.
>   C. Limitations would violate the right of free expression.

pro–con division: organizes a speech according to arguments for and against some policy, position, or action.

Mnemonic or Gimmick Division

A final organizational strategy you can consider for a speech to inform is **mnemonic or gimmick division.** The most common use of this strategy develops and words the key ideas in such a way that the first letter of each key idea forms a word. As a student, you have been using gimmicks for years to help you retain information you need to know. In elementary school, you may have learned to spell *geography* by memorizing the sentence, "George Eliot's old grandmother rode a pig home yesterday." In a science class, you may have memorized the order of colors in the visible spectrum by remembering the name Roy G. Biv: red-orange-yellow-green-blue-indigo-violet.

Gimmicks work so well as memory devices that even advertisers and public service groups occasionally use them. If you can recall what the "four C's" of diamond grading refer to, you probably memorized that information according to a gimmick. The four C's stand for cut, color, clarity, and carat weight. We have heard several students use this gimmick to organize informative speeches on diamonds.

Another student, Heather, spoke on the topic of breast cancer and urged her listeners to adopt a LIFE plan: to learn the facts about breast cancer, to support the need to invest more resources for research, to follow through with monthly self-examinations, and to encourage others to do the same. She concluded her speech with the statement: "[Y]ou need to adopt plans like LIFE—L–Learn, I–Invest, F–Follow through, and E–Encourage—to prevent breast cancer from taking your life or that of someone you love."[2]

> **Applying Mnemonics**
> http://www.demon.co.uk/mindtool/memory.html
> To learn more about memory techniques and a variety of mnemonic devices that you could use to organize a speech or to study, visit this site. Its links to brief articles give you access to methods of improving your memory.

If you were giving a speech explaining how to improve listening, you could use the gimmick developed by Robert Montgomery (giving him credit in your speech, of course).[3] Montgomery suggests six guidelines for better listening:

L — Look at the other person.
A — Ask questions.
D — Don't interrupt.
D — Don't change the subject.
E — Express emotions with control.
R — Responsively listen.

No doubt, the word *ladder* would help you remember your major points as you prepared and delivered such a speech. More important, though, the gimmick would help your listeners retain what you had said.

At times, the gimmick pattern of organizing a speech may seem corny or trivial to you. If you feel that way about this pattern, you probably should avoid it, as your speech delivery may seem self-conscious. When used well and with confidence, however, the gimmick helps your audience remember not only what points you have covered, but also the order in which you have covered them. That is a major accomplishment! In the next section of this chapter, we use a gimmick as we introduce you to our "4 S's" of developing the ideas of the speech. See if it helps you remember these important points.

Problem–Solution Division

The **problem–solution division** is a simple, rigid, organizational approach for a persuasive speech. In this approach the major divisions of your speech and their order are predetermined: You first establish a compelling problem and then present a convincing solution. Because you advocate a plan of action, this method is by nature persuasive.

mnemonic or gimmick division: organizes a speech according to a special memory device, such as alliteration, rhyme, or initial letters that spell a word.

problem–solution division: a rigid organizational pattern that establishes a compelling problem and offers one or more convincing solutions.

A speaker discussing rape prevention could divide the problem area into physical and psychological effects of rape. The solution phase could include a six-step plan to prevent rape. Speeches that call for a law or some action often use a problem–solution format, as in the next example:

Specific Purpose: To persuade the audience to support reform of our national park system.

Key Ideas: I. Our national parks are threatened.
         A. Political influence is a threat.
         B. Environmental pollution is a threat.
         C. Inadequate staffing is a threat.
      II. Our national parks can be saved.
         A. The National Park Service should have greater independence.
         B. Environmental laws should be stricter.
         C. Funding should be increased.

A common alternative to the problem–solution division is to divide the speech into a discussion of problems, causes, and solutions. Notice how Matthew uses this approach:

Specific Purpose: To persuade the audience that involuntary psychiatric commitment laws should be reformed.

Key Ideas: I. The problems caused by involuntary commitment laws are serious.
         A. Many are potential victims of being wrongfully committed.
            1. The elderly are especially at risk.
            2. The poor are at risk.
            3. All of us are at risk.
         B. Victims face physical and financial dangers.
      II. Two factors perpetuate these problems.
         A. Medicare policies indirectly encourage hospitals to commit patients regardless of their actual health.
         B. Involuntary commitment laws are too vague.
    III. To remedy this problem, we must act on three levels.
         A. The federal government must reform involuntary commitment procedures.
         B. The psychiatric industry must establish greater control over mental hospitals.
         C. We, as individuals, must take action as well.[4]

Need–Plan Division

The **need–plan division** is a variation of the problem–solution division. This fourfold approach (1) establishes a need or deficiency in the present system, (2) presents a proposal to meet the need, (3) demonstrates how the proposal satisfies the need, and (4) suggests a plan for implementing the proposal. Business executives and managers often intuitively employ the need–plan organizational strategy. For example, a company president informs the board of directors of the problem of being located in a town not having an airport. Documenting a loss of sales due to unnecessary driving time, the president proposes relocating company headquarters to a city having a major airport. This would permit the company to cover more territory without expanding its sales force. Finally, the president distributes to the board a detailed plan of action for selecting the appropriate city for relocation.

Salespeople also use the need–plan strategy. They demonstrate or create a need, supply the product or service to meet that need, demonstrate or describe how well it will work, and often even arrange an easy payment plan to help guarantee your purchase. This fundamental sales approach is prevalent for one simple reason: It works! You can use this strategy when you want to prompt an audience to action.

need–plan division: a variation of problem–solution organization that (1) establishes a need or deficiency, (2) offers a proposal to meet the need, (3) shows how the plan satisfies the need, and (4) suggests a plan for implementing the proposal.

Suppose the specific purpose of your speech is to persuade your audience that employers should provide health promotion programs for their employees. Using the need–plan pattern, you could make four arguments. First, employee illness results in absenteeism, lost productivity, and increased health care costs. Second, employers should establish on-site health and fitness centers for their employees. Third, when health promotion programs have been tried, they have reduced absenteeism, increased productivity, and capped health care costs. As your final step, you could suggest an implementation strategy to include exercise and conditioning programs, alcohol- and drug-awareness education, stress-management workshops, antismoking clinics, and health status testing and evaluation.

Develop the Key Ideas

Assume that your speech is divided into the key ideas, that you have selected the most appropriate pattern to organize them, and that you have decided their order in the speech. Now you need to develop each major point. Obviously, the number of major points you can develop in a speech depends on the time you have been allocated to speak, the complexity of the topic, and the audience's level of education and knowledge of the subject. There is no fixed rule, but most speech instructors recommend that you develop at least two but not more than five main points. Many speakers find that a three-point structure works best.

Regardless of the number of points you select, your responsibility is to explain and support each one sufficiently. The organizational strategy we suggest is one we call the "4 S's." Your listeners will better comprehend and remember your speech if you *signpost*, *state*, *support*, and *summarize* each idea.

The "4 S" Strategy of Developing Key Ideas	
1. Signpost the idea.	3. Support the idea.
2. State the idea.	4. Summarize the idea.

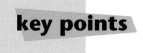

key points

Signpost the Idea

Just as a highway signpost tells travelers where they are in their journey, so a signpost in a speech tells the audience where they are in the speaker's message. A **signpost** is a word such as *initially, first, second*, and *finally*. Signposts enable listeners to follow your organizational pattern and hence increase the likelihood that they will remember your key ideas.

State the Idea

Each major idea needs to be worded precisely and with impact. In her persuasive speech, mentioned earlier, Esperanza argued the benefits of a multicultural college experience. Her specific purpose was to persuade the audience that ethnic studies (ES) courses should be required for all students. Her organizing question was, "Why should all students be required to take ES courses?" Using a topical organization, Esperanza presented three reasons to support her proposal. Before we tell you how she actually worded those ideas, let's take a look at how a less experienced student might have stated them:

1. ES courses promote cultural awareness.
2. I would like to discuss ES courses and what research and expert opinions says about the way they affect conflict that may be ethnic or racial.
3. Third, social skills.

signpost: numbers (*one*) or words (*initially, second,* or *finally*) that signal the listener of the speaker's place in the speech.

Do these points seem related to each other? Are they easy to remember? No, they're a mess!

To avoid clutter, keep the following suggestions in mind when wording your key ideas.

1. *Main headings should clearly state the point you will develop.* The first statement listed on the previous page does that; the others do not.

2. *Main headings should usually be worded as complete sentences.* Think of the main heading as a statement that you will prove with your supporting materials. Listeners would probably remember the wording of statement 1 on the previous page. As a result, they would remember the point of the speaker's evidence. That is not true of either of the other two statements.

3. *Main headings should be concise.* You want listeners to remember your key ideas. The first statement is easier to remember than the second. The third statement is the shortest, but it isn't a complete sentence. Remembering it doesn't help you understand the point the speaker made.

4. *Main ideas should be parallel to other main ideas.* Parallel wording gives your speech rhythm and repetition, two qualities that help listeners remember your points.

5. *Main ideas should summarize the speech.* When you state your main points, listeners should see how those points answer the organizing question and contribute to achieving your specific purpose.

Now let's see how Esperanza worded each of her key ideas.

Specific Purpose: To persuade the audience that ES courses should be required for all students.

Key Ideas: I. ES courses promote cultural awareness.
              II. ES courses reduce ethnic and racial conflict.
             III. ES courses improve social skills.

Each of these main headings clearly states a distinct point that Esperanza will argue. Each statement is a concise, complete sentence. All three sentences are grammatically parallel. Notice, too, that each of the three key ideas directly answers Esperanza's organizing question: Why should ES courses be required for all students?

You can usually accomplish the first two S's, signposting and stating your idea, in one sentence. Suppose the specific purpose of your speech is to persuade the audience to oppose mandatory drug testing in the workplace. If you say, "The first reason mandatory drug testing is harmful is that it is cost-prohibitive," you are signposting—"first"—and stating your idea—"mandatory drug testing is cost-prohibitive."

An alternative to introducing your key idea as a declarative sentence is to ask a question. For example, the specific purpose of Elly's speech was "to persuade the audience that the U.S. should continue to fund the space station *Freedom.*" She organized her supporting materials to answer three questions: (1) What will we gain scientifically? (2) What will we gain technologically? (3) What will we gain economically? She introduced each of these ideas with a signpost, for example: "A third question we must answer to determine the merits of the space station is: What do we have to gain economically?" She was then ready to answer that question using various types of supporting materials.

Support the Idea

This third S is the meat of the 4 S's. Once you have signposted and stated the idea, you must support it. Several categories of supporting materials are at your disposal, limited only by the amount of research you have done and by time limits on your speech. Some of those categories of supporting materials, discussed in detail in Chapter 8, are examples, definitions, comparisons, and statistics.

How would you support your statement that mandatory drug testing is cost-prohibitive? Your strongest form of support will likely be statistics—statistics on the average cost of a single drug screening test, estimates of the number of people currently employed in the United States, and projections of the total cost of testing the entire American workforce for drug use. The figures will be high and will serve as persuasive support for your claim.

Notice how Mike applied the first 3 S's in this section of his speech:

> When prescription drug cartels switch our prescriptions, it hurts us in two ways. First, prescription drug switching is harmful to your health. A November 4, 1997, report from CNN explains that our health insurance companies are allied with health maintenance organizations, or HMOs, and pharmacy benefit managers, or PBMs. The result, according to the October 4, 1997, *New York City Public Advocate,* [is that] almost half of all available prescription drugs are limited by each individual HMO's approved list. So if you end up getting prescribed a drug not on your HMO's list, you'll get your HMO's closest equivalent. As the March 15, 1998, *Observer* states, though 80 percent of all prescription drug switches will not harm a patient, they may not help them. Well, this puts us in danger, because our new drug may not cure our problem. And for at least 20 percent of us, the side effects caused by the new drug could be worse than our original ailment. Take Marie Williams, a school bus driver in Richmond, Virginia. Last January, her pharmacist told her that in order to stay covered Marie would need to begin taking Pritivil instead of Zestril. Because Marie couldn't afford the $208 uninsured bottle of Zestril, she went with the cheaper Pritivil. Three days later she blacked out as she pulled out of her school bus parking lot due to an adverse drug reaction with her appropriate substitute. Motivated by the fear of cost, patients like Marie Williams are forced to accept drug switches.[5]

Summarize the Idea

A summary at the end of each major division helps wrap up the discussion and refocus attention on the key idea. These periodic summaries may be as brief as one sentence. Avoid "Forrest Gump" summaries, however: "That's all I have to say about that." Early in the course our students sometimes summarize a point by saying, "So I've told you a little about ___." What you say in these summaries within the body needs to be more substantial and more varied than that. To continue with our drug testing example, you could summarize your first subpoint by saying, "Clearly, then, the enormous costs of mandatory drug testing would make it an unreasonable burden on the economy." Such a statement reinforces your point by repeating it—"the cost of drug testing would be too high"—and also provides a note of closure, suggesting that you have said all you plan to about the economics of mandatory drug testing. Now you are ready to introduce your second point, that drug testing results in lost work time—again by signposting, stating, supporting, and summarizing.

If you introduced your idea as a question, your summary should provide the answer. Remember, your point is lost if the audience remembers only your question; they must remember your answer. Elly summarized her point this way: "So the answer to our third question is clear and convincing. What do we have to gain economically from continued funding of the space station? A brighter economic future for American workers, American communities, and the American economy."

For an informative speech assignment requiring the use of visual aids, our student Jennifer decided to speak about Victorian homes, America's "painted ladies." Using spatial organization, she focused her speech on interior details and decoration, taking her listeners on a "virtual tour" of a Victorian home. To illustrate the maximum number of

> The *first* room we will visit on our tour of a Victorian home is *the parlor, the woman's domain.* With the growing middle class, Victorian women were expected to be the artistic hearts of the home, and they adopted many of the decorative details of European gentility.
>
> The parlor in Conglomeration House is done in the Rococo revival style, which is almost exclusively used in interior design. In their book *The Secret Lives of Victorian Homes,* Elan and Susan Zingman-Leith, who restore Victorian houses, give us this wonderful example of this style. [Jennifer shows the photograph.] Typical of the Rococo theme, the walls are painted white or a pastel color and are broken into panels decorated with wooden moldings or even artwork painted directly onto the wall. Around the windows and ceiling are intricately carved wooden details that are influenced by botanical or seashell designs. These are painted to match the color of the walls, but are heavily accented with gilt, or gold-colored paint. Following the pale color scheme, the mantle is made of marble. It is also intricately carved in a botanically inspired design and has cherubs worked into it as well.
>
> So the parlor gives us a wonderful example of the Rococo revival architectural style: very feminine, very ornate, and very French.
>
> In sharp contrast to the parlor is the library, the man's retreat in the home. This is the second room we will visit on our tour.

Signpost of key idea

Statement of key idea

Support for key idea

(example)

(citation)
(source)

(visual example)

(definition)

Summary of key idea

Transition to second key idea

interior styles, she called her imaginary dwelling "Conglomeration House," and used a series of enlarged photographs to depict a different style in each room. Her first photograph is shown on page 213. In the excerpt from her speech above, notice how Jennifer applied the 4 S's to her first main point.

We believe that use of the 4 S's is fundamental to effective organization within the body of any speech. As you begin to master and apply this four-step strategy, it may seem to be a cookie-cutter approach to public speaking. It *is* exactly that. The 4 S's are to speech organization what the required movements are to gymnastics—basics that you must learn before you are able to develop your own style or flair. As you master the 4 S's and gain confidence in public speaking, clear organization will become almost a reflex reaction performed without conscious effort. As your ability to organize ideas clearly becomes second nature to you, you will find that the structure of your thinking, writing, and speaking have greatly improved.

Connect the Key Ideas

A speech is composed of key ideas, and you have just seen how to develop each one according to the 4 S approach. Those key ideas form the building blocks of your speech. In order for your speech to hang together, however, you must connect those ideas, just as a mason joins bricks and stones with mortar. A speaker moves from one idea to the next—puts mortar between the units—with the aid of a transition. A **transition** is a statement connecting one thought to another. Without transitions, the ideas of a speech are introduced abruptly. As a result, the speech lacks a smooth flow of ideas and sounds choppy.

transition: a statement that connects parts of the speech and indicates the nature of their connection.

To introduce listeners to Victorian interior decorating styles, Jennifer, a student speaker, led them on virtual "walks" through photos of period rooms such as this Rococco revival parlor.

A transition not only connects two ideas but also indicates the nature of the connection between the ideas. Transitions are usually indicated by *markers,* words or phrases near the beginning of a sentence that indicate how that sentence relates to the previous one.[6] Transitions can indicate four basic types of connections: complementary, causal, contrasting, and chronological.

A **complementary transition** adds one idea to another, thus reinforcing the major point of the speech. Typical transitional markers for complementary transitions include:

also	likewise
and	next
in addition	not only
just as important	

Each of the following transitions uses the complementary approach to reinforce the speaker's thesis.

> Not only does PAC money undermine the concept of equal representation, it also undermines the concept of local representation.

> It is clear, then, that golf courses have sociological effects on communities where they are located. Just as important, however, are their environmental effects.

> Vocal cues, however, are not the only source of information that may help you determine if someone is lying. You may also look for body cues.

A **causal transition** emphasizes a cause-and-effect relation between two ideas. Words and phrases that mark a causal relationship include:

as a result	consequently
because	therefore

In his speech, Victor documented problems resulting from excessive noise. As he shifted his focus from cause to effect, he used the following transition:

> We can see, then, that we live, work, and play in a noisy world. An unfortunate result of this clamor and cacophony is illustrated in my second point: Excessive noise harms interpersonal interaction.

complementary transition: adds one idea to another.

causal transition: establishes a cause–effect relation between two ideas.

A **contrasting transition** shows how two ideas differ. These transitions often use markers such as:

although	nevertheless
but	on the contrary
in contrast	on the other hand
in spite of	

Patricia used a contrasting transition in her speech on theories of alcoholism:

> Although some researchers argue that alcoholism is caused by biological factors, others reject this theory, arguing instead that the cause is cultural.

A **chronological transition** shows the time relationships between ideas, and uses words or phrases such as:

after	at last	later
afterward	at the same time	while
as soon as	before	

Will informed his classmates on the SQ3R system of studying and remembering written material. He organized his five main points around five key words: survey, question, read, recite, and review. His transitions emphasized the natural sequence of these stages, as in:

> After surveying, or overviewing, what you are about to read, you are ready for the second stage of the SQ3R system: to question.

A second example of a chronological transition is:

> If thorough preparation is the first step in a successful job interview, the second step is to arrive on time.

A good transition serves as a bridge, reminding listeners of the idea just presented and preparing them for the one to come. It smooths the rough edges of the speech and

contrasting transition: shows how two ideas differ.

chronological transition: shows how one idea precedes or follows another in time.

ethical decisions

> Rosa has delayed working on her speech until the night before it is due. She plugs into the Internet and begins to download articles relating to her topic: How to avoid harming yourself with prescription drugs. The next morning she sorts through the material, jotting down examples, statistics, and testimony she finds interesting. However, by the time she needs to leave for class, Rosa's speech is still not well organized, and she admits that her listeners may not be able to follow some of the information she plans to present. Rosa is torn between two courses of action. She does not want to get a failing grade on the speech, and she'd like to get some practice speaking in front of a group, so she is tempted to "wing it" and see what happens. "I can always clear up any confusion by answering questions later," she thinks. "After all, I have done the research." However, because she knows that some people in the audience may get lost and even misinterpret the information she presents, Rosa considers telling her instructor that she is not prepared and suffering the consequences.
>
> What would you do if you were Rosa? Would she be violating any ethical standards if she were to forge ahead and deliver her speech? Do you think that delivering a disorganized speech is an abuse of the power a speaker wields over an audience? Put your thoughts in writing, and be prepared to discuss them with your classmates.

enhances the cohesiveness of your ideas. The preceding lists of key words signal different types of transitions. However, you must do more than simply insert a word or phrase between two ideas. If you find yourself always using a single word such as *now, next,* or *OK* to introduce your ideas, you need to work on your transitions. Avoid using weak and pedestrian phrases as transitions, such as, "Moving on to my next point," or, "The next thing I would like to discuss." Instead, work on composing smooth, functional transition statements as one of our students did in the following example.

In her persuasive speech, Bonnie advocated voluntary school uniforms for students in kindergarten through high school. She previewed her ideas in her introduction by stating that pilot programs demonstrate that "voluntary uniforms would help create a safer school environment, enhance academic achievement, and promote a positive social climate." In the body of her speech, Bonnie explained and supported each of these points, connecting them by using smooth transitions. Bonnie used the following excellent transition as she moved from her first to her second idea:

> Every student has a right to learn in a safe environment, and school uniforms help eliminate one cause of school violence. But schools should do more than ensure safety, they should promote learning. A second benefit of school uniforms is that they enhance academic achievement.

As Bonnie moved from her second to her third idea, she said:

> In addition to creating a safer environment and enhancing academic achievement, voluntary school uniforms promote a positive social environment.

If you follow the guidelines and examples in this chapter, the body of your speech will be well organized. You should now know how to generate an organizing question and use it to select an organizational pattern that is appropriate to your topic, your purpose, and your audience. You should also know how to develop each main idea in the body of your speech according to the 4 S's, and how to connect those main ideas with appropriate transitions. In Chapter 10 you will learn how to extend this excellent organization to the introduction and conclusion of your speech.

Summary

Being sure of your speech organization gives you confidence as a speaker; communicating your information in a well-organized manner makes it much easier for the audience to remember what you have said. The chief goal of speech organization is to assist your listeners in understanding and retaining your information.

The three parts of a speech are the *introduction, body,* and *conclusion.* You should organize the body first because it is the most substantial part of the speech and because its content determines the content of the introduction and the conclusion.

To help you evaluate the information you have researched and select an appropriate organizational pattern, you should formulate an *organizing question.* Answering this question will tell you what main ideas and information you need in order to develop your topic for your listeners. Your answer should also suggest possible ways of organizing the body of your speech.

Depending upon your purpose in speaking, you may select any of eight organizational patterns for the body of the speech. *Topical division* narrows a broad topic by limiting it to certain subtopics chosen by the speaker. *Chronological division* organizes a historical topic or a speech explaining a process into a time sequence. *Spatial division* lets the geography or physical structure of a place or thing organize the speech for you. *Causal division* allows a speaker to explore a condition or action from its causes to its effects, or from effects back to causes. *Pro–con division* presents the arguments for and against some policy, position, or action, and with the addition of a final assessment step becomes a persuasive speech pattern. *Mnemonic or gimmick division* uses a memory device such as the letters of a word to organize key points in the speech and help the audience recall them.

Two final organizational patterns are appropriate only for persuasive speeches. *Problem–solution division* presents a compelling issue and then advocates a course of action to resolve it. *Need–plan division,* a variation of problem–solution division, establishes a need, presents a proposal for satisfying that need, demonstrates how the proposal satisfies the need, and then suggests a plan for implementing the proposal.

After choosing a general organizational pattern and establishing your main points, you are ready to organize the presentation of each major idea in the body of your speech. To do this, we recommend a memory device we call the 4 S's: *signpost* the idea, *state* the idea, *support* the idea, and *summarize* the idea. Apply these four steps to each major idea in the speech.

Each of the main points you develop needs to be connected to the others by *transitions.* Effective transitions indicate the nature of the relation between the ideas: *complementary, causal, contrasting,* or *chronological.*

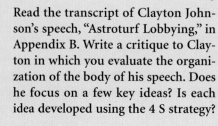

Evaluating Organization

Read the transcript of Clayton Johnson's speech, "Astroturf Lobbying," in Appendix B. Write a critique to Clayton in which you evaluate the organization of the body of his speech. Does he focus on a few key ideas? Is each idea developed using the 4 S strategy? Are these ideas connected with smooth transitions? What suggestions can you offer to improve Clayton's speech in any of these areas? Provide specific examples from the speech to support your comments.

Exercises

1. How should the organization of a speech be similar to the organization of a written essay or report? How may they differ?

2. Read the student speeches in Appendix B, and formulate organizing questions each speaker might have used.

3. Look at the list of self-generated topics in Chapter 6, and select several that would lend themselves to topical organization. What subtopics could each include?

4. Look at the list of self-generated topics in Chapter 6, and select a topic that would lend itself to spatial division. What are some subtopics a speech on this topic could include?

5. Generate a list of three medical conditions that a speaker would likely organize causally (e.g., Tourette's syndrome, Alzheimer's disease, Marfan syndrome).

6. Brainstorm for possible topics about processes of which you have a working knowledge (how to conduct a library computer search, the best way to study for an exam, etc.). Select one of these topics, and develop three to five key ideas, organizing them according to a time sequence.

7. Select one topic, and show how it could be developed using three different organizational patterns. Which do you think would make the best speech? Why?

8. What memory devices or gimmicks have you used recently to help you remember materials in this or another class? For example, you may have used "IRS" to help you remember the elements of the triangle of meaning in Chapter 1.

9. Brainstorm some speech topics that could be developed according to a pro–con division. Select one, and write a specific purpose statement. List the divisions you could use in the body of the speech.

10. Select an organizational pattern you think would be appropriate for speeches with the specific purposes listed below. Could the specific purpose be achieved using other patterns? Are there some patterns that would clearly be inappropriate?
    a. To inform the audience about relaxation techniques.
    b. To inform the audience about the history of Groundhog Day.
    c. To inform the audience about the advantages and disadvantages of raising money for charitable causes by telethons.
    d. To inform the audience about marriage rituals in various cultures.
    e. To persuade the audience that illiteracy is seriously harming national productivity.
    f. To persuade the audience that the health benefits from one exercise program are greater than those from another.

11. Using the 4 S's, develop one major point in the body of a speech. Signpost and state your key idea. Document and cite your source(s) in the support step. Summarize the idea.

12. Locate and identify the types of transitions in Lyn Carley's speech in Chapter 15. Discuss their strengths and weaknesses.

Notes

1. Robert Half, "Memomania," *American Way* 1 November 1987: 21.
2. Heather Larson, "Stemming the Tide," *Winning Orations, 1994* (Mankato, MN: Interstate Oratorical Association, 1994) 118.
3. Robert L. Montgomery, *Listening Made Easy* (New York: AMACOM, 1981) 65–78.
4. Matthew Whitley, "Involuntary Commitment Laws," *Video User's Guide for the Allyn & Bacon/AFA Student Speeches Video I* (Boston: Allyn, 1997) 43–45.
5. Mike Wagner, "The American Drug Cartel," *Video User's Guide for the Allyn & Bacon/AFA Student Speeches Video III* (Boston: Allyn, 1999) 35.
6. Glenn Leggett, C. David Mead, Melinda Kramer, and Richard S. Beal, *Prentice Hall Handbook for Writers*, 11th ed. (Englewood Cliffs, NJ: Prentice, 1991) 417–18. We have drawn on examples these authors use in their excellent section on connecting language.

I think the end is implicit in the beginning. It must be. If that isn't there in the beginning, you don't know what you're working toward. You should have a sense of a story's shape and form and its destination, all of which is like a flower inside a seed.

—Eudora Welty

chapter 10

Introducing and Concluding Your Speech

Consider some good beginnings: the first notes of a favorite piece of music; the opening shots of a favorite film; a cool early morning start for a long, summer road trip; an appetizer before a meal when you're really hungry. Each of these beginnings marks a boundary between what you've been doing or paying attention to and some new activity. Each refocuses your energy or concentration. Whether you are the speaker or a listener, the opening of a speech has the potential to achieve these same effects.

Famed Southern writer Eudora Welty was talking specifically about beginning and ending a short story or novel in the quotation at the beginning of this chapter. However, other writers and speakers share her concerns. Your first words allow you to make a positive impression on your audience, capture their attention, prepare them to listen more effectively, and enlist their support. Those first words are crucial, of course, because they can occur only once in a given speech.

In Chapter 9 you learned how to organize the most substantial part of your speech, the body. In this chapter we'll examine how you frame the body by discussing the objectives of speech introductions and conclusions as well as specific strategies you can use at these important points.

Introductions and Conclusions
http://www.abacon.com/pubspeak/organize/begend.html
Allyn & Bacon's "Write an Introduction and a Conclusion" Web site offers speakers a list of strategies for beginning a speech effectively. It also provides links to memorable quotations, meaningful statistics, and appropriate humor. With *RealAudio,* you can also listen to examples of speech introductions.

Organize the Introduction of the Speech

After you work on the body of your speech, you are ready to turn your attention to the introduction and conclusion. An introduction should be constructed to achieve five objectives: (1) Get the attention of your audience; (2) state your topic; (3) establish the importance of your topic; (4) establish your credibility to speak on your topic; and (5) preview the key ideas of your speech. Studying these objectives and the ways to achieve them will enable you to get your speech off to a clear, interesting start.

key points

Functions of a Speech Introduction

1. Get the attention of your audience.
2. State your topic.
3. Establish the importance of your topic.
4. Establish your credibility to speak on your topic.
5. Preview the key ideas of your speech.

Get the Attention of Your Audience

Your first objective as a speaker is to secure the audience's attention. If you are fortunate enough to have a reputation as a powerful, captivating speaker, you may already have the attention of your listeners before you utter your first word. Most of us, however, have not yet achieved such reputations. Consequently, it is important to get the audience quickly involved in your speech. The strategy you select will depend on your personality, your purpose, your topic, your audience, and the occasion. Your options include the following seven possible techniques for getting the audience's attention.

Question Your Audience. A speaker can get an audience involved with the speech through the use of questions, either rhetorical or direct. A **rhetorical question** stimu-

rhetorical question: a question designed to stimulate thought without demanding an overt response.

direct question: a question that asks for an overt response from listeners.

lates thought but is not intended to elicit an overt response. For example, consider the following opening questions:

- How did you spend last weekend? Watching television? Going to a movie? Sleeping late?
- If you learned that your best friend had AIDS, how would you respond?
- Do you remember when you first suspected that there really wasn't a Santa Claus?

A speaker who asks any of the above questions does not expect an overt audience response. In fact, it would probably disrupt the rhythm of the presentation if someone answered orally. A question is rhetorical if it is designed to get the audience thinking about the topic.

A **direct question** seeks a public response. Audience members may be asked to respond vocally or physically. For example, the following questions could all be answered by a show of hands:

- How many people have worked as a volunteer for some charitable group within the last year? The last six months?
- Last week the Student Government Association sponsored a blood drive. Who in this class donated blood?

Like the rhetorical question, a direct question gets the audience thinking about your topic. But the direct question has the additional advantage of getting your listeners physically involved in your speech and, consequently, making them more alert. This strategy may be especially appropriate if your class meets at 8:00 A.M. and you are the first speaker, or if you have an evening class and are the last speaker, or if you give your speech during midterm week when your classmates are especially tired.

Sometimes a direct question may invite an oral response. In his speech urging classmates to volunteer their efforts at charitable agencies, Lou discovered by a show of hands that only a few people volunteered regularly. He then asked the rest of the class why they did not. Several complained of lack of time. One person said she did not know how to locate groups that need volunteers. Lou continued, incorporating these excuses into his speech and refuting them.

When you ask a direct question and you want oral responses, you need to pause, look at your listeners, and give them sufficient time to respond. If you want your direct question answered by a show of hands, raise your hand as you end the question. In this way you indicate nonverbally how you want the question answered. If you seek and get oral responses, however, make sure that you neither lose control nor turn your public speech into a group discussion. Practice this technique as you rehearse in front of friends before making it part of your speech.

A few final cautions about using a question to get the audience's attention. First, avoid asking embarrassing questions of your listeners. "How many of you are on

(Source: Bunny Hoest and John Reiner. From *Parade* September 24, 1995. Copyright © 1999. Reprinted courtesy of Bunny Hoest and PARADE Magazine.)

"I didn't answer No. 11, because I thought it was a *rhetorical* question."

scholastic probation?" "Has anyone in here ever spent a night in jail?" Common sense should tell you that most people would be reluctant to answer direct questions such as these. Second, make sure that you don't answer your opening question nonverbally before asking it. We remember one student who lined up a number of different tennis racquets—wood, aluminum, and aluminum and graphite—on the chalk tray under the blackboard. He then turned to the audience and asked, "What would you guess is the fastest-growing sport in the United States?" By asking a silly question in a sincere manner, he got a laugh he did not expect and surely did not want. That student's experience leads us to a final caution: Don't use a question without first considering its usefulness to your speech. Many questions are creative and intriguing. Remember, asking a valid question that listeners answer either openly or to themselves gets them immediately in-

speaking with confidence

For my speech advocating the Canadian model of national health care, I began by telling a story about Little Joe, a child who jumped off a swing and hurt his arm. Because they were uninsured, the family couldn't afford adequate medical care. Through vivid narration, I tried to draw a mental picture of the accident and get my classmates emotionally involved in the speech. I wanted them to feel Little Joe's pain. How much the audience gets interested in what you're saying depends on how well you do your introduction. Using the five steps of an introduction gave me a logical format to follow and helped me feel better about my speech. I also tried to be conversational in my delivery, using everyday language so everyone would understand what I was saying and could concentrate on the story. If I can "connect" with my audience at the beginning of my speech, I feel less nervous and that helps me throughout the rest of my speech.

In my conclusion, I returned to the story of Little Joe and his injured arm and told how he ended up having his arm amputated. I tapped into those feelings created from the mental picture I used in my attention-getter. It definitely gave my speech closure and made me feel confident about my speech after I finished.

—Benjamin Wilson, Radford University

volved and thinking about your speech topic. Just don't rely on a question because you haven't developed or found a more creative attention-getter.

Arouse Your Audience's Curiosity. A lively way to engage the minds of your listeners is the technique of suspense. Get them wondering what is to come. Consider the combination of humor and suspense our student David used at the beginning of the following introduction:

> "You what? . . . When? . . . Why? . . . Here, talk to your father!"
>
> "Hey, what the hell's the matter with you, you nuts or what? . . . A perfectly good airplane for no reason at all? . . . What, are you crazy?"
>
> These were the initial responses I received from my mother and father when I called to tell them that I had just gone skydiving for the first time. Growing up I always said that you couldn't pay me to jump out of an airplane. Well, as it turned out, I ended up paying to jump out of one. This morning I would like to share with you three of the things I paid for: a three-hour class, a fifteen-minute airplane ride, and a five-minute fall to Earth.

His mother's comments made us wonder what David's subject was. By the end of his father's questions, we had an inkling, which David confirms in the final part of his introduction.

Amy and Kari chose to keep their listeners in suspense about their topics by referring to "they" and "bed partners," rather than being more specific. Only after they aroused audience curiosity did they identify their topics.

> They can smell you from 65 to 115 feet away. They have 150 different disguises. They are located in all 50 states and abroad. They also have an appetite for blood. The newest Mafia? Aliens? Nope, these monsters are mosquitoes, and they are out to get you.[1]

> Because of STDs we've been told to choose our bed partners more carefully. However, it seems that this advice has gone unheeded. It is estimated that each of us crawls into bed with about two million bed partners each night. We tend to forget about them. And we can hardly see them. But dust mites have taken up residence in our bedrooms, carpets, and homes in record number in recent years, according to the *Guardian* of August 30, 1997.[2]

You can also arouse curiosity by what you do as well as what you say. Our student David began one speech by carrying a small ice chest to a table holding a portable CD player at the front of the room. Without saying a word, he placed a folded towel on the table, opened the chest, and lifted a Bose™ speaker from the water in which it had been soaking. His classmates were completely silent. David's first words were, "I put this in here to soak last night, so it will take a few seconds to drain." By the end of his speech on outdoor speaker technology, he had hooked the speaker up to his portable CD player and played a few seconds of crystal clear music by Candy Dulfer.

Another student, speaking on sign language, began her speech in silence, signing the question, "Can you understand what I am saying?" She paused and then said, "I said, 'Can you understand what I am saying?'," signing as she spoke. She tapped her audience's feelings by arguing that they, undoubtedly, felt the same way a deaf person may feel in a hearing world.

Quotations
http://www.geocities.com/~spanoudi/quote.html
"The Quotations Homepage," an established Web site since 1994, touts more than 20,000 entries in 30 categories. Entries include quotations, definitions, and satire often appropriate for speeches and presentations, either as attention-getters, closing comments, or to emphasize a point. Though the site lacks a search engine, you can search alphabetically by topic to find a quotation of some type for almost any subject.

Stimulate Your Audience's Imagination. Another way to engage the minds of your listeners is to stimulate their imaginations. To do this, you must know what referents they share, and this requires some good audience analysis on your part. Notice in the following example how Patricia introduces her topic by relating a personal experience with which many in the audience could probably identify:

> I can remember as a child the excitement of swinging high on the swings, walking on the teeter totter to balance it, and playing squeeze the lemon on the slide at recess. I can also remember breaking my nose because I was standing too close to the teeter totter, falling off the slide to lie unconscious for half an hour, and spraining my neck after falling off the monkey bars. All of these incidents left me a little bruised and feeling stupid for being such a klutz, but nothing a trip to the hospital couldn't fix. Unfortunately, not all children are as lucky as I was.[3]

Noting that 200,000 children suffer injuries caused by playground equipment each year, Patricia then discussed the reasons and remedies for the problem.

Our student Lori introduced one of her speeches in the following way:

> Imagine yourself on a beach, at night. Through the moonlight you see the palm trees swaying as the warm tropical breeze comes in from the sea. There's an undercurrent of excitement as you all load into the boat. Moonlight shimmers off the waves as you approach your unmarked destination. The boat stops. Backwards, with gear intact, you fall into the pitch black water. There are no words to express the sensation of your first night dive. You hear only the sounds of your own breathing. You see only the brilliantly colored marine life that swims in and out of the scope of your flashlight; all else is a black abyss.

In spite of what she says, we would argue that Lori did find some words to express the sensation of night scuba diving. Notice her strong appeals to our senses of sight and hearing in this example. In Chapter 12, we discuss the use of language to create these and other sensory impressions in your audience.

Promise Your Audience Something Beneficial. We listen more carefully to messages that are in our self-interest. In Chapter 5, we recommended that you consider your listeners' needs using Maslow's hierarchy or the VALS2 typology. If you can promise your audience something that meets one or more of their needs, you secure their attention very quickly. For example, beginning your speech with the statement, "Every person in this room can find a satisfying summer internship related to your major field of study" immediately secures the attention of your listeners—at least those not currently working in their dream jobs. Other effective examples are ones in which a speaker promises that her information can save audience members hundreds of dollars in income tax next April, or in which a speaker says, "The information I will give you in the next ten minutes will help you buy an excellent used car with complete confidence." Job satisfaction, savings, and consumer confidence—the promises of these three attention-getters—are directly related to the interests of many audience members.

> Quotations
> **http://www.columbia.edu/acis/bartleby/bartlett**
> If you're searching for a profound or funny quotation to get your listeners' attention, the venerable *Bartlett's Familiar Quotations* is available at this site. You can search by keyword or author, or just browse a chronological list of authors. Keep in mind, however, that this Web version of the classic source stops at the end of the 19th century.

In addition to promising a benefit that meets your listeners' self-interests, you can also appeal to their selflessness. Notice how David taps his audience's altruism in the following speech attention-getter:

> When Tricia Matthews decided to undergo a simple medical procedure, she had no idea what impact it could have on her life. But more than a year later, when

she saw five-year-old Tommy and his younger brother Daniel walk across the stage of *The Oprah Winfrey Show,* she realized that the short amount of time it took her to donate her bone marrow was well worth it. Tricia is not related to the boys who suffered from a rare immune deficiency disorder treated by a transplant of her bone marrow. Tricia and the boys found each other through the National Marrow Donor Program, or NMDP, a national network which strives to bring willing donors and needy patients together. Though the efforts Tricia made were minimal, few Americans make the strides she did. Few of us would deny anyone the gift of life, but sadly, few know how easily we can help.[4]

Amuse Your Audience. The use of humor can be one of a speaker's most effective attention-getting strategies. Getting the audience to laugh with you makes them alert and relaxed. You can use humor to emphasize key ideas in your speech, to show a favorable self-image, or to defuse audience hostility. However, any humor you use should be tasteful and relevant to your topic or the speaking occasion. As a speaker, you must be able to make a smooth and logical transition between your humorous opening and the topic of your speech. Telling a joke or a funny story and then switching abruptly to a serious topic trivializes the topic and may offend your listeners. Imagine the effect if, as in the cartoon above, Lincoln had actually started the Gettysburg Address with, "A guy walks into a bar. . . ."

Carl Wayne Hensley, professor of speech communication at Bethel College, used humor to introduce his speech on effective communication:

> A woman went to an attorney and said, "I want to divorce my husband." Lawyer: "Do you have any grounds?" Woman: "About 10 acres." Lawyer: "Do you have a grudge?" Woman: "No, just a carport." Lawyer: "Does your husband beat you up?" Woman: "No, I get up about an hour before he does every morning." Lawyer: "Why do you want a divorce?" Woman: "We just can't seem to communicate."
>
> This woman's problem is not unique. Many husbands and wives, many parents and children, many managers and employees, many professionals and clients can't seem to communicate.[5]

Few of us are able to elicit a laugh as successfully as Robin Williams, but we can try to use tasteful humor to build a rapport with listeners and make them more responsive to our messages.

Clyde Prestowitz, Jr., president of the Economic Strategy Institute, used humor to introduce the key points of his speech on economic policy:

> Some of the major problems underlying the U.S. economy are well illustrated by a recent story about the hiker in California who ate a condor, a protected species of bird. It seems that the hiker was apprehended and taken before a judge, who sentenced him to life at hard labor. Before leaving the courtroom, however, the defendant asked the judge to listen to his side of the story because he felt there were exonerating circumstances. The hiker explained that he had been lost in the wilderness and had been hiking for three days and three nights without food or water, and just by chance had spotted this bird sitting on a rock, had thrown a rock at it, killed it and ate it, and then walked for three more days and three more nights before getting to civilization. Said the hiker, "If I hadn't eaten that bird, I wouldn't be alive to be here today." The judge responded by saying that those certainly were unusual circumstances and in view of the fact that the hiker's life had been in danger he, the judge, would suspend the sentence. The defendant thanked him and began to leave the courtroom, but as he did the judge asked, "Oh, by the way, what did that condor taste like?" The hiker paused for a moment and then responded, "Well, it was kind of between a bald eagle and a spotted owl."
>
> The point is, you see, that the judge was operating on the basis of a false premise. He was assuming that he and the hiker adhered to similar premises and views about protected species. In the same way, the United States has been operating on a basis of three false premises for most of the past forty-five years with regard to its economic policies.[6]

Notice how the speaker in each of these examples used humor to provide a smooth transition to the main topic of the speech.

Similarly, Stacey encouraged her classmates to study a foreign language, introducing her classroom speech with the following attention-getting riddle:

> What do you call someone who is fluent in many languages? A polylingual. What do you call someone who is fluent in two languages? A bilingual. What do you call someone who is fluent in only one language? An American!

This is a joke commonly told among the Japanese. Behind the apparent humor of this joke are some embarrassing truths.

Stacey combined humor and rhetorical questions to get her listeners' attention. She then discussed those "embarrassing truths" and the price we pay for speaking only one language.

Energize Your Audience. Sometimes, speakers can command attention simply by their "presence." Elizabeth Dole demonstrated this at the Republican national convention in August 1996, doing what no featured convention speaker had ever before done. She moved from behind the lectern on the stage and walked among people on the convention floor, speaking without using notes or the TelePrompTer. When the radio frequency microphone she was using failed at one point, Dole didn't miss a beat. She accepted another microphone handed to her as naturally as a relay runner accepting a baton. Although not everyone can achieve such dynamism, most speakers can work to enliven their delivery. A positive attitude, appropriate dress, a confident walk to the platform, direct eye contact, a friendly smile, erect posture, a strong voice, and forceful gestures give an introduction as much impact as any of the preceding strategies. Conversely, the absence of these elements can destroy the effect of even the best-worded opening statement. The advantages of an "energized" presence, however, extend far beyond a speech introduction. In Chapter 13, we give you specific suggestions for achieving a dynamic delivery throughout your speech.

Acknowledge and Compliment Your Audience. At some point in your life, you will probably be called upon to deliver a formal, public speech to an assembled group. Perhaps you will be the keynote speaker for a convention, or maybe you will accept an award from a civic group. The group inviting you to speak may even be paying you, anything from a small honorarium to a substantial fee. Such an occasion usually requires that you begin by acknowledging the audience and key dignitaries.

Notice how David Dinkins, then mayor of New York City, included his audience in the introduction of a speech he gave at the University of California at Berkeley:

> I am deeply grateful to former Chancellor Ira Heyman and his successor, Chancellor Chang-Lin Tien, for inviting me to address the distinguished students, faculty, staff, and alumni at this great center of learning, the University of California at Berkeley, a symbol of freedom for universities throughout the world.
>
> To step onto these historic grounds today is to fulfill an American pilgrimage. The most basic human impulse is to communicate; the Free Speech movement rescued the life of the mind of our country, and neither America nor the academy has been the same since.
>
> It was at Berkeley that the academy emerged as America's searing conscience; it was from Berkeley that students spread throughout the Deep South to aid the Negro struggle for civil rights; and it was again at Berkeley that the first Asian-American was appointed to lead a major American university. Congratulations, Dr. Tien.[7]

In this class, your classmates make up your audience. You have interacted with them and, by now, probably know them pretty well. To begin your speech formally by acknowledging and complimenting them would seem stiff and insincere. You should not have to compliment fellow classmates; in fact, if you have prepared well, they should be thanking you for providing excellent information. For your assigned speeches, therefore, you should probably choose one of the other attention-getting strategies.

State Your Topic

Once you have the attention of your audience, state the topic or purpose of your speech directly and succinctly. For an informative speech, your statement of purpose typically takes the form of a simple declarative sentence. "Today, I will show you how you can improve your study skills" clearly informs the audience of your topic.

This second goal of a speech introduction is vitally important, even though the actual statement of purpose will take only a few seconds for you to say. Consider the following beginning section of a speech introduction:

> How many of you have had a cholesterol count taken in the last year? Do you know what your numbers are and what they mean? It seems like we have all recently become much more aware of good cholesterol and bad, high-density lipoproteins and low-density ones, the dangers of high-fat diets and how difficult they can be to avoid in these fast-food, nuke-it-till-it's-hot times. People who never really considered exercising are spending a lot of money to join health clubs and work out. They know that a high cholesterol count can mean you are in danger of developing arteriosclerosis and finding yourself a candidate for surgery. Even if you don't have a heart attack, you may be hospitalized for one of several new procedures to clean out arteries clogged with plaque.

Now answer the following question: This speaker's purpose was to

(a) discuss the interpretation of cholesterol tests.
(b) explain sources of cholesterol in popular foods.
(c) encourage exercise as a key to reducing serum cholesterol.
(d) explain new nonsurgical procedures for opening clogged arteries.
(e) I can't tell what the speaker's purpose was.

Unfortunately, in this case, the correct answer is e. What went wrong? The speaker started off well enough by using two legitimate questions—the first direct, the second rhetorical—as an attention-getter. But then things got out of control; for almost a minute of speaking time, the speaker lapsed into a series of generalizations without ever stating the purpose of the speech. This excerpt represents a minute of wasted time! In a five- to seven-minute speech, that minute represents one-fifth to one-seventh of total speaking time. The speaker has confused the audience with vague statements and

ethical decisions

Yvonne has decided on a specific purpose for her persuasive speech: to convince her classmates that same-sex marriages should be legal. As she analyzes her audience's attitudes, she concludes that most of her classmates disagree with her position, some quite strongly. She is fearful that if she reveals her specific purpose in the introduction, many in her audience will stop listening to her speech objectively and will either begin formulating counterarguments or simply tune her out. She decides that, instead, she will delay the announcement of her purpose and present some basic criteria for a good marriage. After securing agreement on these criteria, she will then reveal her purpose for speaking—to an audience that is primed to listen.

Is Yvonne's strategy ethical? Is it acceptable for a speaker to conceal his or her purpose in an introduction in order to keep an audience's attention? If you think this strategy is legitimate, write a few examples of situations in which it would be justifiable. Try to list and explain the ethical guidelines speakers should follow in making decisions about this strategy.

has lost their confidence. The real shame is that any of the four purposes just listed could be the goal of a good speech. Prepare properly and you will know your purpose. Then, state that purpose clearly as the second step of your introduction.

Establish the Importance of Your Topic

This third goal in organizing the introduction to your speech should convince the listeners that the topic is important to them. You want to motivate them to listen further. Notice how this speaker, Suzanne, stressed the significance of her topic for her college audience in the following part of her introduction:

> For Ramsey Bittar, a typical day involves private nursing, physical therapy sessions, and communicating simple messages such as "hello" or "Mom" on his computer keyboard. Ironically, however, three years ago Bittar was a gifted chemistry student. What happened? An accident that could and should have been prevented. Three years ago Bittar was performing a dangerous chemistry experiment when his flask exploded and an artery in his neck was severed. Before paramedics were summoned, he had lost enough blood to cause serious brain damage.
>
> Ramsey Bittar is just one example of shocking lack of safety in student chemical labs. Academic laboratories. We're all familiar with them, from taking a lab class ourselves or knowing someone who did. Academic labs in high schools or universities are where curious students fearlessly learn about acids and bases or watch photos develop. The thrill of mixing a few milliliters of this with a few milliliters of that, however, easily becomes pain when a lab accident occurs.[8]

Suzanne's topic choice shows how audience-centered she is. She goes beyond that, however, to stress its significance for her listeners.

Establish Your Credibility to Speak on Your Topic

The fourth goal of a speech introduction is to establish your credibility to speak on your topic. Your listeners should understand why you selected your topic and should believe that you are qualified to speak on it. Establishing your credibility begins in the introduction and should continue throughout the rest of your speech. Introducing relevant supporting materials and citing their sources are two ways to demonstrate that you have carefully researched and considered your topic. You can also enhance your credibility by drawing on your own experience with your topic. Our student, Liz, mentioned her nursing degree and her work as a nurse in the introduction to her speech on physician-assisted suicide. In the body of her speech she also mentioned sources that she had studied in a bioethics class. We have had students who have started their own investment firms discuss the importance of early investment. A student who spoke about the importance of wearing auto safety belts reminded us of her work as an emergency medical technician. If you have a similar vantage point from which to speak on your topic, let your audience know that in your introduction.

Preview Your Key Ideas

A final objective in organizing your introduction is the **preview**, in which you "tell us what you're going to tell us." The preview, working like a map, shows a final destination and reveals how the speaker intends to get there. As a result, the audience can travel more easily through the body of the speech. A person discussing the political, economic, and medical implications of national health insurance should inform the audience of these three divisions. A speaker addressing the issue of urban decay could preview her speech by saying, "In order to better understand the scope of this problem, we must look at four measurable conditions: the unemployment rate, housing starts,

preview: a statement that orients the audience by revealing how the speaker has organized the body of a speech.

the poverty level, and the crime rate." That preview lists the four topics to be covered in the body of the speech and prepares the audience to listen more intelligently.

Preview statements are usually from one to three sentences in length. Rarely do they need to be longer. Each of the following examples is appropriately brief and specific in preparing the audience for the key ideas and the organizational pattern of the speech.

> Assuming that you have the necessary materials, the three steps to constructing a piece of stained glass are first, selecting or creating a design; second, cutting the glass; and third, assembling and fixing the individual pieces.

> An enhanced self-concept benefits us in at least three ways. Specifically, it improves our social interaction, our academic achievement, and our chances for career success.

> A person suffering from narcolepsy, then, experiences unexpected attacks of deep sleep. This little-known sleep disorder is better understood if we know its symptoms, its causes, and its treatment.

> Having a *quinceañera* serves two main functions for a young girl and her family. The first is to mark the transition from adolescence to adulthood. The second is to allow the parents to present their daughter to society.

> Today the *charreada* often draws both participants dressed in their traditional costumes and protestors carrying signs. To understand both sides of this issue, we'll look at those who say that the *charreada* is a valid sport that deserves to be practiced and at those who insist that the *charreada* is cruel and inhumane.

> To understand why some species of sharks are endangered today, let's look, first, at the myth that sharks are man-eaters. Next we'll examine the myth that sharks are good for nothing. Then we'll explore the myth that the seas are full of sharks. Finally, we'll look at what we can do to help the plight of the shark today.

> So, today, in order to better understand how the HEV [Hybrid Electric Vehicle] will revolutionize both the auto industry and our own lives we will first examine what an HEV is and how it works. Then we'll take a look at some of the differences between HEVs and other types of electric car technologies. And, finally, we'll explore some of the amazing benefits that these cars can provide, for both our planet and our pocketbooks.[9]

If you've written a thesis statement for your speech, you'll have no trouble constructing a preview statement. Preview statements, however, are often are bland and predictable. Use your creativity to accent the ideas that will follow. For example, Bond could have used the following preview statement in his speech on staged auto accidents: "To better understand this problem, we will look at the harms, costs, and solutions of staged auto accidents." Although this statement is simple and direct, it conveys little creativity. Instead, Bond opted for a longer statement to reinforce the ideas of his speech:

> To get a better understanding of this problem, however, we will initially take a crash course on the harms staged auto accidents present. We're going to shift gears and examine a few of the costs. And finally, we'll go cruising for some solutions at both the societal and the individual level.[10]

How does the introduction sound when all five of its functions are working together? Our student, Rose, showed us that she certainly knows how to develop a complete and effective introduction:

> According to an old Indian saying, every person dies three times. The first time is the moment your life ends. The second is when your body is lowered into the

ground. The third is when there is no one around to remember you. I'm going to talk to you today about death, or rather the celebration of death. This is a special celebration that comes from a Mexican tradition called *Dia de los Muertos,* or Day of the Dead. Now it may seem strange and morbid to speak of celebration and death in the same breath, but in the Mexican culture, death is embraced and worshipped just as much as life is. After I give you a little background on *Dia de los Muertos,* I'll explain the different ways this holiday is celebrated and show you some of the traditional objects used in the celebration.

Our student, Shannon, began one of his speeches in this way:

Scene one: It's late at night. You've been up since 6:00 A.M. Your roommate has the thermostat set on 102 degrees, and you need to start reading that stack of materials you copied at the library for your upcoming persuasive speech. Exhausted, you start to reach for that ice-cold bottle of Jolt Cola™ for a quick infusion of caffeine. Hold it! There may be a better alternative.

    Scene two: It's the day of your persuasive speech. As you walk to class, the stress builds. With each step, your heart beats more rapidly. By the time you arrive at your classroom, those butterflies have taken flight in your stomach. Before reaching for that bottle of Inderal™ or some other drug, stop! Just say no! There may be a better alternative.

    What is this better alternative? Is it a new, just-discovered miracle drug? Well, actually, this remedy has been around for more than 5,000 years and is still used among many cultures. This alternative form of medicine is known as aromatherapy. In its precise definition, aromatherapy is treatment by smelling some odor. *Aromatherapy Quarterly* defines this treatment as "the skillful use of essential plant oils for medical, psychological, and spiritual applications." In this speech, I will discuss three personal benefits of aromatherapy: increased alertness, reduced stress, and even weight control.

In his first two paragraphs, Shannon uses several strategies to get his audience's attention and establish the relevance of his topic to his listeners. (1) His word choice lets his listeners visualize the scenes. (2) His examples tap experiences familiar to any student in a public speaking class. (3) He arouses audience curiosity by not immediately revealing what the "better alternative" is. He heightens this suspense in the third paragraph when he asks the question,"What is this better alternative?" but does not immediately provide the answer. (4) He energizes his delivery by using language that calls for purposeful movement and gesture. He walks as he says "as you walk to class." He reaches out his hand when he says the words "reach for" and "reaching for," and then moves his hand up (creating a "stop" gesture) on the words "Hold it!" and "stop!"

Shannon finally satisfies his audience's curiosity when he introduces the topic of aromatherapy in the third paragraph. Throughout his introduction, Shannon tried to establish his credibility to speak on the topic by demonstrating: (1) preparation—he followed the steps of an introduction outlined in his textbook; (2) concern for his audience—he did not rely on his notes but interacted with his listeners and tapped experiences that were important to them; and (3) accuracy—he referred to history and quoted from a source. And at the end of his introduction he clearly previews the three ideas he will develop in the body of his speech.

Notice how Ryan used each of the five functions of an introduction in his speech on the problems of inexperienced drivers:

One warm July evening in 1996, just two months after receiving his driver's license, Dick Simmons was on his way to see his older brother at the University of Southern California. He never made it to campus. Halfway there, his brown Ford minivan swerved suddenly into oncoming traffic, killing Dick and crippling the other [passenger]. Icy roads? No. Alcohol? No. Inexperience? Yes. As his father told *Quality Progress* in January 1997, he was looking for a cassette [tape] that had fallen on the floor.

Ryan uses a dramatic example followed by a series of questions to get his listeners' attention and introduce his topic.

Ryan uses statistics to demonstrate that the problem of inexperienced drivers is everywhere and could affect all of us. He uses documentation and source citation to help establish his expertise on the topic.

Ryan previews the key ideas he will discuss in the body of his speech.

Although this may seem like an isolated incident in a far-off place, stories of undertrained and inexperienced teenage drivers happen everywhere, including your neighborhood. According to the *National Safety Council's 1996 Report,* driving accidents are the leading cause of teenage deaths in America. Unfortunately, they don't just involve teenagers. Undertrained drivers also kill over 15,000 other people annually and permanently disable some 500,000 more. Even scarier, according to the 1996 *Current Population Report,* in the next eight years the number of teenage drivers will increase 25 percent across the nation. Not only will more teenagers be driving but, considering Congress OK'd higher speed limits last summer, they'll be driving even faster. Since all of us have to share the road with these drivers, it's important that we remedy this problem now before another avoidable accident, possibly involving one of us, happens.

So in order to protect ourselves and our youth from their newfound freedom, we need to first stop and examine the threat undertrained teenage drivers pose to themselves and us; second, see why they continue to be the number one threat on the streets; and finally get a green light on how both a new program of graduated driver's licenses and our own personal involvement can make the road a safer place for all of us.[11]

If you achieve the five objectives we have outlined for a speech introduction, your audience should be attentive, know the purpose of your speech, be motivated to listen, know the major ideas you will discuss, and trust your qualifications to speak on the topic. The only remaining part of the speech is the conclusion. Although it is often briefer than the introduction, your conclusion is vitally important to achieving your desired response. The conclusion is the last section your listeners hear and see and must be well planned and carefully organized.

Organize the Conclusion of the Speech

In John Guare's play *Six Degrees of Separation,* the character Flan, a high-stakes New York art dealer, recalls learning something about art in an unexpected place:

> When the kids were little, we went to a parents' meeting at their school and I asked the teacher why all her students were geniuses in the second grade. Look at the first grade. Blotches of green and black. Look at the third grade. Camouflage. But the second grade—your grade. Matisses everyone. You've made my child a Matisse. Let me study with you. Let me into second grade! What is your secret? And this is what she said, "Secret? I don't have any secret. I just know when to take their drawings away from them."[12]

Knowing when and how to conclude your speech is an art you must master without the luxury of having someone watching over your shoulder. This last division of a speech will be easier to develop, however, if you work to achieve three goals: summarize your key ideas, activate audience response to your speech, and provide closure.

key points

Functions of a Speech Conclusion

1. Summarize your key ideas.
2. Activate audience response.
3. Provide closure.

summary: a statement or statements reviewing the major ideas of a speech.

Summarize Your Key Ideas

In the **summary** you "tell us what you told us." Of all the steps in the process of organization, this should be the easiest to construct. You have already organized the body of the speech and, from it, constructed a preview statement. The summary parallels your preview. If your speech develops three key ideas, you reiterate them. If your speech is on self-concept enhancement, for example, you may simply say, "A good self-concept, therefore, benefits us in three ways. It enhances our social interaction, our academic achievement, and our career success." A speech on dying might be summarized: "Denial. Anger. Bargaining. Depression. Acceptance. These are the five stages of dying as described by Kübler-Ross."

An excellent summary step, however, does more than just repeat your key ideas. It also shows how those ideas support the goal of your speech. Remember Stacey's humorous attention-getter to her speech encouraging her classmates to study a foreign language? In the speech she discussed three harms from the nation's failure to promote bilingualism: "First, we lose economically. . . . Second, we lose scholastically. . . . Third, we lose culturally." Notice how Stacey reiterates and reinforces these points in the summary step of her conclusion:

> Clearly, these three points show us that by being monolingual we lose *economically, scholastically,* and *culturally.* Becoming proficient in another language and its culture may help us reduce our deficit and increase our competitiveness in world trade by recognizing possible problems in marketing campaigns. We will gain intellectually by increasing our vocabulary and expanding our minds. We will gain culturally by breaking barriers and possibly eliminating misunderstandings that occur as a result of being unfamiliar with another language, its people, and its culture.

The summary step gives the listener one last chance to hear and remember the main points of your presentation. Thus, the summary step reinforces the ideas of the speech and brings it to a logical conclusion.

Activate Audience Response

What do you want your audience to do with the information you have provided or the arguments you have proved? The second function of a speech conclusion is to activate an audience response by letting your listeners know whether you want them to accept, remember, use, believe, or act upon the content of your speech. Whether your speech is informative or persuasive, you want the audience to have been involved with your information and ideas. The conclusion is your last opportunity to ensure your audience's involvement. If you have provided practical information that can make your listeners smarter, healthier, happier, or wealthier, encourage them to remember and use what they learned. If you have educated them about a problem and proposed a solution to it, remind them of the significance of not acting. If you have spoken on a topic that you find inherently interesting, hoping to generate audience interest by communicating your enthusiasm as well as your information, this is your last opportunity to invigorate or animate your listeners about the subject. Speechwriter and consultant Elinor Donahue echoes this advice:

> Be sure to wrap up with feelings as well as fact. . . . If you charge an audience with a sense of elevated purpose, if you show them possibilities for growth and new perspective, you will magnify the effect of your speech—and maybe make a difference in some lives.[13]

This second function of a conclusion should certainly do something other than say, "I hope you enjoyed my speech," or "I hope you'll find this information about Gutzon Borglum, the sculptor of Mount Rushmore, useful." Rather than saying, "I hope you'll find what I've said about the film scores of Philip Glass useful," you might say something like this: "The next time you find your attention drawn to a movie's soundtrack because you like the music or feel that it could stand on its own, think about the painstaking process of matching sight and sound that an acclaimed composer like Philip Glass has to go through."

Dan's speech argued for a moratorium on the use of electroshock weapons. He began his speech with examples of three individuals who had been tortured by these stun guns. In his conclusion, he reiterated his key ideas: "As we've seen, not only are electroshock weapons dangerous and psychologically damaging, but they have a high inherent potential for abuse. Despite all of this, they are becoming increasingly popular." Dan then tried to activate audience outrage by encouraging them to speak out:

> This is an atrocity that can no longer be allowed to continue. Until we, as a nation, speak out against this terrible abuse of human rights, people like Mediha Curabaz will be tortured by foreign secret police—using American-made weapons. Until we speak out against this cruel and unusual punishment, prisoners across our nation will meet the same cruel fate as Scott Norberg. And until we speak out for public awareness, consumers will not realize the true danger these weapons pose—and more innocent people, like baby Brandon Jordan, will become tragic victims."[14]

In his conclusion, Dan highlighted for his listeners the commitment he sought from them: to speak out for justice.

Provide Closure

While a final summary of your key ideas is important, ending a speech on the summary step is unsatisfying. Such a strategy is what we call, to borrow from Porky Pig, the "b'dee, b'dee, b'dee, that's all folks" conclusion. You should not have to tell your listeners that the speech is finished. Your wording, as well as your delivery, should make this clear.

If your summary concludes your speech *logically*, your activation and closure statements end the speech *psychologically*. An effective final statement ties the speech together and provides a strong note of finality or closure. The audience should know that you are about to finish, and they should have the feeling that you have said exactly as much as you need to say. Without resorting to saying, "In conclusion," or, "To

Providing closure means moving beyond your summary to present a satisfying conclusion to ideas or issues you have raised. Referring to your speech introduction, calling for action, or posing a provocative question are all effective strategies for ending a speech.

conclude," you should mark the end of your speech by slowing your rate, maintaining direct eye contact with your listeners, and pausing briefly before and after your final sentence.

An example from literature may clarify what we mean by a psychological conclusion. Remember for a moment Catherine and Heathcliff, the main characters in Emily Brontë's *Wuthering Heights.* Though they roamed the moors together in their youth and later fell in love, circumstances kept them apart during the rest of their lives. The book ends after both have died. Novelist and short story writer Katherine Anne Porter once wrote: "One of the most perfect and marvelous endings in literature—it raises my hair now—is the little boy at the end of *Wuthering Heights,* crying that he's afraid to go across the moor because there's a man and woman walking there."[15] The final step of your speech conclusion does not have to be dramatic, but it should seem as satisfying as Brontë's final pages.

Sometimes a speaker employs what is called a **circular conclusion,** in which the final statement echoes or refers to the attention-getting step of the introduction. Bonnie used a circular conclusion in her speech advocating voluntary school uniforms. Notice how she refers in her conclusion to the examples she presented in her attention-getter.

Attention-getting step:

In Los Angeles, a little girl dressing for school puts on her favorite red sweater. Her choice of color results in her being attacked and hit on the head with a rock. The reason: Red is the color worn by one gang, and a member of a rival gang retaliated upon seeing red.

Calvin Wash enjoys football and shows his loyalty to his favorite team by wearing a Cincinnati Bengals jacket. Calvin was shot when he tried to escape from a man who demanded his jacket.

An eighteen-year-old was shot and killed by someone who wanted his Triple F.A.T. Goose parka and his $70 Nike shoes.

There's an old saying: "Clothes make the person." One thing clothes should not do, however, is make the person a target.

Conclusion:

Currently, Virginia's House of Delegates is considering a bill that would require public schools to implement a voluntary school uniform program. I encourage you to call or write your representative and voice your support of this bill. In addition, if your local school does not already have such a program, contact the school board and urge them to implement one. Remember to tell them that voluntary school programs will help create a safer school environment, enhance academic achievement, and promote a positive social climate.

When a little girl is trying to decide what to wear to school, she shouldn't be faced with a life-or-death decision. When a boy puts on his jacket and shoes, he shouldn't be preparing for combat. A voluntary school uniform is one way of helping schools become what they should be: a place where children can learn and grow.

Our student Steve also used a circular conclusion. He began his informative speech by saying: "It is one of the most dreaded, incurable diseases facing humankind today. Everyone in this room knows someone who has it. The disease is diabetes mellitus." In his conclusion, he summarized the main points he had covered and then ended the speech this way:

At the beginning of this presentation I said that each of you knows someone who has diabetes. The reason I could say that without hesitation is that for the past ten

circular conclusion: a conclusion that repeats or refers to material used in the attention-getting step of the introduction.

years I have been an insulin-dependent diabetic taking three shots a day. The good news is that I'm able to lead almost as normal a life as each one of you. The *best* news is that each day we come closer to finding a cure!

Your final statement does not have to allude to your attention-getting step. Any of the specific techniques we discussed for gaining audience attention can help bring your speech to a strong, clear, psychologically satisfying conclusion. You can ask a question, even the same one you began with or a variation of it. Or you can answer the question you initially asked. Once you arouse your audience's curiosity in your speech, you must satisfy it in order to provide closure. You could stimulate their imaginations through vivid imagery, or promise them that the information you have provided can bring them benefits. You could conclude with a joke or humorous story relevant to your topic. Through lively delivery you could energize the audience to act on the information you have provided them. In a speech presented on more formal occasions than a classroom assignment, you may end by complimenting and thanking the audience.

All three functions of the conclusion are important. The summary step reinforces the *ideas* of the speech, while the final two functions reinforce the *impact* of the speech. Consider how Terry accomplished these three functions at the end of her persuasive speech. In the body she had discussed problems caused by the lack of adequate after-school care for older children and teenagers. She proposed expanding existing programs that had been successful in reducing crime, illegal drug use, and other social problems. These programs, she argued, could be staffed, in large part, by volunteers. In her closing statements, Terry said the following:

Terry restates her key ideas.

> We have an ongoing problem of inadequate after-school care in our country. The lack of appropriate care leaves our children vulnerable to crime and drugs, social problems which affect us all. But as responsible members of a community, we can make a difference.

Terry requests audience action.

> Every one of us is capable of planting a seed which will sprout into [an] appropriate after-school care program or volunteering to participate in an existing program. While my own children have never been left home alone, they've also never had a mother who was home waiting for them every school-day afternoon. My husband and I have taken steps to ensure their safety during the after-school hours. You can do the same thing for children in your community.

Terry provides closure.

> You know, local television stations no longer run the old public service announcement at 10 P.M., asking us if we know where our children are—perhaps because, as Jonathan Alter suggests, the question simply is no longer appropriate. But with a little help from all of us, the parents of some seven million children will be able to relax, knowing that they know the answer to today's most important question: "It's 4 P.M.; do you know where your children are?"[16]

A diagram of the individual steps in a well-organized speech would contain the following:

1. Attention-getting step
2. Statement of topic
3. Emphasis on importance of topic
4. Emphasis on speaker credibility
5. Preview
6. Body of speech
7. Summary
8. Activation of audience response
9. Closure

This is the correct sequence to follow as you deliver a speech. In your preparation, however, you will follow the sequence we discussed in Chapter 9 and in this chapter. You

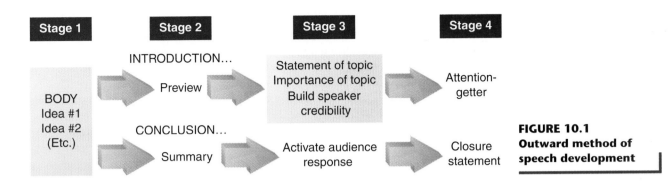

Stage 1	Stage 2	Stage 3	Stage 4

BODY
Idea #1
Idea #2
(Etc.)

INTRODUCTION...
Preview

Statement of topic
Importance of topic
Build speaker
credibility

Attention-
getter

CONCLUSION...
Summary

Activate audience
response

Closure
statement

**FIGURE 10.1
Outward method of
speech development**

should prepare the body of your speech first. Some instructors recommend that you develop your introduction next and your conclusion last. Others suggest that you prepare your introduction last. Remember, there is no one correct way of constructing a speech. Select the method that works best for you.

We suggest an alternative strategy that is divided into four stages (see Figure 10.1). In Stage 1, you construct the body of your speech, determining the key ideas and developing them using the 4 S's. After completing this stage, you then work outward.

Rather than going just to the introduction or just to the conclusion, you work on both simultaneously, focusing on elements that have similar purposes. With your key ideas determined, you can easily word your preview and summary statements. These two objectives are similar because they highlight key ideas of a speech. As you complete Stage 2, you have fulfilled the overall organizational strategy we mentioned at the beginning of Chapter 9: You are ready to "tell us what you're going to tell us," "tell us," and "tell us what you told us."

In Stage 3, you decide how you will state your topic, explain its importance, build your credibility to speak on it, and activate audience response. This should not be difficult. You have already thought through these steps when you selected your topic. Your choice of words and supporting materials should lead naturally to your preview statement, which you have already worded. In the final stage of your preparation, you devise your attention-getting and closure statements, two crucial steps at the furthest extremes from the speech body. Developing the attention-getter and the final statement at the same time should increase the total unity of the speech, and this is particularly important if you are using a circular conclusion.

Speakers who begin preparing speeches by starting with the introduction often end up trying to fit the rest of their speech to the introduction. Speakers who write their introduction, body, and conclusion separately often produce three parts rather than a unified whole. The outward method of development we suggest helps you avoid these pitfalls and enables you to present your ideas clearly, cohesively, and convincingly.

Summary

The introduction and conclusion are brief parts of the speech, but they must be well organized and practiced since they are, respectively, your first and last chances to create a favorable impression for yourself or your topic. The introduction should achieve five goals: (1) Get the attention of your audience; (2) state your topic or purpose; (3) stress the importance or relevance of your topic; (4) establish your credibility to speak on your topic; and (5) preview the key ideas you will be developing in the body of the speech. To get your audience's attention, you can question your listeners, arouse their curiosity, stimulate their imaginations, promise them something beneficial, amuse them, energize them, or acknowledge and compliment them. An effective conclusion must do three things: (1) Summarize your key ideas, or bring your speech to a logical conclusion; (2) secure your listeners' commitment to your information and ideas; and (3) provide closure, or bring the speech to a satisfying psychological conclusion.

Rather than organizing the introduction, body, and conclusion of your speech separately, we recommend that you organize the body first and then work outward from that center. Once you have determined the main ideas of the body, you can easily construct your preview statement for the introduction and your summary statement for the conclusion. Next, amplify your introduction by stating your purpose clearly, emphasizing the significance of your topic, and building your credibility to speak on your topic. Decide how to activate an audience response in your conclusion. Finally, work on your attention-getter and your closure statement simultaneously to help ensure that your speech holds together as a satisfying, cohesive unit.

If you follow the suggestions in Chapters 9 and 10, your speech should be well organized. That clear organization will, in turn, make your information easier for the audience to remember, and that's a major goal of public speaking.

Evaluating Introductions

You have just been appointed judge for a public speaking contest. Your task is to present the award for "best introduction" from among the four student speeches in Appendix B. Read these speeches, and evaluate their introductions using the guidelines presented in this chapter. Select the introduction you think is best, and explain the reasons for your selection.

Exercises

1. Evaluate the openings of chapters you have read thus far in this book. Which are most and least successful at getting your attention? What made them effective or ineffective?

2. Select a magazine, and examine the various ways journalists begin their stories. Which of the seven attention-getting devices discussed in this chapter do the stories employ? Are there other attention-getting techniques you can identify?

3. Examine the attention-getting step of Emelyn Carley's speech in Chapter 15. Rewrite the attention-getter using two strategies other than the one Carley uses.

4. Suppose the specific purpose of a speech is to persuade an audience to contribute money for needed playground equipment for a local elementary school. Write a statement establishing the importance and relevance of the topic for each of the following audiences:
   a. Parents of children who attend the school
   b. Senior citizens on limited, fixed incomes whose children and grandchildren no longer attend the school
   c. Single college students

5. Locate the preview statements in the introductions of the student speeches in Appendix B.

6. Prepare three introductions for the same body of content. Discuss the advantages and disadvantages of each. Select the one you think is best and explain why.

7. Rewrite the closure statement of Emelyn Carley's speech in Chapter 15 using two strategies other than the one Carley uses. Discuss the strengths and weaknesses of each closure statement. Which closure strategy do you prefer? Why?

8. Prepare three conclusions for the same body of content. Discuss the advantages and disadvantages of each. Select the one you think is best, and explain why.

9. How are the introduction and conclusion of a speech similar? What purposes do they have in common?

 Notes

1. Amy Jones, "The Big Sting," *Winning Orations, 1998* (Mankato, MN: Interstate Oratorical Association, 1998) 52.

2. Kari Lou Frank, "Dust Mites," *Video User's Guide for the Allyn & Bacon/AFA Student Speeches Video III* (Boston: Allyn, 1999) 54.

3. Patricia A. Cirucci, "Grounds for Disaster," *Winning Orations, 1991* (Mankato, MN: Interstate Oratorical Association, 1991) 102.

4. David Slater, "Sharing Life," *Winning Orations, 1998* (Mankato, MN: Interstate Oratorical Association, 1998) 63.

5. Carl Wayne Hensley, "What You Share Is What You Get: Tips for Effective Communication," *Vital Speeches of the Day* 1 December 1992: 115.

6. Clyde Prestowitz, Jr., "In Search of Survival: Why Haven't We Done Anything?" *Vital Speeches of the Day* 1 September 1992: 698.

7. David N. Dinkins, "In Praise of Cities," *Representative American Speeches 1990–1991* (New York: Wilson, 1991) 133.

8. Suzanne Landowski, "Academic Laboratories: Risking Life and Limb for Credit," *Winning Orations, 1988* (Mankato, MN: Interstate Oratorical Association, 1988) 64.

9. Lauren McGarity, "The Hybrid Electric Vehicle," *Video User's Guide for the Allyn & Bacon/AFA Student Speeches Video III* (Boston: Allyn, 1999) 22.

10. Bond Benton, "Staged Auto Accidents," *Video User's Guide for the Allyn & Bacon/AFA Student Speeches Video I* (Boston: Allyn, 1997) 67.

11. Ryan Hershberger, "Teenage Drivers," *User's Guide: The Allyn and Bacon/AFA Student Speeches Video II* (Boston: Allyn, 1998) 49–50.

12. John Guare, *Six Degrees of Separation* (New York: Random, 1990) 46.

13. Elinor Donahue, "Writing Your Own Speeches," *Fund Raising Management* (Feb. 1996), 7 July 1999 <http://web4.infotrac.galegroup.com/itw/i_5!xrn_49_0_A18711219?sw_aep= viva_radford>.

14. Dan Alban, "A Stunning Speech," *Winning Orations, 1998* (Mankato, MN: Interstate Oratorical Association, 1998) 21.

15. Katherine Anne Porter, "The Art of Fiction XXIX," *The Paris Review* 29 (Winter–Spring 1963): 102.

16. Terry Tiller, "It's 4 PM: Do You Know Where Your Children Are?" *Winning Orations, 1999* (Mankato, MN: Interstate Oratorical Association, 1999) 103–04.

Order and simplification are the first steps toward the mastery of a subject.

—*Thomas Mann*

Outlining Your Speech

How long would it take you to memorize and be able to repeat the following 26 letters: *c-p-s-y-n-i-r-t-y-m-v-i-e-m-r-t-o-i-p-o-e-m-o-m-e-m*? A typical learner would need a good deal of practice to remember more than the first four to seven letters you just read.[1] Would it help you if the letters were rearranged as follows: *y-m-c-o-i-t-p-s-i-p-t-y-m-m-v-e-n-e-o-i-r-r-m-e-o-m*? Unless you have an eidetic or photographic memory, such a shuffling of letters is likely no help at all. But what if the letters were scrambled again: *m-y-t-o-p-i-c-i-s-p-t-y-m-m-v-e-n-e-o-i-r-r-m-e-o-m*? Those first nine letters are now recognizable as the English words *my, topic,* and *is,* and you can easily repeat them in correct sequence. Those three words would be even more obvious if we eliminated the dashes and used a familiar pattern of grouping and spacing: *my topic is.* If the last seventeen letters were also reorganized as *m-e-m-o-r-y-i-m-p-r-o-v-e-m-e-n-t,* or *memory improvement,* you could master the entire sequence of 26 letters in correct order, orally or in writing, without much effort.

Notice that we did not add or delete any letters. We merely reorganized them until they formed a pattern that is easy to recognize and repeat. When you outline, you perform essentially the same task. You organize and reorganize material into a pattern easy to recognize and remember. As you prepare your speech, you will find that outlining is an indispensable element of speech organization.

In Chapters 9 and 10, we discussed the importance of organization to the delivered speech and suggested some ways of achieving a well-organized presentation. Outlining your speech is the preliminary written work necessary to foster clear organization of your oral message. In this chapter, you will learn why outlines are important to your speech, examine some different types of outlines, and finally, study how to write an excellent outline.

Functions of Outlining

A well-prepared outline serves five important functions for a speaker:

1. It tests the scope of the speaker's content.
2. It tests the logical relations among parts of the speech.
3. It tests the relevance of supporting ideas.
4. It checks the balance or proportion of the speech.
5. It serves as notes during the delivery of the speech.

Tests Scope of Content

The first purpose of outlining is to test the scope of the speaker's content. Have you narrowed the topic sufficiently to cover your key ideas in some depth? Or are you trying to cover too much material, so that you will merely skim the surface of the subject, repeating things your audience already knows? In Chapter 9, we stated that a speaker should ordinarily have no more than two to five main points in a speech. Outlining allows you to use paper and pen to organize your main ideas, and then add, delete, regroup, shuffle, condense, or expand these ideas so you approach your topic in a manageable way. In other words, outlining is a process of setting goals for the speech.

Tests Logical Relation of Parts

Second, outlining allows speakers to test the logical relations among the various parts of the speech. Does one idea in the outline lead to the next in a meaningful way? Do the arguments or subtopics under each of your main points really develop that point? In order to answer these questions, you must understand the concepts of coordination and subordination. **Coordinate ideas** are those of equal value or importance in the overall pattern of the speech. The following hypothetical example illustrates the relation between coordinate and subordinate ideas.

Suppose you find in the library Wilson Bryan Key's books *Subliminal Seduction, Media Sexploitation,* and *The Clam Plate Orgy,* works claiming to show evidence of subliminal messages in print advertisements. Intrigued, you do further research on the topic of subliminal messages. You learn that audio subliminal messages have increased sales and reduced shoplifting in stores where they have been played under background music. If you delivered an informative speech on subliminal messages, you might arrange your speech topically and focus on those two areas:

I. Visual subliminals
II. Audio subliminals

These two topics are coordinate because they are of equal value. You may have more information on one of them than on the other and consequently spend more time in the speech discussing that topic, but neither is a subtopic of the other. Under that first main topic, you would list **subordinate ideas,** subtopics that support it. Two subordinate points for visual subliminals could be:

I. Visual subliminals
   A. Subliminals in print advertising
   B. Subliminals in movies

Notice that A and B above are not only subordinate to the main idea, visual subliminals, but are also coordinate with one another since they seem to be equally important. Subordinate ideas for the second main point, audio subliminals, could include:

II. Audio subliminals
   A. Subliminals to increase sales
   B. Subliminals to reduce theft

Your outline is not yet complete, but you can begin to ask yourself the following questions at this point: Are my main ideas different enough to qualify as separate points? Do those subordinate points really support the main ideas? At this stage, the answers to both of those questions seem to be yes. In this way, the visual form of the outline helps you test the logical connections between parts of your speech. You continue this process to further refine and add to the outline.

Tests Relevance of Supporting Ideas

Third, an outline helps the speaker test the relevance of supporting ideas. To understand how this works, assume that you had written the following portion of an outline for a speech on roller coasters:

I. Famous roller coasters
   A. Coney Island's "Cyclone"
   B. Montreal's "Le Monstre"
   C. Busch Gardens' "Kumba"
   D. New design technology

Notice that the fourth subpoint, "new design technology," is out of place because it is irrelevant to the main point. How do you solve this problem? Careful study of this portion of the outline should signal you to make "new design technology" a separate main point if you can gather adequate supporting material on it; if you can't, eliminate it.

coordinate ideas: ideas that have equal value in a speech.

subordinate ideas: ideas that support more general or more important points in a speech.

Checks Balance of Speech

A fourth function outlining serves for the speaker is to check the balance or proportion of the speech. If you look back to the outline on subliminal messages we used earlier, you will notice that two subpoints support each of the main ideas. As a result, the division of the speech looks balanced, even though a speaker could actually spend more time on one of those main ideas than on the other. The speech would still be balanced if one main point contained three subpoints and the other included two. Yet if the main point of "visual subliminals" contained five subpoints and "audio subliminals" had only two, the outline may not be balanced. This lack of balance in the outline will be reflected in the speech.

How can you fix an imbalance in your speech? In the speech on subliminal messages, the speaker might focus only on visual subliminals rather than have the second topic seem undeveloped or tacked on hastily. As you can see, your outline tests the balance of your speech and can even lead you to alter your specific purpose.

Serves as Delivery Notes

Fifth, and finally, a special type of abbreviated outline can serve as notes for the speaker during the actual delivery of the speech. This outline, called a speaking outline and discussed later in this chapter, has only one rule: It must be brief. If you have prepared adequately for your speech, you should need only key words and phrases to remind you of each point you want to discuss. Moreover, having your notes in outline form rather than arranged randomly on notecards or sheets of paper will constantly remind you of the importance of clear organization as you are delivering the speech.

Principles of Outlining

complete sentence outline: an outline in which all numbers and letters introduce complete sentences.

key word or phrase outline: an outline in which all numbers and letters introduce words or groups of words.

Correct outlines take one of two possible forms: the **complete sentence outline** and the **key word or phrase outline.** In a complete sentence outline, each and every item is a sentence; each item in a key word or phrase outline is a word or group of words. These two forms of outlines should be kept consistent and distinct. Combine them only in the speaker's outline from which you deliver your speech. So far in this chapter, we have used only phrase outlines. More word or phrase outlines and an example of a complete sentence outline will follow.

As you construct your outline, you will work more efficiently and produce a clearer outline if you follow a few rules, or principles.

key points

Principles of Outlining

1. Each number or letter in the outline should represent only one idea.
2. Coordinate and subordinate points in the outline should be represented by a consistent system of numbers and letters.
3. If any point has subpoints under it, there must be at least two subpoints.
4. Each symbol in a sentence outline should introduce a complete sentence. Each symbol in a word or phrase outline should introduce a word or phrase.
5. Coordinate points throughout the outline should have parallel grammatical construction.

First, each number or letter in the outline should represent only one idea. Remember that a chief goal of outlining is to achieve a clear visual representation of the connections between parts of the speech. This is possible only if you separate the ideas. For example, suppose a speaker preparing a speech on color blindness has worded a key idea as "causes of and tests for color blindness." The phrase contains two distinct ideas, each requiring separate discussion and development. Instead, the speaker should divide the statement into two coordinate points: "causes of color blindness" and "tests for color blindness."

Consistency

Second, coordinate and subordinate points in the outline should be represented by a consistent system of numbers and letters. Main ideas are typically represented by Roman numerals: I, II, III, and so forth. Don't worry about brushing up on those higher Roman numerals because you will not have more than five or so main points! Label subpoints under the main points with capital letters: A, B, C, and so forth. Beneath those, identify your supporting points with Arabic numerals: 1, 2, 3, and so on. Identify ideas subordinate to those with lowercase letters: a, b, c, and so on. Using this notation system, the labeling and indentation of a typical outline may appear as follows:

I. Main point
  A. Subpoint
    1. Sub-subpoint
    2. Sub-subpoint
    3. Sub-subpoint
  B. Subpoint
    1. Sub-subpoint
    2. Sub-subpoint
      a. Sub-sub-subpoint
      b. Sub-sub-subpoint
II. Main point
  A. Subpoint
  B. Subpoint
    1. Sub-subpoint
    2. Sub-subpoint
  C. Subpoint

One major thing I learned and improved on in this class was outlining. My high school English teachers always made their students outline, and I never really understood the whole point, but now I am an absolute firm believer in outlines. I would sit down with all this information floating around in my head and not know where to start. The obvious answer was to start that outline. After I wrote my outline everything fell into place. It really taught me to organize my thoughts in a logical way and make my points clear. Even now I have some kind of an outline format in my head for everything I write. If I were asked to give a speech in five minutes, I would write down an outline first and organize what I would want to say before I would ever step onto the stage, whereas before I would have had no idea where to start my speech. Outlining is the *KEY!*

—Elizabeth Cleaver, Clark College

speaking with confidence

Adequacy

A third principle is that if any point has subpoints under it, there must be at least two subpoints. A basic law of physics is that you cannot divide something into only one part. If you have an A, you must also have a B. (You may, of course, also have subpoints C, D, and E.) If you have a 1, you must also have at least a 2.

Uniformity

Fourth, each symbol in a sentence outline should introduce a complete sentence. Each symbol in a word or phrase outline should introduce a word or phrase. In other words, keep the form of the outline consistent. Sentences and phrases should be mixed only in your speaking outline.

Parallelism

Finally, coordinate points throughout the outline should have parallel grammatical construction. For example, a key phrase outline of a speech on how to write a résumé begins with a first main point labeled "Things to include." The second point should be "Things to omit," rather than "Leaving out unnecessary information." The first point is worded as a noun phrase and, therefore, you must follow it with another noun phrase ("Things to omit") rather than a predicate phrase ("Leaving out unnecessary information"). This does not mean that you must choose noun phrases over verb phrases, but rather that all points match grammatically. In this next example, all coordinate points have parallel grammatical construction.

I. Including essential information
   A. Address
   B. Career objective
   C. Educational background
   D. Employment history
   E. References
II. Omitting unnecessary information
   A. Marital status
   B. Religious denomination
   C. Political affiliation

As you can see, coordinate main points I and II are verb phrases, while the coordinate subpoints are all nouns or noun phrases.

Stages of Outlining

Do you have difficulty generating or discovering the main points for a speech topic you have chosen? Don't worry, you are not alone. Many people are intimidated by the prospect of selecting and organizing ideas, particularly for a first speech. We especially worry if an organization plan doesn't come to us quickly. When we get a plan, we worry that it is not the right organizational pattern to use. You can avoid these self-defeating lines of thinking if you keep in mind four guidelines to organizing and outlining.

First, organization is not something that comes to you, but rather it is something that you must go after. Structuring a speech requires you to invest time and thought, investments whose dividends may not be apparent until you deliver the speech. Second, there is no one right way of organizing all speeches on a particular topic. True, some topics logically lend themselves to certain patterns of organization. As you learned in Chapter 9, speeches about processes often almost organize themselves according to a chronological pattern. Speeches about people may be arranged chronologically or topically. Persuasive speeches on social issues are perhaps most logically organized according to a problem–solution format. Yet different speakers may use different structures. You have to determine what works best for you, your topic, and your audience.

Outlining
http://www.abacon.
com/pubspeak/exercise/
5wtopic.html
This interactive site by
Allyn & Bacon offers a
step-by-step exercise to
help you define your
speaking goals and formu-
late, organize, and outline
ideas for a speech. You can
print your work immedi-
ately, e-mail it to an address you specify, or
forward it to your instructor for follow-up.

Third, the early stages of organizing and outlining a speech are filled with uncertainty. You may find yourself asking these questions: Do I have enough main points, too many, or too few? Can I find adequate information to support all of those main points? Am I overlooking other main points the audience would be interested in hearing me discuss? Rather than feeling pressured by such questions, look on the early stages of outlining as a period of flexibility. Remember that the early, informal versions of your working outline are all provisional—temporary and open to change. Don't be afraid to experiment a little. Fourth, and finally, identifying the main points in a speech is also easier than many people imagine. In the remainder of this chapter we will guide you through the process of outlining, from those first tentative ideas a speaker puts on paper to the final outline used as speaking notes.

The Working Outline

The first step in preparing an outline is to construct what we like to call a **working outline,** a list of aspects of your chosen topic. Such a list may result from research you have already conducted, or it may simply be a result of some productive brainstorming. Once you have spent significant time researching the subject, you will notice topics that are repeated in different sources on the subject. If, for example, you had selected Graves' disease as the topic for an informative speech and had conducted adequate research, your list of possible aspects of the topic would include:

Cause	Diagnosis	Prevention
Symptoms	Treatment	

Notice that these same topics could be applied to any disease, physical illness, or mental condition.

You can also generate topic areas through brainstorming and visual brainstorming, techniques we discussed in Chapter 6. Not only can brainstorming help you generate topics, it can also help you explore areas of the topic you finally select.[2] Your creative brainstorming might even reveal interesting areas of your topic that have not been adequately treated in the existing research. This discovery provides you an opportunity to conduct original research or experimentation.

As you can see, at this stage the term *outline* is very loose; the list of key ideas you are developing does not have any numbers or letters attached to it. That's fine, since these notes are for your benefit alone. This working outline is not so much a finished product as it is a record of the process you go through in thinking about a speech topic.

To illustrate these first steps in outline preparation, consider the experience of a speaker, John, who came up with a speech topic in the following manner:

> Several years ago I saw a small picture in *Newsweek* of a really weird-looking building located in some European country. It was made up of two towers. I

working outline: an informal, initial outline recording a speaker's process of narrowing, focusing, and balancing a topic.

remember that the brief story with it said that apartment dwellers in an adjoining building had complained that one of the towers blocked their view of a nearby river and castle. So the architect just twisted one of the towers a little so that it no longer blocked anyone's view. It was really cool looking, and I remember reading that people had started calling the twin towers "Fred and Ginger" after the dance team of Fred Astaire and Ginger Rogers.

Then later I saw a segment of *Nightline* about the Guggenheim Museum in Bilbao, Spain. I liked the video so much that I ordered a copy by calling 1–800-CALL ABC. I found out from that video that the architect of the Guggenheim was Frank O. Gehry. Then when I did some research about him on the Internet, I found links to a structure called "Fred and Ginger" and realized that the same person had designed both of these buildings that had impressed me. When I got the assignment for an informative speech using presentational aids, I knew that I wanted to talk about one or both of these buildings and Gehry's designs for them. I think people in class will be interested in them, and there's a lot of information about both, especially the new Guggenheim Museum.

Notice that at this point John was not sure whether he wanted to speak just about Gehry, just about the Guggenheim Museum, just about "Fred and Ginger," or about some combination of the three topics. Using the visual brainstorming technique discussed in Chapter 6, however, he generated the topics related to Frank O. Gehry shown in Figure 11.1.

John's working outline therefore began with just the following main points:

Biography	Designs
His theories	Work methodology
Critical reactions to his works	

After some preliminary research on Gehry, John expanded his working outline with the following subpoints:

Biography
  Early life
    Birth in Canada, 1929
    Family move to California, 1947
  Education
    Bachelor of Architecture, USC, 1951
    Harvard University Graduate School of Design, 1957
  Marriage and family
    Wife Berta
    Sons Alejandro and Sam
  Work history
    Gruen, Pereira & Luchman, Los Angeles
    Andre Remondet, Paris
    Frank O. Gehry & Associates, Santa Monica
Designs
  Commercial
    Guggenheim Museum, Bilbao, Spain, 1997
    Rasin Building ("Fred and Ginger"), Prague, 1996
    American Center, Paris, 1993
    University of Toledo Art Building, Toledo, Ohio, 1992
    Festival Disney, Marne-la-Vallee, France, 1992

Chiat/Day Building, Venice, California, 1991

Vitra International Furniture Manufacturing Facility/Museum, Germany, 1989

Edgemar Complex, Venice, California, 1987

Loyola Law School, Los Angeles, 1984

Residential

Norton House, Venice, California, 1983

Howell House, Atlanta, 1981

Gehry House, Santa Monica, 1978

Harper House, Baltimore, 1976

Janss House, Los Angeles, 1974

Ron Davis House, Malibu, 1972

Steeves House, Brentwood, 1959

His theories

Feels intense need to change and transform

Finds beauty in buildings under construction

Sees connections between architecture, painting, and sculpture

Involves clients in the design process

Work methodology

Sketching

Relies on others for use of computer

Uses CATIA program developed to design fighter planes

Uses a 3D computer modeling program, Pro/ENGINEER

Provides contractors with AutoCAD 3D translations of designs

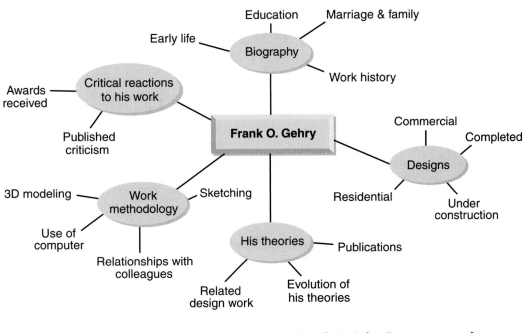

FIGURE 11.1 Visual brainstorming on the subject "Frank O. Gehry"

Relationships with colleagues
 Collaborates with structural engineers
 Maintains working friendships with many contemporary artists
Critical reactions to his works
 Published criticism
  Receives lavish praise by architectural critics in numerous publications
  Prince Charles attacked "Fred and Ginger"
 Awards received
  RAIC Gold Medal, 1994
  National Academy of Design, 1994
  Lillian Gish Award for Lifetime Contribution to the Arts, 1992
  Fellow of the American Academy of Arts and Sciences, 1991
  Pritzker Architecture Prize, 1989
  Fellow of the American Academy of Arts and Letters, 1987
  Fellow of the American Institute of Architects, 1974
  Over 100 national and regional A.I.A. awards

Obviously, this is far too much material for a typical short classroom speech. How do you decide what to include and what to eliminate? First, consider your interests, those of your audience, and the quantity of research materials you have found on each of these topics.

This is how John focused the topic from his working outline:

So many facts about Frank Gehry interest me. Several of the books and magazine articles I read say that he is now one of the top five to seven really influential architects in the United States, but I had never heard of him before hearing about these couple of unusual buildings of his. He is also amazingly modest. In his early seventies, he says that he doesn't even know how to turn his computer on, but his designs could never be built without the use of computer modeling.

I am sure that I could do an entire speech on Gehry's career, using photographs of some of his designs to illustrate his accomplishments. But the more I read, the more interested I became in Gehry's collaborations with artists like Robert Rauschenberg and sculptors like Claes Oldenberg. Many critics call Gehry an artist, in particular a sculptor. His Guggenheim Museum seems to me to be a cubist painting in 3D form.

I've decided that instead of trying to give the class a picture of Gehry's career, I'm going to focus on those two buildings that stuck with me after I saw pictures of them the first time. I'm going to talk about the Guggenheim and the Rasin Building ("Fred and Ginger") and what they reveal about this architect's vision.

As you can see, John is really most interested in just one section of his working outline:

Designs
 Commercial
  Guggenheim Museum, Bilbao, Spain, 1997
  Rasin Building ("Fred and Ginger"), Prague, 1996

So was all of that research and time spent on his initial working outline wasted? "Not at all," he says. "Even though I'm not going to have time to talk about all of those other topics, they help me know Gehry better and have given me a lot of confidence. If someone asks a question about Frank Gehry, I think I'll either know the answer or know where to go to find the answer."

After some more detailed research on the specific topic area he had chosen, John devised another working outline:

I. Frank O. Gehry commercial designs
   A. The Guggenheim Museum, Bilbao
      1. Completed on time and within $100 million budget
      2. Joint project of Basque government and Guggenheim Foundation
      3. Hailed as "first great building of the 21st century"
      4. Composed of various materials
         a. Titanium purchased from Russia
         b. Limestone
         c. Glass
      5. Design possible only with computerized 3D modeling
      6. Composed of various galleries and other spaces
   B. The Rasin Building, Prague
      1. Designed in collaboration with architect Vlado Milunic
      2. Owned by International Netherlands Group
      3. Occupies a site on the Vltava River with a view of Prague Castle
      4. Composed of a rectilinear building with two towers
         a. A nine-story tapered solid tower with windows, "Fred"
         b. A nine-story twisted tower covered in glass, "Ginger"
      5. Design possible only with computerized 3D modeling

This early version of the outline has several problems, but that's OK. Remember, the real function of the working outline is to test the waters of your topic and reveal any problems in your approach. The most obvious problem with this working outline is that it has only one main point, one Roman numeral. As we discussed earlier, you cannot divide something into only one part. John will have to correct that problem in subsequent versions of the outline. He also felt that a speech following this outline would end on a weak note because the Rasin Building, though interesting, is smaller and less important than the Guggenheim Museum.

With some shifting, John developed a stronger outline. Convinced that his classmates would find the story of "Fred and Ginger" immediately interesting, he decided to begin the body of the speech by discussing the Rasin Building. He had much more information about the Guggenheim and decided to focus the remainder of the speech on it. Therefore, he chose to devote his second main point to describing the museum and then to develop the critical reaction to it as a third and final main point. John's revised working outline was as follows:

I. The Rasin Building, Prague
   A. Designed in collaboration with Czech architect Vlado Milunic
   B. Owned by International Netherlands Group
   C. Occupies a site on the Vltava River with a view of Prague Castle
   D. Composed of a rectilinear building with two towers
      1. A nine-story tapered solid tower with windows, "Fred"
      2. A nine-story twisted tower covered in glass, "Ginger"
      3. Design possible only with computerized 3D modeling
II. The enormity of the Guggenheim project and building
   A. Joint project of Basque government and Guggenheim Foundation
   B. $100 million budget
   C. 257,000 square feet
   D. Composed of various galleries and other spaces
      1. Nineteen galleries, the largest 425×260 feet
      2. 165-foot-tall atrium

3. 300-seat auditorium
4. Administrative offices
5. Restaurant
6. Museum store
7. Water garden
   E. Composed of various materials
1. Titanium purchased from Russia
2. Spanish limestone
3. Glass
   F. Technological innovations
1. Use of CATIA computer modeling to determine precise shapes of metal pieces for skin of the building
2. Each piece of metal numbered and detailed
3. Gehry's software used to produce contractors' shop drawings
III. Responses to the Guggenheim Museum
   A. Metaphors for the building
1. "Metallic flower"
2. "Cubist sculpture of a ship"
3. "Ghost of a gigged ship"
4. Tinsmith's shop after an earthquake
5. "Castle of ice"
6. "A stage set"
   B. Published criticism
1. Overwhelming enthusiasm
2. Concerns about the space dwarfing the art to be shown

This second version of the working outline develops three main points rather than just one. It also begins with a point that John thinks will be immediately interesting to his listeners and relatively simple for him to explain. From there, the outline develops more unusual and complicated ideas.

You may think that as a speaker prepares a speech, the outline will become longer and more complex. To a certain point this is true. As you flesh out your ideas over a period of time, your outline does grow more detailed. What finally evolves is called your formal outline. Once you have decided for certain on the number of main points you can cover in the allowed time, what those points are, and how you will support them, you then select words and phrases from the formal outline to make up your much briefer speaking outline.

The Formal Outline

Your **formal outline** is a complete sentence outline reflecting the full content and organization of your speech. In its final form, it is the finished product of your research and planning for your speech. A stranger, picking up your formal outline, should be able to read how you have organized and supported all your main points. If you keep that goal in mind, you should have no trouble deciding what needs to be included.

formal outline: a complete sentence outline written in sufficient detail that a person other than the speaker could understand it.

Your instructor may require you to include any or all of the following items at the beginning of your formal outline: your speech title, a statement of your specific purpose, and your thesis statement, appropriately labeled. The actual outline should follow the accepted pattern of symbols and indentation, with each item in the outline making up a complete sentence. Your instructor may ask you to label the superstructure of the speech—introduction, body, and conclusion—by inserting these words at the appropriate places in the outline but without Roman numerals or other symbols attached to them. Finally, the formal outline should be followed by a bibliography listing the sources you have used in the development of the speech.

Now let's see how John developed his formal outline for his speech on Gehry's buildings. The final version of John's formal outline, together with his bibliography, looked like this:

Speech title: "Lourdes for a Crippled Culture": Two Designs by Frank O. Gehry

Specific purpose: To inform the audience about two buildings designed by architect Frank O. Gehry.

Thesis statement: Frank O. Gehry's designs for the Rasin Building in Prague and the Guggenheim Museum in Bilbao, Spain, make them structures that are easy to love or to hate, but difficult to ignore.

Introduction

Pablo Picasso once painted a portrait of the writer Gertrude Stein. When someone pointed out that it didn't really look like her, Picasso replied, "Don't worry. It will." Art critic Robert Hughes has called the new Guggenheim Museum in Bilbao, Spain, "the first great building of the 21st century." Yet when ABC's Forrest Sawyer asked Hughes on *Nightline,* October 6, 1997, if the Guggenheim was what the 21st century would look like, Hughes replied, "No, the 21st century would be bloody lucky to look like this. It won't." Before the new Guggenheim Museum Bilbao opened late in 1997, Frank O. Gehry, its architect, completed another much smaller building in Prague. One of the twin towers of that building was going to block some apartment tenants' views of a river and a castle, so Gehry used the computer to pinch and twist the design. He started calling that tower "Ginger," and, as you might expect, other people began to refer to the straight tower beside it as "Fred." Today "Fred and Ginger," or "The Dancing Building" is an immensely popular landmark. These two buildings of the 1990s have made Gehry a world-renowned architect. They also prove that a creative 70-year-old who claims he's not able to turn his computer on can push architecture to the limits of computer technology.

Today I want to inform you about these two Gehry designs by looking first at the Rasin Building ("Fred and Ginger"), second at the Guggenheim Museum Bilbao, and finally at the responses these two buildings have evoked.

Body of speech

I. The Rasin Building in Prague increased Frank Gehry's visibility in the mid-1990s.
   A. A series of fortunate events made the project possible.
      1. The building site in a historic section of Prague had been vacant since it was bombed by the United States in 1945.
      2. The Velvet Revolution that brought an end to communism in Czechoslovakia in 1989 revived national spirit and optimism.
      3. Czech president Vaclav Havel, who lived adjacent to the building site, wanted a world-class building constructed there.
      4. Havel enlisted Czech architect Vlado Milunic for design input.
      5. An insurance company, International Netherlands Group, purchased the land and asked Milunic to suggest a distinguished architect as collaborator.
         a. Havel recommended Gehry, whose work he admired.
         b. All parties involved were eager for a revolutionary design that would somehow mesh with the various architectural periods and styles in the area.

John's well-crafted title not only gets attention but also hints at his speech topic. To check the goal of his speech, John then clearly states his specific purpose and thesis.

Note that John writes out his entire introduction, gaining audience attention by arousing curiosity with his unusual opening comparison. Quoting and citing a source explains the significance of John's topic and also begins to build his credibility to speak on it. His preview promises a closer look at two Gehry designs and the reactions they have evoked.

The Rasin Building in Prague,
The Czech Republic.

B. The Rasin Building occupies an important and challenging site in Prague.
   1. The historic site on the Vltava River has a view of Prague Castle.
   2. The site called for an asymmetrical structure to correct the alignment of a busy intersection.
C. The Rasin Building is composed of a rectilinear structure with two towers at one corner.
   1. "Fred" is a nine-story tapered stucco tower with staggered windows.
   2. "Ginger" is a nine-story twisted tower covered in glass.
      a. The flaring skin of this tower—Ginger's dress—is made of double panes of glass set in a steel frame.
      b. The shape and curve of each pane required Gehry to use software created to design airplane fuselages.
   3. Final design of the towers was possible only with computerized 3D modeling.

The body's three parts match the points in the thesis and preview statements. Each item in the outline is a declarative sentence expressing one idea, and each level has at least two headings. Many subordinate points are grammatically parallel.

II. The Guggenheim Museum in Bilbao, Spain, was an enormous undertaking.
   A. The building was a joint project of the Basque government and the Guggenheim Foundation.
   B. The Guggenheim Museum Bilbao had a $100-million budget.
      1. Gehry brought the project in under that budget.
      2. Gehry completed the project on time.
   C. The building contains a total of 257,000 square feet.
   D. The Guggenheim Museum is composed of various galleries and other spaces.
      1. There are nineteen galleries, the largest 425×260 feet.
      2. The building's atrium is 165 feet tall.
      3. The building contains a 300-seat auditorium.

*The Guggenheim Museum
in Bilbao, Spain.*

      4. The building contains administrative offices.
      5. The building contains a restaurant.
      6. The building contains a museum store.
      7. The site design includes a water garden.
  E. The building is composed of various materials.
      1. The most unusual building material is titanium.
         a. Gehry purchased the titanium from Russia as that country disman-
            tled most of its nuclear weaponry.
         b. Much of the building is covered with a thin titanium "skin."
            (1) The reflective property of the titanium, like the dull side of tin
                foil, makes the building look different with changing light and
                weather conditions.
            (2) The thin titanium panels move and "breathe" in high winds.
      2. The building features intricately fitted native Spanish limestone.
      3. The atrium and various towers and walls are made of glass.
      4. The building contains 300,000 steel beams in 250,000 different sizes.
  F. Gehry's design utilized some important technological innovations.
      1. Gehry's staff used CATIA computer modeling to determine the precise
         shapes of the titanium pieces for the skin of the building.
      2. Gehry's staff detailed the contact points for each numbered piece of
         metal.
      3. Gehry provided contractors with his software to produce their shop
         drawings.
III. These two Gehry buildings evoke a variety of responses.
  A. Popular reaction to the Rasin Building has been largely positive.
      1. Prague citizens who saw either of two exhibits of the proposed design
         approved it by more than a four-to-one margin.
      2. Sixty-eight percent of voters in a 1993 national referendum approved
         the design.
      3. The building has become a tourist attraction.
  B. Academic and professional criticism has been more divided.
      1. The rector of Prague's Academy of Fine Arts has dismissed the design
         as "superfluous" and "contrived."
      2. Most say that Ginger is the most inspired part of the design.
      3. Some criticize the limitations that the towers' designs place on the way
         space can be used on each floor.

C. Popular and professional reactions to the Guggenheim have been overwhelmingly positive.
1. Projected to attract 450,000 visitors during its first year, the museum actually attracted nearly one and a half million people.
2. Many call the building an instant landmark.
3. Some call the building the most important structure since the death of Frank Lloyd Wright.
4. Writers have used various metaphors to describe the building.
  a. Several have called it a "metallic flower."
  b. One writer called it both a "cubist sculpture of a ship" and a tinsmith's shop after an earthquake.
  c. Another writer called it the "ghost of a gigged ship," "a stage set," and a "castle of ice."

Conclusion

In his conclusion, John summarizes Gehry's accomplishments as an architect by recapping the descriptions of the two buildings and the responses people have had to them. He activates audience response by introducing the notion of a world where imagination and technology merge. John then provides a strong sense of closure by quoting the stark contrast of critic Anthony Lewis.

A small, quirky building in the historic heart of Prague, Czechoslovakia, and a sprawling, quirky complex on the banks of the Nervion River in Bilbao, Spain: Both the Rasin Building and the Guggenheim Museum are creations of American architect Frank O. Gehry. A modest, unassuming man, he is also, according to critic Herbert Muschamp in the September 7, 1997, *New York Times,* "an architectural intelligence of unequaled stature."

Technology has finally caught up with architects' imaginations. If they can think it, chances are that someone somewhere can figure out a way to build it. By freeing architecture from the structural grid, Gehry and other contemporary architects are creating buildings that inspire optimism and convey great freedom. The Guggenheim Bilbao inspired Muschamp to call the structure a "Lourdes for a crippled culture." Two years later, in the April 17, 1999, issue of the *New York Times,* Anthony Lewis reflected that the building also reminds us of the extremes of human behavior: "In another corner of Europe, people are dying because of one man's lust for power. Here [in Bilbao] they live more fully because of an architect's genius for beauty."

Bibliography

A formal outline should include a complete bibliography; it's an important reference for interested listeners, including your instructor.

Arnell, Peter, and Ted Bickford, eds. and comps. *Frank Gehry: Buildings and Projects.* New York: Rizzoli, 1985.
Churchill, Bonnie. "Laying the Cornerstone for a City's Dream." *Christian Science Monitor* 2 July 1997: 13.
"Dancing-Masters: Czech Architecture." *The Economist* 11 Dec. 1993: 98.
Giovannini, Joseph. "Fred and Ginger Dance in Prague." *Architecture* Feb. 1997: 52. 2 Nov. 1999 <http://web5.infotrac.galegroup.com/itw/in . . . M_0_A19209775& dyn=4!ar_fmt?sw_aep=sancle>.
Jodidio, Philip. *New Forms: Architecture in the 1990s.* Cologne: Benedikt Taschen, 1997.
Lewis, Anthony. "Engine for Change." *New York Times* 17 Apr. 1999: A17.
Ouroussoff, Nicolai. "Gehry's Guggenheim: An Instant Landmark." *Los Angeles Times* 2 June 1997: F1, F8.
Steele, James. *Los Angeles Architecture: The Contemporary Condition.* London: Phaidon, 1993.
Ward, Timothy Jack. "The Towers in Prague that Swirl and Waltz." *New York Times* 1 Feb. 1996: C3.

speaking outline: a brief outline for the speaker's use alone and containing source citations and delivery prompts.

The Speaking Outline

The **speaking outline,** the one you actually use to deliver your speech, is a pared-down version of your full formal outline. You construct the formal outline for an interested reader having no necessary prior knowledge of your topic. However, you write the speaking outline for yourself as a unique speaker. As we mentioned earlier, the only rule for the speaking outline is that it be brief.

Why is the speaking outline briefer than the formal outline? Chances are that your instructor will want most or all of your speeches delivered from notes rather than from a written manuscript. Your brief speaking outline, made up of essential words and phrases, meets the requirements of the assignment while also serving as your speaking notes. But more important, if you spoke from a complete sentence outline, you might be tempted to read the speech, sacrificing eye contact and other vital interaction with your audience. Alternatively, you might try to memorize the formal outline, another dangerous tactic because you then face the prospect of forgetting part of the speech. If, instead, you speak using the outline having just key words and phrases to jog your memory, your delivery will seem more natural and conversational, and you will find yourself freer to interact with your audience.

Though the speaking outline leaves out a lot of what the formal outline includes, it also contains some important items not found in the formal outline. For example, you can include directions to yourself about the delivery of the speech. A speaker with a tendency to speak too softly could write reminders in the margins, such as "volume" or "Speak up!" You might also want to note in your speaking outline places where you want to pause, to slow down, or to use presentational aids. Some speakers find it particularly helpful to make these delivery notes in a color of ink different from the rest of the outline.

Second, most speaking outlines include any supporting material you plan to use. Quotations and definitions should be written in complete sentences, even though the rest of the outline is in words and phrases. When you quote others, you must be exact. For that reason, you'll also want to insert notations about the exact sources you want to cite. Examples, illustrations, and statistics could be noted in only a few words or numbers. Any symbols or abbreviations you are comfortable with are likely appropriate in your speaking outline.

For his speech on Gehry's designs, John condensed his formal outline and added the following notations for the actual delivery of the speech:

I. Rasin Building, Prague
   A. Fortunate events (*Economist,* Dec. 11, 1997)
      1. Site vacant
      2. Velvet Revolution, 1989
      3. Vaclav Havel
      4. Czech architect Vlado Milunic
      5. International Netherlands Group
         a. Gehry enlisted
         b. Revolutionary design needed
   B. Important, challenging site
      1. Vltava River, Prague Castle
      2. Asymmetrical to align intersection
   C. Rectilinear structure + two towers   SHOW PHOTO
      1. "Fred"—nine-story, stucco, staggered windows
      2. "Ginger"—nine-story, twisted, covered in glass
         a. Double paned, steel frame
         b. Software for design of airplane fuselages
      3. 3D modeling
PAUSE
(Rasin—small site . . .)

Delivery prompts are in capital letters so that John can see them at a glance and will not confuse them with content prompts.

Although the entries in a speaking outline are abbreviated, they are still parallel in structure.

II. Guggenheim Museum Bilbao
   A. Basque government + Guggenheim Foundation
   B. $100 million
      1. Under budget
      2. On time
   C. 257,000 sq. ft.
   D. Galleries, other spaces
      1. 19 galleries, largest 425 × 260 ft.
      2. Atrium 165 ft. tall
      3. 300-seat auditorium
      4. Offices
      5. Restaurant
      6. Store
      7. Water garden
   E. Building materials   SHOW PHOTO
      1. Most unusual—titanium
         a. Purchased from Russia
         b. Thin titanium "skin"
            (1) Reflective property of titanium, like the dull side of tin foil, changes building look in different light, weather (*NY Times,* Sept. 7, 1997)
            (2) Panels "breathe" in high winds
      2. Limestone
      3. Glass
      4. 300,000 steel beams, 250,000 sizes (*NY Times,* April 17, 1999)
   F. Technological innovations
      1. CATIA modeling
      2. Metal pieces numbered, detailed
      3. Gehry provided software for shop drawings (*CS Monitor,* July 2, 1997)
PAUSE
(Buildings for people . . .)
III. Responses

John's speaking outline contains specific supporting materials such as statistics and quotations, along with information about each source he needs to cite.

   A. Popular reaction to Rasin largely positive
      1. > 4–1 approval (*Economist,* Dec. 11, 1993)
      2. 68% approval, national referendum (*NY Times,* Feb. 1, 1996)
      3. Tourist attraction
   B. Academic, prof. criticism divided
      1. Rector of Acad. of Fine Arts—"superfluous," "contrived"
      2. Ginger—most inspired part
      3. Limits on space use (*Architecture,* Feb. 1997)
   C. Guggenheim—overwhelmingly positive
      1. 450,000 expected, nearly 1 & ½ million
      2. Instant landmark (*LA Times,* June 2, 1997)
      3. Most important since death of FLW
      4. Metaphors
         a. "Metallic flower"
         b. "Cubist sculpture of a ship," tinsmith's shop after an earthquake (*Economist,* Oct. 25, 1997)
         c. "Ghost of a gigged ship," "stage set," "castle of ice" (Tometa Web site)
PAUSE BEFORE CONCLUSION

Someone who knew nothing of the subject and had not seen John's organization evolve in those earlier outlines might not be able to make much sense of his speaking outline. That's OK. As long as your notes make sense to you, you're fine. For example, John's note in parentheses (Rasin—small site . . .) probably makes little sense to you. For John, though, those two words triggered the following transition: "If the Rasin Building attracted some attention to its small site in Prague, it did not prepare most people for the revolutionary Gehry design that was taking shape on a much larger site in the Spanish town of Bilbao." Similarly, John's note "Buildings for people . . . " reminded him to say, "Buildings are made for the people who visit them, work in them, even for those who live near or drive by them. What do people have to say, then, about these two Gehry buildings?" If you plan and practice your transitions as carefully as John did, you too should need only a few words to remind you of what you planned to say in those important sections of your speech.

Summary

Outlining serves five main purposes for a speaker preparing a speech. First, it allows the speaker to check the scope of the topic. Is the topic too broad? Are you trying to cover too much or too little? Second, the outline permits a speaker to test the logical relations between main points and subpoints. Are the points related and yet distinctive enough to qualify as separate ideas? Third, outlining provides a check of the relevance of subpoints. Supporting ideas should all be related to the main idea under which they are listed. Fourth, a speaker can use an outline to gauge the balance of the speech. Does it look as though you will be spending too much time on one of your points and too little on others? Should you eliminate the points that have little support and reorganize those with a great deal of support? Finally, an outline can function as speaking notes, jogging the speaker's memory with key words in correct order.

Outlines can take one of two possible forms: the *complete sentence outline* or the *key word or phrase outline.* In the first of these outlines, each item introduced by a number or letter is a complete sentence. The key word or phrase outline avoids complete sentences. The two forms of outlines should generally not be combined.

Effective outlining is greatly simplified if the speaker keeps in mind these traditional principles or rules. First, each symbol—number or letter—in the outline should represent only one idea. Second, coordination and subordination should be represented by a consistent system of letters and numbers properly indented. Third, any point divided into subpoints must have at least two subpoints. Fourth, complete sentences and key words should be mixed only in the speaking outline. Finally, coordinate points throughout the outline should have simple, parallel grammatical construction.

The first phase of outlining is a *working outline,* an informal list of different aspects of the selected speech topic. From there, the speaker should develop a complete sentence outline, or *formal outline,* that is clear and thorough enough to communicate the essence of the speech to any reader. Having checked the scope of the topic and the logical connections, relevance, and balance of the subpoints, the speaker can then select key words and phrases for a *speaking outline.* That outline may also include transitions, quotations, and source citations, as well as personal directions or prompts for the delivery of the speech.

A speaking outline provides a visual test of the organization of a speech. While effective outlining does not guarantee clear organization in the delivered speech, chances are good that any well-organized speech has been carefully outlined at some stage in its development.

practice critique

Evaluating a Speech Outline

Read the transcript of Susan Chontos's speech, "The Amish: Seeking to Lose the Self," which appears in Appendix B. As you read, write down an outline of the three main ideas that she develops, including the subpoints. Then, using this outline, write brief answers to the following questions and be prepared to discuss them with your classmates: (1) Did Susan narrow the topic sufficiently to develop her key ideas in some depth? (2) Does one idea in the outline lead to the next in a meaningful way? (3) Do the subtopics under each main idea develop that point? (4) Are the three ideas balanced? In summary, does the outline reveal a well-organized speech? If you were advising Susan, would you offer any suggestions to help her present her ideas more clearly and support them more effectively?

Exercises

1. Test your understanding of coordination and subordination by outlining the following statements:
   a. Blind artists draw objects from a single perspective.
   b. Blind artists use lines to represent surfaces.
   c. Blind artists draw distant objects smaller than close ones.
   d. Blind artists use many of the same visual devices as sighted artists.

   Which of the above statements is the key idea? Which statements are subordinate to it? Which statements are coordinate? [This example is based on John M. Kennedy, "How the Blind Draw." *Scientific American* January 1997: 76+.]

2. Susan Chontos's informative speech on the Amish in Appendix B is clearly organized. Prepare a formal outline of the body of that speech.

3. Select one of the speeches in Appendix B, and prepare a key word or phrase outline of the speech. Identify three ways the outline reveals whether the speech was well organized, whether the ideas are balanced, and whether each point directly relates to the specific purpose of the speech.

4. Using the outline you constructed above, reword it as a complete sentence outline. When is it better to develop a key word or phrase outline? When is a complete sentence outline preferred?

5. Listen to a speech in person or on radio, television, or videotape, and outline its main and supporting ideas. Review the outline. Did the speaker try to cover too many points? Are the main points and subpoints relevant, balanced, and logically sequenced? Based on the outline, what suggestions could you give the speaker to improve the speech?

6. Select one of the following topics: superstitions, hiccups, mandatory retirement, or amusement parks. Without doing any research, brainstorm ideas you could include in a speech. Prepare a key word or phrase outline developing coordinate and subordinate ideas.

7. Using the entries below, construct an outline of four major points on the topic of "Latin music." The major headings are included in the entries.

mariachi	Ruben Blades
small folk band	countries
Cuba	*merengue*
styles	Jennifer Lopez

Marc Anthony	*salsa*
artists	*mariachi* band
Puerto Rico	Mexico
rumba	Enrique Iglesias
Latin big band	Elvis Crespo
instrumentation	Brazil
Spain	*mambo*

[This information is from two Web sites: http://www.latinmusicspecialists.com and http://cd.dj.net.]

1. E. D. Hirsch, Jr., *Cultural Literacy: What Every American Needs to Know* (New York: Vintage-Random, 1988) 34.

2. Many people who teach creative writing prefer visual brainstorming, or "branching," to the traditional, linear outlines such as the ones we illustrate. For interesting discussions of how outlining by visual brainstorming draws on both sides of the brain, see Henriette Anne Klauser, *Writing on Both Sides of the Brain: Breakthrough Techniques for People Who Write* (San Francisco: HarperSanFrancisco, 1987) 47–55, and Gabriele Lusser Rico, *Writing the Natural Way: Using Right-Brain Techniques to Release Your Expressive Powers* (Los Angeles: Tarcher, 1983).

A word is not crystal, transparent and unchanged; it is the skin of a living thought and may vary greatly in color and content according to the circumstances and time in which it is used.

—Oliver Wendell Holmes, Jr.

Wording Your Speech

Socrates was a famous Greek teacher who went around giving people advice. They killed him. Socrates died from an overdose of wedlock. After his death, his career suffered a dramatic decline.

—*From a student paper*[1]

If the people don't want to come out to the park, nobody's going to stop 'em.

—*Yogi Berra*

Sisters Reunited after 18 Years in Checkout Line at Supermarket

—*Newspaper headline*[2]

A congressman was concerned about the costs of unnecessary medical tests and warned his constituents, "They might take you in there and perform a C-SPAN."

—*Jeffrey McQuain*[3]

Speakers of English have access to the richest vocabulary on earth, largely because we have adopted words so freely from other languages. In fact, three out of four words in English come from a foreign tongue.[4] As a result, the revised *Oxford English Dictionary* is huge, containing 615,000 words. That is more than three times as many words as the German language contains, and more than six times the number of words available to the French.[5] People who speak English can achieve degrees of subtlety and nuance that are impossible in most languages. So you would think we could manage to be clearer than the speakers and writers in the examples above.

Socrates died of an overdose of hemlock, not wedlock. Baseball great Berra is famous for "Yogiisms" such as the one above. He is so good-natured that it's easy to believe he knows what he means, even if it doesn't come out clearly. We doubt that those sisters had to wait in the supermarket checkout line for 18 years, even if there were lots of double-coupon days! As for the final example, we can assume the congressman meant to say "CAT scan," a medical test often utilized by physicians during the diagnostic process. C-SPAN is a cable television network.

Examples of language abuse, both spoken and written, are all around us. Their effects can be comic or serious. More important for our purposes are examples of words used correctly, precisely, powerfully, and memorably. How we use words makes us stand out from others. Language empowers us, and we can employ it to serve both ethical and unethical purposes. One speaker explains the power of words this way:

> Words, as symbols of ideas and ideals, have the power to make people fall in love or out of love, to be faithful or unfaithful to their vows and pledges. . . .They can produce tears or laughter, success or disaster. They can bring luster or brightness to the face of a child or send him to bed sobbing and sorrowful. . . .

Words can change the face of a city, build churches, schools, playgrounds, boys' clubs, scout groups, civic forums, Little Theaters, Civic Music organizations, garden clubs, and better governments. . . .

The force of words is great, good, glorious, or terrifying.[6]

In this chapter you will learn five functions language serves for us. We will also discuss four principles of effective language use and offer suggestions for adhering to them. The study of language is important, because the more you know about language, the greater control you will have as you communicate in public.

Functions of Language

Language fulfills at least five functions for those who use it.[7]

Functions of Language

1. Language communicates ideas.
2. Language sends messages about the people using it.
3. Language strengthens social bonds between groups of people.
4. Language can be an instrument of play.
5. Language checks and controls our use of language.

key points

Communicate Ideas

Our language can communicate an infinite number of ideas because it has a structure of separate words. Unlike the sounds most animals make to signal danger, for example, our language allows us to specify the type of threat, the immediacy of the danger, and any number of other characteristics of the situation.[8] However, we must remember that the speaker's language is effective only if it communicates to the listeners. As we mentioned in Chapter 1 in discussing the "triangle of meaning," as long as the speaker and the listener attach similar referents to the words they use, the two can communicate indefinitely.

> Like coins, words get their value from the community at large, which must agree on what they represent. The word *dog* may mean a furry creature with four legs and a wagging tail, for instance, but *hippopotamus* or *ziglot* would serve just as well, as long as both speaker and listener agreed on its meaning.[9]

Send Messages about User

Our vocabulary reveals aspects of our educational background, our age, and even what area of the country we call home. Consider the following exchange from the award-winning sitcom *Frasier:*

> *Frasier, to his brother Niles:* "If you were stranded on an island, what would you choose as your favorite meal, aria, and wine?
> *Niles:* The Coulibiac of Salmon at Guy Savoy. "Vissa d'arte" from *Tosca.* And the Cotes du Rhone, Chateau Neuf du Pape, '47.
> *Frasier:* You're so predictable."[10]

Even if you've never seen the TV show, you probably form a vivid picture of who these brothers are—or think they are.

In addition, language expresses the feelings or emotions of the speaker. The words we select communicate how we feel about both our listeners and the subject under discussion. Which of these terms suggests the strongest emotion, for example?

> fire   blaze   inferno

Inferno obviously suggests a stronger emotional response from the speaker than either of the other terms. Consider another example:

> crisis   dilemma   problem

In this case, *crisis* suggests a more powerful feeling than do the other terms. Language can carry considerable emotional impact, and the words you select carry messages—sometimes obvious, sometimes subtle—about your background and the nature and strength of your emotions.

Strengthen Social Bonds

Precisely because it communicates ideas and emotions between people, language serves a social function. For example, we often use language to identify ourselves as part of a particular group. Think of the slang expressions you used around friends when you were younger to signal that you were a member of a certain group and in the know. Many of these utterances are fun and harmless. Others can provoke unexpected responses. For example, it became popular a few years ago for teenagers to refer to someone or some idea as "phat." For some, that word was interpreted as an insult, especially if they were just hearing the word. But those who understood the jargon knew that it meant "really cool."

Other forms of language serve a more positive function. A group of kindergarten students reciting the alphabet or counting from one to twenty strengthen their group identity and celebrate the group's accomplishment. Adults repeating a pledge, oath, or prayer experience similar group feelings. Or consider the words we use to greet one another. The exchange, "Hi, how are you?" and, "Fine, how are you doing?" may be a hollow, automatic social ritual. Nevertheless, such rituals acknowledge the social bond that exists even between strangers.

Serve as Instrument of Play

Our language not only works, it also entertains. For example, movie history buffs tell the story of the famed gossip columnist of the 1950s, Hedda Hopper. As part of her research on him, Hopper sent Cary Grant the following telegram: "How old Cary Grant?" Grant responded by telegram: "Old Cary Grant fine. How old Hedda Hopper?"

We use language not only for such verbal dueling, but also for the pleasure of its sounds. Many linguists believe we all vocalize as children partly because it just feels and sounds good. Luckily, we do not entirely lose that capacity for play as we mature. The "Ob-la-di, ob-la-da" refrain in the Beatles song of the same name and the forced rhymes in a lot of rap music are but two examples of language used for the sheer fun of its sounds.

Check Language Use

When in doubt, we as speakers will sometimes check with our listeners to see whether they are decoding a message similar to the one we intended: "Do you understand?" "Get it?" As listeners during interpersonal communication, we may even interrupt a speaker to signal our misunderstanding: "Wait a minute. I don't follow you."

Garrison Keillor is able to make the fictional characters in Lake Wobegon come alive through the colorful language, stories, and poems he tells about them in his Prairie Home Companion *radio broadcasts.*

These five functions of language should be obvious to you by this point in your public speaking class. The fact that most of your classmates understood the speeches you have given so far testifies to the power of language to carry a speaker's ideas. Yet your listeners have learned more about you than the ideas you communicated. From your language during your speeches and while commenting on others' speeches, they have learned about your likes and dislikes. They may have even made accurate guesses about aspects of your background. During the semester or quarter, the language you used in your speeches and in class discussion has also established and strengthened the social bonds between you and your classmates. Anytime speakers used humor or showed any verbal virtuosity, they invited you to play with language. Whenever you used an interjection such as "Get this" or "This is important," or whenever you questioned a speaker after a speech, you used language to check and measure your understanding.

Selecting the right words to express your ideas is essential to your speaking success. You can have a great topic, but if your language isn't correct, clear, vivid, and conversational, you won't capture your listeners' attention. In my speeches I used language to connect myself and my message with my audience. For a few of my speeches, I began with a question to get my listeners thinking. I also tried to create vivid pictures and images with my words by using metaphors, personification, and other imagery.

In addition to using vivid language, I also used friendly, conversational language. I wrote my speeches the way I talk to my friends. I used pronouns like *we* and *you* to show that I was really interested in my audience. Practicing my speech out loud helped me develop an oral rather than written style. And, of course, practicing my speech in front of my friends and getting their input was really valuable. Knowing that my language was correct, clear, vivid, and conversational helped make giving my speeches fun, and that made me feel more confident.

—Allison Holt, Eastern Illinois University

speaking with confidence

Language has many registers, from chatty and confidential to simple and direct, complex and technical, lofty and formal. You speak differently to different people, depending upon the environment, the subject under discussion, and your relationship with your listeners. Though public speaking is generally more formal than casual conversation, the precise level of language you use will depend on what you want your speech to accomplish.

At times, we want our language to be "transparent," almost to disappear. In these instances, we focus on getting our meaning across to our listeners quickly and clearly. If you were reporting a fire, a gas leak, or some other emergency to a group of people and advising them to vacate their building, you would try to communicate that information directly, simply, and quickly, without causing panic. You would not waste time mentally editing and practicing the message to make it more clever or more memorable. In giving instructions or issuing a warning, you would never want to use language your audience did not know. Because your goal in these circumstances is getting your message across to a listener, you would use language with clear denotations. **Denotation** is the dictionary definition of a word.

On other occasions, you speak to get a message across but also to convey it in an especially vivid way. At such times, you pay particular attention to the way you encode the message, choosing words as carefully as you might select a birthday gift for an important friend. When your purpose is to signal your feelings about a subject, to strengthen the social bonds between you and your listeners, or to engage them in verbal play, you will likely use language that is "opaque" and has strong connotations.[11] **Connotation** is the emotional association that a particular word has for an individual listener. The word *fire* may have pleasant connotations for you if you spent some time around a campfire recently. The same word will have negative connotations for someone whose home was burned down.

Your choice of language depends on the purpose of your speech. Usually, you will use a combination of denotative and connotative language registers. Whether the wording of your speech is straightforward or evocative, direct or highly embroidered, however, you must use language carefully. The following section offers guidelines for using language correctly, clearly, vividly, and appropriately.

denotation: the literal meaning or dictionary definition of a word or phrase.

connotation: the emotional associations that a word or phrase may evoke in individual listeners.

Principles of Effective Language Use

Words are sometimes compared to tools and weapons, and, in a sense, you draw from that arsenal every time you speak. The words you choose help determine your success in informing, persuading, and entertaining your audience. Four principles should guide your use of language and make you a more effective speaker.

key points

Principles of Effective Language Use

1. Use language correctly.
2. Use language clearly.
3. Use language vividly.
4. Use language appropriately.

Use Language Correctly

When you use language incorrectly in your speech, you run the risk of sending unintended messages, as well as of undermining your credibility and the causes you support. Poorly worded ideas are sometimes evaluated as poor ideas, although this may not be the case. For example, in a speech on how to dress and groom for an interview, a student of ours recently advised, "Men should not wear long hair to a business interview. Long hair has a real astigmatism attached to it." The speaker's advice may be sound, but he has worded it incorrectly; the student meant that long hair has a *stigma* attached to it. Another student, concerned about the increase of sexually transmitted diseases, encouraged her listeners to commit to "long-term monotonous relationships." She should have used the word *monogamous*.

If you hear examples of incorrect language in your class, they will likely be more subtle than the examples given above. Nevertheless, it is important for speakers to rid their speeches of all unnecessary intrusions. Speakers perceived to care about how they state their ideas are also perceived to care about what they say.

The following examples illustrate some common language errors we have heard in student speeches:

1. The first criteria for selecting a good wine is to experience its bouquet. (The speaker should use the singular noun *criterion*.)
2. If our school is to remain financially solvent, we must choose between three options: (1) increasing tuition, (2) laying off faculty and staff employees, or (3) forgoing the planned construction of a new athletic complex. (*Among* is the correct word when more than two options are included.)
3. Because she failed to wear her seat belt, she was hurt bad: a broken leg, fractured ribs, and a mild concussion. (She was *badly* hurt.)
4. Because they conduct most of their missions at night, a drug trafficker often alludes our understaffed border patrol. (*They* is plural, so the speaker should use *drug traffickers*. Also, the correct word is *elude*, not *allude*.)
5. Less than twenty students attended the lecture given by Dr. Hinojosa last Wednesday. (Use *fewer* when people or items can be counted. Yes, those supermarket check-out lane signs that say "10 Items or Less" are wrong!)
6. Members of our legislature voted theirselves a pay raise at the same time they voted down an increase in the state's education budget. (*Theirselves* is not a word. The correct word is *themselves*.)

Some of these errors may seem less severe to you than others. Remember, though, that your language is an important part of the delivery of your speech. Your language, like your physical and vocal delivery, should be free of all distractions. Errors in subject/verb agreement, misplaced modifiers, and incorrect word choice immediately attract the attention of everyone who recognizes these errors. You won't upset anyone if your language is grammatically correct, but even small errors run the risk of monopolizing some people's attention. In turn, they stop listening carefully to *what* you say because they are paying attention to *how* you speak.

You can speak correctly if you follow a few simple guidelines. First, make a note of grammatical mistakes you hear yourself and other people make in casual conversation. Attentive listening is a first step to improving your use of language. Second, when you are unsure of a word's meaning, consult a dictionary. Third, if you have a question

Remember the word "choice." Every speaker, every writer, every user of language, chooses the words that he or she wants to use. . . . Imprecise or weak words detract from the meaning of the message, while the choice of exact words empowers language. Stronger English comes from making stronger choices, and exact wording, when it becomes a habit, can become fun as well as fascinating.

—*Jeffrey McQuain*[12]

about proper grammar, refer to a handbook for writers. Fourth, when practicing your speech, record it and play it back, listening for mistakes you may not have noticed as you were practicing. Fifth, practice your speech in front of friends and ask them to point out mistakes. These strategies will help you detect and correct errors. Not only will your speaking improve, but you may also save yourself some embarrassment. As Mark Twain noted, "The difference between the right word and the almost right word is the difference between lightning and the lightning bug."

Use Language Clearly

How would you respond if a friend said to you, "Let's work on our project for a while after dinner. Could you bring a quire with you?" You would probably ask several questions because your friend failed to communicate clearly. What specifically is "our project"? How long is "for a while"? What time is "after dinner"? Where will this meeting take place? Your friend would have communicated the first part of the message more clearly if she had said, "Let's meet in my room from 6:00 to 7:00 this evening to work on our group report for Psychology 100." You might also ask, "Did you say something about a choir?" After being corrected, you would probably ask, "OK, what's a *q-u-i-r-e*?" Though it is specific, the word *quire* is not common and may be confusing unless you know that it means 24 sheets of paper.

Language use must not only be correct, it must also be clear. In order to achieve clarity, a speaker should use language that is specific and familiar. If you sacrifice either criterion, your language may confuse your listeners.

Use Specific Language. In Chapter 1, we mentioned that many of our communication problems spring from the fact that there are always two messages involved whenever two people are communicating. There is, first, the message that the speaker intends. In addition, there is the message that the listener infers or interprets. If you tell your instructor that you missed an assignment deadline because you were "having some problems," you leave yourself open to a wide range of possible interpretations. Do you have health problems, family troubles, or stress from a personal relationship? You could be having trouble juggling a work schedule with your study time or having car problems. You could be grieving over the loss of a loved one or struggling with one particularly difficult course. These and other interpretations are possible because *problem* is an abstract term.

To clarify your ideas, use the lowest level of abstraction possible. Words are not *either* abstract or concrete, but take on these qualities in relation to other words. Look at the following lists of terms, for example.

theater

Western theater

twentieth-century Western theater

documentary theater

plays of Michael Hastings

The Silence of Lee Harvey Oswald

class

college class

college communication class

Comm 110: Introduction to Public Speaking

Comm 110 at Montana State University

Comm 110 with Prof. Tom Diamond at Montana State University

The terms at the top of these lists are more abstract than those at the bottom. As we add those limiting, descriptive words, or *qualifiers,* the referent becomes increasingly specific. The lower the level of abstraction used, the more clearly the listener will understand the speaker.

Suppose you were giving a speech on how citizens can protect their homes from burglaries, and you made the following statement:

> Crime is rampant in our city. Burglary alone has gone way up in the past year or so. So you can see that having the right kind of lock on your door is essential to your safety.

What is wrong with this statement? The language is vague. What does "rampant" mean? How much of an increase is "way up"—15 percent, 50 percent, 400 percent? Is "the past year or so" one year, two years, or more? What is "the right kind of lock"? As a speaker you should help your audience by making these ideas more concrete. After some research, you might rephrase your argument like this:

> Last week I spoke with Captain James Winton, head of our City Police Department's Records Division. He told me that crime in our city has increased by 54 percent in the last year, and the number of burglaries has doubled. We can help deter crime by making our homes burglar-proof, and one way of doing this is to make sure that all doors have solid locks. I brought one such lock with me: It's a double-keyed deadbolt lock.

Notice the improvement in the second paragraph. Your message is clearer, and with that clarity you would gain added credibility as a speaker.

Use Familiar Language. Anyone who has purchased a video cassette recorder has suffered through the complicated instructions that usually accompany these machines. According to Karen Schriver, English professor at Carnegie Mellon University, those awkward, unclear instructions are usually written by entry-level engineers who are much more concerned with the capabilities of the equipment's features than with the poor consumer who will be using the VCR. Mitsubishi Electronics America recently recruited Schriver to help rewrite their VCR user manuals. A sample of her changes follows:

> *Before:* "This VCR employs direct function switching where any playback mode may be directly entered from any other playback mode (normal playback, still frame, speed search, etc.) simply by pressing the appropriate buttons."

> *After:* "When you use a feature (like Play or Rewind), you can go directly to another feature (like Speed Search) without first pressing Stop."[13]

Both sentences are specific, but the second communicates the message in a language style more familiar to nonengineers.

Your language may be specific but still not be clear. If listeners are not familiar with your words, communication is impaired. The statement "The Sultan of Swat was famous for his batboy shots" is specific but probably unclear to most listeners. Some may know that the Sultan of Swat is a nickname for baseball great Babe Ruth. Probably only the most avid baseball enthusiast, however, knows that the term *batboy shot* refers to a home run hit so powerfully that the batter knows instantly that it is out of the park and has time to hand the bat to the batboy (no batgirls in Babe Ruth's time) before rounding the bases.

Occasionally we hear speeches in which students try to impress listeners with their vocabularies. We suspect they drafted their remarks with a pen in one hand and a thesaurus in the other. Phrases such as "a plethora of regulations," "this obviates

The chief virtue that language can have is clearness, and nothing detracts from it so much as the use of unfamiliar words.

—*Hippocrates*

271

Principles of Effective Language Use

the need for," "the apotheosis of deceit," and "the anathema of censorship" detract from rather than enhance the speaker's message. "We must ever be mindful to eschew verbosity and deprecate tautology" is good advice and fun to say. But if you are trying to communicate with another person, it's probably better simply to say, "Avoid wordiness."

The use of jargon can also undermine clarity. **Jargon** is the special language of a particular activity, business, or group of people. What, for example, are the meanings of the following acronyms used in Internet chat rooms?

BRB	ROFL
BTDTGTS	NRN
GAL	PMFJI
HAND	TTYL[14]

Endnote 14 on page 286 contains the answers. If you know these acronyms, just a few letters enabled you to interpret entire phrases. However, if this jargon was unfamiliar, it thwarted effective communication. Real estate agents will say that a particular house has a good "drive up," meaning that it makes a good first impression. Stockbrokers and their clients discuss "bear markets," "selling short," and "buying on the margin." Say you tell your audience that Orlando, Florida, will have the first high-speed train using maglev technology in the United States. You will probably also need to tell your listeners that *maglev* is short for "magnetic levitation," and then explain what that means.

If you are certain that the people you are addressing know such terms, jargon presents no problem. In fact, it is usually quite specific and can save a lot of time. Jargon can even increase your credibility by indicating that you are familiar with the subject matter. If you have any doubts about whether your listeners know the jargon, however, either avoid such terms or define each one the first time you use it.

jargon: the special language used by people in a particular activity, business, or group.

Use Language Vividly

In addition to selecting language that is correct and clear, speakers should choose language that is colorful and picturesque. Vivid language engages the audience and makes

---

ethical decisions

In his book *The New Doublespeak*, William Lutz writes about the unclear and misleading language used in our society. In recent speeches and public statements, politicians have used phrases such as "revenue enhancement," "receipt proposals," and "wage-based premiums" when they mean *taxes*. Business leaders have referred to "laying off workers" as "work reengineering." Military spokespersons sometimes speak of "neutralizing the opposition" to avoid using the word *killing*. The phrase "economical with the truth" has even been used to cushion the impact of the word *lying*.

Lutz argues that the use of such phrases is unethical because "The clearest possible language is essential for democracy to function, for it is only through clear language that we have any hope of defining, debating, and deciding the issues of public policy that confront us." Do you agree with Lutz's position, or do you think it is legitimate for speakers to use this kind of language if it helps them achieve their purposes? Can you think of a time when the use of such "doublespeak" would be appropriate? In general, what ethical guidelines should speakers use to govern their choice of language?

The Reverend Jesse Jackson is renowned for his moving speeches. He paints vivid images and visions for listeners, using clear, specific language that resonates across social, economic, and racial and ethnic lines.

the task of listening easier. Read the following critiques of the speeches of our twenty-ninth president, Warren Harding:

1. Warren Harding was not an effective public speaker. His speeches often were confusing and uninspired. He did not make his points well.

2. "His speeches left the impression of an army of pompous phrases moving over the landscape in search of an idea; sometimes these meandering words would actually capture a straggling thought and bear it triumphantly a prisoner in their midst, until it died of servitude and overwork." William G. McAdoo, Democratic party leader[15]

3. "He writes the worst English that I have ever encountered. It reminds me of a string of wet sponges; it reminds me of tattered washing on the line; it reminds me of stale bean soup, of college yells, of dogs barking idiotically through endless nights. It is so bad that a sort of grandeur creeps into it. It drags itself out of the dark abysm (I was about to write abscess!) of pish and crawls insanely up to the topmost pinnacle of posh. It is rumble and bumble. It is flap and doodle. It is balder and dash." H. L. Mencken[16]

Which of these three statements did you most enjoy reading? Which characterization of Harding's speaking did you find the most colorful? Which paragraph contains the most vivid images? Which would you most like to read again? While we don't know your answers to these questions, we're fairly certain that you did *not* select the first statement. Why?

The language of the first critique communicates an idea as simply and economically as possible without calling attention to itself. To use a term we introduced earlier in this chapter, its language is transparent. It is also drab and colorless and displays little creativity. The language style of the first example is not nearly as lively and its images are not as vivid as the other two. The language of the second and third statements is opaque; it calls attention to its sounds, textures, and rhythms. Vivid language helps listeners remember both your message and you.

One of the fiercest enemies of vivid language is the **cliché**, a once-colorful expression that has lost most of its impact through overuse. Many clichés involve comparisons. For example, complete the following phrases:

Cute as a _____.

Dead as a _____.

Between a rock and a _____.

Burning the midnight _____.

cliché: a once-colorful figure of speech that has lost impact from overuse.

Did you have any trouble completing those expressions? Probably not. In fact, button, doornail, hard place, and oil most likely popped into your mind without much thought. Each of these sayings is a cliché, an overworked expression that doesn't require (or stimulate) much thinking. Clichés are bland and hackneyed. Avoid them!

Now that you have seen some of the effects of dull wording, what techniques can you use to make your language more vivid? The answer to this question may be limited only by your imagination. We offer three strategies for your consideration: (1) use active language; (2) appeal to your listeners' senses; and (3) use figures and structures of speech. Following these suggestions will give you a good start on making your speeches more colorful and, thus, more memorable.

Use Active Language. Which of the following statements is more forceful?

> It was decided by the Student Government Association that the election would be delayed for one week.

> The Student Government Association decided to delay the election for one week.

The second one, right? The first sentence uses passive voice; the second active. Active voice is always more direct because it identifies the agent producing the action and places it first in the sentence. In addition, active voice is more economical than passive voice; the second sentence is shorter than the first by five words.

Active language, however, involves more than active voice. Active language is language that works. It has energy, vitality, and drive. It is not bogged down by filler phrases such as "you know," "like," and "stuff like that." Rather than being cliché-ridden, it may convert the commonplace into the unexpected. Language that is lively and active can also be humorous. For example, a *Time* magazine reporter wrote that contemporary Dutch-born architect Rem Koolhaas "likes to consider himself an architect without style. For him, form not only doesn't follow function; the two are barely on speaking terms." [17] Notice how the following two students twist familiar expressions to achieve more dramatic results in their speech conclusions.

> Writing Resources Online
> http://www.garbl.com
> Garbl's Writing Resources Online provides speech writers with lots of practical information, from basic grammar to style and usage. Especially helpful to persuasive speakers is the active writing link, which provides information on how to write persuasively. The links to reference materials are also helpful, as well as the option of contacting an online expert for answers to writing questions.

> Cherie spoke of injuries, even deaths, children suffer from playing baseball. After detailing some ways the game could be made safer, she concluded, "[C]hildren may be dying to play baseball, but they should never die because of it." [18]

> Joni claimed there was gender bias in medical research and called for greater attention to women's health issues. She gave an interesting twist to a familiar saying in her final statement: "The old cliché no longer holds true. What's good for the gander is no longer good for the goose." [19]

Coining a word or phrase is another way of making your language work for you. The widespread popularity of e-mail has led us to distinguish it from "snail mail." A well-turned phrase also actively engages the minds of your listeners as they hear the interplay of words and ideas. Indian nationalist leader Mohandas Gandhi, for example, urged his listeners to "live simply so others might simply live."

Appeal to Your Listeners' Senses. Another way you can achieve impact with language is by appealing to your listeners' senses. The obvious and familiar senses are sight, hearing, touch, taste, and smell. To these we can add the sense of motion or movement and the sense of muscular tension. Colorful language can create vivid images that appeal to each of these various senses. Those sharp images in turn heighten audience involvement in the speech, inviting listeners to participate with their feelings and thereby increasing their retention of what you have said.

Assume that you are a roller coaster enthusiast and have decided to deliver an informative speech on roller coasters. Such a topic certainly begs for language to create or recreate the various sensations of a coaster ride for your audience. But what if you are not confident about your ability to appeal to your audience's various senses in your speech? You can always do some research on this topic and use the words of others, as long as you accurately attribute your quotations. We easily found four magazine articles on roller coasters. Figure 12.1 lists and defines the different kinds of sensory images and provides examples from two of these articles.[20] Notice how many of these examples of sensory impressions are not only evocative but also funny and fun to say. Active language and appeals to the senses are not your only techniques for enlivening your speech language, however. Public speaking gives you an opportunity to use some special language structures and to devise some of the figures of speech you may have studied before in English classes.

Use Figures and Structures of Speech. Important ideas are easier to remember if they are memorably worded. Drawing attention to the way you phrase your thoughts—making your language "opaque"—can produce memorable effects in your listeners. To enliven your language, you can use various figures and structures of speech. Some of the most common figures of speech are simile, metaphor, and personification. Common structures of speech are alliteration, parallelism, repetition, and antithesis.

Simile and **metaphor** are comparisons of two seemingly dissimilar things. In simile the comparison is explicitly stated using the words *as* or *like;* for example, "Trying to pin the Senator down on the issue is like trying to nail a poached egg to a tree." In his speech on the need to reform the "enhanced" E-911 emergency telephone system, Bill quoted the following use of simile: "As Congressman Elliot Engel stated in House testimony on September 8, 1998, 'relying on E-911 in an emergency is like relying on [the] *Titanic* to take you to New York.' "[21]

simile: a comparison of two things using the words *as* or *like.*

metaphor: an implied comparison of two things without the use of *as* or *like.*

Can you think of an image or a comparison that would help you communicate what New York's Guggenheim Museum looks like?

This sensory impression . . .	achieves this effect.	Example:
Visual image	recreates the sight of something.	"The Cyclone differs from other roller coasters in being (a) a work of art and (b) old, . . . decrepit, rusting in its metal parts and peeling in its more numerous wooden parts."
Auditory image	suggests the sound of something.	"Yes it may be anguishing initially . . . terrifying, even, the first time or two the train is hauled upward with groans and creaks and with you in it. At the top then—where there is a sudden strange quiet but for the fluttering of two tattered flags. . . ."
Tactile image	recreates the feel of something.	"I should mention that a heavy, cushioned restraining bar locks down snugly into your lap and is very reassuring, although, like everything upholstered in the cars, it may be cracked or slashed . . . "
Thermal image	creates impressions of heat or cold.	"It was an awful moment, with a sickening sense of betrayal and icy-fingered doubt."
Gustatory image	recreates the taste of something.	Nothing matches the faint metallic taste of fear as you feel the train set free to begin falling from the top of that first hill.
Kinetic image	creates feelings of motion or movement.	"At nearly 65 mph, the train shot into a tunnel and spun 540 degrees around a banked helix . . . "
Kinesthetic image	suggests states of muscular tension or relaxation.	"My teeth clenched and my knuckles locked bone-white around the lap bar."
Olfactory image	suggests the smell of something.	We are brought to a "quick, pillowy deceleration in the shed, smelling of dirty machine oil . . . "
Synesthesia	combines two or more sensory impressions.	Riding a coaster is "like driving your car with your head out the window at 70 miles per hour. But to get the full effect, you have to drive it off a cliff."

FIGURE 12.1
Types of sensory images

In metaphor, the comparison is not explicitly stated but is implied, without using *as* or *like.* Metaphor making is an ancient activity. Scholars who have studied the earliest language that gave rise to English and dozens of other languages have discovered the phrase *wekwom texos,* or "weaver of words." This title distinguished the tribal poets who preserved stories and legends by weaving them into sung or chanted verse.[22]

Some of the earliest metaphors probably originated as speakers extended human physiology, as in "the mouth of the river" and "the bowels of the earth."[23] Today our language is full of metaphorical comparisons. If you're tired of waiting to see how things "pan out," so you decide to "take the bull by the horns" because you know that boredom is your "Achilles heel," you are thinking in terms of three distinct metaphors. As you can see, many metaphors lose impact from overuse. We may even lose sight of the original, underlying comparison.

Metaphor helps us accommodate the new in terms of the familiar. As a nation, we have moved from being "couch potatoes" to "channel surfers." At the same time, television executives and advertisers may conceive of us, remote controls in hand, as a nation of "grazers."

> If we think of ourselves as channel surfers, perhaps we are compensating heavily for sitting in front of the television actually doing nothing. If the industry calls us grazers, perhaps they don't have too high an opinion of us. The metaphors people use give us insights into their conceptual and fantasy worlds. More than that, the metaphors shape how we perceive our "real world," and what we are doing in it.[24]

The difference between simile and metaphor is greater than just the presence or absence of *as* or *like*, however. While simile makes a comparison that can sometimes be fairly ordinary and reasonable, metaphor achieves a "qualitative leap . . . to an identification or fusion of two objects" with the characteristics of both.[25] To produce metaphors is to extend meanings, to improvise, to let your imagination go.[26]

Fresh metaphors have the power to surprise us into new ways of seeing things. If you've ever visited or even seen a photograph of the Solomon R. Guggenheim Museum, you'll recognize the brilliance of the following metaphor: "Art museums were stodgy buildings until 1958, when Frank Lloyd Wright plopped a concrete cupcake on New York's Fifth Avenue."[27] Theodore Roosevelt created a memorable metaphor when he made the following comparison, "A good political speech is a poster, not an etching."[28] Peter Schjeldahl, author of one of the articles on Coney Island's Cyclone, uses metaphor when he compares that roller coaster to a poem:

Language Use
http://www.abacon.
com/pubspeak/organize/
style.html
This Allyn & Bacon Web site offers insight into using various figures and structures of speech, such as alliteration, metaphor, and personification. These and other terms are defined and explained. Audio examples are used to reinforce your understanding of these language tools. *RealAudio* is required to hear these examples.

> The coaster is basically an ornate means of falling and a poem about physics in parts or stanzas, with jokes. The special quality of the Cyclone is how different, how *articulated*, all the components of its poem are, the whole of which lasts a minute and thirty-some seconds—exactly the right length, composed of distinct and perfect moments. By my fifth ride, my heart was leaping at the onset of each segment as at the approach of a dear old friend, and melting with instantaneous nostalgia for each at its finish.[29]

Notice that near the end of the description the roller coaster begins to take on human characteristics.

Personification gives human qualities to objects, ideas, or organizations. One speech teacher used personification as the organizing concept of her speech titled "The Anatomy of an Association." In her address, she argued that an association's muscle is its unity, its brains are the knowledge it generates, its lifeblood is its ability to renew its membership, and its heart is its people.[30]

Virginia Postrel, editor of *Reason* magazine, began her speech on the environmental movement using personification this way:

personification: a figure of speech that attributes human qualities to a concept or inanimate object.

On Earth Day, Henry Allen of the *Washington Post* published a pointed and amusing article. In it he suggested that we've created a new image of Mother Nature:

"A sort of combination of Joan Crawford in *Mildred Pierce* and Mrs. Portnoy in *Portnoy's Complaint,* a disappointed, long-suffering martyr who makes us wish, at least for her sake, that we'd never been born.

"She weeps. She threatens. She nags. . . .

"She's a kvetch who makes us feel guilty for eating Big Macs, dumping paint thinner down the cellar sink, driving to work instead of riding the bus, and riding the bus instead of riding a bicycle. Then she makes us feel even guiltier for not feeling guilty enough.

" 'Go, ahead, use that deodorant, don't even think about me, God knows I'll be gone soon enough, I won't be here to see you get skin cancer when the ozone hole lets in the ultraviolet rays. . . .' "[31]

In addition to these figures of speech, you can also employ language structures, such as alliteration, parallelism, repetition, and antithesis. **Alliteration** is the repetition of beginning sounds in adjacent or nearby words. A speaker who asks us "to dream, to dare, and to do" uses alliteration. The sounds of words give your speech impact. A student speaking on the topic of child abuse described the victims as "badly bruised and beaten." Not only did these words themselves convey a severe problem, but the repetition of the stern, forceful *b* sound vocally accentuated the violence of the act.

In his "I Have a Dream" speech in Appendix B, Martin Luther King, Jr., used alliteration to describe his dream of a nation where people "will not be judged by the color of their skin but by the content of their character." Holocaust survivor Elie Wiesel used alliteration in a speech entitled "The Shame of Hunger" when he spoke of "faith in the future," "complacency if not complicity," and "hunger and humiliation."[32]

Speaking on the subject of educational reform, Vincent Ryan Ruggiero, professor of humanities at State University of New York at Delhi, complained of "mindstuffing," a current practice in education "which renders students passive and transforms the 3 Rs into Receiving, Recalling, and Regurgitating information."[33]

Speakers use **parallelism** when they express two or more ideas in similar language structure. When they restate words, phrases, or sentences, they use **repetition.** Parallelism and repetition work in concert to emphasize an idea or a call for action. President Ronald Reagan's moving tribute to the shuttle crew killed in the *Challenger* disaster effectively connected ideas by using parallelism. Near the beginning of the speech, Reagan used repetition to introduce the goal of his speech: "The best we can do is remember our seven astronauts, our *Challenger* seven, remember them as they lived. . . ." Reagan then combined repetition and parallel structure as he issued a final roll call of the ill-fated crew:

We remember Dick Scobee, the commander who spoke the last words we heard from the space shuttle *Challenger*. He served as a fighter pilot in Vietnam earning many medals for bravery and later as a test pilot of advanced aircraft before joining the space program. Danger was a familiar companion to Commander Scobee.

We remember Michael Smith, who earned enough medals as a combat pilot to cover his chest, including the Navy Distinguished Flying Cross, three Air Medals, and the Vietnamese Cross of Gallantry with Silver Star in gratitude from a nation he fought to keep free.

We remember Judith Resnick, known as J. R. to her friends, always smiling, always eager to make a contribution, finding beauty in the music she played on her piano in her off-hours.

The list continued, "We remember Ellison Onizuka," "We remember Ronald McNair," "We remember Gregory Jarvis," "We remember Christa McAuliffe," each repetition of "we remember" like the forlorn tolling of a bell.[34]

Another excellent example of the use of parallel construction is Martin Luther King, Jr.'s, "I Have a Dream" speech. King repeats the phrase "one hundred years later"

alliteration: the repetition of beginning sounds in words that are adjacent or near one another.

parallelism: the expression of ideas using similar grammatical structures.

repetition: restating words, phrases, or sentences for emphasis.

to dramatize the "shameful condition" of inequality. He prefaces his hopes for the future with the phrase "I have a dream." And near the end of his speech he uses parallelism and repetition to create a dramatic climax:

> So *let freedom ring* from the prodigious hilltops of New Hampshire. *Let freedom ring* from the mighty mountains of New York. *Let freedom ring* from the heightening Alleghenies of Pennsylvania! *Let freedom ring* from the snowcapped Rockies of Colorado!
>
> But not only that. *Let freedom ring* from Stone Mountain of Georgia! *Let freedom ring* from Lookout Mountain of Tennessee! *Let freedom ring* from every hill and molehill of Mississippi. From every mountainside, *let freedom ring*.
>
> And when this happens . . . we will be able to join hands and sing, in the words of the old Negro spiritual, *"Free at last! Free at last!* Thank God almighty, we are *free at last!"*

Antithesis uses parallel construction to contrast ideas. You can probably quote from memory John Kennedy's statement: "Ask not what your country can do for you, ask what you can do for your country." The fact that it is so memorable attests to its power. Mario Cuomo used antithesis in his keynote address to the 1984 Democratic National Convention:

> We must get the American public to look past the glitter, beyond the showmanship—to reality, to the hard substance of things. And we will do that not so much with speeches that sound good as with speeches that are good and sound. Not so much with speeches that bring people to their feet as with speeches that bring people to their senses.[35]

In 1999 Sarah Meinen of Bradley University won the national speech tournament of the Interstate Oratorical Association with her speech "The Forgotten Four-Letter Word." She carefully researched and organized her speech on the problem of compassion fatigue, "the inability to care anymore about social issues." She crafted her language carefully, using the figures and structures of speech we've just discussed. Sarah's work paid off. She captured the attention and tapped the concern of her listeners, encouraging them to rekindle a passion for AIDS awareness and activism.

> With statistics and expert opinions, Sarah reminded her listeners of the "savage spread" of this "vicious virus" [alliteration]. "AIDS has been too grim, too overwhelming, and it's been around too long" [parallelism and repetition]. She lamented that "despite our exposure to death and destruction, facts and figures, names and Quilt squares, AIDS has slowly faded from our national consciousness . . . " [alliteration and antithesis]. Sarah concluded, "Our well of compassion has run dry . . . " [metaphor].
>
> Sarah urged her listeners to become advocates for change on a national and personal level. "[C]losing our eyes won't make a monster of this magnitude go away" [personification]. "We may be over AIDS, but AIDS is not over . . . [antithesis]. "We may be immune to the stories and statistics, but none of us is safe from the reality of AIDS" [alliteration and antithesis]. Sarah exhorted her audience to do "whatever you have to do to be shocked, to be scared, to be involved, to be compassionate, and to keep this pandemic from being ignored, dismissed, and forgotten" [parallelism].

A transcript of Sarah's full speech is reprinted in Appendix B. Read it, noting her careful attention to language. We think you will admire the way she used language to tap the values of her audience and sharpen her message.

Simile, metaphor, personification, alliteration, parallelism, repetition, and antithesis enable speakers to create vivid language and images. One note of caution, however: Always remember that your objective as a speaker is not to impress your listeners with your ability to create vivid language. Vivid language is not an end in itself but rather a means of achieving the larger objectives of the speech. As language expert William

antithesis: the use of
parallel construction to
contrast ideas.

Safire notes, "A good speech is not a collection of crisp one-liners, workable metaphors, and effective rhetorical devices; a good speech truly reflects the thoughts and emotions of the speaker. . . ."[36]

Use Language Appropriately

As we have discussed throughout this book, appropriateness has several dimensions. Your language should be appropriate to you, your topic, your audience, and the occasion. Sometimes it may seem impossible to achieve all four of these goals. We have heard speakers criticized for poor grammar or incorrect pronunciation respond, "But that's the way I talk." They apparently believe it's more important for language to reflect their speaking style than for it to be correct. Some listeners may neither detect nor be offended by your incorrect language use, but others will. They are the ones who should concern you. The safest rule for you to follow is this: Correct language never offends, and incorrect language is never appropriate.

If your language is correct, clear, and vivid, you have a good start on achieving appropriateness. However, spoken language that is in good form should possess two other characteristics: oral style and inclusive language.

Use Oral Style. In order to speak appropriately, you must recognize that your oral style differs from your written style. Unless your instructor asks you to deliver some speeches from a manuscript, we believe that you will be better off if you think of "developing" speeches rather than "writing" them. We can give you two good reasons for avoiding writing your speeches. First, you will likely try to memorize what you have written, and the fear of forgetting part of the speech will add to your nervousness and make your delivery seem stiff and wooden.

The second and more important reason for not writing out a speech is that the act of writing itself often affects the tone of the communication. **Tone** is the relationship established by language and grammar between a writer or speaker and that person's readers or listeners. Many of us think of writing as something formal and correct. In fact, many of us are intimidated by writing specifically because we think it must be formal and correct. For that reason, we tend not to write the way that we speak. Novelist and screenwriter Richard Price speaks from his own experience about the crucial difference between the written and the spoken word:

> It's amazing how much stuff looks dazzlingly authentic and true and beautiful on the page, but dies in someone's mouth . . . and it's amazing how little is too much. . . .
>
> That's the importance of a read through for the writer and the director. Because when the actors at a big round table read all the parts of a script, what doesn't work is going to pop up so obviously. And there's no substitute for that. There's no other way you can learn that except to hear it in somebody's mouth.[37]

If you compose parts of a speech on paper, make certain that you read what's on the page out loud to see if it sounds oral rather than written. How can you tell the difference?

Our oral style differs from our written style in at least four important ways. First, in speaking we tend to use shorter sentences than we write. Speakers who write out their speeches often find themselves gasping for air when they try to deliver a long sentence in one breath.

Second, when we communicate orally, we tend to use more contractions, colloquial expressions, and slang. Our speaking vocabulary is smaller than our writing vocabulary, so we tend to speak a simpler language than we write. Speakers who write out their speeches often draw from their larger written vocabularies. As a result, their presentational style seems formal and often creates a barrier between them and their listeners.

tone: the relation established by language and grammar between speakers and their listeners.

> **Inclusive Language**
> http://owl.english.
> purdue.edu/Files/26.html
> The Purdue University On-
> line Writing Lab provides
> useful information on how
> to make your language
> more inclusive. Their sec-
> tion on nonsexist language
> provides guidelines en-
> dorsed by the National
> Council of Teachers of
> English for using pronouns
> and referring to various
> occupations.

Third, oral style makes greater use of personal pronouns and references than written style does. Speakers must acknowledge the presence of their listeners, and one way of doing this is by including them in the speech. Using the pronouns *I, we,* and *you* makes your speech more immediate and enhances your rapport with your listeners. You may even want to mention specific audience members by name: "Last week John told us how to construct a power résumé. I'm going to tell you what to do once your résumé gets you a job interview." Notice how the name of the student, coupled with several personal pronouns, brings the speaker and audience together and sets up the possibility for lively interaction.

A fourth difference between oral and written style is the frequency of repetition. Oral style uses more repetition. As we discussed in Chapter 4, "Responding to Speeches," readers can slow down and reread the material in front of them. They control the pace. Listeners do not have that luxury. Speakers must take special care to reinforce their messages, and one way of accomplishing this is by using repetition. Figure 12.2 summarizes key differences between written and oral styles.

Use Inclusive Language. If you are speaking to a diverse audience, or if you are referring to people in general, it makes sense to include as many people as possible. Select language that is inclusive rather than exclusive. As an ethical speaker, you would never

Oral Style Checklist	Instead of This	Say This
Use Active Voice	A tuition increase was enacted by our college last year.	Last year, our college increased our tuition.
Use Familiar Language	Such an action would not be prudent at this juncture.	I don't think we should do that.
Use Personal Pronouns	People need to stand up and say, "Enough is enough."	We must stand up and say, "Enough is enough."
Use Contractions	You will not find him in a library on a weekend if his personal computer is working.	You won't find him in a library on a weekend if his computer's working.
Use Short Sentences	According to Nigel Hawkes in his book *Structures: The Way Things Are Built,* an accidental discovery by well diggers in 1974 has led archaeologists in central China to unearth an army of possibly 8,000 terra-cotta figures of warriors and horses in the tomb of China's first emperor.	According to Nigel Hawkes in his book *Structures: The Way Things Are Built,* well diggers in central China discovered pieces of broken terra-cotta in 1974. Since then, archaeologists have unearthed what may be a total of 8,000 figures. They are terra-cotta figures of warriors and horses guarding the tomb of China's first emperor.

FIGURE 12.2
Keys to an effective oral style

want to include racial slurs in any speech. You should also avoid language that perpetuates stereotypes about people based on other characteristics, such as their age. "Old goat," "old fogey," and "old hag" are insulting metaphors for people who happen to be old. Expressions such as "dirty old man" and "old maid" manage to be both sexist and ageist at once: They criticize one gender for being sexually active and the other for not.[38]

Language is sexist if it "promotes and maintains attitudes that stereotype people according to gender. It [**sexist language**] assumes that the male is the norm—the significant gender. **Nonsexist language** treats all people equally and either does not refer to a person's sex at all when it is irrelevant or refers to men and women in symmetrical ways when their gender is relevant."[39]

Notice the gender identification in each of the following two statements:

> One of the most important qualities a company executive must possess is effective communication. In fact, the higher he advances in the company, the more important it is that he be able to speak clearly and convincingly.

> A secretary is no longer only a receptionist and a typist. Today she performs the role of information manager for the office.

Both of these examples are sexist. The first one implies that executives are male, and the second one suggests that all secretaries are female. Nonsexist language acknowledges that either gender can assume the roles of executive or secretary.

You can eliminate sexist language in these statements if you replace each "he" and "she" with "he or she." This remedy, however, can be wordy and intrusive at times, especially when a sentence includes several third-person singular pronouns. You can solve this problem by using the plural form if it is appropriate. Note how the statements change when they are reworded with this approach:

> One of the most important qualities company executives must possess is effective communication. In fact, the higher they advance in their companies, the more important it is that they be able to speak clearly and convincingly.

> Secretaries are no longer only receptionists and typists. Today they perform the role of information manager for the office.

A more serious form of sexism occurs when language creates special categories for one gender, with no corresponding parallel category for the other gender. *Man* and *wife*, for example, are not parallel terms. *Man* and *woman* or *husband* and *wife* are parallel. Other examples of nonparallel language are *nurse* and *male nurse, chairman* and *chairperson*. A colleague tells us that when she worked at a television station, she was called a weather girl, even though a male employee of the same age was referred to as a weatherman.

Speakers exhibit fairness when they express their ideas and examples in language that treats all members of the audience equally and fairly. If you have difficulty selecting a gender-free term for one that may be considered sexist, consult a dictionary such as *The Bias-Free Word Finder: A Dictionary of Nondiscriminatory Language*, by Rosalie Maggio. Figure 12.3 features examples of sexist terms and nonsexist alternatives from Maggio's book.

No matter which of the world's roughly 5,000 languages you speak, the words you choose telegraph messages about your background, your involvement with your topic, and your relationship with your listeners.[40] Like the unique voice and body you use to deliver your speeches, your language is an extremely important part of your delivery. If

Inclusive Language
http://www.rpi.edu/dept/llc/writecenter/web/text/gender.html
The Writing Center at Rensselaer Polytechnic Institute offers information on how to use "gender-fair" language. This article, written by Jenny Redfern, presents specific ways to avoid the sexist use of the words *he* and *man*.

sexist language: language that excludes one gender, creates special categories for one gender, or assigns roles based solely on gender.

nonsexist language: language that treats both genders fairly and avoids stereotyping either one.

Sexist Term or Phrase	Nonsexist Alternative(s)
anchorman	news anchor, anchor person
city fathers	city leaders
craftsman	artisan
fireman	firefighter
garbageman	garbage collector
mailman	mailcarrier, letter carrier, postal worker
manpower	workers, workforce
man-size(d)	large-size(d), large, big
mother country	homeland, native land
night watchman	guard, security guard
old wives' tale	superstition, misconception
salesmanship	sales ability, sales expertise
weatherman	weathercaster, meteorologist

FIGURE 12.3
Alternatives to sexist language
[from Rosalie Maggio, *The Bias-Free Word Finder: A Dictionary of Nondiscriminatory Language* (Boston: Beacon, 1991) 7.]

you are conscientious, you must know when to speak simply and directly and when to embellish your language with sensory images, figures of speech, and unusual structural devices. In short, you don't have to be a poet to agree with poet Robert Frost, "All the fun's in how you say a thing."[41]

Summary

Language is a distinctly human instrument, no less important than any other tool we have developed for building and creating. Although other animals produce sounds and noises, the human language alone is articulated into words and alone is capable of expressing an infinite variety of thoughts.

Language serves five functions. First, it communicates ideas between speaker and listener. Second, language sends messages, either intentional or unintentional, about the person who uses it. Your choice of language may reveal your age, your background, and your attitudes about the subjects you discuss. Third, language establishes and strengthens social bonds between groups of people. Fourth, language is an instrument of play because it is the arena for joking and battles of wits. Fifth, we use language to monitor and check our use of language.

As a speaker you use different language on different occasions, depending on the environment, the topic, and your relationship with your listeners. Four principles should guide your use of language: (1) Use language correctly, (2) use language clearly, (3) use language vividly, and (4) use language appropriately.

As a speaker, your first obligation is to use language *correctly*. Select the right word for the thought you wish to convey, and then phrase the thought correctly. Incorrect language may communicate unintended messages as well as undermine a speaker's credibility. Five guidelines will help you detect and correct language errors. First, listen to the language you and others use, and focus on how it can be improved. Second, consult a dictionary when you are unsure of the meaning of a word. Third, refer to a writing handbook when you have a question about proper grammar. Fourth, use a tape recorder to help you detect incorrect language use. Fifth, practice your speech in front of friends, and ask them to point out your mistakes.

A second principle of language use is to use language *clearly.* You achieve clarity when you use specific and familiar language. The more concrete your language, the more closely your referents will match those of your listeners. In addition to being specific, language must also be familiar. Listeners must know the meanings of the words you use. One type of language that may undermine clarity is *jargon,* a special language of a particular activity, business, or group of people. If you doubt that your listeners know the jargon, either avoid such terms or else define each one the first time you use it.

A third guideline is to use language *vividly.* Colorful language makes the task of listening easier and the message more memorable. Three strategies for making your language more vivid are to use active language, appeal to your listeners' senses, and use figures and structures of speech. Active language avoids *clichés* and filler phrases, using instead active voice, coined words, and well-turned phrases.

A speaker can use any of eight types of sensory images to appeal to listeners' senses. *Visual images* appeal to the sense of sight. *Auditory images* suggest sounds. *Tactile images* recreate the feel of an object. *Thermal images* suggest temperatures. *Gustatory images* appeal to the sense of taste. *Kinetic images* suggest movement or motion. *Kinesthetic images* recreate states of muscular tension or relaxation. *Olfactory images* appeal to the sense of smell. *Synesthesia* is the combination of two or more sensory appeals in a single image.

A third way to achieve vividness is to use figures and structures of speech. *Simile* and *metaphor* are figures of speech comparing two dissimilar things. In simile the comparison is explicit, using words such as *like* and *as.* These words are omitted in metaphors because the comparison is implied. *Personification* attributes human qualities to objects, ideas, or organizations. *Alliteration* is the repetition of beginning sounds. *Parallelism* expresses two or more ideas in similar language structure. *Repetition* is the restatement of words, phrases, or sentences. Like parallelism, *antithesis* uses parallel construction, but it does so to contrast ideas.

A final criterion for effective language is to use language *appropriately.* You should select language that is appropriate to you, your topic, your audience, and the occasion. Two additional dimensions of appropriateness are oral style and inclusive language. *Oral style* differs from written style in at least four important ways. First, in speaking we tend to use shorter sentences. Second, when we communicate orally we use more contractions, colloquial expressions, and slang. Third, oral style makes greater use of personal pronouns and references. Fourth, we use more repetition when we speak than when we write.

Inclusive language incorporates audience diversity and avoids stereotypes about people based on characteristics such as race, ethnicity, age, and gender. Nonsexist language, for example, treats both genders symmetrically and fairly. It does not create special categories or assign roles based solely on gender. Speakers who have difficulty selecting gender-free language should consult a dictionary of nonsexist terms.

practice critique

Analyzing Language Use in a Powerful Speech

Speech experts consider Martin Luther King, Jr.'s, "I Have a Dream" to be one of the most powerful speeches of the twentieth century. Dr. King combined the integrity of his ideas with strong imagery and a masterful delivery to create a memorable speech. Read the transcript of the speech in Appendix B, and then write a brief analysis of the language he used to express his ideas and arouse emotions. Note examples of how Dr. King appealed to his listeners' senses and how he used alliteration, parallelism, repetition, antithesis, and metaphor. Comment on Dr. King's use of gender-specific language. If the speech were being delivered today, how might it be rewritten to make the language more inclusive?

Exercises

1. Generate examples of words and phrases that identify a speaker as being from a particular region of the country. Examples could include the pronoun *y'all*, the salutation *yo!*, or the use of *pop* for carbonated soft drinks. Do these examples also suggest stereotypes about the educational levels of the speakers?

2. What features of this book or other textbooks you are reading help you reinforce, clarify, and remember what you read? Compare the organization of textbooks you are currently using. How does clear organization in a textbook affect your study?

3. Linguists believe that Shakespeare invented one-tenth of the words he used. According to Richard Saul Wurman in *Information Anxiety,* the Stanford University admissions form asks applicants to invent and explain a new word. Invent, define, and illustrate the use of a new word in a one- to two-minute practice speech.

4. Select a one- or two-paragraph passage from a book or magazine. Using the guidelines listed in this chapter, rewrite the passage for a speech, incorporating elements of oral style.

5. Decide on nonsexist words that could be substituted for each of the following examples:
   a. Policeman
   b. Enlisted men
   c. Fatherland
   d. Tomboy
   e. Clothes make the man.
   f. Man's best friend
   g. All men are created equal.
   h. Brotherly love

6. Listen to an album, cassette tape, or compact disc of your favorite vocal recording artist or group. Try to identify at least one example of each of the following language devices in the song lyrics:
   a. Alliteration
   b. Metaphor
   c. Simile
   d. Personification
   e. Visual image
   f. Tactile image
   g. Olfactory image
   h. Gustatory image
   i. Auditory image
   j. Kinesthetic image
   k. Kinetic image

7. Select a speech from *Vital Speeches of the Day* or another published source. Identify examples of as many types of the language devices listed in Exercise 6 as possible.

8. Test your understanding of principles discussed in this chapter by answering the following questions:
   a. What sensory appeal is featured in paragraph 18 of Martin Luther King, Jr.'s, "I Have a Dream" speech in Appendix B?
   b. What are the first two examples of alliteration in paragraph 1 of the preface to this book?
   c. What figure of speech does William McAdoo develop in the second quotation under the heading "Use Language Vividly" in this chapter?
   d. What extended figure of speech did Martin Luther King, Jr., develop in paragraphs 4 through 6 of his "I Have a Dream" speech in Appendix B?

1. Richard Lederer, *Anguished English: An Anthology of Accidental Assaults upon Our Language* (Charleston, SC: Wyrick, 1987) 8.

2. Gloria Cooper, ed., *Red Tape Holds Up New Bridge, and More Flubs from the Nation's Press* (New York: Perigee, 1987) n. pag.

3. Jeffrey McQuain, *Power Language: Getting the Most Out of Your Words* (New York: Houghton Mifflin, 1996) 6.

4. Gerald Parshall, "A 'Glorious Mongrel,' " *U.S. News & World Report* 25 Sept. 1995: 48.

5. Bill Bryson, *The Mother Tongue: English & How It Got That Way* (New York: Avon, 1990) 13.

6. E. C. Nance, "The Power and the Glory of the Word: Civilization Is Where It Is Today by the Force of Words," *Vital Speeches of the Day* 1 April 1957: 382.

7. This discussion of functions of language is based on Roman Jakobson, "Closing Statement: Linguistics and Poetics," in *Style in Language,* ed. Thomas A. Sebeok (Cambridge, MA: MIT P, 1964) 350–74.

8. Charles L. Barber, *The Story of Speech and Language* (New York: Crowell, 1965) 9–10.

9. William F. Allman, "The Mother Tongue," *U.S. News & World Report* 5 November 1990: 62.

10. Jefferson Graham, *Frasier* (New York: Simon-Pocket, 1996) 116–17.

11. This discussion of two different ways of responding to language is based on Louise M. Rosenblatt, *The Reader, the Text, the Poem: The Transactional Theory of the Literary Work* (Carbondale: Southern Illinois UP, 1978), particularly Chapter 3, "Efferent and Aesthetic Reading."

12. McQuain 3–4.

13. Jeffrey Blair, " 'Techno-dolts' Face Obstacle of Electronic Manuals," *San Antonio Light* 14 October 1990: Classified 44.

14. *Usenet Acronyms Dictionary,* 11 October 1999 <http://homepages.ihug.co.nz/~tajwileb/dictionary.html>. The following are acronyms commonly used on Usenet and their meanings:

BRB	Be Right Back
BTDTGTS	Been There, Done That, Got the T-Shirt
GAL	Get A Life
HAND	Have A Nice Day
ROFL	Rolling on the Floor Laughing
NRN	No Reply Necessary
PMFJI	Pardon Me For Jumping In
TTYL	Talk To You Later

15. Miriam Ringo, *Nobody Said It Better!* (Chicago: Rand, 1980) 201.

16. Ringo 201.

17. Belinda Luscombe, "Making a Splash," *Time* April 1996: 63.

18. Cherie Spurling, "Batter Up—Batter Down," *Winning Orations, 1992* (Mankato, MN: Interstate Oratorical Association, 1992) 12.

19. Joni Oakley, "Inequality in Medicine," *Winning Orations,* 1992 (Mankato, MN: Interstate Oratorical Association, 1992) 22.

20. Peter Schjeldahl, "Cyclone! Rising to the Fall," *Harper's* June 1988: 68–70. Examples of visual, auditory, tactile, thermal, and olfactory sensory impressions are from Schjeldahl's article. Other examples are from Richard Conniff, "Coasters Used to Be Scary, Now They're Downright Weird," *Smithsonian* August 1989: 84–85.

21. Bill Gallagher, "E-911: A 'Call' for Reform," *Winning Orations, 1999* (Mankato, MN: Interstate Oratorical Association, 1999) 114.

22. Robert Claiborne, *Loose Cannons & Red Herrings: A Book of Lost Metaphors* (New York: Norton, 1988) 13.

23. "Speech, Figure of," *Encyclopædia Britannica Online,* 30 July 1999 <http://eb.com:180/bol/topic?thes_id=503404&pm=1>.

24. Raymond Gozzi, "Metaphors around the TV Remote Control," *ETC.: A Review of General Semantics* Winter 1998: 441.

25. "Metaphor," *Encyclopædia Britannica Online,* 30 July 1999 <http://eb.com:180/bol/topic?cu=53596&sctn=1>.

26. Gozzi 438.

27. "A Beauty Is Born," *The Economist* 25 Oct. 1997: 94.

28. Elyse Sommer and Dorrie Weiss, eds., *Metaphors Dictionary* (Detroit: Gale, 1995) xi.

29. Schjeldahl 68.

30. Maridell Fryar, "The Anatomy of an Association," address, First General Sess., Texas Speech Communication Association Convention, Dallas, 30 September 1983.

31. Virginia I. Postrel, "The Environmental Movement: A Skeptical View," *Vital Speeches of the Day* 15 September 1990: 729.

32. Elie Wiesel, "The Shame of Hunger," *Representative American Speeches: 1990–1991,* ed. Owen Peterson (New York: Wilson, 1991) 70–74.

33. Vincent Ryan Ruggiero, "The Role of Business in Educational Reform: Pessimism and Popular Culture," *Vital Speeches of the Day* 15 February 1989: 287.

34. Ronald Reagan, Remarks at the Johnson Space Center in Houston, TX, January 31, 1986, *Weekly Compilation of Presidential Documents* 3 February 1986: 118.

35. Mario Cuomo, Keynote Address, Democratic National Convention, *Vital Speeches of the Day* 15 August 1984: 647.

36. William Safire, "On Language: Marking Bush's Inaugural," *New York Times Magazine* 5 February 1989: 12.

37. Richard Price, interview with Terry Gross, *Fresh Air,* Natl. Public Radio. WHYY, Philadelphia. 9 May 1995.

38. Sol Saporta, "Old Maid and Dirty Old Man: The Language of Ageism," *American Speech* Fall 1991: 333.

39. Rosalie Maggio, *The Bias-Free Word Finder: A Dictionary of Nondiscriminatory Language* (Boston: Beacon, 1991) 7.

40. Allman 60.

41. Qtd. in George Plimpton, ed., *The Writer's Chapbook: A Compendium of Fact, Opinion, Wit, and Advice from the 20th Century's Preeminent Writers* (New York: Viking, 1989) 176.

A printed speech is like a dried flower: the substance, indeed, is there, but the color is faded and the perfume gone.

—Paul Lorain

13

Delivering Your Speech

If a speech were a style of dress, it would be somewhere between a tuxedo and a flannel shirt. Not stiff. Not sloppy. . . . A speech is more like conversation than formal writing. Its phrasing is loose—but without the extremes of slang, the incomplete thoughts, the interruptions that flavor everyday speech.

—*Elinor Donahue*[1]

In Chapter 1 we quoted communication scholar Karlyn Kohrs Campbell: "Ideas do not walk by themselves; they must be carried—expressed and voiced—by someone." Each of us has a unique voice, body, and way of wording ideas. Your manner of presenting a speech—through your voice, body, and language together—forms your style of delivery. In other words, *what* you say is your speech content, and *how* you say it is your **delivery.** If you and a classmate presented a speech with the same words arranged in the same order (something we don't recommend), your listeners would still receive two different messages. This is because your delivery not only shapes your image as a speaker but also changes your message in subtle ways. Having expended the energy and effort necessary to choose, research, organize, and word your message, on most occasions your goal should be delivery that seems effortless. The irony of working hard to make some act look easy is distilled in a song lyric by Ben Watt and Tracey Thorn: "And all the effort that it took to get there in the first place / and all the effort not to let the effort show."[2]

Sometimes events seem to conspire to make your effort glaringly obvious: The room is too hot, and you begin to perspire; distracted for a moment by some noise, you lose your train of thought; allergens in the air have made your voice sound forced or nasal. No one is immune to such incidents, not even people with extensive public speaking experience.

Delivery Advice for Academics
http://www.si.
umich.edu/~pne/
acadtalk.htm
Visit this Web site to see the delivery suggestions one academician gives to other "academics" who give "talks." See the "Usually Better—Usually Worse" chart for a delivery checklist, with explanations that follow.

On the night of September 22, 1993, President Bill Clinton delivered one of the most important speeches of his first term to members of the House and Senate, his cabinet, Supreme Court justices, and a prime-time television audience. That speech, introducing his controversial vision of national health care reform, was the culmination of thousands of hours of research, meetings, and deliberation by the president's health care task force and hundreds of other people.

As he waited for the sustained applause to fade, Clinton looked into the TelePrompTer and saw the text of an economic address he had made to Congress and the nation eight months earlier! An aide programming the computer had accidentally merged the text of Clinton's current speech with that of the February speech, still in the system.[3] For the seven minutes that it took to load the correct manuscript and program the computer to catch up with the president, Clinton spoke using only the written text he had carried to the lectern. Clinton would tell ABC's Ted Koppel during a national forum the next night, "I thought to myself, 'That was a pretty good speech, but not good enough to give twice.' " The fact that Clinton could speak fluently and calmly under that unexpected stress is a testament to his significant delivery skills.

Speech delivery is so important that one of the criticisms of televised presidential debates is that they turn into "beauty contests," emphasizing looks, poise, and person-

delivery: the way a speaker presents a speech, through voice qualities, bodily actions, and language.

ality while minimizing the importance of what the candidates say. Strong delivery can no doubt mask weak content for some listeners. More important, though, effective delivery can bolster important, well-organized ideas, and poor delivery can diminish the impact of those same ideas.

As Paul Lorain suggests, your delivery gives color and fragrance to your words. To help you understand how that invigoration occurs, we discuss the qualities and various elements of effective delivery in this chapter. Before we examine those individual elements that constitute physical and vocal delivery, let's first consider some rules that apply to all nonverbal communication and four possible methods of delivering a speech.

Principles of Nonverbal Communication

Your nonverbal behavior communicates a great deal of information concerning your feelings about what you say. Recall Albert Mehrabian's formula from Chapter 1 (see page 14). In particular, four principles of nonverbal communication help account for the importance of speech delivery. These principles provide a framework we will use later to evaluate the specific elements of vocal and physical delivery.

1. *Part of our nonverbal communication is conscious and deliberate, while another part is unconscious and unintentional.* You do certain things deliberately to make other people feel comfortable around you or attracted to you. You dress in colors and fabrics that flatter you or make you feel comfortable. You cut your hair in a style that is fashionable, traditional, or uniquely flattering. When speaking or listening to others, you look them directly in the eyes. You smile when they tell you good news and show concern when they share a problem.

On the other hand, you may have habits of which you are unaware. You fold your arms, assuming a closed and defensive body position, or jingle your keys when nervous. You tap your fingers on the lectern when anxious or look down at the floor when embarrassed. You can control only those things you know about. Therefore, the first step toward improving your speech delivery is to identify and isolate any distracting nonverbal behaviors you exhibit.

I spend a lot of time trying to select a speech topic that's interesting. If I'm interested in the topic, I'm definitely more motivated to research, organize, and present my ideas. It's more fun to speak on a topic I enjoy and think is worthwhile. When I delivered my speeches, I used direct eye contact, good facial expressions, and lively gestures to convey my interest in the topic and my desire to communicate that information to my audience. The more physically involved I got in my delivery, the less I thought about being nervous. When I saw my classmates smiling, nodding in agreement, or just paying attention to what I was saying, that made me feel that they were listening to what I was saying and not focusing on how nervous I was. I remember presenting a visual aid that made one of my points in a humorous way, and my classmates and instructor laughed. They seemed relaxed and to be enjoying my speech. That helped me feel relaxed and enjoy giving my speech.

—Joey Bell, Radford University

speaking with confidence

In this chapter, we discuss the following nonverbal elements of speech delivery: rate, pause, volume, pitch, inflection, voice quality, articulation, pronunciation, appearance, posture, facial expression, eye contact, movement, and gestures. Of these elements, only one—vocal quality—is difficult to change or control. The others are much easier to modify. But how can you learn whether you have annoying and distracting habits? Feedback from your instructor and your classmates can show you areas in which you need to improve. If you have access to a cassette recorder, you can listen to your voice as you practice your speech, and a video camera will enable you to observe and assess your physical delivery. Keep in mind that discovering and improving your delivery weaknesses is not a quick, one-shot event but continues with each successive speech you deliver in class.

2. *Few if any nonverbal signals have universal meaning.* Standing at a bakery in Paris, France, you can't resist the aroma of long, golden loaves of bread hot from the oven. Unable to speak French, you get the clerk's attention, point to the loaves, and hold up two fingers, as in a V for victory. The clerk nods, hands you three loaves, and charges you for all three. Why? The French count from the thumb, whether it is extended or not. The same thing would happen if you used an identical gesture to order another two drinks in a German tavern. The French and German people simply apply different rules to their counting gestures than we do.

Just as the meanings of gestures and movements can change from one culture to the next, nonverbal delivery that is appropriate and effective in one speaking situation may be inappropriate and ineffective in another. Smiling and lively gesturing are appropriate if you are informing your audience on the history of clowning. On the other hand, your body should show more tension and your face more concern if you were persuading others of the devastating effects of unnecessary surgery. Though this chapter focuses on improving delivery of your classroom speeches, you can adapt many of our suggestions to your delivery in other speaking situations.

3. *When a speaker's verbal and nonverbal channels send conflicting messages, we tend to trust the nonverbal message.* A used car sales representative rushes you into signing a purchase agreement while saying, "Man, this is the best deal on the lot. You are so lucky!" A supervisor at work tells you privately that she is impressed with your work but then doesn't allow you to speak at staff meetings. A person keeps saying, "I love you," but never does anything to show consideration for you. Would you doubt the sincerity of these people? If you are typical, you certainly would.

We have each been interpreting and responding to other people's nonverbal communication for so long that we lose sight of its significance. But we are reminded of the importance of nonverbal communication when someone breaks a nonverbal rule. One of those rules demands that a person's words and actions match. Suppose Doris walks reluctantly to the front of the classroom, clutches the lectern, stands motionless, frowns, and says, "I'm absolutely delighted to be speaking to you today." Do you believe her? No. Why? Doris's speech began not with her first words, but with the multiple nonverbal messages that signaled her reluctance to speak. Nonverbal messages should complement and reinforce verbal ones. When they do not, as in Doris's case, actions speak louder than words. In such instances, we tend to trust the nonverbal message to help us answer the question, "What's really going on here?" As a result of this, one final principle of nonverbal communication becomes extremely important.

4. *The message you intend may be overridden by other messages people attach to your nonverbal communication.* You stare out the window while delivering your speech because you feel too nervous to make eye contact with your listeners. The audience, however, assumes that you are bored and not really interested in speaking to them. Because we cannot read one another's minds, your audience's perception that you are disinterested is the more important one in this case, even though it may be far from the

truth. Eliminate distracting behaviors that mask your good intentions if you care about presenting the best speech you can.

This chapter is about the process of presenting your speech vocally and physically. Before we survey the individual elements that make up delivery, it's important to know the possible methods of delivering a speech and the qualities that should mark the method you choose or are assigned.

Methods of Delivery

The four basic ways you can deliver your public speech are (1) impromptu, or without advance preparation; (2) from memory; (3) from a manuscript; or (4) extemporaneously, or from notes. The impromptu and the memorized methods have very limited applications, particularly for an important speech, but they deserve at least brief attention.

Speaking Impromptu

We engage in **impromptu speaking** whenever a teacher, a colleague, or a boss calls on us to express an opinion on some issue, or whenever someone unexpectedly asks us to "say a few words" to a group. We deal with those special occasions and offer specific guidelines for impromptu speaking in Chapter 18 (see pages 427–29). In those informal situations, other people do not necessarily expect us to be forceful or well organized, and we are probably more or less comfortable speaking without any preparation. Yet the more important the speech is, the more inappropriate the impromptu method of delivery. Although impromptu speaking is excellent practice for anyone, no conscientious person will risk a grade, an important proposal, or professional advancement on an unprepared speech.

Selecting Methods
of Delivery
http://www.abacon.
com/pubspeak/deliver/
deliver.html
Use the link on this page
to compare the merits of
manuscript, memorized,
and extemporaneous
speech delivery.

Speaking from Memory

Speaking from memory is similarly appropriate only on rare occasions. We speak from memory when we prepare a written text and then memorize it word for word. At its best, the memorized speech allows a smooth, almost effortless-looking delivery because the speaker has neither notes nor a manuscript and can concentrate on interacting with the audience. For most of us, however, memorizing takes a long time. Our concentration on the memory work we've done and our fear of forgetting part of the speech can also make us sound mechanical or programmed when reciting. For these reasons, the memorized method of delivery is usually appropriate only for brief speeches, such as those introducing another speaker, or presenting or accepting an award.

Speaking from Manuscript

Speaking from manuscript, or delivering a speech from a complete text prepared in advance, not only ensures that the speaker will not be at a loss for words, but is also essential in some situations. An address that will be quoted or later published in its entirety is typically delivered from a manuscript. Major foreign policy speeches or State of the Union addresses by U.S. presidents are always delivered from manuscript, because the premium is not just on being understood but on not being misunderstood.

impromptu speaking:
speaking without advance preparation.

speaking from memory:
delivering a speech that is recalled word for word from a written text.

speaking from manuscript: delivering a speech from a text written word for word and practiced in advance.

Speeches of tribute and commencement addresses are also often scripted. Any speaking situation calling for precise, well-worded communication may be appropriate for manuscript delivery. Having every word of your speech scripted should boost your confidence, but it does not ensure your effective delivery. When you write the manuscript, you must take care to write in an oral style. In other words, the manuscript must sound like something you would say in conversation. The text of your speech thus requires a good deal of time to prepare, edit, revise, and type for final delivery. In addition, if you do not also take time to practice delivering the manuscript in a fluent, conversational manner and with appropriate emphasis, well-placed pauses, and adequate eye contact, you are preparing to fail as an effective speaker.

Speaking Extemporaneously

The final method of delivery, and by far the most popular, is **speaking extemporaneously,** or from notes. Assuming that you have researched and organized your materials carefully, and that you have adequately practiced the speech, speaking from notes offers several advantages over other methods of delivery. You don't have to worry about one particular way of wording your ideas, because you have not scripted the speech. Neither do you have to worry that you will forget something you have memorized. With your notes before you, you are free to interact with the audience in a natural, conversational manner. If something you say confuses the audience, you can repeat it, explain it using other words, or think of a better example to clarify it. Your language may not be as forceful or colorful as with a carefully prepared manuscript or a memorized speech, but speaking from notes helps ensure that you will be natural and spontaneous.

The freedom, naturalness, and spontaneity of extemporaneous speaking make this method of delivery particularly attractive. John Kao, professor of entrepreneurship and creativity at Harvard Business School, compares an effective presentation to a successfully performed piece of music. Your content and organization provide the "reference point from which the presentation is going to spring." Your outline and speaking notes are therefore like sheet music. Just as a piece of music can be played in a variety of styles, skillful extemporaneous speaking always involves a degree of improvisation. Perhaps jazz music and extemporaneous speaking have the clearest similarities. Kao notes that

> . . . improvisation in music has a lot to do with keeping to certain themes that are reinforced. If there isn't that sense of form even through the improvisation, the music won't sound good. . . . And the more one knows the tune, the more one feels comfortable with an audience, the more one feels free to experiment.[4]

As that last sentence makes clear, you can't experience the freedom that extemporaneous speaking permits unless you have taken the time to develop your speech content and organization and to know your audience. In the words of the great jazz trumpeter Harry "Sweets" Edison, "If you don't know the tune, you can't improvise."[5]

Former New York governor Mario Cuomo, skilled in various methods of delivery, reveals that he speaks extemporaneously whenever possible because of its advantages:

> Spontaneity is one. Audience contact is another. Because you're not tied to a text, your eyes scan the audience and you can detect signs of agreement that encourage you to elaborate effective points. Or you see impatient fidgeting, the sidelong glances of disapproval, and occasionally, the sure sign of abject failure—eyes closed, chin on chest, a customer not only declaring "no sale," but making it clear he or she is no longer shopping. Alerted, the speaker can then change pace, improvise, move on to a more interesting proposition. It's easier to engage the audience when you have both eyes in direct contact with the people you're addressing, both arms drawing pictures in the air, adding punctuation, fighting off the glaze. It's more fun, too. It has an adventurous quality that one misses when the assignment is just to read a prepared text.[6]

speaking extemporaneously: delivering a speech from notes or from a memorized outline.

When speaking either from a manuscript or from notes, you need to keep several practical points in mind:

1. Practice with the notes or manuscript you will actually use in delivering the speech. You need to know where things are on the page so that you have to glance down only briefly.

2. Number the pages of your manuscript or your notecards so that you can check their order just before you speak.

3. Determine when you should and when you should not look at your notes. Looking at your notes when you quote an authority or present statistics is acceptable. In fact, it may even convey to your audience your concern for exactness in supporting your ideas. However, do not look down while previewing, stating, or summarizing your key ideas. If you cannot remember your key points, what hope is there for the audience? Also, avoid looking down when you use personal pronouns such as *I, we,* and *you,* or when you address members of the audience by name. A break in your eye contact at those points suddenly distances you from the audience and creates the impression that the speech is coming from a script rather than from you.

4. Slide the pages of your manuscript or notes rather than turning them. So that you won't have to pick them up and turn them over, avoid writing on the backs of notecards or sheets of paper that hold your notes. As a rule, if you use a lectern, do not let the audience see your notes after you place them in front of you. The less the audience is aware of your notes, the more direct and personal your communication with them will be.

5. Devote extra practice time to your conclusion. The last thing you say can make a deep impression, but not if you rush through it or deliver it while gathering up your notes and walking back to your seat. Your goal at this critical point in the speech is the same as your goal for all of your delivery: to eliminate distractions and to reinforce your message through your body, voice, and language.

The most satisfactory way of delivering your classroom speeches combines all four of the methods we have discussed. We have advised you not to look at your notes during the preview of your introduction or the summary step of your conclusion. We stressed the importance of the introduction and conclusion in Chapter 10. To demonstrate that you are well prepared and to ensure contact with your audience, you may even want to have your introduction and conclusion memorized. That won't be difficult, because they are brief sections. You may decide or be assigned to deliver the body of your speech extemporaneously, looking at your notes occasionally. Just don't look at your notes while you are stating or summarizing each main point. If you quote sources at different points in your speech, you are, in effect, briefly using a manuscript. Finally, as an audience-centered speaker, you should be flexible enough to improvise a bit. You speak impromptu whenever you repeat an idea or think of a better example to increase your clarity or your persuasiveness. If you are well prepared, this combination of delivery methods should look natural to your audience and feel comfortable to you.

Qualities of Effective Delivery

As you begin to think about the way you deliver a speech, keep in mind three characteristics of effective delivery. First, effective delivery helps the listeners as well as the speaker. If you are well prepared for a particular speech, you have probably spent a good deal of time formulating and rehearsing it. You know what you want to say, but your audience does not. Your audience has only one chance to receive your message.

A delivery style as natural-looking as this speaker's comes with confidence and practice. Record and view yourself on videotape or rehearse in front of friends to try out gestures and movements that will enhance your effectiveness.

Just as clear organization makes your ideas easier to remember, effective delivery can underscore your key points, sell your ideas, or communicate your concern for the topic.

Second, understand that the best delivery looks and feels natural, comfortable, and spontaneous. Former tennis great Helen Wills Moody once said, "If you see a tennis player who looks as if he is working very hard, then that means he isn't very good."[7] The same thing could be said of a speaker's delivery. No one should notice how hard you are working to deliver your speech effectively. Some occasions and audiences require you to be more formal than others, of course. Speaking to a large audience through a stationary microphone, for example, will naturally restrict your movement. For a presentation in this class, on the other hand, you may find yourself moving, gesturing, and using visual aids extensively. You want to orchestrate all these elements so that your presentation looks and feels relaxed and natural, not strained or awkward. You achieve spontaneous delivery such as this only through practice.

Third, and finally, delivery is best when the audience is not aware of it at all. Your goal should be delivery that reinforces your ideas and is free of distractions. When the audience begins to notice how you twist your ring, to count the number of times you say "um," or to categorize the types of grammatical mistakes you make, your delivery is momentarily distracting them from what you are saying. Your delivery has now become a liability rather than an asset. If you eliminate distractions from your delivery and use the elements of delivery to reinforce your purpose in speaking, you help your audience pay attention.

key points

Characteristics of Effective Delivery

1. Effective delivery helps everyone—the listener as well as the speaker.
2. The best delivery looks and feels natural, comfortable, and spontaneous.
3. Delivery is best when the audience is not aware of it.

How can you help ensure effective delivery? Concentrate on your ideas and how the audience is receiving them, rather than on how you look or sound. If you are really interacting with your listeners, you will pay attention to their interest in your speech, their understanding of your message, and their acceptance or rejection of what you are saying. If you notice listeners checking their watches, reading papers, whispering to friends, or snoozing, they are probably bored. At this point you can enliven your delivery with movement and changes in your volume. Such relatively simple changes in your delivery may revive their interest.

But what if you notice looks of confusion on your audience's faces? You want to make certain your listeners understand the point you are making. Slow down your rate of delivery, and use descriptive gestures to reinforce your ideas. If you observe frowns or heads shaking from side to side, you've encountered a hostile audience! There are ways to help break down the resistance of even an antagonistic group. Look directly at such listeners, establish a conversational tone, incorporate friendly facial expressions, and use your body to demonstrate involvement with your topic. These helpful tips take practice. Start with the basics. Once you have mastered the essentials of speech delivery, you will be flexible and able to adapt to various audiences. Your delivery will complement your message, not detract from it.

Any prescription for effective delivery will include three basic elements: the *voice*, or vocal delivery; the *body*, or physical delivery; and *language*. In Chapter 12, we discussed how your language contributes to your delivery style. In the remainder of this chapter we focus on vocal and physical delivery. Vocal delivery includes rate, pause, volume, pitch, inflection, voice quality, articulation, and pronunciation. The elements of physical delivery are appearance, posture, facial expression, eye contact, movement, and gestures. Let's consider, first, how vocal delivery can enhance your speech.

Elements of Vocal Delivery

Elements of Vocal Delivery

1. **Rate and pause**
2. **Volume**
3. **Pitch and inflection**
4. **Voice quality**
5. **Articulation and pronunciation**

Rate and Pause

You have probably heard the warning, "Look out for him; he's a fast talker," or words to that effect. Such a statement implies that someone who talks fast may be trying to put something over on us. At the other end of the spectrum, we often grow impatient with people who talk much slower than we do, even labeling them uncertain, dull, or dense. Though these stereotypes may be inaccurate, we have already noted that the impressions people form based on our nonverbal communication can become more important than anything we intend to communicate.

Your **rate** or speed of speaking can communicate something, intentionally or unintentionally, about your motives in speaking, your disposition, or your involvement with the topic. Your goal in a speech, therefore, should be to avoid extremely fast or slow delivery; you should instead use a variety of rates. Your various rates should, in turn, reinforce your purpose in speaking and make you seem conversational.

In Chapter 4, "Responding to Speeches," you learned that the typical American speaker talks at a rate between 125 and 190 words per minute. To test your own rate of speaking, read the following words from a speech by our student, Steven. Read the

rate: the speed at which a speech is delivered.

paragraphs once silently. Then read them aloud at a rate that seems natural and conversational, using pauses to mark transitions from one idea to the next. Ignore the slash marks. Make a note of the word you have reached after one minute:

> The fourth step to studying a language is learning that language's culture. Culture and language are interdependent. Very few languages spoken today are not supported by a culture, and the few that are, such as Esperanto and Latin, are not widely known.
>
> Methods you can use to study a culture are reading books, watching films, reading travel guides, and reading magazines. Reading books written originally in your target language and then translated into English lets you understand the thought processes of the people who speak your target language. Watching films shot in your target language and later subtitled will allow / you to hear the language while at the same time getting a ready translation for any words you don't understand. As you learn the language more thoroughly, you can eventually start watching films that don't have subtitles.
>
> Travel guides are also useful in studying culture. They provide you with information // about the people in a certain area and their ways of life. They also show you pictures of their architecture, art, and other aspects of their lives. My favorite aid to studying a culture is reading comic books and cartoons. They contain short sentences that are usually easily understood. Humor /// can be one of the greatest differences between cultures, and reading comic books really gives you insight into your target culture's humor. So combining all of these processes—reading books, watching movies, reading cartoons and comics—will support you while you're performing the fourth step of studying your target culture.

How fast did you read? The first slash mark (/) indicates 100 words, and you probably passed that mark easily. The double slash (//) indicates 150 words, the triple slash 200, and the final word of the third paragraph is number 250. You probably did not finish the final paragraph if you were truly pausing and reading conversationally. Chances are that your final word falls somewhere between the single and triple slash marks, or between 100 and 200 words per minute.

This exercise cannot accurately measure your normal speaking rate and is not intended to do so. You may, after all, speak faster or slower than you read aloud. But you now have some idea of how easy it is to speak more than 100 words a minute. To get an idea of how slow a rate of 100 words per minute actually is, try taking exactly one minute to read up to the first slash mark. You probably feel that you are plodding along sluggishly.

Although we can process information at rates faster than people speak, our comprehension depends on the type of material we are hearing. You should slow down, for example, when presenting detailed, highly complex information, particularly to a group that knows little about your subject. Our student René did just that in his informative speech, detailing the history of political and religious conflict in the Middle East. Not only did he speak slower than he had in other speeches, but he also used a clearly labeled map of the area and a timeline showing the splintering of groups into smaller factions. His reduced rate of delivery and his repetition of information in visual form showed his concern for his audience's comprehension. This can work both ways, however. In other situations, speaking slightly faster than the rate of normal conversation may actually increase your persuasiveness by carrying the message that you know exactly what you want to say.

Assessing Vocal Delivery
http://www.historychannel.com/speeches/index.html
The History Channel's rich index of more than 100 speeches and verbal messages that changed the world gives you a chance to appreciate the vocal deliveries of historical and contemporary figures. With a downloadable *RealAudio* plug-in, just click on a link in the alphabetical listing to listen.

Pauses or silences are an important element in your rate of delivery. You pause to allow the audience time to reflect upon something you have just said or to heighten suspense about something you are going to say. Pauses also mark important transitions in your speech, helping you and your audience shift gears. World-renowned violinist Isaac Stern was once asked why some violinists were considered gifted and others merely proficient or competent when they all played the correct notes in the proper order. "The important thing is not the notes. It's the intervals between the notes," he responded.

To test the importance of pauses, let's look at a section near the beginning of a powerful speech Bob Dole delivered upon resigning from the U.S. Senate in May of 1996.[8] Try reading these three sentences without any internal punctuation or pauses, ignoring even the periods.

> You do not lay claim to the office you hold it lays claim to you. Your obligation is to bring to it the gifts you can of labor and honesty and then to depart with grace. And my time to leave this office has come and I will seek the presidency with nothing to fall back on but the judgment of the people and nowhere to go but the White House or home.

The sentences make sense only if you insert appropriate pauses. Speakers reading from a written text sometimes mark their manuscripts to help them pause appropriately. Now try reading Dole's sentences again, pausing a beat when you see one slash (/) and pausing a bit longer when you encounter two (//).

> You do not lay claim to the office you hold, / it lays claim to you. // Your obligation is to bring to it the gifts you can, / of labor and honesty, / and then to depart with grace. // And my time to leave this office has come, / and I will seek the presidency with nothing to fall back on but the judgment of the people, // and nowhere to go but the White House or home.

If the pauses marked were meaningful for you, the statement should have gained power. You may even disagree with the placement and length of the pauses we chose. You might say the sentences differently, and that's fine. Public speaking is, after all, a creative and individual process. Remember, though, that to be effective in a speech, pauses must be used intentionally and selectively. If your speech is filled with too many awkwardly placed pauses, or too many vocalized pauses, such as "um" and "uh," you will seem hesitant or unprepared, and your credibility will erode quickly.

Volume

Your audience must be able to hear you before they can listen to your ideas. **Volume** is simply how loudly or softly you speak. A person who speaks too loudly in a classroom speech may be considered boisterous or obnoxious. In contrast, we often label the inaudible speaker unsure, timid, "wimpy." The truth could be that you speak too loudly because of a hearing loss, and you are not aware that your volume is uncomfortable to your listeners. The frustratingly quiet speaker may have grown up in a household with six other children and parents who were constantly yelling, "Quiet!" But your audience will not know about your history. What they will know is that you are shouting or whispering your speech, and they will judge you by that behavior. Remember that hearing is the first step in listening. If you frustrate your audience or divert their attention with inappropriate volume, your chances of getting them to listen carefully to your message are slim.

Make sure you adapt your volume to the size of the room where you speak. In your classroom, you can probably use a volume just slightly louder than your usual conversational level. When you speak before a large group, a microphone may be helpful or even essential. If possible, practice beforehand so that the sound of your amplified

pause: an intentional or unintentional period of silence in a speaker's vocal delivery.

volume: the relative loudness or softness of a speaker's voice.

When you speak to a large audience, it is especially important to articulate clearly and adapt your volume to ensure that all in your audience can catch every word. If you are using a microphone, try to listen to your amplified voice before delivering your speech.

voice does not startle you. You may even be called upon to speak before a large audience without a microphone. This is not as difficult as it sounds. In fact, your voice will carry well if you support your breath from your diaphragm. To test your breathing, place your hand on your abdomen while repeating the sentence "Those old boats don't float" louder and louder. If you are breathing from the diaphragm, you should feel your abdominal muscles tightening. Without that support, you are probably trying to increase your volume from your throat, a mistake that could strain your voice.

At times, you may have to conquer not only a large space but also external noise, such as the chattering of people in a hallway, the roar of nearby traffic, or the whoosh of the air conditioning system. That may require hard work. If you can, use a microphone in such a situation, speak at normal volume, and let the public address system do the work for you. If a microphone is unnecessary, don't use it; in a small room, a microphone distances you from the audience. We discuss the use of two different types of microphones in more detail in Chapter 18 (see pages 431–32).

Pitch and Inflection

Pitch is a musical term, and when we talk about vocal pitch we are referring to the highness or lowness of vocal tones, similar to the notes on a musical staff. Every speaker has an optimal pitch range, or key. This is the range in which you are most comfortable speaking, and chances are good that in this range your voice is also pleasant to hear. People who speak in unusually high or low voices are rare, and in these cases work with speech therapists helps them to achieve a flexible, useful pitch range.

Speakers who are unusually nervous sometimes raise their pitch. Other speakers think that if they lower their pitch, they will seem more authoritative. (If you have seen the *Mary Tyler Moore Show,* you will recognize this as the Ted Baxter factor.) In truth, speakers who do not use their normal pitch usually sound artificial.

The following practice technique may help you retain or recapture a natural, conversational tone in your delivery. Begin some of your practice sessions seated. Imagine a good friend sitting across from you, and pretend that she asks you what your speech is about. Answer her question by summarizing and paraphrasing your speech: "Mary, I'm going to talk about the advantages of mandatory school uniforms in elementary and middle schools. I've divided my speech into three main arguments. School uni-

pitch: the highness or lowness of a speaker's voice.

forms will enhance student self-esteem; they will reduce discipline problems; and they will save parents money." Listen closely to the tone of your voice as you speak. You are having a conversation with a friend. You're not tense; you feel comfortable.

Now, keeping this natural, conversational tone in mind, stand up, walk to the lectern, and begin your speech. Your words will change, but the tone of your speech should be comfortable and conversational, as it was before. In a sense, you are merely having a conversation with a larger audience. We have found this technique helpful for students whose vocal delivery sounds artificial or mechanical. Not only do they find their natural pitch range, but they also incorporate more meaningful pauses.

A problem more typical than an unusually high- or low-pitched voice is vocal delivery that lacks adequate **inflection,** or changes in pitch. Someone who speaks without changing pitch delivers sentences in a flat, uniform pitch pattern that becomes monotonous. Indeed, the word *monotone* means "one tone," and you may have had instructors whose monotonous droning invited you to doze. People whose voices sound monotonous are usually actually using three tones: one in the middle, one slightly higher, and one lower. That's still too little vocal variety, however. Your inflection is an essential tool for conveying meaning accurately. A simple four-word sentence such as "She is my friend" can be given four distinct meanings by raising the pitch and volume of one word at a time:

"She is my friend." (Not the young woman standing with her.)

"She **is** my friend." (Don't try to tell me she isn't!)

"She is **my** friend." (Not yours.)

"She is my **friend.**" (There's nothing more to our relationship than that.)

Did you ever make a comment jokingly only to have people take you seriously? Chances are that you did not adequately signal with your inflection that it was a joke. In public speaking, women can generally make wider use of their pitch ranges than men can without sounding affected or unnatural. For this reason, men often find that they need to vary other vocal and physical elements of delivery—volume, rate, and gestures, for example—to compensate for a limited pitch range.

Voice Quality

Voice quality or **timbre,** the least flexible of the vocal elements discussed here, is the characteristic that distinguishes your voice from other voices. You may have called a friend on the phone and had difficulty telling him from his father, or her from her mother or sisters. Most of the time, however, even through the telephone, an instrument causing a lot of distortion, you recognize the voices of friends easily. In general, our individual voices are easily recognized as distinct. In fact, you may have heard that police investigators often use voice prints to identify and distinguish individual voices on tape recordings.

Sometimes the clarity and resonance of your voice can be temporarily affected by colds, by allergies, or by strain after you spend hours screaming support for a favorite team. That temporary change should not cause alarm. However, if many people describe your voice as strident, harsh, nasal, breathy, or hoarse over a long period of time, you may want to consult a speech therapist.

Articulation and Pronunciation

The final elements of vocal delivery we will discuss are articulation and pronunciation. **Articulation** is the mechanical process of forming the sounds necessary to

inflection: patterns of change in a person's pitch level while speaking.

voice quality or **timbre:** the unique characteristics that distinguish one person's voice from others.

articulation: the mechanical process of forming the sounds necessary to communicate in a particular language.

communicate in a particular language. Most articulation errors are made from habit. You tell your parents that you're going to the "libary," for example. Even though you know how to spell the word and would say it correctly if pressed to do so, you have fallen into a habit of misarticulating it. Sometimes our articulation errors are reinforced by people around us who make the same mistakes. Sometimes illness or fatigue affect our articulation temporarily.

Articulation errors take four principal forms: deletion, addition, substitution, and transposition. One of these, represented by the example of "libary," is the *deletion* or leaving out of sounds. Saying "goverment" for "government" is another example of a deletion error. If you have heard someone say "athalete" for "athlete," you've heard an example of an articulation error caused by the *addition* of a sound. Examples of errors caused by the *substitution* of one sound for another are "kin" for "can" and "git" for "get." The final type of articulation error is one of *transposition,* or the reversal of two sounds that are close together. This error is the vocal equivalent of transposing two letters in a typed word. Saying "lectren" for "lectern" or "hunderd" for "hundred" are examples of transposition errors.

Articulation errors made as a result of habit may be so ingrained that you can no longer identify your mistakes. Your speech instructor, your friends, and your classmates can help you significantly by pointing out articulation problems. You may need to listen to tape recordings of your speeches to locate problems and then practice the problem words or sounds to correct your articulation.

Pronunciation, in contrast to articulation, is simply a matter of knowing how the letters of a word sound and where the stress falls when that word is spoken. We all have two vocabularies: a speaking vocabulary and a reading vocabulary. Your speaking vocabulary—the group of words you use in day-to-day conversation—is much smaller than your reading vocabulary. To test this, think of the times you have been reading something and encountered a word you have never spoken or even heard spoken: "Her *vitriolic* parting words stung him," for example. You may have seen the word before in print. Even though you may have never looked up its pronunciation or meaning in a dictionary, you probably feel that you know more or less what it means in the context of the sentence. Such a word is part of your reading vocabulary.

Most of us make errors in pronunciation primarily when we try to move a word from our reading vocabulary to our speaking vocabulary without consulting the dictionary. In a public speech, the resulting pronunciation error can be a minor distraction or a major disaster, depending upon how far off your mispronunciation is and how many times you make the error. If you have any doubt about the pronunciation of a word you plan to use in a speech, look it up in a current dictionary and then practice the correct pronunciation out loud before the speech. Apply this rule to every word you select, including those in quotations. If you follow this simple rule, you will avoid embarrassing errors of pronunciation.

Pronunciation of proper nouns, the names of specific people, places, and things, can also pose difficulties. Suppose that for your speech on mountain climbing you want to quote from a fine book entitled *Flow: The Psychology of Optimal Experience.*[9] You copy an excellent passage about the psychology of dangerous sports onto a notecard. Then you turn to the title page to find the author's name: Mihaly Csikszentmihalyi! Don't tear up the notecard.

Obviously, proper nouns should be pronounced the way that the people who have the name (or who live in the place, or who named the thing) pronounce them. The large city on the Texas Gulf Coast is pronounced "HEW stun"; the street in New York City spelled the same way is pronounced "HOW stun." The surname Koch can be pronounced "Kotch" (as in former New York mayor Ed Koch) or "Koke" (as in poet Kenneth Koch). But many people with the last name Koch pronounce it "Cook." When you

pronunciation: how the sounds of a word are to be said and which parts are to be stressed.

see the name Schroeder, you may think of the *Peanuts* character and mentally pronounce the word with a long *o* sound. Yet the late William Schroeder, world's first artificial heart recipient, pronounced his family's name as though the *oe* were a long *a*.

If you refer to people who are well known, make sure that your pronunciation corresponds to common usage. If you quote or refer to a person who is unfamiliar to your audience—as Csikszentmihalyi may well be—your listeners will not know that you have mispronounced the name unless you appear to stumble uncertainly over it. You could be lucky enough to read an article that tells how the person pronounces his or her name; *Psychology Today* says Csikszentmihalyi is pronounced Chick-sent-me-HIGH.[10] The only other way to confirm your pronunciation of a name like "Csikszentmihalyi" would be to locate the person, place a long-distance call, and ask. No one expects you to do that. Instead, decide on a reasonable pronunciation, practice it, and deliver it with confidence in your speech. For names of places, consult the *Pronouncing Gazetteer* or list of geographical names found at the back of many dictionaries.

Once you have mastered these elements of vocal delivery, your speech will be free of articulation errors and mispronounced words. Your unique voice quality will be pleasant to hear. Your voice will be well modulated, with enough inflection to communicate your ideas clearly. You will speak loudly enough that all your listeners can hear you easily. You will adapt your rate to the content of your message, and you will pause to punctuate key ideas and major transitions. In short, your sound will be coming through loud and clear. Now let's consider the picture your listeners will see by examining the aspects of physical delivery.

Elements of Physical Delivery

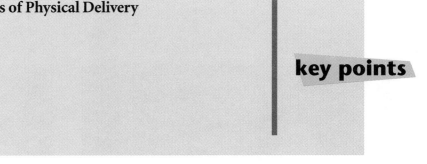

Elements of Physical Delivery

1. Appearance
2. Posture
3. Facial expression
4. Eye contact
5. Movement
6. Gestures

key points

Appearance

As we mentioned earlier in this text, we all form quick impressions of people we meet based on subtle nonverbal signals. **Appearance,** in particular our grooming and the way we dress, is an important nonverbal signal that helps people judge us. Why is appearance so important? You may ask, "What about the inner me? Does it really come down to 'it's not who you are but what you wear'?" Of course, that is not the case. But you would be foolish to underestimate the power of first impressions and the initial reactions people have to your appearance.

Studies demonstrate that people we consider attractive can persuade us much more easily than can those we find unattractive. In addition, high-status clothing carries more authority than does low-status clothing. For example, studies show we are more likely to jaywalk behind a person dressed in a dark blue suit, a crisp white shirt, and a dark tie, and carrying an expensive black-leather briefcase, than we would behind a person dressed in rags or even in jeans. We will also take orders more easily from that

appearance: a speaker's physical features, including dress and grooming.

well-dressed person than we would from someone poorly dressed. These studies reinforce the adage that "clothes make the person," a saying any public speaker would do well to remember.

Since John T. Molloy's first book, *Dress for Success,* came out in 1975, we have all been getting plenty of advice about the best colors, fabrics, and styles of clothing for the business office. Dressing for success has become big business. Today, "image consultants" across the country teach men and women how to dress for increased productivity and influence. Some of this may seem unrealistic or inappropriate for you as a public speaker. But some commonsense tips will help you choose clothing that eliminates problems and adds impact to your speech.

The safest advice we can offer the public speaker on appearance is to avoid extremes in dress and grooming. Use clothes to reinforce your purpose in speaking, not to draw too much attention to themselves. Every moment that the audience spends admiring your European-cut navy blue suit or wondering why you wore the torn Old Navy T-shirt is a moment they are distracted from your message.

Here are some "Dress for Address" guidelines for you to follow. In selecting your attire, take into consideration the occasion, audience, topic, and speaker.

1. *Consider the Occasion.* The formality or informality of your clothing is dictated in part by the speaking occasion. A student delivering a valedictory would dress differently from one delivering an impromptu campaign speech in the school cafeteria. A speech in your classroom permits you more informality than would a business presentation to a board of directors, a sermon to a congregation, or an acceptance speech at an awards ceremony.

2. *Consider Your Audience.* Some of your listeners dress more casually than others. In any audience, there is a range of attire. As a rule, we suggest that you dress at the top of that range. For speeches outside the classroom, traditional, tasteful, and subdued clothing is your wisest choice. Your aim is to appear as nicely dressed as the best dressed

When it comes to public speaking, think about "dressing for address" rather than "dressing for success." Each of these speakers chose clothing suited to her topic, audience, speaking occasion, and the image she wants to project.

people in your audience. In other words, when in doubt, dress "up" a little. An audience is more easily insulted if you appear to treat the speaking occasion too casually than if you treat it too formally. Remember, your listeners will make judgments based on your appearance before you even open your mouth.

3. *Consider Your Topic.* Your topic may also affect your choice of clothes. While the public speech is not a costumed performance, clothing can underscore or undermine the impact you want your speech to have. A hot pink dress or lime green shirt would be appropriate for a speech on the festival of Mardi Gras but not for one on the high cost of funerals. On the other hand, you would look foolish presenting a speech on step aerobics if you demonstrated exercises dressed in a business suit.

4. *Consider Your Image.* Finally, the image you want to create as a speaker should shape your selection of clothing. Darker colors, for example, convey authority. Lighter colors establish a friendlier image. A student perceived as the class clown could dress more formally on the day of his or her speech to help dispel this image.

Clothing not only influences our perceptions of others, it also shapes our self-perception. Just think of your own experiences. You probably have certain clothes that give you a sense of confidence or make you feel especially assertive or powerful. You feel differently about yourself when you wear them. Dressing "up" conveys your seriousness of purpose to your listeners. It also establishes this same positive attitude in your own mind.

As a practical matter, we suggest that you decide what you will wear before the day of your speech and that you practice, at least once, in those clothes. You will discover that this benefits you in three ways. First, you reduce by one the number of decisions you must make on the day of your speech. Second, you will be more comfortable as you deliver your speech. If you wear a suit coat and are not used to doing so, you will have practiced gesturing with it on. You will have decided if it is best buttoned or unbuttoned. Third, practicing in what you actually plan to wear alerts you to problems and enables you to correct them. Make sure that what you plan to wear is clean and pressed. You may also discover, for example, that a favorite bracelet creates a distracting sound as it taps on the lectern when you move your arm. One of our students complained that she was distracted during her presentation because every time she moved her arms to gesture her coat made a rustling sound. She could have eliminated this distraction had she practiced in that suit coat before the day of her speech. Whatever the problems, it's best to encounter and fix them before the speech. You can then concentrate fully on the speech itself.

Posture

A public speaker should look comfortable, confident, and prepared to speak. You have the appropriate attire. Your next concern is your **posture,** the position or bearing of your body. In posture, the two extremes to avoid are rigidity and sloppiness. Don't hang on to or drape yourself across the lectern, if you are using one. Keep your weight balanced on both legs, and avoid shifting your weight back and forth in a nervous swaying pattern. Equally distracting is standing on one leg and shuffling or tapping the other foot. You may not realize that you do those things. Other people will have to point them out to you. Remember that before your delivery can reinforce your message, it must be free of annoying mannerisms.

Facial Expression

Researchers estimate that the human face is capable of 250,000—a quarter of a million—different facial expressions.[11] That's a vast amount of communication potential!

posture: the position or bearing of a speaker's body while delivering a speech.

Yet, ironically, many people giving a speech for the first time put on a blank mask, reducing their **facial expression** to one neutral look. We have often seen our students do this, and we know why it occurs. Inexperienced speakers are understandably nervous and may be more concerned with the way they look and sound than they are with the ideas they are trying to communicate.

To articulate clearly you must open your mouth freely; as you speak, your face must move. However, your facial expression must match what you are saying. The speaker who smiles and blushes self-consciously through a speech on date rape will simply not be taken seriously by the audience and may offend many listeners. If you detail the plight of earthquake victims, make sure your face reflects your concern. If you tell a joke and your listeners can't stop chuckling, you certainly should break into a smile rather than a frown. In other words, your face should register the thoughts and feelings that motivate your words.

> Studying Facial Expression
> http://mambo.ucsc.edu/psl/fanl.html
> This graphics-heavy site may take a few moments to load but can be worth the wait. It links to a number of sites with bibliographies, annotated bibliographies, and images on research in facial expression. Many of these sites use computer modeling to measure facial movements or to teach speech recognition.

The way to use facial expression appropriately to bolster your message is really simple: Concentrate as much as possible on the ideas you present and the way your audience receives and responds to them. Try not to be overly conscious of how you look and sound. This takes practice, but your classroom speeches provide a good forum for such rehearsal. You will learn to interact with the audience, maintain eye contact, and respond with them to your own message. Chances are that, if you do those things, your facial expression will be varied and appropriate and will reinforce your spoken words.

Eye Contact

We've all heard the challenge, "Look me in the eye and say that." We use direct eye contact as one gauge of a person's truthfulness. **Eye contact** can also carry many other messages: confidence, concern, sincerity, interest, and enthusiasm. Lack of eye contact, on the other hand, may signal deceit, disinterest, or insecurity.

Try this simple experiment. The next time you talk to a good friend, look at a spot on that person's hair rather than looking him or her in the eyes. What will happen? Chances are good that your friend will either ask you, "What's the deal?" or use one of those nervous, self-directed, preening gestures we all have to make sure that there's nothing wrong with our hair. Your friend may even do both, because the speaker who avoids eye contact with us, or who looks beyond us, will frustrate or anger us or at least make us very self-conscious.

Your face is the most important source of nonverbal cues as you deliver your speech, and your eyes carry more information than any other facial feature. As you speak, you will probably look occasionally at your notes or manuscript. You may even glance away from the audience briefly as you try to put your thoughts into words. Yet you must keep coming back to the eyes of your listeners to check their understanding, interest, and evaluation of your message.

As a public speaker, your goal is to make eye contact with as much of the audience as much of the time as possible. The way to do that is to make sure that you take in your entire audience, from front to back and from left to right. Include all those boundaries in the scope of your eye contact, and make contact especially with those individuals who seem to be listening carefully and responding positively to your message. Whether you actually make eye contact with each member of the audience is immaterial. You must, however, create that impression. Again, this takes practice before you feel comfortable.

facial expression: the tension and movement of various parts of a speaker's face.

eye contact: gaze behavior in which a speaker looks at listeners' eyes.

Movement

Effective **movement** benefits you the speaker, your audience, and your speech. First, place-to-place movement can actually help you relax. Moving to a visual aid, for example, can help you energize and loosen up physically. From the audience's perspective, movement adds visual variety to your speech, and appropriate movement can arouse or rekindle the listeners' interest. Most important, though, physical movement serves your speech by guiding the audience's attention. Through movement, you can underscore key ideas, mark major transitions, or intensify an appeal for belief or action.

Remember that your speech starts the moment you enter the presence of your audience. Your behavior, including your movement, sends signals about your attitudes toward the audience and your speech topic. When your time to speak arrives, approach your speaking position confidently, knowing that you have something important to say. Addressing a large audience through a microphone mounted on the lectern will naturally restrict your movement. If the lectern is there as a matter of convenience, and particularly if you are speaking to a relatively small audience, don't automatically box yourself into one position behind the lectern. Remember that even the smallest lectern puts a physical barrier between you and your audience. Moving to the side or the front of it reduces both the physical and the psychological distance between you and your listeners and may be especially helpful whenever you conclude your speech with a persuasive appeal.

Make certain that your movement is selective and that it serves a purpose. Avoid random pacing. Movement to mark a transition should occur at the beginning or the end of a sentence, not in the middle. Finally, bring the speech to a satisfying psychological conclusion, and pause for a second or two before gathering your materials and moving toward your seat in the audience.

Gestures

Gestures, movements of a speaker's hands, arms, and head, seem to be as natural a part of human communication as spoken language. Deaf communities throughout the world spontaneously develop various sign languages. "Indeed, children exposed from an early age only to sign language go through the same basic stages of acquisition as children learning to speak, including a stage when they 'babble' silently in sign!"[12] Among adults, gestures not only punctuate and emphasize verbal messages for the benefit of listeners but apparently also ease the process of encoding those messages for speakers. Various studies show that people asked to communicate without gestures produce labored speech marked by increased hesitations and pauses. Such speakers also demonstrate decreased fluency, inflection, and stress, and they use fewer high-imagery words.[13] Hand gestures, then, seem to help speakers retrieve elusive words from their memories.[14]

Gestures are important adjuncts to our verbal messages; at times, they can even replace words altogether. As a public speaker, you can use gestures to draw a picture of an object, to indicate the size of objects or the relationships between them, to re-create some bodily motion, to emphasize or underscore key ideas, to point to things such as presentational aids, or to trace the flow of your ideas. If you don't normally gesture in conversation, force yourself to include some gestures as you practice your speech. At first you may feel self-conscious about gesturing. Keep practicing. Gestures that are natural and spontaneous are well worth whatever time you spend practicing them. Not only do they reinforce your ideas and make you seem more confident and dynamic, but gestures, like movement, can help you relax.

To be effective, then, gestures must be coordinated with your words and must appear natural and spontaneous. In addition, any gesture should be large enough for the

movement: a speaker's motion from place to place during speech delivery.

gestures: movements of a speaker's hands, arms, and head while delivering a speech.

audience to see it clearly. The speaker who gestures below the waist, or whose gestures are barely visible over the top of a lectern, may appear timid, unsure, or nervous. Speakers who gesture too much—who talk with their hands—may also be perceived as nervous, flighty, or excitable. The two extremes to avoid, therefore, are the absence of gestures (hands clenched in a death-grip on the sides of the lectern) and excessive gestures (gestures emphasizing everything, with the result that nothing stands out). Remember, if your audience is waiting for you to gesture or counting your many gestures, they are distracted from your message.

The following two generalizations from research on gestures are particularly helpful for the public speaker. First, people who are confident, relaxed, and have high status tend to expand into the space around them and use gestures that are wider than those of other people. Speakers who wish to emphasize their authority, or to seem more authoritative, can therefore help do so by increasing the width of their gestures. Second, a wide, palm-up gesture with both hands creates an openness that is entirely appropriate when a speaker is appealing for a certain belief or urging the audience to some action. A palm-down gesture with one or both hands carries more force and authority and can be used to command an audience into action or to exhort them to a certain belief. Stand up and deliver the following statement, gesturing with both hands palms-up: "We need to communicate our message to the university administration: It's time to get serious about adequate funding of our library. Give us

> **Testing Your Delivery**
> http://www.abacon.com/pubspeak/exercise/delex.html
> Click "yes" or "no" to answer seven questions about your perception of some of your speech delivery habits. Upon submitting the questionnaire, you get advice based on your answers.

the resources we deserve!" Now repeat those sentences gesturing with both hands palms-down. Did you feel a subtle difference in tone and intensity?

As a speaker, adapt the size of your gestures to the size of your audience. On stage before a crowd of several thousand, your gestures should be more expansive than when you stand at the front of a small classroom. In a cavernous auditorium, you must adjust your gestures, as well as your facial expression and eye contact, so that they will be clear to those in the back rows.

These, then, are the tools of vocal and physical speech delivery, from rate of speaking to hand gestures. Your goal throughout this class and in your future public speaking experience will be to eliminate any distracting elements and then work toward delivery that is conversational, forceful, and as formal or informal as your audience and subject require.

One traditional saying is "If it's worth doing, it's worth doing well." That's wise counsel for the public speaker. Your gestures, rate of delivery, and grammar may seem trivial until they begin to interfere with your communication, undermine your credibility, and erode your persuasiveness. Delivery is a vital part of your public speech, and effective delivery is an asset worth cultivating.

Summary

Speech *delivery* is composed of a speaker's voice qualities, bodily actions, and language. This chapter focused on vocal and physical delivery, aspects of a speech presentation that are subject to four principles of nonverbal communication. First, part of our nonverbal communication is intentional, while another part is unconscious and unintentional. Second, few if any nonverbal signals have universal meaning. Third, when a speaker's verbal and nonverbal channels send conflicting messages, we tend to trust the nonverbal message. These three principles contribute to a fourth: The message you intend may be overridden by other messages people attach to your nonverbal communication.

As a speaker, you can select any of four methods of delivery: *impromptu speaking,* or speaking without advance preparation; *speaking from memory; speaking from manuscript;* and *speaking extemporaneously,* or from notes. While each of those types of delivery is appropriate under certain public speaking circumstances, impromptu speaking and speaking from memory should almost certainly be avoided for prepared, graded classroom speeches. Speeches from a manuscript and, particularly, from notes have far fewer limitations and more applications than the other two methods of delivery. Those who can speak clearly and emphatically from a few notes after the necessary period of practice have gone a long way toward ensuring success, not only in the public speaking classroom but also in any future public speaking situations.

The nonverbal elements of delivery include everything about your speech that could not be captured and recorded in a manuscript of the speech. *Vocal delivery* is comprised of your rate, use of pauses, volume, pitch and inflection, voice quality, articulation, and pronunciation. Your appearance, posture, facial expression, eye contact, movement, and gestures make up the elements of your *physical delivery*. With each of these elements, your goal as a speaker should be to eliminate distractions and to work for variety so that you look and sound natural. Once you are aware of unconscious mannerisms you may have and of the characteristics of effective delivery that you should have, you can make significant improvements in the way you deliver a speech.

You exercise a good deal of control over most of these physical and vocal elements of delivery. With the confidence that comes from practice, you should be able to adapt your delivery to different speaking situations and audience sizes. Though this chapter examined several different elements of delivery, speech delivery is best when none of those elements makes an impression on the audience. Instead, delivery should reinforce the clear, forceful communication of your ideas.

practice critique

Pairing Gestures and Movements with Words

Read the transcript of Sarah Meinen's speech "The Forgotten Four-Letter Word" in Appendix B. Focusing on Sarah's use of language, write suggestions for places in the speech where she might incorporate movement and gestures to enhance her delivery. Describe the types of gestures and movements you recommend. Also, using the markings discussed on page 299, note where Sarah could incorporate meaningful pauses to give her ideas emphasis.

Exercises

1. Make a list of famous people you think are exciting speakers and ones you find boring. Or list instructors who have reputations for being exciting or boring lecturers. How do these individuals' vocal and physical deliveries add to or detract from their ideas? Which of these techniques could you adapt to make your own speaking more dynamic?

2. Using the guidelines discussed in the "Rate and Pause" section of this chapter, mark pauses for paragraphs 15–19 of Martin Luther King, Jr.'s "I Have a Dream" speech in Appendix B. Practice reading this excerpt aloud to convey its meaning with the greatest impact.

3. Select a short passage from a novel, short story, speech, or other prose selection, and photocopy it. Study the meaning and emotion of the excerpt. After marking the copied text, read the passage aloud, emphasizing key words and phrases and using pauses to enhance the message's impact.

4. Record your speech on audiotape, and listen to it. Analyze your use of rate, pauses, volume, pitch, inflection, articulation, and pronunciation. What can you do to ensure that your delivery is lively and reinforces the message of the speech?

5. Record your speech on videotape. Watch and listen to it. Analyze your physical delivery, focusing on those aspects discussed in this chapter. What are your strengths? What are your weaknesses? What can you do to improve the physical delivery of your message?

6. Attend a speech, and analyze the speaker's vocal and physical delivery. Was the message delivered effectively? What nonverbal elements enhanced and what detracted from the speech? What suggestions could you give the speaker to improve the delivery of the speech?

Notes

1. Elinor Donahue, "Writing Your Own Speeches," *Fund Raising Management* (Feb. 1996), 7 July 1999 <http://web4.infotrac.galegroup.com/itw/i. . . 5!xrn_49_0_A18711219?sw_aep=viva_radford>.

2. Ben Watt and Tracey Thorn (Everything but the Girl), "Downhill Racer," *Temperamental,* Atlantic, 1999.

3. "Tale of the TelePrompTer," *Newsweek* 4 Oct. 1993: 4.

4. John Kao, *Delivering Successful Presentations,* FYI Video, American Management Association, 1992.

5. Myron H. Wahls, "The Moral Decay of America," *Vital Speeches of the Day* 15 July 1996: 604.

6. Mario Cuomo, "Introduction," *More than Words: The Speeches of Mario Cuomo* (New York: St. Martin's, 1993) xiv–xv.

7. Laurence J. Peter, *Peter's Quotations: Ideas for Our Time* (New York: Bantam, 1979) 476.

8. Bob Dole, "The Full Text: 'My Time to Leave,' " *USA Today Election 96.* Online. Internet. 16 March 1996.

9. Mihaly Csikszentmihalyi, *Flow: The Psychology of Optimal Experience* (New York: Harper-Perennial, 1990).

10. Mihaly Csikszentmihalyi, "How to Shape Our Selves," *Psychology Today* January/February 1994: 38.

11. Ray Birdwhistell, *Kinesics and Context: Essays on Body Motion Communication* (Philadelphia: U of Philadelphia P, 1970) 8.

12. Michael C. Corballis, "The Gestural Origins of Language," *American Scientist* March–April 1999: 140.

13. Donna Frick-Horbury and Robert E. Guttentag, "The Effects of Restricting Hand Gesture Production on Lexical Retrieval and Free Recall," *American Journal of Psychology* Spring 1998: 45–46.

14. Sharon Begley, "Living Hand to Mouth," *Newsweek* 2 November 1999: 69.

Using Presentational Aids

A three-year-old boy with bangs and short pants saluting at his father's funeral. . . .

Two helmeted figures saluting an American flag staked into a desolate, gray landscape. . . .

A space shuttle exploding in a cloudless azure sky. . . .

A young man standing motionless in a street in front of four tanks. . . .

People dancing and spraying champagne all night from atop a wall. . . .

Sheet-metal buildings erupting in flames on a windswept Texas prairie. . . .

A firefighter cradling the limp, bloodied body of a one-year-old girl. . . .

A bloody teenaged boy dropping from a second-story window into the arms of EMTs standing on the roof of an ambulance. . . .

If you form a vivid mental image at the description of any of these events, you prove the haunting power of pictures.[1] We have all grown up in a visually oriented society. Even our language reflects the power of the visual message. Consider these familiar sayings:

"A picture is worth a thousand words."

"Don't believe anything you hear and only half of what you see."

"I wouldn't have believed it if I hadn't seen it with my own eyes."

Today, television and film are our primary entertainment media. Most Americans get the majority of their news from television. Even our newspapers are filled with pictures, black and white or color. When the news is bad, we expect to see pictures or videotape of the airplane wreckage, the flooding, or the aftermath of the earthquake. When the news is good, we expect to see pictures of the winning team, the successful space mission, or the heroic rescue. We are, indeed, people for whom "seeing is believing."

Because pictures are such an important part of life, delivering a public speech without considering using presentational aids is a little like playing tennis with your racquet hand tied behind your back. As a speaker, you need not rely only on words to communicate your ideas precisely and powerfully. You can add force and impact to your message by incorporating a visual dimension as well.

The Importance of Using Presentational Aids

A well-designed, appropriate presentational aid can add significantly to the effectiveness of the speech and the speaker. Such aids serve four important functions. First, they add clarity to a speaker's message. Second, they reinforce the impact of the message. Third, they can increase the dynamism of a speaker's delivery. Finally, effective presentational aids used well can enhance a speaker's confidence. Consider these four functions as you determine whether to include presentational aids in a particular speech.

Increases Message Clarity

First, presentational aids give your speech greater clarity. They can specify the demographic breakdown of voters in the past presidential election, for example, or illustrate how a hologram is constructed, or explain the steps in the new university registration procedure. Detailed statistical information is more clearly conveyed in a simplified line graph than through a recitation of data. Speeches that use a spatial organizational pattern in particular often benefit from visual reinforcement.

Reinforces Message Impact

Second, presentational aids give your speech greater impact. Seeing may encourage believing; certainly, it aids remembering. "The introduction of visual communication to a presentation, which was previously communicated via the audio channel, has been shown to increase audience retention *at least fivefold.*"[2] In addition to making a message more memorable, however, presentational aids have other benefits:

> A study conducted by the University of Minnesota . . . showed that when computer-generated overhead transparencies or slides were used to present an idea, the presenter was perceived to be 43 percent more persuasive than in meetings with unaided presentations. The study also concluded that the use of visuals could reduce the length of a typical meeting by 28 percent.[3]

Studies draw different conclusions as to the degree of impact presentational aids give to a speech. They all conclude, however, that a well-constructed presentational aid helps listeners remember more of your speech for a longer period of time. Because they both hear and see the message, listeners are more fully involved in the speech. This greater sensory involvement with the message lessens the opportunity for outside distractions and increases retention.

Increases Speaker Dynamism

Third, presentational aids make you seem more dynamic. In Chapter 13, we discussed the importance of gestures as part of your delivery. Most speakers, unfortunately, have difficulty incorporating meaningful gestures into their delivery. They remain behind a lectern, their hands resting on, or clutching, their notes. Consequently, they may appear uninvolved, perhaps even bored, with their speech. Using presentational aids forces you to move, to point, to become physically involved with your speech. Your gestures become motivated and meaningful, and, consequently, you appear more dynamic and forceful.

Enhances Speaker Confidence

A fourth benefit of using presentational aids in your speech is that it can increase your confidence as a public speaker. In Chapter 3 we argued that one way to build your confidence is to identify characteristics of effective speakers, then to incorporate those behaviors into your speaking. Clear, attractive presentational aids that you have practiced using can help you relax in three ways. First, knowing that your presentational aids will enhance the clarity and impact of your message should increase your confidence. Second, revealing your presentational aids will give purpose to your movement and gestures, and this will help burn off some of your nervous energy. Finally, if you become nervous when you see the listeners' eyes focused on you, you can use your presentational aids to divert their attention to your speech content. Just remember that the purpose

Using a variety of visual aids can make your speech more dynamic and boost the clarity and impact of your message.

of your presentational aids should not be to divert attention from you but to enhance the impact of your message.

Before you plan presentational aids to clarify and enliven your speech, ask yourself, "Will such aids make my presentation more effective?" This question is important because any presentational aid, no matter how well designed and planned, involves some distractions for both speaker and audience. It may require setup time, for example. When you uncover the aid for audience view and cover it later, you create a visual break in the speech. In addition, presentational aids remove part of a listener's focus from the speaker. In short, *use presentational aids only if they are necessary to the speech,* and be prepared for possible distractions.

As powerful as presentational aids can be, remember that they are supplements to, not replacements for, your spoken words. As a speaker, you communicate; your pre-

speaking with confidence

The visual aids for my informative speech were designed to keep my listeners interested in my topic of check fraud. One of my aids was a large check. I purchased a large white sturdy posterboard and outlined in simple colors the details of the check. I made the check out to my speech teacher to the tune of $1000. Needless to say, it caught the attention of everyone in the room including my teacher. I then pointed out where forgeries occur on a check.

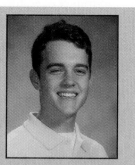

I also wanted to generate my listeners' interest by using an actual example of a fraudulent check. Since I work at a bank, I called the fraud department and was faxed a copy of a check with a signature that had been altered. I also received a copy of the depositor's real signature. Using an overhead projector, I displayed the bad check next to the good one. The audience could see that the signatures were indeed not identical. Using exciting visual aids was a way of getting my audience interested in my topic, and this made me feel more confident giving my speech.

—Jacob Casey, Clark College

sentational aids simply illustrate. "Whether your presentation hinges on flipping a few charts or running a multimedia computer, the three secrets to effective presentations remain: communication, communication, communication." [4] To test what you are actually going to be communicating, ask yourself:

> How would the presentation "play" if it were stripped of visual tools and presented in a face-to-face meeting across a bare wooden desk? Looking at a presentation this way strips away the decoration and focuses on content. It may also serve as contingency planning in disguise—preparation for a mechanical failure or a collapsed schedule. [5]

A guiding rule for using visual aids is surely to exercise restraint. [6] As a speaker, you have the burden of making the case for using presentational aids in a particular speech. As accessible, common, and relatively easy to produce as presentational aids are today, their presence in a public speech is not a default setting.

If you add an aid to your speech at the last moment because you realize that a presentational aid is part of the speech requirement, you may be on shaky ground. A presentational aid should never be an afterthought. The requirement for a presentational aid should have guided your topic selection, research, and practice of the speech. In addition, you should never employ a presentational aid just to add length to a presentation that you fear is too short. Don't incorporate a visual aid just to show that you know how to use the technology or to demonstrate your artistic skills. In this chapter we will tell you that a presentational aid should serve as your speaking notes during the time you are revealing and discussing it in your speech. This does not mean, however, that any time you require speaking notes to deliver your speech you must present them as bulleted lists on a chart. Would Martin Luther King, Jr.'s "I Have a Dream" speech, reprinted in Appendix B, really have required an electronic slide show, if that technology had been available to him? More important, how different would the effect of the speech have been with slides projected on some jumbo screen for his thousands of listeners?

Now that you understand how presentational aids can enhance your speech, some of the problems they may pose, and some of the circumstances in which you should not use them, let's examine the various types of aids you might consider using in a speech.

Types of Presentational Aids

Once you have decided to use presentational aids, you need to determine the type most appropriate to your presentation. Presentational aids come in many forms, but they can generally be divided into four classifications: objects, graphics, projections, and handouts.

Objects

Objects may be either actual, such as a 35-millimeter camera, or scaled, such as an architect's model of the new campus library. Other three-dimensional presentational aids are, for instance, a scuba diver's oxygen tank and breathing regulator, a deck of tarot cards, a replica of the Statue of Liberty, or a new model of computer hardware. Our student James presented an informative speech on product packaging design. Among other objects he used were several Pepsi cans of a design used in 1990. In a matter of seconds he showed how the lines on the cans clearly spelled out the word *sex* when two cans were stacked and aligned in a certain way.

Also included under the category of objects are people or animals you employ in delivering a speech. You might enlist a volunteer to help you demonstrate tests for color blindness or bring in a Jack Russell terrier for a speech on that breed of dog. Objects used effectively give your speech immediacy and carry a great deal of impact.

object: an actual item or three-dimensional model of an item used during the delivery of a speech.

Graphics

The term **graphics** includes a variety of two-dimensional presentational aids used to clarify or illustrate a point being made orally. Five types of graphics to consider are pictures, diagrams, graphs, charts, and maps.

Pictures can make a speaker's oral presentation more concrete and vivid. It is difficult to imagine how a speech on the artistic styles of Georgia O'Keeffe or Edward Hopper could be effective without pictures or prints of some of their paintings. A speaker trying to persuade the audience that subliminal messages are common in advertising would be both vague and unconvincing unless he or she presented actual examples.

Speakers can also use pictures to dramatize a point, as with photographs showing the extent of tornado damage in a particular area. Our student, Nena, delivered an informative speech on Barcelona's *La Sagrada Familia* (The Sacred Family) cathedral, a site she had visited. Under construction since 1882 and long thought to be unfinishable, the cathedral is the vision of eccentric architect Antonio Gaudí, who died in 1926. Nena used a color enlargement of a photograph (Figure 14.1a) to show her listeners how the 328-foot towers of the cathedral's east facade dominate the landscape. Later, as she described how the cathedral reflected Gaudí's changing views of architecture, Nena showed a photographic detail (Figure 14.1b) of

graphic: a two-dimensional visual aid, including pictures, diagrams, graphs, charts, and maps, used during the delivery of a speech.

picture: a photograph, painting, drawing, or print used to make a point more vivid or convincing.

Using Audio-Visual Aids
http://www.uakron.edu/
schlcomm/Turner/
avgen.htm
Maintained by Professor Dudley Turner of the University of Akron, this site links to brief discussions of general considerations about using audio-visual aids. Topics include types and benefits of presentational aids, as well as when and how to use them.

(a)

(b)

FIGURE 14.1

(a) *La Sagrada Familia* cathedral, east facade; **(b)** *La Sagrada Familia* cathedral, detail.

the façade's elaborate ornamentation.[7] By citing her sources and using enlarged photographs that were easy to see, Nena expanded her description and gave her classmates a clear, vivid glimpse of this architectural wonder.

When you use pictures, make sure that you select them with size and clarity in mind. A small snapshot of the Palace of Versailles or a picture from an encyclopedia held up for audience view detracts from, rather than reinforces, the speaker's purpose. Pictures used as visual aids often must be enlarged. Luckily, color laser copiers found at many copy shops today make enlarged copies of pictures quickly and inexpensively. You can also check the library for books with large pictures. The picture you want to show may even be available as an inexpensive poster from a local museum gift shop or a bookstore. For very large audiences, you may need to project pictures for easy viewing. Here again, you may be able to borrow slides from your school's art department library or to purchase them from a museum gift shop.

Diagrams are graphics, typically drawn on posterboard or designed on computer, showing the parts of an object or organization or the steps in a process. Posterboard is ideal for diagrams used in classroom speeches because its large size makes it easy for audience members to see. It is also thick and rigid enough to make handling easy. A diagram could show the features of a new aircraft design, the organizational structure of the U.S. judicial system, or the steps in the lost-wax method of casting jewelry. The best diagrams achieve their impact by simplifying and exaggerating key points. For example, no diagram of manageable size could illustrate all the parts of a six-cylinder engine clearly enough for the audience to see easily. A carefully constructed diagram could isolate and label key parts of that engine design, however.

Paul, a nursing student, was interested in why Japanese people live longer lives than anyone.[8] Figure 14.2 shows two diagrams Paul used in an informative speech comparing the diets of people in different ethnic groups and geographic areas. He showed the USDA food pyramid first, reminding his listeners of these daily recommendations. He then showed the Asian pyramid, with its different proportions and far different recommended frequencies for eating foods in some categories. To underscore the differences

diagram: a graphic, usually drawn on posterboard, showing the parts of an object or organization or the steps in a process.

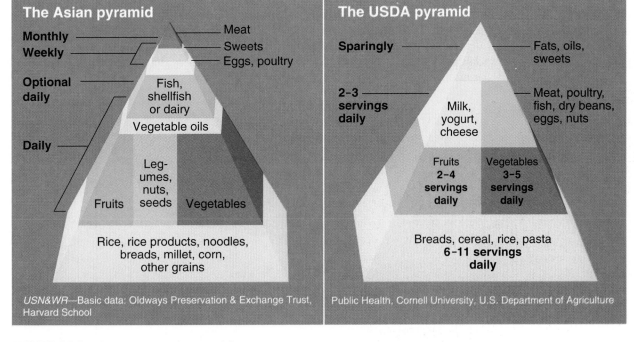

FIGURE 14.2 Diagrams: Food Pyramids
(Source: U.S. News & World Report, January 8, 1996. Copyright © 1996 by U.S. News & World Report. Reprinted by permission.)

between the two diets, he placed the two pyramids side by side as he compared and contrasted them.

Graphs can take several familiar forms and can be used as presentational aids to illustrate some condition or progress. A **line graph** is useful in depicting trends and developments over time. A speaker might convincingly use a line graph to illustrate the rising cost of a college education over the past twenty years. Some line graphs trace two or more variables—income and expenditures, for example—in contrasting colors.

Genna used a line graph (Figure 14.3) in her informative speech on the aging of America. In a Department of Labor publication, she found a table that listed by decade the percentage of the U.S. population falling into two age groups: 65 to 74 years, and 75 years and older. She constructed a chart using this information and practiced her speech in front of her roommates. However, they found the chart cluttered and confusing, and Genna agreed. She decided that a line graph would more clearly and vividly make her point that the U.S. population was aging and would continue to do so.

A **bar graph** is useful in comparing quantities or amounts. We can measure the economic health of an institution, a company, or a nation, for example, by learning whether it is "in the red" or "in the black." A bar graph contrasting deficits and profits, showing their relative size, provides us a clear, visual indication of economic health, particularly when income is represented in black and deficits in red.

While researching for a speech on the use of Internet metasearch engines, Octavio began to discover some interesting information about the percentage of the Web that is currently indexed. He came across a link to http://searchenginewatch.com, a site that collects statistical information about the growth of the Web and access to it.[9] He knew that his classmates were familiar with and used search engines such as FAST, AltaVista, Excite, Lycos, Infoseek, and WebCrawler. But he had never heard of Northern Light, and he found that it indexed almost as many Web pages as FAST, the leader, and more than AltaVista. Octavio reasoned that a number of his classmates would find this comparison of search engine sizes interesting, so he adapted and used a bar graph (Figure 14.4) from *Search Engine Watch* in his speech, being sure to cite the source for his graph.

A third type of graph, the **pie** or **circle graph,** is helpful when you want to show relative proportions of the various parts of a whole. If you are analyzing the federal budget, for example, a pie graph could illustrate the percentage of the budget allocated for defense. Pie graphs can show proportions of how people spend their time in a typical day, the causes of cancer deaths, how the average grocery dollar is spent, and the com-

line graph: a diagram used to depict changes among variables over time.

bar graph: a diagram used to show quantitative comparisons among variables.

pie or **circle graph:** a diagram used to show the relative proportions of a whole.

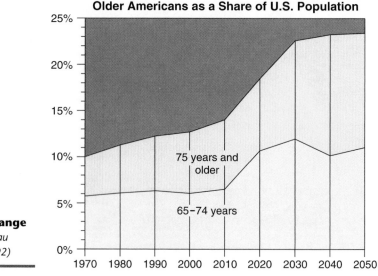

**FIGURE 14.3
Line Graph:
Population Change**
*(Source: U.S. Bureau
of the Census, 1992)*

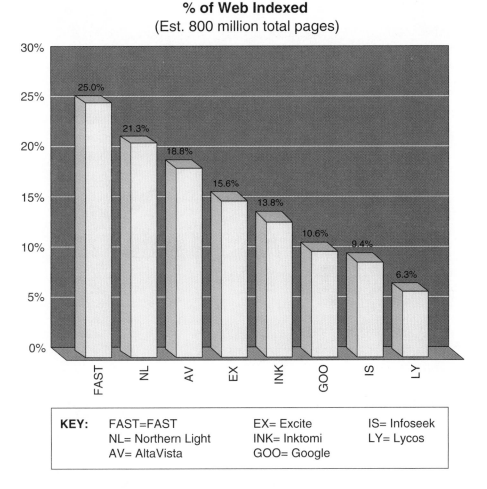

% of Web Indexed
(Est. 800 million total pages)

KEY:
FAST=FAST
NL= Northern Light
AV= AltaVista

EX= Excite
INK= Inktomi
GOO= Google

IS= Infoseek
LY= Lycos

FIGURE 14.4
**Bar Graph: Search
Engines—% of
Web Indexed**

position of your university according to the majors chosen by the student population. When using a pie graph, emphasize the pertinent "slice" of the pie graph with a contrasting color.

Todd chose as a speech topic the business side of the music industry. In his research he found several articles that included interesting and informative graphics. He adapted and used two of them in his speech, citing the source for each. Figure 14.5 shows one of those graphics, a pie graph showing the cost breakdown of a compact disc.

Similar to diagrams and graphs, **charts** condense a large amount of information into a small space. For visibility and ease of handling, charts are often drawn on posterboard when used as presentational aids for a small audience. Speakers introducing an audience to new terms will sometimes list those words on a chart. This strategy is particularly effective if the words can be uncovered one at a time in the order they are discussed. Using charts, you could list the top ten states in per capita lottery ticket sales or rank professional sports according to players' average salaries. Charts are particularly appropriate for medical and other technical topics. A speaker detailing the solution phase of a problem–solution speech could list steps advocated on a chart and introduce them in the order they are discussed.

As a speaker, you can either prepare charts in advance or draw them during the speech. For example, charts could show how regular investment in an Individual Retirement Account can lead to financial security in later life, and those calculations could be done ahead of time or during the course of the presentation. If you plan to draw one or more charts during your speech, rehearse the drawing. Make sure that you can

chart: a graphic, usually drawn on posterboard or transparency, used to condense a large amount of information, to list the steps in a process, or to introduce new terms.

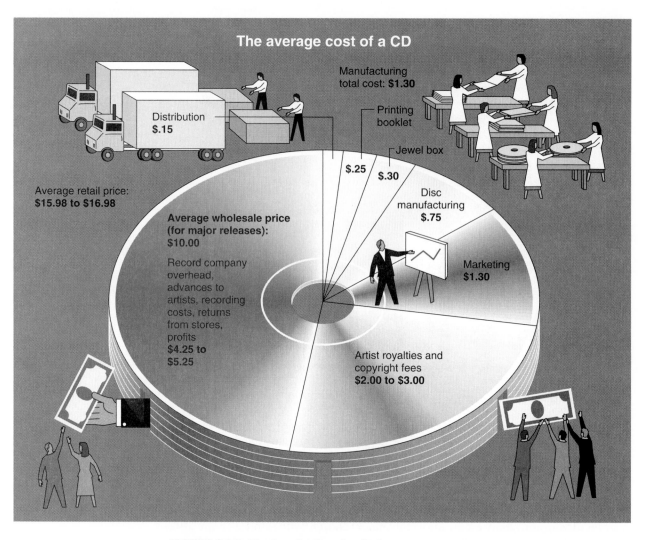

The average cost of a CD

Manufacturing total cost: $1.30

Distribution $.15

Printing booklet $.25

Jewel box $.30

Disc manufacturing $.75

Average retail price: $15.98 to $16.98

Average wholesale price (for major releases): $10.00

Record company overhead, advances to artists, recording costs, returns from stores, profits $4.25 to $5.25

Marketing $1.30

Artist royalties and copyright fees $2.00 to $3.00

FIGURE 14.5 Pie Graph: Cost Analysis
(Source: U.S. News & World Report, *September 25, 1995. Copyright © by U.S. News & World Report, Inc. Reprinted by permission.)*

continue to speak as you draw, so that your speech is not marred by long gaps of silence. If a chart is so complex that you cannot draw it as you speak, prepare it in advance.

Keira thought her classmates would be interested in learning about job prospects after graduation. She logged onto the Internet and accessed the Bureau of Labor Statistics, where she found a list of occupations with projected job growth. She adapted the information on the Web site to make her chart (Figure 14.6) more focused and less complicated.

You can use a flip-chart, a large sketch pad bound at the top, to accommodate a series of charts. Available at most art supply stores, flip-charts have a sturdy backing that will stand up straight on an easel. They allow you to flip each visual aid back after using it. If you need to show one chart briefly, speak for a while, and then show another chart, simply leave a blank page between charts that need to be separated.

Maps, the final type of graphic presentational aid, lend themselves especially well to speeches discussing or referring to unfamiliar geographic areas. Speakers informing an audience on the islands of Hawaii, the Battle of Gettysburg, or threats to the Alaskan wildlife refuge would do well to include maps to illustrate their ideas. Although commercial maps are professionally prepared and look good, they may be either too small

Occupations with the Largest Job Growth
1996–2006

Occupation	Number of New Jobs (in thousands)	Increase
1. Cashiers	530	17%
2. Systems analysts	520	103%
3. General managers/top executives	467	15%
4. Registered nurses	411	21%
5. Salespersons, retail	408	10%
6. Truck drivers	404	15%
7. Home health aides	378	76%
8. Teacher aides/educational assistants	370	38%

**FIGURE 14.6
Chart: Occupations with the Largest Job Growth**
(Source: U.S. Bureau of Labor Statistics, 1998)

or too detailed for a speaker's purpose. If you cannot isolate and project a section of the map for a larger audience, you will probably want to prepare a simplified, large-scale map of the territory in question.

Colleen became interested in the geography of cyberspace after a guest lecturer presented a multimedia presentation on this topic in her computer class. Colleen wanted to learn more about these virtual geographies and, with some guidance from her computer professor, began researching the topic. She accessed a Web site that displayed maps of cyberspaces. There, she learned that Emmanuel Frécon had developed a tool called WebPath that visually maps users' trails as they browse the Web.[10] She downloaded and printed a color copy of one of these Surf maps. She took it to the library's Media Resource Center, where she had the map enlarged (see Figure 14.7).

map: a graphic representing a real or imaginary geographic area.

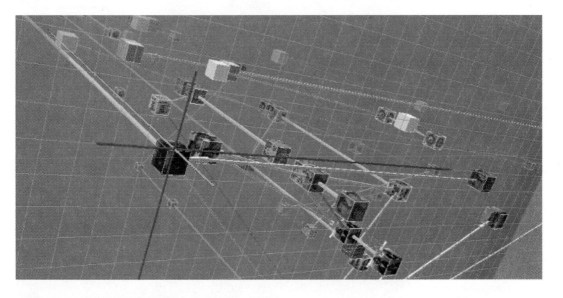

FIGURE 14.7 Map: Surf Map of Web Browsing

Colleen had a challenging task of making a technical topic understandable for her listeners, but her presentational aid made her goal easier. After the speech her classmates and the instructor seemed genuinely interested in her topic and asked several questions. Several students even stayed after class to look at her visual aid.

Projections

Projections refer not so much to a type of presentational aid as to a manner of presentation. Any of the graphics mentioned earlier—pictures, diagrams, graphs, charts, or maps—can be projected. This is especially appropriate when your audience is too large to see the presentational aid easily and clearly. In such a case, you may want to use projections, such as slides, transparencies, or opaque projections. For convenience, we can group projections into two categories: *still projections* (slides, opaque projections, and transparencies) and *moving projections* (films and videotapes).

Still and moving projections can be critical to business and other public presentations. They may not, however, always serve the purpose of the public speaker and, particularly, the student of this class. Two notes of caution are in order. First, films and videotapes are lengthy, and their organization is predetermined. It is important that you, not a presentational aid, organize and present the ideas of your speech. Second, as a beginning public speaker, you need to control and be the primary focus of the public speaking event. When you stand at the back of the room, with lights dimmed, and narrate a slide show, you get little experience in speaking before an audience. For this reason, your instructor may not allow you to give a slide show, although you may be able to present a few relevant slides. Presentational aids must always support, not become, your speech.

Still Projections. **Slides** are small mounted transparencies projected one at a time, and most of us associate slides with photographs or pictures. Yet any of the graphics we discussed earlier can be photographed and developed into slides. Whereas maps, charts, graphs, and diagrams may be cumbersome and subject to wear, slides of those graphic presentational aids are easily transported and easily reproduced. However,

projection: a manner of presenting visual aids by casting their images onto a screen or other background.

slide: a small transparency mounted in a frame for projection.

Using today's computer technology, you can easily produce a wide array of professional-looking charts, graphs, and even drawings. In addition, traditional projection methods are giving way to high-tech devices that offer greater flexibility.

you should be aware of two disadvantages. One, slides require projection equipment that is frequently noisy and intrusive. The second disadvantage is that slides must be projected in darkness to be easily visible, and this, of course, takes the focus away from you, the speaker.

The **opaque projection** is an image that can be projected directly from a sheet of paper. Noisy, cumbersome opaque projectors of the past are gradually being replaced by high-tech visual presenters such as the ELMO. This equipment offers the advantage of enlarging and projecting visual aids without the work of preparing transparencies. However, such systems can also project transparencies, video, computer slide shows and computer animation, as well as images of three-dimensional objects. Many models feature auto-focus and power zoom magnification controlled by wireless remotes.

Transparencies are clear or tinted sheets of plastic with words or images drawn or printed on them. Shown with an overhead projector, the transparency may be either prepared in advance or drawn with a felt-tip marker during the presentation. Many computer graphics programs can generate professional-looking transparencies. Overhead transparencies allow you to work through a problem, for example, without turning your back to the audience, thus helping you maintain audience involvement and interaction. If you plan to use transparencies in your very first speech, prepare them beforehand. You will be nervous enough without having to worry about drawing your presentational aid as you speak.

Each of these types of still projections can visually enhance a presentation. They help ensure that the images are big enough for even the largest audiences to see clearly. All require special projection equipment, however. You may need to reserve that equipment through the audio-visual department of your school library. Your instructor may have some basic equipment in the department. Check all of this in advance, and practice with the equipment so that you know how to operate it and how to minimize any noise it makes. On the day of your speech, you will need to be extremely well organized and punctual because projection equipment requires time for setup and focusing and is subject to mechanical failure. Your diligence can pay off handsomely, however. If you are sure that the visual aid is important enough to project, its contribution to your speech will probably outweigh these potential disadvantages and reward your extra effort.

Moving Projections. Moving projections include **films** and **videotapes,** and they are appropriate whenever action will enhance a visual presentation. Moreover, with the widespread popularity of video cassette recording equipment, this particular type of presentational aid is becoming easier and cheaper to use. The choice between films and videotapes is dictated both by the projection equipment available to you and by the size of the audience. Images are clearer and can be projected larger from film than from videotape, making film a wise choice for presentations to large groups. Videotapes are entirely appropriate for presentations to small audiences or before larger groups that have multiple viewing monitors. Again, use only short clips from videotapes to illustrate the ideas of your speech. Do not let the presentational aid monopolize your presentation.

Videotapes have one obvious advantage over films: They do not require you to darken the room for projection. Though both film and videotape carry with them possible distractions, their potential impact is undeniable. Many speeches on social problems are significantly more compelling if the audience not only hears about but also sees graphic evidence of the problem.

Using PowerPoint
http://plato.acadiau.ca/sandbox/ppt/ppt.htm
http://www.microsoft.com/powerpointdev/p-tips.htm
The first site, from Acadia University in Nova Scotia, contains a page of links to sound, video, and graphics files for use in PowerPoint presentations. With its basic how-to links, it's also appropriate for novice users. The Microsoft site contains numerous links for users who already have a working knowledge of PowerPoint.

opaque projection: an image cast directly from a sheet of paper by use of an opaque projector.

transparency: a sheet of clear or tinted plastic with drawn or printed images projected using an overhead projector.

film and videotape: moving projections used to enhance a speaker's point.

ethical decisions

Nicole, a student with a dance background, delivered a speech on the structure and symbolism of *Riverdance* a week before the touring company arrived in town for a series of performances. She illustrated a point in her speech by showing a sequence of less than two minutes from a commercial videotape she had rented of a *Riverdance* performance at Radio City Music Hall. That presentational aid certainly made her speech livelier and more vivid for her listeners. Was it, however, a violation of copyright? Using the four guidelines discussed in Chapter 2 (see pages 34–35), determine whether Nicole's use of this material constituted fair use or copyright infringement. Be prepared to defend your answer. Are there other conditions that, had they occurred, would change your answer? If there had been time at the end of class, for example, could Nicole have ethically fulfilled students' requests to see more of the tape?

Video and film can also introduce viewers to aspects of various cultures. One of our students, Henry, delivered an informative speech on the topic of Sufism, an Islamic tradition that is both mystical and multicultural. He informed his listeners how this tradition combines dance and music to express spiritual ecstasy. He played a videotape of the dance of the "whirling dervishes" of the Mevlevi Order, pointing out the religious significance of the dancers' gestures and movements.

Electronic Aids

Computer technology has revolutionized the production and display of prsentational aids. Today, if you have access to a computer and any of the wide spectrum of graphics software, you can produce a variety of high-quality, professional-looking presentational aids. If you know how, you can use the computer not only to design visual aids but also to display them. Popular presentation graphics software includes Microsoft's PowerPoint™ and Lotus's Freelance Graphics. PowerPoint™ is the more popular of these, and it features "cue cards" that you can call up from the Help menu. These brief step-by-step instructions remain onscreen, prompting you to accomplish certain tasks. With PowerPoint™ you can create slides using more than 100 color and design templates. These slides can contain titles, text, graphics, clip art, drawn art, and even video. You can then organize these slides for manual or automatic display on a computer monitor as you speak. For large audiences, you can project your electronic slide show from a liquid crystal display panel attached to an overhead projector. You can also print the slides as color or black-and-white transparencies or have them printed as 35-millimeter slides. PowerPoint™ also lets you outline speaking notes to accompany each slide. You can even print smaller versions of your slides one, two, or six to a page to distribute as handouts.

Software like PowerPoint™ will produce graphics such as pie graphs that are more accurate than you could produce freehand. All you need to do is program the numbers and the identifying labels that you want represented. You can change one type of graph into another—a line graph into a bar graph, for example—with just a couple of clicks of the mouse. With a color laser copier, you can tint the sections of the graph different colors or produce a line graph that shows two variables in contrasting colors.

Graphics software will also let you create on the computer screen any image that you can draw, scan, or photograph. Software like PowerPoint™ allows you to import such digital images and then manipulate them: You can simplify a graph or diagram, for example, or isolate and enlarge one section of a map or photograph. Digital cameras allow you to take photographs, display them immediately on a Video Graphics Adaptor (VGA) computer screen, then enlarge sections of them, adjust their color, or even superimpose images to your satisfaction.

The computer-generated image or text that you print on a laser printer or color laser printer will probably be the size of a sheet of typing paper. That size would be appropriate for handouts given to each audience member but would be too small to display to an audience during your speech. What are your other options? You can enlarge that image up to 150 percent on most color laser copiers at print shops. If the image is still too small for easy audience viewing, you'd probably be wise to project it from a transparency, a slide, or a computer.

Rapid innovations in the field of computer graphics are exciting. But be sure that any presentational aids you produce this way enhance your message, rather than just showcase what the software can do. Avoid the temptations to overload or complicate your computer-generated visual by using all the bells and whistles of the program you choose. The same qualities that we've discussed for freehand presentational aids—clarity, simplicity, and contrast—should be evident in any computer graphic you use.

Handouts

A final method of visually presenting material is the **handout.** Copies of any graphic presentational aid—pictures, diagrams, graphs, charts, or maps—may be handed out to individual audience members.

Handouts are appropriately used under two conditions: (1) when the information cannot be effectively displayed or projected, or (2) when the audience needs to study or refer to the information after the speech. Gwen, a student presenting a speech on "The Power Résumé," used a handout to great benefit. She distributed a sample power résumé and referred to it at key intervals in her speech: "If you look at line fifteen, you will see. . . ." She had numbered the lines of the résumé in the margin so that the audience could find the references without fumbling. Not only could the audience refer to the résumé as Gwen discussed its key features, but many also probably saved it to use later as they prepared to enter the career world upon graduation. Gwen's speech and her presentational aid made a convincing argument for the importance of the power résumé. In a similar way, if you try to persuade your audience to contribute time and money to local charities, you will more likely achieve your goal if you distribute a handout with the name, address, telephone number, and brief description of each charity.

If you are distributing handouts to listeners who are likely to receive handouts from other speakers on the same day you speak, use colored paper to distinguish your materials. If you are the only speaker and are distributing several handouts, consider putting each one on a different color. It's easier to identify which handout you want your listeners to look at if you can say, "On the blue sheet . . . ," for example.

Audio and Other Aids

Audio aids include records, tapes, and compact discs, and certainly there is an audio dimension of films and videotapes. Certain speech topics lend themselves to audio reinforcement of the message. A speech on Janis Joplin, for example, would be more vivid and informative if the audience could see and hear a videotaped clip of one of her performances. Lindahl, a student whose research we mentioned in Chapter 7, began her speech on the savant syndrome by playing half a minute of a taped piano performance of Chopin's Polonaise no. 6 in A-Flat Major. Her first words were, "The person who was playing that music is considered handicapped, but he heard this piece of music for the first time only minutes before sitting down to play it." The audiotape was a compelling example of one form of the savant syndrome. A speech comparing the jazz styles of Branford Marsalis and Hugh Masakela could hardly be effective without letting listeners hear examples from each of those artists. A speech comparing and contrasting the protest music of World War I with that of the Vietnam War would certainly be more powerful with audio examples.

handout: any graphic visual aid distributed to individual audience members.

audio aid: a cassette tape, compact disc, or record used to clarify or prove a point by letting listeners hear an example.

Audio aids need not be confined to music topics, however. An audience listening to a speech on Winston Churchill could benefit from hearing his quiet eloquence as he addressed Great Britain's House of Commons and declared, "I have nothing to offer but blood, toil, tears, and sweat." A speaker analyzing the persuasive appeals of radio and television advertisements could play pertinent examples. Dan, a criminal justice major and intern with the police department, began his speech by playing an audiotape recorded in a police squad car. The officers were deciding whether they should stop a motorist suspected of driving under the influence (DUI). The audience heard the law enforcement officials describe what they saw that alerted them to a possible DUI and heard them discuss criteria for stopping the motorist. As the siren sounded, Dan stopped the tape. He used the audio aid to introduce his topic on the criteria for making a DUI arrest.

You may want to appeal to senses other than sight and hearing. For example, a student of ours gave each audience member an envelope before her speech on aromatherapy. When she discussed the effects of certain scents on behavior, she had students open the envelopes and remove strips of lavender- and vanilla-scented paper, two of the scents she discussed. Think creatively as well as critically as you consider ways of supporting what you say.

We have discussed the importance and major types of presentational aids. Remember, though, that even the most brilliant presentational aid cannot salvage a poorly planned, poorly delivered speech. Visuals can aid, but they cannot resuscitate a weak speech. On the other hand, even the most carefully designed and professionally executed visual aid can be spoiled by clumsy handling during a presentation. The effect of public speaking is cumulative, with each element contributing toward one final effect. If you use presentational aids, you cannot afford to use them poorly. The following section offers some practical guidelines on how to prepare and use presentational aids in your public speech.

Guidelines for Designing Presentational Aids

Whether you are preparing a slide show to project from a laptop computer, transparencies, or handouts to distribute to audience members, your presentational aids can have a positive impact only if they are clear and readable. Before preparing your presentational aids, consider the guidelines in the following categories.

Focus

- Focus on a few key points. Resist the temptation to present all of your information visually. Select ideas that are the most important or that can best be made through the use of presentational aids.
- Present ideas one at a time. Don't put two visual aids on one posterboard. If you are discussing the first of a five-step list of solutions for road rage, keep steps two through five covered. Don't let the audience get ahead of you. If you are using a transparency, for example, you can cover the steps not yet discussed with a sheet of paper and reveal the next point when you get to it.

Layout

- Use a landscape (horizontal) page format rather than a portrait (vertical) format when displaying transparencies, 35-mm slides, and posterboard. Text displayed horizontally is easier to read. A horizontal orientation also gives you a better chance of expressing an idea in a single line.

- Compose your text in the top half or two-thirds of your transparency, slide, or posterboard to ensure better viewing by those in the back of the classroom.
- Use left-margin alignment. It is easier to read than full- or right-margin justification.

Highlighting

- Use bullets or numbers to highlight your key points. If you have several key ideas, number them. Listeners can more readily focus on the appropriate part of the visual aid if they see a number when they hear you say, "My third suggestion . . . "
- Use no more than six words per line. Longer sentences are more difficult to read and remember. Also, speakers craft their speaking skills as they learn how to condense and simplify their messages.
- Use no more than four to six lines per page. Listeners in the back of the room may have difficulty seeing the lower portion of a transparency projection or a posterboard.

Fonts

- Use strong, straight fonts such as Ariel, Helvetica, and Times New Roman. Ornate fonts are more difficult to read.
- Use no more than two fonts per transparency or screen. Too many fonts can make your presentational aid more difficult to read.
- Select a font size large enough to be read easily from the back row. Minimum font size will vary according to the size of the classroom and the distance between the projector and the screen. Check out the font size prior to the time of your presentation.

Color and Art

- Use color to enhance your presentational aids. Research suggests that color can increase the audience's understanding and retention of information. Select colors that highlight the ideas you present. For example, a red line may reinforce a line graph showing a decline in student contributions to charitable organizations. To show growth a speaker might use a green line. Color can also complement the mood of a speech. A presentational aid for an informative speech on the celebration of Mardi Gras might use brighter colors than a graph showing the number of college students who die each year in automobile accidents.
- Limit the number of colors you use in your presentational aid. Presentational software provides you with the possibility of selecting from 16.8 million colors, so you'll need to be selective.[11] In fact, too many colors make reading a visual aid more difficult. You should probably use no more than six colors per presentational aid and even fewer if the aid contains only text.
- Avoid *chartjunk,* irrelevant graphics and art that clutter and detract from your visual aid. An effective presentational aid draws the reader's attention to key points being made in the speech.[12]

Strategies for Using Presentational Aids

Strategies for Using Presentational Aids

key points

Before the Speech

1. Determine the information to be presented visually.
2. Select the type of aid best suited to your resources and speech.
3. Ensure easy viewing by all audience members.
4. Make sure that the aid communicates the information clearly.
5. Construct an aid that is professional in appearance.
6. Practice using your aid.
7. Arrange for safe transportation of your aids.
8. Carry back-up supplies with you.
9. Properly position the aid.
10. Test your presentational aid.

During the Speech

1. Reveal the aid only when you are ready for it.
2. Talk to your audience—not to the aid.
3. Refer to the aid.
4. Keep your aid in view until the audience understands your point.
5. Conceal the aid after you have made your point.
6. Use handouts with caution.

Before the Speech

Determine the Information to Be Presented Visually. Sections of a presentation that are complex or detailed may be particularly appropriate for visualization. Be careful, however, not to use too many visual aids. The premium in a speech is on the spoken word. Multimedia presentations can be exciting; they may also be extremely difficult to coordinate. Handling too many charts and posters quickly becomes cumbersome and distracting.

Select the Type of Presentational Aid Best Suited to Your Resources and Speech. The aid you select will be influenced by the information you need to present, the amount of preparation time you have, your technical expertise at producing the aid, and the cost involved. If preparing quality presentational aids to illustrate your speech will take more time, money, or expertise than you have, you are probably better off without them. A presentational aid that calls attention to its poor production is a handicap, no matter how important the information it contains.

Ensure Easy Viewing by All Audience Members. A speaker addressing an audience of 500 would not want to use a videotaped presentation displayed on a single television or computer monitor. A bar graph on posterboard should be visible to more than just the first four rows of the audience. If possible, practice with your presentational aids in the room where you will speak. Position the aid and then sit in the seat of your farthest possible audience member. (In an auditorium, make it the back row; people will not move forward unless forced to.) If you can read your presentational aid from that distance, it is sufficient in size. If you cannot, you must either enlarge the aid or eliminate it.

Make Sure That the Presentational Aid Communicates the Information Clearly.
Simplicity should be your guiding principle in constructing your visual aid. Michael
Talman, a graphics design consultant, compares a graphic in a presentation to "going
by a highway billboard at 55 miles per hour. Its effectiveness can be judged by how
quickly the viewer sees and understands its message."[13] Too much information may
clutter or confuse. For example, speakers sometimes construct posters in technicolor
to make them lively and interesting. But, remember that the purpose of visual aids is
to inform, not to impress, the audience. You may use red to indicate a budget deficit,
but, as a rule, black or dark blue on white is the most visually distinct color combination for graphics.

Construct a Presentational Aid That Is Professional in Appearance. In the business
and professional world, a hand-lettered poster, no matter how neatly done, is inappropriate. Professionals understand the importance of a good impression and are willing
to pay graphics designers to help them create polished presentational aids. Today, however, the computer puts a galaxy of inexpensive, professional-looking design options at
the fingertips of anyone willing to learn the programs. If you have access to a computer
and are familiar with a computer graphics program that meets your needs, by all means
use it. If you can't use a computer and doubt your freehand skills, hiring an art student
to draw and letter a presentational aid you have designed is another alternative.

If you throw together a chart or graph the night before your speech, that is exactly
what it will look like. Your hastily prepared work will undermine an image of careful
and thorough preparation.

Practice Using Your Presentational Aid. A conscientious speaker will spend hours
preparing a speech; presentational aids are a part of that presentation. Just as you rehearse the words of your speech, you should rehearse referring to your aid, uncovering
and covering charts, advancing slides, and writing on overhead transparencies. In
short, if you plan to use presentational aids, learn how *before* your speech; no audience
will be impressed by how much you learn during the course of your presentation.

Arrange for Safe Transportation of Your Presentational Aids. Aids worth using are
worth transporting safely. The laptop computer you've bought or borrowed needs obvious care. Posterboards should be protected from moisture and bending. Cover your
presentational aid with plastic to protect it from a freak rainstorm or that flying Frisbee
you encounter just before speech class. Do not roll up paper or posterboard charts, carrying them to different classes or leaving them in a car trunk throughout the day, and
then expect them to lay flat when you speak. You will have a cylinder, not an effective
presentational aid.

Carry Back-Up Supplies with You. An exciting and informative presentation can be
ruined when a projector bulb blows as you are preparing to speak. Make an inventory
of equipment you may need, such as extension cords, bulbs, and batteries, and then
take them with you.

Properly Position the Presentational Aid. Get to the place where you will give your
speech *before* the audience arrives. Check out the equipment you will use. Check the
height of the easel if you are using a flip-chart or posterboards. If you are plugging in
an overhead projector or a laptop computer, make sure that the equipment works and
that you can place electrical cords so that you won't trip over them. Position your presentational aid in the most desirable location. Make sure that the maximum number of
people will see it and that nothing obstructs the audience's view. If you are not to be the
first speaker, have your presentational aid and any necessary equipment out of the way
but located so that you can set up quickly and with little disruption.

Test Your Presentational Aid. Finally, if you are using transparencies, make sure that they are in focus and in the correct order. Use a test transparency. If there are people already in the room, you may not want to "give away" your topic by displaying one of your presentational aids. Some speakers use a transparency with the words *Test Transparency* on it. Although this keeps the audience from seeing part of the speech before you deliver it, it reveals little thought or creativity. A transparency with a creative title for your speech can create interest in your topic without revealing key information. In fact, it could motivate your audience to listen even before you utter your first word.

During the Speech

Not even the most careful preparation of a presentational aid guarantees that it will work for you as you deliver your speech. Keep the following commonsense guidelines in mind as you practice incorporating the aid into your delivery.

Reveal the Presentational Aid Only when You Are Ready for It. A presentational aid is designed to attract attention and convey information. If it is visible at the beginning of the speech, the audience may focus on it rather than on what you are saying. Your aid should be seen only when you are ready to discuss the point it illustrates.

If your presentational aid is on posterboard, cover it with a blank posterboard, or turn the blank side to the audience. At the appropriate time, expose the visual aid. If you are using projections, have someone cued to turn the lights off and the projector on at the appropriate time.

Occasionally, a speaker will stop speaking, uncover a presentational aid, and then continue. This is where rehearsal can really help you. You want to avoid creating unnecessary breaks in the flow of your speech. With practice you will be able to keep talking as you uncover your aid.

Talk to Your Audience—Not to the Presentational Aid. Remember, eye contact is a speaker's most important nonverbal tool. Sustained visual interaction with your audience keeps their attention on you and allows you to monitor their feedback regarding your speech. Turning your back to your listeners undermines your impact. For this reason, use prepared graphics rather than a dry erase board.

Refer to the Presentational Aid. Speakers sometimes stand at the lectern using their notes or reading their manuscript, relatively far from their aid. This creates two lines of vision and can confuse your audience. It may also give the impression that you must rely on your notes because you do not fully understand what the presentational aid conveys.

Other speakers carry their notes with them as they move to the aid, referring to them as they point out key concepts. This is cumbersome and again reinforces the image of a speaker unsure of what he or she wants to say.

A well-constructed presentational aid should be used as a set of notes. The key ideas represented on the aid should trigger the explanation you will provide. You should not need to refer to anything else as you discuss the point your visual aid illustrates. When you practice using your presentational aid, use your aid as your notes.

If you use a metal, wooden, or light-beam pointer to refer to the aid, have it easily accessible, use it only when pointing to the presentational aid, and set it down immediately after you are finished with it. Too many speakers pick up a pen to use when referring to their aid and end up playing with the pen during the rest of the speech.

Finally, point to your presentational aid with the hand closer to it. This keeps your body open and makes communication physically more direct with your audience.

Keep Your Presentational Aid in View until the Audience Understands Your Point.
Remember that you are more familiar with your speech than is your audience. Too

often, a speaker hurries through an explanation and covers or removes an aid before the audience fully comprehends its significance or the point being made. Just as you should not reveal your aid too soon, do not cover it up too quickly. You will have invested time and effort in preparing the aid. Give your audience the time necessary to digest the information it conveys. As you discuss and describe the presentational aid, check your audience response. Many will likely signal their understanding of the presentational aid by nodding their heads or changing their posture.

Conceal the Presentational Aid after You Have Made Your Point. Once you proceed to the next section of your speech, you do not want the audience to continue thinking about the presentational aid. If the aid is an object or posterboard, cover it. If you are using projections, turn off the projector or clear the computer screen, and turn on the room lights.

Use Handouts with Caution. Of all the forms of presentational aids, the handout may be the most troublesome. If you distribute handouts before your remarks, the audience is already ahead of you. Passing out information during a presentation can be distracting, especially if you stop talking as you do so. In addition, the rustling of paper can distract the speaker and other audience members. Disseminating material after the presentation eliminates distractions but does not allow the listener to refer to the printed information as you are explaining it. In general, then, use handouts in a public speech only if that is the best way to clarify and give impact to your ideas.

You will encounter some speaking situations, such as the business presentation, that not only benefit from but may also demand handout material. Those audiences are often decision-making groups. During an especially technical presentation, they may need to take notes. Afterward, they may need to study the information presented. Handouts provide a record of the presenter's remarks and supplementary information the speaker did not have time to explain.

Presentational aids—objects, graphics, projections, and handouts—can make your speech more effective. By seeing as well as hearing your message, the audience becomes more involved with your speech and more responsive to your appeals.

Summary

We live in a visually oriented world, expecting not only to hear about events around the globe but also to see color pictures and videotapes of them. Various studies show that presentational aids complement the spoken word by increasing audience involvement with a speech and aiding listeners' retention of the information presented. Presentational aids can contribute to the clarity and impact of a speaker's message and, when handled well, can make a speaker's delivery seem more dynamic.

The six categories of presentional aids discussed in this chapter are objects, graphics, projections, electronic aids, handouts, and audio and other aids. *Objects* are three-dimensional and may be either actual items or models of large or small items. *Graphics* refers to a large group of two-dimensional presentational aids, including pictures, diagrams, graphs (line, bar, or pie graphs), charts, and maps. If you have access to a computer and any of the wide range of graphics programs, you can produce electronically generated graphics. *Projections* may be either still or moving. Still projections include slides, opaque projections, and transparencies. Any type of graphic may be shown by a still projection. Moving projections include films and videotapes. *Handouts* of any type of graphic may be given to audience members when no other method of presentation is possible. In addition to these strictly visual supports, a speaker may choose *audio aids* such as records, tapes, and compact discs of music, spoken words, and other sounds.

To design graphics that have maximum impact, a speaker should *focus* on just a few key points and should present these points one at a time. For graphics that contain text, the *layout* should be horizontal, with text placed in the top half or two-thirds and left-margin aligned. Graphics should have no more than six words per line, no more than four to six lines per page, with bullets or numbers *highlighting* key points. A speaker should use strong, straight *fonts,* with no more than two different fonts on each graphic. Finally, a speaker should select *color and art* that amplify the impact of the graphic without cluttering it.

To use these graphics or other presentational aids for maximum impact, a speaker needs to prepare them carefully using the following steps as guidelines: (1) Determine the amount of information to be presented; (2) select the type of aid best suited to the speaker's resources and topic; (3) ensure easy viewing by all audience members; (4) ensure that the aid communicates its information clearly; (5) construct an aid that appears carefully or professionally done; (6) practice using the aid; (7) arrange for safe transportation of the aid; (8) carry back-up supplies in case of equipment failure; (9) properly position the aid before beginning the speech; and (10) test the aid before using it.

During the actual delivery of the speech, the speaker using presentational aids needs to remember the following: (1) Reveal the aid only when ready to use it; (2) talk to the audience, not to the aid; (3) refer to the aid; (4) keep the aid in view until the audience understands the point it makes; (5) conceal the aid after making your point with it; and (6) use handouts with caution.

Presentational aids can greatly enhance many speeches, and some speeches would be difficult to deliver without appropriate audio or visual aids. Effective use of those aids, however, requires careful planning and practice to integrate them into your speech delivery without distraction.

practice critique

Evaluating Presentational Aids

Read the transcript of Emelyn Carley's speech "A Stitch in Time" in Chapter 15, and look at the copies of the visual aids she used to illustrate her ideas. Do these aids make the speech clearer and more memorable than just your reading the speech? What suggestions would you give Lyn to guide her presentation of these aids? Are there other presentational aids you think would make her speech more effective?

Exercises

1. Select a graph, diagram, or chart that you find in a magazine article. Describe how you would adapt it as a presentational aid for a speech.

2. Compile a list of memorable television advertisements. Discuss the visual elements of the ads. What strategies do they use to reinforce the message? Can some of these techniques be adapted to a speech? Are there elements in any of the ads that detract from viewers' remembering the product or brand name? How can a public speaker avoid this pitfall when designing and presenting a presentational aid?

3. Using information you obtain from the Department of Transportation's National Highway Traffic Safety Administration Web site (http://www.nhtsa.dot.gov) or from a site linked to it, prepare one PowerPoint™ slide that illustrates the "Guidelines for Preparing Presentational Aids" discussed in this chapter and one slide that violates one or more of those guidelines. Be sure to include a source line indicating where you got this information. Save the slides to a disk, or print them in color. Display your printed slides in class, or project them if multimedia equipment is available, showing the problem slide first. After classmates correctly

identify the problems you have illustrated, show the improvements you made on the second slide.

4. Select a statistical table from an almanac, a government report, the *Gallup Poll Monthly, American Demographics,* or some other source. Decide how you could convert the information to a line, bar, or pie graph. Construct the graph on a sheet of paper, posterboard, or transparency film.

5. Sketch a presentational aid you could construct for one of the speeches in Appendix B. Describe how the aid would make the message of the speech clearer and more memorable.

6. Describe at least two different types of presentational aids you could use for a speech having the following specific purposes:
   a. To inform the audience about techniques of handwriting analysis.
   b. To inform the audience about "the look" of a Quentin Tarantino film.
   c. To inform the audience about the process of photograph restoration.
   d. To persuade the audience that more money should be spent on AIDS research.
   e. To persuade the audience that the government should invest more money in the U.S. space program.
   f. To persuade the audience that [name of building on campus] should be razed and replaced with another facility.

7. Go the library, and consult a recent book on graphic design, or read a chapter on the topic in a recent advertising textbook. What suggestions concerning layout and illustrations are appropriate for a speaker's presentational aids? What suggestions seem unsuited to the medium?

Notes

1. We adapted this chapter opening from four images described in an effective Nikon advertisement we saw for the first time in *American Photo* March/April 1991: 19.

2. Kit Long, *Visual Aids and Learning,* 12 Aug. 1997, U of Portsmouth, 17 June 1999 <http://www.mech.port.ac.uk/av/ALALearn.htm>.

3. Michael Antonoff, "Meetings Take Off with Graphics," *Personal Computing* July 1990: 62.

4. Ellen Braun, "Visual Presentation Tools Sharpen Communication Style," *The Office* June 1993 <http://web4.infotrac.galegroup.com/itw>.

5. Braun.

6. Joyce Kupsch and Pat R. Graves, *Create High Impact Business Presentations* (Lincolnwood, IL: NTC Learning Works-NTC/Contemporary, 1998) 49.

7. Nigel Hawkes, *Structures: The Way Things Are Built* (New York: Collier-Macmillan, 1993) 70–72.

8. Susan Brink, "Secrets of the Pyramids," *U.S. News & World Report* 8 Jan. 1996: 58–59.

9. Danny Sullivan, "Coverage of the Web," *Search Engine Sizes,* 1 Sept. 1999, Search Engine Watch, 14 Nov. 1999 <http://searchenginewatch.internet.com/reports/sizes.html>.

10. Martin Dodge, "Surf Maps: Visualizing Web Browsing," *An Atlas of Cyberspaces,* 9 May 1999, Centre for Advanced Spatial Analysis, University College London, 14 Nov. 1999 <http://www.cybergeography.org/atlas/surf.html>.

11. Kupsch and Graves 95.

12. This list of guidelines is adapted from two sources: Ann Luck, *Visual Aid Checklist for Interactive Video Presentation* (1997). Used by permission of the author. Also from Joyce Kupsch and Pat R. Graves, *Create High Impact Business Presentations* (Lincolnwood, IL: NTC Learning Works-NTC/Contemporary, 1998) 89–90, 95–96, 107–09.

13. Michael Talman, *Understanding Presentation Graphics* (San Francisco: SYBEX, 1992) 270.

We are drowning in information and starving for knowledge.

—John Naisbitt

chapter 15

Speaking to Inform

As the 20th century ebbed and the 21st century dawned, certain patterns in our consumption of information became clearer. Between 1995 and 1999, for example, the number of Americans who reported "using the Internet regularly (defined as four times a week or more)" jumped from 7 percent to 34 percent.[1] At the same time, reliance on national and local TV news broadcasts dipped significantly (from 68 to 60 percent for national news, 70 to 59 percent for local news). The fact that reliance on daily newspapers dipped less during this same period (from 59 to 54 percent) has lead to speculation that the Internet may actually be spawning a generation who read more than their predecessors.

Many observers note that we are still getting plenty of news and information, just from different sources. Increasingly, we are turning from broadcasting to "narrowcasting." Now that every possible interest group has a Web site (or many of them), we can use our computers to select and gather information tailored to our individual interests: "Okay, get me political news, health news, Chicago Cubs scores, IBM stock price updates, and anything about Everything But The Girl." As *Time* magazine puts it, "The *Daily Me* has arrived on our doorstep, not with a thump but with a polite mechanical chime."[2]

Unfortunately, these changes in our news and information consumption patterns are undoubtedly eroding our sense of community. People are "less likely to share a common pool of information, or the same idea of which events and trends are important, than they were when nearly everyone in town read the same paper and watched the same newscasts."[3]

An informative speech assignment allows you to take a small step toward restoring this lost sense of community in your classroom, as each student in turn shares information with the same classmates. However, in preparing an informative speech, you also face three challenges. First, you must be able to select an appropriate informative topic. You don't want to repeat information that your audience already knows. Yet you may worry that a topic you find personally interesting might seem irrelevant to your listeners. Once you select a topic, you face a second challenge: to find information that will make you well informed about the topic and ultimately will be useful in constructing your speech. Finally, to determine what supporting material is most suitable for your audience and relevant to your purpose, you must organize your information in the most fitting manner. These three tasks form the essence of informative speaking, the subject of this chapter.

Characteristics of a Speech to Inform

Dr. Jones, your geology professor, enters the classroom, takes out a folder of notes, puts up the first of a series of slides, and begins to lecture on the differences between active and inactive volcanoes. At the morning staff meeting, Dr. Mendez explains how the hospital will implement its new policy to secure the confidentiality of patient records. Scott, a classmate in your business communication class, spends half the period summarizing his outside reading on factors that shape a company's corporate culture. The lecture, briefing, and oral report these people deliver are three of the forms informative speeches can take. In this chapter we focus on the variety of subject areas for a **speech to inform.**

At the most fundamental level, we seek knowledge for three reasons: We want to *know, understand,* and *use* information. The goals of any informative speaker, in turn, are to impart knowledge, enhance understanding, or permit application. Suppose you decided to prepare an informative speech on the general subject of advertising. You could select as your specific purpose to inform the audience about advertising in ancient times. Your listeners probably know little about this topic and you can readily assume that your speech would add to their knowledge. Alternatively, you could have this as your specific purpose: to inform my audience on how effective advertising succeeds. Using examples your audience already knows, you could deepen their under-

speech to inform: a speech to impart knowledge, enhance understanding, or facilitate application of information.

standing of advertising strategies and principles. A third specific purpose could be to inform your listeners about how they can prepare effective, low-cost advertisements when they want to promote a charity fund-raising project or a garage sale. In this instance you would help the audience apply basic advertising principles.

Speakers inform us, then, when they provide us with new information, when they help us understand better some information we already possess, or when they enable us to apply information. When you prepare an informative speech, however, you must make sure that you don't slip into giving a persuasive speech. How can you avoid this problem? After all, a persuasive speech also conveys information. In fact, the best persuasive speeches usually include supporting material that is both expository and compelling.

Some topics, of course, are easy to classify as informative or persuasive. A speaker urging audience members to sign and carry an organ donor card is clearly trying to persuade; the speaker is attempting to intensify beliefs and either change or reinforce behavior. On the other hand, a speech charting the recent increases in organ transplant procedures is a speech to inform. A speech on the history of computers is informative, while a speech advocating an IBM clone as the best computer buy for the college student is persuasive. A speech describing different forms of alcohol addiction is informative, whereas a speech advocating the Alcoholics Anonymous program to overcome addiction would be persuasive.

Many speakers, both beginning and experienced, at times have trouble distinguishing between informing and persuading. The reason is that speakers sometimes begin preparing a speech with the intention to inform, only to discover that somewhere during the speech construction process their objective has become persuasion. In other instances, speakers deliver what they intended to be an informative speech only to find that their listeners received it as a persuasive message. How can this happen? Let's look at the experience of one speaker, Sarah.

> Sarah designed a speech with the specific purpose of informing the audience of the arguments for and against allowing women to serve in military combat. In her speech, she took care to represent each side's arguments accurately and objectively. After her speech, however, Sarah discovered that some listeners previously undecided on the issue found the pro arguments more persuasive and now supported permitting women to serve in combat roles. But Sarah also learned that others in the audience became more convinced that women should be excluded from such roles. Did Sarah's speech persuade? Apparently for some audience members the answer is yes; they changed their attitudes because of this speech. Yet Sarah's objective was to inform, not to persuade.

In determining the general purpose of your speech, remember that both speakers and listeners are active participants in the communication process. As we discussed earlier in this text, listeners will interpret what they hear and integrate it into their frames of reference. Your objectivity as a speaker will not stop the listener from hearing with subjectivity. As a speaker, though, you determine the motive for and manner of your presentation. Your goal in your informative speech is not to advocate specific beliefs, attitudes, and behaviors on controversial issues. Your objective is to assist your hearers as they come to know, understand, or apply an idea or issue. As you word the specific purpose of your speech, you should be able to determine whether your general purpose is to persuade or to inform.

Informative Speech Topics

Experts identify several ways of classifying informative speeches. We have chosen a topical pattern that we think will work well for you. This approach is based on the types of topics you can choose for your speech. As you read about these topic categories, keep two guidelines in mind. First, approach each category of topics with the broadest possible perspective. Second, recognize that the categories overlap; the boundaries between them are not distinct. Whether you consider the Great Pyramid of Cheops an object or a place, for example, is much less important than the fact that it's a fascinating informative speech topic. The purpose of our categories is to stimulate, not to limit, your topic selection and development. As you begin brainstorming, consider information you could provide your listeners regarding people, objects, places, events, processes, concepts, conditions, and issues. In the following sections, we discuss these eight major topic areas for informative speeches and the patterns of organization appropriate for each.

---

key points

Topic Categories for Informative Speeches

1. Speeches about people
2. Speeches about objects
3. Speeches about places
4. Speeches about events
5. Speeches about processes
6. Speeches about concepts
7. Speeches about conditions
8. Speeches about issues

Speeches about People

Activities and accomplishments of other people fascinate us. We gravitate toward books, magazine articles, television programs, films, and even supermarket tabloids that reveal the lives of celebrities. We are interested in the lives of the rich and the famous. We are also interested in the lives of the poor and the not-so-famous. Lifetime TV's *Intimate Portrait* series features the lives of influential women. A&E's *Biography* has been so popular and so critically acclaimed that it has spawned its own cable channel.

> Online Biographies
> http://www.biography.com
> http://www.lifetimetv.com
> Visit these sites for thousands of ideas for speeches about people. At Biography.com you can search paragraph-length biographies of 25,000 people. At LifetimeOnline, click on Intimate Portrait, then on Intimate Portrait Archive to search alphabetically for longer biographies of hundreds of influential women.

People, then, are an obvious and abundant resource of topics for your informative speech. Choosing to inform about a person lets you be as historical or as contemporary as you wish. A speech about a person allows you the opportunity to expand your knowledge in a field that interests you while sharing those interests with your listeners. If you are majoring in computer and information sciences, you could speak on Bill Gates, founder of Microsoft, as a contemporary leader, or Thomas J. Watson, founder of IBM, as a historical figure. If you are studying art, speeches on Claude Monet or Mary Cassatt are just two of hundreds of options available to you. If you are an avid photographer, an informative speech assignment gives you the opportunity to discover and communicate something about the life and accomplishments of Ansel Adams, Diane Arbus, Alfred Stieglitz, or Annie Leibovitz, for instance.

Of course, you don't need to confine your topic to individuals associated with your major or areas of interest. You could interest and inform audiences by discussing the lives and contributions of people such as:

Lance Armstrong	Sally Hemings	Jackie Robinson
Cesar Chavez	Jimi Hendrix	Eleanor Roosevelt
e. e. cummings	Alfred Kinsey	Andy Warhol
Clarence Darrow	Gary Larson	Eudora Welty
D. W. Griffith	Margaret Mead	Frank Lloyd Wright

You may choose to discuss not one person but a group of people, such as the Marx Brothers, FDR's brain trust, the Four Horsemen of Notre Dame, or the rock group Aerosmith. You could even compare and contrast two or more individuals to highlight their philosophies and contributions. The following pairs of noted figures could generate lively exposition:

Rachel Carson and Ralph Nader
Mark McGwire and Sammy Sosa
The Dalai Lama and Pope John Paul II
J. Edgar Hoover and Elliott Ness
Whitney Houston and Thelma Houston
Thurgood Marshall and Clarence Thomas
Edward R. Murrow and Joseph McCarthy
Malcolm X and Martin Luther King, Jr.

In considering an informative speech about a person, you must decide not only what is important but also what the audience will remember. Too often, students organize speeches about people so that the speeches resemble biographical listings in an encyclopedia. The speech amounts to a seemingly limitless compendium of dates. This is a mistake. Even the most attentive listener will remember few of the details in such a speech.

If you selected the life of Thomas Jefferson as your speech topic, for example, you would need to narrow and focus that subject. Listeners would probably not remember that Jefferson was born on April 13, 1743, according to the modern calendar and April 2 according to the old calendar; that he entered the College of William and Mary in 1760; that he was admitted to the Virginia bar in 1767; and that he married Martha Wayles Skelton on January 1, 1772. On the other hand, an audience probably would remember that Jefferson died on the fiftieth anniversary of the Declaration of Independence, July 4, 1826.

Speeches about people are often organized either chronologically or topically. One chronological pattern for a speech about Jefferson could be:

I. Jefferson's Early Life
II. Jefferson's Middle Years
III. Jefferson's Last Years

So many fascinating speech topics, so little time! With such an abundance of interesting topics to choose from, it's difficult to narrow it down to one. But I found that being as specific as possible was a key element for success whenever I delivered an informative speech. When a speech topic is too general, it loses impact and can lose the audience's attention.

For my three informative speeches I chose topics that I was passionate about: trainhopping, the *kisaeng*, and Tuvan throatsingers. In the first, I was careful to stress that I wasn't trying to persuade anyone to go hop on a train, because that is both illegal and very dangerous. But I knew that my limited experience riding the rails would intrigue my classmates. Then there were the *kisaeng*, Korean courtesans about whom I have a romantic view. Discussing them and their writings, I felt sure that I would be able to break people's hearts. Tuvan throatsingers, my third topic, amaze me! I first heard them while living in Austin many moons ago when a group of them were touring. I couldn't believe my eyes—or my ears!

By following the guidelines for speaking to inform and letting my enthusiasm for my topics propel me, I was able to deliver informative speeches with confidence, making the experience enjoyable for both my listeners and myself.

—Amy Landry, San Antonio College

speaking with confidence

You could organize your speech topically based on the epitaph Jefferson wrote for his tombstone:

I. Author of the Declaration of Independence
II. Author of the Statute of Virginia for Religious Freedom
III. Father of the University of Virginia

If you wanted to focus on the three major roles Jefferson assumed in different stages of his life, you could develop your speech topically and chronologically, as in the following example:

I. Jefferson as Revolutionary
II. Jefferson as President
III. Jefferson as Elder Statesman

Speeches about Objects

A second resource of informative topics is objects. Speeches about objects focus on what is concrete rather than on what is abstract. Again, consider objects from the broadest perspective possible so that you can generate a maximum number of topic ideas. Topics for this type of speech could include the following:

the Acropolis	Fabergé eggs
coffee	the Great Pyramid of Cheops
crocodiles	the Great Wall of China
electric cars	smart roads
endangered species	volcanoes

Speeches about objects can use any of several organizational patterns. A speech on the Cathedral of Notre Dame or the Statue of Liberty could be organized spatially. A speech tracing the development of cyclones and anticyclones evolves chronologically. A speech on condors discussing (1) the Andean condor and (2) the California condor is organized topically. A speaker discussing the origins, types, and uses of pasta also uses a topical division. If the speech focused only on the history of pasta, however, it may best be structured chronologically.

Emelyn Carley's informative speech on quilts near the end of this chapter uses a topical organization to discuss quilts as historical records, quilting as an art form, the investment value of quilts, and an example of a personal history quilt.

Speeches about Places

One of the favorite pastimes for many of us is the summer vacation. Families pack their suitcases and, maps in hand, take to the road in search of historical, cultural, and recreational sites. Returning with souvenirs, pictures, postcards, and informational literature, we are able to relive our vacation.

Places are an easily tapped resource for informative speech topics. These speeches introduce listeners to new locales or expand their knowledge of familiar places. Topics may include real places, such as historic sites, emerging nations, national parks, famous prisons, and planets. Topics may also include fictitious places, such as the Land of Oz, the Island of the Lord of the Flies, and the Sea of Frozen Words. Speeches about places challenge speakers to select words that create vivid images.

> **Researching Historical Topics**
> http://memory.loc.gov/ammem/amhome.html
> If you're interested in discussing an informative topic from a historical perspective, check out *American Memory: Historical Collections for the National Digital Library,* maintained by the Library of Congress. The site contains more than 70 collections, with topics including the African-American odyssey, early baseball cards (1887–1914), Civil War photographs, Hispanic music and culture, historic buildings, and sound recordings of speeches from World War I.

A visit to a museum, a historic site, a natural attraction, or even a mural painted on the side of a building might provide inspiration for an informative speech topic.

To organize your speech about places you would typically use one of three organizational patterns: spatial, chronological, or topical. A speech about the Nile, the world's longest river, is organized spatially if it discusses the upper, middle, and lower Nile. A presentation about your college could trace its development chronologically. A speech on Poplar Forest, Thomas Jefferson's getaway home, could use a topical pattern discussing Jefferson's architectural style.

Suppose you selected as your informative speech topic Ellis Island, the site of the chief U.S. immigration center from 1892 to 1954. You could choose any of the following patterns of development.

> *Pattern:* Spatial
> *Specific Purpose:* To inform the audience about Ellis Island's Main Building.
> *Key Ideas:* I. The Registry Room
> II. The Baggage Room
> III. The Oral History Studio

> *Pattern:* Chronological
> *Specific Purpose:* To inform the audience of the history of Ellis Island.
> *Key Ideas:* I. Years of Immigration, 1892–1954
> II. Years of Dormancy, 1954–84
> III. Years of Remembrance, 1984–present

> *Pattern:* Topical
> *Specific Purpose:* To inform the audience of the history of Ellis Island.
> *Key Ideas* I. The Process of Immigration
> II. The Place of Immigration
> III. The People Who Immigrated

Notice that each of these outlines is organized according to a distinct pattern. The key ideas in the first outline are organized spatially. Although the specific purposes of the second and third speeches are identical, the former is organized chronologically and the latter topically.

If you choose to speak about a place, be aware of a couple of common pitfalls. First, avoid making your speech sound like a travelogue. The speaking occasion is not an opportunity to show a captive audience slides you took during your last vacation ("And here are my cousins Lois and Louie. If you look closely, you can see part of Berkeley Plantation, the site of the first Thanksgiving and the birthplace of William Henry Harrison and Benjamin Harrison."). Your speech should identify and develop ideas that contribute to the general education of your listeners.

A second pitfall to avoid is inappropriate presentational aids. We have too often seen speakers illustrate their ideas visually by holding up postcards or books and magazines containing pictures of places. This strategy is a mistake. These pictures are too small to be seen. As we advised in the previous chapter, use presentational aids that are large enough to be viewed by all audience members. On other occasions, students speaking about places have distributed photographs or postcards to be passed among audience members during the speech. Although listeners could see the presentational aids clearly as they held them, they often became preoccupied with the pictures and missed much of what the speaker was saying at the time. Remember, your presentational aids should not distract your audience from the main attraction: you, speaking to inform.

Speeches about Events

Events are important or interesting occurrences. Speeches about events focus on these occurrences, personal or historical, and seek to convey knowledge so that an audience can better understand them. Examples of topics for this type of speech include:

the Chautauqua movement	the sinking of the *Titanic*
D-Day	the *War of the Worlds* broadcast
the explosion of the zeppelin *Hindenburg*	the Woodstock festivals

For a speech assignment that does not require you to conduct research, you could speak about an event in your life you consider important, funny, or instructive. Examples of such topics could include "the day I registered for my first semester in college," "the day my first child was born," or "my most embarrassing moment."

Speeches about events typically use a chronological or topical pattern. For example, if your topic is the daring Great Train Robbery that took place in Britain in 1963, you could organize your speech chronologically, describing what happened before, during, and after those famous fifteen minutes. If your specific purpose is to inform the audience about aerial sports, you could use a topical pattern and discuss (1) gliding, (2) ballooning, and (3) skydiving.

A speaker wanting to inform the audience about the Scopes "Monkey" Trial could use any of the following developmental patterns:

Pattern: Topical
Specific Purpose: To inform the audience of the theological dispute in the trial.
Key Ideas: I. The literal interpretation of the Scriptures
          II. The figurative interpretation of the Scriptures

Pattern: Topical
Specific Purpose: To inform the audience of the key players of the drama.
Key Ideas: I. John T. Scopes, the defendant
          II. Clarence Darrow, the defense attorney
        III. William Jennings Bryan, the prosecutor

Pattern: Chronological
Specific Purpose: To inform the audience of the background and outcome of the controversy.
Key Ideas: I. The law
          II. The challenge
        III. The verdict

The first two speeches are organized topically; the third is structured chronologically. Notice how each organizational strategy neatly matches the specific purpose of the speech.

Speeches about Processes

A process is a series of steps producing an outcome. Your informative speech about a process could explain or demonstrate how something works, functions, or is accomplished. Our students have given informative speeches on such how-to topics as how to read a food packaging label, detect plagiarism, write an effective term paper, administer first aid for burns, suit up and enter a "clean room," and tie-dye T-shirts. Informative topics such as how batik materials are made, how Doppler radar works, and how to make children "waterproof" (a speech on the process of teaching water safety) are all process speeches. Speeches on critical path analysis, global positioning systems, the Nielsen ratings, nuclear medicine, and cryptography (encoding and decoding messages in a code known only to those who understand) are also potentially good informative topics about processes.

Because a process is by definition a time-ordered sequence, speeches about processes commonly use chronological organization. They are not, however, confined to this pattern. As we have argued earlier, the best organization is the one that achieves the purpose of the speech. A student presenting a speech on colorization of black-and-white movies might choose a chronological pattern if the specific purpose is to explain how the process works. A pro–con division detailing the arguments for and against colorization would also be informative if the speaker discussed both sides in an unbiased manner.

Suppose you select cartooning as a topic area for a speech to inform. You would choose the organizational pattern best suited to your specific purpose. Let's look at some examples illustrating how you can narrow your topic on cartooning and what organizational patterns fit each topic.

> *Pattern:* Topical
> *Specific Purpose:* To inform my audience on cartooning.
> *Key Ideas:*   I. Definition of cartoons
>   II. Purposes of cartoons
>   III. Types of cartoons

> *Pattern:* Chronological
> *Specific Purpose:* To inform my audience on the process of creating a comic strip.
> *Key Ideas:*   I. Designing a comic strip
>   II. Drawing a comic strip
>   III. Producing a comic strip

> *Pattern:* Spatial
> *Specific Purpose:* To inform my audience on how to draw a cartoon character.
> *Key Ideas:*   I. Drawing the head
>   II. Drawing the upper body
>   III. Drawing the lower body

Notice that each of the speeches outlined above is progressively narrowed. Each organizational pattern is also suitable for the specific purpose, whether the pattern is topical, chronological, or spatial.

Speeches about Concepts

Speeches about concepts, or ideas, focus on what is abstract rather than on what is concrete. Whereas a speech about an object such as the Statue of Liberty may focus on the history or physical attributes of the statue itself, a speech about an idea may focus on the concept of liberty. Other topics suitable for informative speeches about concepts include eco-tourism, concrete poetry, nihilism, traumatic obsessions, the Doppler effect, nirvana, and religious dualism.

Speeches about concepts challenge you to make specific something that is abstract. These speeches typically rely on definitions and examples to support their explanations. Appropriate organizational patterns vary. A speech on Norse mythology could use a topical division of materials and focus on key figures.

Drew, a student of ours, entertained all his listeners with a speech on onomastics, or the study of names. Notice how his introduction personalizes his speech and quickly involves his listeners. You can also see from his preview statement that he, too, used a topical organization for this speech about a concept:

> These are some actual names reported by John Train in his books *Remarkable Names of Real People* and *Even More Remarkable Names.* Let me repeat: These are actual names found in bureaus of vital statistics, public health services, newspaper articles, and hospital, church, and school records: E. Pluribus Eubanks, Loch Ness Hontas, Golden Pancake, Halloween Buggage, Odious Champagne, and Memory Leake.
>
> Train says in *Even More Remarkable Names* that "what one might call the free-form nutty name—Oldmouse Waltz, Cashmere Tango Obedience, Eucalyptus Yoho—is the one indigenous American art form."
>
> We're lucky. No one in here has a name as colorful as any of those. But we all have at least two names—a personal and a family name. Today, I'll tell you, first, why personal names developed, and second, the legal status of names. Finally, I have something to tell each of you about the origin of your names.

Speeches about theories, particularly if they are controversial, sometimes use a pro–con division. A discussion of the merits and shortcomings of Felice Schwartz's "mommy track" theory of career advancement reflects a pro–con development.

Speeches about Conditions

Conditions are particular situations: living conditions in a third-world country or social and political climates that give rise to movements such as witchcraft hysteria in Salem, Civil War in the United States, McCarthyism, the women's movement, labor movements, the civil rights movement, and national independence movements.

The word *condition* can also refer to a state of fitness or health. Speeches about conditions can focus on a person's health and, indeed, medical topics are a popular source of student speeches. Informative speeches about crush syndrome, Williams syndrome, and Treacher Collins syndrome, for example, can educate listeners about those interesting medical conditions. A speaker could choose as a specific purpose "to inform the audience about the causes and treatment of repetitive stress injuries." Topical organization such as this is appropriate for many speeches about specific diseases or other health conditions. Another excellent topic for a speech to inform is *affluenza,* a word coined to denote chronic psychological disorders afflicting the wealthy. States of health also characterize the economy, individual communities, and specific institutions. Recession, depression, and full employment are terms economists use to describe the health of the economy. Speakers inform their listeners about conditions when they describe the state of the arts in their communities, assess the financial situation of most college students, or illustrate how catch limits have affected the whale population, for example.

Speeches about Issues

Speeches about issues deal with controversial ideas and policies. For example, some people today are investing in "viatical companies" that make large cash payments to

Preparing for a speech about a person might begin with a personal interview. However, if your subject is well known, like Lady Bird Johnson, you may be able to rely on information gleaned by professional journalists such as Katie Couric.

people having terminal illnesses. The patients, many of them too ill to work, can thus keep their homes and afford medical care. In return, each cash recipient must name the company involved as sole beneficiary of his or her life insurance policies. People who invest in such viatical companies can receive returns of up to 25 percent each year.[4] Financial profit from the deaths of others is certainly a controversial issue and would make an interesting speech topic.

Other topics appropriate for informative speeches on issues include the use of polygraphs as a condition for employment; uniform sentencing of criminals; freedom of expression vs. freedom from pornography; fetal tissue research; and systematic instruction vs. child-oriented activities in preschools. Any issue being debated in your school, community, state, or nation can be a fruitful topic for your informative speech.

You may be thinking that controversial issues are better topics for persuasive speeches, but they can also be appropriate for speeches to inform. Just remember that an informative speech on a controversial topic must be researched and developed so that you present the issue objectively.

Two common organizational patterns for speeches about issues are the topical and pro–con divisions. If you use a topical pattern of organization for your speech about issues, it will be easier for you to maintain your objectivity. If you choose the pro–con pattern, you may run the risk of moving toward a persuasive speech. A pro–con strategy—presenting both sides of an issue—lets the listener decide which is stronger. If your informative speech on an issue is organized pro–con, guard against two pitfalls: lack of objectivity and lack of perspective.

Speakers predisposed toward one side of an issue sometimes have difficulty presenting both sides objectively.

> Carl presented a speech on the increasingly popular practice of adopting uniforms for public schools. He presented four good reasons for the practice: (1) Uniforms are more economical for parents; (2) uniforms reduce student bickering and fighting over designer clothes; (3) uniforms increase student attentiveness in the classroom; and (4) uniforms identify various schools and promote school spirit. Carl's only argument against public school uniforms was that they limit students' freedom of expression. His speech was obviously out of balance. Though the assignment was an informative speech, Carl's pro–con approach was ultimately persuasive.

If, like Carl, you feel strongly committed to one side of an issue, save that topic for a persuasive speech.

A second pitfall that sometimes surfaces in the pro–con approach is lack of perspective. Sometimes a speaker will characterize an issue as two-sided when, in reality, it is many-sided. For example, one of our students spoke on the issue of child care. He mentioned the state family leave laws that permit mothers of newborn infants to take paid leaves of absence from work and fathers to take unpaid leaves while their jobs are protected. The speaker characterized advocates of such bills as pro-family and opponents as pro-business. He failed to consider that some people oppose such laws because they feel the laws don't go far enough; many state laws exempt small companies with fewer than 50 employees. If you fail to recognize and acknowledge the many facets of an issue in this way, you lose perspective and polarize your topic.

In the preceding sections, we have discussed eight types of informative speeches. As you begin working on your own informative speech, remember to select a topic that will benefit your listeners and then communicate your information clearly and memorably. Use these eight subject categories to narrow and focus your topic. As you go through each category, use the self-, audience-, occasion-, and research-generated strategies we discussed in Chapter 6 on pages 124–31 to help you come up with many topics to consider for your informative speech.

As you review this list you will, no doubt, find several persuasive topics. Before excluding them, see if there are related topics suitable for an informative speech. For example, you may have some strong feelings about intercollegiate athletic programs and their role in colleges and universities. To argue their merits or to suggest that they be scaled back would make your speech persuasive rather than informative. However, you could change your focus to a more informative topic related to the issue of intercollegiate athletics. You could inform the audience of the history and intent of Proposition 48, the National Collegiate Athletic Association's statement of academic entrance requirements for college athletes. You could explain the reasons behind the breakup of the Southwest Conference or trace the history of the athletic conference to which your school belongs.

As you go about selecting your topic, keep in mind this question: "How will the audience benefit from my topic?" Remember, your informative speech must help your audience know, understand, or apply information you provide. A speech detailing what employers look for in an employment résumé, for example, is clearly relevant to a class of students ready to enter the job market.

What about topics such as the golden age of vaudeville, the origins of superstitions, the history of aviation, the effect of music on livestock production, or the psychological aspects of aging? Maybe you think that these topics are not relevant to your audience. But part of the process of becoming an educated individual is learning more about the world around you. We are committed to this perspective and believe it is one you should encourage in your listeners. For example, in his speech on kites and competitive kite flying, our student Ken informed us about the use of kites in ancient religious worship. After a bountiful harvest, early tribes would tie a handful of the first wheat harvested to the tail of a kite and literally offer it up to the gods in thanks. After this historical background, Ken traced the evolution of kite designs. He showed exam-

Choosing and Researching Informative Topics http://vos.ucsb.edu Whether you are generating ideas for informative speeches or researching a topic you have already chosen, you ought to look at this site if your subject is in the area of the humanities. *The Voice of the Shuttle: Web Page for Humanities Research,* maintained by Alan Liu of the University of California at Santa Barbara, contains numerous links in areas from anthropology to women's studies. The site also contains a huge group of links on its Reference Page and links to fascinating, offbeat sites on its Laws of Cool Page.

ples of the large, colorful, aerodynamic kites he takes to the coast to fly on weekends. Speeches on such subjects are interesting and fun, and they also contribute to an audience's general education.

Once you have selected a topic that meets criteria discussed in Chapter 6, ask yourself the following three questions: (1) What does the audience already know about my topic? (2) What does the audience need to know to understand the topic? (3) Can I present this information in a way that is easy for the audience to understand and remember in the time allotted? If you are satisfied with your answers to these questions, your next step is to begin developing the most effective strategy for conveying that information. Use Figure 15.1 as you select an appropriate organizational pattern.

Speeches about	Use	If your purpose is to
People	Topical organization	Explain various aspects of the person's life
	Chronological organization	Survey events in the person's life
Objects	Topical organization	Explain various uses for the object
	Chronological organization	Explain how the object was created or made
	Spatial organization	Describe various parts of the object
Places	Topical organization	Emphasize various aspects of the place
	Chronological organization	Chart the history of or developments in the place
	Spatial organization	Describe the elements or parts of the place
Events	Topical organization	Explain the significance of the events
	Chronological organization	Explain a sequence of actions or events
	Causal organization	Explain how one event produced or resulted from another
Processes	Topical organization	Explain aspects of the process
	Chronological organization	Explain how something is done
	Pro–Con organization	Explore the arguments for and against the procedure
	Causal organization	Discuss the causes and effects of the process
Concepts	Topical organization	Discuss aspects, definitions, or applications of the concept
Conditions	Topical organization	Explain aspects of the condition
	Chronological organization	Trace the stages or phases of the condition
	Causal organization	Show the causes and effects of the condition
Issues	Topical organization	Discuss aspects of the issue's significance
	Chronological organization	Show how the issue evolved over time
	Pro–Con organization	Present opposing viewpoints on the issue

FIGURE 15.1
Organizing Informative Speeches

Guidelines for Speaking to Inform

In the remainder of this chapter, we suggest ten guidelines for the informative speech. Use them as a checklist during your speech preparation, and you will deliver a better informative speech than you would have otherwise.

Stress Your Informative Purpose

The primary objective of your informative speech is to inform. It is important for you to be clear about this, especially if your topic is controversial or related to other topics that are controversial. For example, if you are discussing U.S. immigration policy, political correctness, or the role of women in religion, you must realize that some in your audience may already have some pretty strong feelings about your topic. Stress that your goal is to give additional information, not to try to change anyone's beliefs.

Be Specific

At times we have had students tell us they will deliver a brief informative speech on "sports." This topic is far too broad and reflects little or no planning. Many of us know a little about a lot of subjects. An informative speech gives you the perfect opportunity to fill in the gaps by telling your audience a lot about a little. Narrow your topic. To help you do that, we have suggested in this chapter that you focus on specific people, objects, places, events, processes, concepts, conditions, and issues. Your "sports" topic could be narrowed to sports commentators; the history of AstroTurf; Forest Hills, former home of the U.S. Open Tennis Championships; competitive team sports and male bonding; and so on. The more specific you are about your topic, your purpose, and the materials you use to support your speech, the more time you will save during your research. Your specific focus will also make your speech easier for the audience to remember.

Be Clear

If you choose your topic carefully and explain it thoroughly, your message should be clear. Do not choose a topic that is too complex. If your speech topic is Boolean polynomials or the biochemistry of bovine growth hormone, you run the risk of being too technical for most audiences. You would never be able to give your audience the background knowledge necessary to understand your presentation in the limited time you have. At the same time, be careful about using jargon. Impressing the audience with your vocabulary is counterproductive if they cannot understand your message. The purpose of informative speaking is not to impress the audience with complex data but to communicate information clearly.

Be Accurate

Information that is inaccurate does not inform; it misinforms and has two negative consequences. First, inaccuracies can hurt your credibility as a speaker. If listeners recognize misstatements, they may begin to question the speaker's credibility: "If the speaker's wrong about that, could there be other inaccuracies in the speech?" Accurate statements help you develop a positive image or protect one you have established earlier.

Second, inaccurate information can do potential harm to listeners. Such harm can be mental or physical. For example, you give an informative speech on the life-threatening reactions some people have to sulfites, a common ingredient in certain food preservatives. Your audience leaves the class worried about their health and the damage they may have suffered. You neglected to mention that these reactions are rare. Your misinformation has harmed your audience. In another example, you give a speech on how to apply and check a tourniquet but discuss outdated methods. If people in your audience later try your method, they could do serious physical damage. As you can see, if audience members are unaware of factual errors, they may form beliefs that are not valid or make decisions that are not wise.

Not only should your information be accurate, but you must accurately cite any sources you have used to develop your speech. Some speakers assume that because they do not take a controversial stand in an informative speech, they need not cite sources. An informative topic may require fewer sources than you would use to establish your side of a debatable point. Demonstrating the truth of your ideas and information is nevertheless important. Also, as we mentioned in Chapter 2, you must cite the sources for any quotations you use.

Limit Your Ideas and Supporting Materials

Perhaps the most common mistake speakers make in developing the content of their speeches is including too much information. Do not make the mistake of thinking that the more information you put into a speech, the more informative it is. As we have mentioned previously, listeners cannot process all, or even most, of what you present. If you overload your audience with too much information, they will stop listening. Remember the adage that less is more. To spend more time explaining and developing a few ideas will probably result in greater retention of these ideas by your listeners than the "speed and spread" approach.

Be Relevant

As you research your topic, you will no doubt discover information that is interesting but not central to your thesis. Because it is so interesting, you may be tempted to include it. Don't. If it is not relevant, leave it out.

> One student, Larry, delivered an intriguing informative speech on the Jains, a tribe of monks in India whose daily life is shaped by reverence for all living things. As you might guess, the Jains are vegetarians. But they don't eat vegetables that develop underground because harvesting them may kill insects in the soil. Larry had done a good deal of research on this fascinating topic, including his own travels in India. His firsthand knowledge was both a blessing and a curse. Listening to a speaker who had visited the Jains' monasteries certainly made the topic immediate and compelling. But because he knew so much about the country, Larry included a lot of information about India that was interesting but irrelevant to his main point. His speech became much too long.

To avoid this problem and to keep yourself on track, write out your central thesis and refer to it periodically. When you digress from your topic, you waste valuable preparation time, distort the focus of your speech, and confuse your audience.

Be Objective

One of the most important criteria for an informative speech is objectivity. If you take a stand, you become a persuader. Informative speakers are committed to presenting a balanced view. People representing political parties, charitable organizations, business associations, and special interest groups are understandably committed to the objectives and policies of their groups. Your research should take into account all perspectives. If, as you develop and practice your speech, you find yourself becoming a proponent of a particular viewpoint, you may need to step back and assess whether

**ethical
decisions**

Leon is president of a campus fraternity. He feels he is an expert on the subject of Greek life at his school, so he decides to use his observations and personal experiences as the basis for an informative speech on the pros and cons of joining fraternities and sororities. However, Leon fears that if he reveals that he is a fraternity president, his listeners will assume that he is not presenting objective information—so he does not mention it.

Is it ethical for Leon to avoid mentioning his fraternity affiliation or the fact that he is a fraternity president? Is it possible for him to give an unbiased presentation of both sides of the issue? In general, is it ethical for speakers who are strongly committed to an organization, cause, or position to give informative speeches on related topics? If so, what obligations do they have to their audience? What guidelines should these speakers follow to ensure that they will deliver objective information rather than a persuasive speech? Write some suggestions that you can discuss with your classmates.

your orientation has shifted from information to persuasion. If you do not think you can make your speech objective, save the topic for a persuasive speech.

In Chapter 12, "Wording Your Speech," we discussed the use of language. Nothing betrays the image of objectivity that is essential in an informative speech as quickly as the inappropriate use of language. For example, in an informative speech on the pros and cons of juvenile curfew laws, one of our students used language that telegraphed his personal opinion on the issue. Even when explaining the arguments for such laws, he described them as "silly," "costly," and "unenforceable." In an informative speech, your language should be descriptive rather than evaluative or judgmental.

Use Appropriate Organization

As we stated earlier, there is no one best organizational pattern for informative speeches. You choose the pattern that is most appropriate to your topic and specific purpose. However, some patterns are inappropriate for an informative speech. While a pro–con approach is appropriate, a pro–con-assessment strategy moves the speech into persuasion. Problem–solution and need–plan patterns are also inherently persuasive. The motivated sequence strategy, to be discussed in Chapter 17, is also traditionally used for persuasive, not informative, speeches. Again, Figure 15.1 offers suggestions for selecting an appropriate organizational pattern. If you have any doubt that your organization is informative rather than persuasive, check with your instructor.

Use Appropriate Forms of Support

As with persuasive speeches, speeches to inform require appropriate supporting materials such as those we discussed in Chapter 8. These materials should come from sources that are authoritative and free from bias. If you discuss a controversial issue, you must represent each side fairly. For example, if your specific purpose is to inform your audience on the effects of bilingual education, you must research and present information from both its proponents and its critics.

Use Effective Delivery

Some speakers have a misconception that delivery is more important for a persuasive speech than for an informative speech. Regardless of the type of speech, show your involvement in your speech through your physical and vocal delivery. The suggestions we offered in Chapter 13, "Delivering Your Speech," are appropriate for the speaker who informs as well as the speaker who persuades. Your voice and body should reinforce your interest in and enthusiasm for your topic. Your delivery should also reinforce your objectivity. If you find your gestures, body tension, or voice conveying an emotional urgency, you have likely slipped into persuasion.

Guidelines for Informative Speaking

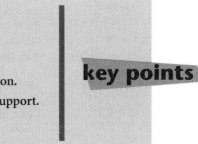

1. Stress your informative purpose.
2. Be specific.
3. Be clear.
4. Be accurate.
5. Limit your ideas and supporting materials.
6. Be relevant.
7. Be objective.
8. Use appropriate organization.
9. Use appropriate forms of support.
10. Use effective delivery.

We hope that after reading this chapter you know the principles and characteristics of informative speaking, that you understand how they contribute to effective speaking, and that you will be able to apply them as you prepare your speeches. Our student Lyn Carley understood and used these principles when she delivered the following speech to her classmates. Notice how her organization of the introduction, body, and conclusion contributed to a seamless, organic whole. Members of her class seemed particularly impressed with Lyn's presentational aids, and we are grateful to Judy Martin for her permission to reprint them here. In the marginal annotations we have indicated the major strengths of Lyn's speech, as well as some improvements she might make.

Annotated Sample Speech

"A Stitch In Time"[5]

Emelyn Kathryn Carley, San Antonio College, San Antonio

1 How would you like to go to bed tonight with a dear old friend and find you've woken up with a millionaire? Well, the quilt your great-grandmother made, the one you toss over your bed on those cold winter nights, the quilt you carelessly throw into the washing machine, probably won't be worth a million dollars, but it could be worth a small fortune. Some antique quilts have been valued between $35,000 and $50,000—and some have sold for more than $150,000!

2 Quilts were treasured in their own day for their beauty, utility, and craftmanship. Today they are perhaps even more highly regarded as documents of our American heritage. They tell us a lot about ourselves, and many of them are just beautiful to look at. But if you're absolutely unsentimental and don't have trouble eventually parting with them, quilts can also be solid investments.

3 So first, I would like to tell you how quilts are viewed as historical records. Second, I will describe quilting as an art form. Third, I will discuss a quilt's investment value. And finally, I will describe and show you a personal history quilt I've put together for a member of this class.

4 One of the most interesting ways of looking at antique quilts is as historical records. "Quilts are among the few tangible objects that reflect the role women played in the building of America," says Patricia Wilens, editor of the Better Homes and Gardens book, *America's Heritage Quilts.* She notes, "Pilgrim women brought to the New World [the] skills and styles of their European homeland." They also brought memories of those homelands. They created quilt patterns that they

Lyn begins with a rhetorical question. Her topic is apparent by the time she finishes her second sentence. The surprising prices she mentions here certainly give the audience a reason to listen.

This section of the introduction builds the importance of Lyn's subject further.

Her third paragraph clearly previews the ideas she will develop in the body of her speech.

Here Lyn begins to apply the 4 S's to her first point. She signposts ("One") and states her idea (quilts are historical records). She quickly introduces a source to support the idea.

These brief, vivid examples show that the names of quilt blocks tell a history and evoke images of pioneer life. "As you can see" begins a very brief summary of the point Lyn has made so far.

"In addition" begins a complementary transition. Lyn defines "crazy quilt" and reminds her listeners of the dates of the Victorian era. She uses "if you find" to introduce two brief hypothetical examples.

This quotation serves as an effective summary of Lyn's first point.

The information from *Harper's* serves as Lyn's transition to her next point. In the final sentence, Lyn signposts and states her second point.

Lyn gives no author for this source, nor did she for the booklet she quoted earlier.

Lyn mentions her own experience as a quilter at this point. If her topic had been controversial, she would have needed to build her credibility earlier in the speech.

Lyn's use of *I, you* and *we* throughout the speech helps her involve her listeners and establish a warm, friendly interaction with them. At this point, Lyn used several quilt blocks as visual aids. One was partially quilted so that the audience could see the layers she mentions. Lyn's second point lacks a summary.

called "Windmill Blades" and "Dresden Plate," for example. Wilens says that as quiltmakers designed individual blocks for their patchwork quilts, they frequently chose names to commemorate important people or events. Early pioneer women traveling across America named their quilt blocks "Kansas Troubles," "Road to California," "Oklahoma Wonder," or "Rocky Mountain Chain." As their families settled down, the women made quilts out of blocks with names like "Barn Raising" and "Straight Furrow." Blocks with names like "Hands-All-Around" and "Swing-in-the-Center" remind us how important the country dance was to them. With fabric scarce during the Civil War, the "Log Cabin" block, made of thin strips of material, became popular. As you can see, the names early Americans gave their quilt patterns tell us something about their lives.

5 In addition to telling us about individual lives, certain styles of quilting also identify particular historical periods. Today, if you find a "crazy quilt" made of odd shaped scraps of velvet, satin, silk, and ribbons, it may have been made in the Victorian era, from 1870 to 1900. If it's in good shape, that's probably because it was made to be thrown over a sofa or chair. It was decorative rather than useful. If you find a quilt made of bright, solid colors on a dark background, it could have been made by Amish women whose families settled in Pennsylvania or Kansas. Because their austere religious beliefs prohibited them from using printed fabrics, the Amish put together strong, solid colors that look very contemporary to us.

6 In the 1920s, quilts reflected the new "modern woman," and Wilens says that the widespread publication of quilt patterns for the first time greatly popularized quiltmaking. The Depression marked another change; quilters again were quilting out of necessity, like their colonial predecessors. Two sentences in a little booklet entitled *Quilts: Heirlooms of Tomorrow,* summarize quilts as historical records: "Today we treasure as part of our American culture the innumerable variety of patchwork patterns that have recorded gallant lives, the growth of our nation, and the symbols of a new society. Thousands of people take pride in preserving and further enriching this heritage by making quilts of beauty that generations to come will prize."

7 Quilting took a back seat during World War II and through the '50s and '60s. In fact, according to Beth Sherman, in an article in the February 1989 *Harper's Bazaar,* it wasn't until New York's Whitney Museum of American Art exhibited sixty pieced quilts in 1971 that people began to look at quilting as something more than a useful craft. And that second way of appreciating quilts is as a fine art.

8 *Aunt Martha's Favorite Quilts Magazine* notes, "For a 'Prize Winning' quilt, design is most important. The selection and combination of materials and colors, the skill of the needle worker, and artistic quilting all go to make the quilt a thing of beauty."

9 The most important step in achieving a beautiful quilt is the fabric selection. Cotton is the most popular fabric and the most durable of textiles. Cotton's color retention is exceptional as well. I have worked with denim and silk in the past and always return to cotton. Any fabric store will have a large selection of colors and prints to choose from. It takes practice to get the right combinations, but once you get the hang of it, you are on your way. I mentioned Amish quilts earlier, and Amish quilters were experts at combining colors. What they lost in the detail of printed fabric that was forbidden to them they made up for in color. The neon colors of Amish quilts remind many people of the pop art of the 1960s.

10 You may be curious as to the actual construction of a quilt. Maggie Malone, author of *500 Full-Size Patchwork Patterns,* says, "Quilt patterns consist largely of geometric pieces; it is the different sizes of those pieces and their arrangements that give patchwork its tremendous variety." A quilt top is either pieced together from blocks or is a solid fabric with other materials sewn, or appliquéd, to it. Shirley Thompson, who has a special interest in throws and crib quilts, writes in her book *Think Small,* "Quilts consist of three layers: top, batting, and backing. Quilting stitches hold the three layers together while adding ornamental surface interest to the quilt." The stitch count on a finely crafted quilt should be eight to twelve stitches per inch, and no area larger than the palm of your hand should be left unquilted. You will often see an obvious mistake somewhere in the pattern of an old quilt. Members of strict religious orders often made these mistakes on purpose as a sign of humility, a recognition that only God is perfect.

11 If you have absolutely no appreciation of craftsmanship and no eye for color and design, you may still be interested in quilts because of those dollar figures I mentioned at the beginning of my speech. Yes, a third way of looking at quilts is as investments. In their book *Quilts, Coverlets, Rugs, & Samplers,* Dr. Robert Bishop, director of New York's Museum of American Folk Art, and his coauthors tell the story of one quilt. They relate, "In the fall of 1980, an important collection of American textiles was sold at auction in New Hampshire." One particular quilt, signed by its maker and dated 1837, fetched only $85 at that time. However, the buyer then sold it to a museum curator in New York City for $650. "Today," they note, "it is one of the most prized examples of Americana in the museum's permanent collection and is valued at $6,500. This is not an isolated incident."

12 An article in *Business Week,* March 6, 1989, tells of the investment potential of unique quilts. For example, a "1930 quilt depicting interracial scenes, such as a black doctor caring for a white patient, sold for a few dollars in the 1960s. Despite the quilt's ordinary workmanship, a collector purchased it last year for more than $50,000."

13 Sherman says in her *Harper's Bazaar* article that today, "Quilts generally cost between $500 and $2,000, but in urban areas they may sell for $25,000 or more. The record for a quilt sold at auction was set [in 1987] at Sotheby's when a dealer paid $176,000 for a Baltimore album quilt," made around 1840. As you can see by these examples, these bed covers can be anything but ordinary. But even seemingly ordinary early twentieth-century quilts seem to be appreciating at about 10 percent a year, according to the *Business Week* article. A trip to an antique dealer's shop, a quilt shop, or to an organization such as the Greater San Antonio Quilt Guild might give your great-grandmother's quilt a new value, and even a new lease on life. If it's an heirloom, its value will increase steadily throughout the years.

14 But you don't have to be made out of money to get yourself a quilt today. With some skill and patience, you can make a special type of quilt, the personal history quilt. That's the final topic I'll briefly discuss today.

15 Quilters seem to take special joy in selecting blocks not only for their aesthetic qualities, but also for the blocks' names. Your quilt can tell a story. It can be a personal history or family sampler quilt. A quilter simply selects blocks with names that have special meaning for the person who is to receive the quilt.

16 I interviewed classmate Norma Falkner and asked her a few questions about herself. We came up with blocks representative of the special people, places, things, and times that are important to her. These are the blocks I selected for Norma's quilt and why they are significant in her life:

Night Owl—Norma rarely gets to bed before midnight.

Emerald Isle—The emerald is her birthstone.

Sister's Choice—Norma has two sisters.

Collector's Block—Antique collecting is a hobby of hers.

Texas Two-Step—She is a native Texan.

Mother's Day—This must be better than Christmas! Not only was Norma born and married on this day, but she's also the mother of a little boy.

Puppy Dog Tails—She is a pet lover.

Chocolate Lover—Need I say more?

Vagabond—Norma enjoys traveling and plans to see a lot of the world.

Baby Boomer—Without giving away her age, I'll just say that Norma qualifies.

Baby's Breath—For her two-year-old son.

Mexican Star—This final block proudly reflects Norma's heritage.

In paragraph 11, Lyn begins her transition to her third point. She signposts and states her next idea with "a third way of looking at quilts is as investments."

Lyn's citation of Bishop is her best job of explaining a source's qualifications. Again, she quickly uses a source to support the idea she has just introduced.

These three actual examples from three different sources seem well organized because the dollar amounts ($6,500, $50,000, $176,000) increase with each one.

Mentioning a local quilt guild localizes the topic and tells listeners where they may go to learn more about the subject.

Here, Lyn introduces the idea of the personal history quilt and then signposts it as her "final" point.

The fact that Lyn had developed a quilt based on the life of one of her listeners gives an immediacy to this final point.

At this point, Lyn introduced a large visual aid composed of enlarged color copies of quilt blocks. As she mentioned the twelve blocks in Norma's quilt, Lyn pointed to each.

Night Owl

Emerald Isle

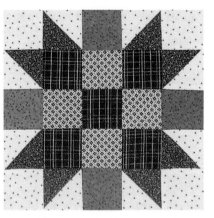

Sister's Choice

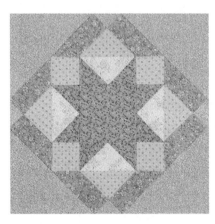

Collector's Block

Texas Two-Step

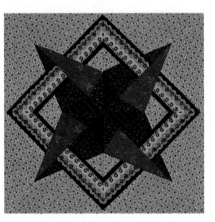

Mother's Day

Lyn shows excellent audience adaptation by mentioning other members of her classroom audience and their interests. Each of these people had spoken on the subject Lyn indicates.

Here Lyn acknowledges the source of the quilt blocks she used in her visual aid.

Lyn summarizes her points in reverse order.

Delivered from memory and with appropriate pauses, Lyn's final quotation brings her speech to a solid psychological conclusion.

17 A quilt made up of those blocks and using fabrics I chose would be as unique as Norma herself. I could also make a personal history quilt for a group of people—a family or a group of friends. From speeches I've heard given in class this semester, I could create a class quilt. Let's start with the block "Classmates." How about "Carnival Ride" for Dianne Bloom's love of the roller coaster? Housebuilder Darin Turner would be well represented with a block entitled "Carpenter's Wheel." "Acrobats" might be the best block to describe our exercise guru John Caballero. To represent Sonja Heldt's expertise in photography, I'd choose a block named "Photo Album." My own block would be "Quilter's Dream." And to date our quilt, how about "Yellow Ribbons," signifying the safe return of our Desert Shield participants? Judy Martin, who was for eight years senior editor of *Quilter's Newsletter Magazine,* lists numerous quilt block patterns in her *Ultimate Book of Quilt Block Patterns,* my source for the blocks I've used in Norma's quilt. You can see the endless possibilities available to quilters today. You need only a subject and a little imagination to create a historical record, treasured for years to come.

18 Today, I've shown you a personal history quilt fashioned after classmate Norma Falkner's life. I've demonstrated how a quilt can be a valuable investment. I've described quilting as an art form and told you a little about the historical significance of quilts. Personal history quilts are an excellent way to preserve family histories, as they would be handed down from generation to generation. As Dr. Bishop points out, "A quilt is often made as a document of love. It's a record of being in a certain place at a certain time. It's craftsmanship. It's emotional. It's art."

Puppy Dog Tails

Chocolate Lover

Vagabond

Baby Boomer

Baby's Breath

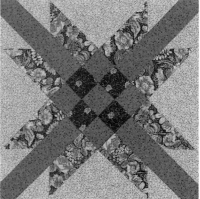

Mexican Star

Summary

As part of your work in this class, you will present at least one *speech to inform*. An informative speech assignment provides you with the opportunity to be the sender rather than the receiver of information; it requires you to research a subject of your choice, synthesize data from various sources, and pass it on to your listeners. Your goals as an informative speaker are to expand listeners' knowledge, assist their understanding, or help them apply the information you communicate.

Classifying informative speeches by subject gives you an idea of the range of possible topics and the patterns of organization each subject typically uses. Speeches about *people* are often arranged chronologically but may explore subtopics, such as aspects of the subject's life. Speeches about *objects* use spatial organization if your purpose is to describe various parts of the object, chronological organization if your purpose is to explain how the object was created, and topical organization if your purpose is to explain how the object is used. Speeches about *places* use chronological organization if your purpose is to explain the history or stages of development of the place, topical organization if you want to emphasize various aspects of the place, and spatial organization if your purpose is to describe the parts of the place. Speeches about *events* also use any of the following three methods of organization: Chronological organization to explain a sequence of events, topical organization to explain the significance of events, and causal organization to show how one event produced or led to another.

Speeches about *processes* can use chronological organization to tell listeners how to do something or how something is done, pro–con organization to explore the arguments for and against the process, or causal organization to discuss what caused or causes some process and the effects that result. Speeches about *concepts* typically use topical organization as the speaker discusses various aspects, definitions, or applications of the concept.

Speeches about *conditions* may use topical organization to discuss various aspects of the condition, chronological organization to trace the stages or phases of a condition, or causal organization to show the causes of the condition and the effects that the condition has. Finally, speeches about controversial *issues* may use a pro–con organization if your purpose is to explore opposing viewpoints on the issue, topical organization if your purpose is to discuss the significance of the issue, or chronological organization if your purpose is to discuss how the issue has evolved.

As you begin to prepare an informative speech on a subject from one of these categories, ask yourself three questions: (1) How much does the audience already know about this topic? (2) What does the audience need to know in order to understand this topic? (3) Can I present this information in the allotted time so that the audience will understand and remember it? When you answer these questions, you can be sure that your topic is sufficiently narrow and appropriate to your listeners.

Finally, we offer ten guidelines to help you develop and deliver an effective informative speech. (1) Begin with an overall picture; let your audience know that your purpose is to inform. (2) Be specific; narrow the topic you have chosen. (3) Be clear; remember that your audience probably knows much less about this topic than you do. (4) Be accurate; misinformation can harm your listeners. (5) Limit the ideas and supporting material that you try to include. Covering a few ideas in depth is usually more informative than discussing many ideas superficially. (6) Be relevant; do not be sidetracked by interesting but irrelevant information. (7) Be objective in your approach to the topic and the language you use. (8) Use the pattern of organization best suited to achieving your specific purpose. (9) Use appropriate forms of support. (10) Use lively, effective speech delivery.

Evaluating and Comparing Three Informative Student Speeches

Lyn Carley's speech "A Stitch in Time" (pages 353–56), Daniel Sarvis's speech "A Ship in a Bottle" (pages 457–59), and Susan Chontos's speech "The Amish: Seeking to Lose the Self" (pages 464–66) are three examples of informative speeches delivered by students in a public speaking class. Read these transcripts, and, using the guidelines you have learned in this and previous chapters, compile a list of strengths and weaknesses in each speech. Suppose you were judging these three speeches in a competition. Which speech would you select for the first place award? In writing, provide the reasons for your decision.

Exercises

1. Write and bring to class five specific purpose statements for speeches on any topics you choose. Do not identify the general purpose in these statements, for example: "To _____ the audience on the effects of fragrance on personal health, worker productivity, and product sales." Two or three of these statements should

be for informative speech topics; the remainder for persuasive topics. Be prepared to exchange your paper with another classmate. Each person should write "inform" or "persuade" in the blank provided in each specific purpose statement. Return the papers, and discuss the answers.

2. Using techniques of brainstorming and research, generate a list of two informative speech topics for each of the following categories: people, objects, places, events, processes, concepts, conditions, and issues. Place an asterisk (*) by the five topics you think are most appropriate for a speech in this class.

3. Using the list you generated in Exercise 2, select one topic from each of four categories, and write a specific purpose statement for each. Think about how you could develop each specific purpose, and then discuss what organizational pattern you think would be most appropriate.

4. Suppose you are asked to speak to a group of incoming students on the topic "Using the Campus Library." Your objective is to familiarize new students with the physical layout of the library so that they can research more efficiently. Outline the key ideas you would develop in your speech. What types of presentational aids would you use to reinforce your message?

5. Select an emotionally charged issue (sexual harassment, hiring quotas, and legalization of drugs, for example). Brainstorm aspects of the issue that would be appropriate for an informative speech. State the specific purpose of the speech and briefly describe what you could discuss. In discussing your topic, point out what makes the speech informative rather than persuasive.

6. Select an informative speech from *Vital Speeches of the Day,* from some other published source, or from the Internet. Analyze the speech to see if it adheres to the guidelines discussed in this chapter. If it does, show specifically how it fulfills the goals of each of these guidelines. If it does not, list the guidelines violated, and give examples of where this occurs in the speech. Suggest how the speaker could revise the speech to meet the guidelines.

7. Using the speech you selected in Exercise 6, identify and write down the specific purpose of the speech. Does it meet the characteristics of a speech to inform? Why or why not? What method of organization is used in the speech? Do you think this is the best pattern to achieve the speech's specific purpose? Why or why not?

8. Analyze a lecture by one of your instructors to see if it adheres to the guidelines listed in this chapter. Which guidelines for informative speeches do you think also apply to class lectures? Which do not apply? If the instructor violated any guidelines you think apply to lecturing, how might the instructor remedy this?

Notes

1. Joseph P. Bernt, Thomas Hargrove, and Guido H. Stempel III, "Relation of Growth of Use of the Internet to Changes in Media Use from 1995 to 1999." Unpublished manuscript, 1999.
2. Richard Zoglin, "The News Wars," *Time* 21 Oct. 1996: 62.
3. Zoglin 61.
4. Mark Miller, "Taking on 'Death Futures,' " *Newsweek* 21 March 1994: 54.
5. Emelyn Kathryn Carley, "A Stitch in Time." San Antonio College, Texas, Fall 1990. Reprinted with permission of the author.

The humblest individual exerts some influence, either for good or evil, upon others.

—Henry Ward Beecher

The Strategy of Persuasion

Media specialist Tony Schwartz, producer of political commercials for presidential and other political candidates, combined the words *manipulation* and *participation* to create a new word—*partipulation*. He argues that voters are not simply manipulated by campaign and advertising strategists. Voters do, after all, have the option of rejecting the messages politicians present them. So Schwartz contends, "You have to participate in your own manipulation."[1]

Persuasion is similar to Schwartz's concept of partipulation. The persuasive speaker tries to move the audience to his or her side of an issue. But, as we discussed in Chapter 2, you, the critical listener, have a right and an ethical responsibility to choose whether you are persuaded. Speakers should view listeners as active participants in the communication process. As a speaker, your goal should be to establish a common perspective and tap values your listeners share, not to manipulate, cajole, or trick your audience. Charles Larson echoes this speaker–listener orientation:

> [T]he focus of persuasion is not on the source, the message, or the receiver, but on *all* of them equally. They all *cooperate* to make a persuasive process. The idea of *co-creation* means that what is inside the receiver is just as important as the source's intent or the content of messages. In one sense, *all* persuasion is *self-persuasion*—we are rarely persuaded unless we participate in the process.[2]

In this chapter and in Chapter 17, we examine the three elements Larson mentions—source, message, and receiver—that interact to co-create persuasion. Persuasion and persuasive speaking are complex activities, so we have divided our discussion into two separate chapters. In this chapter we introduce you first to the *strategy* of persuasion. Why is persuasive speaking important? How does the persuasive process work? What are some principles and strategies you can use as you prepare your message? The answers to these questions provide a blueprint for your speech. In the next chapter, we introduce you to the *structure* of persuasion. You will use your blueprint as you build your persuasive speech. You will study how to organize and test the arguments of your speech. You will then discover how to integrate those arguments into a clear and convincing message.

The Importance of Persuasion

It is impossible to isolate yourself from persuasive messages, either as a receiver or as a sender. Each day, we are bombarded by appeals from political, business, education, and religious leaders, among others, who try to enlist our support, sell us products or services, and change our behaviors. Persuasive speaking is both inescapable and consequential. While we can all cite examples of messages that are intentionally misleading and patently unethical, we can also list persuasive messages that benefit us as senders and receivers.

In this public speaking course, you will probably be asked to deliver a persuasive message to your classmates, and that will challenge and benefit you in several ways. First, it will require you to select an issue you think is important and to communicate your concern to your audience. Voicing your beliefs will demand that you confront their logic and support; in other words, you must test your ideas for their validity. That process, in turn, will require that you gather supporting materials and draw valid inferences from them as you develop your arguments. Approached seriously and researched energetically, a persuasive speech assignment can develop both your critical thinking and speech-making skills. Finally, you may also use it as an opportunity to improve your school or community. Change can occur when people speak and audiences are moved. You can be an instrument of constructive social and political change.

As a listener, you also benefit by participating in the persuasive process. A speaker can make you aware of problems around you and show how you can help solve them.

Christopher Reeve, a persuasive voice on behalf of people who are disabled, bases many of his arguments on factual information and statistics. He is seen here testifying on Capitol Hill in regard to insurance limits.

You hear other points of view and, consequently, may better understand why others have beliefs different from yours. A speech that challenges your beliefs often forces you to reevaluate your position. Your "partipulation" can correct erroneous beliefs or confirm valid beliefs you hold. Regardless, participating as a listener also heightens your critical thinking and improves your ability to explain and defend your beliefs. Finally, as a listener you have an opportunity to judge how others use persuasive speaking techniques, thus enabling you to improve your own persuasive speaking.

A Definition of Persuasion

Persuasion is the *process of influencing another person's values, beliefs, attitudes, or behaviors.* Key to understanding persuasion is the concept of influence. Too often, we equate persuasion with power, but as you will learn, persuasion does not necessarily mean power. Power implies authority or control over another. For example, employers wanting you to be on time will state that policy and then issue reprimands, withhold promotions, and even terminate your employment to ensure that you obey the policy. They do not need to persuade you. Likewise, in this class, you probably speak on the days assigned because failing to do so would hurt your grade. In each of these instances, your behavior is shaped, at least in part, by the power residing in the other person's position.

Persuasion, however, is more accurately equated with influence than with power. As a speaker you try to influence the audience to adopt your position. You probably have little power over your listeners, and they have the freedom to reject your intended message. Suppose, for example, that your speech instructor wants your class to attend a lecture given on campus by author Tom Wolfe. You are not required to attend, and there is no penalty or reward. To influence you, however, your instructor emphasizes the importance of this opportunity by telling you about Wolfe's background. To make certain that you know who Wolfe is, your instructor lists some of Wolfe's best-known books: *A Man in Full, The Bonfire of the Vanities,* and *The Right Stuff.* Your instructor outlines the

Applying Principles of Persuasion

http://www.salesdoctors. com/diagnosis/3pers.htm

This site features an article for *SalesDoctors Magazine* by consultants Gary and Teresa Cosnett. "The Art of Persuasion in Selling" argues that sales representatives need to combine *ethos, logos,* and *pathos* and offers specific examples of how those principles work in effective sales presentations.

persuasion: the process of influencing another person's values, beliefs, attitudes, or behaviors.

relevance of Wolfe's topic to work you are doing in English, journalism, or sociology classₑs, and also mentions Wolfe's reputation as a lively, entertaining speaker, quoting some of Wolfe's controversial views of modern novels.

In each of these cases, your instructor is using influence rather than power to persuade. The concept of persuasion as influence means that you can bring about change whether or not you are the more powerful party in a relationship. You can also see that compared to power, influence requires more effort, creativity, and sensitivity, but in the long run is probably more effective. If persuasion is our attempt to influence others, let's look more closely at the types of influence we can achieve.

Types of Influence

Our definition of persuasion suggests three types of influence. You can change, instill, or intensify your listeners' values, beliefs, attitudes, and behaviors. Your goal is to move your listeners closer to your position. It may help you to think of this process as a continuum:

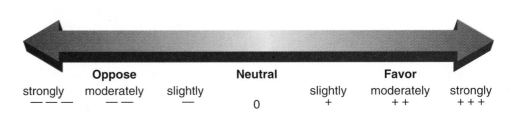

	Oppose			Neutral		Favor	
strongly	moderately	slightly			slightly	moderately	strongly
— — —	— —	—	0		+	+ +	+ + +

Remember, when you speak to persuade, you are speaking to listeners who may oppose, be indifferent to, or support your position. What strategy will you adopt to reach them? The information you gather and the assumptions you make about your audience before your speech determine the strategy you use as you develop your remarks.

Many students preparing persuasive speeches make the mistake of thinking that they must change their audiences' opinions from "oppose" to "favor," or vice versa. Take the example of Chris, who argued in his persuasive speech that the National Collegiate Athletic Association should adopt a playoff system to determine each year's college football champion. After his speech, only one classmate who opposed a playoff system said that Chris had persuaded her to support the proposal. Chris thought he had failed to persuade. Further class discussion, however, proved him wrong. A few listeners said they had changed their position from strong opposition to mild opposition. In addition, several who already supported the playoff system said that Chris's arguments had strengthened their opinion. And several listeners who were neutral before the speech found that Chris persuaded them to agree with him. As you can see, even though Chris persuaded only one audience member to move from "oppose" to "favor," his speech was quite successful. Persuasion occurs any time you move a listener's opinion in the direction you advocate, even if that movement is slight.

The most dramatic response you can request of your listeners is that they *change* a value, belief, attitude, or behavior. The response you seek is dramatic because you attempt to change opposition to support, or support to opposition. For example, if you know your audience opposes putting rating labels on music albums, tapes, and CDs, you could argue in favor of such a policy. You would be asking them to change an attitude. If you discover that the majority of listeners eat foods laden with cholesterol, you could give a persuasive speech encouraging them to alter their diets. In each of these cases, you would be trying to change your audience's values, beliefs, attitudes, or behaviors.

Second, you can attempt to *instill* a value, an attitude, a belief, or a behavior. You instill when you address a particular problem about which your listeners are unaware or undecided. If you persuade your audience that a problem exists, you have instilled a belief.

> Yolanda discussed how language and culture affect access to medical care. She quoted from one source that for non-English-speaking hospital patients "language differences may cause treatment to take almost 25 to 50 percent longer than treatment for English-speaking patients."[3] She pointed out that people from different cultures respond to medical treatment in different ways. She supported this point with specific examples. Near the end of her speech, Yolanda argued that hospital staffs needed to include "culture brokers"—medical interpreters who understand not only the language but also the culture of non-English-speaking patients. After the speech, several listeners said they had not been aware of the problem and were now concerned about it. Yolanda had successfully moved those individuals from a neutral to a supportive position. In short, she had instilled an attitude.

Finally, you may try to *intensify* values, beliefs, attitudes, or behaviors. In this case you must know before your speech that audience members agree with your position or behave as you will advocate. Your goal is to strengthen your listeners' positions and actions. For example, your audience may already believe that recycling is desirable and may even do it occasionally. If your persuasive speech causes your listeners to recycle more frequently, you have intensified their behavior. Your persuasive speech may even encourage them to persuade family and friends to adopt similar behavior. When you change believers into advocates and advocates into activists, you have intensified their attitudes and behavior.

The Pyramid of Persuasion

You cannot know *how* to change your audience until you know *what* you want to change. As our definition of persuasion implies, you can target one of several changes in those listening to your persuasive speech. You can seek to influence their values, beliefs, attitudes, behaviors, or a combination of these. Recall that we discussed these four concepts in Chapter 5 and illustrated them as a pyramid (see Figure 5.1, p. 103). In that discussion, we suggested that our behavior is typically shaped by our attitudes, which are based on our beliefs, which are validated by our values. Figure 16.1, the Pyramid of Persuasion, reproduces that model. This figure emphasizes that persuasive speaking is an audience-centered activity. To be a successful persuader, you must connect with your audience. Organizing values, beliefs, attitudes, and behaviors into a pyramid can help you visualize your speaker–listener connection as you work on your persuasive speech.

This pyramid can help you formulate the specific purpose of your speech by identifying what you seek to change in your audience. Do you want to influence what they believe, how they feel, or how they act? More specifically, do you want to influence their values, beliefs, attitudes, or behaviors? Perhaps you want to affect more than one or all of them. For example, if you convince an audience that a new convention center would help revive the economy of your city (belief), they may consequently favor its construction (attitude) and vote for the necessary bond issue to pay for it (behavior).

As the Pyramid of Persuasion suggests, our values and beliefs interact to affect our attitudes; attitudes, in turn, affect our behavior. The upward arrows in the model reflect this traditional view of how we produce change. A speaker trying to persuade you not to smoke could argue in the following way: You shouldn't smoke because it is a bad habit. It is a bad habit because it increases your chances of getting cancer. Getting

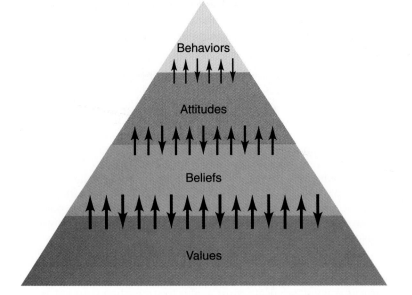

FIGURE 16.1
The Pyramid of Persuasion

cancer is bad because it imperils your health, and you should value your health. Notice that the speaker uses values the listener is presumed to possess in order to justify the behavior sought. The pyramid helps you visualize the process of persuasion and develop your arguments accordingly. As you prepare your persuasive speech, use this pyramid to help you develop your strategy.

When you develop your persuasive strategy, begin by clarifying why you feel strongly about an issue. Providing reasons for your feelings moves you to consider the first and second levels of the pyramid—in other words, your values and beliefs. The example of Tony, whose persuasive speech called for a boycott of a department store, illustrates how you can use the pyramid for your persuasive speech.

Tony was bothered when his friend Mike told him about the hiring and promotion policies at the department store where Mike worked. Men and single women were given priority over married women whose husbands were employed. When a newspaper investigated and reported the charge, Tony decided to make this issue the topic of his persuasive speech. Using the pyramid structure, Tony sorted out his feelings and planned his persuasive strategy. He first asked himself, "Why do I think this topic is important to discuss?" His answer was that the store's policies were unfair. Knowing this, he worked through the various levels of the pyramid as follows:

Statement of values: I value equality and fairness.
Statement of belief: The local department store has discriminated against married women in its hiring and promotion decisions and policies.
Statement of attitude: No one should be denied employment on account of gender or marital status. I disapprove of the store's employment practices.
Statement of behavior sought: Therefore, I will not shop at this store, and I will urge others to join in the boycott.

Once he identified the values and beliefs underlying his and his listeners' attitudes and behaviors, Tony was able to generate the materials he needed to construct his persuasive appeal. Tony reminded his audience of their respect for the values of equality and fairness. He then quoted from a newspaper article to document that the local department store had indeed discriminated against two married women. Arguing that an injustice had been committed, Tony declared that everyone should be incensed by the store's employment practices and he urged a boycott.

The examples we have shown so far suggest that our beliefs affect our attitudes and our attitudes affect our behavior. The Pyramid in Figure 16.1 shows this clearly. But persuasion and influence do not move in only one direction—up. If you turn back to page 54 in Chapter 3, you will remember the discussion of self-perception. Just as beliefs and attitudes influence behavior, so too can behavior influence beliefs and attitudes. As the arrows in the pyramid suggest, influence moves up and down. Our behavior may filter down and affect our attitudes. This principle is practiced in a variety of contexts, as illustrated in the following examples.

Business executives assume that dressing the part of a "company person" will help create a company attitude. Parents assume that teaching children to share with others will develop a respect for others. At behavior modification clinics, clients sometimes speak publicly about their addiction. The clinic staff believes that this public behavior will bolster the speaker's attitudes and beliefs. In each of these instances, the persuader targets a change in behavior and assumes that a change or reinforcement in beliefs and attitudes will follow. The philosophy behind this assumption is simple: People are often uncomfortable when what they believe and what they do are inconsistent. One way to resolve that dissonance is to modify their beliefs.

Are you wondering how these examples relate to you as a public speaker? Certainly, you do not want to force your audience into a public declaration and demonstration of support at the conclusion of each persuasive speech. You can, however, use the basic principle to your advantage. Take a close look at the following example.

Beverly worked as a volunteer for a community literacy project and decided to use this experience as the basis for her persuasive speech. She realized that many people consider illiterate adults to be either stupid or lazy. Beverly decided that the best way to get them to change their belief would be to concentrate on convincing them to volunteer a few hours to work at the adult literacy center or in a tutorial program. From her own experience, Beverly knew that the volunteers would see how hard these adults worked to improve themselves. She believed that through this volunteer work, her classmates might also begin to understand the social, economic, and language barriers that keep some of these adults from becoming literate in English. By securing a behavior (getting listeners to work with an adult literacy program), she would give her classmates a firsthand experience that, she hoped, would change their beliefs and attitudes in a more permanent way than any speech alone could accomplish.

You can also use behavior to effect change by pointing out an existing behavior that is inconsistent with an existing belief or attitude. Note how Mike used this strategy in his persuasive speech.

Two weeks before his persuasive speech, Mike distributed a short questionnaire to his classmates regarding their beliefs and attitudes about a state lottery. Mike supported a state lottery but found that almost half of his audience opposed it, believing that gambling is morally wrong. In his speech he pointed out that bingo and the office sports pool were technically gambling and, like buying lottery tickets, done on a voluntary basis. Mike discovered some audience members' commitment to the behavior (gambling) was stronger than their commitment to their attitude (gambling is wrong). They adjusted their attitude to accommodate their behavior, and ended up thinking, "Some forms of gambling are worse than others." While these audience members might still oppose a state lottery on other grounds, Mike successfully weakened the argument that it was immoral. Other audience members had beliefs that were apparently stronger than their behavior. At the end of Mike's speech they still opposed the lottery and said they would quit the forms of betting he had pointed out.

As you see from these examples, your persuasive speech will target your audience's thoughts and actions. It's true that we sometimes act without fully considering the consequences of our actions; we also sometimes think about taking certain actions without ever acting. For this reason, your persuasive speech may aim to change your listeners' thoughts, actions, or both. Your goal determines the type of persuasive speech you will be giving, so let's consider your options in more detail.

Types of Persuasive Speeches

Persuasive speeches are generally classified according to their objectives. An effective persuasive speech may change what people believe, what people do, or how people feel. Persuasive speeches, then, may be divided into speeches to convince, to actuate, or to inspire, and our discussion in this chapter centers on these three divisions. Understanding these divisions can help you determine your primary objective as you work on your speech, but keep in mind that persuasive speeches often include two or more objectives. For example, if your purpose is to get your audience to boycott fur products, you must first convince them of the rightness of your cause. We usually act or become inspired after we are convinced.

Speeches to Convince

In a **speech to convince,** your objective is to affect your listeners' beliefs or attitudes. Each of the following specific purpose statements expresses a belief the speaker wants the audience to accept:

> To convince the audience that "hate speech" is constitutionally protected.
> To convince the audience that exit polls harm the balloting process.
> To convince the audience that air travel is safer than ground travel.
> To convince the audience that there is a constitutional right to privacy.
> To convince the audience that sealed adoption is preferable to open adoption.
> To convince the audience that Robert E. Lee was a better general than Ulysses S. Grant.

The speaker's purpose in each of these speeches is to establish belief. While a speech to convince does not require listeners to act, action may be a natural outgrowth of their belief. So be aware that you may need an action step in your speech. For example, if you convince your audience that exit polling harms democracy but you suggest no remedy for the problem, you may leave your audience frustrated. In this case, you can suggest a simple action step, such as urging your listeners to express their views to their elected representatives. When a speech includes this step, it becomes a speech to actuate.

Speeches to Actuate

A **speech to actuate** may establish beliefs, but it always calls for the audience to act. The specific purpose statements listed here illustrate calls for action:

> To move, or actuate, the audience to donate nonperishable food to a local food bank.
> To move the audience to investigate charities before making cash donations.
> To move the audience to spay or neuter pet cats and dogs.
> To move the audience to begin a low-impact aerobic workout program.
> To move the audience to equip their homes with carbon monoxide detectors.

Speeches to Inspire

A third type of persuasive speech is the **speech to inspire.** The speech to inspire attempts to change how listeners feel. Examples include commencement addresses,

---

speech to convince: a persuasive speech designed to influence listeners' beliefs or attitudes.

speech to actuate: a persuasive speech designed to influence listeners' behaviors.

speech to inspire: a persuasive speech designed to influence listeners' feelings.

*Appealing to your listeners'
emotions can be a legitimate
way to persuade your audience
to support an ethical cause.
Marian Wright Edelman,
founder and president of the
Children's Defense Fund, often
relates moving stories about the
boys and girls for whom she is
advocating in order to spur her
audience to action.*

commemorative speeches, eulogies, and pep talks. Some specific purposes of speeches
to inspire are:

> To inspire the audience to respect those who volunteer their time to help others.
>
> To inspire the audience to honor the journalistic integrity of Edward R. Murrow.
>
> To inspire the audience to appreciate those who made their education possible.
>
> To inspire audience members to give their best efforts to all college courses
> they take.

The purposes of inspiration are usually noble and uplifting. These speeches typically have neither the detailed supporting material nor the complex arguments characteristic of speeches to convince or actuate.

Thus far, we have seen the importance of audience involvement in the important
process of persuasion. We have provided a definition of persuasion and discussed the
various goals that persuasive speakers can have. In the following section we will discuss
six important strategies that apply to all persuasive speeches.

Persuasive Speaking Strategies

As far back as the era of Ancient Greece, we can find evidence of people giving advice
on how to be an effective persuasive speaker. Aristotle, for example, devoted much
space in his classic work *The Rhetoric* to the subject. Aristotle discussed three modes of
persuasion speakers have at their disposal: *ethos, logos,* and *pathos.*[4] These three modes

remain an important foundation today for our understanding of persuasive speaking. What do these terms mean and how can they help you as you prepare a persuasive speech?

Ethos, or speaker credibility, derives from the character and reputation of the speaker. *Logos*, or logical appeal, relies on the form and substance of an argument. *Pathos*, or emotional appeal, taps the values and feelings of the audience. Like Aristotle, we have emphasized throughout this text that any speech is shaped by the speaker, the message, and the audience. Each of these variables affects the finished product. After all, no two people will give the same speech on the same topic to the same audience. Therefore, no person can give you a simple formula to make your persuasive speech effective. Your strategy for each speech must be based on your unique situation and on your own creativity. Nevertheless, we can give you some strategies, or guidelines, to follow as you prepare your persuasive speech.

Persuasive Speaking Strategies

key points

1. **Establish your credibility.**
2. **Focus your goals.**
3. **Connect with your listeners.**
4. **Organize your arguments.**
5. **Support your ideas.**
6. **Enhance your emotional appeals.**

Establish Your Credibility

As a speaker, your first available source of persuasion is your own credibility, or *ethos*. **Credibility** is simply your reputation, and it helps determine how your listeners evaluate what you say. Research confirms what you already probably believe: The higher your perceived credibility, the more likely the audience is to believe you.[5]

Speaker credibility is fluid, varying according to your listeners. You possess only the credibility your listeners grant you. If you pepper your speaking with humor, for example, some listeners may see you as lively and interesting while others may think you frivolous. You probably have as many different images as you have audience members.

Credibility also varies according to time. Your credibility can be divided chronologically into the time before, during, and after your speech. These chronological divisions are sometimes referred to as initial, derived, and terminal credibility.[6] Your image or reputation prior to speaking comprises your **initial credibility**, sometimes called **antecedent** *ethos*. The more the audience knows about you, the firmer your image.

But what if your listeners do not know you personally? Even in this case, you still bring varying images to the speaking occasion. For example, if you are a spokesperson for an organization, you may assume the image of that organization in the minds of your audience. What if someone asked you to describe the kind of person who belongs to the Democratic Party, the Republican Party, the Sierra Club, or the National Rifle Association? An image probably comes to your mind for each group. If a representative from one of those associations were to speak to you, you would make certain assumptions about the individual based on what you know about that organization. Just as you do with strangers, you form impressions of your classmates based on what they say in

ethos: speaker credibility.

logos: logical appeal.

pathos: emotional appeal.

credibility: the degree to which listeners believe a speaker.

initial credibility or **antecedent** *ethos:* a speaker's image or reputation before speaking to a particular audience.

Readings on Rhetoric
http://www.rpi.edu/ dept/llc/webclass/web/ project1/group4/ index.html
Visit this student-generated Web site for easily understood explanations of the concepts of *ethos, logos,* and *pathos*. The site includes links to examples and dictionary definitions of each rhetorical form.

Readings on Rhetoric
http://www.lcc.gatech.
edu/gallery/rhetoric/
terms.html
The Rhetoric Resources
Web site at the Georgia
Institute of Technology includes student essays on
topics related to the study
of rhetoric and communi-
cation. Enhance your un-
derstanding of *ethos, logos,*
and *pathos* (and other
communication concepts)
by reading these essays.

class, how they dress, whether they arrive at class on time, their age and appearance, and any organization to which they belong. They have also formed impressions of you, of course. Such images constitute your initial credibility.

Derived credibility is the image the audience develops of you as you speak. The moment you enter the presence of your listeners, you provide stimuli from which the audience can evaluate you. As you begin your speech, the number of stimuli multiplies quickly. If you begin your speech with an offensive joke, listeners' images of you will become more negative. However, when you appeal to your listeners' values and present reasoned arguments to advance your position, you enhance your image. The credibility you derive during your presentation is a function of many factors. Your information, of course, helps your audience judge your credibility. Your audience will also judge your nonverbal behaviors (see Chapter 13), such as gestures, posture, eye contact, and appearance, to name a few. If you convey confidence, authority, and a genuine concern for your listeners, you will enhance your credibility.

Terminal credibility is the image the audience has of you after your speech. Even this credibility is subject to change. The listener may be caught up in the excitement and emotion of your speech and end up with an elevated opinion of you. As time passes, that evaluation may moderate. As you can see, the process of generating and maintaining credibility is ongoing. In this class, for example, your credibility at the conclusion of one speech will naturally shape your initial credibility for your next speech.

Studies demonstrate that a speaker having high credibility can more successfully persuade than a speaker having low credibility. Clearly, you need to pay careful attention to your credibility at each stage in order to deliver a successful persuasive speech. How do you enhance your image? Communication theorists agree that speakers who appear competent, trustworthy, and dynamic are viewed as credible speakers.[7] If your audience believes you possess competence, trustworthiness, and dynamism, you can be effective in persuading them.

Convey Competence. In this class you are among peers, and so your audience probably considers you a fellow student rather than an expert on your chosen topic. How can you get them to see you as knowledgeable and worthy of their trust? Your task is to establish an image of **competence** on your subject. Four strategies will help you do that.

derived credibility: the image listeners develop of a speaker as he or she speaks.

terminal credibility: the image listeners develop of a speaker by the end of a speech and for a period of time after it.

competence: listeners' views of a speaker's qualifications to speak on a particular topic.

Guidelines for Enhancing Your Image of Competence

1. Know your subject.
2. Document your ideas.
3. Cite your sources.
4. Acknowledge personal involvement.

key points

First, the obvious: *Know your subject.* From which of these people would you be more likely to buy a new video disc player: a salesperson who can answer all your questions about the product or someone who doesn't know the answers and doesn't care to find out? The answer is obvious, isn't it? In a persuasive speaking situation, you as speaker are a salesperson, and your audience members are consumers. To speak ethically, you must be well informed about your subject. You will discover that the more you read and listen, the easier it is to construct a message that is both credible and compelling.

Not only should you know your specific topic, but you should also understand how it interacts with related topics. Just as the salesperson must know the video disc player and how it will operate with other equipment you own, you should comprehend both the content and the context of your persuasive message. Persuading your classmates to begin recycling low-density plastics (LDPs) does you little good if your area has no processing plant for LDPs and thus recyclers will not accept them. In addition, you will feel foolish if an audience member asks after your speech, "Did you know that no recycling center will accept those plastics?" This is where your research helps you by enhancing your expertise on your subject. A well-researched speech increases persuasion by contributing to your image as a well-informed individual. In a public speaking course such as this, the image building you do is cumulative. Thorough, quality research not only enhances your credibility on the immediate topic but also generates positive initial credibility for your next appearance before the same group.

Second, you can bolster your image of competence if you *document your ideas*. You document ideas by using clear, vivid, and credible supporting materials to illustrate them, as we discussed in Chapter 8. Unsupported ideas are mere assertions. Though your listeners don't expect you to be an expert on your topic, they need assurance that what you say is corroborated by facts or by experts. Providing documentation supports your statements and increases your believability.

A third strategy for enhancing your credibility is to *cite your sources*. Simply presenting the data upon which your conclusions are based is insufficient. Remember, your audience is not going to have the opportunity to read your bibliography. You need to tell your listeners the sources of your information. Citing sources enhances the credibility of your ideas by demonstrating that experts support your position. Of course, it also requires that your sources be unbiased and of good quality. We remember one student who cited *Hustler* magazine as the source for his contention that soft-core pornography does not exploit women and thereby destroyed his credibility. That same fate befell a student who tried to enlist contributions of time and money to the American Red Cross using only Red Cross promotional literature as her sources.

Fourth, *acknowledge any personal involvement* or experience with your subject. Listeners will probably assume that you have an edge in understanding color blindness if you let them know you are color blind. They will probably make the same positive assumption if you are diabetic and speaking on diabetes, or if you are a child of an alcoholic and are speaking on codependency. If you have worked with terminally ill patients and are speaking on hospice care, mentioning your experience will add authority to your ideas.

Convey Trustworthiness. A second criterion of speaker credibility is **trustworthiness,** and it should tell us two things about you. First, we should trust you as an individual: You are honest in what you say. Second, we should trust you with your topic: You are unbiased in what you say. A speaker can demonstrate trustworthiness in two simple, practical ways.

1. *Establish common ground with your audience.* If listeners know that you understand their values, experiences, and aspirations, they will be more receptive to your arguments. When you let them know you identify with those values, experiences, and aspirations, you increase your persuasiveness.

2. *Demonstrate your objectivity in approaching the topic.* The information and sources you include in your speech should demonstrate thorough, unbiased research. One student gave his speech on cigarette smoking, arguing that its harmful effects were greatly exaggerated. In presenting his arguments, he re-

trustworthiness: listeners' views of a speaker's honesty and objectivity.

lied on studies sponsored by the tobacco industry. Few in the audience were persuaded by his evidence. He undermined his image of trustworthiness because he limited his research to sources the audience considered biased on the topic, sources that had a financial interest in supporting one side of the issue.

Convey Dynamism. A third element of credibility is **dynamism.** Competence and trustworthiness are obviously legitimate criteria used to determine speaker credibility, but you may wonder why we include personal dynamism on this list. Dynamism is more closely associated with delivery than with content. We enjoy listening to speakers who are energetic, vigorous, exciting, inspiring, spirited, and stimulating. But should speakers whose delivery is static, timid, and unexciting be considered less credible than their more exuberant counterparts? Perhaps not, and the ethical listener will focus more on the content than on the form of the message. Yet you should know that studies continue to document dynamism as an element of speaker credibility, and it would be wise for you to develop this attribute.

Dynamism contributes to persuasion because it conveys both confidence and concern. You show confidence largely through your speech delivery. If you appear tentative or unsure of yourself, the audience may doubt your conviction. To the extent that you can strengthen your verbal, vocal, and physical delivery, you can enhance your image of confidence and, hence, your credibility. No one expects you to give a professional-level performance. Remember that mastering public speaking is a process that involves study and practice. If you take yourself and your speech seriously, you will do fine.

Dynamism also demonstrates a concern for the audience and a desire to communicate with them. If your delivery seems flippant, distracted, or detached from the audience, your listeners will assume that you are not concerned about the topic or about them. On the other hand, conveying enthusiasm for your topic and your listeners communicates a strong positive message.

As a speaker, then, present a well-researched and documented message and communicate it in an honest and unbiased manner. Your verbal, vocal, and physical delivery should show you to be a fluent, forceful, and friendly individual serious about the issue you address. If listeners perceive you to be competent, trustworthy, and dynamic, you will have high source credibility and, hence, be an effective persuader.

dynamism: listeners' views of a speaker's confidence, energy, and enthusiasm for communicating.

Janet Reno's straight-talking, no-nonsense style gives people in her presence confidence that they can believe in her message, though others have questioned her forthrightness.

Limit Your Goals. A common mistake many beginning speakers make is to seek dramatic change in the values, beliefs, attitudes, and behaviors of their listeners. In our experience, it is the rare speaker who can accomplish this, particularly if he or she seeks change on highly emotional and controversial issues such as abortion, gun control, capital punishment, religion, or politics. Keep in mind that the more firmly your audience is anchored to a position, the less likely you are to change their attitudes. It is unrealistic for you to expect dramatic change in a person's beliefs and values in a one-shot, five- to ten-minute speech. Instant conversions occur, but they are rare. Rather than try to convince your audience to support (or oppose) the death penalty, try convincing them of a limited goal, a smaller aspect of the topic; for example, argue that capital punishment deters crime (or does not). Once a listener accepts that belief, you or another speaker can build on it and focus on a successive objective: support for (or opposition to) the death penalty.

Which specific purpose statement in the following pairs is the more limited and reasonable goal?

Specific purpose: To persuade the audience to oppose the use of all animals in laboratory tests, *or*

Specific purpose: To persuade the audience to oppose the use of animals in laboratory tests of cosmetics and cleansers.

Specific purpose: To persuade the audience that violence on television promotes aggression in viewers, *or*

Specific purpose: To persuade the audience that violence in television programs aimed at children promotes aggression in children.

Specific purpose: To persuade the audience that actively involving students in classroom learning is desirable, *or*

Specific purpose: To persuade the audience that team learning is a cost-effective way to promote student learning.

In each case, the second statement is the more limited and potentially more persuasive. To be successful as a persuasive speaker, you must view persuasion as a process of moving a listener incrementally through a range of positions. Your speech may be only one part of this process. Select a realistic goal, and channel your efforts toward achieving it. Remember the persuasive principle: *Persuasion is more likely if your goals as a speaker are limited rather than global.*

Argue Incrementally. A second principle builds on the first one: *Persuasion is more permanent if you achieve it incrementally.* To be effective and long-lasting, persuasion should occur incrementally, or one step at a time. This principle becomes more important if your audience is likely to hear counterarguments to your argument. In any speech, you speak for a fixed amount of time. The greater the number of points you must prove, the less time you have to support and explain each. Because you must move through several steps, your limited time may force you to abbreviate your support of some of these steps. When your listeners hear another speaker attack one of those steps later, they may lack sufficient evidence to counter those attacks; as a result, what you accomplished may be only temporary. Your goal should be to "immunize" your listeners to possible counterarguments. The stronger your arguments, the greater the likelihood that you will bring about enduring change in the opinions of your audience. If you know your audience has been exposed to counterarguments, you may need to address those arguments before introducing your own.

Which source advising you to "take Carolyn DeLecour for public speaking; she's a great teacher" would you find more persuasive: a friend who is also a college student or a counselor at your school? If you are typical, your answer is "my friend," particularly if that friend has already taken a public speaking class with Professor DeLecour. The counselor may have taken DeLecour's public speaking class, may know DeLecour personally, or may have heard many complimentary remarks about DeLecour from her former students. But the counselor may also just be trying to fill a class that other students are avoiding.

Persuasion is more likely if a speaker establishes common ground with the audience. The example above illustrates this concept. You are probably more easily persuaded by people similar to you than by those who are different. Your friends, for example, are credible sources not because they possess special expertise but because they share your values and interests. We all reason that individuals having backgrounds like ours will view situations and problems as we would. Furthermore, we believe that people who share our beliefs will investigate an issue and arrive at a judgment in the same manner we would if we had the time and the opportunity.

One way to increase your persuasion, then, is to identify with your listeners. Sonja, a weekend news anchor for a local television station, was asked to speak to a college television production class on employment opportunities in television. Notice how Sonja used the strategy of identification in her introduction as she focused on experiences she shared with her listeners.

> Seven years ago a timid freshman girl sat in a college classroom much like this. Just like you, she was taking a TV production class. And like some of you, I suspect, she dreamed of being in front of a camera someday, sitting at an anchor desk, reporting the news to thousands of families who would let her come into their homes through the magic of television.
>
> There was little reason to predict that this girl would achieve her dreams. In many ways she was rather ordinary. She didn't come from a wealthy family. She didn't have any connections that would get her a job in broadcasting. She was a B student who worked part-time in the university food service to help pay for her education. But she had a goal and was determined to attain it. And then one day, it happened. An instructor announced that a local TV station had an opening for a student intern. The instructor said the internship would involve long hours, menial work, and no pay. Hardly the opportunity of a lifetime! Nevertheless, after class, she approached the instructor, uncertain of what she was getting into. With her instructor's help, she applied for and received the internship. It is because of that decision that I am now the weekend anchor of the city's largest television station.

The rest of Sonja's speech focused on the importance of student internships in learning about the reality of the broadcast media and making contacts for future references and employment. Her opening comments made Sonja a more believable speaker by bridging the gap between her and her listeners. Sonja's suggestions had more impact on her audience because she had established common ground with them.

Four principles of persuasion should guide how you establish common ground with your audience. Each of these principles requires that you understand your listeners as a result of some careful audience analysis.

Assess Listeners' Knowledge of Your Topic. Persuasion is more likely if the audience lacks information on the topic. In the absence of information, a single fact can be compelling. The more information your listeners possess about an issue, the less likely you are to alter their perceptions. Duane applied this principle in a speech designed to persuade his audience that the little known, sexually transmitted HPV, or Human Papillomavirus, is as serious a national health threat as AIDS. Early in his speech, Duane cited the Spring 1995 *HPV News,* which claimed that up to 50 percent of the sexually active population might be carrying the HPV virus. He then went on to cite credible studies linking HPV to cervical, anal, and prostate cancer.[8] Duane gave his audience information that was new and surprising, and it had great persuasive impact. This principle, of course, has significant ethical implications. Ethical speakers will not exploit their listeners' lack of knowledge to advance positions they know are not logically supported.

Assess How Important Your Audience Considers Your Topic.

Ken, Andrea, and Brad gave their persuasive speeches on the same day. Ken's purpose was to persuade the audience to support the school's newly formed lacrosse team. He urged his listeners to show their support by attending the next home game. Andrea's topic concerned the increasing number of homeless adults and children in the city. She told the class about Project Hope, sponsored by the Student Government Association, and asked everyone to donate either a can of food or a dollar at designated collection centers in campus dining halls or in the Student Center. Finally, Brad advocated legalization of marijuana, citing the drug's medical and economic potential.

Which speaker do you think had the most difficult challenge? In answering this question you must consider the audience. A significant factor is how important the audience considers the topic.

The importance of a topic can increase the likelihood of persuasion. Audience members in the above example probably agreed with both Ken and Andrea, and both may have been successful persuaders. Listeners who viewed combating hunger as a more important goal than supporting the lacrosse team were probably more persuaded by Andrea and may have contributed to Project Hope.

Just as the importance of a topic can work for you as a persuasive speaker, it can also work against you and decrease the likelihood of persuasion. It is surely easier, for example, for someone to persuade you to change brands of toothpaste than to change your religion. The reason is simple: Your religion is more important to you. Brad probably had a tougher time persuading his listeners than did either Ken or Andrea. Legalizing marijuana probably ran counter to some deeply held audience opinions, and the intensity of those beliefs and values may have made them more resistant to Brad's persuasive appeals. The importance of an issue will vary according to each audience member, and you need to take this into account as you prepare your persuasive appeal.

Motivate Your Listeners.
A third principle of persuasion is that persuasion is more likely if the audience is self-motivated in the direction of the message. People change their values, beliefs, attitudes, and behaviors because they are motivated to do so. To be an effective persuader, you must discover what motivates your listeners. This requires an understanding of their needs and desires. How can you do this? You can enhance your persuasive appeal by following three steps. First, identify as many of the needs and desires of your listeners as possible. Second, review your list, and select those that your speech satisfies. Third, as you prepare your speech, explain how the action you advocate fulfills audience needs. If you discover that your speech does not fulfill the needs or desires of your listeners, then you have probably failed to connect with these listeners. They may receive your speech with interest, but such listeners will probably not act on your message. What you intended as a persuasive speech may in fact be received as informative.

Relate Your Message to Listeners' Values. Finally, persuasion is more likely if the speaker's message is consistent with listeners' values, beliefs, attitudes, and behaviors. We have discussed the importance of consistency elsewhere in this text, but we think it important enough to mention here. People want to establish consistency in their lives. We expect coherence between our beliefs and actions, for example. In fact, we will call someone a hypocrite who professes one set of values but acts according to another. Your ability to persuade is thus enhanced if you request an action that is consistent with your audience's values.

Use this principle of consistency in constructing your persuasive appeal. For example, we have had students who persuaded their classroom audience to oppose the use of animals in nonmedical product testing. They first identified the beliefs that would cause a person to challenge such tests—for example, product testing harms animals and is unnecessary. Next they showed their audience that they share these beliefs. Once they accomplished that, the speakers then asked their listeners to act in accordance with their beliefs and boycott companies that continue to test cosmetics on animals, because continuing to buy such products would be inconsistent with their beliefs.

Organize Your Arguments

In Chapter 3 you learned that most of us are inefficient listeners. Immediately after your speech, chances are that your classmates will remember only 50 percent of what they heard. Two days later that figure drops to only 25 percent. And a speech that is poorly organized in the first place has even less of a chance of surviving in the minds of audience members. Using the organizational strategies presented in Chapters 9 and 10 can increase the longevity of your message in the minds of your listeners. This is especially important if you seek long-term changes in your audience's attitudes and behaviors, or if you want your listeners to deliver your message to a larger audience.

In addition to what you've already learned about structuring your speech, we offer one more organizing principle: *Persuasion is more likely if arguments are placed appropriately.* Once you have determined the key arguments in your speech, you must decide their order. To do that, you must know which of your arguments is the strongest. Assume for a moment that your persuasive speech argues that the public defender system needs to be reformed. Assume, too, that you are using a problem–solution organization, discussed in Chapter 9. Your first main point and the arguments supporting it could be:

1. The public defender system is stacked against the defendant.
   A. Public defenders have too heavy caseloads.
   B. Public defenders have too little experience.
   C. Public defenders have inadequate investigative staffs.

One of these three arguments will probably be stronger than the other two. You may have more evidence on one; you may have more recent evidence on it; or you may feel that one argument will be more compelling than the other two for your particular audience. Assume that you decide point B is your strongest. Where should you place it? Two theories of argument placement are the primacy and recency theories.

Primacy Theory. **Primacy theory** recommends that you put your strongest argument first in the body of your speech to establish a strong first impression. Because you are most likely to win over your listeners with your strongest argument, this theory suggests that you should win your listeners to your side as early as possible. Primacy theorists would tell you to move your strongest argument to the position of point A.

primacy theory: the assumption that a speaker should place the strongest argument at the beginning of the body of a speech.

Recency Theory. Recency theory, on the other hand, maintains that you should present your strongest argument last, thus leaving your listeners with your best argument. They would have you build up to your strongest argument by making it point C. If you had only two supporting points, A and B, your stronger point could be in either position. But what do you do if you have three arguments, as in the public defender example, or even more?

Though the primacy and recency theorists argue whether the first or last position is stronger, they generally agree that the middle position is the weakest. Therefore, do not place your strongest argument in the middle position. When you sandwich a strong argument between weaker ones, you reduce its impact.

Support Your Ideas

Well-supported ideas benefit your speech in two ways. First, they provide an ethical underpinning for your position. Ethical speakers test their ideas for validity and support and share that support with their listeners. Second, as we mentioned in discussing credibility, well-supported ideas enhance your *ethos*. Research demonstrates that using quality evidence, citing your sources, and employing valid reasoning increase your credibility as a speaker.[9]

Two sections of this book will help you construct a convincing case for your position. In Chapter 8, we discussed the types of supporting material and tests of evidence that you can use to prove your arguments. Speakers may use examples, definitions, narration, comparison and contrast, statistics, and testimony to give their ideas credibility. In Chapter 17, we will introduce you to the elements of an argument, describe five types of arguments you can use in your persuasive speaking, and define several categories of faulty reasoning you should avoid.

Enhance Your Emotional Appeals

As we indicated near the beginning of this chapter, *pathos* is the appeal to emotions. Among the emotions speakers can arouse are your anger, envy, fear, hate, jealousy, joy, love, or pride. When speakers use these feelings to try to get you to believe something or act in a particular way, they are using emotional appeals.

recency theory: the assumption that a speaker should place the strongest argument at the end of the body of a speech.

ethical decisions

In this chapter, we noted that a speaker's ability to influence an audience depends, in part, on his or her credibility. Credibility, in turn, is a function of an audience's perception of the speaker's competence, trustworthiness, and dynamism. Dynamic speakers convey confidence; they also communicate a sense of concern for their audiences, a desire to make a connection with their listeners.

Unfortunately, dynamism sometimes masks a speaker's questionable motives. Both Hitler and Mussolini, for example, were dynamic speakers. So were many other leaders throughout the ages who led their followers into battle for unjust causes. How can listeners separate a speaker's dynamism from his or her trustworthiness and competence? If a dynamic speaker *seems* to care about the audience, how do listeners determine whether the speaker's feelings are sincere? Moreover, what ethical responsibility do listeners have to evaluate the credibility of speakers whose delivery is timid and unexciting? Is it legitimate to tune out a speaker's message if he or she is not effective at making an emotional connection with the audience? In general, what guidelines should listeners follow when they evaluate a speaker's dynamism and credibility? Write your answers to the questions above, and be prepared to discuss them in class.

Many of the feelings listed above seem negative—anger, fear, hate, and jealousy, for example. Consequently, you may consider emotional appeals as unacceptable or inferior types of proof. Perhaps you have even heard someone say, "Don't be so emotional; use your head!" It is certainly possible to be emotional and illogical, but keep in mind that it is also possible to be both emotional and logical. Is it wrong, for example, to be angered by child abuse, to hate racism, or to fear chemical warfare? We don't think so. The strongest arguments combine reason with passion. *Logos* and *pathos* should not conflict but complement each other.

In his persuasive speech Chris examined problems caused by inadequate vaccination. He presented data gathered by the Centers for Disease Control showing that measles, rubella, tetanus, mumps, influenza, and pneumonia cause much unnecessary suffering. After these discussions, Chris concluded:

> All told, every year diseases that we can prevent kill an estimated 70,000 people, take over 20 billion dollars worth of lost productivity and so-called free medical benefits from our pockets as taxpayers, and cause pain and suffering to hundreds of thousands of others.[10]

In this speech Chris's specific purpose was to advocate a nationwide vaccination campaign to save lives, reduce suffering, and conserve tax dollars. Did Chris construct a logical argument? Yes. He used statistics from a reliable source and explained how they supported his position. Did Chris construct an emotional argument? Again, yes. He appealed to his listeners' fear of death and their compassion toward others. *Logos* and *pathos* coalesced to form a compelling argument.

As you can see, when properly constructed, emotional appeals make your listeners active participants in the development of your message. By tapping their feelings, you involve them psychologically and physiologically. The following four guidelines will help you develop and enhance the *pathos* of your persuasive speech.

Tap Audience Values. The first, and probably most important, guideline for developing emotional appeals is to *tap audience values*. As we have mentioned repeatedly, you must conduct careful audience analysis before you can deliver an effective speech. Demonstrate in your speech how your audience's values support your position. In Chapter 5, "Analyzing Your Audience," we discussed how you can relate your topic to audience needs (see pages 105–09). Try some of the strategies discussed in that section. The more attached listeners are to the values a speaker promotes, the more emotional is the appeal. Part of your responsibility as a speaker is to make that connection evident to your listeners.

Use Vivid Examples. A second strategy for enhancing emotional appeals is to *use vivid, emotionally toned examples*. The example may not be sufficient to prove your point, but it should illustrate the concept and generate a strong audience feeling. Dan used this strategy in his speech on the harms of electroshock weapons.

> Mediha Curabaz, a young Turkish nurse; Scott Norberg, an inmate in Maricopa County Jail; and seven-month-old Brandon Jordan of nearby Peoria, Illinois, all share a common tragic link—they have all been abused by electroshock weapons. The *Lancet* of April 26, 1997, reports that Turkish secret police using stun weapons repeatedly tortured Ms. Curabaz—at one point violated her with an electric truncheon. While the 1996 *Phoenix News-Times* tells of how prisoner Scott Norberg was dragged from his cell, strapped to a chair, and gagged with a towel. As he struggled to breathe, correctional officers stepped back and fired stun guns 21 times into his helpless body—electrocuting him. And the *New York Times* of November 25, 1994, reports how tiny Brandon Jordan was brutally killed as his aunt shocked him repeatedly with a stun gun to prevent him from crying. Sadly, events like these are becoming all too common.[11]

Who can listen to Dan's examples without feeling compassion or anger?
Visual and audio aids can also enhance a speaker's *pathos*.

Duncan selected as the specific purpose of his speech to persuade the audience to become members of Amnesty International. He had joined the organization because he felt that as an individual, he could do little to help end torture and executions of prisoners of conscience throughout the world. As part of a concerted worldwide effort, however, he saw the opportunity to further social and political justice. His speech included ample testimony of persecution coupled with statistical estimates of the extent of the problem. Duncan wanted to infuse his speech with convincing emotional appeals to support the data. After presenting the facts, he paused and spoke these words to his listeners: "In the last four minutes you've heard about the anguish, the pain, the suffering, and the persecution experienced by thousands of people, simply because they want to be free and follow their consciences. I want you not only to *hear* of their plight, but also to *see* it." Duncan pushed the remote control button of a slide projector and proceeded to show five slides of people brutalized by their own governments. He did not speak, but simply showed each slide for ten seconds. After the last slide, he spoke again: "They say a picture is worth a thousand words. Well, these pictures speak volumes about man's inhumanity to man. But these pictures should also speak to *our consciences*. Can we stand back, detached, and do nothing, knowing what fate befalls these individuals?" Duncan then told the audience how they could become involved in Amnesty International and begin to make a difference. Duncan's speech had a powerful effect because he touched his audience's emotions with vivid examples.

Use Emotive Language. Duncan also employed *pathos* by using a third technique: he *used emotive language*, such as "the anguish, the pain, the suffering, and the persecution. . . ." In Chapter 12, "Wording Your Speech," we discussed the power of words. Nowhere can words be more powerful than when they work to generate emotional appeals. Consider the following passage from Bill Clinton's 1997 inaugural speech. Notice how he begins with fairly neutral language and builds to a crescendo with increasingly emotive words.

The divide of race has been America's constant curse. Each new wave of immigrants gives new targets to old prejudices. Prejudice and contempt, cloaked in the pretense of religious or political conviction, are no different. They have nearly destroyed us in the past. They plague us still. They fuel the fanaticism of terror. They torment the lives of millions in fractured nations around the world.[12]

Destroyed, plague, fuel, fanaticism, terror, torment, and *fractured* are all words carefully chosen to evoke strong feelings among the audience.

Use Effective Delivery. As a final method, you should *use effective delivery* to enhance emotional appeals. As we discussed in Chapter 13, "Delivering Your Speech," when a speaker's verbal and nonverbal messages conflict, we tend to trust the nonverbal message. For that reason, speakers who show little physical and vocal involvement with their speeches usually come across as uninterested or even insincere. When you display emotion yourself, you can sometimes generate audience emotion.

Before leaving the subject of *pathos*, a few parting comments are in order. Emotional appeals are powerful persuasive tools. They can stir passions, intensify beliefs, and impel actions. Speakers have an ethical responsibility to use emotional appeals wisely. Emotional appeals are never in order if the speaker disregards the logical basis of the speech. Emotion and logic are best used in concert with each other.

It is important to remember that these three modes of persuasion—*ethos, logos,* and *pathos*—all work to enhance your persuasive appeal. The best persuasive speeches combine all three. Effective persuaders are credible, present logically constructed and supported arguments, and tap the values of their listeners.

Persuasion is a dynamic activity requiring the participation of a speaker, a message, and at least one listener. Politicians, educators, businesspeople, and religious leaders flood us with persuasive appeals daily. In order to benefit from sound persuasion and avoid the pitfalls of flawed or unethical persuasion, speakers and listeners must understand what persuasion involves.

Persuasion is the process of influencing another person's values, beliefs, attitudes, or behaviors. *Influencing* can mean changing attitudes or actions, instilling new beliefs, or simply intensifying people's feelings about their existing beliefs or behaviors. The Pyramid of Persuasion helps you determine the specific purpose of your speech and generate arguments you can use to achieve that purpose. A persuasive speech aimed at changing beliefs and attitudes, but not requesting any overt behavior of listeners, is called a *speech to convince*. A *speech to actuate* seeks to change behaviors. A *speech to inspire* encourages positive changes in the way listeners feel about their beliefs or actions.

Three modes of persuasion, discussed at least as early as the time of Aristotle, are *ethos, logos,* and *pathos. Ethos,* the first source of persuasion available to speakers, is their credibility or believability. *Logos* is a logical appeal based on the form and substance of the message. It appeals to the listener's intellect and reasoning. *Pathos,* or emotional appeal, relies on the audience's feelings for its persuasive impact.

Whether you target values, beliefs, attitudes, behaviors, or a combination of these, your job as an effective persuader will be easier if you're aware of some persuasive strategies. First, the higher your perceived credibility, the more likely the audience is to believe you. A starting point for persuasion, then, is to establish your credibility. Some speakers have *initial credibility* or *antecedent ethos* with a particular audience, based on the listeners' prior knowledge of the speaker. An unknown speaker may take on the credibility of the organization he or she represents. All speakers have *derived credibility,* developed from the ideas they present in their speech and their speech delivery, and *terminal credibility,* based on the audience's evaluation of speaker and message after the speech.

Competence, trustworthiness, and *dynamism* are three components of a speaker's credibility. To build images of competence, speakers should know their speech subjects, document their ideas, cite their sources, and mention any special experience or involvement that they have with their topics. To demonstrate trustworthiness, speakers should establish common ground with their audiences and show evidence of objectivity through thorough, unbiased research. Because listeners associate dynamism with the energy, vigor, and friendliness of a speaker's delivery, developing a dynamic image requires showing confidence about speaking and concern for the well-being of the audience.

A second persuasive strategy deals with your goals as a speaker. You are more likely to persuade if your goals are limited rather than global. In addition, your persuasiveness with an audience will be more permanent if you achieve it incrementally, or step by step.

A third persuasive strategy is that persuasion is more likely if a speaker establishes common ground with the audience. Connecting with your listeners requires careful analysis of your audience's knowledge, values, and motivation. You are more likely to persuade an audience if your listeners lack information on your subject. Persuasion is also related to how important the audience considers your topic. Its importance (or relative unimportance) can boost your persuasiveness for listeners who are self-motivated in the direction of your message. Persuasion is also more likely if your message is consistent with listeners' values, beliefs, attitudes, and behaviors.

A fourth persuasive strategy deals with the organization of your message. Persuasion is more likely if the speaker's arguments are appropriately placed within the speech. *Primacy theory* asserts that you should place your strongest argument first in the body of your speech. *Recency theory* maintains that you should build up to your strongest argument, placing it last in the body of your speech. The lesson for public speakers is to avoid placing a strong argument between weaker ones.

A fifth persuasive strategy is to provide solid support for the ideas you present. Well-supported ideas provide an ethical underpinning for your speech and enhance your *ethos* for the audience. Use a variety of quality supporting materials, cite your sources, and reason logically to increase your persuasiveness.

Finally, you can increase your persuasiveness by enhancing the emotional appeals of your message. To develop powerful emotional appeals, a speaker should tap audience values; use vivid, emotionally toned examples; use emotive language; and display emotion in the physical and vocal delivery of the speech. *Pathos* should complement rather than replace the logical structure of a speech.

practice critique

Analyzing Persuasive Appeals in a Powerful Speech

Martin Luther King, Jr., delivered his "I Have a Dream" speech on August 28, 1963. The speech helped elevate a national debate on equal access to employment opportunities, public accommodations, home ownership, and voting rights. In 1964, 1965, and 1968, the Congress and President Lyndon Johnson approved legislation that prohibited racial discrimination in these areas. Some historians claim that Dr. King's powerfully persuasive speech spurred creation of a coalition to support this legislation.

As you read the transcript of Dr. King's speech in Appendix B, note how he directed his arguments to several diverse audiences: black and white; rich and poor; powerful and powerless; nonviolent and militant. Identify appeals that are designed to convince, actuate, and inspire listeners. What values and beliefs did Dr. King tap to influence his listeners' attitudes and behaviors? How did he seek to establish common ground with such diverse audiences?

Exercises

1. List on a sheet of paper messages aimed at persuading you that you have heard, read, or seen during the past 24 hours. These messages may come from friends, family members, boyfriends or girlfriends, politicians, religious leaders, advertisers, newspaper or magazine columnists, television commentators, and so forth.

2. Select three print, broadcast, or Internet advertisements for the same kind of product (soft drinks, insurance, automobiles, and so on). Discuss the persuasive appeals of each ad. Which one do you think is the most effective? Why? Could any of these strategies of persuasion be incorporated in a speech? Provide some examples.

3. Select a copy of an editorial from your campus newspaper, a local or national paper, or *Editorials on File*. Identify the beliefs, attitudes, and values implicit in the editorial, as well as any behaviors the writer advocates.

4. Select a topic, and write a specific purpose statement that seeks dramatic change in the behavior or attitude of your audience. Divide the change you seek into several incremental steps. Discuss what you would need to prove to achieve each step. Could any of these steps be the basis for a speech by itself?

5. Listen to a speaker on C-SPAN, *The NewsHour with Jim Lehrer, Nightline,* a news interview show, or some other broadcast. Keep a chronology of the speaker's initial, derived, and terminal credibility. What changes occurred in your impression of the speaker? What accounted for those changes? What might the speaker have done to improve his or her credibility?

6. Write a self-profile that includes an analysis of how you believe your audience views you as an advocate of the position you plan to take in an upcoming persuasive speech. Include both positive statements (e.g., "My classmates probably think I'm a creative speaker based on my previous speeches, and therefore may listen attentively") and equivocal statements (e.g., "My audience has no reason to believe that I have any special expertise in understanding the topic of environmental racism"). Discuss how you plan to overcome any negative perceptions.

7. Brainstorm a list of values you think the majority of your class holds. You might use the PERSIA framework (political, economic, religious, social, intellectual, and artistic) to get you thinking about a broad range of values. Refer to this list as you discuss how you could develop an audience-centered persuasive speech for an upcoming assignment.

8. Bring to class a picture from a magazine, newspaper, or some other printed source. Construct and present an argument that uses the picture to tap your listeners' emotions.

9. Read Martin Luther King, Jr.'s "I Have a Dream" speech in Appendix B. Identify examples of how the speaker tapped audience values, using vivid examples and using emotive language.

10. Locate a speech that you feel includes examples of unethical emotional appeals. Many political campaign speeches are a good source of these examples. Explain why the emotional appeals are questionable.

Notes

1. "The 30-Second President," narr. Bill Moyers, *A Walk through the 20th Century,* exec. ed. Bill Moyers, PBS, 1984.

2. Charles U. Larson, *Persuasion: Reception and Responsibility,* 8th ed. (Belmont, CA: Wadsworth, 1998) 11.

3. Jill L. Shearer, "Crossing Cultures: Hospitals Begin Breaking Down Barriers to Care," *Medical Staff Leader* July 1993: 3.

4. *The Rhetoric of Aristotle,* trans. Lane Cooper (New York: Appleton, 1960) 8.

5. James Benjamin, *Principles, Elements, and Types of Persuasion* (Fort Worth, TX: Harcourt, 1997) 122, 124.

6. James C. McCroskey, *An Introduction to Rhetorical Communication,* 7th ed. (Boston: Allyn, 1997) 87–88.

7. McCroskey 89. McCroskey credits D. K. Berlo and J. B. Lemmert with labeling these three dimensions of credibility in "A Factor Analytical Study of the Dimensions of Source Credibility," a paper they presented at the 1961 convention of the Speech Association of America, New York.

8. Duane W. Smith, "The Human Papillomavirus," *Winning Orations,* 1995 (Northfield, MN: Interstate Oratorical Association, 1995) 5–6.

9. Benjamin 129. See also Robert H. Gass and John S. Seiter, *Persuasion, Social Influence, and Compliance Gaining* (Boston: Allyn, 1999) 89.

10. Chris Thomas, "Better Safe than Sorry," *Winning Orations, 1989* (Northfield, MN: Interstate Oratorical Association, 1989) 61.

11. Dan Alban, "A Stunning Speech," *Winning Orations, 1998* (Mankato, MN: Interstate Oratorical Association, 1999) 18.

12. William J. Clinton, Inaugural Address, 1997. *New York Times.* 20 Jan. 1997. Online. America Online/Newsstand. 21 Jan. 1997.

Good argument, like good architecture, reveals its structural elements so that what is being said and how it is being supported lie open to the consideration of all.

—Perry Weddle

The Structure of Persuasion

In the space of one hundred and seventy-six years the Lower Mississippi has shortened itself two hundred and forty-two miles. That is an average of a trifle over one mile and a third per year. Therefore, any calm person, who is not blind or idiotic, can see that . . . just a million years ago next November, the Lower Mississippi River was upwards of one million three hundred thousand miles long.

—*Mark Twain*[1]

oes Twain's argument seem unconvincing to you? Does it strike you as more humorous than persuasive? If so, you have probably detected a flaw in it and would not be persuaded by a speaker who said it. In order to be an effective and ethical speaker, you must be able to construct sound arguments and organize them in a convincing fashion. Speakers who knowingly use faulty reasoning act unethically. Understanding how to reason also benefits you as a listener. In order to make rational decisions, you must be able to analyze and assess what you hear.

The ability to structure sound arguments and detect flawed reasoning is an important skill for the public speaker. Thomas Gilovich, associate professor of psychology at Cornell University, explains:

> Thinking straight about the world is a precious and difficult process that must be carefully nurtured. By attempting to turn our critical intelligence off and on at will, we risk losing it altogether, and thus jeopardize our ability to see the world clearly. Furthermore, by failing to fully develop our critical faculties, we become susceptible to the arguments and exhortations of those with other than benign intentions. In the words of Stephen Jay Gould, "When people learn no tools of judgment and merely follow their hopes, the seeds of political manipulation are sown." As individuals and as society, we should be less accepting of superstition and sloppy thinking, and should strive to develop those "habits of mind" that promote a more accurate view of the world.[2]

Developing your own persuasive arguments and responding to others' persuasive appeals exercises all of your critical thinking skills. Your research involves *information gathering* as you formulate questions and collect data to answer them. As you develop new lines of inquiry based on the research you have conducted, you will use your *generating* skills. As you develop your arguments from various sources, you'll be *remembering, integrating,* and *organizing.* Throughout the process you'll be *analyzing* and *evaluating* your evidence, discarding weaker sources, and *focusing* your speech more sharply.

In the previous chapter we discussed the *strategy* of persuasion. You learned what persuasion is and also some strategies you can use to develop a convincing message. In this chapter we discuss the *structure* of persuasion. We will show you how to construct an argument and how to detect faulty arguments. In addition, you will

Constructing Arguments
http://owl.english.purdue.edu/Files/123.html
This section of the Purdue University Online Writing Lab Web site provides both examples and exercises to help you understand logic and to practice constructing arguments. It also includes information on various types of fallacies.

study characteristics and types of persuasive propositions and special organizational patterns you can use in your persuasive speeches.

Making Arguments

Aristotle's description of the effective persuasive speech sounds simple, doesn't it? Before you can prove your case, however, you must understand the structure of arguments and how those arguments are organized in your speech. In the previous chapter, we referred to this type of persuasive appeal as *logos*. Let's see how all this works.

> *A speech has two parts. Necessarily, you state your case, and you prove it.*
> —Aristotle[3]

Steps of an Argument

Suppose you make the following statement: "I am more confident about public speaking now than I was at the beginning of this course." If someone asked you to justify your statement, you could respond in this way:

> Well, I experience fewer symptoms of nervousness. I seem to worry less about facing an audience. The night before my speech, I sleep better than I used to. I establish eye contact with my audience now rather than avoiding looking directly at them, as I did in my first speech. I no longer nervously shift my weight from foot to foot, and I've stopped playing with my high school class ring and have started gesturing.

Your statement and response together constitute an argument. You have made a claim ("I am more confident about public speaking now") and then supported it with evidence—in this case, examples from personal observation. Aristotle would be pleased!

At its simplest level, an argument includes three steps:

1. You make a claim.
2. You offer evidence.
3. You show how the evidence proves the claim.[4]

The *claim* is the conclusion of your argument. It is a statement you want your listeners to accept. Some examples of claims are:

The influence of race undermines the accuracy of eyewitness testimony.

Textbook prices are too high.

Alcoholism is a disease.

The most important thing you can learn in college is how to learn.

Pornography is not a constitutionally protected form of free expression.

Visual aids make ideas easier to remember.

Pizza is the ultimate health food.

The validity of any claim depends on the evidence supporting it. **Evidence** is the supporting material you use to prove a point. As an advocate, you have an obligation to support your position with valid arguments. In other words, you must offer your listeners reasons to accept your conclusion.

Ty always took special interest in any information on asthma because his younger brother had suffered from asthma attacks since the age of five. He knew from reports he had read and heard that rates of asthma attacks were increasing and that the medical community was puzzled and somewhat alarmed by this trend. Ty decided to

evidence: supporting material a speaker uses to prove a point.

research the topic for a persuasive speech, and he used the following materials to make the first point in his speech:

Makes a claim

> You'd think that with all the advances in medicine an illness like asthma would have already been stopped, or at least that it would be getting rare. Unfortunately, it's not. In fact, the problem of asthma has increased significantly in recent decades.

Offers evidence

> According to an article in the June 16, 1999, issue of *The Journal of the American Medical Association,* the Centers for Disease Control and Prevention (CDC) notes that the number of people self-reporting asthma grew 75 percent between 1980 and 1994. Those are unconfirmed, self-reported cases. But the CDC reports a 61 percent increase in diagnosed cases between 1982 and 1994. The result, according to the "Asthma Fact Sheet" on the American Lung Association Web site in 1998, is that an estimated 14.6 million people in the United States have asthma.
>
> The American Lung Association also estimates that more than 5,600 people now die of asthma in the United States each year, a mortality increase of 45.3 percent in the years from 1985 to 1995.

Shows how the evidence proves the claim

> Just remember: Diagnosed cases of asthma are up 60 percent in the last 20 years, and the death rate has increased more than 45 percent since 1985. As you can see, asthma is clearly a growing problem.

In his speech, Ty followed the three steps in constructing and presenting an argument. First, he stated his claim (the problem of asthma has increased significantly in recent decades). Second, he supported his claim with evidence from the American Lung Association and *The Journal of the American Medical Association.* Finally, he focused his listeners' attention on the key statistics that proved his point.

Refuting an Argument

In Chapter 9 we offered the 4 S strategy for developing your key ideas in a speech. In a persuasive speech you signpost your claim, state your claim, support your claim with quality evidence, and summarize, showing how your evidence proves your claim. That's how you develop and present a persuasive argument. But how do you refute, or

speaking with confidence

When I started researching my topic on home schooling, I looked for information to support my opinion. My opinion was based on a few examples of home schooling I had seen. I guess I was guilty of the hasty generalization fallacy. As I researched, I found information that challenged what I thought. I also learned that it was not an either-or issue. I ended up not opposing or supporting home schooling, but arguing that it should be better regulated.

I learned that it's important to start your research with an open mind. You need to look for facts and not just opinions that support what you already think. It's hard sometimes to find unbiased sources, but if you don't do this, you've blown it! Knowing that I avoided fallacies such as hasty generalization and false dilemma in my argument and that my sources were unbiased experts helped me feel confident about what I advocated. This made me feel more credible, and I hope my classmates thought so too. Consequently, I was less nervous as I delivered my speech.

—Rometta Carrico, Radford University

dispute, another's argument? The question is relevant because topics you and your classmates select for your persuasive speeches will involve a spark of controversy. There is always another side, perhaps several sides, in addition to the one presented by the speaker. You may even select a topic because you read or heard a statement with which you disagreed. Persuasive speakers and critical thinkers must know both how to prove arguments and how to refute them. For each argument you **refute,** you may want to use the following four-step **refutational strategy:**

1. State the position you are refuting.
2. State your position.
3. Support your position.
4. Show how your position undermines the opposing argument.

Joel became interested in the topic of irradiated food (food treated with gamma rays) when a classmate warned the class of the dangers of eating foods processed this way. After researching the topic, Joel decided that irradiation was a safe and beneficial process. He presented the following argument in his speech. Notice the marginal comments that show how Joel used each of the four steps of refutation.

> One argument opponents make against irradiated foods is that they harm consumer health. Some have even claimed that these foods become radioactive and can cause death.
>
> Well, before you're taken in by these claims, let's replace the fear with facts. Rather than harming consumer health, irradiation actually protects it.
>
> In a 1992 issue of *Public Health Reports,* James Mason, Assistant Secretary of Health, writes: "More than 40 years of research involving literally hundreds of studies plainly demonstrate that foods processed with radiation using the permitted sources do not become radioactive. . . ." Comparing irradiation with pasteurization, Dr. Mason says: "Not only does the technology extend the shelf life of produce by inhibiting ripening or sprouting, it kills or renders noninfective many harmful food-borne organisms. . . ."
>
> In the October–December 1992 issue of *Food Review,* three USDA [U.S. Department of Agriculture] economists point out how irradiation can be extremely helpful for poultry products. Salmonella is just one disease commonly associated with poultry, and of the 2 million cases each year, between 1,000 and 2,000 result in death. The U.S. Economic Research Service estimates that if just 15 percent of chickens were irradiated, approximately $100 million could be saved in reduced medical costs and lost productivity.
>
> As consumers, we must be guided by facts, not fears. The experts, 40 years of research, and statistics clearly demonstrate that irradiated food does not harm your health—it protects it!

States position to be refuted

States speaker's position

Support speaker's position

Shows how speaker's position undermines opposing argument

Statesman and diplomat Adlai Stevenson proclaimed, "Freedom rings where opinions clash." Democracy and education are about making and testing arguments. The quality of our decisions—indeed, the quality of our lives—depends on what we know and how we use that information. You can use five types of argument as you select and develop the ideas for your speech and refute arguments you encounter. Knowing how to construct and test arguments will also help you as you listen to the speeches of others.

refute: to dispute; to counter one argument with another.

refutational strategy: a pattern of disputing an argument by (1) stating the position you are refuting, (2) stating your position, (3) supporting your position, and (4) showing how your position undermines the opposing argument.

Types of Argument

Speakers can justify their claims by using any of five types of argument. You may offer proof by arguing from example, analogy, cause, deduction, or authority. The type of argument you select will depend on your topic, the available evidence, and your listeners. You may combine several types of argument in a single persuasive speech. In fact, the

Trial lawyers know that cases–and arguments–cannot be won by eloquent language alone. The validity of any claim depends on the quality of the evidence supporting that claim.

best speeches usually do combine types of argument. Let's look in more detail at these five basic types of argument available to you as a persuasive speaker.

Argument by Example. **Argument by example** is an inductive form of proof. **Inductive argument** uses a few instances to assert a broader claim. For example, if you have struggled through calculus and analytic geometry, you may conclude that math is a difficult subject for you. You arrive at this conclusion by generalizing from the few specific math classes you have taken.

We form many of our opinions through proofs provided from argument by example. We read of several murders in Chicago and assume that the city is plagued with violence. We hear a few friends complain of electrical problems with a particular make of car and decide not to buy that model. A speaker relates several examples of corruption in city hall, and we conclude that political corruption is widespread. Those are all examples of inductive reasoning.

Notice how Lindsay cited a series of examples to establish her assertion that burglar bars can be deadly in cases of fires:

> Anyone who has ever been victimized by fire . . . knows that numbers cannot tell of the emotional and sentimental toll a fire can take. Dollar figures alone can't begin to describe the human tragedy associated with burglar bars. In their *1997 Report on Home Security and Fire Safety,* the NFPA [National Fire Protection Associ-

argument by example or **inductive argument:** says that what is true of a few instances is true generally.

ation] identify three separate groups which are particularly endangered by fire. These same three groups are most likely to be victimized by burglar bars. They are the young, the elderly, and the poor.

The April 23, 1997, *San Jose Mercury-News* tells the tragic story of 47-year-old Yvette Michael and her 11-year-old daughter Halthine. A neighbor recounts, "The little girl was at the window, crying 'Help me, help me.' She tried to break the bars . . . but she couldn't." Firefighters attempted to rescue the girl using crowbars, but failed.

The June 6, 1997, *Atlanta Journal-Constitution* tells the story of 71-year-old Eugene Roemnick's death. The elderly man was found lying fully clothed next to a window where burglar bars had prevented his escape.

The May 14, 1997, *Los Angeles Times* chronicles the plight of seven people packed into a Palo Alto home. All were victims of a deadly combination of arson and burglar bars. The *Times* reported that the bars kept a majority of the family from escaping.

And in case you feel as though these are isolated incidents, check out the April 23, 1997, edition of the *San Jose Mercury-News.* They detailed 30 separate incidents which claimed the lives of 89 people from all over the country. These stories include testimony from firefighters themselves, including "Had those bars not been there, we might have been able to save her," and "If they hadn't had those bars, we would have been able to save them all."[5]

Perhaps as you read the preceding arguments, you questioned the validity of some of them. How can you test whether the examples used to support an argument are sound? The validity of argument by example hinges on the quality of the examples a speaker chooses. Ask yourself the following four questions to test the validity of argument by example. Keep in mind that argument by example is valid only if you can answer yes to each of four tests of argument.

Tests of Argument by Example

1. Are the examples true?
2. Are the examples relevant?
3. Are the examples sufficient?
4. Are the examples representative?

key points

1. Are the examples true? The first test of argument by example is to determine if the examples are true. In Chapter 8, we noted that hypothetical or imaginary examples can clarify a point, but they do not prove it. Only when true examples are presented should you proceed to the next question.

2. Are the examples relevant? Suppose a speaker presented evidence that three murders were committed during the past weekend in a major city and concluded, "So you can see that it is not safe to walk the streets of this city." Do these examples relate to the claim? If these three homicides resulted from domestic violence, they would not relate to street crime and, thus, would not prove a threat to the city's visitors. The examples, in this case, are not relevant.

3. Are the examples sufficient? Three murders in one weekend are statistically significant for a small town such as London Mills, Illinois, but, even though tragic, that number is actually below the average number for several of our larger cities. In general, the greater the population for which you generalize, the more examples you need.

4. Are the examples representative? The examples you use as evidence should be typical, not exceptions. Was this weekend typical, or was the number of murders abnormally high?

Argument by Analogy. An analogy is a comparison. **Argument by analogy** links two objects or concepts and asserts that what is true of one will be true of the other. Arguing that computerized phone registration would work at your college because it works at State U is an example of reasoning by analogy.

Argument by analogy is appropriate when the program you advocate or oppose has been tried elsewhere. Some states have lotteries, no-fault insurance, and the line-item veto; others do not. Some school systems allow corporal punishment, offer magnet programs, and require a passing grade for participation in extracurricular activities; others do not. A speech defending or disputing one of these programs could demonstrate success or failure elsewhere to establish its position.

Marcus wanted to persuade his classmates that Virginia should reform its welfare system. He researched experimental programs that other states had tried and found several articles describing Wisconsin's program. In his speech, he explained some of the facets of that program: investments in job training, job placement, and child care for welfare recipients. Citing an August 1996 issue of *Newsweek,* he argued that this approach to welfare reform had reduced Wisconsin's caseload by nearly 45 percent compared to a decade ago. Marcus then argued that because the states have similar welfare populations and total populations, with Virginia the twelfth largest and Wisconsin the sixteenth largest state, Wisconsin's program had a good chance of achieving similar beneficial results in Virginia.

The preceding example illustrates the persuasive appeal of argument by analogy. You introduce a situation that is familiar to the audience and explain why we respond to it as we do. You then assert that your idea or proposal is analogous and, therefore, deserves a similar response. The key to this pattern of argument is the similarity between the two entities. In testing the validity of your argument by analogy, you need to answer this question: "Are the two entities sufficiently similar to justify my conclusion that what is true of one will be true of the other?" If not, your reasoning is faulty. This question can best be answered by dividing it into two questions.

---

key points

Tests of Argument by Analogy

1. Are the similarities between the two cases relevant?
2. Are any of the differences between the two cases relevant?

---

1. Are the similarities between the two cases relevant? If you decide to argue by analogy for a computerized phone registration system, you may find many similarities between your college and State U. However, the fact that both schools have similar library facilities and the same mascot is irrelevant to registration. Equivalent student enrollments, advising procedures, and periods for registration are highly relevant and can be forceful evidence as you build your case.

2. Are any of the differences between the two cases relevant? If so, how do those differences affect your claim? If you discover that, unlike State, your college has neither an integrated computer network nor the technical staff to program it, these differences are relevant to your topic and will undermine the validity of your claim.

Argument by Cause **Argument by cause** connects two elements or events and claims that one is produced by the other. Causal reasoning takes two forms—reasoning from effect to cause and from cause to effect. The difference between the two is their chronological order. An *effect to cause argument* begins at a point of time (when the effects are evident) and moves back in time (to when the cause occurred). When you feel ill and

argument by analogy: says that what is true in one case is or will be true in another.

argument by cause: says that one action or condition caused or will cause another.

go to the doctor, the doctor will usually identify the symptoms (the effects) of the problem and then diagnose the cause. The doctor is problem solving by reasoning from effect to cause. In contrast, *cause to effect argument* begins at a point of time (when the cause occurred) and moves forward (to when the effects occurred or will occur). Doctors reason from cause to effect when they tell their patients who smoke that this habit may result in emphysema or lung cancer.

In her speech promoting good oral hygiene, Tammy presented evidence that linked gum disease to life-threatening medical problems. She urged her listeners to reduce their medical risks by developing the habit of flossing their teeth at least once a day. Tammy argued from effect to cause as she explained why too many people failed to floss.

> But, why do so many of us have such bad dental hygiene habits? Or more to the point, why will 63 percent of us, according to the *Detroit Free Press* of July 15, 1997, not floss sometime today? After all, brushing once a day is a habit for nearly all Americans. Why don't we have this same habit when it comes to flossing?
>
> On the most basic level, from our childhood, we are told to brush, and while we may not be the ones making the commitment to forming a habit of brushing, our parents are more than ready to provide that commitment for us. By nature of habit, we continue to brush. On the other hand, since most parents aren't flossers, they don't instill this habit in their children either. And until now, very few of us have had incentive to form a habit. Because while your dentist and hygienist may encourage you to floss, all the media messages you receive are from toothbrush, toothpaste, and mouthwash manufacturers who portray the scourge of gingivitis as bad breath. Leaving all of us to reason that if I brush and use mouthwash, don't have extremely painful gums, and don't have bad breath, well then I don't need to worry about gum disease. And besides, for some Americans flossing can be a pain—literally. Faced with something we find unpleasant we choose to do it not at all or at best occasionally.[6]

Effect

Cause

Tammy focused on an effect (failure to floss) and then discussed several causes. Once her audience understood these specific causes, she explained how her proposed solution would remedy the problem.

The following speech excerpt demonstrates cause to effect argument. Ellen Wartella, Dean of the College of Communication at the University of Texas at Austin, spoke on the context of television violence:

> In the past fifteen or so years, a remarkably cavalier, vicious, wanton, and senseless pattern of violence entered society and the American psyche. Drive-by shootings and gangbanger crimes, fueled by a trade in handguns and crack cocaine, ushered in fears of an epidemic of violence we may not fully comprehend. The violence panic of this time, unlike that of the 1960s, seems much more to surround children and youth, as both the victims and the perpetrators of violence . . .
>
> [This] cycle of violence has helped us become the most violent industrialzed nation on earth. A lot of numbers gird that conclusion. But the numbers that tell the most tragic story concern children and adolescents:

Cause

Effect

- Among young people in the age group from 15–24 years old, homicide is the second leading cause of death and for African-American youth is number one.
- Adolescents account for 24 percent of all violent crimes leading to arrest. The rate has increased over time for those in the 12–19 year old age group, while it is down in the 35 and older age group.
- Every five minutes a child is arrested in America for committing a violent crime; gun-related violence takes the life of an American child every three hours.
- A child growing up in Washington D.C. or Chicago is fifteen times more likely to be murdered than a child in Northern Ireland.[7]

When you argue by cause, test your reasoning to make certain it is sound. In order to do this, ask yourself the following three questions.

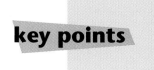

Tests of Argument by Cause

1. **Does a causal relationship exist?**
2. **Could the presumed cause produce the effect?**
3. **Could the effect result from other causes?**

1. Does a causal relationship exist? In order for an argument from cause to effect or effect to cause to be valid, a causal relationship must exist between the two elements. As we will discuss later in this chapter, just because one event precedes another does not mean that the first caused the second. One of our students argued that the scholastic decline of American education began with, and was caused by, the Supreme Court's decision outlawing mandatory school prayer. We doubt the connection.

2. Could the presumed cause produce the effect? During the highly inflationary times of the late 1970s, one of our students gave a speech in which she argued that various price hikes had contributed to the high inflation rate. She provided three examples of price increases: The cost of postage stamps had increased 87.5 percent, chewing gum 100 percent, and downtown parking meter fees 150 percent. While she was able to document the dramatic percentage increase in the prices of each of these products, her examples had more interest than impact. Her examples did not convince her audience or her instructor that these increases by themselves could produce a significant influence on the inflation rate.

3. Could the effect result from other causes? A number of causes can converge to produce one effect. A student who argues that next year's increased tuition and fees are a result of the college president's fiscal mismanagement may have a point. But a number of other factors may have made the tuition increase necessary: state revenue shortfalls, decreased enrollment, cutbacks in federal aid, major spending on campus building projects, and so on. Speakers strengthen their arguments when they are able to prove the following: that the alleged cause contributed substantively to producing the effect, and that without the cause the effect would not have occurred or the problem would have been much less severe.

Argument by Deduction. Ben began his speech on time management with the following statement:

> All of us are taking courses that require us to be in class and to study outside class. In addition, many of us are members of social, academic, religious, or career-oriented clubs and organizations. Some of us work. All of us like to party! Crowded into our school and work schedules are our responsibilities to friends and family members. In short, we're busy!
>
> College is a hectic time in our lives. Sometimes it seems that we're trying to cram 34 hours of activity into a 24-hour day. In order to survive this schedule and beat the stress, college students need to develop effective time-management skills. You are no exception! If you listen to my speech today, you will learn how to set realistic goals, meet them, and still have time to socialize with friends and get a good night's sleep. Sound impossible? Just listen closely for the next eight minutes.

Ben used two types of arguments in his introduction. He opened by arguing from example, providing several instances to make his case that college life is busy. He then used deductive reasoning to make the speech relevant to each member of the audience. A **deductive argument** moves from a general category to a specific instance. In this sense, deductive arguments are the reverse of argument by example. To see why that's true, consider the structure of a deductive argument.

Deductive arguments consist of a pattern of three statements: a major premise, a minor premise, and a conclusion. This pattern of deductive argument is called a **syllogism.** The **major premise** is a claim about a general group of people, events, or conditions. Ben's major premise was this: "College students need to develop effective time-management skills." The **minor premise** places a person, event, or condition into a general class. Ben's minor premise could be phrased like this: "You are a college student." The **conclusion** argues that what is true of the general class is true of the specific instance or individual. Ben concluded that each college student in his audience needed to develop effective time-management skills.

Use the following steps to check the structure and flow of your deductive argument:

1. State your major premise.
2. Say "because," and then state your minor premise.
3. State your conclusion.

The resulting two sentences should flow together easily and make sense. This strategy tests the interconnectedness of the parts of your deductive argument. Ben could have tested the clarity of his argument by saying the following: "College students need to develop effective time-management skills. *Because* you are a college student, you need to develop effective time-management skills." Notice that if the two premises are true and relate to each other, the conclusion must also be true.

Major premises sometimes embody principles that shape our beliefs and guide our actions. A speaker who makes the following statement is using deductive reasoning: "Judge Shady committed an ethical violation when she accepted a campaign contribution from the defendant in a case scheduled for her court." A diagram of this argument is as follows:

Major premise: It is unethical for judges to accept campaign contributions from individuals involved in cases in their courts.

Minor premise: Judge I. M. Shady accepted a contribution from the defendant in a case scheduled for her court.

Conclusion: Judge Shady is guilty of unethical judicial conduct.

In order for deductive arguments to be valid, they must meet certain tests. Whether you are listening to others' arguments or evaluating arguments in your own speech, keep in mind three questions.

deductive argument: says that what is true generally is or will be true in a specific instance.

syllogism: the pattern of a deductive argument, consisting of a major premise, a minor premise, and a conclusion.

major premise: a claim about a general group of people, events, or conditions.

minor premise: a statement placing a person, an event, or a condition into a general class.

conclusion: the deductive argument that what is true of the general class is true of the specific instance.

Tests of an Argument by Deduction

1. **Do the premises relate to each other?**
2. **Is the major premise true?**
3. **Is the minor premise true?**

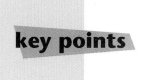
key points

1. Do the premises relate to each other? "All men are created equal. Equal is an artificial sweetener. Therefore, all men are artificial sweeteners." This statement doesn't make much sense, does it? The first sentence uses the word *equal* to mean "equivalent."

The second uses *Equal* as a product name for a sugar substitute. In order for an argument to be valid, the premises must relate to each other. In this case they clearly do not.

Let's construct another example. Suppose John prepares a speech trying to persuade his classmates to apply for a new academic scholarship named after his father, James Burke. In his speech, John makes the following statement:

> Any student enrolled in State U who is a U.S. citizen can apply for the Burke Scholarship. That includes everyone in this class. Just think, next year you could have your entire tuition and fees paid, and you can spend your money for something you've been wanting but were unable to afford. Maybe even that new CD player!

Before John convinces his classmates to apply for the scholarship, he first tells them that they are eligible. His argument may be depicted as follows:

Major premise: Any State U student who is a U.S. citizen can apply for the Burke Scholarship.

Minor premise: Every student in this class is a State U student who is a citizen of the United States.

Conclusion: Therefore, every student in this class can apply for the Burke Scholarship.

The terms in the minor premise fall within the scope of the major premise. Both premises relate to each other, and the conclusion seems logical.

2. Is the major premise true? Before John's classmates head to the financial aid office to begin filling out a scholarship application form, they should ask the question, "Is the major premise of the argument true?" Suppose two prerequisites for application are full-time student status and good academic standing. The statement "any State U student who is a U.S. citizen can apply for the Burke Scholarship" is then false. Part-time and probationary students cannot apply. The conclusion of the argument ("Every student in this class can apply for the Burke Scholarship") would therefore not necessarily be true. You must be able to prove your major premises before you draw conclusions.

3. Is the minor premise true? A false minor premise is just as damaging to an argument as a false major premise. Let's suppose that John's major premise is true, and that any State U student who is a U.S. citizen can apply for the Burke Scholarship. What if his class includes some foreign students? His minor premise ("Every student in this class is a State U student who is a citizen of the United States") is then false. Those students are not eligible for the scholarship, and John's conclusion is false. Arguing a position entails ethical considerations. You must know your facts and reason logically from them.

Argument by Authority. Argument by authority differs from the four other forms of argument we have discussed. To see how it is different, consider the following example from Lynn's speech:

> I believe that every student should be allowed to vote for Outstanding Professor on Campus, rather than having the award determined by a select committee of the faculty. And I'm not alone in my opinion. Last year's recipient of the award, Dr. Linda Carter, agrees. The President of the Faculty Senate spoke out in favor of this proposal at last week's forum, and the Student Government Association passed a resolution supporting it.

argument by authority: uses testimony from an expert source to prove a speaker's claim.

Argument from authority uses testimony from an expert source to prove a speaker's claim; its validity depends on the credibility the authority has for the audience. In this example, Lynn did not offer arguments based on example, analogy, cause, or deduction to explain the validity of her position. Instead, she asserted that two distinguished professors and the SGA agreed with her. She asked her audience to believe her position based on the credentials of the authority figures who endorsed her claim. Her rationale was that her sources had access to sufficient information and had the expertise to interpret it accurately; thus, we should trust their conclusions.

An argument based on authority is only as valid as the source's credibility. To test your argument, ask and answer two questions: (1) Is the source an expert? (2) Is the source unbiased? Our discussion of these questions, as well as other tests of evidence in Chapter 8, "Supporting Your Speech," will help you select the best authority for your claim.

In this section, we have identified and discussed five types of argument. You will want to select as many of these forms as are appropriate to your topic and audience. We have also illustrated how to test these arguments so that they work to make your speech more believable.

Testing the arguments you use and hear others use is crucial to effective, ethical speaking and listening. When you analyze the arguments you use, you strengthen them and can save yourself the embarrassment of being caught using illogical or invalid proof. It is just as important to check the validity of persuasive arguments you hear, however. By doing this, you avoid being duped into misguided thoughts and actions.

In spite of these tests, persuasive speakers sometimes incorporate certain errors of proof into their speeches. These errors are so widely used that they have been named and studied. In the following section, we take a look at some of these mirages of persuasion—arguments that appear, but only appear, to say something authoritative. We want you to be able to identify these errors so you can avoid them.

Fallacies of Argument

A **fallacy** is "any defect in reasoning which destroys its validity."[8] Remember the Mark Twain argument we presented at the beginning of this chapter? Twain assumed that what had occurred in the past 176-year history of the Mississippi River could be projected farther back in time. The example is humorous because of its obvious distortion of figures. Unfortunately, not all distortions of logic we hear are so obvious, nor are they always used for humorous effect. In fact, fallacies are often persuasive and dangerous for the same reason: Because they resemble valid reasoning, we often accept them as legitimate. They can produce bad decisions leading to harmful consequences.

> *He who will not reason is a bigot; he who cannot is a fool; and he who dares not is a slave.*
>
> —*William Drummond*

We want to stress that fallacies are flawed patterns of reasoning that you will want to avoid as both speaker and listener. As you construct your persuasive speech, make sure that the arguments you encounter in your research are valid. Then, use your research to develop sound arguments to support the ideas in your speech. As a listener, you have an ethical responsibility to evaluate critically the ideas other persuasive speakers present to you. Be alert for those arguments based on sound reasoning and for those based on flawed reasoning. Consider the valid arguments, and reject fallacious ones. How can you tell the difference?

Fallacies come in many different varieties. In fact, *The New York Public Library Desk Reference* notes that "there are now over 125 separate fallacies, most with their own impressive-sounding names, many of them in Latin."[9] For our purposes, we will discuss ten of the most common fallacies. Some you will readily recognize while others may be new to you. As you read them, notice how many of them resemble the patterns of argument we have just discussed.

fallacy: a flaw in the logic of an argument.

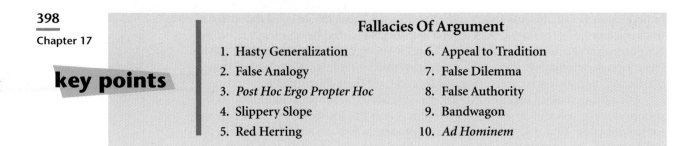

key points

Fallacies Of Argument

1. Hasty Generalization
2. False Analogy
3. *Post Hoc Ergo Propter Hoc*
4. Slippery Slope
5. Red Herring

6. Appeal to Tradition
7. False Dilemma
8. False Authority
9. Bandwagon
10. *Ad Hominem*

Hasty Generalization. People who jump to conclusions commit the fallacy of **hasty generalization,** a faulty form of argument by example. What distinguishes valid from fallacious inductive proof is the quantity and quality of examples. When speakers make claims based on insufficient or unrepresentative instances, their reasoning is usually flawed. For example, a speaker uses examples of two students convicted of plagiarism and concludes that cheating is widespread on campus. A senator notes that gasoline prices are increasing and warns of impending spiraling inflation. An advertisement shows a dentist recommending a particular brand of toothbrush, and the consumer assumes that it carries the endorsement of dentists in general. A student concludes that a public speaking course will not be helpful based on a hectic first class meeting. People who rely too much on first impressions, who do not read widely, or who spend little time researching are prime candidates for reasoning from hasty generalization. They often develop beliefs and opinions that later prove erroneous. Just as dangerous, such people will often reason from hasty generalization in the speeches they deliver.

False Analogy. Speakers argue by analogy when they link two items and assert that what is true of one will be true of the other. If the two items are sufficiently similar, the speaker's claim may be valid. However, if the items differ in critical ways, the persuader may be guilty of using a **false analogy,** and the claim may be fallacious. You've probably heard someone respond to an argument by saying, "That's like comparing apples and oranges." That person just detected a faulty comparison. Read some of the arguments we've heard in students' speeches and see if you can detect some faulty reasoning:

> We license drivers; why shouldn't we license parents? You can't take to the road until you learn how to drive and pass a test. Aren't children more important than cars?
>
> Part of being an adult includes the right to make choices and accept the consequences of your actions. If it's legal to purchase tobacco, shouldn't it also be legal to buy marijuana?
>
> We prohibit cigarette advertising on television, why shouldn't we prohibit ads for beer?
>
> If you're old enough to vote and even go to war when you're 18, you're old enough to drink a beer.

What do you think of these arguments? Which comparisons are valid arguments by analogy? Which are fallacies? Your answers may differ from your friends' and classmates'; detecting fallacies is not always easy. Researchers are careful about making claims that a diet that reduced cancer in laboratory animals will produce the same result in humans. Policy makers are cautious about assuming that traffic laws appropriate for New York City are suitable for those living in the plains of Montana. You

hasty generalization: a fallacy that makes claims from insufficient or unrepresentative examples.

false analogy: a fallacy that occurs when an argument by analogy compares entities that have critical differences.

need to exercise your critical thinking skills as you read, listen to, and develop arguments by analogy.

Post Hoc Ergo Propter Hoc. This fallacy uses the Latin title and literally means "after this, therefore because of this." A chronological fallacy, *post hoc* (as it is usually called) assumes that because one event preceded another, the first caused the second. Perhaps you have heard a friend comment, "I should have known it would rain; I just washed my car!" Your friend is probably making a joke based on the *post hoc* fallacy. People exhibit *post hoc* reasoning when they expect something good to happen if they carry a lucky charm while gambling in a Las Vegas casino, wear a lucky shirt to a football game, or cross their fingers as a teacher returns a graded exam.

During the 1996 presidential election, some people used an obscure baseball fact to predict a Republican victory. What was the basis for their conclusion? The New York Yankees won the World Series that year. These *post hoc* pundits noted that since the end of World War II, whenever the Yankees played in and won the World Series, the Republicans had captured the White House. When the Yankees played in and lost the Series, however, the Democratic candidate was victorious. In fact, in 1996 these pundits were wrong. President Clinton was reelected. It is unwise to mistake coincidence for causality.

These examples may seem absurd, with obvious defects in reasoning. Yet, other examples of confusing coincidence with causation are more subtle and potentially more damaging. For example, a person rejects medical treatment, relying instead on an unresearched cure because someone else tried it and subsequently got well. An individual refuses to exercise and diet, citing the example of his Uncle Bert who "drank like a fish, smoked like a chimney, ate anything he wanted, never worked a day in his life, and lived to be 93!" An incumbent mayor takes credit for every city improvement that occurred since she took office; her opponent blames her for everything bad that happened during this time. An event may have more than one cause. It is also preceded by occurrences having no effect on it whatsoever. As a result, determining the relationship between two events or conditions is often difficult. But you must examine that relation if you are to avoid the *post hoc ergo propter hoc* fallacy.

> Fallacies of Reasoning
> http://www.
> intrepidsoftware.com/
> fallacy/toc.htm
> For an explanation of the ten fallacies of reasoning discussed here and many others, visit Stephen Downes's Guide to Common Logical Fallacies. This site provides definitions, examples, and explanations of the missing proof of more than 60 fallacies.

Slippery Slope. Envision yourself at the top of a hill on a wintry day. You take one step, slip on a patch of ice, lose your footing, and begin sliding down the hill. You try to regain your balance, but you continue your slide, stopping only when you reach the bottom of the hill. This visual image depicts the slippery slope fallacy. **Slippery slope** is a fallacy of causation that asserts that one action inevitably sets in motion a chain of events or indicates a trend. This defect in reasoning is exemplified in the following two arguments:

> If you amend the Constitution to prohibit flag burning, you open the door to other amendments to our Bill of Rights. Ultimately, you destroy the freedoms upon which our nation is based.

> If we begin to control the sale of guns by restricting the purchase of handguns, where will it end? Will shotguns be next? And then hunting rifles? Soon the right to bear arms will disappear from the Constitution, and sportsmen and -women will be denied one of their basic freedoms.

post hoc: a chronological fallacy that says that a prior event caused a subsequent event.

slippery slope: a fallacy of causation that says that one action inevitably sets a chain of events in motion.

These speakers' arguments imply that a single act will set in motion a series of events that no one will be able to stop, but that is not necessarily the case. Just because legislators support one constitutional amendment or one law doesn't necessarily mean that they must support subsequent reforms. Most of the time, a slide down the slope is preventable. Each journey involves a series of decisions, and it is possible to retain or regain your footing.

Red Herring. The name of the **red herring** fallacy apparently originated with the English fox hunt. When the hunt was over, the hunt master would drag a red herring—a type of fish that is smoked and salted—across the path of the hounds. The pungent scent would divert the dogs from their pursuit of the fox, and they could then be rounded up. This diversionary tactic was also supposedly used by escaping criminals to throw dogs off their trails. If you love to read murder mysteries, you may have trained yourself to be on guard for some incidental twist in the plot that seems to be there just to throw less attentive readers off track. Such devices have come to be called red herrings.

A red herring fallacy is an example of a faulty argument by deduction. An arguer makes a claim based on an irrelevant premise. How does the red herring fallacy work in a speech? Bruce Waller provides a vivid example and analysis of this defect in reasoning using the issue of gun control:

> If the debate is over whether handguns should be banned, it is relevant to consider how many people have been killed in handgun accidents. But suppose someone asserts, "Everybody talks about handgun accidents! But think of how many people are killed each year in auto accidents! Why don't we ban automobiles?" You must hold your breath and cover your nose and stay on the trail, for a red herring has just been dragged across the argument. The danger of auto accidents is certainly serious, and perhaps on another occasion we should discuss how to reduce that danger—but that has nothing to do with the question of banning handguns. Whether there are other unacceptable dangers in society is not the issue; the question is instead whether handguns pose an unacceptable risk. Perhaps they do, perhaps they do not, but no progress will be made on that issue if the arguers are distracted by irrelevant reasons.[10]

In essence, then, a speaker guilty of the red herring fallacy introduces an irrelevant issue to deflect attention from the subject under discussion. The following speakers each attempted to divert discussion from germane issues to irrelevant concerns:

A politician answers charges that she accepted illegal campaign contributions by noting her service on the state's ethics advisory board.

When asked about rumors of excessive drinking, a legislator declares, "Madam, my father was a Methodist minister. That should answer your question."

A student responds to a charge of plagiarism with the statement, "I was a Boy Scout throughout high school."

red herring: a fallacy that introduces irrelevant issues to deflect attention from the subject under discussion.

appeal to tradition: a fallacy that opposes change by arguing that old ways are always superior to new ways.

When you present a persuasive speech, you are an advocate for the position you present. As such, you have an ethical responsibility to defend your arguments. Answer criticisms of your argument with evidence and logic; don't deflect criticism by diverting your audience to another track.

Appeal to Tradition. This fallacy is grounded in a respect for traditional ways of doing things. On the surface, respect for tradition seems reasonable. But the fallacy commonly called **appeal to tradition** defends the status quo and opposes change by arguing that old ways are always superior to new ways. A speaker who argues against admitting men to her college because of the school's history as a women's school commits this fallacy unless she offers additional support for the claim. Its most common form of expression—"We've always done it that way"—is merely descriptive. It discourages discussion and reevaluation of our traditions.

As important as many traditions are to us, they should not be used to thwart needed change. Our nation's founders created a glorious document that gave us many of the freedoms we enjoy. Yet that document also precluded non-European Americans and women from full participation in our society. The fight to secure the right to vote for all citizens challenged that tradition, and we all agree that this change is for the better. Keep in mind that the old ways are not always the best ways.

False Dilemma. When forced to choose between alternatives, you face a dilemma. Dilemmas can be actual or false. In an actual dilemma, the alternatives you face are real; there is no room for compromise. For example, suppose you are asked to choose between going to a movie with friends and going to the library to research your upcoming speech. If the library and theater hours coincide, your dilemma is real and you must forfeit either entertainment or study.

A **false dilemma** exists when you have more than the two options presented. For example, if there is a late showing of the movie, perhaps you can convince your friends to meet you at the theater after you finish your research. In this instance, the dilemma is false because you do not have to choose between studying and seeing the movie; you can do both. Woody Allen's quotation is an example of a false dilemma. Certainly, humans face alternatives other than utter hopelessness and total extinction.

The fallacy of false dilemma, sometimes called the either-or fallacy, presents the listener with two choices when, in reality, there are more. Characterized by a "bumper sticker" mentality, the dilemma usually polarizes issues into two mutually exclusive categories, such as "America—love it or leave it!" and "When guns are outlawed, only outlaws will have guns!" Neither of those slogans allows for middle-ground positions. As cartoonist Charles Schulz noted with wry understatement, "There's a difference between a philosophy and a bumper sticker."

Listeners should be especially attentive to all "either-or" and "if-then" statements they hear. These grammatical constructions lend themselves to the fallacy of false dilemma, as in the following examples:

> A person is either a Republican or a Democrat. Because I know Carolyn isn't a Republican, she must be a Democrat.
>
> The issue is very simple: Either you support the Constitution on which this nation was founded, or you're not a patriotic American.
>
> That's the policy of this company. If you're not with us, then you're against us.
>
> I don't support a cutback in defense spending. I don't want to see a weakening of America's strength.

Each of these examples presents the listener with only two choices. However, they disregard other legitimate options: Carolyn may be a Libertarian, a Socialist, a

More than at any time in history, mankind faces a crossroads. One path leads to despair and utter hopelessness, the other to total extinction. Let us pray we have the wisdom to choose correctly.

—*Woody Allen*

false dilemma: a fallacy that confronts listeners with two choices when, in reality, more options exist.

member of some other political party, or an independent. We can exhibit patriotism and company loyalty and still question the laws and policies of nations and companies. Eliminating unnecessary defense spending does not necessarily weaken the country. Using that money for other important projects—like major road and bridge repair—may actually make America stronger.

False Authority. The fallacy of **false authority** is an invalid form of argument by authority. This fallacy occurs when advocates support their ideas with the testimony of people who have apparent but not real expertise. Before deciding to accept someone's opinion or testimony, ask the question, "Is the person an objective expert on this topic?" Celebrity endorsements of commercial products frequently illustrate this fallacy. The famous sports personality who urges you to buy that 260-horsepower sedan with an all-aluminum, high-output, 3.5 liter, 24-valve, V6 engine may know only what she's reading from a script. Celebrities are often used more for their popularity or status than for their credibility.

It is important to exercise your critical thinking skills to avoid using the fallacy of false authority. If you cite information from a Web site without checking its authority and accuracy, or if you quote from authors of books and articles without knowing their credentials, you have used the fallacy of false authority, most likely unintentionally. The statement "I couldn't find any information about the author" is a recipe for irresponsibility. You can avoid the fallacy of false authority by using only information you believe to be expert and credible.

Bandwagon. In the 1800s and early 1900s, political candidates held parades to meet the people. A band rode on a wagon leading the parade through a town. As the wagon passed, local leaders would jump on the bandwagon to show their support. The number of people on board was considered a barometer of the candidate's popularity and political strength.

The **bandwagon** fallacy is faulty argument by authority. It is based on the assumption that popular opinion is an accurate measure of truth and wisdom. The Latin name

false authority: a fallacy that uses testimony from sources who have no real expertise on the topic in question.

bandwagon: a fallacy that determines truth, goodness, or wisdom by popular opinion.

During the 2000 presidential primary debates, Republican candidates Governor George W. Bush, Gary Bauer, and Senator John McCain sometimes lapsed into ad hominem *argument, attacking one another's personal shortcomings.*

for this appeal to popular opinion is *argumentum ad populum.* Frequently referred to as the "everybody's doing it" fallacy, bandwagon arguments commonly use phrases such as "everyone knows" or "most people agree." Door-to-door salespeople or intrusive phone solicitors who tell you that all your friends and neighbors are purchasing their encyclopedia or portrait package use the bandwagon appeal. They base their sales pitch on the product's popularity, not on its merits.

Speakers who defend the rightness of their positions by pointing to polls showing popular support similarly exploit the bandwagon fallacy. While agreement regarding a belief or action may be reassuring, it is no guarantee of accuracy or truth. "Truth is not always democratic."[11] History is cluttered with popularly held misconceptions. Remember, most people once believed that the world was flat; that the sun revolved around the Earth; and that leeching, or bleeding, patients was state-of-the-art medical treatment. You decide the validity of an argument by its form and substance, not merely by how many people agree on it.

Ad Hominem. *Ad hominem,* literally meaning "to the man," arguments ask listeners to reject an idea because of the allegedly poor character of the person voicing it. Political speeches, especially those delivered at national conventions, are peppered with *ad hominem* arguments. These statements often evoke applause, cheers, and laughter, but they provide little insight into issues. When Rush Limbaugh refers to feminists as "feminazis," he is making an *ad hominem* attack rather than engaging in reasoned discourse. A club member commits this fallacy when he argues that Bryan's proposal for an alcohol-free party should not be taken seriously because Bryan has two DUI (driving under the influence) convictions.

> *If you can't answer a man's argument, all is not lost; you can still call him vile names.*
>
> —*Elbert Hubbard*

In its most obvious form, this fallacy is name calling. For some people, simply knowing that a speaker is liberal, conservative, feminist, or fundamentalist is sufficient to close their minds. They disregard the merits of an idea because of the person giving the message. But, as we stated in Chapter 2, an ethical listener has a responsibility to give all ideas a fair hearing.

To be an effective and ethical persuader, you must know how to construct valid arguments and avoid defective ones such as those we have just discussed. Once you have mastered this ability, you can use your arguments to achieve the overall goal of your speech. In the remainder of this chapter, we will show you how to develop a persuasive proposition and how you can effectively organize your arguments.

Selecting Propositions for Persuasive Speeches

In Chapter 6, "Selecting Your Speech Topic," we explained that your first steps in constructing a speech are to select your topic, focus or narrow it, determine your general purpose, formulate your specific purpose, and construct a thesis statement. In persuasive speaking, you can add one additional step: State your proposition. Let's make sure that we understand the difference between a proposition and a thesis statement.

For example, if you speak on the topic of improving education, you may narrow this broad subject and select as your specific purpose to persuade the audience that teacher salaries should be increased. Your basic position—"teacher salaries should be increased"—can be thought of as a proposition. A **proposition** is a declarative sentence expressing a judgment you want the audience to accept. Notice that this proposition *expresses a judgment* that *is debatable* and that *requires proof.* We will discuss these three characteristics of propositions in the next section.

ad hominem: a fallacy that urges listeners to reject an idea because of the allegedly poor character of the person voicing it; name calling.

proposition: a declarative sentence expressing a judgment a speaker wants listeners to accept.

Your thesis statement, in contrast, lists the reasons you offer to prove your proposition. In the preceding example, your thesis statement could be this: Higher teacher salaries would recruit better teachers, retain better teachers, and improve student learning. The following example also demonstrates the difference between a proposition and a thesis statement:

Proposition: The new campus classroom building should be named Richter Hall.

Specific Purpose: To persuade the audience that the new classroom building should be named for Louise Richter.

Thesis Statement: The new classroom building should be named for Louise Richter, an outstanding teacher, advisor, and friend.

Key Ideas: I. The name of the new classroom building should honor an outstanding educator.

II. Louise Richter deserves this recognition.
A. She was an outstanding teacher.
B. She was an outstanding advisor to student organizations.
C. She was a cherished friend.

Notice again that this proposition expresses a judgment, while the thesis statement includes the reasons the speaker will offer to prove the proposition.

Characteristics of Propositions

If you formulate a well-worded proposition early in preparing your persuasive speech, you will be sure of your persuasive goal and can keep it firmly in mind. Your proposition also helps you to focus your persuasive speech and test the relevance of supporting ideas as you develop them. Devising your proposition can be relatively easy. As we suggested before, propositions are marked by three characteristics.

key points

Requirements of Propositions

1. Propositions express a judgment.
2. Propositions are debatable.
3. Propositions require proof.

Propositions Express a Judgment. A proposition for a persuasive speech states the position you will defend. Consequently, it should be worded as a declarative sentence expressing your position. If you advocate statehood for Puerto Rico, you could word your proposition like this: The United States should grant Puerto Rico statehood. This simple declarative sentence clearly states your position on the issue.

Sometimes, however, you may be interested in a topic but lack enough information to have developed a position on it. In this case, you may first want to phrase a question to guide your research. Once you answer the question, you can then develop your proposition.

Mark was a criminal justice student interested in the issue of the death penalty. He had read an article discussing the pros and cons of capital punishment for juveniles convicted of capital crimes, but he had not developed his own position on the issue. To guide his research, Mark worded the following question: Is the death penalty for juveniles cruel and unusual punishment? He researched the topic, reading articles by scholars and jurists on both sides of the issue. He made a list of arguments for and against capital punishment for juveniles. Although Mark supported capital punishment for adult offenders, his research convinced him to oppose it for juveniles. The proposition he subsequently decided to defend was "The death penalty for juveniles is cruel and unusual punishment." By phrasing his position statement, writing it out, and keeping it in front of him as he continued researching and assembling his arguments, Mark was able to keep his speech focused on arguments against capital punishment for juveniles.

Propositions Are Debatable. Propositions are appropriate for persuasive speeches only if they are debatable. In other words, the judgment must include some degree of controversy. The proposition "The earth revolves around the sun" is not a good proposition for a persuasive speech because you are unlikely to find any qualified authority today opposing that statement. We now accept it as fact. Once we accept a proposition as fact, it ceases to be an appropriate topic for persuasive speeches. However, in the sixteenth century, when Copernicus's heliocentric theory opposed governmental and religious teaching as well as popular opinion, the topic was debatable. It was then a proposition appropriate for persuasive speaking.

Another example of a proposition that probably is not debatable is "Jack Ruby killed Lee Harvey Oswald." Millions of people watched the shooting live on television or saw it rebroadcast. The filmed account of the shooting convinced most people to accept the statement as fact. On the other hand, the proposition "Lee Harvey Oswald killed John F. Kennedy" is debatable and has been the subject of much discussion. Despite the findings of the Warren Commission Report, several theories of the assassination remain.

Propositions Require Proof. Finally, propositions require proof. A proposition is an assertion, and assertions are statements that have not yet been proven. Your objective as a persuasive speaker is to offer compelling reasons for listeners to accept your proposition. As we discussed earlier in this chapter, you may support your proposition with arguments from example, analogy, cause, deduction, or authority.

Types of Propositions

Propositions for persuasive speeches are of three types: fact, value, and policy. The type of organization and support materials you will use depends on the type of proposition you defend.

Propositions of Fact. A **proposition of fact** focuses on belief. You ask the audience to affirm the truth or falsity of a statement. The following are examples of propositions of fact:

Electric automobiles are commercially feasible.

Conversion to a cashless society would reduce sales of illegal drugs.

Access to math tutors increases students' grades in mathematics courses.

Gun control laws violate the second amendment of the U.S. Constitution.

An aspirin a day can reduce the risk of heart disease.

Jennifer's speech on random drug testing was a speech on a proposition of fact. Jennifer defended this proposition: Random drug testing on the job decreases workplace drug use. Her specific purpose and key ideas were as follows:

Specific Purpose: To convince the audience that random drug testing (RDT) decreases workplace drug use.

Key Ideas: I. RDT deters casual drug use.

II. RDT helps decrease drug addiction.

A. Users are identified.

B. Users are encouraged to seek therapy.

proposition of fact: an assertion about the truth or falsity of a statement.

Propositions of Value. A proposition of value requires a judgment on the worth of an idea or action. You ask the audience to determine the "goodness" or "badness" of something, as in this proposition: "Corporal punishment in schools is wrong." Remember Mark's speech defending the proposition "The death penalty for juveniles is cruel and unusual punishment"? That too was a proposition of value. Propositions of value can also ask you to compare two items and determine which is better, as in Sir William Blackstone's statement, "It is better that ten guilty persons escape than one innocent suffer." Other propositions of value include:

Censorship is a greater evil than pornography.

Minority rule is morally indefensible.

Retribution is a more important goal of criminal justice than rehabilitation.

Civil disobedience is justifiable in a democracy.

Educational tracking of students by ability perpetuates social and racial inequality.

Suppose you decided to persuade your audience that free agency is bad for professional sports. You could develop your speech on this value proposition as follows:

Specific Purpose: To persuade the audience that free agency is hurting professional sports.

Key Ideas: I. It destroys the competitive balance of teams.

II. It undermines the financial solvency of teams.

III. It creates bad role models for kids.

Another example of a speech on a proposition of value is Cary's speech on "infotainment," the media's blending of news and entertainment:

Specific Purpose: To persuade the audience that "infotainment" harms the public's right to know.

Key Ideas: I. News reenactments mislead the public.

II. Docudramas misinform the public.

Propositions of Policy. A proposition of policy advocates a course of action. You ask the audience to endorse a policy or to commit themselves to some action. These statements usually include the word *should*. Here are some examples of policy propositions:

College athletes should be paid.

Nonviolent offenders should be excluded from "three strikes and you're out" sentencing.

There should be a ban on advertising of all tobacco products.

Students should be able to repay student loans through community service.

The United States should convert to the metric system.

Duane wanted to persuade his classmates and instructor to support the student government association's proposal to change from a quarter to a semester academic calendar. Organizing his speech topically, he presented three benefits to a semester system.

Specific Purpose: To persuade the audience that this college should adopt a semester calendar.

Key Ideas: I. Semesters allow more time for research in theory courses.

II. Semesters allow more time for skill development in performance courses.

III. Semester credits are easier to transfer to other institutions.

proposition of value: an assertion about the relative worth of an idea or action.

proposition of policy: a statement requesting support for a course of action.

Monroe's Motivated Sequence

In Chapters 9 and 10 we discussed how to organize the introduction, body, and conclusion of a speech. Those guidelines apply to the organization of persuasive, as well as informative, speeches. One type of persuasive speech, the speech to actuate, provides an interesting challenge to speakers. They must move their listeners to action using a progression of motivated steps. One of the most popular patterns for organizing the superstructure of a speech to actuate was developed by Alan Monroe in the 1930s.[12] Called "the motivated sequence," this pattern uses strategies you've already studied and applied in your speeches. The motivated sequence is particularly appropriate when you discuss a well-known or easily established problem. Monroe drew from the conclusions of educator and philosopher John Dewey that persuasion is best accomplished if a speaker moves a listener sequentially through a series of steps.[13] **Monroe's motivated sequence,** then, includes the following five steps, or stages: attention, need, satisfaction, visualization, and action.

Monroe argued that speakers must first command the *attention* of their listeners. Suppose your geographic area is experiencing a summer drought. You could begin your speech with a description of the landscape as you approached your campus a year ago, describing in detail the green grass, the verdant foliage, and the colorful, fragrant flowers. You then contrast the landscape of a year ago with its look now: bland, brown, and blossomless. With these contrasting visual images, you try to capture the attention and interest of your audience.

A speaker's second objective is to establish a *need*. This step is similar to the problem and need steps in the problem–solution and need–plan patterns of organizing a speech. For example, your speech on the drought situation could illustrate how an inadequate water supply hurts not only the beauty of the landscape but also agricultural production, certain industrial processes, and, ultimately, the economy of the entire region.

When you dramatize a problem, you create an urgency to redress it. In the *satisfaction* step of the motivated sequence, you propose a way to solve, or at least minimize, the problem. You may suggest voluntary or mandatory conservation as a short-term solution to the water shortage crisis in your area. As a longer-range solution, you may ask your audience to consider the merits of planting grasses, shrubs, and other plants requiring less water. You may advocate that the city adopt and enforce stricter regulations of water use by businesses, or that it develop alternative water sources.

However, Monroe argued that simply proposing a solution is seldom sufficient to bring about change. Through *visualization*, Monroe's fourth step, a speaker seeks to intensify an audience's desire to adopt and implement the proposed solution. You could direct the audience to look out the window at their campus and then ask if that is the scenery they want. More often, though, you create word pictures for the audience to visualize. Without adequate water, you could argue, crops will die, family farms will be foreclosed upon, industries will not relocate to the area, and the quality of life for everyone in the area will be depressed. In contrast, you could refer to the landscape of a year ago, the image you depicted as you began your speech. The future can be colored in green, red, yellow, and blue, and it can represent growth and vitality.

The final step of the motivated sequence is the *action* you request of your listeners. It is not enough to know that something must be done; the audience must know what you want them to do, and your request must be within their power to act. Do you want them to join you in voluntary conservation by watering their lawns in the evening when less water will evaporate, or by washing their cars less frequently? Are you asking them to sign petitions pressuring the city council to adopt mandatory conservation

Monroe's motivated sequence: a persuasive pattern composed of (1) getting the audience's attention, (2) establishing a need, (3) offering a proposal to satisfy the need, (4) inviting listeners to visualize the results, and (5) requesting action.

measures when the water table sinks to a designated level? Conclude your speech with a strong appeal for specific, reasonable action.

Dolly decided that her final speech would be a speech to actuate; she wanted her classmates to decide to study a foreign language. She researched articles she found in the library and on the Internet. She interviewed a professor in the foreign languages department and borrowed some brochures published by the Modern Language Association. After taking extensive notes, she opened a new computer file and typed five phrases: Attention Step, Need Step, Satisfaction Step, Visualization Step, and Action Step. She then began to draft the framework for her speech. Using the motivated sequence helped Dolly move her listeners step-by-step to her final request for action.

Attention Step

In January 1997 Diane Crispell, executive editor of *American Demographics*, observed that "America is a linguistic paradox. Even as it boasts a richly diverse population speaking a host of languages, it encourages immigrants to forsake their mother tongues and doesn't encourage native English speakers to acquire foreign-language skills." Those who reject opportunities to connect with other cultures do so at their personal and professional peril. Studying a foreign language can give you a competitive edge. Learning a foreign language develops your communication skills, your analytical skills, and your employment opportunities.

Need Step

College students need a variety of competencies for personal, academic, and career success.

A. Communication skills are essential in each of these areas.
B. Problem-solving skills are necessary to function successfully in life.
C. An understanding of other cultures is increasingly important in a global society.

Satisfaction Step

Studying a foreign language can give you a competitive edge.

A. It improves your communication skills.
B. It develops your analytical skills.
C. It provides employment advantages.

Visualization Step

Wouldn't it be nice to take a friend to a romantic French movie and be able to understand the dialogue without having to read the translation? Or, when visiting another country, to be able to pick up a newspaper and to read the headlines? Or, when you land that dream job, to be able to negotiate an important business deal with that client from another country, in part because you spoke her language and understood the customs of her culture?

Action Step

Before the semester is over, I want you to take that step that will give you a competitive edge in your personal, academic, and professional life.

A. Enroll in a foreign language class while you are in college.
B. Visit the International Programs Office, and sign up for a study abroad program.
C. Buy some foreign language self-study learning tapes.
D. Begin learning a foreign language from a friend from another culture.

Annotated Sample Speech

Wesley Schawe delivered the following persuasive speech and placed second at the 1999 Interstate Oratorical Association National Speech Contest. As you read his speech, notice how he used Monroe's motivated sequence to frame his problem–solution discussion of diploma mills.

Diploma Mills[14]

Wesley Schawe

Kansas State University

1 In one of the first college classes I ever took, the professor thought he was funny when I handed him my paper and he said, "Oh, B–." There are some days when that would be just fine. But more often, it feels good to know that I'm actually earning my degree. Apparently not everyone feels that way. Hundreds of thousands of college students are taking part in one of the fastest growing trends in education—paying money to not get one.

2 The February 11, 1999, *Houston Chronicle* points out that diploma mills, or universities that offer degrees all the way up to a doctorate just by sending in money and a short paper, are popping up all over the country. These colleges sound legitimate—like Frederick Taylor University in California or the American International University in Alabama—but in truth have no campus, usually no faculty, and nothing close to legitimate accreditation. The "dean" of one of these colleges told the December 12, 1998, *20/20* that they really did weigh their papers to assign grades.

3 As the rest of us work to get our degrees the old-fashioned way, *20/20* tells us that just one of these diploma mills handed out over 30,000 degrees in six years. Considering that the March 12, 1999, *St. Louis Post Dispatch* points out that among them are firefighters, police officers, and building inspectors who we count on for protection on a daily basis, but who don't even have a recognized degree in that area, these phony universities have managed to threaten our education and public safety at the same time. We need to shut down diploma mills by first learning how big of a problem they are, secondly what caused them to become so popular, and finally what we can do to make sure they don't stay that way.

4 First, we have to get some grasp on the two problems associated with diploma mills—the mills themselves and the students who take advantage of them. First, the February 22, *Boston Globe* states that there are over 350 diploma mills worldwide—schools like Columbia State University, or Trinity College and University.

5 Nina Nielsen saw an ad for Columbia State and was excited to know that there was a way she could work toward her doctorate, but still keep her teaching job in Omaha, Nebraska. She told the *U.S. News and World Report* on September 9, 1998, that she couldn't believe it—every time she sent in a chapter of her dissertation, she got it back without any comments. She didn't know her work was that good—probably because it wasn't. In the January 1, 1999, *Atlanta Journal and Constitution,* Louisiana Attorney General Richard Leyoub points out that Columbia State has no faculty. If you send in $2,000, they promise you a bachelor's degree in 27 days. A doctorate isn't so easy. It costs $2,800, and you have to write a 12-page dissertation.

6 Some of them don't even worry about distinguishing themselves from others. As the April 5, 1998, *Pittsburgh Post-Gazette* points out, a degree from Washington University sounds pretty impressive, until you find out that it's not the one in St. Louis, but one in Bryn Mawr, Pennsylvania. The President of Washington University laughed as he told the *Gazette,* "I'm not in it for education. I'm in it for money."

7 And this is where the second big problem with diploma mills arises. If you were given the chance to get your degree by paying a fourth or even a tenth of

Attention

In his introduction (paragraphs 1–3), Wesley focuses his audience's *attention* on the problem of diploma mills. He seeks to motivate their concern for this topic by asserting that these phony institutions "threaten our education and public safety." He appeals to his listeners' self-interest to protect the integrity of their academic degrees.

Need

Wesley discusses the problems of and causes for diploma mills in paragraphs 4–12. He establishes the *need* for reform by documenting that hundreds of these schools exist, that they mislead unsuspecting students who enroll, and that they foster an inadequately trained workforce.

what you're paying now, then just reading a book and writing a report over it, wouldn't you think something was a little strange? Carl Pack, a state inspector told *20/20* that there may be a few people who are robbed by diploma mills. But there are far more who know exactly what they're doing. In many instances, the employer doesn't even know the difference.

8 Washington University was more than happy to send me a list five pages long of the companies who have hired their graduates—including Boeing, Coca-Cola, American Express, and even our own military. For an employer who doesn't know the difference, we're the ones who are losing out: losing pay raises, job offers, promotions. More fundamentally, the degree that we're working so hard to attain is being diminished by those who can get the exact same thing with just a big check.

9 So how did we arrive at the point where a diploma is easier to get with a credit card than with a good GPA? Secondly, it's important to see what has led to this increased enrollment at our diploma mills. The cause is two-fold: the increase in distance education and the educational demands we've set for ourselves.

10 First, the rise of the World Wide Web has lead to more and more courses being taught outside of the classroom. At my college, we have some degrees you can get entirely over the Internet. So now that an actual campus is no longer required to get a diploma, it doesn't take more than a good-looking Web page to appear to be a legitimate institution.

11 I visited the home page of Monticello University, named by the *Irish Times* on November 24, 1998, as one of the twelve biggest diploma mills in the U.S. The page was incredibly professional, complete with an original school seal and even a section titled accreditation—usually a dead giveaway for diploma mills. And sure enough, Monticello is accredited by the International Commission for Excellence in Higher Education. But if you read the fine print on another page, you'd see that the International Commission for Excellence in Higher Education was formed by the Board of Trustees at Monticello so they could turn around and accredit themselves. I'll be the first to admit that there's nothing illegal about this. But as National Public Radio's *All Things Considered* stated on October 3, 1998, when real colleges and diploma mills both offer degrees online, the differences between the two are sometimes hard to find.

12 But distance education isn't the only reason diploma mills are successful, as we must secondly take a look at the emphasis we're placing on getting an advanced degree. I'm not about to say that that's entirely a bad thing. But how many businesses throughout the country reward advanced degrees with pay raises and better promotions? The March 3, 1999, *Hartford Courant* points out that nearly the entire firefighting department in Hartford, Connecticut, received a raise after buying degrees from a diploma mill in Missouri. The June 11, 1998, *Chicago Sun-Times* points out that if a master's degree is going to get you a bonus no matter where it comes from, people are going to take shortcuts, and usually they're going to get away with it.

13 It'd be easy to say that if someone's dumb enough to fall for a diploma mill or an employer's not smart enough to check, then that's their problem. But how many of us here are willing to set aside four or more years of our life and money that we can't even afford to watch someone come out with the same degree in three months from a university that's nothing more than a mailbox and a fancy name?

14 It's time that we take some action and stop letting diploma mills set the educational standard. There are three steps that need to be taken, and our state governments can lead the way with step one: shutting down the illegal diploma mills. Now granted, there's nothing the states can do if I want to name myself the dean of the newest Wesleyan College and get my accreditation from my grandparents. But as the October 27, 1998, *Times-Picayune* points out, when schools like Columbia State and Cambridge State falsely claim accreditation from the real

Visualization

In paragraph 13, Wesley encourages his listeners to consider solutions to the problem by *visualizing* how they may be harmed if nothing is changed.

Satisfaction

In paragraphs 14–16, Wesley seeks to *satisfy* the need for a change by presenting a three-step solution of government and individual action.

agencies, then they've gone too far. The *U.S. News & World Report* points out that so many of these colleges were setting up in Louisiana that the first thing you heard if you called the Attorney General's office was, "To report a diploma mill, press 1." Louisiana responded by shutting down Columbia State and Cambridge, but Cambridge has already reopened in Hawaii. Every state must aggressively track down illegal diploma mills, because until they do, there will always be at least one more place to go.

15 While this will help stop the illegal diploma mills, it won't affect the majority of legal ones—no matter how unethical. That's why it's up to us to take the second step. If you're looking at colleges online, the best thing to do is check for legitimate accreditation. As the *Boston Globe* states, the one thing that most people don't know is that national accreditation by the Department of Education no longer exists, except in certain fields. The November 11, 1998, *New York Times* points out that there are eight regional accrediting agencies. To see if your prospective school is legitimate, call the Department of Education in the state where the school is located, and they can tell you for sure.

16 But let's face it, most diploma mill graduates know exactly what they're doing. But other than telling them that they're an embarrassment to the educational system, what can we do? If the reason employers are hiring these graduates, even paying for their degrees, is because they don't know any better, then the best thing we can possibly do is step three: letting people know the difference. We may never be in the position to directly hire anybody. But as employees, even as students, we're often a formal or informal part of the selection process. For example, this semester I'm serving on a search committee for a new faculty member in my department. If a potential employee's degree comes from a college you've never heard of, check it out. In all fairness, you may learn several good things about the employee and the college. But at the same time, a simple call to the state of California could tell you that CULA—the City University of Los Angeles—is not the same thing as UCLA, and more importantly, is not accredited. If companies would just tell their employees from the start that a diploma mill won't get them a promotion, then they won't even try.

17 Among the diploma mill graduates I read about were a medical engineer, a judge, a police officer, and a jailed Hamas terrorist. When they claim to have a degree for everything, they may not be kidding. But when it comes to offering an education, it's a completely different story. By examining diploma mills, what caused their success, and how we can stop them, we've seen that these schools may get a kick out of weighing your paper for a grade; but by shutting these diploma mills down, we can finally tip the scales in our favor.

Visualization

After presenting his solution to the problem, Wesley asks his audience (in paragraph 16) to *visualize* how they can become part of the solution. They can become agents of change as students and future employees to help stop the harms caused by diploma mills.

Action

In paragraphs 15 and 16, Wesley requested some specific actions from his audience. Wesley concludes his speech with a final call for action—action that will close the diploma mills and "tip the scales in our favor."

Summary

Persuasion is the art of affecting other people's values, beliefs, attitudes, or behaviors. The logical impact of a persuasive speech springs from a speaker's *evidence* and reasoning. To be an effective persuader, you must know how to structure a valid argument, how to detect flaws in reasoning, and how to word propositions. If you are delivering a speech to actuate, you also need to have a clear grasp of the motivational superstructure of your message. The three steps of structuring an argument are (1) to make a claim you want the audience to accept, (2) to supply evidence supporting that claim, and (3) to explain how the evidence proves the claim. The validity of any claim ultimately depends on the quality of the evidence supporting it.

Speakers sometimes select a particular persuasive topic because they hear or read an argument they wish to oppose. The act of countering one argument with another is called refutation. To refute an argument, follow this four-step *refutational strategy*. First, state the position you are refuting. Second, state your own position. Third, support your position with evidence. And fourth, show how your position undermines the argument you oppose.

To give listeners a reason to accept a persuasive claim, speakers may use any of five types of arguments. First, *argument by example* uses specific instances to support a general claim. In order for an argument by example to be valid, the speaker must use examples that are true, relevant to the claim, sufficient in number, and representative. Second, *argument by analogy* links two concepts, conditions, or experiences and claims that what is true of one will be true of the other. The validity of argument by analogy depends upon the quality of the comparison a speaker develops. To test that analogy, ask two questions: (1) Are the similarities between the cases relevant? and (2) Are any differences between the two cases relevant?

Argument by cause, the third type of argument, links two concepts, conditions, or experiences and claims that one causes the other. A speaker arguing by cause can move listeners' attention forward from cause to effect or can trace effects back to their causes. To test the validity of the cause–effect relationship, speakers and listeners should consider three questions: (1) Does a causal relationship exist? (2) Could the presumed cause produce the effect? and (3) Could the effect result from other causes?

A fourth type of argument, *deductive argument,* employs a pattern called a *syllogism,* consisting of three parts. The major premise is a claim about a general group of people, events, or conditions. The minor premise places a person, event, or condition into that general class. And the conclusion argues that what is true of the general class is also true of the specific instance. In order for an argument by deduction to be valid, both the major and minor premises must be true and they must be related.

Finally, *argument by authority* uses testimony from an expert source to prove a speaker's claim. The validity of this type of argument depends upon the credibility the authority has with the audience. To be credible, the source should be competent and unbiased.

Both speakers and listeners must watch out for logical flaws or *fallacies* in persuasive arguments. Fallacious arguments are particularly dangerous because they may resemble sound reasoning as we read or listen to them. Unfortunately, ten fallacies of argument are common. The fallacy of *hasty generalization* involves making claims on the basis of insufficient or unrepresentative examples. *False analogy* occurs when an argument by analogy compares entities that have critical differences. *Post hoc ergo propter hoc* falsely argues that because event A preceded event B, A caused B. It confuses chronology with causation. The *slippery slope* fallacy asserts that one event inevitably unleashes a series of events. The *red herring* fallacy introduces irrelevant issues to deflect attention from the true question under discussion. The fallacy called *appeal to tradition* asserts that old ways of doing things are correct or best, simply because they are traditional. A *false dilemma* argues that we must choose between two alternatives, when in reality we may have a range of options. The fallacy of *false authority* uses testimony from sources who have no real expertise on the topic in question. The *bandwagon* fallacy argues that we should behave or think a particular way because most people do. Finally, the *ad hominem* fallacy urges listeners to reject an idea because of allegations about the character, politics, religion, or lifestyle of the person voicing the idea.

All persuasive speeches advocate *propositions,* position statements the speaker wants listeners to accept. Persuasive propositions must be stated as a declarative sentence expressing a judgment, must be debatable, and require proof in order to be accepted. The three types of persuasive propositions are propositions of fact, propositions of value, and propositions of policy. *Propositions of fact* ask the audience to accept the truth or falsity of a statement. *Propositions of value* ask the audience to determine the relative worth of an idea or action. *Propositions of policy* ask the audience to support a course of action.

A persuasive speech must move listeners through a series of steps. *Monroe's motivated sequence* is a formal, five-step pattern for moving listeners to belief or action. It consists of (1) getting the attention of your listeners, (2) clarifying the need, (3) showing how to satisfy that need, (4) visualizing the solution, and (5) requesting action.

Identifying a Claim and Evaluating Evidence

Read the transcript of Wesley Schawe's speech, "Diploma Mills," in this chapter. Before offering a solution, Wesley discusses the problems and causes of diploma mills. As you read through his speech, make a list of the problems and causes he defines, then analyze how he develops each one. What is the claim? What supporting materials does Wesley offer to support that claim? Does the evidence prove the point? Why or why not? Write down a few suggestions you could offer Wesley to make his arguments stronger and more persuasive.

practice critique

Exercises

1. You have been asked to visit your former high school to speak to a group of college-bound students. The school's counselor has asked you to speak on the topic "College Years Are the Best Years of Your Life!" Construct three arguments that support this position. Give an example of how your speech could use each of the types of argument: example, analogy, cause, deduction, and authority.

2. Using argument by analogy, construct a short speech on one or more of the following topics. What similarities between the two entities make your analogy credible? What differences undermine the believability of each statement?
   a. Being in college is like being in a demolition derby.
   b. Life is like an athletic contest.
   c. Studying for an exam is like tying your shoe.
   d. Marriage is like gardening.
   e. A job interview is like an audition for a role in a film.

3. Determine whether each of the following statements is a proposition of fact, value, or policy.
   a. The university should build a new library.
   b. A new library would cost the university seven million dollars.
   c. It is more important to build a new library than to expand our athletic facilities.
   d. Sex education encourages sexual activity among schoolchildren.
   e. The FDA should reduce required testing for experimental drugs to fight life-threatening illnesses.
   f. Workers in high-stress jobs should be subject to random periodic drug testing.
   g. *Citizen Kane* is the best American film ever made.
   h. It is more important for a country to do good than to feel good.
   i. If the proposed tuition increase is adopted, the university may lose up to 500 students.
   j. U.S. K–12 schools should adopt a 12-month schedule.

4. Identify the major premise, minor premise, and conclusion in each of the following groups of statements:
   a. *Inquiring Minds* should be aired on the Trashy Cable Network.
      Inquiring Minds is a fluffy news show.
      All fluffy news shows should be aired on the Trashy Cable Network.

    b. A high grade-point average is important to Charlotte.
       Today's college students value high grade-point averages.
       Charlotte is a college student.
    c. A lot of the dance music of the 1990s sounded like disco music of the 1970s.
       A lot of dance music of the 1990s was awful.
       The disco music of the 1970s was awful.

5. Find an editorial from a recent campus, local, or national newspaper. Identify the different types of arguments the writer used.

6. Locate examples of each of the fallacies discussed in this chapter. Examine advertisements in newspapers, in magazines, on radio, on television, and on the Internet. Read editorials, letters to the editor, and transcripts of speeches.

7. Apply the three criteria for well-worded propositions by writing specific propositions on the following topics:
   a. Affirmative action
   b. Lotteries
   c. Funding of the National Endowment for the Arts
   d. Feminism
   e. Living wills

8. Write a proposition analysis thinkpiece on the topic you have selected for a persuasive speech.
   a. Write the proposition you intend to support or oppose.
   b. Define key or ambiguous terms.
   c. Determine the important debatable issues.
   d. Suggest types of supporting materials necessary to prove your points.

9. Write a proposition of fact, value, and policy for each of the following topic areas.
   a. Term limits for elected officials
   b. Electric cars
   c. A foreign language requirement for all college students
   d. Competency tests for teachers
   e. Funding for cancer research

10. Consider the topic "This college should use only a pass-fail grading system." Prepare an argument for this topic using the 4 S structure. Then refute your argument using the four-step refutational strategy.

11. Select a topic not discussed in this chapter, and describe how you might go about developing it using each step of Monroe's motivated sequence.

Notes

1. Mark Twain, *Life on the Mississippi* (New York: Harper, 1917) 156.
2. Thomas Gilovich, *How We Know What Isn't So* (New York: Free, 1991) 6.
3. Aristotle, *The Rhetoric of Aristotle*, trans. Lane Cooper (New York: Appleton, 1932) 220.
4. For a more elaborate discussion of the structure of an argument, see Stephen Toulmin, *The Uses of Argument* (New York: Cambridge UP, 1974).
5. Lindsay Wolfgang, "Burglar Bars," *Winning Orations, 1998* (Mankato, MN: Interstate Oratorical Association, 1998) 22–23.
6. Tammy Frisby, "Floss or Die," *Winning Orations, 1998* (Mankato, MN: Interstate Oratorical Association, 1998) 68–69.
7. Ellen Wartella, "The Context of Television Violence," Arnold Lecture presented at the Speech Communication Association Annual Convention, Marriott Hotel & Marina, San Diego, 23 Nov. 1996.

8. John M. Ericson and James J. Murphy with Raymond Bud Zeuschner, *The Debater's Guide,* rev. ed. (Carbondale, IL: Southern Illinois UP, 1987) 139.

9. *The New York Public Library Desk Reference,* 2nd ed. (New York: Stonesong-Simon, 1993) 273.

10. Bruce N. Waller, *Critical Thinking: Consider the Verdict* (Englewood Cliffs, NJ: Prentice, 1988) 30.

11. W. Ward Fearnside and William B. Holther, *Fallacy—The Counterfeit of Argument* (Englewood Cliffs, NJ: Prentice, 1959) 92.

12. Raymie E. McKerrow, Bruce E. Gronbeck, Douglas Ehninger, and Alan H. Monroe, *Principles and Types of Speech Communication,* 14th ed. (New York: Addison-Longman, 2000) 153–61. See also: Alan H. Monroe, *Principles and Types of Speech* (Chicago: Scott, 1935).

13. See our discussion of Dewey's Steps to Reflective Thinking in Chapter 19, pp. 443–46.

14. Wesley Schawe, "Diploma Mills," *Winning Orations, 1999* (Mankato, MN: Interstate Oratorical Association, 1999) 47–50.

If we use common words on a great occasion, they are the most striking, because they are felt at once to have a particular meaning, like old banners, or everyday clothes, hung up in a sacred place.

—George Eliot

c h a p t e r **18**

Speaking on Special Occasions

On the morning of July 23, 1999, Senator Ted Kennedy delivered the eulogy for his nephew, John F. Kennedy, Jr. Woven with a combination of witty anecdotes, vivid images, and emotional eloquence, it was the type of speech the senator has unfortunately had reason to perfect. He had previously eulogized two other nephews, in 1997 and 1984. In 1995, he delivered the eulogy for his mother, Rose. A year before that he spoke at a memorial service for sister-in-law Jacqueline Kennedy Onassis. In 1990, he eulogized his brother-in-law Steve Smith; in 1969, his father Joseph Kennedy. In 1968, he spoke for his family and the nation for the first time when he eulogized his slain brother Robert F. Kennedy. In light of all those memorials, his words near the end of his remarks about JFK, Jr., take on special poignancy: "We dared to think . . . that this John Kennedy would live to comb gray hair, with his beloved Carolyn by his side. But like his father, he had every gift but length of years" (see Appendix B).

In November of 1995, sports commentator Bob Costas delivered a eulogy at the funeral of baseball great Mickey Mantle. He spoke, in part, about "the sheer grace of that ninth inning—the humility, the sense of humor, the total absence of self-pity, the simple eloquence and honesty of his pleas to others to take heed of his mistakes."[1]

In April 1993, Elie Wiesel, 1986 winner of the Nobel Prize for Peace, spoke at ceremonies to dedicate the United States Holocaust Memorial Museum in Washington, D.C. He described a Jewish woman from the Carpathian mountains who was confused when she read about the Warsaw Ghetto uprising. "Treblinka, Ponar, Belzec, Chelmno, Birkenau; she had never heard of these places. One year later, together with her entire family, she was in a cattle-car traveling to the black-hole of history named Auschwitz." Many in the audience were quietly weeping as Wiesel revealed at the end of his speech, "She was my mother."[2]

Sample Speeches
http://www.
executive-speaker.
com/spchlist.html
Visit this site, maintained by the Executive Speaker Company, to browse the texts of more than 20 speeches by business executives speaking on a variety of special occasions.

Though none of us has the celebrity or visibility of the individuals mentioned in these examples, you can count on being called upon to deliver a speech on some special occasion: a speech introducing a guest speaker at a club meeting, a speech accepting an award from a civic group, or a eulogy at the funeral of a relative or friend. In addition to these "ordinary" special occasions, remember some of the truly special occasions we mentioned in Chapter 1: speaking to accept a Heisman Trophy, a Tony, or an Academy Award, or to present important research findings to a national convention and to the media.

To speak your best on any of these special occasions, you must consider the customs and audience expectations in each case. In this chapter, we will discuss eight special occasions or special circumstances for public speeches: the speech of introduction, the speech of presentation, the acceptance speech, the speech of tribute, the speech to entertain, the impromptu speech, the question-answer period, and the videotaped speech. You will learn guidelines for each of these types of speeches and read examples of many of them. This information can serve you well beyond the classroom and prepare you for any occasion when you are requested, invited, or expected to speak.

The Speech of Introduction

One of the most common types of special-occasion speeches is the **speech of introduction.** Some people use that phrase to indicate speeches by people introducing themselves to an audience. As we use the phrase in this chapter, however, we mean a speech introducing a featured speaker. The following guidelines will help you prepare such a speech of introduction.

speech of introduction: a speech introducing a featured speaker to an audience.

Guidelines for the Speech of Introduction

1. Focus on the featured speaker.
2. Be brief.
3. Establish the speaker's credibility.

4. Create realistic expectations.
5. Set the tone for the speech.

key points

The first guideline to remember is to *keep the focus on the person being introduced.* The audience has not gathered to hear you, so don't upstage the featured speaker. Keep your remarks short, simple, and sincere.

In order to achieve the first guideline, you will want to follow the second: *Be brief.* If you can, request and get a copy of the speaker's résumé. This will give you a body of information to select from when preparing your introductory remarks. The key word in that last sentence is *select.* Your listeners will tune out quickly if your introduction is a lengthy chronology of jobs or events in a person's life. Highlight key information only.

A third guideline is to *establish the speaker's credibility on the topic.* You do this by presenting the speaker's credentials. As you prepare your speech of introduction, ask and answer questions such as these: What makes the speaker qualified to speak on the subject? What education and experiences make the speaker's insights worthy of our belief?

Fourth, remember to *create realistic expectations.* Genuine praise is commendable, just be careful not to oversell the speaker. Can you imagine walking to the microphone after the following introduction: "Our speaker tonight is one of the great speakers in this country. I heard her last year, and she had us laughing until our sides hurt. She will keep you spellbound from her first word to her last. Get ready for the best speech you've heard in your entire life!"

Finally, you should phrase your remarks to *establish a tone consistent with the speaker's presentation.* Would you give a humorous introduction for a speaker whose topic is "The Grieving Process: What to Do When a Loved One Dies"? Of course not. On the other hand, if the evening is designed for merriment, your introduction should help set that mood.

Communication professors should certainly know how to introduce a featured speaker. In the following example, Professor Don Ochs of the University of Iowa did an exemplary job of introducing his longtime colleague, Professor Samuel L. Becker. Becker was the keynote speaker at the Central States Communication Association convention in Chicago on April 12, 1991. You'll see that Ochs uses some communication jargon because he is speaking to a group of communication professionals. Notice, though, how Ochs's brief, cordial remarks focus on Becker, establishing his credibility and setting the tone for Becker's informative and inspirational speech:

> Thirty years ago I walked out of an Iowa City store onto the main street and noticed Sam Becker walking about twenty feet ahead of me. His youngest daughter was alongside Sam but she was terribly upset about something; crying, and obviously hurt about something. Sam put his arm around his daughter and, in the space of two blocks, said something that comforted and fixed the problem. She was smiling when they parted company.
>
> I share this snapshot of Sam with you because, for me, it captures Sam's approach to life, higher education, scholarship, and our profession.
>
> Sam Becker has figuratively put his arm around difficulties and problems for his entire career. He's made all of us as teachers and scholars better persons and better professionals with his intellect, his vision, his energy, and his instinctive willingness to help.

As a rhetorician I would much prefer to introduce Sam with figures and tropes, with synechdoche, litotes, and hyperbole. But Sam is a social scientist, so I will be quantitative instead.

How much has Sam helped us? Sam has taught at four universities; written six books; been active in eight professional associations; authored ten monographs; served on twelve editorial boards; worked on evaluation teams for thirty-two colleges and universities; served on thirty-six university committees; lectured at fifty colleges and universities; directed fifty-five PhDs; and authored 105 articles. Without doubt, he has helped and assisted and supported all of us. Our speaker today, Sam Becker.[3]

The Speech of Presentation

The **speech of presentation** confers an award, a prize, or some other form of special recognition on an individual or a group. Such speeches are typically made on special occasions: after banquets or parties; as parts of business meetings or sessions of a convention; or at awards ceremonies such as the Tony Awards, the Academy Awards, or the Grammy Awards, during which many people will be recognized.

We will restrict our discussion of the speech of presentation to prepared statements commenting on and presenting an award to an individual or group. Thus, remarks made by a presenter about an actor honored with the American Film Institute's Lifetime Achievement Award would qualify as a speech of presentation; opening the envelope and reading the winner of the Grammy Award for Song of the Year is really an announcement rather than a prepared speech. When you give a speech of presentation, let the nature and importance of the award being presented, as well as the occasion on which it is being presented, shape your remarks. The following guidelines will help you plan this special-occasion speech.

key points

Guidelines for the Speech of Presentation

1. **State the purpose of the award or recognition.**
2. **State the recipient's qualifications.**
3. **Adapt your speech's organization to audience knowledge.**
4. **Compliment finalists for the award.**

First, as a presenter, you should *state the purpose of the award or recognition.* If the audience is unfamiliar with the award—if it is a new or special award—or if they know nothing about the organization making the award, you will probably want to begin by briefly explaining the nature of the award or the rationale for presenting it. This is especially important if you as the speaker represent the organization making the award. In contrast, an award having a long history probably needs little if any explanation.

A second guideline is to *focus your speech on the achievements for which the award is being made;* don't attempt a detailed biography of the recipient. Because you are merely highlighting the honoree's accomplishments, the speech of presentation will be brief, rarely more than five minutes long and frequently much shorter.

Third, *organize a speech of presentation primarily according to whether your listeners know the name of the recipient in advance.* If they do not know the name of the individual you are honoring, capitalize on their curiosity. If you begin by announcing the name of the recipient and then explaining why that person was selected, the bulk

speech of presentation: a speech conferring an award, a prize, or some other recognition on an individual or group.

of your speech will be anticlimactic. Instead, let ambiguity about who will receive the honor propel the speech and maintain the audience's attention. Begin by making general comments that could refer to several or many people; as the speech progresses, let your comments get more specific. If the person receiving your award is from a group containing both men and women, use gender-neutral descriptions ("this person" or "our honoree") rather than using "he" or "she." In this way, you keep your audience guessing and allow them the pleasure of solving a puzzle. If the audience knows in advance the name of the person being recognized, your strategy changes. In this case, begin the speech with specifics and end with more general statements that summarize the reasons for the presentation.

Finally, if a group of individuals has been nominated and you are announcing the winner with your speech of presentation, briefly *compliment the entire group of people who have been nominated for the award.*

The following speech was delivered at an annual convention of the Texas Speech Communication Association (TSCA) to honor a person giving lengthy and outstanding service to that organization. Notice how the speaker focuses on the reasons for the award and the honoree's qualifications. In addition, the speaker's organization carefully creates suspense for this surprise award.

> The key word in "TSCA Outstanding Service Award" is "service." We who have been privileged to serve this association as officers soon learn that what we accomplish is not primarily a function of our own talents and hard work, but a function of the expertise and efforts of many individuals like you—individuals who understand what is important in making the Texas Speech Communication Association a vibrant and vital organization. . . .
>
> Important to TSCA is networking. Through letters, phone calls, and testifying, this year's recipient helped make our voice heard in her local community and in Austin. . . .
>
> Important to TSCA is service on the Executive Committee. As editor of the *TSCA Newsletter,* this year's recipient gave life to this instrument of communication, establishing the professional format it continues today.
>
> Important to TSCA are the many programs which comprise our convention. Many of you have attended and learned from programs and workshops this year's recipient has conducted.
>
> A Piper Professor and a Danforth Scholar, she was honored by her institution this year as the first recipient of the Dr. and Mrs. Z. T. Scott Fellowship for Excellence in Teaching. This award recognizes excellence in teaching, advising, and support for student organizations.
>
> I have long believed that an important criterion for professional service is that an individual is not offended by doing the menial. This year's recipient is not offended by doing the menial and is capable of accomplishing the significant. She is professional, gracious, amiable, and hard-working.
>
> I suspect that there is only one person in this room who will be surprised at this year's choice for the Outstanding Service Award—and that person is the recipient herself, for she will feel that she was just fulfilling her professional obligations. We know better. She represents the best of our association, the best of our discipline, and the best of our profession.
>
> At the beginning of my remarks I said that this introduction is a personal privilege, for the individual we honor today is perhaps the most significant colleague in my professional life. It is with pleasure that I present to you this year's recipient of the TSCA Outstanding Service Award: Frances Swinny.[4]

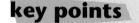
ethical decisions

King is president of the Porridge Players, an organization that stages musical comedies on his campus. This season, the Players have performed *South Pacific,* and the actress who played Nelly Forbush is Maria MacIntosh, an enormously talented singer, dancer, and actress with a horrible temper and an insufferably arrogant attitude. As president of the Players, King has been called on time after time to mediate disputes between this woman and other members of the cast and crew. By the time the season is over, he has little respect for her, despite her considerable talents.

At the end of each season, the faculty advisory board for the Players votes on awards for the best performers, director, technical people, and so forth. No one is very surprised when Maria is chosen to receive the award for best actress. King, however, is dismayed to learn that he has to present it, along with a short introductory speech. He wonders what to do. Should he simply praise Maria's performance and not mention the difficulties she caused, or is it his responsibility to make the faculty board aware of her flaws and negative impact on the company? What kind of information do you think King should include in his speech? Be prepared to discuss your answer with the class.

The Acceptance Speech

At some point in your life, you may be commended publicly for service you have given to a cause or an organization. You may be presented a farewell or retirement gift from your friends or coworkers. You may receive an award for winning a sporting event, an essay contest, or a speech contest. Although these are different occasions, they have at least one thing in common—each requires a response. To accept a gift or an award without expressing appreciation is socially unacceptable. An **acceptance speech,** then, is a response to a speech of presentation. When a recipient acknowledges the award or tribute, he or she provides closure to the process. A gracious acceptance speech usually includes four steps.

key points

Guidelines for the Acceptance Speech

1. Thank those who bestowed the award.
2. Compliment the competition.
3. Thank those who helped you attain the award.
4. Accept the award graciously.

First, *thank the person or organization bestowing the award.* You may wish to name not only the group sponsoring the award but also the person who made the speech of presentation. In addition, you may want to commend what the award represents. Your respect for the award and its donor authenticates your statement of appreciation.

Second, if you are accepting a competitively selected award, and especially if your competitors are in the audience, acknowledge their qualifications and compliment them. This step need not be lengthy; you can *compliment your peers* as a group rather than individually.

Third, *thank those who helped you achieve the honor.* Seldom do we achieve things by ourselves. Whether you are an accomplished pianist, vocalist, artist, athlete, or

acceptance speech: a speech responding to a speech of presentation by acknowledging an award, a tribute, or recognition.

Sample Acceptance Speech
http://home.sol.no/
~solhanse/wiesel.htm
Visit this site for an excellent example of an acceptance speech that was both inspirational and persuasive. On December 10, 1986, Elie Wiesel graciously accepted the Nobel Peace Prize. In this famous speech he blended examples and evocative language to remind his audience of suffering and injustice, and to call them to action, "the only remedy to indifference."

writer, you have usually had someone—parents, teachers, or coaches—who invested time, money, and expertise to help you achieve your best.

Finally, *accept your award graciously.* James Burrows, cocreator of *Cheers* and director of situation comedies including *Taxi, Cheers, Frasier,* and *Friends,* is renowned for his warmth and kindness as well as his great talent. When Burrows received the Creative Achievement Award at the tenth annual American Comedy Awards ceremony in 1996, Kelsey Grammar narrated a videotaped tribute that concluded with the line, "So it is that James Burrows has brought a little more humanity to humor, and has helped bring a little more humor to humanity." Following in the footsteps of his father, Abe Burrows, an illustrious Broadway writer and director who died in 1985, James Burrows began his career as a theatrical stage manager. After interning at MTM productions, he left to help create and direct 250 episodes of *Cheers.*[5] As you read his acceptance speech, notice how Burrows acknowledges his debt to his father and to the television people who gave him the chances he needed. At the end, he jokes about being confused with producer James L. Brooks.

It's wonderful to accept an award for something you enjoy doing. . . . I can't believe I'm getting this for making people laugh. Who knew when I told the Mr. Ribbit joke in the third grade it was a sign. . . .

I'd like to thank the American Comedy Awards for including me in this illustrious company of previous winners. I'm honored to be the first situation comedy director to be chosen for the Creative Achievement Award, and I hope I'm not the last because we are good, and maybe this is the beginning of getting the recognition we deserve.

I'd first and foremost like to thank Desi Arnaz for inventing the form. Thanks to Mr. [Grant] Tinker for taking a chance . . . and letting me share in the glory of MTM. To Mr. [Jay] Sandrich, thanks for taking me under your wing and showing me you can get aggressive on the stage, and what a horn high ace deuce is. To Mr. [Brandon] Tartikoff, thanks for calling me on Saturdays in the early years to tell me that the *Cheers* shares were moving up to the teens. To Broder, thanks for letting me worry only about what is funny and showing me a first name is unimportant. To Glenn and Les Charles for teaching me comic rhythms that I could only dream about, and for having faith to include me as a creator based solely on the fact that I had a famous father.

To the actors, all of you, there's a lot of you here tonight. Thanks for the trust to take it to the comic limit. And when a scene works, giving me the credit, and when it doesn't, giving me the credit. To all the writers, thanks for the words, for without them I would not be up here. And for choosing from all my notes the ones that actually make the piece better, thereby making me look better. To my crews, all of them, thanks for learning how to shoot a show from the hip and thus capturing the moment.

To my family, thanks for finding me funny even when there is trouble with the act break, and for being diplomatic with the phrase, "Daddy, don't work too hard." To my Mom, for being my greatest fan and not starting a fan club. To my father, who taught me images I use every day, who listened to rhythms and paced while he worked. And told me, you can do what you want with your life, but first try the theater for a few decades. [Laughter] Thanks for the set up, Dad. I hope somewhere you're laughing at my punchline. When I was in New York, I was Abe's son. When I first came to L.A., I was Mr. Brooks. I hope this award makes me Jim Burrows.[6]

The Speech of Tribute

A **speech of tribute** honors a person, a group, or an event, and it can be one of the most moving forms of public address. Vivid and memorable examples include Edward Kennedy's eulogy of his nephew John F. Kenndy, Jr., in 1999 (see Appendix B), Ronald Reagan's tribute to the crew of the *Challenger* after the shuttle's explosion in 1986, and Abraham Lincoln's Gettysburg Address.

A special form of the speech of tribute is the **eulogy**, a speech of praise usually given for those who have recently died. Peggy Noonan, speechwriter for presidents Ronald Reagan and George Bush, captures the power of eulogies:

> They are the most moving kind of speech because they attempt to pluck meaning from the fog, and on short order, when the emotions are still ragged and raw and susceptible to leaps. It is a challenge to look at a life and organize our thoughts about it and try to explain to ourselves what it meant, and the most moving part is the element of implicit celebration. Most people aren't appreciated enough, and the bravest things we do in our lives are usually known only to ourselves. No one throws ticker tape on the man who chose to be faithful to his wife, on the lawyer who didn't take the drug money, or the daughter who held her tongue again and again. All this anonymous heroism. A eulogy gives us a chance to celebrate it.[7]

Five guidelines will help you write a eulogy or any other speech of tribute.

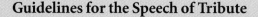

key points

Guidelines for the Speech of Tribute

1. Establish noble themes.
2. Provide vivid examples.
3. Express audience feelings.
4. Create a memorable image.
5. Be genuine.

First, *establish noble themes*. As you begin developing the eulogy, ask "Why is this person worthy of my respect and praise?" Answer this question by developing themes you want the audience to remember. Remember to focus on the positive. A speech of tribute celebrates what is good about a person; it is not an occasion for a warts-and-all biography. You must be careful, however, not to exaggerate a person's accomplishments. To do so may undermine your speech by making it seem insincere or unbelievable.

Second, *develop the themes of your speech with vivid examples*. Anecdotes, stories, and personal testimony are excellent ways of making your speech more vivid, humane, and memorable.

Third, *express the feelings of the audience assembled* or those whom you represent. The audience needs to be a part of the occasion for any speech of tribute. If you are honoring a former teacher, you may speak for yourself, but you can also speak for your class or even all students who studied under Mr. Crenshaw. If the honoree is present, he or she should feel that the tribute expresses more than one person's view.

Your use of noble themes, vivid examples, and audience feelings should combine to *create a memorable image of the person being honored*. Your speech not only honors someone, it also helps audience members focus on that person's importance to them.

Finally, *be genuine*. If you are asked to deliver a speech of tribute about someone you do not know, you may want to decline respectfully. The personal bond and interaction you develop in getting to know someone well is essential for a speech of tribute. Also, the person being honored may find the tribute more meaningful if it comes from a person he or she knows well.

speech of tribute: a speech honoring a person, group, or event.

eulogy: a speech of tribute praising a person who has recently died.

The Speech to Entertain

As we discussed early in this text, the three main purposes of speaking are to inform, to persuade, and to entertain. Although many informative and persuasive speeches contain elements of humor, the speech designed specifically to entertain is a special case because it is often difficult to do well.

The **speech to entertain** seeks to make a point through the creative, organized use of the speaker's humor. The distinguishing characteristic of a speech to entertain is the entertainment value of its supporting materials. It is usually delivered on an occasion when people are in a light mood: after a banquet, as part of an awards ceremony, and on other festive occasions.

A *speech to entertain* is different from *speaking to entertain.* In their opening monologues, Jay Leno and David Letterman are both speaking to entertain. Their purpose is to relax the audience, establish some interaction with them, and set the mood for the rest of the show. Their remarks are not organized around a central theme, something essential to a speech to entertain. If you combine the following five guidelines with what you already know about developing a public speech, you will discover that a speech to entertain is not only challenging but also fun to present.

Guidelines for the Speech to Entertain

1. Make a point.
2. Be creative.
3. Be organized.
4. Use appropriate humor.
5. Use spirited delivery.

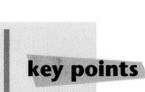

key points

The first requirement for a speech to entertain is that it *makes a point,* or communicates a thesis, no less than does the most carefully crafted informative or persuasive speech. Frequently, the person delivering a speech to entertain is trying to make the audience aware of conditions, experiences, or habits that they take for granted. Here are examples of topics on which we have heard students present successful speeches to entertain:

The imprecision and incorrectness of language, especially that used in some advertisements.

Many doctors' failure to speak language that their patients can understand and many patients' failure to ask their doctors the right questions.

Our interest in or curiosity about tabloid news stories.

"Momilies," familiar homilies or sayings that mommies (and daddies) tell their children.

The routine, expensive date versus creative, less expensive dating options.

In some of these speeches, the speaker had stated the main point fairly bluntly by the end of the speech: Take a careful look at the language used to sell you things; you owe it to your health to ask questions of your doctor; you do not have to spend a fortune to have an interesting time on a date. In other speeches, speakers simply implied their thesis: Think about what you say to correct or otherwise manipulate your children. Each of these speeches did make a point, however.

Second, *a speech to entertain is creative.* To be creative you must make sure that your speech to entertain is your product, and not simply a replay of a Rosie O'Donnell or a Jerry Seinfeld monologue. A replay like this is not creative, no matter how great a

speech to entertain: a speech used to make a point through the creative, organized use of the speaker's humor.

job you think you do delivering the other person's lines. Moreover, if you copy Rosie's or Jerry's words and don't credit them, you are plagiarizing. Your speech to entertain should be original and creative. It should give your audience a glimpse of your unique view of the world.

Third, *a speech to entertain is organized.* It must have an introduction, body, and conclusion just as informative and persuasive speeches do. In other words, the speech to entertain must convey a sense of moving toward some logical point and achieving closure after adequately developing that point. Failure to organize your materials will cause you to ramble, embarrassing both you and your audience. You will feel, quite literally, like the novice comic caught without a finish, a sure-fire joke that makes a good exit line. The audience will sense that you are struggling and will have trouble relaxing and enjoying your humor.

Use of appropriate humor is the fourth guideline for a speech to entertain. The speech to entertain is difficult to do well for a simple reason: Most people associate entertainment with lots of laughter and feel that if the audience is not laughing a good deal, they are not responding favorably to the speech. But stop to consider for a moment the range of things that entertain you, from the outrageous antics of Carrot Top to the quiet, pointed barbs of Bill Maher. Your humor should be adapted to your topic, your audience, the occasion, and your own personal style. Four suggestions should guide your use of humor.

1. Be Relevant. Good humor is relevant to your general purpose and makes the main ideas of your speech memorable. Humor not related to the point you are making should still be relevant to your general purpose: to entertain. Michael's speech to entertain discussed the ways we label products and people. One of his points was that the product warnings printed on packaging tell us about various companies' views of their customers. His examples at this point in the speech were relevant to that main idea and added humor to his speech by helping him show the absurdity of many product labels.

> For example, the first thing I saw on the box my toaster came in was a warning. Warning—do not submerge in water, especially when the plug is connected to an electrical outlet. Now just at a practical level, I'm pretty sure that almost anyone should be able to figure out that the chances of getting your Pop Tart to turn brown at the bottom of a Jacuzzi are pretty slim to begin with. But as far as this whole electrocution thing is concerned, I'm not entirely sure how much damage 500 volts could do to these people. I mean let's face it, if you're going to plug in your toaster just so you can take it into the shower with you, a little shock there may not be such a bad idea.[8]

2. Be Tasteful. Important to any speech, audience analysis is vital for a speech to entertain. Taste is subjective. What delights some listeners may offend others. Do the best job you can in analyzing your audience, but when in doubt, err on the side of caution. Remember, humor that is off-color is off-limits.

3. Be Tactful. Avoid humor that generates laughter at the expense of others. There may be times when good-natured ribbing is appropriate, but humor intended to belittle or demean a person or group is unethical and unacceptable. For that reason, most sexist or ethnic humor should also be off-limits.

4. Be Positive. The tone for most occasions featuring speeches to entertain should be festive. People have come together to relax and enjoy each other's company. Dark, negative humor is usually inappropriate as it casts a somber tone on the situation.

Finally, *a speech to entertain benefits from spirited delivery.* We have often heard good speeches to entertain and looked forward to reading transcripts of them later. We were usually disappointed. The personality, timing, and interaction with the audience that made the speech lively and unforgettable could not be captured on paper. We have also read manuscripts of speeches to entertain that promised to be dynamic when presented, only to see them diminished by a monotonous, colorless, and lifeless delivery.

The Impromptu Speech

You are sitting at a staff meeting listening to your coworkers argue about office assignments in the company's new building. Your boss suddenly turns to ask how you would solve the problem. Or you are standing in the back of a crowded orientation session when, to your surprise, your supervisor introduces you and says, "Come up here and say a few words to these folks." Or you receive an award you didn't know you were being considered for. As people begin to applaud and whistle, you start walking to the front of the room to accept an attractive plaque. These are but three situations in which you would deliver an impromptu speech.

The **impromptu speech,** one with limited or no advance preparation, can be intimidating. You have not had time to think about the ideas you want to communicate. You begin speaking without knowing the exact words you will use. You have not practiced delivering your speech. Don't panic! All is not lost. By now you have a pretty good understanding of how to organize, support, and deliver a speech. You have practiced these skills in prepared classroom speeches. All this practice will help you in your impromptu speech. With experience comes confidence. You already know what it feels like to stand before an audience. "But this is different," you might be saying right about now. "In those cases I had time to prepare." Well, if you follow these four guidelines, you should be ready for almost any impromptu speech that comes along.

Guidelines for the Impromptu Speech

1. Speak on a topic you know well.
2. Make the most of the preparation time you have.
3. Focus on a single or a few key points.
4. Be brief.

key points

First, if you have a choice, *speak on a topic you know well.* The more you know about your topic, the better you will be able to select relevant ideas, organize them, and explain them as you speak. You will also be more comfortable talking about a subject you know, and your confidence will show in your delivery.

Even though your preparation time is limited or nonexistent, *make the most of the time you have.* Don't waste "walking time" from your seat to the front of the room worrying. Instead, ask yourself, "What do I want the audience to remember when I sit down? What two or three points will help them remember this?"

Third, *focus on a single or a few key points.* This may be easier if you think a bit like the character Charlie Fox in David Mamet's play *Speed-the-Plow.* A movie producer, Charlie's test of a screenplay is whether he can condense it to one sentence so that *TV Guide* can print a blurb about it. As silly as it may seem, this strategy could help you focus on the few ideas you want to get across to your listeners. If you have been asked to explain why you support building a new library instead of renovating the existing facility, think of the two or three most important reasons underlying your position. And remember to use the 4 S's as you present those reasons to your audience.

Finally, *be brief.* One public speaking axiom is, "Stand up! Speak up! Shut up!" Although this can be carried to an extreme, it is probably good advice for the impromptu

impromptu speech: a speech delivered with little or no advance preparation.

The skills you develop in business and social conversations will come to your aid when you are called upon to deliver an impromptu speech.

speaker. An impromptu speech is not the occasion for a long, rambling discourse. Say what you need to say, and then be seated.

One of us gave an impromptu speech to his public speaking students the second day of class. He had assigned an ungraded speech of self-introduction for that day, and he wanted students to think of the assignment as an important practice opportunity. As he walked to class, he considered how he could set a proper tone and relax his students. He remembered hearing that baseball spring training was just 30 days away. A baseball fan, he decided to illustrate his point with an analogy between baseball and the class. Three aspects of baseball spring training were similar to what he expected in his class. By the time he walked into the class, he was ready to deliver the following impromptu speech:

> In less than a month, major league baseball players will pack their bags and head to Florida and Arizona for spring training. As part of their training, they do three things. They receive instruction from their coaches. They work on fundamental skills. And they play exhibition games in which they practice putting it all together. Spring training is important because it helps baseball players prepare for the regular season, when games really count.
>
> I want you to think of the first weeks of this class as your spring training in public speaking. You will learn from your coach—that's me—public speaking strategies and techniques. You will work on fundamental skills such as supporting, organizing, and delivering your speech. And you will give ungraded, practice speeches to your classmates. If you take this spring training seriously, you'll be ready when it's your turn to walk to the front of the room, look at your audience, and begin giving your first graded speech.

Later he reflected on the speech. He had included the nonspecific word *things* at the end of his second sentence where a more specific word would have served better. The last sentence seemed OK, but maybe something with a baseball image would have been more catchy. What about coming to the plate and hitting a home run? Despite these weaknesses, he was satisfied with his impromptu remarks. Judging from the reactions of the class and their comments, he had succeeded in relaxing them before they gave their first speech to the class. If the instructor uses the strategy in subsequent semesters, he will reflect on his first attempt, polish his language, and improve his speech.

Notice how the instructor used the guidelines listed previously for the impromptu speech. He selected two topics he knew well: public speaking and baseball. He was comfortable talking about both topics. He collected his thoughts and outlined the body of the speech in his mind as he walked to class. He focused on a single idea: The ungraded speaking assignments in this class give you an opportunity to prepare for future speeches. He established this position by developing three simple points. The speech was brief and to the point, just eleven sentences. And after the speech was over, he evaluated it in order to do a better job next time.

The Question-Answer Period

If time permits, seize the opportunity to answer your listeners' questions. Holding a **question-answer period** following your speech offers you an opportunity to interact directly with your audience. This usually results in a natural, lively delivery and makes for better speaker–listener rapport.

Almost any question asked can help you. If questions are friendly, that is a high compliment: The audience is genuinely interested in you and your topic. If questions stem from audience confusion about your presentation, you have an opportunity to clarify. If someone asks you a combative and contentious question, you've just been given a second chance to win this person over to your point of view.

Guidelines to Answering Questions

1. Restate or clarify the question.
2. Compliment the question.
3. Answer the question.
4. Check the response with the questioner.

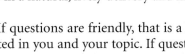
key points

Before tackling the Q-A period, study the guidelines in the box. You will find them helpful when you stand in front of an audience and ask, "Are there any questions?"

The first step, *restating or clarifying the question,* is important for three reasons. First, repetition makes sure that the entire audience has heard the question. Second, repeating the question allows the questioner the opportunity to correct you if you misstate it, saving you the embarrassment of beginning to answer a different question. Third, if the question seems confusing to you or somehow misses the point, you can rephrase the question to make it clearer, more focused, and more relevant. Never answer a question you don't understand.

A second step in answering a question is to *compliment the question* whenever possible. We have all heard speakers say, "I'm glad you asked that." Of course, you cannot repeat that same remark after each question. But without seeming insincere you can say, "That's a good (or perceptive or interesting) question," or "I was hoping someone would ask that."

This applies even to hostile questions. Sincerely complimenting a hostile question or questioner can defuse a tense situation and focus attention on issues rather than on personal antagonism.

You are now ready for the third step: *answering the question.* Of course, the content and the form of your answers depend on the specific questions; nevertheless, the following suggestions may be helpful.

1. *Know Your Topic Thoroughly.* Your success during the Q-A period will depend, in large part, on your research and preparation for your speech. You should always

question-answer period: a time set aside at the end of a speech for audience questions of the speaker.

know more than you included in your speech. Most of the time, poor answers reflect poor preparation.

2. *Be as Brief as Possible.* Obviously, some questions require longer, more thoughtful answers than others. The question, "How much did you say it will cost to complete Phase II of the new library?" can be answered simply, "Two and a half million dollars." The question, "What will that $2.5 million provide?" will require a much longer answer. There are two reasons for making your answers as succinct as possible. First, short answers are easier to remember than lengthy ones. Second, the shorter each answer, the greater the number of questions you can field.

3. *Be Methodical when Giving Lengthy Answers.* When you need to give a detailed answer, use the "frame it, state it, and explain it" approach. Suppose you were asked the question, "How will the $2.5 million budgeted for Phase II of the new library be spent?" You could answer as follows:

> In order to answer that question, we need to look at three categories of costs: construction, furniture and equipment, and instructional materials.
>
> Mike Phillips, the director of buildings and grounds, estimates cost breakdowns as follows: $1.7 million for construction, $300,000 for furniture and equipment, and $500,000 for instructional materials.
>
> Unlike many institutions, we're fortunate that we can provide a sizable amount of money—half a million dollars—in addition to our regular annual budget of $200,000 for instructional resources. This is a one-time infusion of money. You should also know, however, what these figures do not include. Not included are personnel costs, energy costs, and costs for purchases of materials and equipment beyond the first year.

4. *If You Don't Know an Answer, Admit It.* Making up an answer is unethical. Fabricated answers can not only undermine your credibility, but the audience may also act on incorrect information you have provided. There is nothing wrong with saying, "I don't know," or, "I don't know, but I'll check on it and let you know." If you give the second response, make sure you follow up promptly.

5. *Be Careful about What You Say Publicly.* Remember that in a public gathering, there is no such thing as an off-the-record statement. Don't say, "It's not official and I would not want it reported yet, but we expect that the vice-president will be our commencement speaker." You will probably read the following headline in the next issue of your school paper: "Vice-President Possible Commencement Speaker." If the press is present, what you say may indeed be reported. As a rule, never say anything that would embarrass you or slander others if it were to appear in the next morning's paper.

The final step in answering a question is to *check the response with the questioner.* Did you answer the question to his or her satisfaction? Is there a follow-up question? Remember two drawbacks to this approach, however. If each person is allowed a question and a follow-up, you will be able to answer fewer people's questions. Second, if questioners are argumentative, asking them if you answered the question to their satisfaction gives them an opportunity to keep the floor and turn the Q-A period into a debate.

The Videotaped Speech

In Chapter 1, we introduced you to the components of the communication process: speaker, message, listener, channel, feedback, environment, and noise. Channel, you remember, refers to the way the message is sent. Messages may be written or spoken. If spoken, they may be delivered in person or transmitted electronically. Videotape is one popular electronic medium. Even though you still see and hear the speaker, videotape introduces a new dynamic to the public speech, and that dynamic affects how audience members receive the message.

The **videotaped speech** is increasingly common, for both practice and presentation. If you have access to a camcorder, you may want to use it as you practice your speeches for this class. If you are nervous about your speech and self-conscious practicing in front of another person, just set up a camera, turn it on, walk to the front of the room, and deliver your speech. You can then watch yourself on the videotape and note what you do well and what still needs work. After viewing yourself, you may even ask some friends to look at the tape with you and offer their comments and suggestions. If you use the videotape strategy, keep a copy of your final practice tape for each of your speeches in this class. After you have a few examples, review them. You will probably be surprised to see how much you have improved since your first effort.

Videotaping actual presentations is also increasingly common. Speeches given to community groups or before governmental bodies are often taped for possible broadcast on local news. Speakers can now include videotape in multimedia peripherals. Your instructor may have played tapes of great speeches for you or speeches other students gave when they took a public speaking class. These examples may have been particularly helpful, because videotape re-creates the event better than a lifeless manuscript does. In this section we discuss videotaping an entire speech for playback, and we offer three guidelines to help you meet this challenge.

Guidelines for the Videotaped Speech

1. Adapt your delivery to your audience(s).
2. Adapt your delivery to your microphone.
3. Adapt your delivery to your camera shots.

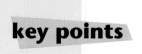

Your first consideration in preparing for a videotaped or filmed speech is your *audience.* Are you speaking primarily to the immediate group assembled or to those who will view the videotape later? Which is your primary audience and which your secondary? Or are both equally important? Unlike traditional speaking situations requiring analysis of one audience, the videotaped speech often requires you to analyze several audiences. If these audiences differ in significant ways, the task of constructing your speech is more difficult.

The audience you expect to view your videotape should also guide the way you respond to the camera. If you are videotaping your speech for your own analysis, you want the camera to see what any audience member in the camera's location would see. In that case, don't look directly into the camera during your entire speech. Make eye contact with all parts of your audience as you practice, treating the camera as just another audience member. If you are speaking only to an external audience, as the president does when speaking to the public from a desk in the Oval Office, you will want to make eye contact only with the camera, treating it as your only listener. As a rule, if audience members viewing a videotape see another audience in the speaker's presence, they will expect the speaker to be interacting with those people. If audience members watching a videotape believe themselves to be the speaker's only audience, they will expect to receive the full measure of the speaker's eye contact.

A second concern is the *microphone* you will use. A lapel microphone clips to your shirt, blouse, tie, dress, or jacket. It moves with you. A fixed, or stationary, microphone is often fastened to the lectern or held in place by a microphone stand. You may or may not be given a choice of microphones. What are the advantages and drawbacks of each?

videotaped speech: a speech taped during practice for the speaker's review or during actual delivery for viewing by another audience.

A *lapel microphone* allows you freedom of movement. You can walk and keep the same voice level. Some media experts believe that, because it is attached near the chest cavity, it adds resonance to your voice, making your vocal delivery richer. This mike is also unobtrusive, as it is not easily seen by you or your audience. Speakers who experience "mike fright" usually prefer the lapel to the fixed microphone because it is out of their sight. However, if you use a lapel mike that has a cord, you will need to watch your movement, being careful not to become entangled in the cord. You will also want to select your clothing carefully. If your jacket and shirt or blouse rustle as you move, the mike will pick up distracting noise.

Even a *fixed microphone* attached to the lectern sometimes picks up distracting noises, such as nervous tapping of fingers on the lectern or shuffling of paper as you move your speaking notes. In order to do your best job as a speaker, you need to be aware of all that the audience hears. A disadvantage of the fixed microphone is that it restricts movement. As you walk away from the mike, your volume may fade. Most fixed microphones today, however, are multidirectional, or able to pick up sound from many directions. You do not need to stand rigidly twelve inches away from the fixed mike, speaking without turning your head from side to side. You may (and should) move your head as you make eye contact with various sections of your audience. Avoid looking at the mike and becoming preoccupied with its presence.

A third factor you should consider when planning and practicing your speech is the *camera*. Where is it positioned? What is its angle of vision? Will it record close-up or long shots? What the camera sees should help determine your delivery. If the camera takes only head shots, your facial expressions become more important and gesturing less so. Glancing down at your notes will be more noticeable. In a full body shot, you will be able to gesture and move about more freely. If the camera sees you from chest up, you will want to ensure that your gestures are high enough to convey your dynamism visibly. Someone videotaping your speech rehearsal or actual presentation may use the camera's zoom lens to get a variety of shots. If possible, find out this person's plans before you speak.

Here are some other tips to make your videotaped presentation more effective:

1. Avoid wearing predominantly white or black clothing. Pastel clothing is usually preferred.
2. Avoid wearing finely striped clothing, or other busy patterns.
3. Avoid wearing large or excessive jewelry.
4. Keep make-up simple and natural. Shiny facial and head areas should be treated with powdered makeup. Men who have "5 o'clock shadows" should shave or use corrective makeup before they speak.
5. Don't blow into or tap on a microphone.
6. Don't make exaggerated movements in front of the camera.
7. Exercise caution in using overhead projectors, slides, or other types of visual aids that require lights to be turned off. The camera may not be able to videotape these projections efficiently.

In summary, try to determine what the viewing audience will see. If possible, find out how your speech will be taped beforehand so that you can practice accordingly. If this is not possible, be prepared to adapt during the event. Arrive early and talk to the camera operator; you may even want to suggest how you would like the speech recorded. Let the camera operator know if and when you will use a visual aid so that he or she can zoom in on the chart or graph at the appropriate time. If your primary audience is the tape-viewing audience and if you are given a choice, request many close-up shots. Remember, your eyes and face are the most expressive parts of your body.

Emphasizing those aspects of your physical delivery can make the speaker–viewer relationship more personal.

As with any speech, practice is the key to effective delivery. Videotaping adds another dynamic to that delivery. You must be concerned not only with how your body and voice carry your message, but also with how the medium of transmission affects the message your listeners receive.

Summary

The *speech of introduction* presents a featured speaker to an audience. If you are called on to introduce another speaker, your speech should not compete with the one you are introducing. Be brief, focus your remarks on the featured speaker, establish that person's credibility, create positive but realistic audience expectations, and match the tone of the featured speech.

The *speech of presentation* confers an award, prize, or special recognition on an individual or group. Such a speech should state the purpose of the award or recognition, particularly if it is new or unfamiliar to the audience. The speaker should state the recipient's qualifications to reveal why the person deserves the award. If the audience does not know the name of the recipient in advance, the speech of presentation should create suspense, revealing the recipient's name only late in the speech. If the person being honored has been selected from nominees known to the audience, the speech of presentation should compliment those other individuals.

The *acceptance speech* is an honoree's response to a speech of presentation. Social custom dictates that you thank at least briefly any group presenting you an award, prize, or other recognition. When accepting an award, you should thank the people bestowing the award, compliment your competitors if you know them, and thank those who helped you attain the award. Your acceptance speech gives you a chance to say thanks humbly and sincerely.

The *speech of tribute* honors an individual, a group, or a significant event. A *eulogy*, spoken to honor a person who has recently died, is one of the most familiar speeches of tribute. In delivering a speech of tribute, you should establish noble or lofty themes built upon vivid examples from the subject's life. As a speaker, you should attempt to express the collective feelings of the audience. You should create a memorable image of the subject, and you should be genuine.

The *speech to entertain* seeks to make a point through the creative, organized use of the speaker's humor. Usually delivered on a light, festive occasion, your speech to entertain should make a point, be creative, be well organized, use appropriate humor, and be delivered in a spirited manner. The humor you use in a speech to entertain should be relevant to your point, tasteful, tactful, and positive.

An *impromptu speech* is one delivered with little or no advance preparation. You speak impromptu whenever someone asks you a question or calls on you to speak with only a moment's notice. Under these circumstances, speak on a subject you know well, if possible, and use your limited preparation time in a positive way. Ask, "What do I want the audience to remember from what I say?" Then focus your remarks to achieve that goal. Cover only a few key points and be brief. To improve your impromptu speaking, reflect on each speech to see how you could have improved its content, organization, and delivery.

The *question-answer period* after your speech gives you the opportunity to interact with your audience. Answering questions from audience members will be easier if you follow four steps. First, restate or clarify the question. Second, compliment the question or the questioner. Third, answer the question. Finally, check your response with the person who asked the question.

The *videotaped speech* is becoming increasingly common, both for practice and for actual presentation of the speech. Videotaping requires speakers to adapt their delivery to their various audiences, to the microphone, and to the camera. The presence of a video camera will influence your eye contact, movement, gestures, and other elements of your vocal and physical delivery.

practice critique

Evaluating a Eulogy

In the summer of 1999 John F. Kennedy, Jr., died alongside his wife and sister-in-law in an airplane crash. A week later his uncle, Ted Kennedy, delivered the moving eulogy we mentioned at the beginning of this chapter. Read the transcript of Senator Kennedy's eulogy of his nephew John F. Kennedy, Jr., in Appendix B. Then, using the five guidelines discussed on page 424 in this chapter, write a brief critique of the speech, noting places where the senator did or did not follow each of the guidelines.

Exercises

1. Pair up with another member of the class. Discuss each other's speech topics and relevant personal background. Following the guidelines discussed in this chapter, prepare a speech introducing your partner on the day of his or her speech. Your partner will introduce you when you speak.

2. Watch all or a portion of an awards ceremony (the Oscars, Grammies, or the Tony awards, for example). Select the best and worst acceptance speeches; justify your choices.

3. Pair up with someone, and discuss what each of you does well. Create an award that one of you will receive. One of you will give a speech of presentation and the other a speech of acceptance.

4. Prepare and deliver a speech of tribute for someone you admire who is known to the class. This person may be a campus, local, national, or international figure.

5. View a speech that was constructed for both public and mass communication. Examples include speeches at political conventions, inaugural addresses, State of the Union addresses, and State of the State addresses by governors. Analyze the speech in light of the different audiences. Did one audience seem more important to the speaker than the other? If so, what led you to this conclusion? Do you think the speaker adapted well to each audience? If so, what strategies and techniques did the speaker use well? If not, what could the speaker have done better?

6. Listen to a formal speech of introduction. The speech may be one you see on television, as in a C-SPAN broadcast of a National Press Club address. Or you might attend a campus or community meeting during which a speaker is introduced. Using the guidelines in this chapter, critique the speech of introduction. What did the introducer do well? What could he or she have done better? Did the introducer prepare the audience to listen intelligently to the speech that followed?

7. Select a humorous magazine article or newspaper column. Discuss how you might edit, revise, and adapt the article for a speech to entertain, as well as how you would cite the source. Write a thesis statement, outline the key ideas, and develop entertaining examples to support those points.

8. Listen to or read a transcript of a question-answer period following a speech or at a press conference. Sources may include network broadcasts of presidential press conferences; C-SPAN broadcasts of interviews, National Press Club addresses,

conference proceedings, news briefings, and call-in shows; and transcripts of presidential press conferences published in *Weekly Compilation of Presidential Documents* and *Public Papers of the Presidents of the United States.* Analyze the speaker's strategies and effectiveness in responding to audience questions.

1. Bob Costas, "Text of Bob Costas' Eulogy at the Funeral," speech, 7 Nov. 1995. Online. ESPNet SportsZone, 13 Nov. 1995.

2. Diana Jean Schemo, "Holocaust Museum Hailed as Sacred Debt to Dead," *The New York Times* 23 April 1993, natl. ed.: A1, 24.

3. Don Ochs, "Introduction of Samuel L. Becker, Central States Communication Association Convention, April 12, 1991," *The CSCA News* (Spring 1991): 2.

4. George L. Grice, "Remarks at the First General Session, Texas Speech Communication Association Convention, October 4, 1986," *TSCA Newsletter* (January 1987): 12.

5. Rick Marin, "The Spielberg of Sitcoms," *Newsweek* 11 Sept. 1995: 73.

6. James Burrows, acceptance speech, 10th Annual American Comedy Awards Ceremony, Shrine Auditorium, Los Angeles, 11 Feb. 1996.

7. Peggy Noonan, *What I Saw at the Revolution* (New York: Random, 1990) 253.

8. Michael McDonough, "Untitled Speech," *1990 Championship Debates and Speeches* (Annandale, VA: Speech Communication Association, 1990) 86.

Never doubt that a small group of thoughtful, committed citizens can change the world. Indeed, it's the only thing that ever has.

—Margaret Mead

Speaking in and as a Group

ake out a sheet of paper and start listing all the small groups to which you belong. Think of committees, subcommittees, boards, and councils on which you serve. Include your network of close friends. Add your family to the list. What about athletic teams, honor societies, fraternities or sororities, the chess club, the debating society, the arts council, study groups, and other groups? After a few minutes of this brainstorming, you will probably be surprised at the length of your list. In light of that discovery, you probably won't be surprised that one survey estimated that "35 to 60 percent of the average manager's day is taken up by meetings."[1] In fact, groups are so prevalent in our society that it is estimated that there are more groups in America than there are people.[2]

Not only are groups plentiful, they are also influential. They shape our society and our behavior. Government, businesses, educational institutions, and other organizations depend on groups to gather information, assess data, and propose courses of action. Our families and our close friends give us counsel and support in times of need. We do so much planning, problem solving, and recreating in small groups that we can all relate to the humorist's remark that "there are no great people, only great committees."

Because groups significantly influence our lives, it is essential that groups communicate effectively. Unfortunately, small group communication seems not to be a skill most of us master easily. For example, a communication professor and a consultant note that "poor meeting preparation, ad hoc scheduling, and lack of participant training in meeting management are causing many companies to lose the *equivalent of thirty man-days and 240 man-hours a year for every person who participates in business conferences.*"[3] Clearly, poor group communication can be costly. You will work more effectively in groups if you understand the subjects covered in this chapter: the relationship between small group communication and public speaking, the characteristics of a group, the types of groups, the principles of group decision making, the responsibilities of group leaders and members, and the most frequently used formats for group presentations.

Small Group Communication and Public Speaking

Why study group work as an adjunct to public speaking? The answer is twofold: (1) Groups of people often make presentations, either internally or to the public; and (2) the quality of those presentations depends on how well group members have functioned together.

For most of your work in your public speaking class, you have operated alone. You selected your speech topics. You researched as much as you wanted and at your own convenience. You organized your speeches as you thought best and practiced them as much as you thought necessary. Your individual work continues in a group. You must still present, support, and defend your ideas. As you'll see in this chapter, group communication involves a variety of speeches, from the chairperson's orientation speech, to internal reports to other group members, to public presentations about the group's work. Each time you share your ideas and opinions with other group members, you will, in effect, be giving an impromptu speech. The more you know about effective speech content, organization, and delivery, the better your individual speeches within the group will be.

As part of a group solving a problem and preparing a presentation, your work is more complex, however. On-the-spot interaction in a group elevates the importance of listening and critiquing. You will need to utilize all of the critical thinking skills we discussed in Chapter 1. You'll also be challenged to provide feedback to other group members. Using the guidelines for critiquing that we discussed in Chapter 4 will help you do your part to create and maintain a constructive, supportive communication environment. Group processes will truly test your ability to work productively and congenially with other people.

Small Groups Defined

A **small group** is a collection of three or more individuals who interact with and influence each other in pursuit of a common goal. This definition includes four important concepts: individuals, interaction, influence, and goal.

The number of *individuals* in a group may vary. At a minimum, there must be three. Two people are not a group but rather an interpersonal unit, sometimes called a dyad. The addition of a third person adds a new dynamic, a new perspective. Paul Nelson describes the new relationship in the following way:

> Something happens to communication when it involves more than two people: It becomes much more complex. For example, imagine two people, A and B, having a conversation. There is only *one* possible conversation, A-B. Add one more person, C, however: Now there are *four* possible interactions, A-B, A-C, B-C, and A-B-C. Add another person, D, and there are *eleven* possible interactions. And so on.[4]

Although we can all agree that three is the minimum number for a small group, we do not always agree on the maximum number. Even communication experts disagree, with some using seven as a workable maximum and others stretching the range to twenty. What characterizes a small group is not a specific number of participants but the *type* of communication they undertake. A group that is too large cannot maintain meaningful interaction among members and may have to be divided into smaller working groups.

A group's size, then, affects a second characteristic of a small group: *interaction*. A small group offers each participant an opportunity to interact with all other members of the group. A group cannot function if its participants fail to interact, and it functions ineffectively when a few members dominate. Generally, the larger the group, the fewer opportunities for any one member to participate and the greater the likelihood that a few members will dominate the flow of communication, making certain that meaningful interaction does not take place.

A third characteristic of small groups is *influence*. Members of a group interact in order to influence others. As journalist Walter Lippman observed, "When all think alike, no one thinks very much." Groups function best when members express differences of opinions openly and try to persuade others with data and arguments.

Finally, a group has a purpose. As we noted in Chapter 1, a group is more than simply a collection of individuals who interact; it exists for a reason. Members interact and influence each other over a period of time in order to achieve a *goal*. The group process fails when members are unsure of their goal or when they fail to resolve conflicting perceptions of that goal.

Types of Groups

People form groups for two reasons: because they enjoy interacting with each other or because they need to accomplish a task. Therefore, we can classify groups into two general types: socially oriented and task-oriented. A **socially oriented group** is one that

small group: a collection of three or more people influencing and interacting with one another in pursuit of a common goal.

socially oriented group: a small group that exists primarily because its members enjoy interacting with one another.

exists primarily because its members enjoy interacting with one another. Group members may not have a major task in mind but rather be concerned mainly with relationships, enjoying time spent with other members of the group. A **task-oriented group** is more formal. Members interact having a specific goal in mind. For example, you and a few classmates may form a study group to review for examinations and to be an audience for each other as you practice your speeches.

The objectives of socially and task-oriented groups often intermingle. Say you and your friends decide to go to a movie. Clearly, this is a social occasion, but you still must accomplish certain tasks: What movie does the group want to see? When is the best time for everyone to see it? Will you carpool or will everyone meet at the theatre? Do you want to get a bite to eat before or after the movie? At times you have probably been frustrated when your social group was unable to make some of these "easy" task decisions.

While socially oriented groups may have task objectives, the converse is also true. You form a study group to accomplish certain tasks, but as you get to know the others in the group you discover that you enjoy their company. As social objectives emerge, the group meets more frequently and functions more effectively. If social purposes predominate, however, you may find that your group sacrifices studying for socializing. Even though most groups have both social and task objectives, one purpose usually takes precedence according to the situation. That purpose determines the structure of your group and the nature of the communication among its members.

In this chapter, we will focus on task-oriented groups, sometimes called working groups. These include study groups, problem-solving groups, and action groups. The objective of a **study group** is to learn about a topic. It gathers, processes, and evaluates information. When you and your classmates work together to prepare for an exam, you are a study group. A **problem-solving group** decides on courses of action. This type of group explores a problem, suggesting solutions to remedy it. The objective of an **action group** is, as its name implies, to act. It has the power to implement proposals. These

> **Task Force and Team Work**
> http://www.resultgp.com/news_task_force.htm
> Visit this page for a discussion of a particular type of work group, the task force. It includes a brief description of the four stages teams go through (forming, storming, norming, and performing), as well as tips for enhancing the function of a task force.

task-oriented group: a small group that exists primarily to accomplish some goal.

study group: a task-oriented group devoted to researching and learning about a topic.

problem-solving group: a task-oriented group devoted to deciding on courses of action to correct a problem.

action group: a task-oriented group devoted to implementing proposals for action.

Although a task-oriented group functions more effectively if members enjoy one another's company, social interactions should not take precedence over the group's basic objective: to accomplish the task.

categories may overlap. In fact, you may be a member of a group that studies a situation, devises a solution, *and* implements it.

Successful athletic teams recognize the importance of working together as a group of individuals to accomplish their goals. The football quarterback, for example, is on the sidelines when the opposing team has the ball. When on the field, the quarterback depends on teammates to make the plays called in the huddle. It's not surprising, then, that successful quarterbacks reward members of their offensive lines with gifts at the end of the season.

Successful sports teams rely on individual responsibility and shared leadership. A pitcher's role is uniquely different from that of the second baseman, but both are critical to team success. Being able to strike out a power hitter is no less important than the ability to turn a flawless 6-4-3 double play. Business and professional organizations are increasingly using **work teams** to accomplish their objectives. Communication scholars Thomas Harris and John Sherblom argue, "Teams differ substantially from many small groups, because the teams themselves, rather than the leader, control the group process."[5] These sports analogies are particularly apt because team leaders gradually assume the role of coach, similar to the athletic coach.

A type of action group becoming increasingly common in the business world is the **self-directed work team.** Such work teams manage themselves, in addition to getting work done. Responsibilities and characteristics of self-directed work teams include:

- sharing management and leadership roles;
- planning, controlling, and improving their own work;
- setting team goals, creating schedules, and reviewing group performance;
- identifying and securing necessary training;
- hiring and disciplining team members; and
- assuming responsibility for products and services produced.[6]

Work teams obviously require that traditional leadership responsibilities gradually shift to team members. Many teams rotate the role of team leader, with members occupying the position for a designated length of time.

As you go through this chapter, you will find that participating in task groups and delivering public speeches are similar in several ways. Both usually involve research, analysis of information and ideas, and the presentation of that information to others. In small groups your presentation may be to other group members, although sometimes a group will present its findings to an external body. Yet despite these similarities, there are notable differences between public speaking and group communication. The effective communicator will seek to master both sets of skills.

Group Discussion and Decision Making

One of the most important reasons we form groups is to make decisions. We may seek a friend's guidance because we believe that two heads are better than one. The philosophy behind this decision is the foundation of group decision making. You may have heard the expression that in communication "the whole is greater than the sum of its parts." This is particularly true in group communication. What this means is that, if a group of five functions effectively, its product will be qualitatively or quantitatively superior to the total product of five people working individually. But a group is able to work most effectively when members follow certain principles of group decision making.

work team: a team or group of people who perform all activities needed to produce the product, service, or other goal specified by an outside leader, supervisor, or manager.

self-directed work team: a group of people who manage themselves by identifying, conducting, and monitoring all activities needed to produce a product or service.

Principles of Group Decision Making

1. Group decision making is a shared responsibility.
2. Group decision making requires a clear understanding of goals.
3. Group decision making benefits from a clear but flexible agenda.
4. Group decision making is enhanced by open communication.
5. Group decision making requires adequate information.

Principles of Group Decision Making

Group Decision Making Is a Shared Responsibility. It's true that the group leader plays a special role in the group. As a matter of fact, we include separate sections in this chapter about the responsibilities of the group leader as well as of members. The presence of a group leader does not necessarily establish a leader-follower, or even an active-passive, association. In fact, this relationship is usually better represented as a partnership. Group decision making requires the active participation of all members performing mutually reinforcing responsibilities.

Group Decision Making Requires a Clear Understanding of Goals. As we have stated earlier, every group has a goal. Sometimes that goal is predetermined. Your instructor may, for example, divide your class into small groups, assigning each group to generate a list of 25 topics suitable for a speech to inform. In your career, you may be part of a small group having the task of studying specific job-related problems and proposing workable solutions. In both of these instances, the group has a clear statement of its objective. In other situations, the goal of your group may be less clear. If that is the case, you will have to clarify, specify, or even determine your goals.

Group Decision Making Benefits from a Clear but Flexible Agenda. Every group needs a plan of action. Because a group's process affects its product, it is vital that members spend sufficient time generating an action plan. The leader can facilitate this process by suggesting procedures that the group may adopt, modify, or reject. The best plan, or agenda, however, is one not dictated by the leader but rather developed by both the leader and the members of the group. Remember, the leader and the group members form a partnership.

A group's agenda should be both specific and flexible. Group participants must know what is expected of them and how they will go about accomplishing the task at hand. Raising $1,000 for charity could be accomplished by dividing the membership into five teams, each having the responsibility for generating $200. These teams would need to communicate and coordinate to avoid unnecessary overlap as they decided on their fund-raising projects. Groups also need to be flexible as they pursue their goals. Unexpected obstacles may require revising the agenda. The group needs a backup plan, for example, if its car wash is canceled because of rain.

Group Decision Making Is Enhanced by Open Communication. If all members of a group think alike, there is no need for the group. One person can simply make the decision. Diversity is what gives a group breadth of perspective. Both the group leader and individual members should protect and encourage the expression of minority views.

What a group wants to avoid is the problem of *groupthink,* a term coined by Irving Janis. **Groupthink** occurs when group members come to care more about con-

groupthink: excessive agreement among group members who value conformity more than critical evaluation.

forming and not making waves than they do about exercising the critical evaluation necessary to weed out bad ideas.[7] Groupthink reduces open communication and adversely affects the quality of decision making. In order to be effective, a group must encourage each member to exercise his or her independent judgment.

Groupthink
http://sol.brunel.ac.
uk/~jarvis/bola/
communications/
groupthink.html
This Web site discusses Irving Janis's concept of *groupthink*. You can learn seven symptoms of groupthink, as well as suggestions for enhancing effective group decision making.

Group Decision Making Requires Adequate Information. Access to information that is sufficient and relevant is extremely important. A group suffers if its information is based on the research of only one or two of its members. To avoid this problem, a group should follow a few simple steps. First, the leader should provide essential information to the group as a starting point. Second, each member of the group should contribute critical knowledge to the group. Third, the group should divide the gathering of information in a way that is efficient and yet provides some overlap. Later in this chapter, we provide some suggestions for gathering information. Now that we understand the principles of group decision making, let's take a look at how the group makes decisions.

The Process of Group Decision Making

In his celebrated book *How We Think,* published in 1910, John Dewey argued that decision making should be a logical, orderly process.[8] His "Steps to Reflective Thinking" have provided one of the most useful, and we think one of the best, approaches to problem solving. Authors and theorists differ in their adaptations of the reflective thinking model, organizing it around five, six, or seven steps. We prefer a seven-step approach.

If you are a member of a problem-solving discussion group or a task-oriented group and you have not been assigned a topic, the group will need to select a topic and word it. A good discussion topic is current, is controversial, and has a body of data and opinion from which to construct and refute positions. Once you select a topic meeting these criteria, you must word the topic according to the following guidelines.

First, it should be worded as a question the group will seek to answer. "The campus parking problem" fails to meet this criterion and, consequently, does not direct participants in the discussion toward a goal. Better wordings are evident in the examples presented in the second criterion.

Second, the question should be open rather than closed. Open wording might include "What can be done to alleviate the parking problem on campus?" or "How should this college solve the campus parking problem?" These questions are open because they do not direct the group to one particular solution. They invite a variety of solutions and can generate lively and productive discussion. The question "Should the campus build a multistory parking facility to solve the campus parking problem?" is an example of a closed question, because it focuses attention on only one solution. This yes-or-no question limits discussion of alternative proposals. Because it forces individuals to choose sides, a closed question is probably more appropriate for a debate than for a discussion format.

After members have agreed upon a topic question, the group should begin answering it in a logical, methodical manner. The following seven-step process, based on Dewey's model, will aid your group. It is important that you go through these steps chronologically and not jump ahead in your discussion. Solutions are best discussed and evaluated only after a problem is thoroughly defined and analyzed.

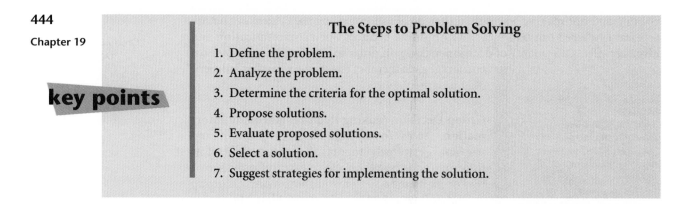

The Steps to Problem Solving

1. Define the problem.
2. Analyze the problem.
3. Determine the criteria for the optimal solution.
4. Propose solutions.
5. Evaluate proposed solutions.
6. Select a solution.
7. Suggest strategies for implementing the solution.

Define the Problem. Before you can solve a problem, you must first define it. By defining the key terms of the question, group members decide how they will focus the topic, thus enabling them to keep on track and to avoid extraneous discussion. Suppose your college asks you to be part of a student advisory committee to address the issue, "What can be done to alleviate the parking problem on campus?" In order to answer the question, members must agree on what constitutes "the parking problem." Are there too few parking spaces? If there are sufficient spaces, are they not geographically located to serve the campus best? Is there congestion only during certain times of the day or week? Is the problem how the spaces are designated—for example, is there adequate parking for faculty but not for students? Is the problem not the number of spaces but the condition of the parking lots? How your group defines the problem determines, to a large extent, how you will solve it. If there is not a problem with the condition of the lots or the number of spaces for faculty, you can safely delete these considerations from your discussion agenda.

Analyze the Problem. In analyzing any problem, a group looks at both its symptoms and causes. We gauge the severity of a problem by examining its *symptoms*. For example, the group needs to know not only the approximate number of students unable to find parking spaces, but also why that is detrimental. Students may be late for class or may avoid going to the library because of parking congestion; accidents may occur as cars crowd into small spaces; the college may spark resentment from students who pay to attend but have no place to park; students may transfer to another school having more convenient access; students walking to dimly lit and distant parking spaces after an evening class may worry about physical attacks. These symptoms point to the magnitude of the problem. Certainly, some symptoms are more serious than others, and group members must identify those needing immediate action.

However, the group is still not ready to propose remedies. The group must now consider the *causes* of the problem. By examining how a difficulty developed, a group may find its solution. The parking problem may stem from a variety of causes, including increased enrollment, parking spaces converted to other uses, lack of funds to build new parking lots, too many classes scheduled at certain times, inadequate use of distant parking lots, and some student parking spaces earmarked for faculty and administrators.

Determine the Criteria for the Optimal Solution. Decision-making criteria are the standards we use to judge the merits of proposed solutions. It is wise to state these criteria before discussing solutions. Why select an action plan only to discover later that sufficient funding is unavailable? The group studying campus parking worked to avoid this pitfall. Some of the criteria they considered were as follows:

Criteria	Explanation
Economics	The proposal should be cost effective.
Aesthetics	The proposal should not spoil the beauty of the campus.
Legality	The proposal cannot force residents and businesses adjacent to campus to sell their land to the college.
Growth	The proposal should account for future increases in enrollment.
Security	Students should be safe as they go to and from parking lots.

The group could also have considered ranking parking privileges according to student seniority or giving students parking status equal to faculty.

Propose Solutions. Only after completing the first three steps is the group ready to propose solutions. This is essentially a brainstorming step with emphasis on the quantity, not quality, of suggestions. At this stage, the group should not worry about evaluating any suggested solutions, no matter how farfetched they may seem. This group's brainstorming list included the following:

Building a multistory parking lot in the center of campus.

Constructing parking lots near the edge of campus.

Reclaiming some faculty spaces for student use.

Lighting and patrolling lots in the evening.

Initiating bus service between apartment complexes and the campus.

Encouraging students to carpool or to ride bicycles to campus.

Evaluate Proposed Solutions. Now the group is ready to evaluate each of the proposed solutions using the criteria listed in the third step. Next, the group considers the advantages of the proposed solution. Finally, they assess its disadvantages. The centrally located, high-rise parking garage may not be cost effective and may intrude on the beauty of the campus but may use valuable land efficiently and limit the extent of late-night walking.

Select a Solution. After evaluating each proposed solution, you and your fellow group members should have a pretty good idea of those solutions to exclude from consideration and those to retain. You will then weigh the merits and deficiencies of each. Your final solution may be a combination of several of the proposed remedies. For example, the group working on the campus parking problem could issue a final report advocating a three-phase solution: short-range, middle-range, and long-range goals. A short-term approach may involve converting a little-used athletic practice field to a parking facility, creating more bicycle parking areas, and encouraging carpooling. A middle-range solution could involve creating a bus system between student apartment houses and the campus or trying to get the city transit system to incorporate new routes. The proposal for the long term could involve building a well-lit multistory parking facility, not in the middle of campus but near the athletic complex, to be used during the week for general student parking and on weekends for athletic and entertainment events.

Suggest Strategies for Implementing the Solution. Once the small group has worked out a solution, members would normally submit their recommendations to another body for approval, action, and implementation. Sometimes, however, decision makers should not only select feasible and effective solutions but also show how they can be implemented. How would the small group incorporate suggestions for implementing its solution? Members would probably recommend coordinating their plan with the long-range master plan for the college. Other administrators would have to be included. The group would probably also suggest a timetable detailing short-term and long-term projects, and might also identify possible funding sources.

In summary, the reflective thinking model enables a group to define a problem, analyze it, determine the criteria for a good solution, propose solutions, evaluate solutions, select a solution, and suggest ways to implement it. Decisions made by following this process are generally better, and group members are more satisfied with their work. Not only can this model benefit groups in business, government, education, and other organizations, it can also improve your individual decision making.

The Responsibilities of Group Members

Whether your group is a self-directed team or an assembly of members with a traditional leader, the ideal leader–member relationship is not an active-passive partnership. In order to enhance the quality of the group's product, all members must participate actively. What do group members do? If you reflect on our example of the group tackling the campus parking problem, you can see how those group members handled their responsibilities. Productive group members undertake five key responsibilities.

key points

Responsibilities of Group Members

1. Inform the group.
2. Advocate personal beliefs.
3. Question other participants.
4. Evaluate ideas and proposals.
5. Support and monitor other group members.

Inform the Group. Group members should enlarge the information base upon which decisions are made and action taken. As we have said elsewhere, a decision is only as good as the information upon which it is based. If the group does not know all the causes of a problem, for example, its proposed solution may not solve it. The greater the number of possible solutions a group considers, the greater its chance of selecting the best one.

Just the facts, ma'am.
—Sgt. Joe Friday, Dragnet

You enlarge the group's information base in two ways. First, you contribute what you already know about the issue being discussed. Hearsay information is worth mentioning at this stage, as long as you acknowledge that it is something you have heard but cannot prove. Another member may be able to confirm or refute it, or it can be put on the agenda for further research. Dispelling popular misconceptions so that they do not contaminate the decision-making process is important.

Second, group members contribute to a group's understanding of a topic by gathering additional relevant information. Ideas surfacing during a group meeting may help shape the agenda for the next meeting. You may hear ideas that you want to explore further. You may need to check out facts before the group can clarify the dimensions of a problem or adopt a particular plan of action. The research and thought you give to a topic before a meeting will make the meeting itself more efficient and productive.

Advocate Personal Beliefs. Group members should not only provide information to help make decisions, but they also should use that data to develop positions on the issues being discussed. Participants should be willing to state and defend their opinions.

A good participant is open-minded, though—willing to offer ideas and then revise or retract them as additional facts and expert opinion surface. Your opinions may change as they are challenged throughout the discussion.

Question Other Participants. Effective participants not only give but also seek information and opinions. Knowing how and when to ask an appropriate question is an important skill for group members. As one advertisement claims, "When you ask better questions, you tend to come up with better answers." The ability to ask effective questions requires active listening, sensitivity to the feelings of others, and a desire to learn. Group members should seek clarification of ideas they do not understand and encourage others to explain, defend, and extend their ideas.

Evaluate Ideas and Proposals. Too often we either accept what we hear at face value or remain silent even though we disagree with what is said. Yet challenging facts, opinions, and proposals benefits the quality of discussion. As Adlai Stevenson proclaimed, "Freedom rings where opinions clash." It is the obligation of the group to evoke a range of positions on the issue being discussed and then separate the good ideas from the bad. Each idea should be discussed thoroughly and analyzed critically. A decision based on incorrect information or faulty reasoning may be ineffective or even counterproductive. Thus, all group members are obligated to evaluate the contributions of others and to submit their own positions to rigorous testing. This is sometimes difficult to do. Yet participants should not be defensive about their ideas, but instead be open to constructive criticism.

Support and Monitor Other Group Members. A group is a collection of individuals having different personalities. Some may be less assertive than others and may have fragile egos. Reluctant to express their ideas because they fear criticism, they may cause the group to lose important information and to rush into a decision. They may even foster the groupthink we discussed earlier. In addition to providing support for reticent individuals, members should also take note of possible dysfunctional, self-oriented behaviors that impede the group's progress. Ronald Adler and Jeanne Elmhorst describe some of these roles and behaviors:

- *The blocker:* Prevents progress by constantly raising objections.
- *The attacker:* Aggressively questions the competence or motives of others.
- *The recognition-seeker:* Repeatedly and unnecessarily calls attention to self by relating irrelevant experiences, boasting, and seeking sympathy.
- *The joker:* Engages in joking behavior in excess of tension-relieving needs, distracting others.
- *The withdrawer:* Refuses to take a stand on social or task issues; covers up feelings; does not respond to others' comments.[9]

The climate of the group should encourage openness and acceptance. It is the job of both the leader and the group members to create and reinforce a climate of openness and acceptance.

The Responsibilities of Group Leaders

When individuals complain about the lack of cohesiveness and productivity of their group, much of their criticism is often directed toward the group's leader. Just as effective leadership depends on effective membership, so does effective membership depend on effective leadership. Leaders have certain responsibilities that, if fulfilled, will help the group meet its goal.

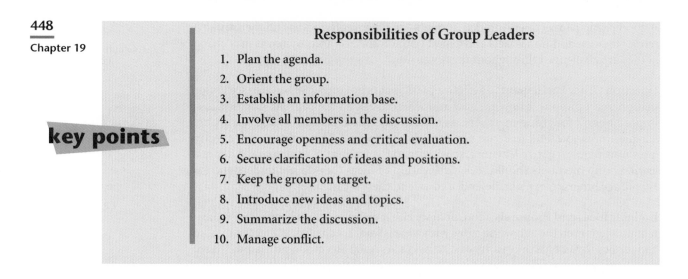

key points

Responsibilities of Group Leaders

1. Plan the agenda.
2. Orient the group.
3. Establish an information base.
4. Involve all members in the discussion.
5. Encourage openness and critical evaluation.
6. Secure clarification of ideas and positions.
7. Keep the group on target.
8. Introduce new ideas and topics.
9. Summarize the discussion.
10. Manage conflict.

Plan the Agenda. A group leader has the primary responsibility for planning an agenda. This does not mean dictating the agenda; rather, the leader offers suggestions and solicits group input into the process.

Orient the Group. How a meeting begins is extremely important in setting expectations that affect group climate and productivity. A leader may want to begin a meeting with some brief opening remarks to orient the group to its mission and the process it will follow. In analyzing business meetings, Roger Mosvick and Robert Nelson conclude, "The chairperson's orientation speech is the single most important act of the business meeting." They describe this speech as follows:

> It is a systematically prepared, fully rehearsed, sit-down speech of not less than three minutes nor more than five minutes (most problems require at least three minutes of orientation; anything over five minutes sets up a pattern of dominance and control by the chairperson).[10]

For some groups that you lead, it will not always be appropriate or even desirable to begin a meeting with a structured speech. Still, leaders should try to accomplish several objectives early in the group's important first meeting. They should (1) stress the importance of the task, (2) secure agreement on the process the group will follow, (3) encourage interaction among members, and (4) set an expectation of high productivity.

Establish an Information Base. Leaders may wish to introduce background information to the group in an opening statement or to forward some relevant articles with background information to members before the first meeting. This sometimes makes the initial meeting more productive by establishing a starting point for discussion. Leaders should encourage input from all members, however, as the primary means of ensuring sufficient information for making decisions.

Involve All Members in the Discussion. A leader must make certain that participation among group members is balanced. A person who speaks too much is as much a problem as one who speaks too little. In either case, the potential base of information and opinion is narrowed. Leaders can encourage more thoughtful and balanced discussion by asking members to think about a particular issue, problem, or solution prior to the discussion, then asking each member to share his or her ideas with the group before discussing each. This strategy often promotes a more thoughtful analysis of the topic and encourages each member to participate in the discussion. Remember our position that all members share the responsibility of group leadership. If someone is not contributing to the discussion, any member of the group can ask the silent person for his or her opinion.

Encourage Openness and Critical Evaluation. After the group has shared information and ideas, the leader must guide the group in evaluating them. The leader may do this by directing probing questions to specific individuals or to the group as a whole. To achieve and maintain a climate of free and honest communication, the group leader must be sensitive to the nonverbal communication of participants, encouraging them to verbalize both their reluctance and their excitement about the ideas other members are expressing. At the same time, the sensitive leader will keep criticism focused on ideas rather than on personalities.

Secure Clarification of Ideas and Positions. Effective leaders are good at getting members of the discussion to make their positions and ideas clearer and more specific. They do this in two ways. First, the leader may encourage a member to continue talking by asking a series of probing follow-up questions ("So what would happen if . . . ?"). Even the use of prods ("Uh-huh." "Okay?") can force discussants to think through and verbalize their ideas and positions. Second, the leader may close a particular line of discussion by paraphrasing the ideas of a speaker ("So what you're saying is that . . ."). This strategy confirms the leader's understanding, repeats the idea for the benefit of other group members, and invites their reaction.

Keep the Group on Target. Effective leaders keep their sights on the group's task while realizing the importance of group social roles. There is nothing wrong with group members becoming friendly and socializing. This added dimension can strengthen your group. However, when social functions begin to impede work on the task, the group leader must "round up the strays" and redirect the entire group to its next goal.

Introduce New Ideas and Topics. We've already mentioned that it is important for leaders to prepare for the first group meeting, either by researching and preparing an orientation speech or by circulating background materials to group members. In addition, the leader should be the most willing researcher among the group. If discussion stalls because the group lacks focus or motivation, the leader must be willing and able to initiate new topics for research and talk. If a lapse in the group's progress signals that research and discussion have been exhausted, the leader must recognize this situation and be willing to move on to the next phase of group work.

Summarize the Discussion. A leader should provide the group periodic reviews of what has been decided and what remains to be decided. These summaries keep members focused on the group's task. Leaders may begin a group meeting with an *initial summary,* a brief synopsis of what the group decided previously. They may offer *internal summaries* during the discussion to keep the group on target. At the conclusion of the group task, leaders should provide a *final summary,* reviewing what the group accomplished.

Manage Conflict. Conflict is not only inevitable in group discussion, it is essential. When ideas collide, participants must rethink and defend their positions. This process engenders further exploration of facts and opinions and enhances the likelihood of a quality outcome. It is important, then, that a group not discourage conflict but manage it.

An anonymous benefactor has contributed funds to sponsor a Career Day on Emily's campus. The president of the Student Government Association appoints Emily, a first-year student, to chair a committee charged with drafting a detailed proposal for Career Day activities. Despite Emily's efforts to encourage open discussion and to distribute the workload, two of the five committee members have contributed little. Kate, a junior, opposes most of the ideas offered by others, seldom volunteers any concrete suggestions of her own, and often wants to discuss issues unrelated to the committee's task. Gary, a senior, seldom attends meetings, and when Emily asks for his input, he usually shrugs and says, "Whatever you decide is fine with me." After three unproductive meetings with all five members present, Emily is concerned that the committee may not meet its deadline for the report. She decides to call a private meeting with the two productive members and draft the report. They finish it in a few hours, then present it to the full committee at the next meeting, allowing all of the members to discuss and vote on it.

Is Emily's strategy an ethical one for a committee chair? When a group is not functioning effectively, should the leader do everything possible to ensure that all members participate in the decision-making process, or is it more important to ensure that the group takes action, even if it means giving more power to selected members? What responsibility do the members have to ensure equal participation?

While conflict of ideas contributes to group effectiveness, interpersonal antagonism may undermine it. When conflict becomes personal, it ceases to be productive. Such conflict disrupts the group. Some members may stop expressing their opinions for fear of attack. If the climate becomes too uncomfortable, members may withdraw from the group. Thus, it is essential that when conflict surfaces, the group responds appropriately. At some point, it may become evident that conflict cannot be solved by the group or in the presence of group members. In this event, the leader may have to meet with the disruptive member one-on-one and discuss the problem.

When a group, following the seven steps of problem solving, is composed of members and a leader fulfilling the various roles we have just outlined, it should produce results quickly. At times, the problem solving will benefit the group alone and no external report is needed. Often, however, the group will be requested or will want to present its findings to a larger group: coworkers, company stockholders, or just an interested public audience, for example. In such cases, the group must continue to work together to plan its presentation.

The Group Presentation

In the following sections of this chapter, we discuss two popular formats for group presentations and provide a systematic checklist to help you develop a first-rate presentation.

Formats for the Presentation

There are several different formats for a group presentation, two of which are the public discussion and the symposium.

The Public Discussion. In a **public discussion,** a group sits, usually in a semicircle, in front of the audience. Members are aware of an audience but usually address others in the group. The audience, in effect, eavesdrops on the group's conversation. If your pub-

public discussion: a small group exchanging ideas and opinions on a single topic in the presence of an audience.

In a symposium, speakers offer their perspectives on a topic and then discuss those issues with other panelists, often answering questions from the audience.

lic speaking class includes group presentations, your small group may be asked to use this format to present its report to the class.

The problem-solving classroom discussion usually requires extensive preparation. The group has researched the topic, planned the discussion, and possibly practiced the presentation. Members have a general idea of the content and organization of their own and other participants' remarks, although the presentation is not memorized or scripted. The presentation is intended to inform and persuade the audience on the issue being discussed. Sometimes a question-answer period follows.

The Symposium. A **symposium** is a series of speeches on a single topic presented to an audience. It differs from a public discussion in at least two ways. First, there is no interaction among the speakers during the presentation, unless a discussion period follows. Each speaker has a designated amount of time to present his or her remarks. Second, speakers address members of the audience directly. Sometimes speakers are seated at a table; often they use a lectern. In most public symposiums, the speakers have not met beforehand to discuss what they will say. If you are assigned to a group for a presentation in this class, you will likely want to meet several times, following some of the guidelines we discuss in the following section.

Preparing a Group Presentation

A group presentation offers you a variety of learning experiences. You can enhance your research, organization, oral communication, and group interaction skills. This assignment, therefore, is a significant learning opportunity. In addition, your group presentation can be a positive learning experience for your classmates.

Although there is no one correct way to prepare for a group presentation, the following suggestions will help you work more efficiently and produce a more effective product. This symbol (•) denotes those steps requiring group interaction; the other steps can be done individually.

symposium: a series of public speeches on a single topic, possibly followed by group discussion or a question-answer period.

Steps in Preparing a Group Presentation

- • 1. Brainstorm about the topic.
  2. Do some exploratory research.
- • 3. Discuss and divide the topic into areas of responsibility.
  4. Research your specific topic area.

(continued)

key points

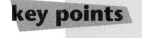

5. Draft an outline of your content area.
- 6. Discuss how all the information interrelates.
- 7. Finalize the group presentation format.
- 8. Plan the introduction and conclusion of the presentation.
  9. Prepare and practice your speech.
- 10. Rehearse and revise the presentation.
- 11. Develop a team look.

- **Brainstorm about the Topic.** If you've read the previous chapters, our first suggestion for preparing a group presentation shouldn't surprise you. Through brainstorming, you will discover knowledge that group members already possess, and you will uncover numerous ideas for further research. In addition to providing content, brainstorming also serves a relationship function. By giving all members an opportunity to participate, brainstorming affords you a glimpse of your peers' personalities and their approaches to group interaction. You get to know them, and they get to know you. Maintaining an atmosphere of openness and respect during this first meeting gets the group off to a good start. Once you have generated a list of areas concerning your group's topic, you are ready for the second step.

Do Some Exploratory Research. Through brainstorming, you discover areas that need further investigation. The second phase of your group process is individual research. While there may be some merit in each person's selecting a different topic to research, research roles should not be too rigid. Rather than limit yourself by topic, you may wish to divide your research by resource. One member may look at popular news magazines, another at government documents, while a third may interview a professor who is knowledgeable on the topic, and so forth. It is important that you not restrict your discovery to the list of topics you have generated. Exploratory research is also a form of brainstorming. As you look in indexes and read articles you find, you will uncover more topics. Each member of the group should try to find a few good sources that are diverse in scope.

- **Discuss and Divide the Topic into Areas of Responsibility.** After exploratory research, your group should reconvene to discuss what each member found. Which expectations were confirmed by your research? Which were not? What topics did you find that you had not anticipated? Your objective at this stage of the group process is to decide on the key areas you wish to investigate. Each person should probably be given primary responsibility for researching a particular area. That person becomes the content expert in that area. While this approach makes research more efficient, it has a drawback. If one person serves as a specialist, the group gambles that he or she will research thoroughly and be objective in reporting findings. If either assumption is not valid, the quantity of information can be insufficient and its quality contaminated. An alternative approach is to assign more than one person to a specific area.

Research Your Specific Topic Area. Using strategies we have discussed in Chapter 7, research your topic area. Your focus should be on the quality of the sources you discover, not on quantity. While your primary goal should be to gather information on your topic, you should also note information related to your colleagues' topics. As you consult indexes, jot down on a card sources that may be helpful to another member in the group. If you are researching a relevant Internet source that gives you the option of forwarding the page to someone, send it to the e-mail address of a group member who might find it useful. Group members who support each other in these and other ways make the process more efficient and, hence, more enjoyable. This usually results in a better product.

Draft an Outline of Your Content Area. After you have concluded your initial research but before you meet again with your group, construct an outline of the ideas and information you've found. This step is important for two reasons. It forces you to make sense of all the information you have collected, and it will expedite the next step when you will share your information with the rest of the members of your group.

• **Discuss How All the Information Interrelates.** You are now ready to meet again with the other members of your group. Members should briefly summarize what they have discovered through their research. After all have shared their ideas, the group should decide which ideas are most important and how these ideas relate to each other. There should be a natural development of the topic that can be divided among the members of the group.

• **Finalize the Group Presentation Format.** The speaking order should already be determined. There are, nevertheless, certain procedural details that the group must decide. Will the first speaker introduce all presenters, or will each person introduce the next speaker? Where will the participants sit when they are not speaking, facing the audience, or in the front row? The more details you decide beforehand, the fewer distractions you will have on the day you speak.

• **Plan the Introduction and Conclusion of the Presentation.** A presentation should appear to be that of a group and not that of four or five individuals. Consequently, you must work on introducing and concluding the group's comments, and you must incorporate smooth transitions from one speaker's topic to the next. An introduction should state the topic, define important terms, and establish the importance of the subject. A conclusion should summarize what has been presented and end with a strong final statement.

Prepare and Practice Your Speech. By this time in the course, you know the requirements of an excellent speech and have had the opportunity to deliver a few. Most of our earlier suggestions also apply to your speech in your group's presentation. Some differences are worth noting, however. For example, as part of a group presentation, you will need to refer to members' speeches and perhaps even use some of their supporting materials. The group presentation may also impose physical requirements you haven't encountered as a classroom speaker, such as using a microphone, speaking to those seated around you in addition to making direct contact with the audience, or speaking from a seated position.

• **Rehearse and Revise the Presentation.** Independent practice of your individual speech is important, but that is only one part of rehearsal. The group should practice its entire presentation. Group rehearsal will not only make participants more confident about their individual presentations, but will also give the group a feeling of cohesion.

• **Develop a Team Look.** A team presentation is more than just a collection of individual presentations on the same topic. Coordinating both the content and the delivery of your presentation enhances impact and credibility. Consider the details that contribute to a polished, proficient image. Your appearance, for example, can reinforce that image. Discuss what you will wear. All presenters should be well groomed and should probably dress up a little rather than "dressing down." Coordinate your presentational aids. You may even want to assign one person to produce all the presentational aids so that they are consistent in design and appearance. You should also decide on signals to provide team members feedback during their individual presentations. What time signals will you use to keep the presentation flowing? How will you signal if a team member is speaking too long or needs to speak louder?

Following the procedures we have described above should result in a group presentation that seems carefully planned, conscientiously researched, adequately supported, and well delivered. More than that, however, your presentation should also demonstrate the spontaneity, goodwill, and camaraderie that will likely have developed if members of your group have functioned effectively and productively together.

Summary

Whether they are part of our business, social, or personal lives, numerous formal and informal groups are important to us because they solve problems, get things done, and provide us with emotional support. A *small group* is a collection of three or more people influencing and interacting with one another in pursuit of a common goal.

Groups usually fulfill both *socially oriented* and *task-oriented* needs for their participants, though one of these types of needs will predominate depending upon the situation. Three types of task-oriented groups include the *study group,* which learns about a topic; the *problem-solving group,* which decides on courses of action; and the *action group,* which implements proposals. The business and professional worlds are relying increasingly on *work teams,* groups of people who perform all activities needed to produce some product, service, or other goal specified by an outside leader, supervisor, or manager. *Self-directed work teams* perform all the activities of work teams but also set their own goals and monitor their own progress. This chapter focused on the ways such groups and teams function and the tasks they accomplish: gathering, analyzing, and spreading information; and formulating, advocating, and implementing courses of action.

Group decisions are usually superior to decisions individuals make by themselves. To ensure valid decisions, groups must abide by five principles. First, group decision making is a shared responsibility and requires active participation of all members. Second, group members must share a goal that is specific and realistic. Third, groups make decisions best under a clear but flexible schedule or agenda. Fourth, groups can avoid *groupthink* and make the best decisions when members are free to express opinions openly. Fifth, group decision making requires and benefits from the research and information shared by all participants.

Problem-solving groups can speed their progress and simplify their task by following a seven-step modification of John Dewey's steps to reflective thinking. First, define the problem. Second, analyze the symptoms and the causes of the problem. Third, determine the criteria that an optimal solution to the problem must satisfy. Fourth, propose various solutions to the problem. Fifth, evaluate each possible solution against the established criteria. Sixth, decide on the best solution, and seventh, suggest ways of putting the solution into action. Following these steps in this order will streamline group problem-solving work.

Group participation involves five functions: sharing information, advocating personal beliefs, questioning other participants, evaluating data and opinions, and supporting other participants in the group. Responsibilities of group leaders include planning the group's agenda; orienting the group to the task at hand; providing background information on the problem to be discussed; involving all members in the group's discussion; encouraging a climate of open, honest critical evaluation; seeking clarification of members' ideas and positions; keeping the group focused on its task; introducing new ideas and topics for discussion; summarizing the discussion at various points; and managing interpersonal conflict. If group members and leaders perform these functions during the seven-step problem-solving process, they should reach a satisfactory conclusion and may then be asked to present their findings in a public presentation.

The presentation may take the form of a *public discussion* before an audience. In this situation, participants speak to one another about aspects of the problem after researching, organizing, and practicing the presentation. Another popular form of group presentation is the *symposium,* a series of formal individual speeches on different aspects of a problem.

When given the opportunity to meet and plan a group presentation before delivering it, members should always do so. Both those experienced and inexperienced in preparing group presentations can benefit from a logical eleven-step approach to developing them. First, brainstorm the topic with colleagues in the group. Second, do some individual exploratory research to gauge the scope of the topic. Third, discuss the topic with group members and divide areas of research responsibility by topic or source. Fourth, individually research your assigned area, noting sources in other group members' areas. Fifth, organize the data your research has yielded. Sixth, discuss with other group members how all the generated information interrelates. Seventh, determine the presentation format. Eighth, plan the introduction of group members and the material to be discussed. Ninth, prepare and practice speeches individually. Tenth, rehearse and revise the entire group presentation. Eleventh and finally, develop a team look to underscore the group's belonging and functioning together.

Analyzing a Group's Interactions

Arrange to attend a meeting of a student, faculty, city, or some other decision-making group. Select a group with a limited number of members so that you can observe interactions among them. Take notes during the meeting and then, using the lists of responsibilities for group members and group leaders on pages 446 and 448 as a guide, write a brief analysis of the group's interactions. Which responsibilities did the group perform well? Which responsibilities seemed to receive little attention? What could the group do to foster more effective interactions? If the group had a leader, what strengths and weaknesses did you observe in his or her communication behaviors?

practice critique

Exercises

1. Complete the brainstorming exercise suggested in the opening paragraph of this chapter. Select one of the groups you listed. Describe the group according to four characteristics: individuals, interaction, influence, and goal.

2. Refer to the list of groups generated in Exercise 1. Classify each of these groups. Which are primarily socially oriented groups? Which are primarily task-oriented groups? Which groups balance both goals?

3. Select someone in a leadership position to interview. The person may be a business executive, an officer in an organization, a school principal, a college president, or any other leader. Construct and ask a series of questions designed to discover his or her views on characteristics of effective and ineffective leaders. Record the answers, and be prepared to discuss them in class.

4. Using the topic areas listed below, select a specific problem area, and word it in the form of a problem-solving discussion question.
   a. crime
   b. education

    c. international relations

    d. political campaigning

    e. pubic health

5. Choose four campus problems you think need to be addressed—for example, class registration. Word the topics as problem-solving questions. Analyze each topic, asking the following questions:

    a. How important is the problem?

    b. What information do you need to analyze and solve the problem?

    c. Where would you find this information?

    d. What barriers keep the problem from being solved now?

    e. Which steps in the problem-solving process do you think will generate the most conflict? Why?

    Based on your answers to these questions, select the best topic for a problem-solving discussion. Justify your choice.

6. Think of a problem you are experiencing that you need to solve. Work through the seven steps of the reflective thinking model to arrive at a solution to the problem. Did the model help you arrive at a decision? If so, which steps were most helpful? If not, what are some limitations of the model?

7. Observe a meeting of a student, faculty, city, or some other decision-making group. What examples did you observe of good and bad group communication skills? Could the meeting have been conducted better? If so, how?

8. Write a summary and evaluation of your participation in an assigned group discussion, using the five criteria for effective group participation. Write a critique of other members in your group using these same criteria.

9. Write a critique of your group leader using the ten criteria for effective leadership. If you served as leader, write a self-critique.

10. Discuss when it would be better for a group presentation to take the form of a public discussion. When would the symposium format be preferable?

Notes

1. *Working Woman* July 1993: 39. The survey was conducted by Goodrich & Sherwood, a New York human-resources consulting firm.

2. Bobby R. Patton and Kim Giffin, *Decision-Making Group Interaction,* 2nd ed. (New York: Harper, 1978) 1.

3. Roger K. Mosvick and Robert B. Nelson, *We've Got to Start Meeting Like This!* (Glenview, IL: Scott, 1987) 4.

4. Paul E. Nelson, "Small-Group Communication," in Lilian O. Feinberg, *Applied Business Communication* (Sherman Oaks, CA: Alfred, 1982) 27.

5. Thomas E. Harris and John C. Sherblom, *Small Group and Team Communication* (Boston: Allyn, 1999) 123.

6. Richard S. Wellins, William C. Byham, and Jeanne M. Wilson, *Empowered Teams: Creating Self-Directed Work Groups That Improve Quality, Productivity, and Participation* (San Francisco: Josey-Bass, 1991) 4–5.

7. Irving L. Janis, *Groupthink: Psychological Studies of Policy Decisions and Fiascoes,* 2nd ed. (Boston: Houghton, 1982) 9.

8. John Dewey, *How We Think* (Boston: Heath, 1910).

9. Ronald B. Adler and Jeanne Marquardt Elmhorst, *Communicating at Work: Principles and Practices for Business and the Professions,* 6th ed. (Boston: McGraw, 1999) 241. These authors, and other scholars, base their discussion of these group roles on Kenneth D. Benne and Paul Sheats, "Functional Roles of Group Members," *Journal of Social Issues* 4 (1948): 41–49.

10. Mosvick 114.

A Classroom Speech and Speaker's Journal

Daniel Sarvis took a public speaking class at San Antonio College, a community college, during the spring of 1996. The first major speech assignment in that course was a six- to eight-minute informative speech focusing on a process or a procedure. The speech required no research; students could explain or even demonstrate a process with which they were already familiar. Daniel delivered an interesting extemporaneous speech on the craft of building a ship in a bottle. We asked him to put his speech on videotape, and we then transcribed it as follows.

A Ship in a Bottle

Daniel Sarvis, San Antonio College, San Antonio

I must go down to the seas again, to the lonely sea and the sky,
And all I ask is a tall ship and a star to steer her by.

1   The opening lines of John Masefield's poem "Sea Fever" strike a chord in many of us. We go down to the water for pleasure, relaxation. We even go down to the water just in wonderment. But we go down to the water. And the craft that ply the seas—the sailing ships, the tall ships of a bygone era—often fascinate us. One way that man has commemorated and memorialized the tall ships is in models. And one of the most interesting types of models is the ship in a bottle.

2   "How did they get that big sailing ship into the neck of that tiny, little bottle?" That's a question that many of us have asked. It's a question many of us answer by saying, "They probably cut the bottom off the bottle, put the ship model in, then put the bottle back together." That's a great idea, but that's not how they're done. Just as we are curious about a magician and how he performs an illusion, we have often wondered how they get that ship in the bottle. Today I will answer the question for you, how to get a ship in a bottle. Along with that I will introduce you to the hobby of making a ship in a bottle. I'll give you some history on how ship in a bottle models were first made, why

they were first made. I'll give you two methods of how you may want to produce one yourself. And then I'll sum up by giving you some ideas as to why you would want to do it and what benefit there may be in it for you.

3 Let's begin by looking at the history of model ships in bottles. According to Guy R. Williams in his book *The World of Model Ships and Boats,* there were no ship in bottle models prior to the middle of the nineteenth century. The reasons for this are probably the big clipper ships used in the Australian grain trade, the American gold rush, and also in the China tea trade. These ships went on long, lengthy voyages, and it was not uncommon for voyages to be over 100 days. The sailors were on board these ships in cramped spaces with plenty of time on their hands. Handicrafts they turned to—ship model building, sewing, whatever else they could find—to occupy their time. Ship models in bottles were made because, not surprisingly, there were plenty of empty bottles found in the forecastle, the living quarters of the sailors in the old ships, and the opportunity to produce something as fragile as a ship model and protect it, encase it in glass, was something that presented itself. The materials were very limited. You had very few spare materials on board an old sailing ship. But, fortunately, very few materials were necessary to produce a ship in a bottle model. There is something about the construction that I will reveal to you later, and it is the same method of construction we use today. It gives us a bit of solidarity with the past to think we can produce a piece of work exactly as it was produced over 150 years ago. To summarize, let's look at what we've got: sailors, cramped spaces, limited materials, and plenty of time on their hands. It's a hobby that they took up and one that you can use today.

4 Now that we know something of the history of sailing ship models in bottles, let me explain to you how you may produce your own if you decide on this hobby. There are two very wonderful methods available. Kits are the best way for a beginner to go. Kits are available nationwide in museum shops and hobby shops. They answer every question you might have: what type of ship, what types of materials? The instructions are very clear. Many of the kits already come with the bottle already washed and with the laborious task of peeling the label off taken care of for you. Kits are a very good choice for beginners.

5 If you decide to build one from scratch, there are wonderful books available. The best I have found is Jack Needham's book, *Modeling Ships in Bottles.* Printed originally in 1972, it is still in print and found in hobby shops and libraries. If you decide to build your own, you'll need to know how to go about it. The method used to build a ship in a bottle is quite simple. You produce a model ship small enough to fit into the bottle [presentational aid]. Only that which is visible above the water line—this part of the hull, the body of the ship—is constructed. The rigging—all of the ropes used to stand the masts and yards up (masts being the vertical poles, yards being the spars on which the sails could be hung)—that's all you need to produce. The rigging is reduced to its most rudimentary form. There is a tenth the amount of rigging on a model this size than there would be on a full-sized, museum-quality model.

6 The materials you need are simple. You'll need some wood, some clay, thread, sewing needles, some wire or small pins, and a lot of patience. You'll need a bottle. One of the joys of producing a ship in a bottle is finding and preparing the bottle to put the model in. There's a distiller in Tennessee that produces a wonderful bourbon and an excellent bottle for putting ships in. It's nice and square, and it accommodates a ship very nicely. As if college students need another excuse for throwing a party, you can always throw a party, empty a few bottles, and then put some ships inside of them.

7 When making a ship in a bottle, you'll need to know the secret of how the ship got into the bottle. It's very simple [presentational aid]. Everything on the ship model is made to hinge. The masts fold backwards. The yards fold flush with the masts and lay back against the deck of the ship, using a package that is small enough to slide into the neck of the bottle. These threads, representing the rigging of the ship, are the controlling lines. They extend out past the neck of the bottle and allow you to raise everything back up in place once the model has been set into the bottle. If we summarize, we'll see we've got a hobby that's over 150 years old. The method of production is the same as used over 150 years ago. The sense of solidarity, touching history with the past, is given.

8 It's a very enjoyable, relaxing hobby. It's an absorbing hobby that can relieve your stress after a long day in class, or after a tough day at the office in the business world. These little models make wonderful gifts. If you only produce one in your entire lifetime and keep it for yourself, you'll have a wonderful sense of satisfaction. They are also sold in crafts shows and trade fairs. I have seen them in museum gift shops selling at very high prices. The enjoyment you'll get out of it is difficult to surpass.

9 I've told you about the secret of putting a ship in a bottle. Once all the controlling lines are brought up, you have produced a ship in a bottle. [presentational aid] I've left this one in this situation so you can see the controlling lines. The ship sits in a bed of clay. Everything is straightened up and brought up. With a long bit of razor blade on the end of a stick, you trim the lines off, cap the bottle, and you've completed the project.

10 The old sailor's pastime of producing ships in bottles is over 150 years old. It's a very enjoyable hobby. You can use kits. You can build from scratch using some of the wonderful books that are available to you. The options are yours. You'll enjoy relaxation and a sense of accomplishment once you get finished. And now that you know the secret of how to put a ship model in a bottle, the next time someone asks you can tell them. Or, better yet, you can keep it to yourself.

Reprinted with the permission of the speaker.

Speaker's Journal

After Daniel delivered his speech in class and later on videotape, we interviewed him about his experiences preparing and delivering it, recording his comments on audiotape. In the following Speaker's Journal, you have a chance to read Daniel's account of his thoughts and actions throughout the speech-making process.

Q: How much previous public speaking experience did you have before taking this college class?

A: I did come to the class with a little public speaking experience, only because I am older than the traditional student, probably as old or older than anyone in our class. I had handled sales and had to speak to small groups in sales presentations. I had no formal training, other than what I had learned out in the field. But the experience of having made speeches before boosted my confidence. I knew I could do this.

Q: The topic you chose seems to cut across audience demographics. It could appeal to people regardless of their age, gender, ethnic background, religion, economic status, or group membership. To what extend did you consider each of those characteristics of your audience? Did you select your topic because it does seem to have wide appeal?

A: My listeners' religious affiliations had absolutely no bearing on this topic; I did not even consider them. Age I did consider, because I felt that these young people might have felt that this is an old fogey's hobby and turned off the minute they heard me announce the topic. But I also thought that the young people might be interested in something they can do that's a little unique. In terms of gender, I felt it's a hobby anyone can do—male or female—and some of the young women seemed quite interested. The ethnic backgrounds of my listeners were not a consideration. Neither were their economic status nor their group memberships. Education was a consideration in the sense that we were all in that college class together. Because of that, I assumed that we had all been exposed to fairly similar kinds of information. I also felt that I was speaking to people who, if I mentioned a book, would perhaps go and find it. I didn't have time to give them complete instructions for the process I was describing. But I gave them enough directions that they could go and find detailed instructions.

Q: What was the specific purpose of your speech?

A: To inform the audience of the age-old hobby of building a ship in a bottle and to reveal the secret of getting the model ship into the bottle.

Q: What was your thesis statement?

A: Building a model sailing ship in a bottle is a centuries-old hobby that people can enjoy today by assembling a model kit or by building from scratch.

Q: Was the topic that you chose for this speech self-generated, audience-generated, occasion-generated, or research-generated?

A: The topic I chose was self-generated; I had built ships in bottles before and always had an interest in them.

Q: Were there other aspects of this topic that you wanted to discuss but couldn't because of time limits? If so, what were they? In other words, how did you focus this topic?

A: I didn't go into much detail on the assembly, how to build the ship in the bottle. I did not start with a block of wood and explain the intricacies of carving the hull. Actually, in building a ship in a bottle from scratch, there are steps as tedious as drilling holes in toothpicks with a watchmaker's drill bit. I didn't explain anything like that. I felt that too much detail would lose some of the audience and probably lead me into a 20-to-25-minute speech. Instead, I thought I would get my listeners interested and let them know where they could go to find out the rest of the details if they were interested.

Q: What did you notice about your audience as you were giving your speech, and how did you respond?

A: I remember one was a young man who seemed like he was not at all interested. So after glancing at him about three times, I tried not to look at him. I felt he wasn't interested, and there wasn't anything I could do. Of the people who were interested, I distinctly remember Shannon saying, in the question-and-answer period after the speech when I said anyone can try this, that she would become too frustrated and would break the bottle. She just felt that it was beyond her.

I also remember that when I was speaking and brought out the bottle, several people seemed very interested, sat up in their chairs, and seemed genuinely interested. I think a lot of people have seen a ship in a bottle but have never been up close to one. And they had just learned the secret of how it got in there and wanted to see for themselves if what I was telling them was true.

Q: You did mention a couple of sources of information in your speech, even though the assignment didn't require you to conduct any research. To what extent did you draw on your personal knowledge of this topic?

A: I had built ships in bottles before, and I remembered the two books that I had used to get me started the first time. I was able to find copies of both books so that I could list them in my bibliography. Even though the assignment didn't require research, I knew that I needed to cite my sources because so much of what I know about this topic came from those books.

Q: As you prepared the speech, were you conscious of trying to use a variety of supporting materials to achieve a balanced presentation?

A: Yes. I began the speech with testimony when I quoted the lines from the John Masefield poem. I also used testimony from the Williams books to explain how model ships in bottles originated. A lot of the early part of the speech involved comparing and contrasting the two building methods: from kits and from scratch. Much of the speech was based on my personal narrative as I described the construction of the models.

In order to explain how a model ship is actually placed in a bottle, I had to be sure that my listeners understood some basic parts of a ship. I thought that visual definition would be the clearest and quickest method of ensuring understanding. I did the line drawing and used it to define the "masts" and the "yards." I think that simple line drawing, labeling the mast, yards, and the hull, gave them enough information so that they knew what I was talking about as I described the process. Then, toward the end of the speech, I showed the actual example of the model ship I was building.

Q: How did you determine the key ideas you would cover in your speech?

A: I had three key ideas. The first one was to explain a little about the history of this obscure topic. I wanted to get my classmates interested in the topic beyond the time it took to deliver my speech. I wanted to get people to say, "Yes, I've seen a ship in a bottle" and to ask, "How did that son of a gun get in there?" Therefore, I decided to begin with the interesting anecdote about the history of the craft. I wanted to explain why ships were originally built in bottles by the old sailors. Then, once I thought I had their attention, my second main topic in the body of my speech was sort of a *New Yankee Workshop/This Old House* kind of approach: Here is how you would go about building one of these model ships, either from scratch or from a kit. I laid that out as clearly as I could within the time frame and without getting out the wood and the knives and starting to carve and build one right before their eyes. For my final key idea, I wanted to point out that this is a relaxing hobby. Everyone in the class was a student, and I found out a long time ago that if you can find some sort of a diversion, you'll study more efficiently. I tried to bring that out as well. "Hey, you're in school. If you need a study break, why not try this?"

Q: How did you decide on what to use as an attention-getter, and what did you think you should stress to show the significance of your topic?

A: So many people in class were starting their speeches with questions, some good and some not so good. I knew that I wanted to do something different, use something other than a question. I've always loved John Masefield's poem "Sea Fever," and for this topic those opening lines were always in the back of my mind.

To stress the significance of the topic, I wanted to tie the present to the past. I wanted to establish a link between my classmates and this 150-year-old hobby. No technology here, no software. It's a quiet, solitary, self-paced activity. That's one of its attractions. With the Masefield lines and the link to the past, I guess I was trying to say, "Look, we've all got this latent interest in water."

Q: Did you make a working outline for your speech? If so, then how did it evolve into a formal outline?

A: I did start with a working outline, which changed a lot as I developed and practiced my speech. Originally, I was going to talk just about the building of the ship model with two main points: (1) building from a kit, and (2) building from scratch. But I found that I had so many subpoints under each of those topics that the speech was too long. Finally, I had to take out quite a bit of the detail. That let me add the history section, though. It's funny, but in order to make the speech short enough, I actually had to lengthen my outline. If I hadn't outlined the speech and then worked through a couple of rough drafts of that outline, my speech would have either been way too long or way too dry except for someone who was already interested in the topic. My formal outline eventually was as follows:

I. Model ships in bottles date back more than 150 years.
   A. Sailors on old sailing ships had plenty of time.
   B. Sailors had limited work space and supplies.
      1. Bottle models were small.
      2. Materials for bottle models were plentiful.
II. Today's hobbyist can choose from two methods of construction.
   A. Kit models are best for the beginning model builder.
      1. Many commercial kits provide all necessary materials.
      2. Kits answer questions concerning choice of wood, ship style, and bottles.
      3. Kits offer detailed instructions for assembly.
   B. Building from scratch is an option for the advanced hobbyist.
      1. Building from scratch is more difficult than building from a kit.
      2. Books on model building offer detailed instructions.
      3. Necessary materials include wood, clay, thread, sewing needles, wire, small pins, and a bottle.
III. The secret of getting the ship into the bottle is simple.
   A. The builder constructs only the part of the hull visible above the clay "sea."
   B. All parts of the rigging are made to hinge.
      1. The rigging folds back against the deck of the ship.
      2. Threads attached to various parts allow the rigging to be raised after the ship is in place.
IV. Building ships in bottles is rewarding.
   A. It is an enjoyable, relaxing hobby that provides a sense of accomplishment.
   B. Selling bottle models at craft shows can be profitable.

Q: Thinking back about the speech, how would you evaluate your use of language?

A: I think my language was correct and clear. I'm not aware of making any grammatical mistakes. I also think the speech sounded oral rather than written. I used personal pronouns and contractions, so the speech sounds like my classmates and I talk. That was important in order to engage my listeners. I tried to be clear by defining words like *forecastle, masts,* and *yards*—words my listeners probably didn't know.

One of the consequences of speaking from notes rather than from a manuscript is that my language may not have been as specific or as vivid as it could have been. For example, I think I said that those tall ships went on "long, lengthy voyages." That's a little wordy. If I had scripted the speech, I probably would have included more visual and sensory appeals to describe what it's like to build a model ship. I suppose there's a trade-off: I had to sacrifice some vividness in order to be sure that my speech sounded conversational.

Daniel delivered his speech extemporaneously, with only a set of notes to guide him. By chance, the videotaping of Daniel's speech presented him with an opportunity to improve on his delivery. Interrupted once by static noise from his wireless microphone and once by simultaneous noise from an airplane and a train whistle, Daniel had to repeat a couple of sections of his speech. His answer to the next question sent us back to transcribe one of those sections that had to be replaced.

Q: How did those sections of your speech change after the interruptions?

A: The words in those sections *seemed* to flow much more smoothly. The second time, I had a better feel for what would be interesting and important to my audience, and my sentences took on a livelier rhythm. Here's how I began the body of my speech before the interruption:

> Let's begin by looking at the history of model ships in bottles. According to Guy Williams in his book *The World of Model Ships and Boats,* no one knows the exact beginning of this craft, but no ship in bottle models existed before the middle of the nineteenth century. The reasons for this are the clipper ships used in the California gold rush and later in the Australian grain trade and the China tea trade. These ships brought on the advent of lengthy, lengthy voyages. Voyages of over 100 days were not uncommon. What you found were sailors on board these ships with limited space and a lot of time on their hands. The opportunity to produce handicrafts was something sailors indulged in often. The reason they began ships in bottles no one knows exactly, probably because there were, not surprisingly, a number of empty bottles around in the boats where the old sailors lived in the ships.

When you compare these sentences with those in paragraph 3 of the transcript, you'll see that my delivery improved the second time around.

Q: What presentational aids did you decide would work best for your speech? Did they present any special problems or concerns?

A: I used two types of visual aids in my speech: a diagram and an object. I felt pretty good about them. I knew the simple diagram was clearly drawn and would be easy to see. I knew the ship in a bottle would be harder for people in the back to see clearly, so I thought I would hold it and walk closer to the audience when I talked about it. The only nervousness I really had was about picking up the bottle, for fear I would drop it in front of everyone. It may sound silly, but I was concerned about sweaty palms and that glass bottle.

Q: You delivered an informative speech about a process. Using Chapter 15's ten "Guidelines for Speaking to Inform," how would you evaluate your speech?

A: I think it was clear that I was trying to inform rather than to persuade. I'm obviously enthusiastic about this craft, but I don't think my speech sounded like an "infomercial" selling some ship model kit. I could have been more detailed and specific by narrowing the topic to building from a kit, for example. I could have brought in a kit and showed models at different stages of completion. But that would have made the speech too long, I discovered. Besides, I wanted to explain the options of either using a kit or building from scratch.

The topic is not particularly technical or complicated, so I think my message was clear. I'm not aware of any inaccuracies in the speech, and I cited my sources.

Probably the toughest thing to do was to limit my ideas and supporting materials. I had to resist going into much detail or telling stories about my model building experiences. I had to streamline, making sure that everything I included was relevant to my topic and purpose.

My organization changed as I worked on and timed the speech. Eliminating some of the detail meant that I was able to give a brief history of how these models originated. My final organization seemed appropriate to my purpose.

The visual aids—the drawing and the model I showed—were important to help me explain the process clearly and vividly. Was my delivery effective? That's hard to say. Wearing the microphone and having the extra lights on me certainly made me more nervous than I thought I would be. Having feedback from some listeners there in the room helped me relax; I would have been a lot more nervous speaking only to the camera and camera operator. I think I felt most relaxed when I was using the visual aids. Watching the videotape enabled me to see whether I looked and sounded the way I felt. If I were to retape the speech, I'd try to make my delivery different in a couple of spots.

The Amish: Seeking to Lose the Self[1]

Susan Chontos, San Antonio College, San Antonio

Susan was impressed with an Amish settlement she visited during her summer vacation. This personal interest is evident in her informative speech. Notice how meticulously Susan applies the 4 S's to each of her main points.

1 Our society is one that caters to the individual. We have seminars on how to be assertive, books on how to better your self-image, and countless articles on how to take control of your life. It seems that everyone today is in a great rush to find themselves. There is, however, a small group of people in our country who are seeking rather to lose themselves. They are the Amish.

2 The Amish were a small group of persecuted immigrants who came to this country 250 years ago seeking religious freedoms. They quietly settled along the northeastern coast of the United States, primarily in Pennsylvania. Last summer, I visited this Pennsylvania settlement and toured an Amish home. So, this morning, I would like to briefly examine the three major tenets of the Amish faith. They are based on Biblical scriptures. They are separation from the world, simplicity in the world, and a strong dedication to their group.

3 The first major tenet of the Amish faith is a desire to be separate from this world. 2 Corinthians 6:17 states, "Therefore come out from them and be ye separate, says the Lord." You can see how the Amish separate themselves from society in many ways. First, they are an endogamous people. That is, they marry within their group. Marriage to non-Amish outsiders is strictly forbidden. Also, they separate themselves in that they speak a Germanic dialect among themselves, and this further distances them from their non-Amish neighbors. In addition, the Amish are separate from what would be considered the public life of most Americans. They don't seek public office. They don't participate in local sports teams or any other community organizations. Most recently, the Amish have separated themselves from our public school system. The Amish believe in attending school only from elementary up through the eighth grade, which they feel is adequate time to learn the basic skills necessary to succeed in Amish culture. In the

1950s, however, states began requiring attendance up through high school. The Amish parents and children protested this, and were fined and even imprisoned. According to the *Encyclopedia of World Cultures,* this controversy was finally resolved in 1972, when the Supreme Court unanimously ruled in favor of the Amish separating themselves on the basis of their religious beliefs.

4 This Amish desire to remain separate from our world—to be in our world but not of our world—has required them to strike many compromises with the rise of modern technology around them. Don Kraybill, in his book *The Puzzles of Amish Life,* describes some of these compromises. For example, the primary mode of transportation for the Amish is the horse and buggy. Today, however, they are permitted to ride in automobiles, although they can't own one. Similarly, they may use a telephone, but they can't have one in their home. In addition, they may use modern farm equipment, but only if it's pulled by their plow horses. Certainly, it is becoming more and more difficult for the Amish to separate themselves from our modern world and its conveniences.

5 The second major tenet of the Amish faith is the desire to be simple, or plain. 1 Peter 3:3–4 states, "Your beauty should not come from outward adornment, such as braided hair or the wearing of gold jewelry or fine clothes. Rather, it should be that of your inner self." Therefore, the Amish don't seek any material possessions at all. Rather, they strive to be plain and simple. Nicknamed "the plain people," nowhere is this plainness more evident than in their dress. In their dress, the Amish don't allow anything that represents style: no buttons, belts, bright colors, or pockets. Instead, they use hooks and ties and straight pins to fasten their clothes. As you can see in this picture [presentational aid], the Amish men are restricted to wearing only black and white. They must always have a wide-brimmed hat to cover their head, and you can tell that this man is married since he has a beard but no mustache. The Amish women are allowed a little more variation in their clothing, and they can wear different combinations of dark solids—dark purples or blues or browns. The Amish women must also wear bonnets to cover their hair, and they must never cut or curl their hair.

6 Not only do the Amish have simple ways of dressing, but they also provide very simple toys for their children to play with. I have here an example of a wooden bear toy [presentational aid]. This toy is very popular among Amish boys, since it has fun marbles and moving parts. The Amish girls, however, as you might expect, like to play with dolls. And here is a traditional Amish doll [presentational aid]. There are two things I'd like for you to notice about this doll. First, her simple dress. Notice again the dark colors and the ties and hooks instead of buttons. The second thing I'd like for you to notice is that she doesn't have a face. The Amish don't believe in putting the human face on any object, or even having their pictures taken. They feel that this represents a graven image and is a sign of personal pride.

7 There are two exceptions to this rule of simplicity for the Amish people, and these are the only two things that they may wear, or hang, or display in their homes. The first exception to the rule of being a simple people is their quilts [presentational aid]. Notice again the dark colors and the simple patterns. John Ruth, in his book *A Quiet and Peaceable Life,* states that quilts began as a way for frugal housewives to use leftover scraps of cloth. Now quilts have grown into a beautiful expression of the artistry and creativity of the Amish women. A second exception to this rule of being a simple people is what's known as *Fraktur* art. And this dates back to the Middle Ages and is characterized by calligraphy writing and bright colors, with hearts or birds or flowers. What the Amish will do is they will write scripture verses in this *Fraktur* style and they will hang these plaques in their homes to remind them to be humble. We can see how this inner desire of the Amish to be a simple people is reflected outwardly in such tangibles as their dress and in their toys.

8 The third and final tenet of the Amish faith is a strong commitment to the group. 1 John 3:16 states, "This is how we know what love is. Jesus Christ laid down his life for us, and we ought to lay down our lives for our brothers." John Hostetler, in his book *Amish Society,* describes some of the ways the Amish care for and are committed to their brothers. Perhaps the most vivid example of this is what would be known as the barn-raising day. If any of you have seen the movie *Witness,* you will recall the barn-raising scene, where the entire community of twenty to thirty families came together to join forces and build a barn. Barn-raising day is a very common occurrence among Amish communities, and they use it to provide new barns, either for newlyweds who are just starting out, or for families whose original barns have been destroyed by fire or rains. And this barn is actually a gift from the entire community to that family, since all of the builders of the barn share in the cost of the materials.

9 A second way we can see how the Amish are dedicated to their group is in times of hardship. For example, if there is a birth in the family or a death in the family, the neighbors of that family will come together and they will cook for the family, care for their children, tend for their crops, and do everything necessary until that family is able to emotionally and physically recuperate.

10 Lastly, we can see how the Amish are dedicated to their group in the way they care for their elderly. The Amish elderly are treated with the greatest respect, and they hold all of the authority and leadership positions in the community. Instead of sending their elderly to nursing homes, they build additions onto their farmhouses, where the elderly grandparents can live comfortably and have their needs provided for. Certainly, this strong dedication to the group has its benefits. John Ruth, in *A Quiet and Peaceable Life,* describes one of these benefits as "a powerful deliverance: to sense the blending of your thoughts and prayers with those who would give their lives for you."

11 This morning we have briefly reviewed the three major tenets of the Amish faith. That is separation from this world, simplicity in the world, and strong dedication to their group. Clearly, the Amish have chosen a different path in life than have most of us: one that is not so fancy, not so modern, not so fast-paced, and, perhaps, one that is not so bad after all.

Reprinted with the permission of the speaker.

AstroTurf Lobbying[2]

Clayton Johnson, Kansas State University

Clayton's well-documented speech demonstrates the wisdom of choosing a novel topic when you are seeking to persuade. The "round" to which he refers was a round of competition at the American Forensic Association's National Individual Events Tournament, where this speech was a finalist in 1998.

1 When the citizens of Florida felt threatened by an onslaught of riverboat gambling, from the furnace of discontent rose Limited Casinos Incorporated, a grassroots coalition proposing a law that would keep out new casinos. Ironically, the *Tampa Tribune* discovered that the sole source of funding for this antigambling, grassroots coalition was the state's own gambling industry. It seems the proposed law would have actually protected all the state's existing casinos by keeping out the competition. Well, luckily, the February 7, 1997, *Tampa Tribune*[*] reports that after discovering the organization's dubious intent, voters shot down the proposal, but the public good isn't out of jeopardy yet. But the only thing rare about this case is that the deception failed. According to the September 15, 1997, *Sacramento Bee,* across every state in this country, corporations have discovered an ethically questionable but extraordinarily effective means of manipulating public policy. It's called AstroTurf lobbying. By

creating the illusion of a real grassroots reform, AstroTurf lobbying convinces us to support legislation we don't understand and wouldn't support if we did. And it's all perfectly legal.

2 According to the March 22, 1997, *Public Relations Review*, AstroTurf lobbying is now the fastest growing segment of the public relations field. So when that same public relations journal calls AstroTurf lobbying a threat to democracy, we should take action. To do so, we'll first clarify the mechanics of AstroTurf lobbying; second, discuss chief criticisms of this legal but controversial practice; and finally, look at what can be done to ensure the legitimacy of grassroots reform.

3 In clarifying the mechanics of this practice it will become clear that in both football and lobbying, AstroTurf has two main advantages over real grass. It's easier to maintain, and it looks a lot prettier. On March 15, 1997, the Associated Press reported that AstroTurf coalitions are easier to maintain because they don't require actual members. In the most popular version of this deceptive practice, corporations devise cool coalition names, like Citizens Against, or The People For . . . and then they contact ordinary citizens giving them a blatantly one-sided version of proposed legislation. Many of us then feel inclined to contact Congress, even though we really don't know anything about the legislation or its impact on the community. For example, since 1994 the Coalition for Energy and Economic Revitalization has been convincing Virginians to allow American Electric Power Company to build a massive power line across the state. Now the Coalition insists that its only concern is the possibility of widespread electrical blackouts. Not so, says the December 7, 1997, *Roanoke Times,* considering that the overwhelming majority of the Coalition's funding, a whopping $700,000 a year, comes from, you guessed it, American Electric Power Company. And it turns out that the Coalition for Energy and Economic Revitalization is nothing more than a trade name for a PR firm called Image Advertising. Legitimate grassroots takes time and energy to coordinate and maintain.

4 But AstroTurf coalitions bypass those constraints. When you've got corporate funding and a PR spin doctor on your side, the coalition is not only easier to maintain, it produces beautiful results. Ameritech, Indiana's largest telephone company, used another version of AstroTurf lobbying when it wanted to pass a controversial telecommunications bill. According to the March 17, 1997, *Indianapolis Star,* Ameritech cranked out computer-generated letters on behalf of some 10,000 Ameritech employees, expressing their support for the bill. And presto, thousands of letters landed on the desks of legislators. And with no reference to the corporation on any of the stationery, it looked like thousands of independently frustrated citizens, the kind of grassroots expression politicians respond to. But Kansas City Chiefs running back Marcus Allen is quick to point out that while AstroTurf is prettier and easier to maintain than real grass, it also yields more injuries.

5 But in the lobbying game, it's not the big-name players getting hurt. So let's, second, discuss chief criticisms of this legal but controversial practice. First, it's a deceptive political tactic. After all, AstroTurf coalitions aren't really coalitions at all. They serve to mask the economic interest of private enterprise in the sheep's clothing of democratization. The March 22, 1997, *Public Relations Review* asserts that when someone receives a phone call from an organization with a name like Coalition for Competitive Long Distance Service, they're likely to support the effort on its face, without looking into the issue any further. California representative Nancy Pelosi told the May 12, 1997, *San Diego News Tribune* that there's nothing more eloquent than having someone from your own district give you a call. But when those callers have been intentionally misled by an AstroTurf campaign, a violation of the public trust has occurred. Second, critics worry that AstroTurf lobbying creates an environment where the law can literally be bought. *Fortune* magazine of December 6, 1997, explains that not long ago, real-life lobbyists looked like their caricatures: bad cigar-smoking men

who stuffed hundred-dollar bills into the pockets of lawmakers. But now it's difficult to tell the lobbyist from a legitimate social reformer. And with an ignorant public so eager to jump on the grassroots bandwagon, a well-funded AstroTurf coalition can accomplish just about anything. Third, AstroTurf lobbying preys on our most fragile citizens. According to the July 17, 1997, *Herald Sun,* if you think stories of AstroTurf lobbying are horrific, consider that these are just the ones that get reported. Without regulation this preferred means of lobbying is yielding untold exploitation, particularly of the elderly. When Blue Cross and Blue Shield of North Carolina wanted to pass a bill that would allow it to convert to a for-profit entity, the company donned a coalition name and called its elderly subscribers telling them that without the bill their premiums would skyrocket. Scared, confused senior citizens were then automatically patched through to their state representatives. As the day wore on it became strikingly clear that these folks knew nothing about the legislation. And what looked like an outcry from the public was really just an AstroTurf gimmick.

6 On the field of public policy, AstroTurf has caused enough damage. It's time to rip it up from the stadium floor and plant the seeds of alternate grassroots by, finally, looking at what can be done to ensure the legitimacy of grassroots reform. In the governmental sphere we can do two things. First, lobbying campaigns should be required to fully disclose all corporate affiliations in every communication they have with the public. Second, those PR firms that offer AstroTurf services should be required to register as the lobbyists they are. North Carolina's Secretary of State, Elaine Marshal, echoed the views of many frustrated policy makers when she told the July 17, 1997, *Herald Sun* that these measures would be perfectly fair for everyone, that while all citizens certainly have the right to petition the government, all citizens also have the right to know when they are the target of professional persuasion. After all, the primary function of lobbying laws is to keep the public informed about who the hired guns are. And in the personal sphere, we can help institute these legislative changes by contacting our congressional representatives. According to the December 26, 1997, *Wall Street Journal,* as long as national efforts at lobbying reform are at a stalemate, the opportunity for localized reform is ripe. And so to speed up the process I've started Concerned Citizens Against AstroTurf Lobbying. After the round I'll make available a stack of postage-paid envelopes addressed to state senators and representatives with a pre-scripted message inside that you need only sign and place in the mail. Just kidding.

7 Before you give your name to any legislation, research it yourself. By using the search terms *AstroTurf Lobbying* and *Corporate Grassroots* you should yield a plethora of information about this topic from a variety of sources. If, after your close personal consideration, you find this is one reform you'd like to give your name to, then write your congressional representatives that letter. It takes some effort, but nobody said democracy was easy. And while we'd like to blame the selfish corporate machine for the whole of this problem, let us not forget the second culprit behind AstroTurf lobbying: a citizenry that's politically apathetic enough to let it happen in the first place. Of course, any one commercial advertisement, telemarketing pitch, or even speech should only be the springboard to persuasion. The rest is entirely up to us.

8 Today, we've examined AstroTurf lobbying, discussed chief criticisms of this legal but controversial practice, and finally, looked at what could be done to ensure the legitimacy of grassroots reform. Grassroots has become quite the God term in American politics. It represents ordinary people banding together in the democratic tradition. When the citizens of Florida realized that Limited Casinos Incorporated was a mockery of that tradition, they stood up and vindicated themselves. Now, it's our turn.

* Date should be February 19

From *Video User's Guide for the Allyn & Bacon/AFA Student Speeches Video III,* ed. Karla Kay Jensen (Boston: Allyn, 1999) 50–52. Reprinted with permission.

The Forgotten Four-Letter Word[3]

Sarah Meinen, Bradley University

In this powerfully worded speech, Sarah seeks to shake our complacency about a too-familiar topic. Notice how her evocative language heightens the emotional impact of this speech, the first-place winner at the Interstate Oratorical Association annual contest in 1999.

1 In 1981, two strange diseases first grabbed the attention of the American public. The first, a mental malaise born of our overabundance of seemingly insurmountable societal ills. We called it compassion fatigue, best described by the July–August 1981 *Utne Reader,* as the inability to care anymore about social issues like refugees, homelessness, famine, natural disasters, the environment, or the Holocaust. The second was a new disease initially brought to our attention by its savage spread through the homosexual community. We called it AIDS and watched in horror as it polarized society and stopped discriminating on the basis of sexual preference, victimizing every demographic group and defying modern medical advances.

2 The July 1998 *Scientific American* reports that AIDS has recently been renamed a pandemic, having left mere epidemic status behind. And compassion fatigue? It's just added HIV to its list, somewhere between homelessness and the Holocaust, as something we just can't find the heart to care about anymore.

3 This speech is not about a freshly discovered, rare disease. It's not about a faulty new technology or an obscure but deadly industrial chemical. Rather, AIDS is familiar, and this familiarity is the problem. Our well of compassion has run dry, and we're all too eager to relegate AIDS to a growing list of historical atrocities.

4 As the February 16, 1998, *Business Week* claims, we don't want to hear that 16,000 people contract HIV every day, that 2.3 million died of AIDS last year alone, that 650,000 Americans are now HIV positive. However, closing our eyes won't make a monster of this magnitude go away. Instead, we must revive our compassion and interest by, first, discovering why we've become immune to this vicious virus; next, detailing the effects of our plague of indifference; and finally, curing ourselves of AIDS compassion fatigue.

5 True, 1997 was a banner year for AIDS research. True, the number of AIDS deaths reached a record low last year. True, scientists scrambled to assemble the sketchy outlines of an AIDS vaccine. But, 1997 was also the year we stopped carrying a banner for AIDS, the year new cases of HIV infection continued to shatter already ominous records, the year we found our own AIDS vaccine: apathy, disinterest, indifference.

6 Despite our exposure to death and destruction, facts and figures, names and Quilt squares, AIDS has slowly faded from our national consciousness chiefly due to hype surrounding an AIDS cure and grossly misleading statistics.

7 "The other day," says columnist Urvashi Vaid in the December 24, 1997, *Advocate,* "someone called to tell me that AIDS had ended. I mean, he'd read it in the *New York Times,* so it had to be true. I wondered if anyone from the *Times* had called to break the news to Neil, who died just three months ago," Vaid says as he recalls reading similar headlines in *Time, Newsweek,* and *U.S. News.*

8 The January 1998 *Scientist* argues that these hype-filled headlines fuel our compassion fatigue, offering us a false sense of security. It's easy to forget about AIDS if we don't consider it a threat anymore. For example, says the February 17, 1998, *Advocate,* media coverage abounds about the development of an AIDS vaccine which promises to eradicate HIV. Lost in the fine print, however, are the vaccine's innumerable problems: It won't be testable for at least five years, will only protect against the most basic, least drug-resistant strains of the quick-to-mutate HIV virus, and will only benefit a fraction

of one percent of AIDS patients, those who have been recently tested and remain un-exposed to any HIV drugs.

9 Misleading AIDS statistics are also fatiguing our AIDS compassion, says the July 1998 *Harper's*. For example, the Centers for Disease Control and Prevention has changed the way it reports AIDS statistics, but it hasn't changed the way it labels them. The CDC used to count cases of HIV infection and full-blown AIDS. Now it only counts full-blown AIDS cases.

10 The August 19, 1998, *JAMA* points out that even though AIDS death rates look lower, HIV infection rates are more important and prove that AIDS continues to claim new victims. "Drugs keep victims alive longer," says Jack Killen, head of the National In-stitute of Allergy and Infectious Disease division, of AIDS, "but these people can't live on AZT cocktails and protease inhibitors forever."

11 The July 11, 1998, *Lancet* reminds us that despite slightly lower United States numbers, the AIDS pandemic has grown out of control in developing countries. In Botswana and Rwanda, HIV lurks in 25 percent of the population and threatens to in-crease infant mortality by 75 percent in the next 10 years. "These are the statistics we don't hear," says Dr. Anthony Fauci, Head of the U.S. Institute of Allergies and Infec-tious Diseases. "But these are the same statistics which prove AIDS is still the greatest threat facing humanity."

12 AIDS has been too grim, too overwhelming, and it's been around too long. We may be over AIDS, but AIDS is not over, and we must focus on both the attitudinal and behavioral effects of compassion fatigue.

13 A Gallup Poll taken in October of 1997 reveals that today, only 29 percent of us consider AIDS a serious problem. Ten years ago, 66 percent of us did. Only 30 percent of us are concerned about contracting the disease, compared to 42 percent of Ameri-cans a decade ago. AIDS simply is old news, yesterday's worry, blasé, passé, overdone, a has-been disease.

14 Additionally, the Spring 1998 *Albany Law Review* claims that we are unwilling to let go of old AIDS stereotypes and prejudices. Our it-can't-happen-to-me mentality is surprisingly resilient, flying in the face of statistics that tell us heterosexual sex is the number-one way to contract AIDS in 1998.

15 Behaviorally, says the July 13, 1998, *MacLean's*, our compassion fatigue has pro-duced both a lack of AIDS champions and an increase in risky behavior. The April 7, 1997, *U.S. News & World Report* argues that lately, AIDS activism is strictly backstage activity for many of Hollywood's elite, who have abandoned red ribbons because, as Gerry Ansel, spokesman for AIDS Project Los Angeles, says, "they have become a cliché." It's no longer chic for movie stars to support AIDS awareness, and sadly where trendy Hollywood goes, the American public follows. AIDS bracelets have been cast aside, and red ribbons are unpinned as we search for a fresh, new cause to champion.

16 But the most alarming result of our compassion fatigue, says the January 5, 1998, *AIDS Weekly Plus,* is the cavalier way we treat the disease. A Yale University School of Medicine study reports that 9 out of 10 adolescents believe they are invulnerable to AIDS, even though 20 percent of those same kids have seen a friend or relative die of the disease, and half of them regularly engage in sex without condoms. "This study is important," says Dr. Michael Merson, Director of Public Health at Yale, "because it tells us that despite the wealth of information that's out there, young people have still not internalized the dangers of AIDS." Have not internalized or just don't care, asks the April 8, 1998, *JAMA*?

17 With this haunting question in mind, we must develop a practical and realistic prescription for our compassion fatigue on both a national and personal level. First, the January 5, 1998, *AIDS Weekly Plus* says that the focus must shift from an AIDS cure to AIDS prevention. "While we don't want AIDS vaccine and drug research to stop," says Michael Shriver of the National Association of People with AIDS, "we believe that more time, research, and money needs to go into feasible prevention programs." These programs, he says, need to begin with awareness and concern. The May 1998 *American Bar Association Journal* agrees, arguing that if we don't shift our focus soon, by the time we find a cure, there'll be no one left to save.

18 Devising utopian research and prevention plans is useless, claims the July 1998 *Scientific American,* unless we as citizens change our attitudes and revive AIDS activism. We need to be critical consumers who refuse to be pacified with optimistic statistics and miracle cures. We need to evaluate AIDS information carefully, analyzing numbers, questioning source validity, and separating hope from hype. Most importantly, we need to find a way to care about AIDS again. Wear a red ribbon. Walk in the John Keats March for AIDS. View the AIDS quilt. Volunteer at a local hospice. Do whatever you have to do to be shocked, to be scared, to be involved, to be compassionate and to keep this pandemic from being ignored, dismissed, or forgotten.

19 By the year 2000, one out of every three of us will know someone infected with the HIV virus. We may be immune to the stories and statistics, but none of us is safe from the reality of AIDS. The July 1998 *Scientific American* claims that the most effective AIDS wake-up calls are made by vocal people in high-risk communities; individualized grassroots efforts that start small make the biggest steps.

20 Is that a loud enough call to action? This time, the solution really is in our hands. This community has the ability to speak passionately, the platform to affect an enormous audience, and the clout to command attention. The forensics community has a choice. We can take a risk and speak out, knowing our voices may be lost but hoping someone hears. Or we can stand idly by, succumb to our compassion fatigue, and watch AIDS claim our best and our brightest.

From *Winning Orations, 1999* (Mankato, MN: Interstate Oratorical Association, 1999) 26–29. Used by permission.

Untitled Speech[4]

Jennifer Deem, Indiana University

Jennifer was a finalist at the 1998 Interstate Oratorical Association national contest held in Springfield, Illinois. That location is important to one of her examples. Notice how Jennifer blends those examples with statistics and expert opinion to highlight dangers that travelers may experience at rest stops.

1 This past summer, Allison Garrett took her young sons, Kevin and Kyle, on a family vacation. Driving down a long stretch of Interstate 65, Ms. Garrett pulled into a rest area just outside of Atlanta. She allowed the boys to use the rest room by themselves. According to the March 1997 *Atlantic,* only Kyle returned. Kevin is still missing, presumably abducted, possibly dead. Unfortunately, stories like the Garretts are all too common. As Col. Ron Tussing of the Nebraska State Police states in the June 7, 1997, *Omaha World Herald,* "Rest areas in this country are becoming more and more dangerous." Violent crime at rest areas is running out of control. In fact, an *Associated Press Newswire* from January 24, 1997, reports that state officials list 77 percent of all rest areas as "highly dangerous." Highly dangerous is defined as a area in which violent crimes such as murder, rape, and attacks are more likely to occur.

2 Whether we're taking a vacation, driving to school, or traveling to a tournament, we rely on those cozy-looking rest areas for a chance to use the rest room, stretch our legs, and simply take a breather from driving. Rest areas exist to provide exactly what they sound like, a place to rest, not a harbor for violent crimes. Yet, as frightening as it sounds, rest areas present one of the greatest hidden dangers to people on the road. The *Buffalo News* of August 18, 1997, sums up the problem, "Rest area crime occurs everywhere." From kidnapping to burglary to rape to murder, it is about time we take steps to restore safety to rest areas. In order to address the problem of rest area safety, we will: first, expose the dangers that travelers face at rest areas; second, determine why these dangers exist; and finally, propose solutions to ensure that rest areas provide the welcome service for which they were created.

3 Often surrounded by nicely wooded picnic areas and furnished with booths of tourist information, the atmosphere of a rest area belies its hidden dangers.

4 Unfortunately, determining the numbers of violent crimes that occur at rest areas is difficult. The *Buffalo News* of August 18, 1997, explains that crime statistics are not designed to record crimes committed at rest stops. However, we can recognize the dangers of rest areas by examining the number of people at risk and how we're vulnerable to violent crimes. First, we do know that many people use rest areas and many rest areas are extremely dangerous. According to the January 24, 1997, *AP Report*, three out of four rest stops are considered high-risk crime areas. In addition, the August 24, 1997, issue of the *Dayton Daily News* tells us that Americans embarked on approximately 188 million car trips during the summer of 1997, many of whom stopped at one of the nation's thousands of rest areas. In fact, the August 23, 1997, *Toronto Star* reveals, odds are nearly every one of us has visited a rest area in the last three months.

5 The danger lies in the fact that when we stop to rest—usually to use the rest room—we're vulnerable to violent crimes. The August 22, 1997, *Washington Post* reports that in Virginia, one criminal shot a man in the rest room; in the same rest area, another criminal robbed a woman at gunpoint while she changed her son's diaper. Criminals can catch us with our pants down—literally. Unfortunately, it's not funny.

6 The September 21, 1996, *St. Petersburg Times* notes that an assailant attacked and raped a woman in a stall at an I-75 rest stop. KNXV-TV reported on April 9, 1997, that at a Tennessee rest area still another unnamed villain shot and killed an entire family. But none of this affects us, right? Unfortunately, it does affect us even here in Springfield, Illinois. The *State Journal Register* of February 12, 1998, explains that two criminals stabbed and killed a man at the Interstate 55 rest area near Sherman, Illinois, only 90 miles from here.

7 Of course, the countless number of crimes committed in rest areas across the country don't do justice to the stories of individual lives marred by tragedy. The May 25, 1997, *CNN Early Prime* program tells the story of a man driving for many hours who stopped at a rest area to use the facilities and give himself a little break. He hoped that by stopping he would feel refreshed enough to drive some more. After helping his disabled sister, he went to use the rest room as well. He was shot and killed. In the words of Cyndi Ward, the special operations director of the Virginia Department of Transportation, "There's no method to the madness. People should be afraid to stop at these rest areas because of the violence." Considering the escalation of violent crimes at rest areas, we must examine why these dangers exist in the first place.

8 Three reasons for the problem stand out: isolated areas, poor security facilities, and inadequate security personnel.

9 First, states locate rest areas in remote areas with wooded picnic areas and large parking lots. If you can find a really large field with nothing but cows and corn, then you bet that you will find a rest area. Lt. Col. W. Gerald Massengill notes in the *Las Vegas Review-Journal* on August 18, 1997, "States place rest areas in isolated areas with not many people around." In addition, states cannot legally build rest areas in conjunction with commercial businesses except on toll roads. As the April 27, 1997, *Newsday* explains, the Federal Highway Act of 1956 prohibits the development of commercial rest areas along interstate highways built with public money. The original idea was to encourage travelers to use the rest areas for bathroom breaks, but for a meal and a refill of gas they needed to get off the interstate and come into the town. However, the outdated bill now forces states to build isolated rest areas where disasters are waiting to happen.

10 Second, compounding the problem, many rest areas have little or no security facilities. The May 29, 1997, *Virginian-Pilot* reveals that rest areas lack decent lighting facilities and surveillance cameras. In case of an emergency, most rest areas have no panic buttons to call for help. Local police provide the only remaining security. The St. Francis County Chief Deputy H. N. Green sums up the dangers in the July 27, 1997, issue of the *Dallas Morning News,* "A police officer may only drive through a couple of times a night. These rest areas are targets of opportunity."

11 Finally, virtually no rest areas employ security personnel. For example, according to the May 26, 1997, *Washington Times,* state officials informed one maintenance man that, along with cleaning the drains, trimming the hedges, and repairing any weather damage to the building, he would also be acting as security. The unnamed security guard/maintenance man explains, "Nobody didn't give me no training. Only thing they gave me a was a manual on security. Give me a phone. Said to dial 911." How comforting. The fact is little or no security exists at our nation's rest areas. In light of the dangers and why they exist, we must enact solutions to ensure our safety.

12 Putting an end to the violent acts at rest stops requires the work of the national government, state highway agencies and every one of us. First, the federal government must repeal The Federal Highway Act of 1956, which bans private business from interstate rest areas. According to the August 18, 1997, *Las Vegas Review-Journal,* many officials agree that commercial rest areas with restaurants and gas stations experience far fewer crime problems because of the well-lit facilities and 24-hour-a-day staff members. What's more, commercial rest stops prove cost effective. Billy Higgins, the spokesman for the American Association of State Highway and Transportation Officials, notes that if the legislation was changed, "the rest areas could be changed from a funding drain to a revenue source." Removing the federal restriction would save money, and more importantly, people's lives.

13 Second, state highway agencies should allocate funds for improving security facilities. The cost is within reach. The May 12, 1997, issue of the *Washington Post* points out that Virginia, for example, would only need to invest $700,000 to provide security cameras, well-lit areas, and full-time security guards for all state-run rest areas. To develop an investment plan, other states should follow the lead of North Carolina. The August 19, 1997, issue of the *Herald-Sun* tells us that North Carolina started a program called "Operation Rest Assured." The program involves putting up warning signs and assigning an armed officer to regularly visit the rest areas. According to Mitzi Powell, a spokeswoman for the North Carolina Department of Motor Vehicles, "The program has virtually wiped out robberies in the rest areas." We must pressure State Highway and Transportation agencies to invest in our safety.

14 In the meantime, we can also play a vital role in our own safety. We need to remember to act with caution and to use our heads. The August 18, 1997, *Indianapolis Star* offers some safety tips when using rest areas. Try to stop at a busy, not deserted, rest area. You may have to wait longer for your 83 oz. of Mountain Dew, but it's worth it. Lock your car when you leave it. Park in a well-lit area. Accompany any children with you to the rest room. Some other suggestions include carrying a cell phone with you and traveling with someone. Rest areas are dangerous, but by taking a few simple precautions, we can protect ourselves.

15 After exposing the dangers of rest areas, determining why these dangers exist, and finally, proposing some solutions, it's clear that we must take action to restore safety to rest areas. Rest areas are a major part of U.S. travel. We deserve protection for ourselves and our loved ones. Fortunately, by working together and taking a few extra precautions, we can insure that stories like Allison Garrett's are never repeated.

From *Winning Orations, 1998* (Mankato, MN: Interstate Oratorical Association, 1998) 31–34. Used by permission.

Eulogy for John F. Kennedy, Jr.[5]

Sen. Edward M. Kennedy

"The whole world knew his name before he did." That startling statement is part of Senator Ted Kennedy's eulogy for his nephew, John F. Kennedy, Jr., delivered at New York's Church of St. Thomas More on the morning of July 23, 1999. Kennedy speaks with an uncle's humor, warmth, and affection, but also voices the sentiments of countless Americans.

1 Thank you, President and Mrs. Clinton and Chelsea, for being here today. You've shown extraordinary kindness through the course of this week.

2 Once, when they asked John what he would do if he went into politics and was elected President, he said, "I guess the first thing is call up Uncle Teddy and gloat." I loved that. It was so like his father.

3 From the first day of his life, John seemed to belong not only to our family, but to the American family.

4 The whole world knew his name before he did.

5 A famous photograph showed John racing across the lawn as his father landed in the White House helicopter and swept up John in his arms. When my brother saw that photo, he exclaimed, "Every mother in the United States is saying, 'Isn't it wonderful to see that love between a son and his father, the way that John races to be with his father.' Little do they know, that son would have raced right by his father to get to that helicopter."

6 But John was so much more than those long ago images emblazoned in our minds. He was a boy who grew into a man with a zest for life and a love of adventure. He was a pied piper who brought us all along. He was blessed with a father and mother who never thought anything mattered more than their children.

7 When they left the White House, Jackie's soft and gentle voice and unbreakable strength of spirit guided him surely and securely to the future. He had a legacy, and he learned to treasure it. He was part of a legend, and he learned to live with it. Above all, Jackie gave him a place to be himself, to grow up, to laugh and cry, to dream and strive on his own.

8 John learned that lesson well. He had amazing grace. He accepted who he was, but he cared more about what he could and should become. He saw things that could be lost in the glare of the spotlight. And he could laugh at the absurdity of too much pomp and circumstance.

9 He loved to travel across the city by subway, bicycle, and roller blade. He lived as if he were unrecognizable, although he was known by everyone he encountered. He always introduced himself, rather than take anything for granted. He drove his own car and flew his own plane, which is how he wanted it. He was the king of his domain.

10 He thought politics should be an integral part of our popular culture, and that popular culture should be an integral part of politics. He transformed that belief into the creation of *George*. John shaped and honed a fresh, often irreverent journal. His new political magazine attracted a new generation, many of whom had never read about politics before.

11 John also brought to *George* a wit that was quick and sure. The premier issue of *George* caused a stir with a cover photograph of Cindy Crawford dressed as George Washington with a bare belly button. The "Reliable Source" in *The Washington Post* printed a mock cover of *George* showing not Cindy Crawford, but me dressed as George Washington, with my belly button exposed. I suggested to John that perhaps I should have been the model for the first cover of his magazine. Without missing a beat, John told me that he stood by his original editorial decision.

12 John brought this same playful wit to other aspects of his life. He campaigned for me during my 1994 election and always caused a stir when he arrived in Massachusetts. Before one of his trips to Boston, John told the campaign he was bringing along a companion, but would need only one hotel room.

13 Interested, but discreet, a senior campaign worker picked John up at the airport and prepared to handle any media barrage that might accompany John's arrival with his mystery companion. John landed with the companion all right—an enormous German shepherd dog named Sam he had just rescued from the pound.

14 He loved to talk about the expression on the campaign worker's face and the reaction of the clerk at the Charles Hotel when John and Sam checked in.

15 I think now not only of these wonderful adventures, but of the kind of person John was. He was the son who quietly gave extraordinary time and ideas to the Institute of Politics at Harvard that bears his father's name. He brought to the Institute his distinctive insight that politics could have a broader appeal, that it was not just about elections, but about the larger forces that shape our whole society.

16 John was also the son who was once protected by his mother. He went on to become her pride—and then her protector in her final days. He was the Kennedy who loved us all, but who especially cherished his sister, Caroline, celebrated her brilliance, and took strength and joy from their lifelong mutual admiration society.

17 And for a thousand days, he was a husband who adored the wife who became his perfect soul mate. John's father taught us all to reach for the moon and the stars. John did that in all he did—and he found his shining star when he married Carolyn Bessette.

18 How often our family will think of the two of them, cuddling affectionately on a boat, surrounded by family—aunts, uncles, Caroline and Ed and their children, Rose, Tatania, and Jack, Kennedy cousins, Radziwill cousins, Shriver cousins, Smith cousins, Lawford cousins—as we sailed Nantucket Sound.

19 Then we would come home, and before dinner, on the lawn where his father had played, John would lead a spirited game of touch football. And his beautiful young wife, the new pride of the Kennedys, would cheer for John's team and delight her nieces and nephews with her somersaults.

20 We loved Carolyn. She and her sister Lauren were young extraordinary women of high accomplishment—and their own limitless possibilities. We mourn their loss and honor their lives. The Bessette and Freeman families will always be part of ours.

21 John was a serious man who brightened our lives with his smile and his grace. He was a son of privilege who founded a program called Reaching Up to train better caregivers for the mentally disabled.

22 He joined Wall Street executives on the Robin Hood Foundation to help the city's impoverished children. And he did it all so quietly, without ever calling attention to himself.

23 John was one of Jackie's two miracles. He was still becoming the person he would be, and doing it by the beat of his own drummer. He had only just begun. There was in him a great promise of things to come.

24 The Irish Ambassador recited a poem to John's father and mother soon after John was born. I can hear it again now, at this different and difficult moment:

> We wish to the new child,
> A heart that can be beguiled,
> By a flower,
> That the wind lifts,
> As it passes.
> If the storms break for him,
> May the trees shake for him,
> Their blossoms down.

In the night that he is troubled,
May a friend wake for him,
So that his time be doubled,
And at the end of all loving and love,
May the Man above,
Give him a crown.

25 We thank the millions who have rained blossoms down on John's memory. He and his bride have gone to be with his mother and father, where there will never be an end to love. He was lost on that troubled night, but we will always wake for him, so that his time, which was not doubled, but cut in half, will live forever in our memory, and in our beguiled and broken hearts.

26 We dared to think, in that other Irish phrase, that this John Kennedy would live to comb gray hair, with his beloved Carolyn by his side. But like his father, he had every gift but length of years.

27 We who have loved him from the day he was born, and watched the remarkable man he became, now bid him farewell.

28 God bless you, John and Carolyn. We love you and we always will.

I Have a Dream[6]

Martin Luther King, Jr.

Speaking from the steps of the Lincoln Memorial on August 28, 1963, Martin Luther King, Jr., delivered the keynote address of the March on Washington, D.C. for Civil Rights. As you read his "I Have a Dream" speech, study the power of its language and see if you agree with many scholars that this is the greatest American speech of the twentieth century.

1 I am happy to join with you today in what will go down in history as the greatest demonstration for freedom in the history of our nation.

2 Five score years ago, a great American, in whose symbolic shadow we stand today, signed the Emancipation Proclamation. This momentous decree came as a great beacon light of hope to millions of Negro slaves, who had been seared in the flames of withering injustice. It came as a joyous daybreak to end the long night of their captivity.

3 But one hundred years later, the Negro still is not free. One hundred years later, the life of the Negro is still sadly crippled by the manacles of segregation and the chains of discrimination. One hundred years later, the Negro lives on a lonely island of poverty in the midst of a vast ocean of material prosperity. One hundred years later, the Negro is still languished in the corners of American society and finds himself an exile in his own land.

4 And so we've come here today to dramatize a shameful condition. In a sense we've come to our nation's Capitol to cash a check. When the architects of our republic wrote the magnificent words of the Constitution and the Declaration of Independence, they were signing a promissory note to which every American was to fall heir. This note was a promise that all men—yes, black men as well as white men—would be guaranteed the unalienable rights of life, liberty, and the pursuit of happiness.

5 It is obvious today that America has defaulted on this promissory note insofar as her citizens of color are concerned. Instead of honoring this sacred obligation, America has given the Negro people a bad check—a check which has come back marked "insufficient funds."

6 But we refuse to believe that the bank of justice is bankrupt. We refuse to believe that there are insufficient funds in the great vaults of opportunity of this nation. And so we've come to cash this check—a check that will give us upon demand the riches of freedom and the security of justice.

7 We have also come to this hallowed spot to remind America of the fierce urgency of now. This is no time to engage in the luxury of cooling off or to take the tranquillizing drug of gradualism. Now is the time to make real the promises of democracy. Now is the time to rise from the dark and desolate valley of segregation to the sunlit path of racial justice. Now is the time to lift our nation from the quicksands of racial injustice to the solid rock of brotherhood. Now is the time to make justice a reality for all of God's children.

8 It would be fatal for the nation to overlook the urgency of the moment. This sweltering summer of the Negro's legitimate discontent will not pass until there is an invigorating autumn of freedom and equality. Nineteen sixty-three is not an end, but a beginning. Those who hope that the Negro needed to blow off steam and will now be content will have a rude awakening if the nation returns to business as usual. There will be neither rest nor tranquility in America until the Negro is granted his citizenship rights. The whirlwinds of revolt will continue to shake the foundations of our nation until the bright day of justice emerges.

9 But there is something that I must say to my people, who stand on the warm threshold which leads into the palace of justice. In the process of gaining our rightful place, we must not be guilty of wrongful deeds. Let us not seek to justify our thirst for freedom by drinking from the cup of bitterness and hatred.

10 We must forever conduct our struggle on the high plane of dignity and discipline. We must not allow our creative protest to degenerate into physical violence. Again and again we must rise to the majestic heights of meeting physical force with soul force.

11 The marvelous new militancy which has engulfed the Negro community must not lead us to a distrust of all white people. For many of our white brothers, as evidenced by their presence here today, have come to realize that their destiny is tied up with our destiny. They have come to realize that their freedom is inextricably bound to our freedom. We cannot walk alone.

12 As we walk, we must make the pledge that we shall always march ahead. We cannot turn back. There are those who are asking the devotees of civil rights, "When will you be satisfied?" We can never be satisfied as long as the Negro is the victim of the unspeakable horrors of police brutality. We can never be satisfied as long as our bodies, heavy with the fatigue of travel, cannot gain lodging in the motels of the highways and the hotels of the cities. We cannot be satisfied as long as a Negro in Mississippi cannot vote and a Negro in New York believes he has nothing for which to vote. No, no, we are not satisfied, and we will not be satisfied until justice rolls down like waters, and righteousness like a mighty stream.

13 I am not unmindful that some of you have come here out of great trials and tribulations. Some of you have come fresh from narrow jail cells. Some of you have come from areas where your quest for freedom left you battered by the storms of persecution and staggered by the winds of police brutality. You have been the veterans of creative suffering. Continue to work with the faith that unearned suffering is redemptive.

14 Go back to Mississippi, go back to Alabama, go back to South Carolina, go back to Georgia, go back to Louisiana, go back to the slums and ghettos of our Northern cities, knowing that somehow this situation can and will be changed. Let us not wallow in the valley of despair.

15 I say to you today, my friends, so even though we face the difficulties of today and tomorrow, I still have a dream. It is a dream deeply rooted in the American dream.

16 I have a dream that one day this nation will rise up and live out the true meaning of its creed, "We hold these truths to be self-evident, that all men are created equal."

17 I have a dream that one day on the red hills of Georgia the sons of former slaves and the sons of former slaveowners will be able to sit down together at the table of brotherhood.

18 I have a dream that one day even the state of Mississippi, a state sweltering with the heat of injustice, sweltering with the heat of oppression, will be transformed into an oasis of freedom and justice.

19 I have a dream that my four little children will one day live in a nation where they will not be judged by the color of their skin but by the content of their character. I have a dream today.

20 I have a dream that one day, down in Alabama, with its vicious racists, with its governor having his lips dripping with the words of interposition and nullification, one day right there in Alabama little black boys and black girls will be able to join hands with the little white boys and white girls as sisters and brothers. I have a dream today.

21 I have a dream that one day every valley shall be exalted, every hill and mountain shall be made low, the rough places will be made plain and the crooked places will be made straight, and the glory of the Lord shall be revealed, and all flesh shall see it together.

22 This is our hope. This is the faith that I go back to the South with. With this faith we will be able to hew out of the mountain of despair a stone of hope. With this faith we will be able to transform the jangling discords of our nation into a beautiful symphony of brotherhood. With this faith we will be able to work together, to pray together, to struggle together, to go to jail together, to stand up for freedom together, knowing that we will be free one day.

23 This will be the day—this will be the day when all of God's children will be able to sing with new meaning, "My country 'tis of thee, sweet land of liberty, of thee I sing. Land where my fathers died, land of the pilgrim's pride, from every mountainside, let freedom ring." And if America is to be a great nation, this must become true.

24 So let freedom ring from the prodigious hilltops of New Hampshire. Let freedom ring from the mighty mountains of New York. Let freedom ring from the heightening Alleghenies of Pennsylvania!

25 Let freedom ring from the snowcapped Rockies of Colorado! Let freedom ring from the curvaceous slopes of California!

26 But not only that. Let freedom ring from Stone Mountain of Georgia!

27 Let freedom ring from Lookout Mountain of Tennessee!

28 Let freedom ring from every hill and molehill of Mississippi. From every mountainside, let freedom ring.

29 And when this happens, when we allow freedom to ring—when we let it ring from every village and every hamlet, from every state and every city—we will be able to speed up that day when all of God's children, black men and white men, Jews and Gentiles, Protestants and Catholics, will be able to join hands and sing in the words of the old Negro spiritual, "Free at last! Free at last! Thank God Almighty, we are free at last!"

1. Susan Chontos, "The Amish: Seeking to Lose the Self," Speech Delivered at San Antonio College, San Antonio, Texas, Summer 1992. Used with permission.

2. Clayton Johnson, "Astroturf Lobbying," in *Video User's Guide for the Allyn & Bacon/AFA Student Speeches Video III,* ed. Karla Kay Jensen (Boston: Allyn, 1999) 50–52. Coached by Craig Brown.

3. Sarah Meinen, "The Forgotten Four-Letter Word," *Winning Orations, 1999* (Mankato, MN: Interstate Oratorical Association, 1999) 26–29. Coached by Dan Smith.

4. Jennifer Deem, Untitled Speech, *Winning Orations, 1998* (Mankato, MN: Interstate Oratorical Association, 1998) 31–34. Coached by Andy Billings.

5. "Text of Eulogy by Sen. Edward M. Kennedy," *New York Times* 23 July 1999, 25 July 1999 <http://www.nytimes.com/library/national/regional/ap-kennedy-eulogy.html>.

6. Martin Luther King, Jr., "I Have a Dream," 28 August 1963, Washington, DC. Reprinted by permission of Joan Daves Agency. Copyright 1963 by Martin Luther King, Jr.

photo credits

Chapter 1: p. 2, © Bob Daemmrich/Stock Boston; p. 8, © Bob Daemmrich; p. 16, © Liaison

Chapter 2: p. 22, AP/Wide World Photos; p. 27, © Brad Markel/Liaison Agency; p. 33, © Bob Daemmrich

Chapter 3: p. 42, © Bob Daemmrich/Stock Boston; p. 50, © Bob Daemmrich; p. 52, Orlando Sentinel/Liaison Agency

Chapter 4: p. 66, © Bob Daemmrich/The Image Works; p. 73, © Bob Daemmrich/Stock Boston; p. 78, © Bob Daemmrich

Chapter 5: pp. 92 and 96, © Bob Daemmrich; p. 99, © Richard Lord/The Image Works; p. 102, © Michael A. Dwyer/ Stock Boston

Chapter 6: p. 120, © David R. Frazier Photolibrary; p. 124, © A. Ramey/Stock Boston; p. 129, © Michael Newman/PhotoEdit

Chapter 7: p. 142, © Bob Daemmrich; p. 149 © Jeff Greenberg/PhotoEdit; p. 158, © Bob Daemmrich/Stock Boston; p. 164, © Elizabeth Crews/The Image Works

Chapter 8: p. 174, © Jeff Greenberg/PhotoEdit; p. 179, © Bob Daemmrich/Stock Boston; p. 185, © Michael Borkoski/Stock Boston

Chapter 9: p. 198, © Esbin-anderson/The Image Works; p. 205, © Bob Daemmrich/Stock Boston; p. 213, © Tim Fields

Chapter 10: p. 218, © Darcy Padilla/Liaison Agency; p. 222, Lora L. Gordon, Office of Public Relations, © Radford University; p. 226, © Barbara Alper/Stock Boston; p. 234, © Michael Dwyer/Stock Boston

Chapter 11: p. 240, © Michael Newman/PhotoEdit; p. 254, © Tim Griffith/ESTO; p. 255, © Raphael Gailarde/Liaison Agency

Chapter 12: p. 262, © Corey Sipkin/Liaison Agency; p. 267, © Steve Wott/Stock Boston; p. 273, © Bob Daemmrich; p. 275, © Barbara Alper/Stock Boston

Chapter 13: p. 288, © Bob Daemmrich/Stock Boston; p. 291, Lora L. Gordon, Office of Public Relations, © Radford University; p. 296, © Dick Blume/The Image Works; pp. 300 and 304 left, © Bob Daemmrich/Stock Boston; p. 304 right, © Bob Daemmrich/The Image Works

Chapter 14: p. 312, © Najlah Feanny/Stock Boston; p. 316, © Bob Daemmrich; p. 318 left, © Rob Crandall/Stock Boston; p. 318 right, © Leslye Borden/PhotoEdit; p. 324, © Charlie Westerman/Liaison Agency

Chapter 15: p. 336, © Najlah Feanny/Stock Boston; p. 343, © Richard Pasley/Stock Boston; p. 347, © Bob Daemmrich/Stock Boston

Chapter 16: p. 360, AP/Wide World Photos; p. 363, © Karin Cooper/Liaison Agency; p. 369, AP/Wide World Photos; p. 373, © Bob Daemmrich/ Stock Boston

Chapter 17: p. 384, © Bob Daemmrich/The Image Works; p. 386, Lora L. Gordon, Office of Public Relations, © Radford University; p. 390, © Jim Bourg/Liaison Agency; p. 402, © Liaison Agency

Chapter 18: p. 416, © Rob Crandall/Stock Boston; p. 428, © Bob Daemmrich/Stock Boston

Chapter 19: p. 436, © Bob Daemmrich; p. 440, © C. J. Allen/Stock Boston; p. 451, © Bob Daemmrich/Stock Boston

name index

subject index

*Boldface page numbers indicate marginal glossary entries.

Criteria for Critiquing a Speech

✦ Content

- What audience needs and motivations did the topic address? Was the speaker's analysis of the audience on target?
- Was the topic appropriate for the occasion? Why or why not?
- Was the topic clearly focused enough to develop and support the speaker's specific purpose?
- Did the speaker use a sufficient array of sources to gather information for each idea?
- What supporting materials gave the speaker's ideas clarity, vividness, and credibility?
- Did the speaker cite the sources for those supporting materials?
- How did the speaker establish the reliability of the sources?
- Did the speaker develop the speech in an ethical way, presenting and supporting ideas that will benefit the audience?
- Did the speaker use presentation aids to make the ideas more clear, vivid, and credible? Did the speaker miss any opportunity to use presentation aids to his or her advantage?
- Were the presentation aids designed and prepared effectively?

✦ Organization and Approach

Introduction

- What strategy did the speaker use to get the audience's attention? Was the opening statement effective?
- Did the speaker clearly state the topic and establish its importance? If not, did you have difficulty understanding the purpose?
- How did the speaker establish his or her credibility to speak on the topic?
- Did the speaker preview the speech's key ideas?

Body

- Did the speaker select a manageable number of key ideas to develop? What were they?
- Were the key ideas relevant to the specific purpose?
- What pattern did the speaker select to organize the key ideas?
- Did the speaker use the 4 S strategy to develop each key idea? If not, then what components were missing?
- What kind of transitions did the speaker use to connect the key ideas?